FACTS ON FILE

Pocket Guide to the World

D0732627

FACTS ON FILE

Pocket Guide to the World

Bernard Stonehouse

Facts On File Publications
New York, New York ● Oxford, England

Facts on File Pocket Guide to the World

Copyright © 1985 by Bernard Stonehouse
Maps © George Philip & Son Ltd 1985

Published in Great Britain by
George Philip & Son Ltd, 12–14 Long Acre, London WC2.

First published in the United States by
Facts On File, Inc.
460 Park Avenue South
New York, New York 10016

Library of Congress Cataloging in
Publication Data

Stonehouse, Bernard
  Facts on File pocket guide to the world.

  1. Handbooks, vade-mecums, etc. I. Facts
on File, Inc.   II. Title
AG106.S76   1984   031'.02   84-8103

ISBN 0-87196-966-1
ISBN 0-87196-975-0 (PK)

Printed in Great Britain
10 9 8 7 6 5 4 3 2 1

Contents

Introduction

The *Philips' Pocket Guide to the World* fills a personal need. I am interested in geography in the old-fashioned sense – the countries of the world, their shapes and sizes, mountains and coastlines, people, products and politics. A world war started my travels, and my career has taken me to more than my share of out-of-the-way places. Like others I scan travel brochures and venture abroad for fun; like others I keep an eye on political events, hear radio commentaries on wars, test matches and famines in foreign parts, and watch TV news to see where the next lot of trouble is coming from. Always I want to know just a little more than they tell me about Afghanistan, Botswana or Cambodia – just a little, not too much – and I want to know it immediately, while the interest is hot.

Public libraries are full of reference books that tell their readers a great deal about the 160-odd countries of the world. Several on my own bookshelves slake the long-term thirst for geographical knowledge, and have helped in compiling the *Guide to the World*. *Encyclopaedia Britannica* is always the stand-by and final authority. *Whittaker's Almanack* tells me much that I want to know about what happened last year and the year before; *Pear's Encyclopaedia* (London, Michael Joseph) has useful comments on the political scene and an excellent quick-reference glossary. For up-to-date information the annually produced *Statesman's Year Book* (London, Macmillan) is hard to fault. Leaders in detailed fact and analysis are the longer regional guides produced annually by Europa Publications, including *Africa South of the Sahara*, *The Far East and Australasia*, and the excellent two-volume *Europa Year Books*, which no serious researcher can be without.

At another level altogether are the technical source books, full of statistical information, that every geographer uses sooner or later but few sit down and scan for immediate gratification. Many are produced by the United Nations Organization and its agencies; those I have drawn on and can recommend for research are listed below.

It is no fault of these publications that they did not meet my requirements for a pocket sourcebook; all were designed for other purposes. Some were too short for my taste, others too long, too expensive for my pocket, more detailed than I needed, or hard to plough through. Some gave me too much history, others not enough physical geography – so in the end I have written my own. While drafting it out, it seemed possible that a pocket or desk-top book of this kind might also serve other armchair geographers, provide a quick reference book for businessmen and travellers, and perhaps serve as a sourcebook for students, teachers, journalists, TV presenters, and others with similar needs. George Philip and Son thought so too, and I thank Lydia Greeves, their editor on the project, for help and encouragement during the months of preparation.

We thank Dr D. Cotton, who was mainly responsible for Section 4, and F.B. Singleton who helped with material for the European entries in Section 1. Ann Stonehouse helped with Section 3, and Fiona Gore with the final stages of the text. We also thank the following for comments and advice: Dr Clive Agnew; Professor K.F. Bowden; Dr Frank Carter; Dr Ian Douglas; Professor T.H. Elkins; David Fox; Professor T.W. Freeman; Professor B.W. Hodder; Professor A.T.A. Learmonth; Dr Keith McLachlan; James Muirden; Dr Judith Pallot; Professor H.B. Rodgers; John Sargent.

Throughout this book areas in km^2 are derived from *UN Statistical Yearbook 1981* (32nd issue, New York, United Nations, 1983). Population projections for most countries are those given in *Demographic Indicators of Countries; estimates and projections as assessed in 1980* (New York, United Nations, 1982); for smaller countries they are calculated from data in *UN Demographic Yearbook 1981* (33rd issue, New York, United Nations, 1983) and other sources. Estimates of Gross National Product per head of population and growth rates for countries outside the communist bloc are based on *1983 World Bank Atlas* (Washington, World Bank, 1983). Those for countries within the bloc are based on data from National Westminster Bank Overseas Economic Reports, which, together with ABECOR Country Reports from the Group Economics Department of Barclay's Bank, have provided useful guides to economic trends. Most values of GNP refer to 1981, most growth rates to the period 1970–80.

Most of the climatic means in Section 3 are derived from the World Meteorological Organization's *Climatological Normals (Clino) for CLIMAT and CLIMAT ship stations for the period 1931–1969*. Others are from *Meteorological Office Tables of Temperature, Relative Humidity and Precipitation for the World* (London, HMSO, 1958). Nearly all represent thirty-year means. The following sources were used in compiling Section 4: *FAO Production Yearbooks* issued in 1981 and 1983; *World Mineral Statistics 1975–80* (Institute of Geological Sciences, London, HMSO, 1982); *FAO Forest Products Yearbook 1980* (1982); *FAO Forest Production Yearbooks 33, 35* (1980, 1982); *FAO Yearbook of Fisheries Statistics 49, 51* (1979, 1981).

Names used in the text and on the maps have English conventional spellings, i.e. the placenames are in English rather than in their indigenous forms (Rome, not Roma; Cairo, not El Qâhira). In the text, placenames in China have been given in their conventional English form followed by the Pinyin transcription in brackets.

Bernard Stonehouse
Cambridge

Section 1
Countries of the World

Europe

Europe is a small continent, defined politically rather than geographically; viewed from the east it is little more than a complex of peninsulas, islands and shallow seas on the western fringe of Asia. Western, northern and southern limits are defined by coastlines and well-established conventions. Of the off-lying islands Iceland, Svalbard, the Faroes and Britain are always included; Greenland and the larger Mediterranean islands are generally regarded as European, though more on the grounds of their occupation by Europeans than from geographical proximity. Europe's eastern boundary is generally drawn by geographers along the eastern flank of the Ural Mountains in the USSR, north of the Caspian Sea and the Caucasus Mountains, and south of the Black Sea; however, this splits the USSR into European and Asian sectors, making little political sense. In this book the border is drawn along the eastern boundaries of Norway, Finland, Poland, Czechoslovakia, Hungary, Romania, Bulgaria and Greece, placing both the USSR and (somewhat arbitrarily) Turkey firmly in Asia. Europe so defined covers an area of 7.26 million km^2 (2.80 million sq miles), with a population approaching 500 million, extending from well north of the Arctic Circle almost to latitude 34° N.

In this section, information is gathered under the following headings:

The Country   Official name; position; bordering states; area; capital (and largest settlement, if different); population (est. 1986 – for projection to 1990 see Section 2).

Organization   Form of government with details of structure; local government; predominant religions and ethnic groups, when significant; languages.

Geography   Main features of physical geography and climate (for climatic statistics see Section 3).

History and Development   Origins, and main events in political and social history (including ethnic background when relevant).

Resources and Economics   Main sources of employment and wealth: relative importance of agriculture and industry. Major products; transportation; tourism.

Recent Developments   Important political, economic or social events and changes.

The length of each article is related to population size.

EUROPE WEST

Belgium

The Country
Belgium is a kingdom on Europe's northwestern flank, bordered by France, Luxembourg, Germany and the Netherlands, and facing southeastern England across the southern North Sea. *Area* 30,513 km² (11,781 sq miles); *capital* Brussels; *population* 9,873,000 (est. 1986).

Organization
A constitutional monarchy, Belgium is governed by a bicameral parliament. The Chamber of Representatives, elected for four years by a system of proportional representation, has 212 members. The Senate includes, in addition to directly elected members, others who are elected by the nine provincial councils. The population, predominantly Roman Catholic, is divided into two main linguistic groups – Dutch (Flemish) in the north and French (Walloon) in the south. There is also a small German minority. Brussels, which lies close to the linguistic boundary, is bilingual.

Geography
Belgium has a low-lying, dune-fringed coastline of 65 km (41 miles) along the North Sea, between the mouth of the River Schelde and the French border. From the coast to the Ardennes mountains in the south, the lowlands form part of the North European Plain. Most of the area is covered by fertile soils which have been intensively cultivated for hundreds of years, but along the Dutch border in Kempenland there is also an area of poor, sandy soil covered by heath, peat-bog and woodland.

The Ardennes, which rise to a height of 700 m (2296 ft), are the northernmost of the Hercynian block mountains of the Rhineland, covered by forests of mixed deciduous and coniferous trees. The main river systems, the Sambre-Meuse (Maas) and Schelde, drain towards the mouths of the Rhine across the Dutch border. The climate is temperate with strong maritime influences.

History and Development
Originally the country of the Belgae, a Gallo-Celtic tribe of northern Europe, Belgium was for long part of a group of feudal states of the North Sea coastlands, subject successively to Spanish, Dutch and French rule. Achieving a considerable degree of autonomy under the Holy Roman Emperor after the Treaty of Utrecht (1713), it was reconquered by France in 1795. After the Napoleonic era it again became linked with the Netherlands, but a revolt in 1830 led to separation, and in 1839 Belgium's independence and neutrality were guaranteed by international agreement under the Treaty of London. With rapid development of industry during the 19th century, Belgium became one of the most densely populated countries in Europe. The acquisition of a colonial empire in Africa began with the establishment of trading posts in the Congo under royal patronage, and eventually led to the colonization of the Belgian Congo, covering an area eighty times larger than the homeland and including the rich copper-mining area of Katanga. Belgium's withdrawal in 1960 led to a major re-orientation of the economy and precipitated an international crisis.

Resources and Economics

Belgian farming is prosperous, with many intensively cultivated smallholdings owned by industrial workers, as well as larger, highly-mechanized farms. Wheat, potatoes, sugar-beet, other vegetables and hay are the main crops. Only 3 per cent of the workforce is employed full-time in agriculture. Belgium was also one of the first countries in Europe to industrialize, its initial development being based on the rich coalfields along the foothills and valleys of the Ardennes, and on the long-established textile industry of Flanders. An important iron and steel industry, dependent upon imported raw materials from Luxembourg and Germany and from overseas, has given rise to metallurgical and engineering industries. Transport of heavy materials is assisted by the excellent canal system across the lowlands. The modern port of Antwerp is a centre of international waterways, linking the canal systems of France, Germany and the Netherlands. Brussels is a major international city with a population of about a million, including a cosmopolitan community of officials serving the headquarters of NATO and the EEC Commission.

Recent Developments

Political instability arising from conflicts between the two linguistic communities, mainly over questions of regional devolution, is exacerbated by the economic problems arising from the run-down of the coal industry and the restructuring of traditional metal and textile industries. There are frequent changes of government as coalitions are formed and disbanded amongst the six major parties, each of which has a Flemish and Walloon wing. Belgium was a founder member of NATO, EEC and the European Coal and Steel Community, and is a partner in the Benelux customs union.

France

The Country

The French Republic, largest in area of the EEC countries, is bordered by Belgium, Luxembourg, Germany, Switzerland and Italy in the east, and Spain in the southwest. *Area* (including the Mediterranean island of Corsica) 547,026 km² (211,207 sq miles); *capital* Paris; *population* 54,426,000 (est. 1986).

Organization

The constitution of the Fifth Republic (1958) gives wide powers to the President, who is elected by universal suffrage for seven years. Ministers are appointed by the President from Parliament, to which they are primarily responsible. Parliament consists of a 491-member National Assembly elected for a maximum of five years by a two-stage system of proportional representation, and a Senate whose 318 members are indirectly elected for nine years, one third retiring every three years. There is no official state religion; Roman Catholics form the largest denomination. The national language is French.

Geography

France has coastlines along the English Channel, the Bay of Biscay and the Mediterranean. Most of its land frontiers are based on natural features – the Pyrenees in the southwest, the Alps in the east and the Rhine in the northeast;

only from Strasbourg to the Channel coast is there no clear geographical divide separating France from its neighbours. Most of the country lies below 300 m (1000 ft); the highest lands lie along the margins, except for the Massif Central (between the Basin of Aquitaine and the Rhône Valley), which includes several extinct volcanic peaks over 1500 m (5000 ft). The most important lowland area is the Paris Basin, drained by the Seine and its tributaries which flow into the English Channel. Ranges of low chalk and limestone form concentric arcs around the basin, their slopes providing ideal sites for the vineyards of many celebrated wine-growing areas, including Champagne. Two large rivers enter the Atlantic Ocean – the Garonne, reaching the sea via the long Gironde estuary, and the Loire, which rises in the heart of the Massif Central and enters the sea at St Nazaire. The main drainage southward to the Mediterranean is via the Rhône-Saône system. This provides a vital route between Paris and Marseilles, which lies at the eastern edge of the Rhône delta.

The climate of France is influenced by its three long coastlines. Maritime air-masses bring moist, equable conditions, typical of the temperate climate of northwest Europe, to the Paris Basin, the peninsulas of Brittany and Normandy, and the warmer lowlands of Aquitaine. Continental influences bring cold winters to the plains of northeastern France and the Argonne. The Mediterranean coast, the island of Corsica and the dune-fringed Landes coast along the Bay of Biscay experience hot, dry summers.

About one fifth of France is forest-covered, with deciduous trees predominating. Coniferous forest characterizes the Vosges, Alps and Pyrenees and the sandy Landes coast. Uplands fringing the Mediterranean carry dense maquis scrub.

History and Development

Consolidated from many loosely-linked provinces under a succession of Bourbon kings, France became the major power in Europe towards the end of the 17th century. After the Revolution of 1789, monarchy was replaced briefly by the First Republic, to be restored when Napoleon declared himself Emperor in 1804. Under Napoleon, French influence spread widely across Europe and into northern Africa. Following his defeat at Waterloo (1815), France continued as a monarchy under a restored Bourbon dynasty until the declaration of the Second Republic in 1848; monarchy returned again four years later when the President, Napoleon's nephew, became Emperor Napoleon III. The Second Empire fell during the Franco-Prussian War of 1870–71, to be replaced after a brief revolutionary episode (the Commune of Paris) by the parliamentary democracy of the Third Republic. This lasted until the German occupation of 1940. A Fourth Republic, with a constitution similar to that of the Third, was established in 1946, but it was overthrown by de Gaulle in 1958, after the regime had failed to cope with the economic problems of France and with French North Africa's struggle for independence. The constitution of the Fifth Republic, currently in force, strengthened the powers of the President and diminished the role of Parliament. After re-election in 1965, de Gaulle retired in 1969 following a wave of unrest by students and workers in 1968.

There have been profound changes in France's economic and social life under the Fifth Republic. The proportion of the population employed in agriculture fell in the late 1950s from 25 per cent to under 10 per cent, and there has been rapid urban growth. Industry has been modernized and greatly expanded, creating a demand for labour which the French population has been unable to satisfy. Population growth from 46.5 million in 1962 to 54 million in 1982 is partly due to an increased birth rate, but also to the inflow of migrants from former overseas possessions, such as Algeria, and from other European countries. About 3.5 million foreigners currently live and work in France.

France became a founder member of NATO in 1948 and of the EEC in 1957, although de Gaulle decided on an independent defence policy and withdrew from the military council of NATO while remaining a member of the alliance. The close association of France and Germany, France's traditional enemy, is an important factor in maintaining the stability of Western Europe. Having granted independence to most of its colonies in recent decades, France maintains links with its former African dependencies through the institution of the French Community.

Resources and Economics

One of the major industrial nations of Europe, France is also a leading agricultural country, with a wide range of products, including fruits and wines, rice, tobacco, cereals, sugar-beet and root crops, dairy produce, cattle and sheep. There is a large export surplus of wine and food products.

The chief coalfields are in northern France, Lorraine and the Massif Central, a source of potential weakness in view of the long history of conflict with Germany. Output has declined in recent years. The formation of the European Coal and Steel Community, which was later merged with the EEC, has made possible the development of heavy industry in cooperation with Germany, Belgium and Luxembourg. Hydroelectric power is well developed in the alpine regions; atomic power is well developed, and oil and natural gas are mostly imported. At Rance in Brittany there is a tidal power station.

Iron ore is mined in Lorraine, and elsewhere there are rich reserves of bauxite, potash, salt and sulphur. Metal-working, engineering and chemical industries based on domestic resources have been expanded greatly since World War II. The traditional iron and steel and textile industries are to be found mainly in the northern coalfield areas.

Newer industries which play an important part in France's exports include motor cars, aircraft, armaments and electronics. Fuel, especially oil, and industrial raw materials are the most significant imports.

The topography of the Paris Basin and northern France has facilitated the construction of a communications network centered on Paris, but with easy access to other regions. Inland waterways play an important part in the transport of goods, and the canal system is linked to the waterways of Belgium and Germany. With over 2500 km (1560 miles) of coastline and several good natural harbours, France is a major seafaring nation, with the world's ninth largest merchant marine and an important fishing industry.

The variety of scenery encourages tourists of all types, and Paris, as one of the cultural capitals of the world, attracts millions of visitors each year.

Recent Developments

The election to the Presidency of the socialist leader, François Mitterand, and the victory of the Left in the Assembly elections in 1981 instituted a new era in French politics. The inclusion of Communist ministers in the new government, for the first time since 1946, caused some alarm in right-wing circles at home and abroad. These fears were exaggerated – Mitterand's foreign and home policies proved similar to those of his predecessor, his avowed Socialism being constrained by the exigencies of the world economic crisis. During 1981 the main banks and iron and steel firms were nationalized, wages were increased and the private sector squeezed, but in 1982, in the face of rising unemployment and inflation, a four-month freeze of pay and prices was ordered. Far-reaching decentralization of local government may be the most important reform instituted by the new regime. The local election results in 1982 indicated a falling-off in support for the government, although its majority in Parliament was not endangered.

French arms sales abroad, especially to Middle Eastern and Latin American states, have given rise to some criticism, especially during the battle for the Falklands in 1982, when French missiles were used by the Argentines to sink British ships.

Ireland

The Country
The Republic of Ireland (Eire) occupies 85 per cent of Ireland, westernmost of the British Isles in the eastern Atlantic Ocean. Its only land boundary is with the Province of Northern Ireland (UK). *Area* 70,283 km² (27,136 sq miles); *capital* Dublin; *population* 3,536,000 (est. 1986).

Organization
A democratic republic, Ireland is governed by a President who is elected by direct vote for a term of seven years. Parliament consists of a lower house (the Dáil Éireann) with 166 members elected for a maximum of five years by proportional representation, and a Senate of 60 members. Four fifths of the population is Roman Catholic. The official languages are Irish and English.

Geography
Geologically Ireland resembles a basin, in which a rim of ancient rock, including quartzites and metamorphosed sandstones, surrounds an interior lowland of glacial and post-glacial deposits overlying strata of Carboniferous age. Ireland's Carboniferous rocks, unlike those of Britain, contain little coal. Lack of this natural fuel is partly compensated for by thick layers of peat which have formed above the glacial clays. The central lowland is drained by the River Shannon and its tributaries, a sluggish system with many long, narrow lakes along its course. The climate is dominated by mild, moist Atlantic air, which brings heavy rain to the mountains along the west coast. The limestone plateau of the Burren in Co. Mayo contains a rich flora, with species more common to the Mediterranean than to the British Isles.

History and Development
The Celtic-speaking tribes who settled in Ireland in pre-Roman times were converted to Christianity by St Patrick in the 5th century. After a period under Norse occupation, the Normans invaded from England, imposing a feudal system under an alien aristocracy. Later English kings attempted to subjugate the Irish chieftains and to settle English and Scottish landowners on the country. In 1801 the parliaments of Great Britain and Ireland were united, but Irish resistance continued, culminating in the development of a militant resistance movement and the rebellion of 1916. In 1921 an Irish Free State, with dominion status, was established in twenty-six of the thirty-two counties of Ireland; the six counties of the northeast, with predominantly Protestant

populations, remained under British rule. Ireland's present constitution, introduced in 1937, freed the country more completely from British influence and claimed Irish sovereignty over the whole of the island. Ireland remained neutral in World War II, and in 1948 severed its last constitutional links with Britain. Its population has declined from 6.5 million in 1841, largely as a result of emigration to Britain, America and the Commonwealth.

Resources and Economics
Despite a shortage of coal, oil and metal ores, manufacturing industry has developed rapidly and at the same time agriculture has been modernized. The proportion of the workforce in agriculture fell from 33 per cent in 1965 to 19 per cent in 1980, but farm workers are still the major occupational group, producing the highest proportion of exports. Livestock – especially pigs and cows – and animal products are the most important exports, and Britain is the chief customer, although since joining the EEC in 1973 trade with Western Europe has increased. European investment has stimulated manufacturing, especially in the textile, electronics and metal industries. Energy resources have been improved by government-financed power stations (fuelled by peat) and by hydroelectric schemes, such as the Shannon barrage. Prospecting for oil and gas has produced no important finds, and large imports of petroleum products are essential. The ten million tourists who visit Ireland every year provide valuable foreign currency.

Recent Developments
Ireland's farmers prospered greatly under the Common Agricultural Policy in the first few years of EEC membership, but by 1980 there was considerable dissatisfaction as the Irish economy suffered from the effects of the world recession, and the farming community claimed that it bore a disproportionate share of the burden. Inflation, unemployment and a balance of payments deficit remain unresolved problems which have led to industrial unrest.

Relations with Britain over Northern Ireland have overshadowed the political scene. The attempts by two Prime Ministers – Mr Haughey of Fianna Fáil in 1980 and again in 1982, and Mr Fitzgerald of Fine Gael in 1981 – to develop an Anglo-Irish rapport have had little success.

Luxembourg

The Country
The Grand Duchy of Luxembourg, an independent sovereign state 80 km (50 miles) long and nowhere more than 50 km (30 miles) across, is bounded by northern France, southeastern Belgium and West Germany. *Area* 2586 km^2 (998 sq miles); *capital* Luxembourg; *population* 356,000 (est. 1986).

Organization
A hereditary Grand Duchy, Luxembourg is governed by a Chamber of Deputies of 59 elected members, with a 21-member advisory Council of State; the Grand Duke's executive power is normally abrogated to a Council of Ministers responsible to the Chamber. Local government is vested in thirteen cantons. The official language is French, the commercial language German, the spoken language Luxembourgeois. Roman Catholicism predominates.

Geography
Northern Luxembourg (the Oesling) lies in the Ardennes whose sandstone uplands provide spectacular forest scenery. The southern scarplands (Gutland), descending toward the Moselle Valley, provide good soils for farming and stock-raising, and, in the southwest, also provide the iron ores on which Luxembourg's industrial prosperity was largely built. The climate is temperate, with long, cold winters and hot summers.

History and Development
Straddling important trade routes between western and central Europe, blessed with good building stone, minerals and farmland, Luxembourg has often found itself dominated and at times even occupied by larger neighbours. Nevertheless, it has retained its identity as a sovereign state for over a thousand years. A pioneer of European federation, Luxembourg was a founder member of Benelux, the customs union that was the forerunner of the EEC.

Resources and Economics
About one third of the land area of Luxembourg is forested, and about half is farmed. The main crops are barley, oats and wheat; vines are grown in the southern valleys, and extensive grasslands provide forage for cattle and sheep. Minerals include limestone and iron ores; however, the iron and steel industry and associated manufacturing industries, in which almost half the country's workforce is employed, are now based largely on imported raw materials. Chemical industries, tourism and international finance and banking are growing in importance.

Recent Developments
Although its early prosperity was based on agriculture, Luxembourg's industrial development expanded rapidly after World War I and has helped to provide its current population with one of Europe's highest standards of living. Like the Swiss, Luxembourgers play prominent roles in international affairs; their capital is the second capital of the EEC and headquarters of several European organizations.

Monaco

The Country
The Principality of Monaco is a tiny independent state on the Mediterranean coast, bounded inland by France. It occupies about 3 km (less than 2 miles) of rocky coast between Nice and the French–Italian border, extending little over $\frac{3}{4}$ km ($\frac{1}{2}$ mile) inland. *Area* 1.5 km^2 (0.6 sq miles); *capital* Monaco; *population* 26,000 (est. 1986).

Organization
A hereditary Principality, Monaco is governed by a National Council of 18 elected members and a Communal Council of 16 members; executive power rests with the Monarch and a Council of Government of four members. Roman Catholicism is the predominant religion. The official language is French; Italian, English and Monegasque are also spoken.

Geography

Monaco occupies a headland and a group of coastal hills at the foot of the Alpes de Provence, on the Côte d'Azur. Its area has been increased by harbour works and coastal extensions. The climate is mild throughout the year, with warm summers and cool, dry winters. Building, landscaping and cultivation replace most of the natural coastal vegetation.

History and Development

Monaco became a Genoese outpost in the 12th century, passing into the possession of the Grimaldi family which aligned its fortunes with those of France. Although relationships have often been strained, Monaco has since then retained almost continuous independence under France's wing, with Grimaldis still occupying the monarchy. Only about one sixth of the current population is native Monegasque; the rest are French or Italian citizens with temporary or permanent residence.

Resources and Economics

With few natural resources apart from a fine climate and scenery, Monaco lives largely on its wits. Most of the national revenue comes from visitors – some 200,000 or more per year – whose spending supports the many hotels, lidos, sports-clubs and entertainments, including the Casino at Monte Carlo. Banking and sale of postage stamps provide further income, and light industries are developing to support the small but slowly-growing population.

Recent Developments

Despite economic depression elsewhere in Europe, the leisure industries continue to bring prosperity to Monaco. Unable to spread in other directions, the Principality is expanding seaward; shortage of space is being overcome by land reclamation along the waterfront for new housing and office space.

The Netherlands

The Country

The Kingdom of the Netherlands (often called Holland) lies on the North Sea coast of Western Europe, bordered by Belgium and West Germany. *Area* 40,844 km^2 (15,769 sq miles); *capital* Amsterdam, *seat of government* The Hague, *largest city* Rotterdam; *population* 14,458,000 (est. 1986).

Organization

The Netherlands is a constitutional monarchy. The parliament, known as the States-General, consists of two Chambers, the first of 75 members, elected by the Provincial States for six years, and the second of 150 members, elected by universal suffrage for four years. There are eleven provinces, each with its own elected council. The national language is Dutch. The Dutch Reformed Church (to which the Royal Family belongs) and other Protestant churches together account for about 45 per cent of those with a religious affiliation; Roman Catholics account for about 50 per cent.

Geography

The Netherlands form part of the North European Plain. Much of the coastal area between the East Schelde and the mouth of the Ems lies below sea level, protected by coastal dunes and man-made dykes; without these sea defences, two fifths of the country would be submerged. The highest point, 684 m (2244 ft), is in the southeast, where Dutch, German and Belgian frontiers meet. The reclamation of the Zuider Zee (the remnant of which now forms the IJsselmeer) began with the construction of the Afsluidijk in 1932. Reclamation work is also proceeding in the Rhine delta, where the huge Europort complex has been built.

The Rhine and its associated mouths, the Schelde and the Maas, cross the southern Netherlands, providing water routes for sea-going ships, and connecting canals give access to the inland waterways of Belgium and Germany.

Although much of the Netherlands is covered by fertile alluvium, in the east and north there are areas of infertile, sandy heathlands, similar to the heaths of northern Germany. Much of this area is planted with conifers. The climate is temperate, with no average monthly temperatures below freezing point, although cold winds from continental Europe occasionally bring severe winter conditions.

History and Development

Formerly a group of semi-independent feudal provinces, the Netherlands came successively under Burgundian and Spanish domination, emerging as the predominantly Protestant United Provinces ruled by the dynasty of Orange-Nassau, which is still the royal house. Its seamen rivalled Britain's in the struggle to establish overseas possessions and world trade. Linked intermittently to Belgium, it was joined with Belgium at the Congress of Vienna (1815). Union with Belgium ended in 1830. The Netherlands remained neutral in World War I, but suffered invasion and privation during World War II. Since 1948 it has re-established close ties with its neighbours through the Benelux customs union and adherence to the Western European Union, NATO and the EEC. The Hague has for long been the seat of the International Court of Justice, established under the League of Nations. Former colonies in the East Indies became independent in 1949 (see Indonesia); links with Suriname were retained until 1975, and the Netherlands Antilles still remain associated with the Dutch Crown. Immigrants from these territories are a visible element in the Netherlands' population.

The Netherlands is one of the most densely populated countries of Europe, with over 350 inhabitants per km^2 (900 per sq mile). The population has grown from 12.6 million in 1968 to over 14 million.

Resources and Economics

The small amount of coal mined in the south was exhausted in the 1970s, just as natural gas and oil from the North Sea and the Groningen area began to be developed. There are few other mineral resources apart from salt, which provides a raw material for the chemical industry, and china clay. Economic prosperity has for long been based on intensive cultivation of the land, and on the commercial opportunities offered by the country's position at the mouth of the Rhine. Rotterdam and the newly-constructed Europort are major European ports of trans-shipment, handling goods for the EEC countries. Industries based on them, including oil-refining, petrochemicals and food-processing, have added to such traditional occupations as shipbuilding, engineering and metal-working. Amsterdam is the world centre of the diamond industry.

Grassland supports a dairy industry and horticultural land produces flowers, bulbs, fruit and vegetables. High productivity is achieved under glass, but field crops – notably potatoes and sugar-beet – are also important. The cultivation of oyster beds and inshore fishing for herring are of local importance.

Recent Developments

Based firmly on world trading, the Dutch economy suffered severely during the world recession of the 1970s and 1980s; while demand for manufactured goods and services outside the Netherlands remained low, balance of trade was achieved only through a poverty-induced reduction in imports. Unemployment rose steadily, standing in the mid-1980s at 10 per cent of the workforce. Inflation, however, is low, and the currency remains stable, due mainly to stringent economic measures which successive governments have adopted to reduce budget deficits.

United Kingdom

The Country

The United Kingdom (often called Britain) lies off the northwest coast of continental Europe. It consists of Great Britain (England, Scotland and Wales), and the separate Province of Northern Ireland. The Isle of Man and the Channel Islands are Crown Dependencies, usually included within the United Kingdom but with a considerable degree of autonomy. *Area* 244,046 km^2 (94,226 sq miles); *capital* London; *population* 55,600,000 (est. 1986).

Organization

Britain is governed by a bicameral parliament. The Sovereign is Head of State. The House of Commons, with 635 elected members, originates much of the legislation; the House of Lords includes hereditary peers (now a minority), life peers, Anglican bishops and law lords. An executive cabinet is headed by the Prime Minister. Local authority is vested in ninety-two counties (England), regions and island areas (Scotland) and districts (Northern Ireland). The official language is English; Welsh and Gaelic are spoken locally. Anglican Christianity is the established religion; there are significant Roman Catholic, Presbyterian, Methodist, Jewish, Moslem and other minorities.

Geography

Britain is geologically complex with oldest and hardest rocks mainly in the north and west, younger sediments in the south and east. Scotland (78,781 km^2, 30,417 sq miles) occupies the northern third of Great Britain. Its Highland Region, including the outlying islands of Orkney, Shetland and the Hebrides, is composed of both ancient sediments and granites and younger volcanic rocks. The Great Glen, which cuts diagonally from northeast to southwest, separates northern moors from the higher but more gently-contoured Grampian Highlands and fertile eastern plains; from the western Grampians rises Ben Nevis (1344 m, 4410 ft), Britain's highest peak. The Central Lowlands to the south form a broad swathe of plains and rolling hills, including the valleys of the Clyde and Forth rivers. The Southern Uplands include some of Scotland's gentlest scenery and finest farmland.

England (130,438 km^2, 50,331 sq miles) has two northern uplands – the Cumbrian Mountains (Lake District), which include Scafell (978 m, 3210 ft), the highest peak, and the sprawling Pennine range, extending from the Cheviot

Hills to the Trent valley. Crags, moorlands and dales are characteristic Pennine scenery, with collieries and quarries acting as reminders of the underlying mineral wealth. Limestones rich in iron ore underlie the plains along the eastern and southern flanks of the Pennines, from the Lincolnshire Uplands to the Quantock Hills. Red sandstones predominate west of the Pennines. Britain's oldest rocks outcrop in the Malvern Hills, and the granites, slates and sandstone of Cornwall and Devon create a resistant outlier in the southwest.

Wales (20,769 km², 8019 sq miles) is largely mountainous, with its highest peaks clustered in the northwest about Snowdon (1086 m, 3563 ft). Ancient sediments and metamorphic rocks predominate in the centre and north; southern Wales is dominated by sandstones (Black Mountains, Brecon Beacons) and carboniferous limestones rich in coal and iron ore. Although the valleys and coastal plains of the south are heavily industrialized, many in central and north Wales retain much of their original beauty.

Northern Ireland (14,120 km², 5452 sq miles) is centered on Lough Neagh, a lake basin with a surrounding ring of uplands. Ancient shales, sandstones and volcanic rocks underlie much of the province, with younger limestones and sandstones in the west and the granitic Mourne Mountains (Slieve Donard 852 m, 2795 ft) in the southeast. Much of the northeast, Antrim, is capped by columnar basalt, forming high cliffs along the northern coast. Glacial soils predominate, yielding good farmland where drainage is adequate.

British climate is damp and anomalously warm, tempered by the North Atlantic Drift. Cyclonic depressions move eastward across the country, prevailing southwesterly winds bringing cloud and rain. Originally a mosaic of forest and moorland, Britain has now lost most of its indigenous vegetation: burning, draining, farming and building have changed the face of the land completely.

History and Development

Britain attracted Angles, Saxons, Danes, Jutes, Celts, Romans and many other invaders from mainland Europe. England had achieved quite a high degree of internal order and culture before falling victim to the last successful invasion, that of the Norman–French under William I in 1066. At this time the population was about two million. Early prosperity was based on wool and woollen cloth exported to the continent, and later on iron and steel locally smelted with charcoal from the extensive forests. An increasing maritime trade was centered on ports developing in the east and south, through which British goods were sold abroad, while imported raw materials stimulated manufacturing.

Of the four nations that evolved in the British Isles, the English quickly gained ascendancy and expanded most rapidly. Wales was first defeated under Edward I (1272–1307), but resistance continued for the next century; it was formally united with England in 1536. Union with Scotland came in 1707, at which time there was a population of some six million English and Welsh, about one million Scots, and probably no more than one million Irish in an unruly, uncensused western colony. The parliaments of Great Britain and Ireland were united in 1801, but Irish resistance resulted in the division of Ireland in 1921, with only the six counties of the northeast remaining under British rule (see also Ireland).

Britain's 18th-century Industrial Revolution preceded those of her continental neighbours. Canal and railway networks spread with the developing industries. Wales, Scotland and Ireland lagged behind England in the race to industrialize; industries play a smaller role in their economies even today, and their populations, depleted by emigration, remain relatively small. To provide cheap raw materials for home industries and markets for manufactured goods, Britain developed the largest empire the world has seen – one that reached its greatest extent in the early 20th century and then fragmented. Although relatively isolated from Europe, Britain was involved in successive European wars which threatened trade, imperial possessions or sovereignty. Playing a prominent role in the two World Wars, Britain emerged victorious but impoverished, having lost many of the economic and political advantages that had previously sustained wealth and progress. Scotland, Wales and Ireland have small, relatively stable populations; England's population shows a slight annual increase. Parts of southeastern England are among the world's most densely populated areas.

Resources and Economics

Agriculture, horticulture, forestry and fishing employ less than 2 per cent of the workforce. Britain raises over half its own food with high yields of cereals, sugar-beet, potatoes, vegetables, fruit, livestock and dairy produce. More than 90 per cent of timber needs are imported. The fishing industry is declining through loss of traditional distant-water fishing grounds and overfishing in waters closer to home. Manufacturing industries occupy a third of the workforce and generate about a third of the annual income. Mechanical, electrical and chemical engineering predominate, producing iron and steel, chemicals, motor vehicles, aircraft, and electronic and other equipment. Heavy engineering (steel production, shipbuilding etc.), centered originally close to the sources of raw materials, has gradually been overtaken by lighter manufacturing based in new locations close to the main centres of population.

Many of Britain's most prosperous industries (including those connected with computer technology), which are not very dependent on sources of raw materials, are concentrated in a corridor extending across southern England from London to Bristol. A shift from coal to oil and natural gas as the main industrial fuels during the 1950s and 1960s, boosted by the development of Britain's own petroleum industry in the North Sea, encouraged industries based on these products to settle away from traditional inland sites and close to ports and estuaries. Increasing costs of oil in the 1970s restimulated coal production, though mining remained concentrated in fewer centres.

Textiles and clothing manufacture and the food and drinks industries employ many Britons, though the service industries (banking, insurance, professional, civil and local authority services and education) are now Britain's major employers; together they occupy about half the workforce and are expanding despite economic recession. Tourism brings about ten million visitors per year, mostly from France, Germany, the Low Countries and the USA, and plays an increasing role in the economy.

Recent Developments

Britain is currently suffering the effects of worldwide depression; traditional heavy industries – steel and shipbuilding especially – have been most heavily hit, but lack of consumer demand at home and overseas has affected sales in lighter industries too. Bankruptcies and cutbacks combined in the early 1980s to produce over three million unemployed – almost 14 per cent of the workforce. Scotland, Wales and Northern Ireland are hardest hit by the industrial recession. The comparative poverty of post-industrial Wales and Scotland encourages ground-swells of opposition to English hegemony, while Northern Ireland continues to be torn between Unionist (mainly Protestant) forces dedicated to close ties with Great Britain, and Republicans (mainly Catholic) seeking union with the Irish Republic.

EUROPE NORTH

Denmark

The Country
The Kingdom of Denmark occupies the peninsula of Jutland and an extensive group of islands in the Kattegat and southern Baltic (see also Faroe Islands, Greenland); southern Jutland borders Germany, and Denmark's easternmost islands lie within 8 km (5 miles) of Sweden. *Area* 43,069 km² (16,629 sq miles); *capital* Copenhagen; *population* 5,170,000 (est. 1986).

Organization
A constitutional monarchy, Denmark has a single-chambered parliament of 179 elected members (Folketing). The Sovereign exercises joint power with the Folketing through the Prime Minister and a small cabinet, which is the executive body. Local authority is vested in the elected councils of 14 counties and, on a smaller scale, over 270 municipalities. The national language is Danish; the established church is the Danish Lutheran.

Geography
Geologically Denmark is the youngest of the Scandinavian countries, made up of sedimentary rocks overlain by glacial deposits of sand and clay. Chalk cliffs are exposed on the island of Møn, off Sjaelland; the granite island of Bornholm is akin to southern Sweden. Mainly low-lying, Jutland is fringed along its western coast by sandy dunes and shallow saline lagoons; the three major islands (Sjaelland, Fyn, Lolland) and many minor ones are similarly flat and featureless, edged with low cliffs or salt marshes. The climate is mild, cloudy and damp, with prevailing westerly winds; low temperatures are experienced in winter when continental influences are strong. Heath and low-growing forest were the original vegetation; reclamation, intensive agriculture and coniferous plantations have now altered the landscape considerably.

History and Development
Aboriginal settlers probably entered Jutland from the south shortly after the retreat of the glaciers over ten thousand years ago. Taking to the sea, they joined the Norwegians in raiding Britain and other southern European lands where the climate was milder and the soils more promising. Under King Knud (Canute), England, Denmark and Norway were briefly joined (1018–42). Later Denmark's position commanding the entrance to the Baltic Sea became strategically important; Danish sea power and political influence spread, allowing the country to join the Kalmar Union with Sweden and Norway (1397) on commanding terms. During the 15th, 16th and 17th centuries Denmark prospered; land reforms and the ending of serfdom later provided a firm foundation for agriculture and stock-raising, which maintained Denmark's prosperity during the 19th century despite substantial losses of territory,

carrying it through to the present day. Neutral in World War I, Denmark suffered occupation by German forces in World War II. Recovering rapidly after the war, its capacity for efficient food production set Denmark quickly back on the road to prosperity.

Resources and Economics

Denmark's agricultural heritage, nurtured in the virtual absence of other wealth or resources, developed most noticeably in the late 19th century with the intensive raising of cattle, pigs and poultry and development of cooperative methods of marketing. Denmark provided bacon, eggs and dairy produce cheaply and effectively for British and North European mass markets, and continues to do so despite mounting customs barriers and competition from other countries. Cereal production is the basis of the industry, with barley the main crop. Coastal and deep-water fisheries are well developed from many small ports, though currently in decline due to overfishing and intense competition. Industries include food-processing, brewing, printing, manufacture of electrical and other light engineering goods, petroleum-refining and chemicals, shipbuilding and the design and manufacture of furniture. Road, rail, sea and air links are excellent, and there is a flourishing tourist trade.

Recent Developments

Though vulnerable because of the narrow base of its prosperity, Denmark continues to enjoy one of the highest standards of living in Europe. Economic setbacks have led to strikes and other manifestations of social unrest, especially among the young, but social welfare acts as a safety net; though unemployment is high, poverty is rare. Attempts to diversify the economy continue, hampered by the need to import most raw materials. North Sea oil and gas now provide an increasing proportion of the country's energy needs, and its economic future seems assured.

The Faroe Islands

The Country

The Faroe Islands are an archipelago in the northeastern Atlantic Ocean between Britain, Iceland and Scandinavia, some 400 km (250 miles) from Scotland and 600 km (375 miles) from Norway. Seventeen of the twenty-two islands are inhabited: Streymoy, the largest, has over a third of the population. *Area* 1399 km^2 (540 sq miles); *capital* Thorshavn; *population* 47,000 (est. 1986).

Organization

A self-governing province of Denmark since 1948, the Faroes have an elected parliament (Lagting) of 32 members, with an executive (Landsstyre) of six members; two members are sent to the Danish Parliament where matters of foreign policy, law etc. are decided. The people are of Danish or Scandinavian stock, mostly Lutheran Christians. Faroese is generally spoken, with Danish an important second language.

Geography

Mostly volcanic basalts and tuffs, the islands are steep-sided and bear ample evidence of glaciation: the highest point is Eysturoy, rising to 882 m (2894 ft).

Soils are thin and wind-blown, fertile in hollows where there is protection from the weather. The climate is cool, windy and damp, with a moderate temperature range controlled by the surrounding ocean; fogs occur often, especially in winter. Trees grow only in sheltered places; grass and bog cover most of the surface, and sea birds are abundant on the cliffs.

History and Development
The Faroes were first occupied by monks in the 8th century, later by Viking settlers. A Norwegian province from 1380, they passed with Norway to Danish sovereignty and came directly under the Danish Crown in 1709. British forces occupied them during World War II, and the islands attained self-government, with their own flag and currency, in 1948.

Resources and Economics
Long noted for their wool production, the islands have a continuing tradition of sheep-farming with associated spinning and handicraft industries. Deep-sea fishing is, however, far more important economically, occupying over a sixth of the workforce and providing over 85 per cent of the community's export income. Ancillary industries (fish-drying and freezing, ship repairs etc.) arising from the fishing industry are also major employers. Sea birds, their eggs and plumage provide additional sources of food and revenue. Brown coal is mined on Sudenoy.

Recent Developments
The high standard of living enjoyed by the Faroese depends precariously on the cod, capelin, whiting, mackerel and other fish taken by their inshore and distant-water fleets. Legislation to protect their home fisheries – including a 370-km (200-mile) protection zone around their islands – has effectively excluded them from membership of the EEC.

Finland

The Country
The Republic of Finland, the most northerly state of mainland Europe, is bordered by Sweden, Norway and the USSR, with a long Baltic Sea coastline. *Area* 337,032 km^2 (130, 128 sq miles); *capital* Helsinki; *population* 4,979,000 (est. 1986).

Organization
Finland's parliament of 200 members (Bduskunta) is elected for four-year terms; the President, elected for six-year terms, appoints a Prime Minister and a small cabinet of ministers with executive powers. Local government is vested in over 460 urban and rural communes, with elected councils and boards. The national languages are Finnish (spoken by over 90 per cent of the population) and Swedish; a Sami (Lapp) minority speak their own dialect. The largest religious group belongs to the Evangelical Lutheran Church.

Geography
Most of Finland is a heavily glaciated plateau of 200 m (650 ft) or lower, dotted with over 60,000 shallow lakes which occupy about a tenth of its surface.

Aligned northwest to southeast, these lakes indicate the direction of flow of the ice sheets that planed the land less than ten thousand years ago. Glacial deposits cover the coastal lowlands behind the Gulfs of Bothnia and Finland. In the north the roots of an ancient mountain system with the same alignment rise gently to a little over 1000 m (3300 ft), their hard crystalline rocks heavily abraded by ice and severe weathering. Over one third of the country lies north of the Arctic Circle. Winters are long and cold, tempered by influxes of warm air from the Atlantic; ice blocks the Baltic ports for several months each year. Summers are short and mild, warmed by long hours of gentle sunshine. Over half the country is forested with birch and conifers, grading to treeless tundra in the far north.

History and Development

Language suggests that the Finnish people migrated towards the Arctic from southern Europe about two thousand years ago, displacing an aboriginal population now represented by the Sami (Lapps). Thinly populated, the country was controlled by Sweden from about 1150 to the early 19th century, when it acted as a buffer zone against neighbouring Russia. Parts of it were lost to Russia in the early and mid-18th century, and in 1809 Finland was forfeited entirely to Russia. Strong nationalist movements developed under Tsarist rule and Finland gained its own parliament in 1906. After the Bolshevik Revolution Finland declared its independence (1917), retaining a conservative democratic government. Invaded by Soviet troops in 1939, Finland lost some of its territory; alliance with Germany in World War II failed to restore its old frontiers, and Finland has found it expedient to form close alliances with the USSR during the post-war years.

Resources and Economics

Agriculture, forestry and fishing were for long the mainstays of the Finnish economy and are still important. Barley, rye and oats are the main crops, grown mostly in small mixed farms with increasingly intensive livestock production. Finland's huge forests support an extensive timber industry, including the manufacture of pulp and paper, plywood and chipboard. Virtually without coal or oil of its own, the country has developed hydroelectric power but relies heavily on imported fuels. Iron, copper and other metal ores are mined and processed, providing the basis for expanding industries. Finland has an established reputation for steel, engineering products and shipbuilding; designs for ice-breaking ships have proved particularly effective. Industrial chemicals, textiles and clothing are also produced for export and home consumption.

Recent Developments

Treading a careful path of neutrality, Finland manages to remain on amicable terms with the USSR while developing trade and friendship with European neighbours. Recent economic expansion based largely on timber products (which make up over 40 per cent of its exports) has been halted by the world depression, and Finland remains vulnerable to rises in the price of fuels. However, for a country with few natural assets beyond its extensive forests, Finland has managed to achieve a remarkably high standard of living for its small population, and appears well set for further expansion when markets for its diversifying products improve.

Greenland

The Country

Greenland is an island complex in the North Atlantic and Arctic oceans, extending from 60°N (the latitude of Shetland) to within 800 km (500 miles) of the North Pole. Much of it lies north of the Arctic Circle. *Area* approx. 2,175,600 km^2 (840,000 sq miles); *capital* Godthaab; *population* 52,000 (est. 1986).

Organization

A self-governing province of Denmark, Greenland has an elected Provincial Council that decides local matters, and returns two members to the Danish Parliament which retains overriding responsibility. Local government is vested in nineteen district (settlement) councils. Greenlanders are Inuit (Eskimos), full-blooded in remote areas, or with European admixtures – mostly Danish – where the cultures have met. Both Eskimo (several dialects) and Danish are spoken. The two principal religions are Lutheran Christianity and Shamanism.

Geography

Several large islands are overlain by a permanent ice-sheet of mean depth 1500 m (5000 ft). Only about 16 per cent of the total area is exposed, including mountains of over 3500 m (11,500 ft) on the east coast; less than 5 per cent is habitable by man. The climate, cold and often stormy, is mildest in the southwest, where birch and dwarf willow scrub grow; in the colder and drier north mosses and lichens predominate.

History and Development

Seal-hunting Eskimos from North America spread to Greenland in several waves, the earliest before 2500 BC. Norse settlers farmed the southwest between the 12th and 15th centuries, but were forced out – possibly by a deteriorating climate. Starting afresh in 1721, Danish missionaries and administrators settled at many points along the coast, colonizing Greenland in stages. The monopolistic Danish Royal Greenland Trading Company allowed some development, excluding other influences. Home rule was granted in 1979.

Resources and Economics

Limited sheep-farming is possible around Julianehaab in the southwest. Much of Greenland's income depends on inshore and deep-water fishing, based on southwestern ports that are ice-free throughout the year. About a sixth of Greenland's workforce is involved in catching and processing fish, mainly cod, capelin, salmon and shrimps. Traditional hunting for furs (seal, fox) continues, mainly in north and east Greenland. Cryolite is mined at Iviglut. Air and sea links keep contact between the scattered communities, and bring in increasing numbers of tourists.

Recent Developments

Heavily subsidized by Denmark, the Greenland community subsists precariously on its fishing income; EEC membership was rejected by ballot in 1981. Efforts to find oil and natural gas have so far failed, but other minerals (lead, zinc, coal) are present; mining and tourism offer hope for economic diversification in the future.

Iceland

The Country
The Republic of Iceland includes one large and several smaller islands lying east of Greenland and northwest of Britain in the North Atlantic Ocean. *Area* 103,000 km² (39,768 sq miles); *capital* Reykjavik; *population* 245,000 (est. 1986).

Organization
Iceland is governed by a parliament (Althing) of 60 elected members, 20 of whom form an Upper House. The elected President and Head of State appoints a Prime Minister and a small cabinet from the Althing. Local authority is vested in town and county councils. Icelanders are mainly of Nordic stock with Celtic admixtures. Their religion is Lutheran Christianity, their language Icelandic.

Geography
Straddling the Mid-Atlantic Ridge (see Section 5), Iceland is of geologically-recent volcanic origin; composed mainly of basaltic lavas and tuffs, it has several active volcanoes and is occasionally augmented by volcanic action. Hot springs appear side-by-side with glaciers – remnants of the last glacial period. Coastal fjords lead inland to broad valleys and high ridges; the highest peak is Öraefajökull (2119 m, 6952 ft) close to the south coast. Summers are cool, winters only slightly cooler, with rain or snow prevalent: moorland vegetation predominates.

History and Development
Iceland was colonized before AD 900 by Irish monks and Norsemen, who founded coastal farming and fishing settlements. The population grew with the centuries, rising during periods of affluence and falling through emigration when climatic or economic changes brought hard times. For long a dependency of Denmark, Iceland achieved independence in 1944.

Resources and Economics
Stock-farming keeps Iceland in fresh meat, poultry and dairy produce; hay, potatoes and greenhouse crops are grown. Inshore and deep-water fisheries provide the main industry, employing one eighth of the workforce directly or indirectly, and earning three quarters of the country's export revenues. Cheap hydroelectricity and geothermal energy provide for aluminium-smelting and other energy-intensive industries. Road, air and sea transport are adequate, and there is a growing tourist industry.

Recent Developments
Based squarely on a single and possibly declining resource (fish), Iceland's current prosperity is real but vulnerable. The need to protect local fish stocks against foreign fleets has to some degree isolated the country politically; Iceland is a member of NATO but not of the EEC. Cheap industrial power – an important resource but as yet under-exploited – offers possibilities for future development.

Norway

The Country
The Kingdom of Norway occupies the western flank of the Scandinavian peninsula, bordered by Sweden, Finland and the USSR (see also Svalbard and Jan Mayen). *Area* 324,219 km² (125,182 sq miles); *capital* Oslo; *population* 4,155,000 (est. 1986).

Organization
A constitutional monarchy, Norway is governed by an elected parliament (Storting) of 155 members representing 19 electoral districts. One quarter of the members forms a separate chamber (Lagting), the remainder the Odelsting, which meet separately when new legislation is under discussion. A Prime Minister and about fifteen other ministers form the cabinet, which exercises the authority of the Sovereign. Local government is provided by district councils and committees. Norwegian is the official language. The Lutheran Church has national status, with clergy nominated by the Sovereign.

Geography
Extending over 1600 km (1000 miles) from north to south, Norway has a central spine of mineral-rich crystalline mountains which rise at their high southern end to over 2400 m (7900 ft). The narrow western coastal plain is deeply indented by long, narrow fjords, and protected by chains of islands which break the main force of the Atlantic swell and provide sheltered coastal channels. In the southeast, low land to west and east of Oslo Fjord provides good farming land. About one third of the country lies within the Arctic Cricle and there are permanent ice-fields on the high plateaus; however, the sheltered valleys are fertile, and the climate is ameliorated by the North Atlantic Drift, which warms the coast and brings warm, moist air well inland; the port of Narvik ($68\frac{1}{2}$°N) is usually ice-free in winter. Summers are warm, winters cool and damp, and rainfall is heavy, reaching 2000 mm (80 in) per year at Bergen. About two thirds of Norway is tundra, bare rock or snowfields; about one fifth is covered by coniferous forest; good agricultural land is scarce and patchy.

History and Development
Inhabited originally by local sea-going tribes, Norway was first united as a country in the 10th century. Norse settlers left to found coastal colonies throughout the rest of Europe, while the homeland developed slowly into a single, though necessarily decentralized state, with well-founded colonies in Greenland and Iceland. During the 14th century Norway became part of the Kalmar Union under Swedish and Danish control, and was ceded to the Swedish Crown in 1814. The union was never a happy one, and in 1905 Norway gained its independence as a separate kingdom. Neutral in World War I and at the start of World War II, Norway was invaded by Germany in 1940; in 1949 it became a founder member of NATO but in 1972 declined by plebiscite to join the EEC.

Resources and Economics
One of Europe's most sparsely populated countries, with only about 3 per cent of its land surface cultivable, Norway traditionally based its economy on the sea. Forestry and dairy-farming prosper in favoured parts of the country, but for

generations the main wealth of the community came from fishing, whaling, shipbuilding and shipping. Minerals are plentiful and have recently come to the fore in the economy. Iron, copper, zinc, lead and nickel ores are mined; aluminium and other metals are processed using cheap hydroelectricity as a power source. Paper and pulp industries have also benefited from plentiful power and water. Metal goods, machinery and ships are the country's main exports, together with timber products and processed foods. Oil and natural gas discoveries in the Norwegian sector of the North Sea have formed the basis of new petrochemical industries which have already brought further prosperity and still have considerable potential for expansion.

Recent Developments
Though a non-member, Norway enjoys favourable trading status with the EEC which, like Sweden, provides ready markets for much of its produce. Economic expansion has slowed considerably since the 1970s and sales of oil have reduced, but Norway continues to develop as one of the world's most prosperous countries, with a high standard of living and the prospect of oil-based wealth that should continue well into the 21st century.

Svalbard and Jan Mayen

Svalbard
Svalbard is an archipelago of Arctic islands in the Barents Sea north of Norway. It comprises five main islands (Spitzbergen, Nordaustlandet, Edgeøya, Barentsøya and Prins Karl Forland), three fringing islands (Kvitøya, Konig Karls Land and Hopen) and many small islands; tiny Bjørnøya well to the south is included. *Area* 62,422 km^2 (24,101 sq miles); *administration centre* Longyearbyen. There is no permanent population, but about 1000 Norwegians and 2000 to 3000 Soviets mine coal, currently at five centres.

Svalbard was noted on maps from the late 16th century, though was probably known to earlier voyagers. Largely ice-capped, and difficult to approach because of floating ice, it was visited only by whalers, sealers and trappers (the Dutch shore-base, Smeerenberg, dating from the 17th century, is currently being investigated) and later by explorers. Mining began in 1904. The sovereignty of the islands was finally settled in 1920 with an international treaty granting Norway possession, and eight other countries equal mineral rights – the ninth country, the USSR, signed in 1925. Other minerals are present apart from coal, including oil and natural gas. There are good harbours, and an airfield within reach of Norway and the USSR. Isolated Bjørnøya, 220 km (137 miles) to the south, is the site of a weather station.

Jan Mayen
Jan Mayen lies 550 km (344 miles) north of Iceland and 500 km (312 miles) east of Greenland – a narrow volcanic island 55 km (34 miles) long, with a single ice-capped mountain rising to 2277 m (7470 ft). Uninhabited except for weathermen and visiting scientists, it is surrounded by rich fishing banks and is an important breeding area for harp seals. It has been a Norwegian possession since 1929.

Sweden

The Country
The Kingdom of Sweden occupies the eastern flank of the Scandinavian peninsula, bordered by Norway in the west and Finland in the northeast; approximately half its border is coastline, extending from the Baltic Sea into the Skagerrak. *Area* 449,964 km^2 (173,731 sq miles); *capital* Stockholm; *population* 8,258,000 (est. 1986).

Organization
A constitutional monarchy, Sweden has a unicameral parliament (Riksdag) of 349 members, elected for three-year terms. The Prime Minister leads a cabinet of about twenty ministers. The Sovereign, though Head of State, has little power or responsibility. Administratively Sweden is divided into 24 counties, each with a governor and elected administrative board. Local government is vested in over 270 municipalities, each with an elected council. The official language is Swedish; Finns and Sami (Lapps) in the north speak their own languages. The established religion is Lutheran Christianity.

Geography
Extending well beyond the Arctic Circle, Sweden is long and narrow, with a low-lying, shelving coast of some 1600 km (1000 miles) forming the Baltic shore; from this the country rises gently at first, then more steeply, to the ridge of ancient mountains that forms the frontier with Norway. Many parallel rivers drain long, upland lakes into the Baltic, and a chain of lakes extends westwards across the country in the latitude of Stockholm, formerly connecting the Baltic with the Skagerrak. South of these lakes the land is low-lying, and covered with glacial drift. Southern Sweden is open to maritime influences which give a relatively mild climate; the centre and north are more open to continental influences. About three quarters of Sweden is covered by coniferous forests; in the mountains and northern lowlands treeless fells with peat-bogs and moss are common, and snow persists for much of the year.

History and Development
Sweden's original inhabitants, the Svear, were warrior tribes who fought their Scandinavian neighbours and extended southeastward over Russia. Playing a dominant role in the Kalmar Union which united Norway, Denmark and Sweden in 1397, the Swedes eventually broke free to form their own kingdom under Gustav I in the early 16th century, further extending their influence over the whole Baltic area during the 16th and 17th centuries. Although Swedish power was broken by wars in the early 18th century, the country continued to develop socially and politically. During the 19th century it remained rural and exported manpower heavily to the USA and other countries of opportunity. From the early 20th century it began to develop as an industrial power. Neutrality during World Wars I and II helped its progress, and Sweden now leads the industrial nations in prosperity, social welfare and labour relations, matching Switzerland in its standard of living.

Resources and Economics
Agriculture, fisheries and forestry, former mainstays of Swedish wealth, now occupy only about 5 per cent of the working population and contribute

33

marginally to the national income. Wheat, oats and other cereals are grown mainly in the south. Forests provide timber, paper, cellulose and other products. Minerals include iron ore, extensively mined in the Arctic and in the south, and exported worldwide; copper, lead, zinc and aluminium ores are also exploited. Fuels are scarce but hydroelectricity provides over half the country's present energy needs. Industrial manufacture includes iron and steel, fine and heavy industrial machinery, building materials, textiles, clothing, chemicals, processed food, automobiles and ships. Well-designed household cutlery, glassware, clothing, furniture and other consumer goods are a feature of Swedish industrial production. Rail, road and air links are excellent throughout the country, and there is a luxury tourist industry.

Recent Developments
Following a prolonged spell of almost uninterrupted growth during the 1960s and 1970s, Sweden currently feels the pinch of world recession. However, the workforce has an enviable level of employment and maintains high living standards, the currency remains stable, inflation remains low and social welfare benefits are unequalled elsewhere. Coalition governments maintain political stability, although the recession led to strikes in 1980 and the breakdown of methods of industrial pay negotiations which had preserved industrial peace for almost half a century.

EUROPE CENTRAL

Austria

The Country
The Republic of Austria is land-locked and bordered by Switzerland, Liechtenstein, West Germany, Czechoslovakia, Hungary, Yugoslavia and Italy. *Area* 83,849 km^2 (32,374 sq miles); *capital* Vienna; *population* 7,448,000 (est. 1986).

Organization
Austria is a federal state: the National Assembly (Bundesversammlung) is made up of a Bundesrat of 63 members (elected for varying terms), representing the nine provinces, and a Nationalrat of 120 members directly elected for four-year terms. The Federal President, elected for six-year terms, acts on the advice of the Federal Chancellor and Council of Ministers. Each province has its own assembly; local government is vested in 98 districts. German is the national language, Roman Catholicism the majority religion: there is a Slovene minority in the area bordering Yugoslavia, and a Croat minority in Burgenland bordering Hungary.

Geography
Two thirds of Austria lies in the eastern Alps, which run in west–east ranges from the Swiss border to the edge of the Hungarian plain; the highest point is Grossglockner 3797 m (12,458 ft). The lowlands north of the Alps, focused on the Danube, accommodate over 60 per cent of the country's population. Northern Austria overlaps onto the southern fringes of the Bohemian Massif.

The lowlands and the larger alpine valleys provide good agricultural land. The alpine valley slopes are covered by coniferous forests, giving place upwards to alpine meadows and then to rocky peaks and glaciers.

History and Development

A cockpit of warring tribes, Austria has been occupied in turn by Celts, Romans, and after AD 100 by Germanic Alemans, Bavarians and Avars. Founded by Charlemagne as the eastern extension of his empire, Austria with European assistance expelled the Magyar invaders after 955, and the Turks in 1529 and 1683. Austria became an important province of the Habsburg Empire, ultimately attaining the central position under its first Emperor Francis and powerful minister Clemens von Metternich in the early 19th century. Vienna became the capital of the Austro–Hungarian Empire, which collapsed in 1918, leaving Austria a small, land-locked republic of 6.5 million people. Economic problems during the 1920s frustrated the development of democracy and led Austria into economic dependence on Germany; in 1938 Austrian-born Adolf Hitler forced the Anschluss, the union of Austria with the German Reich. After World War II Austria was divided between Soviet and US occupation forces, regaining its sovereignty with the Austrian State Treaty of 1955. Austria is pledged to neutrality.

Resources and Economics

Only about 10 per cent of the employed population is still engaged in agriculture and forestry. Arable production (wheat, barley, maize, potatoes, sugar-beet), and also cattle-fattening are concentrated in the lowlands and major Alpine valleys. Wine and fruit production is important around Vienna and elsewhere. Cattle-breeding and milk production are characteristic of the Alps. Forests cover 43 per cent of the country.

Since World War II Austria has been an industrial country, with 40 per cent of all employment in this area. Iron and steel industries, based on rich local ores and imported coal, provide stock for engineering and metal-working industries. There are important deposits of brown coal, also of magnesite, non-ferrous metals, graphite and salt. Water-power is the major source of electricity and there is some oil and gas. About half of Austrian employment is in the tertiary sector; tourism is of particular importance. Tourism and industry alike benefit from a well-developed road, rail and river transport system.

Recent Developments

With one of Europe's highest GNPs and lowest rates of inflation, Austria enjoys unprecedented prosperity. Since 1975 the death rate has exceeded the birth rate, and large numbers of migrant workers have been introduced, mainly from poorer countries to the south, to maintain the Austrian workforce.

Czechoslovakia

The Country

The Socialist Republic of Czechoslovakia is a land-locked state, bordered by East and West Germany, Austria, Hungary, Poland and the USSR. *Area* 127,869 km^2 (49,370 sq miles); *capital* Prague; *population* 15,808,000 (est. 1986).

Organization

Czechoslovakia is a federation of the Czech and Slovak Socialist Republics. Formal political structure involves a Federal Assembly composed of a Chamber of the People (136 Czech, 64 Slovak members) and a Chamber of Nations (75 members from each Republic). The Assembly elects the President for five-year terms; the President appoints ministers. Each Republic is responsible for its own internal affairs; foreign policy, defence and major economic decisions fall to the federal government. Actual political power is exercised by the Communist Party of Czechoslovakia headed by its General Secretary, whose branches parallel the political, economic and social structure of the state at every level. About 70 per cent of the population is Roman Catholic and about 15 per cent Protestant. Czech and Slovak are the chief languages; there are Hungarian and German minorities.

Geography

The Czech lands of the west centre on the Prague Basin, which is drained by the Vltava River, a tributary of the Elbe. They lie within the Bohemian Massif, its mountain fringes rising in the southwest to over 1300 m (4200 ft). Moravia, which lies to the east, drains via the Morava River to the Danube. Bratislava, the Slovak capital, lies at the confluence of the Morava and Danube, only 80 km (50 miles) west of Vienna. Slovakia is bounded in the north by the alpine Beskid Mountains and crossed centrally by the Tatra Mountains, which rise to over 2600 m (8500 ft). To the south, the lower Slovakian Ore Mountains drop away to the Hungarian plain.

The climate is continental, with warm, humid summers and cold, dry winters. There are extensive beech forests in Slovakia, and mixed forests of oak, spruce and pine in Bohemia and Moravia. In the remoter forests of the Slovak mountains bears and wild boar are still found.

History and Development

Czechoslovakia came into existence as a modern state in 1918, formed from the union of Czech lands previously held under Austrian rule, and of Slovakia which had belonged to Hungary. Alone among the states created by the Treaty of Versailles from the ruins of the Austro–Hungarian Empire, Czechoslovakia maintained a strong system of parliamentary democracy during its formative years. Allegations about the ill-treatment of the large German-speaking minority in the Sudetenland along the German border during the 1930s were used by Nazi Germany as an excuse to occupy the area in 1938. In 1939 the rest of the country was dismembered under German supervision, the Czech lands being directly occupied, Slovakia becoming a puppet state, and border areas being occupied by Hungary and Poland.

After World War II Czechoslovakia was reconstituted, except that sub-Carpathian Ukraine was appropriated by the USSR. Most remaining Germans were expelled. A Western-type democracy was briefly established, but the attempt to bridge East and West came to an end with a communist coup in 1948. Since then Czechoslovakia has remained firmly communist; an attempt in 1968 to liberalize the regime and establish 'communism with a human face' was crushed by an invasion of Warsaw-Pact troops.

Resources and Economics

Czechoslovakia has a centrally-planned socialist economy. One of the more industrialized of the East European COMECON countries after World War II, economic growth has been held back by the loss of skilled German labour after 1945, by the need to finance the industrial development of rural Slovakia, and by political tensions. There is good coking and steam coal, especially from the Ostrava field, while brown coal is much used in power generation and chemical production. Oil- and gas-refineries near Bratislava are fed by pipeline from the USSR. Metallic ores include iron and lead, but are inadequate for national needs. Glass sands, pottery clays and graphite are also worked. Steel production is mainly located on the Ostrava field, but the east Slovakian works at Košice, based mainly on Soviet iron ore, typifies the attempt to industrialize this formerly rural region. The old-established Czech engineering industries have been greatly extended in range and geographical location, producing heavy machinery, machine tools, armaments, electrical equipment, cars, commercial motor vehicles and motor cycles. There is a wide range of chemical industries, as well as the traditional textile, footwear, pottery, glass and wood-product industries.

About one seventh of the workforce is still employed in agriculture. 90 per cent of the agricultural land is in cooperative (collective) or state farms. The main crops are wheat, barley, sugar-beet, hops and potatoes. Agriculturally-based industries include brewing (Pilsner beer, for example), woollen textiles, shoe-making and food-processing. Over a third of the country is forested. Czechoslovakia's shape, position and history have militated against the creation of a unified transport system. Electrification has been undertaken on the main 'Friendship' spine rail route (East Germany–Prague–Košice–USSR), and progress made on an East Germany–Prague–Bratislava motorway. The Vltava–Elbe and Danube waterways carry significant traffic. For exporting its produce Czechoslovakia has sought transit rights across neighbouring territories; facilities have been granted at Hamburg, Szczecin and Trieste. There is considerable potential for tourism, but recent political problems have placed restrictions on visitors and internal travel.

Recent Developments
Since 1968, Czechoslovakia has been tightly controlled by the regime of President Husák. The 'Charter 77' movement of intellectual dissent continues to embarrass the government, echoing the dissent in neighbouring Poland. The Polish troubles of 1981 led to a tightening of the regime in Czechoslovakia and affected the economy adversely. The effective welding-together of the Czech and Slovak lands still remains an economic and political problem. In foreign policy Czechoslovakia closely follows Soviet lines. Its technicians are prominent in schemes of technical assistance for pro-Soviet, Third World countries.

East Germany

The Country
The German Democratic Republic (East Germany) is bounded in the north by the Baltic Sea, to the west by West Germany and to south and east by Czechoslovakia and Poland. *Area* 108,178 km² (41,767 sq miles); *capital* East Berlin; *population* 16,885,000 (est. 1986).

Organization
A single-chamber parliament of 500 members, the Volkskammer, is elected for

five-year terms from a list of candidates provided by the communist-led National Front. From the Volkskammer are elected a 26-member Staatsrat (Council of State) with collective presidential functions, and an executive Ministerrat (Council of Ministers). Effective political control is exercised by the Socialist Unity Party, its leading Politburo headed by the First Secretary of the Party, the most powerful political office in the state. Local authority is vested in fifteen districts (Bezirke), closely controlled by the central government and the Party. Some residual restrictions relating to the four-power Allied occupation rights still apply to East Berlin. The national language is German; a small minority of Sorbs (Wends) speak a Slavonic language. About 38 per cent of the population is registered as Protestant, and 4 per cent as Roman Catholic.

Geography

East Germany lies between a line linking the River Elbe with the Harz Mountains and Thuringian Forest in the west, and the Oder and Neisse rivers in the east. Behind the dunes and lagoons of the 250-km (156-mile) Baltic coast, fertile boulder-clay lowlands with beech woods give place southwards to the pine-clad glacial outwash sands of Brandenburg, the district around Berlin. The main arable belt, frequently based on loess soils, is in Thuringia and Saxony, fringed west and south by the spruce and fir woodlands of the Harz Mountains, Thuringia Forest and Erzgebirge (maximum elevations a little over 1000 m (3300 ft). About 40 per cent of the country is forested. The climate is continental, tempered by maritime influences from the west.

History and Development

The territory that is now East Germany was formerly occupied by a number of German states, including Mecklenburg, Thuringia, Saxony and, principally, the central provinces of Prussia. The Prussian capital, Berlin, was capital of Germany from 1871 to 1945. The current boundaries of East Germany were determined after World War II. Following the creation of West Germany (the Federal German Republic) in the west, the Soviet-occupied sector of Germany was proclaimed the German Democratic Republic in 1949. It attained full sovereignty in 1954 and has since been given de facto diplomatic recognition by most Western countries. The presence of West Berlin, a Western enclave in the heart of East Germany, is a constant source of irritation. Following rigorous socialization, over 2.5 million workers escaped from the new state between 1948 and 1960, many of them through Berlin; the building of the notorious Berlin Wall in 1961 almost completely stemmed the flood. Total population declined from 19 million in 1947 to 16.7 million in 1979; with the loss of many young people the age structure became distorted and is only slowly recovering.

Resources and Economics

East Germany has a Soviet-style, centrally-planned socialist economy. The southern part of the country was considerably industrialized before 1945, while Berlin was Germany's largest single industrial city. The creation of state and cooperative (collective) farms, together with the industrialization of the formerly rural north and east, have resulted in the reduction of the proportion of the workforce engaged in agriculture and forestry to 10 per cent. Raw-material resources are few except for extensive deposits of potash and brown coal (lignite), the basis of the country's electricity supply. The expanded chemical industry now relies heavily on imported oil. The industrial significance of East Germany, especially with regard to the other COMECON countries, lies in its ability to manufacture advanced industrial equipment of all kinds: machine tools, control and measuring equipment, electrical equipment, electric locomotives, electronic and optical equipment. Other industries include chemicals, fibres, shipbuilding, motor vehicles, industrial and domestic ceramics, textiles and food products.

There is an excellent system of inland waterways, linking the Elbe and Oder, but the dense rail network and the road system are in need of modernization. New motorway (Autobahn) links have been made to the main port of Rostock and to Hamburg, through which much of East Germany's trade still passes.

Recent Developments
A loyal supporter of Soviet foreign policies, East Germany forms a bulwark between East and West, taking a strong line, for example, against dissident movements in Poland and Czechoslovakia. Relations with West Germany are difficult and fluctuating, compounded by East Germany's insistence on being regarded as a fully independent state, by its dependence on credit and trade privileges given by West Germany, and by the desire of the latter to maximize links between the people of the two German states. East German efforts to increase trade with Western countries in order to pay for essential imports of oil and raw materials have had some success, but the international depression that began in the 1970s caused severe economic difficulties. The regime has internal difficulties with Church leaders, intellectuals and young people, many of whom support general nuclear disarmament and seek greater freedom of action.

Hungary

The Country
The Hungarian People's Republic is a land-locked state bordered by Yugoslavia, Austria, Czechoslovakia, the USSR and Romania. *Area* 93,030 km^2 (35,919 sq miles); *capital* Budapest; *population* 10,890,000 (est. 1986).

Organization
Hungary has a single-chamber National Assembly of 352 members, elected for five-year terms, and a 21-member Presidential Council, chaired by the President. Actual political power is exercised by the Hungarian Socialist Workers' Party, led by the First Secretary of its Cultural Committee. Local government is vested in nineteen counties and five county boroughs, all with local executive councils. The national language is Magyar, spoken by about 90 per cent of the population; there are Serb, Romanian and Slovak minorities. About four million Hungarians are Roman Catholic; all churches have equal status.

Geography
Hungary lies within the drainage basin of the Danube, which enters the country near Bratislava and forms the border with Czechoslovakia for 200 km (125 miles) before turning south. Its principal tributary, the Tisza, follows a parallel course some 100 km (60 miles) to the east. The plain of Hungary is divided by a line of hills, the Bakony Forest, which run in a southwesterly direction from the bend in the Danube near Budapest; to the northwest lies the Little Plain (Kisa föld) and to the southeast the Great Plain (Nagya föld), which occupies the rest

of the country. The highest hills, in the northeast, reach a little over 1000 m (3300 ft). Lake Balaton, 72 km (45 miles) long, lies below the southern slopes of the Bakony Forest. Loess-covered, the plains of Hungary include some of Europe's most fertile soils; there are also infertile areas of marsh and sand dunes. Excluded from maritime influences, Hungary has an extreme continental climate with severe winters and hot summers; rainfall is generally sparse (less than 620 mm (25 in) annually), and most falls in summer. Natural vegetation of the lowlands is steppe grassland and heath, and mixed deciduous forest grows on high ground in the northwest.

History and Development
Emerging as a kingdom in medieval times, Hungary became linked with Austria through the Habsburg dynasty from the 16th century onward. After World War I it became an independent state; civil war and brief communist rule were followed by a long spell of right-wing authoritarian government under Regent Horthy de Nagybanya. Siding with Germany in World War II, Hungary was occupied by Soviet forces; in 1946 the National Assembly declared a republic and in 1949 Hungary became a People's Republic under the communist Hungarian Working People's Party. Discontent under a severe regime led to a revolt which restored to power Imre Nagy, who represented a liberal trend within the communist party. Intervention by Soviet troops led to Nagy's overthrow in 1956 and the installation of János Kádár. Kádár was successful in reconciling rival groups within the party, and promoting reforms which greatly improved living standards. Birth rate and death rate in Hungary are similar, and the population is increasing only very slightly.

Resources and Economics
Hungary is an important producer of food, growing and exporting wheat, maize, fruits and wines; 20 per cent of the working population is engaged in farming, mostly on collective farms. Large cooperatives produce abundant fruit and vegetables in the Budapest area, and the drier plains of Hortobágy in the northeast support extensive cattle-ranching. In many areas irrigation is necessary.

Hungary has coal, and limited oil and gas, insufficient to support its industries; petroleum products are imported by pipeline from the USSR. There are significant resources of copper and manganese; iron ore is supplemented by imports from the USSR to support a steel-making industry; bauxite is plentiful for alumina production. Manufacturing includes rolled steel, machine tools, textiles, vehicles, mining equipment, petrochemicals and large river craft. Heavily dependent on foreign trade, Hungary has growing markets in the West, especially in West Germany. Tourism, which earns substantial foreign currency, is based on historic cities, and on the natural beauty of the countryside – especially the resort areas surrounding Lake Balaton.

Recent Developments
One of the main preoccupations of the Hungarian government in the early 1980s has been to promote economic efficiency, including the imposition of austerity measures; another concern is to avoid the ferment in Poland with its threat of increasing industrial democracy. Concessions to private enterprise, especially in rural areas, have enabled some wine-growers and merchants to achieve moderate wealth. Dissident intellectuals in Budapest are carefully controlled by the authorities, though political trials are currently rare.

Liechtenstein

The Country
The Principality of Liechtenstein, only 24 km (15 miles) long and a little over 8 km (5 miles) wide, stands in the Rhine and Samina valleys of the western Alps, bounded by Austria and Switzerland. *Area* 157 km^2 (61 sq miles); *capital* Vaduz; *population* 27,000 (est. 1986).

Organization
A democratic principality, Liechtenstein is governed jointly by the Prince, who is Head of State, and an elected 15-member parliament (Landtag); the Prince appoints a government of five on the Landtag's recommendations. The country is divided into eleven local communes, six in the industrial southern Triesenberg (Upper Country), five in the northern Eschnerberg (Lower Country). The people are of mixed Germanic and Swiss origin, speaking dialects of German: over 90 per cent is Roman Catholic.

Geography
From the Rhine which forms its western boundary, Liechtenstein extends over a broad flood plain at about 450 m (1500 ft), an intermediate-level plateau containing the capital and most of the population, and the Alps which rise to over 2500 m (8200 ft) at the Austro–Swiss borders. Summers are warm, winters cold and snow-ridden for several months. The mountains are extensively forested with alpine meadows above; the plains, once marshy, are now drained and cultivated.

History and Development
Liechtenstein was settled by Germanic and later by Swiss pastoralists whose descendants still inhabit different areas and speak distinct dialects. Independent since 1719, the principality has avoided being drawn into either of its neighbouring countries. Most links are with Switzerland, whose currency and customs union it shares and whose embassies represent its diplomatic interests. Its economy is heavily dependent on immigrant workers.

Resources and Economics
Only a few per cent of the small workforce is now employed in farming; most are involved in construction and light industry, manufacturing textiles, chemicals, paints, scientific instruments, ceramics, artificial teeth and a range of other small commodities from imported materials. International banking and finance (attracted by the favourable tax structure and legal system), the sale of postage stamps and a flourishing tourist industry bring in overseas revenue. There are good internal and external road and rail links.

Recent Developments
With few assets apart from its natural beauty, business acumen and long-preserved independence, Liechtenstein has in forty years graduated from a peasant economy to a prosperous, modern, outward-looking society.

Poland

The Country
The Polish People's Republic lies on the Baltic Sea, bordered by East Germany, Czechoslovakia and the USSR. Its coastline extends some 400 km (250 miles) from the German to the Soviet border. *Area* 312,677 km^2 (120,725 sq miles); *capital* Warsaw; *population* 37,869,000 (est. 1986).

Organization
Poland's constitution defines it as a socialist state. Its formal political structure consists of a single-chamber parliament of 460 members (the Sejm), elected for four years from an approved list of candidates submitted by the National Unity Front. Each of the 49 provinces has a People's Council whose members are elected for four years. The Sejm elects a 16-member Council of State with the functions of a collective presidency. Effective power lies in the Politburo of the Polish United Workers' Party. Over 90 per cent of the population belongs to the Roman Catholic Church which, exceptionally among communist countries, has freedom of teaching and worship, and great political influence. There are Ukrainian, Belorussian, Slovak, Lithuanian, German and Jewish minorities; Polish is the universally spoken language.

Geography
South of the sandspits and lagoons of the long Baltic coast, the plains of northern and central Poland have a chaotic surface of moraines, lakes, outwash sands and former river valleys, a legacy from the Ice Age. The southern lowland has stretches of fertile loess soil as well as escarpments and hills of older rocks containing valuable minerals. Poland extends southwest to the foothills of the Sudeten Highlands and southeast to the Carpathian Mountains, which reach 2499 m (8199 ft) in the Tatra. Most of Poland drains to the Baltic, in the east by the Vistula system, entering the sea at Gdańsk, and in the west by the Oder system, which enters a wide estuary at Szczecin.

Most of the country has a severe continental climate, with hard winters (mean January temperatures below freezing point) and hot summers; most of the rain falls in summer, though annual totals of precipitation are low (below 650 mm, 26 in). Coniferous woodlands and heath are typical of the sandy northern plains; deciduous forests alternate with intense cultivation in the richer south. About 65 per cent of Poland's total area is farmed.

History and Development
The first Polish state was founded over one thousand years ago when the Poles emerged as the most powerful of several Slavic groups; the Christian Kingdom of Poland dates from 1025. Combining with neighbouring Lithuania, the Poles spread their influence to the Black Sea during the 14th to 16th centuries, but were subsequently weakened by wars with Sweden, Russia and Turkey. Poland disappeared completely into neighbouring states in 1795 but was resurrected under the Congress of Vienna in 1815. It finally emerged as a modern state in 1918, after 150 years of occupation by Austria–Hungary, Russia and Prussia. An authoritarian regime ruled until the German invasion of 1939 when Poland was again partitioned, this time between Germany and the USSR. Subsequently under complete German control, the country lost some six million of its population, including most of its three million Jews. After World War II Poland

lost territory in the east but was compensated with German territory in the west, including the ports of Danzig (Gdańsk) and Stettin (Szczecin).

In 1944 a People's Democracy was set up under Soviet influence and by 1947 communist control of the government was complete. A workers' revolt in 1956 brought to power W. Gomulka, a popular leader who had been ousted in 1948; but Gomulka resigned after bread riots in 1970. Further discontent led in 1980 to the virtual disintegration of the Communist Party and the recognition of the workers' right to an independent trade union ('Solidarity'), which supplanted the subservient communist-dominated trade unions. To avoid direct Soviet intervention the army took over the machinery of the state in 1981. Martial law was declared on 13 December 1981, and although it was lifted in July 1983, severe restrictions on individual freedom remained in force.

Resources and Economics
About 30 per cent of employment is in agriculture, with a third of the land in state or collective farms, and two thirds in private hands. Output, which should allow for export of bacon, eggs, pork, turkeys and geese, does not match potential. Poland is a major coal producer (over 200 million tonnes per annum) and there are also important deposits of lead, zinc, copper, sulphur, potash, salt and natural gas. Heavy industry, including chemicals partly dependent on Soviet oil, is concentrated in Upper Silesia with a postwar extension near Kraków. Lower Silesia (including Wroclaw) has varied machine-building and electrical equipment industries, as does Lódź, the traditional textile centre, and Warsaw (also special steel, food and vehicle industries). About a quarter of the rail network is electrified, and coastal shipping and inland waterway transport have been modernized. Although over a third of Poland's foreign trade is with the USSR, there is also a developing trade with Western countries, especially West Germany. There are attractive holiday resorts in the Tatra Mountains and the Masurian Lakes, but recent political unrest has dealt tourism a severe blow.

Recent Developments
The political, economic and social position of Poland is particularly difficult given its necessary strategic subservience to the USSR and its strong cultural links with the West, particularly by way of the Catholic Church. Loans from Western sources assisted the achievement of economic growth rates of the order of 10 per cent a year in the mid-1970s, but internal political difficulties reduced growth to zero by 1980.

Romania

The Country
The Socialist Republic of Romania is bordered by Yugoslavia, Hungary, the USSR and Bulgaria, and has a short coastline on the Black Sea. *Area* 237,500 km^2 (91,699 sq miles); *capital* Bucharest; *population* 23,322,000 (est. 1986).

Organization
A Grand National Assembly of 369 members is elected for five-year terms; the Assembly elects a President, a 25-member State Council with legislative authority, and a Council of Ministers. Local authority rests with the People's Councils of 40 districts and over 2700 local authorities. Actual political power is

exercised by the Romanian Communist Party, whose General Secretary is also President. Party branches parallel the political, economic and social structure of the state at every level. The official language is Romanian; Hungarian and German are also spoken locally by substantial minority groups. The Romanian Orthodox Church claims the allegiance of over half the population; several other Churches are recognized by the government.

Geography
Relief is dominated by the great southeast-pointing arc of the Carpathians, rising to a little over 2500 m (8000 ft). The Carpathians enclose the hills and lowlands of the Transylvanian Basin to the northwest. The lowland of Moldavia lies to the east, that of Wallachia to the south. The Danube breaks through the mountain chain at the Iron Gates and forms much of the southern frontier until near Silistra it suddenly turns north for almost 200 km (320 miles) before entering the Black Sea through its complex delta below Galati. Between the north-flowing Danube and the splendid Black Sea beaches is the low plateau of the Dobrogea. The climate is continental, with only a narrow coastal zone tempered by the Black Sea. Rainfall is highest in the mountains, with annual totals exceeding 700 mm (28 in), and much lower (400 mm, 15.7 in) at the coast. Vegetation ranges from alpine pastures and dense mixed forests in the mountains to steppe and marshes in the lowlands.

History and Development
Romania acquired its Latin-based language from the Romans, who occupied it briefly in the 2nd century. Goths, Huns, Bulgars, Magyars and Mongols invaded successively, and from the 15th to the early 19th century the lowland areas of Moldavia and Wallachia formed part of the Ottoman Empire, while the uplands came under Hungarian rule. Passing into Russian hands after the Russo–Turkish War (1828–29), the lowland provinces were united under a single prince in 1859, and the state of Rumania was formed in 1862. In 1878 it gained full independence and three years later became a monarchy. Transylvania was added after World War I, together with Bukovina, Bessarabia and the Banat, but the country remained unstable, coming under a royal dictatorship in 1938. Siding with the Germans and Italians during World War II, it was invaded in 1944 by Soviet forces, which appropriated Bessarabia and Bukovina. In 1947 Romania (as it was renamed) became a communist state, but increasingly developed along distinctive national lines, differing markedly from its neighbours on strategic matters and on trade and other relationships with the West.

Resources and Economics
Internally Romania still has a Soviet-style, centrally-planned socialist economy. Agriculture and forestry are important industries, occupying some 30 per cent of the workforce. Lowland Romania is one of the major grain-growing areas of Europe, with rye, maize and wheat the chief crops. Sunflowers provide shelter-belts and edible oil. Sugar-beet and potatoes are important crops, and the vineyards of the south-facing hills provide large quantities of wine for export. Official policy is to process important raw materials rather than to export them to other COMECON countries. Although the largest East European oil producer, supplementary imports support refining and petrochemical industries; there are major natural gas resources. Iron ore production also has to be supplemented, notably by imports to the new Galati

steel plant on the Danube; there are important resources of coal, brown coal, copper, lead, zinc, bauxite, salt and even some gold and silver. In the post-war period the machine-building, vehicle, chemical and food industries have been vigorously expanded. Most electricity is thermally generated from natural gas or brown coal; development of the considerable hydroelectric potential includes the Iron Gates scheme, in cooperation with Yugoslavia. The Danube is navigable for smaller sea-going ships throughout Romania and a new canal is being cut through the delta. Tourism brings in valuable foreign exchange, and has great potential.

Recent Developments

Economic development, which was rapid during the 1960s and 1970s, has slowed considerably; the current five-year plan (1981–85) is failing to reach its relatively modest growth targets in the face of worldwide recession. A substantial debt to international financiers, and the need to buy oil and capital goods, has resulted in a serious imbalance of the country's budget; IMF help over a three-year period (1981–83) has involved cutbacks in domestic consumption and living standards – even local food shortages – which may well continue several years longer. President Ceauşescu retains a firm hold of government, taking a stern line against dissident workers and intellectuals alike.

Switzerland

The Country

The Swiss Confederation is a land-locked republic bordered by France, West Germany, Liechtenstein, Austria and Italy. *Area* 41,288 km² (15,941 sq miles); *capital* Bern, *largest city* Zürich; *population* 6,490,000 (est. 1986).

Organization

The twenty Swiss cantons and six half-cantons are sovereign and independent units, except where the Swiss constitution allocates power to the Federal level, for example in diplomatic relations and defence. The Federal Assembly consists of a 46-member Council of State (Ständerat), representing the cantons and half-cantons, and a National Council (Nationalrat) of 200 members elected directly by proportional representation for four-year terms. A Federal Council (Bundesrat) of seven members holds executive responsibility; its President is elected annually. Each canton and half-canton has its own elected parliament (Kantonsrat). A unique feature of Switzerland is its direct democracy: constitutional amendments must be submitted to a popular referendum, and also new laws and treaties if requested by a defined number of electors. These arrangements are repeated at cantonal and communal (local) level. There are four national languages; German (64%), French (18%), Italian (12%) and Romansch (0.4%). Religious allegiance is equally divided between Roman Catholicism and Protestantism.

Geography

The western Alps in the south and east occupy 60 per cent of the country: the highest peak is Monte Rosa (4634 m, 15,204 ft). Many ranges are permanently snow-covered; glaciers and lakes add to the natural beauty. Between the western Alps and the lower Jura Mountains along the French frontier lies the Mittelland

Plateau where most of the population is concentrated. Much of Switzerland lies in the Rhine Basin, its tributaries providing access to the alpine passes. The climate is continental, but highly dependent on relief. Summers are warm in the valleys, winters are cold and bracing, and rain or snow are plentiful throughout the year. Land-use closely follows relief: the valleys are cultivated or under pasture, the mountain slopes are forested with alpine pastures above the forest.

History and Development

The Swiss Confederation began in 1291 when three cantons – Uri, Schwyz and Unterwalden – formed a defensive league, following a long history of encroachment by neighbouring communities. More cantons joined the league, which defended itself successfully against the Habsburgs in the 14th century and achieved virtual statehood in 1499. Under Napoleonic influence a United Helvetic Republic was formed in 1798, but federal structure was regained in 1803, and in 1815 the Congress of Vienna guaranteed the Confederation permanent neutrality. Switzerland's present constitution dates from 1874. The mountainous character of the country has favoured local rather than national cultural development; hence the highly-localized language groupings and the continuing autonomy of the cantons. The population is stable and prosperous, currently boosted by over half a million foreign workers.

Resources and Economics

About 7 per cent of the active population is still employed in agriculture, principally dairy-farming, stock-rearing and forestry, with vines particularly characteristic of the warmer southern cantons. Agriculture is supported by the state on strategic and social grounds, especially in mountain areas. These have also traditionally supported craft industries such as woodcarving and watchmaking (Jura), and have benefited from the growth of tourism. Switzerland is a centre of advanced industries, notably in the electrical equipment, machine-tool, chemical (especially pharmaceutical), aluminium, textile and food sectors. Typically, Swiss firms have important overseas subsidiaries. Switzerland also derives considerable income from its role as a major centre of international finance, banking and insurance; well over half the employed population is in the tertiary sector. Fuels, heavy machinery and raw materials are the major imports; most trading is with neighbouring EEC countries, particularly West Germany, and with Switzerland's EFTA associates.

Recent Developments

Despite its prosperity, Switzerland has in recent years suffered from serious social tensions. Referendums have been held on a number of controversial social and economic issues, including the imposition of import restrictions and the granting of foreign loans. Internationally, Switzerland maintains its neutral position; though not a member of the United Nations Organization, it houses the World Health Organization, the Economic Commission for Europe, the International Labour Organization and other UN agencies. It is also the home of the International Red Cross, World Wildlife Fund and many other bodies concerned with welfare and worldwide conservation.

West Germany

The Country
The Federal Republic of Germany (West Germany), which includes West Berlin, is bordered by Denmark, East Germany, Czechoslovakia, Austria, Switzerland, France, Luxembourg, Belgium and the Netherlands, with coastlines on the North and Baltic Seas. *Area* 248,577 km^2 (95,976 sq miles); *federal capital* Bonn, *largest city* West Berlin; *population* 59,992,000 (est. 1986).

Organization
West Germany is a democratic, federal state. Executive power is vested in the first instance in the ten constituent states (Länder) plus (with certain limitations) West Berlin. The Federal Parliament consists of a lower house (Bundestag) of 520 members elected for four-year terms by a version of proportional representation, and an upper house (Bundesrat) of 45 members nominated from provincial parliaments in proportion to population. Berlin representatives have limited voting rights. An electoral college from both houses selects the Federal President for a five-year term. The government is headed by the Federal Chancellor who reflects the ruling majority in the Bundestag and who nominates an executive cabinet. The constitution (Basic Law) is suspended in respect of Berlin, reflecting the city's residual four-power occupation status; Berlin effectively functions simultaneously as a Federal State and as a city under its own Burgomaster and Assembly. Local government organization varies from state to state but consists typically of a Kreis (county) level with the larger cities in parallel, plus a lower level of rural districts (Gemeinde). The national language is German; Protestantism and Roman Catholicism are almost equally represented.

Geography
The fertile marshes and boulder-clay plains fringing the 160-km (100-mile) North Sea coast and the 320-km (200-mile) Baltic coast give place southwards to the leached moraine and glacial outwash of the lowlands of Lower Saxony, with generally poor soils and many stretches of forest. South of this a belt of fertile loess soils gives way in turn to the extensive and geographically-varied Central Uplands, frequently consisting of dissected, forested plateaus mostly below 800 m (2600 ft), but rising to over 1000 m (3300 ft) in massifs such as the Harz Mountains or Black Forest. The Central Uplands also contain numerous fertile and sheltered basins and river valleys. Germany's southern boundary includes the northern fringe of the Alps, culminating in the 2968 m (9738 ft) Zugspitze. At the foot of the mountains are numerous lakes, and the broad lowland of the Alpine Foreland, its surface made up of Tertiary rocks and glacial outwash, which stretches north to the line of the Danube.

History and Development
Until well into the 19th century Germany was still merely a conglomeration of independent states, of which the largest and most powerful was Prussia. Under Otto von Bismarck's leadership, Prussia's defeat of Austria in 1866 determined that the non-Austrian states would be united under Prussian hegemony, a development sealed by the proclamation of Wilhelm I as German Emperor in 1871, following the Prussian victory over France. Heavy industry developed rapidly on the coalfields of Upper Silesia, Saar, Aachen and, above all, the Ruhr

district. Imported high-grade ores were supplemented by low-grade ore and pig-iron from annexed Alsace-Lorraine. Existing cities, notably Berlin, experienced explosive industrial and urban expansion. This period of development was halted by the outbreak of World War I in which Germany's defeat resulted in the loss of Alsace-Lorraine and an extensive overseas empire.

A post-war democratic republic (the Weimar Republic) collapsed during a period of acute poverty which, during the world depression of the late 1920s and early 1930s, engulfed the country in economic chaos and social ferment. In 1933 Hitler and the Nazi Party assumed power, and Germany's subsequent eastward expansion into Austria, Czechoslovakia and Poland led to World War II. Germany's second defeat, accompanied by severe devastation and a four-power occupation, resulted in lasting partition: West Germany was forged from the sectors occupied by French, US and British forces. The Federal Republic was declared in 1955, retaining its share of West Berlin as an enclave within East Germany (the German Democratic Republic). The population of West Germany increased during the 1960s and 1970s, initially due to a flood of refugees from the East, and later because of a need for immigrant workers to support its expanding economy.

Resources and Economics

Agriculture now occupies only about 6 per cent of the workforce; there are many uneconomically small farms, especially in the centre and south of the country. The Central Uplands are mostly devoted to mixed arable and livestock farming, with fruit and wine specializations along the valleys of the Rhine and its tributaries. Arable farming is concentrated on fertile soils along the northern fringe of the Central Uplands, milk production in the alpine foothills and coastal marshes. Timber is produced in the Central Uplands and alpine fringe. The Rhine system and many interlinking canals have been progressively improved for the transport of heavy goods: there are also efficient state railways and a motorway (Autobahn) network. Iron, steel and non-ferrous metals are now mainly processed from imported ores. Deep-mined coal and open-pit brown coal (lignite) are still important fuels, but the country depends heavily on imported oil and gas. Electricity generated from fossil fuels is supplemented by hydroelectric production, mostly from southern rivers, and by production from nuclear plants. The chemical industry is also very dependent on imported materials and energy. The country's economic strength depends heavily on its technically-advanced manufacturing industry, which produces motor vehicles, aircraft, machine tools, chemicals, electrical and electronic equipment, computers and varied consumer goods. Since World War II there has been a tendency for manufacturing to move away from traditional centres, notably southwards into Bavaria and Baden-Württemberg. Half of all employment is now in the tertiary sector.

Recent Developments

Although the economy of West Germany has suffered less from inflation and unemployment than that of most other West European countries, heavy dependence on imported oil put it very much at the mercy of rising oil prices during the 1970s. The steady rise in GNP that marked the post-war years of recovery slowed; inflation hovered about the 6 per cent mark and unemployment rose to about two million, more than 8 per cent of the workforce. Tensions between the main political parties hinge on remedies for economic stagnation and West Germany's role in NATO. However, the basic economy remains strong, and living standards are among the highest in Europe.

EUROPE SOUTHWEST

Andorra

The Country
The Principality of Andorra, roughly 24 km (15 miles) across, lies on the border between France and Spain towards the eastern end of the Pyrenees. *Area* 453 km² (175 sq miles); *capital* Andorra la Vella; *population* 36,000 (est. 1986).

Organization
Andorra is a co-principality, governed by a joint delegation of the French government and the Spanish Bishopric of Urgel (see below). Day-to-day administration rests with a 28-member Council General, composed of representatives of the six valley communes, which refers matters to the joint delegation. About one third of Andorrans are native born; the rest are immigrants, mostly from Spain. Roman Catholicism is the major religion. Catalan is the language of the country: French and Spanish are also spoken.

Geography
Lying between 1000 and 2900 m (3300 to 9500 ft), Andorra consists of valleys and mountain ridges converging onto a central valley – that of the Valira River. Summers are warm – usually dry and sunny after spring rainfall; winters are long and cold, with snow lying for several months in the valleys. Forests and alpine meadows cover the mountain slopes.

History and Development
Andorra's status as a co-principality dates back to 1278, when seigneural rights were shared between the French Comte de Foix and the Spanish Bishop of Urgel. French rights have passed to the French President, who delegates them to the neighbouring Prefect of the East Pyrenees; Spanish rights remain with the Bishopric, and both are represented on the permanent joint delegation. The system has helped to keep Andorra a quiet rural backwater, only recently stirred by tourism.

Resources and Economics
Mountain pastures support sheep and cattle, and tobacco, potatoes and cereals grow on the warm lower slopes. Timber, hydroelectricity and water are valuable resources, and Andorra makes full use of its scenic beauty for attracting tourists; winter sports are well catered for. Low personal taxes and duty-free goods are extra incentives for immigrants and visitors. Good year-round roads link Andorra with Spain and France: there are no railways or internal air links.

Recent Developments
Andorra's medieval attractions and willing hospitality ensure its success as a tourist centre. The medieval system of government is proving less adequate for 20th-century needs: Andorrans are concerned to modernize toward a more flexible and democratic system of self-government.

Gibraltar

The Country
Gibraltar, a limestone massif 5 km (3 miles) long and 1.2 km (0.75 miles) wide, forms the eastern flank of Algeciras Bay, off the southern Spanish coast. A British colony and garrison, it is linked to the mainland by a sandy isthmus 1.6 km (1 mile) long. *Area* 6.5 km² (2.5 sq miles); *population* 31,000 (est. 1986).

Organization
A self-governing Crown Colony, Gibraltar has a House of Assembly of eighteen members, fifteen elected, two *ex officio* and a Speaker. The governor (representing the British Crown) has executive authority, advised by a Council of nine ministers of whom five are elected members of the House of Assembly. Native Gibraltarians, of mixed British–Iberian and Mediterranean stock, outnumber transients by about nine to one. Three quarters of the residents are Roman Catholic, with Anglican, Jewish and Moslem minorities also present. English is the official language; both English and Spanish are spoken.

Geography
The Rock, predominantly limestone, shale and sand, rises to a north-south ridge over 400 m (1300 ft) high. It shelves steeply to east and south, where beaches line an indented shore; the gentler western slopes carry the main settlement. Summers are hot, winters mild and damp. The Rock is patchily covered with trees and shrubs, though little original vegetation remains.

History and Development
Gibraltar has been noted and occupied since Neolithic times; its Arabic name Jabal Tariq commemorates the Moorish leader who first conquered it in 711. Captured from the Moors in 1704 and assigned by treaty to Britain in 1713, it has remained a British garrison and colony ever since.

Resources and Economics
For centuries Gibraltar's main value has been its position commanding the Strait of Gibraltar: it has little capacity for agriculture, and barely enough water despite a huge man-made catchment on the ridge. Its western flank, extended by harbour installations and an airport runway, is covered by a small industrial town geared to handle, repair and provision both military and commercial shipping. Roads cross the border to Spain: growing tourist traffic arrives by sea and air, and daily ferries cross to North Africa.

Recent Developments
Spain's reiterated claim to Gibraltar is countered by the Gibraltarians' almost unanimous desire, expressed in a referendum of 1967, to remain British. Incommoded to 1985 by the closed frontier with Spain, the colony continues to prosper with help from Britain and the EEC: tourism is currently its most profitable field for economic expansion.

Portugal

The Country

The Republic of Portugal extends along the west and southwestern coasts of the Iberian peninsula, bordered in the north and east by Spain. The Atlantic islands of the Azores and Madeira are regarded administratively as districts of Portugal, though in many respects autonomous (see Atlantic Ocean Islands). *Area* 92,082 km^2 (35,552 sq miles); *capital* Lisbon; *population* 10,266,000 (est. 1986).

Organization

Portugal is a parliamentary democracy with a National Assembly of 250 members elected for four-year terms. A President, elected five-yearly, appoints the Prime Minister and other ministers. Most of the population are Roman Catholic. The national language is Portuguese.

Geography

Roughly rectangular, Portugal has a low-lying eastern coast, with broad plains that rise gradually towards Spain; the international boundary runs along the faulted edge of the Spanish Meseta, including rolling uplands within Portugal (mainly in the northern half of the country). The highest peaks, in central Serra da Estrêla, rise to almost 2000 m (6600 ft); part of an extensive system of folded mountains, they cross central Portugal in a southwesterly direction, reaching the sea at Cabo da Roca, Europe's most westerly point. Three major river systems drain eastward and south from the mountains – the Douro (with Oporto, Portugal's second city, at its mouth), the Tagus (with Lisbon on its estuary) and the Guadiana, which enters the Gulf of Cadiz. South of the Tagus the land is generally low-lying. The climate is mild, though with cold winters in the northern hills; the southern lowlands and Algarve coast are warm in winter and subtropical in summer, with drought in the hottest months. Cork oaks, pines and chestnuts cover the uplands, grading to scrub in the southwest.

History and Development

Portugal was inhabited originally by Celts from the north, who successively came under the domination of Roman, Germanic and Moorish overlords. Liberated from the Moors during the 12th and 13th centuries, Portugal became a Christian kingdom, finally achieving independence from Spanish domination in the late 14th century. During the 15th and 16th centuries Portuguese navigators sailed the world's oceans, establishing an empire in Africa, southeast Asia, India and South America. Again under Spanish rule from 1580 to 1640, Portugal recovered its independence but slowly declined as a world power; invaded by the French in 1807, it lost its richest colony, Brazil, in 1822 and thereafter became a minor power, impoverished and under weak monarchic government. Revolution in 1910 disposed of the monarchy but did little to alleviate the country's poverty. From 1932 Portugal began to develop economically under the dictatorship of Dr António de Oliveira Salazar, which continued until his enforced resignation in 1968. In 1974 a military coup ousted the authoritarian government and Portugal's first democratic elections were held in the following year. Since then the country has remained constitutionally stable, though with frequent changes of government. Emigration, both temporary and permanent, offsets the relatively high birth rate; the population is currently increasing by less than 1 per cent a year.

Resources and Economics
Portugal's economic development proceeded slowly under Salazar's *Estado Novo* regime, accelerating only after the 1974 coup when social and agrarian reforms took effect: the south is less developed than the north, both socially and industrially. About one third of the workforce is still engaged in agriculture and forestry, often using primitive methods of production; attempts to socialize and modernize farming have had mixed success. Major exports include textiles, timber, cork, canned fish, olive oil, fruit and wines. Grain and other basic foodstuffs are imported, especially during periods of drought when local production falls drastically. Industrial development is hampered by the need to import fuel and raw materials; costs have increased since Portugal lost its remaining colonies during the 1970s. However, chemical and engineering industries are expanding and the more long-established textile and food-processing industries are being modernized; hydroelectric supplies are improving, though still unreliable when the rains fail. Tourism is an important source of overseas income, matched by remittances from expatriate workers.

Recent Developments
Committed by its bloodless revolution to socialism, Portugal retains strong right-wing elements in power; the resulting tensions slow and sometimes reverse both social and economic development. Progress is, however, being made; the country has survived the loss of its colonies and markets, high inflation and unemployment, and other problems associated with rapid modernization. Still Europe's poorest community, it has a long way to go before it can match its economy to those of the EEC countries, which it expects to join on equal terms.

Spain

The Country
The Kingdom of Spain occupies 85 per cent of the Iberian peninsula, bordered in the west by Portugal, in the south by Gibraltar, and in the northeast by France and the small enclave of Andorra. Administratively it includes the Balearic Islands and a number of smaller Mediterranean isles, the Canary Islands (see Atlantic Ocean Islands), and several enclaves including the ports of Ceuta and Melilla on the Moroccan coast. *Area* 504,782 km^2 (194,896 sq miles); *capital* Madrid; *population* 39,313,000 (est. 1986).

Organization
Spain is a constitutional monarchy. Parliament consists of a 350-member Congress of Deputies, elected for four-year terms, and a Senate of 208 elected members, also on four-year terms. The Senate also includes some members elected by regional parliaments. The monarch as Head of State appoints the Prime Minister and Council of Ministers, and has the power to initiate referenda on matters of importance. Local authority is vested in fifty provinces. The national language is Castilian Spanish; Catalan, Andalusian and Galician Spanish and the unique Basque language are also spoken locally. Most Spaniards are Roman Catholic.

Geography
Spain's northern border runs along the Pyrenees, a high range of alpine fold

mountains with peaks rising over 3300 m (10,800 ft). Most of the country is a high, dissected plateau of ancient crystalline rocks (the Meseta), sloping westward toward Portugal. Four of its major rivers – the Guadalquivir, Guadiana, Tagus and Douro – and their extensive tributaries drain into the Atlantic Ocean; only the Ebro and a number of minor rivers drain into the Mediterranean. In the southeast rises a second range of fold mountains, the Sierra Nevada, which includes Mulhacen (3478 m, 11,411 ft), Spain's highest peak. Central Spain has a markedly continental climate with hot summers and cold winters. The northern coastlands of Galicia and Asturias, isolated by the Cantabrian Mountains, have a milder maritime climate, and the south and east coasts have the Mediterranean climate enjoyed by tourists from northern Europe. Vegetation reflects climate; much of the high Meseta is steppe, merging to mattoral (scrub) in the drier south, evergreen oak and pine forests along the warmer coasts, and deciduous forests of beech and oak in the northwest.

History and Development

Inhabited from earliest times, Spain was the home of Basques and Iberians who suffered invasion by Celts, Phoenicians, Greeks, Carthaginians and Romans. In 711 Berber Moors invaded from the south, extending gradually into all but the northern provinces. Just as gradually they were absorbed or driven out during the 13th and 14th centuries, leaving a rich legacy of buildings, craftsmanship and culture; Granada, the last Moorish stronghold, fell in 1492. In the same year Columbus discovered America during a voyage promoted by the Spanish monarchy, and in the following century Spain acquired enormous wealth from exploration and conquest in the Americas and Philippines. In Europe Spanish influence extended over Naples, Milan, France, Portugal and the Netherlands.

Throughout the 17th and 18th centuries Spain's powers declined; from 1808 to 1814 French forces occupied the Spanish homeland, and by 1825 most of the valuable colonies had gained their independence. Social unrest and civil wars continued through the 19th and early 20th centuries, reducing Spain to poverty. Revolution in 1931 deposed the monarchy, and a bloody civil war (1936–9), precipitated by military revolt, introduced a long term of right-wing dictatorship under General Francisco Franco. On Franco's death in 1975 the Bourbon prince Juan Carlos was made King. A democratic constitution was promulgated two years later, accompanied by liberalizing reforms; these have popular support, despite the attempts of right-wing elements to re-impose authoritarianism. Spain's economic development is to some degree hampered by its birth rate; the population continues to grow rapidly despite emigration.

Resources and Economics

Agriculture provides a livelihood for over 17 per cent of the population; grapes, wheat, olives and citrus fruits are the chief crops of the Mediterranean regions, and rice is grown in the wetter river valleys. The Meseta uplands support sheep, which migrate seasonally to the slopes of the Sierras; the richer pastures of the north support cattle. Sea fishing is an important industry on both Mediterranean and Atlantic coasts. Spain is rich in minerals, though lacking adequate coal or oil. The main industrial areas are in the north, especially Asturias and the Basque country, where copper, lead, zinc, iron, silver, mercury and potash are mined. A drive for further industrialization which started in the 1960s has resulted in more of these resources being used locally; American, German and Japanese capital is helping Spain to develop large-scale chemical, metal-working, electrical engineering and motor car manufacturing industries.

Raw cotton, fuels and machinery are imported; major exports include wines, fruits, textiles, shoes, iron ore, automobiles and domestic appliances. Tourism is an important source of foreign currency and round-the-year employment.

Recent Developments
Spain's internal problems have not entirely been solved by its adoption of democracy. An attempted coup by army officers in February 1981 was thwarted by firm action of King and government. No less disruptive is the strong separatist movement among the Basque people; though statutes granting regional autonomy for Basques, Catalans, Galicians and Andalusians were endorsed by referendum between 1979 and 1981, a violent minority of Basques continues to press for independence. Liberalization after the Franco regime, including the modernization of educational and social services, has created further tensions, especially between the new left-wing parties and traditional Roman Catholics. Spain expects to join the EEC in 1985.

EUROPE SOUTHEAST

Albania

The Country
The People's Republic of Albania is a Balkan state on the Adriatic Sea, bordered by Yugoslavia and Greece. *Area* 28,748 km² (11,099 sq miles); *capital* Tiranë; *population* 3,108,000 (est. 1986).

Organization
Government is vested in a People's Assembly of 250 deputies, elected for four-year periods from a list put forward by the communist-dominated Democratic Front; the Assembly meets twice yearly to ratify decisions of a fifteen-member Presidium, under a Chairman who is Head of State. The communist Labour Party controls the cabinet or Council of Ministers, whose Chairman is Premier. Local government is vested in village, town, sub-district and district People's Councils. The national language is Albanian, with regional dialects; many of the population are Moslems, or Christians of Catholic or Orthodox faiths.

Geography
The Adriatic coastal lowlands are backed by parallel ranges of alpine fold mountains, which include both limestones and mineral-rich igneous rocks; the highest peaks rise over 2500 m (8200 ft). Most of the population live on the plains and lower hill slopes, which were formerly forest, grassland and malarial marshes; the higher ground is forested, with poor alpine pastures. Winters on the coast are warm and moist, summers hot and dry; the mountains are intensely cold in winter, with rain and snow.

History and Development
Coastal Albania was dominated successively by Greek, Roman, Byzantine and other neighbouring civilizations, while the mountains bred fiercely independent pastoral tribes. Ottoman Turks took over control of the country from Serbs and Bulgars in the late 15th century, holding power until their defeat in the Balkan

Wars of 1912–13. Declared a kingdom on liberation, a republic in 1925 and a kingdom again in 1928, Albania was invaded by Italy in 1939. During World War II communist-led partisans took control, forming an effective resistance to German and Italian occupying forces, and taking over government at the liberation in 1946. After a period of close association with Yugoslavia, former partisan leader Enver Hoxha led the country into hard-line support of Stalinism, but broke with the USSR in 1961 to link with Chinese communism. More recently Albania has broken with China and now remains in political isolation, gradually establishing diplomatic relations and trade links with neighbouring countries.

Resources and Economics
Agriculture, which is collectivized, employs about 30 per cent of the labour force; the main crops are vines, olives, wheat, maize, cotton, potatoes, tobacco and sugar-beet. Copper, iron and chrome ores are mined; lignite and oil provide fuel, together with timber and important hydroelectric developments which allow Albania to export power. Industry is developing slowly; a growing proportion of exports are manufactured goods including textiles, tobacco and food products, and paper. There is a poorly-developed railway system and there are few good roads. Visits by organized groups of tourists are slowly increasing.

Recent Developments
Ideological as well as economic and geographic barriers keep Albania isolated from the rest of the world. President Hoxha's rigid policy of self-sufficiency, re-emphasized since Albania's break with China in 1977, allows only a slow rate of resource development, and Albania remains Europe's poorest and economically most backward country. Most trade links are with Yugoslavia; as the country's manufacturing industries develop, more trade with Western neighbours is being sought, but the process is slow. A gradually liberalizing policy towards tourism, and a projected rail link across the northern border with Yugoslavia, may help to reduce Albania's isolation.

Bulgaria

The Country
The People's Republic of Bulgaria lies on the shore of the Black Sea, bordered by Romania, Turkey, Greece and Yugoslavia. *Area* 110,912 km^2 (42,823 sq miles); *capital* Sofia; *population* 9,276,000 (est. 1986).

Organization
A National Assembly of 400 members is elected for five-year terms; this in turn elects a 25-member Council of State as the supreme legislative and executive body. All candidates are members of the Fatherland Front, composed of the powerful Communist Party and smaller Agrarian Union. Local authority is vested in People's Councils, which are elected for $2\frac{1}{2}$-year terms at provincial, town and village levels. The national language is Bulgarian, written in Cyrillic script. Many Bulgarians belong to the Orthodox Christian sect, with Roman Catholic and Moslem minorities.

Geography
The River Danube, which forms the northern frontier, has left a fertile alluvial

plain crossed by northward-flowing tributaries. To the south lie the Balkan Mountains, extending east-west across the country and rising to over 2300 m (7500 ft). In the southeast of Bulgaria the Maritsa River forms a broad valley. In the southwest lie the Rhodope Mountains, part of the ancient crystalline core of the Balkans extending across the frontier into Greece; here the highest peaks rise over 2900 m (9500 ft). Bulgaria has a modified continental climate, with cold dry winters and hot, rather moist summers. The high mountains are forested with conifers, the lower ones with deciduous forests that originally extended over the plains.

History and Development

Bulgar tribes from the east and Slavs from the northwest joined forces in the fertile lands south of the Danube to form a Bulgarian state and empire that for two hundred years fought successfully against the Byzantine Empire; conquered in the 11th century it again became powerful in the 12th and 13th centuries, falling to the Ottoman Empire in 1396. Subdued but rebellious for almost five centuries, Bulgaria was liberated with Russian assistance in 1878; initially an autonomous principality, it gained full independence in 1908 under Tsar Ferdinand. Parts of Macedonia and Thrace were intermittently included in Bulgaria but were lost after World War I, and again after World War II when Bulgaria sided with Germany and Italy. Soviet forces occupied the country in 1944, and a communist republic was established following the deposition of the King in 1946.

Resources and Economics

Traditionally agricultural up to World War II, almost 40 per cent of Bulgaria's labour force is still occupied in agriculture and forestry. On the Danube plain wheat, barley, maize and sunflower seeds are important crops, in the warmer Maritsa Valley rice, cotton and tobacco; hill slopes support vines and orchards, and the eastern plains grow crops of roses for the international perfume industries. Sheep, cattle and pigs are reared. Food-processing industries are a post-war development, providing valuable export earnings. Manganese and iron, lead, zinc and aluminium ores are mined; lignite, oil and natural gas are used locally. Bulgaria also processes and exports petroleum products from the USSR and Middle East. Industry has developed within the COMECON framework, which has encouraged Bulgaria to specialize in electrically-powered machinery and develop steel works, fertilizer and industrial chemical plant and non-ferrous metal smelters. Tourism is encouraged, and there is a small but important Black Sea fishing industry. Road and rail links are adequate in lowland areas, where most of the population live.

Recent Developments

Though strongly socialist and closely linked with the USSR, Bulgaria is experimenting with economic reforms designed to decentralize controls, simplify planning and increase production. The most recent five-year plan (1981–5) allows for modest growth targets which are generally being met; particular emphasis is placed on continuing industrial expansion. About 80 per cent of the trading is with COMECON and developing countries; trade links with the West are increasing, and Bulgaria has a substantial but reducing foreign debt.

Cyprus

The Country
The Republic of Cyprus is a large island in the northeast corner of the Mediterranean Sea, 224 km (140 miles) long and 80 km (50 miles) wide, some 90 km (56 miles) from the Turkish coast. *Area* 9251 km² (3572 sq miles); *capital* Nicosia; *population* 641,000 (est. 1986).

Organization
Cyprus's population includes communities of Greek (80%) and Turkish (19%) descent. The 1960 Constitution provides for an elected Greek President and Turkish Vice-President, an elected House of Representatives with 35 Greek and 15 Turkish seats, and a Council of ten Greek and three Turkish ministers. This system is in abeyance: there are currently separate Greek and Turkish administrations. The communities speak their own languages (English too is widely spoken) and are respectively Greek Orthodox Christian and Moslem.

Geography
Cyprus is formed by two gently curving mountain ridges, separated by the Mesaöria Plain. The igneous Troödos Massif in the southwest rises to 1951 m (6400 ft) at Mt Olympus: the limestone and marble Kyrenia Mountains form a lower northern ridge, extending seaward into the Cape St Andreas Peninsula. The island is scored by dry stream valleys that flood during rainstorms. Summers are hot and dry, winters warm and moist on the plains, colder – even frosty – and wetter in the mountains. The hilltops are forested; lower ground carries lush scrub and pasture in spring, drying out in the summer heat.

History and Development
Inhabited since Neolithic times, Cyprus's strategic position in the eastern Mediterranean made it indispensable to a number of empires; it was controlled successively by Assyria, Egypt, Greece, Rome, Byzantium, Venice and Turkey before its occupation by Britain in 1878. By then a Greek-speaking majority was already seeking union with Greece, while a Turkish minority – mostly in the northeast – resisted it. This damaging situation persisted both throughout the British colonial period and after independence (1960). In 1963 the Turkish community withdrew from government: in 1964 UN troops were landed to avert civil war and in 1974, after a decade of continuing strife, Turkish troops invaded to establish a permanent 'Turkish Federated State of Cyprus' in the north, announced as the independent Turkish Republic of Northern Cyprus in 1983.

Resources and Economics
Primarily agricultural, Cyprus employs about one third of its population in farming; grapes, potatoes, cereals and citrus fruit are the main crops, providing 40 per cent of the island's overseas income. Renowned for its minerals since classical times, Cyprus exports asbestos, gypsum and ores of iron, copper and chromite. Cement is manufactured from local limestone, and light industries (food-processing, shoe-manufacture) are starting to diversify the economy. There are adequate road, air and sea links, and a tourist industry that was one of the first casualties of the civil disturbances.

Recent Developments

Despite chronic political problems, Cyprus made good economic progress after independence, backed by international and Commonwealth funding. The trauma of partition and its aftermath set back development programmes, but progress continues. In the Greek sector Emergency Action Plans have helped to develop agriculture, light industry and tourism in what was previously the less developed area of the island. The Turkish sector, which includes much of the best land and tourist facilities, has remained relatively static. There are continuing refugee problems, and reunification talks continue desultorily.

Greece

The Country

The Republic of Greece is the southernmost Balkan state, bordered by Albania, Yugoslavia and Bulgaria in the north and Turkey in the east; it includes many islands in the Ionian, Aegean and Mediterranean seas. *Area* 131,944 km² (50,944 sq miles); *capital* Athens; *population* 9,665,000 (est. 1986).

Organization

Government is vested in a unicameral Parliament of 300 deputies, elected for terms of four years; Parliament elects a President (for five-year terms) who appoints a Prime Minister and cabinet of about twenty-two ministers. He presides also over the Council of the Republic, a group of former Presidents, Prime Ministers and other leaders, which can act should Parliament be deadlocked. Local authority is exercised through 106 prefectures; Mount Athos is a self-governing community of twenty monasteries. The national language is Greek, with formal and demotic forms; most Greeks belong to the Greek Orthodox Church.

Geography

The Pindos Mountains form a limestone backbone to peninsular Greece, extending south from the Dinaric Alps; their line continues through the Peloponnisos and Crete, parallel folds forming the southeastern peninsulas and islands. Several peaks rise above 2400 m (7800 ft). Macedonia, Thrace and the northern Aegean islands are of older crystalline rocks extending south from the Rhodope Mountains. Pockets of lowland, lined with alluvium from the mountain streams, lie between the ranges and extend into narrow coastal plains, where most of the population live. The climate is typically Mediterranean, with long, hot, dry summers and warm moist winters; the central mountains have hard frosts and snow in winter. Greece has lost much of its former forest cover, though secondary forest and scrub cover the uplands; the lowlands are mostly cultivated.

History and Development

Populated for over six thousands years, the islands and peninsula of Greece housed some of Man's earliest cultures, including the Minoan of Crete and Mycenaean of Peloponnisos. City states emerged during the ten centuries before Christ, each developing its own form of government. Athens, the largest, became influential during and after the wars which kept the Persian Empire at bay; Sparta, Corinth, Thebes and Macedonia dominated in turn, the latter under Alexander the Great whose empire extended from India to Western Europe. During the 2nd century BC the Greek states became part of the Roman Empire. Later, from the 4th to the 15th centuries AD, they formed part of the Byzantine Empire (ruled from the former Greek colony of Constantinople), and for four further centuries were a province of the Ottoman Empire. Greece finally fought for and gained independence in 1821–9, becoming a kingdom in 1830 under the patronage of Britain, Russia and France. New territories were added including the Ionian Islands, Thessaly, Macedonia, Thrace and Crete. Although Greece was constantly torn by internal dissent and weak central government, it remainded intact through wars with neighbouring Balkan countries and occupation by German and Italian forces in World War II. Liberation in 1944 brought civil war between monarchists and left-wing republicans; British and US aid supported the monarchists to victory in 1949, but civil strife and military dictatorship followed. Greece became a republic in 1973, finally re-attaining civil democratic government in the following year.

Resources and Economics
Agriculture and fishing are the traditional industries, still occupying about one third of the population. The main crops – wheat, barley, potatoes, tomatoes and sugar-beet – are grown intensively on small family farms; olives, vines and citrus fruits are grown on the hill slopes, and sheep, goats, cattle and poultry are the main livestock. Iron and manganese ores, bauxite and a little lignite are mined; oil in small quantities flows from Aegean wells, but much has to be imported. Industrial development has been slow, hampered by lack of capital and the need to import most raw materials. Fertilizers and cement find ready home markets; processed foods and textiles are the main exports. Greece has a large merchant fleet, and relies heavily on tourism to help in balancing its budget; in terms of income per capita it remains one of the poorest European countries. Road and rail links are adequate between the main centres of population, and many coasters and ferries connect the islands.

Recent Developments
Greece joined the EEC in January 1981; its continuing involvement with NATO is questionable, and its current foreign policy seeks to strengthen ties with non-aligned countries. Tensions with Turkey persist because of disputes over oil-prospecting in the Aegean and the continuing Turkish occupation of northern Cyprus. Inflation and trade imbalance run high, and economic growth is likely to remain slow during the period of adjustment to EEC tariffs and conditions. The country is, however, passing through a period of political stability, with firm government and enviably low unemployment, and the tourism which helps to bolster the economy shows no signs of flagging.

Italy

The Country
The Republic of Italy occupies the long, boot-shaped peninsula between the Adriatic and Tyrrhenian seas in the central Mediterranean Sea, bounded in the north by France, Switzerland, Austria and Yugoslavia; it includes the islands of Sicily and Sardinia. *Area* 301,225 km^2 (116,303 sq miles); *capital* Rome; *population* 57,942,000 (est. 1986).

Organization

A parliamentary democracy, Italy is governed by a 630-member Chamber of Deputies and 315-member Senate, each elected for five-year terms; the President is elected by a joint session of Parliament to serve for seven years. The President appoints a Prime Minister, who directs a cabinet of about twenty ministers. Local government is vested in twenty regional parliaments and governments. Italian is spoken throughout the country; there is a German-speaking minority group close to the Austrian border, and an Albanian-speaking population in the Basilicata region (Gulf of Taranto). The national religion is Roman Catholicism.

Geography

Some 800 km (500 miles) long, the Italian peninsula extends southeastwards from the Lombardy plains; its backbone is the Apennine Mountains, a fold of the main Alpine system rising to peaks above 2900 m (9500 ft) in the central Gran Sasso range. Narrow plains line the coasts, broadening into wider river valleys where the soft mountain limestone has been eroded. The Lombardy plains, drained by the River Po and its tributaries, are ringed by mountains to south, west and north; in the east they open on to the Adriatic Sea, with a coast formed by lagoons and deltas. To the north and west stand the Alps, rising in steep steps from the plains. The highest peaks along the Swiss and French borders include Monte Rosa (4634 m, 15,204 ft), the Matterhorn (4479 m, 14,695 ft) and Mont Blanc (4807 m, 15,771 ft). Sicily, separated from the mainland by the Strait of Messina, 4 km (2.5 miles) wide, includes the limestone massifs of the Nebrodi Mountains and the volcanic cone of Etna (3340 m, 10,958 ft), one of several active or quiescent volcanoes in the region. Sardinia is a rugged island of older crystalline rocks; its central peak, Monti del Gennargentu, rises to 1834 m (6017 ft). Southern Italy has a typically Mediterranean climate, with hot dry summers and warm damp winters; the north has a more continental climate, with much colder winters and hot, rather humid summers. Vegetation ranges from the arid maquis and semi-desert of the south to the richly forested hills and alpine meadows of the north.

History and Development

Etruscan, Latin, Sabine and other tribes occupied central areas of the peninsula from about 1000 BC, possibly earlier. Those centered about Rome gained the ascendancy from about 500 BC, organizing the rest of the peninsula and countries far beyond under the banners of the Roman Empire. Ostrogoths invading from the north and Byzantines from the south defeated Rome in the 5th century AD, though the heart of the city (the Vatican) remained the centre of the Christian Church. Charlemagne was crowned there in AD 800, and Rome became the centre of a papal empire; however, the peninsula was a medley of kingdoms and city states, rich in culture but politically weak, that formed various alliances but failed to unify throughout the medieval period. In the 16th century Sicily, Naples and Milan fell to Spain; in the 18th century Austria took over much of the north, leaving only Sardinia, the Papal States, Venice, Genoa and Lucca as independent states.

Italy was first unified under Napoleon in 1805, though the embryo state was suppressed at the Congress of Vienna. A popular movement for unification – the Risorgimento – grew throughout the 19th century, and in 1870 the country was re-united under King Victor Emmanuel II. Never wealthy, and slow to industrialize, Italy lost population steadily through the late 19th and early 20th centuries. Somaliland and Eritrea were acquired as the basis of an empire in 1889–90, Libya and the Dodecanese were added in 1912, and Trieste became part of Italy after 1918. Falling under Fascist dictatorship in 1923, Italy became organized but militaristic, conquering Ethiopia in 1936, Albania in 1939, and joining forces with Germany in World War II. With the defeat of Italian armies and the death of dictator Benito Mussolini in 1944, Italy left the war, losing all overseas territories; Trieste too was lost, but returned in 1954. The country became a republic in 1948.

Resources and Economics

Lacking coal and mineral resources, Italy has relied heavily on agriculture for its prosperity; some 15 per cent of its workforce is currently agricultural, many on small peasant holdings, especially in the impoverished south. The chief crops in the fertile northern lowlands are wheat, maize, sugar-beet, potatoes and rice; in the centre and south vines, citrus fruits, tomatoes, olives and tobacco are grown. In the north cattle and pigs are raised, in the south goats, donkeys and mules; fruit, wines and vegetables are important exports. Elba and Sardinia produce iron ore; Sardinia, Sicily and Lombardy are sources of non-ferrous metals, notably lead; oil and gas fields have been exploited in Lombardy and the south, though there is still a need for imports. Sulphur and mercury are exported. Textiles, footwear, motor cars, domestic appliances, plastics and chemicals are important industrial products that sell well in export markets, though costs of importing fuel, raw materials and manufactured goods currently exceed export earnings. The tourist trade (catering for 14 million visitors a year) helps to balance payments; another considerable source of national income is money sent home by Italian workers abroad. Inflation and unemployment are chronically high. The country's long coastline encourages coastal shipping trade. There are also good electrified rail links along both flanks of the peninsula, and excellent trunk roads (autostrada): traffic links across the mountains are less satisfactory. The Alps are pierced by several rail and road tunnels into France and Austria.

Recent Developments

Post-war Italian policies have been complex and on the whole ineffectual at providing government. Political life has often been paralysed by revelations of high-level corruption and by the stalemates resulting from uneasy alliances between rival political parties. Most governments have been centre-right coalitions with Christian Democrats predominant; communists, socialists and a number of smaller liberal and right-wing parties provide alternative support or opposition. The Italian Communist Party, the largest in Western Europe, commands one third of the votes. The Red Brigade, a violent urban guerrilla movement prominent in the late 1970s and early 1980s, seems to have been brought under control, but other groups – notably the Mafia – continue to dominate local and regional politics. Questions of womens' rights, abortion and birth control remain divisive issues in this predominantly Catholic country.

Malta

The Country

The Republic of Malta includes three islands of the central Mediterranean Sea –

Malta, Comino and Gozo – and several small islets, lying 170 km (106 miles) south of Sicily. *Area* approx. 316 km² (122 sq miles); *capital* Valletta; *population* 360,000 (est. 1986).

Organization
A democratic republic within the British Commonwealth, Malta is governed by a 65-member House of Representatives. The House elects a President, who nominates a Prime Minister: there is an appointed Cabinet of about twelve ministers. The population, largely island-born, is a mixture of Mediterranean and European stocks. The language is Maltese, with English widely spoken: Roman Catholicism is the recognized religion.

Geography
The islands form a chain of coralline limestone uplands, steep to the north, descending gently to the south, and ranged by lowland plains. Bays on the northern flank form sheltered natural harbours. Hot and dry in summer, with warm damp winters, the Maltese islands have been much modified by terracing and cultivation; little of the original scrub vegetation remains.

History and Development
Settled since Neolithic times, Malta stands at a crossroads of Mediterranean shipping lanes; its deep-water harbours have been welcome havens for over four thousand years. Its civilization dates from the mid-16th century when the Knights Hospitallers fortified Valletta aginst the Turks. Britain obtained possession after the Napoleonic wars (1814), developing it primarily as a naval base. Self-government was first granted in 1921, independence in 1964.

Resources and Economics
Agriculture (mostly in smallholdings) and fishing occupy about 6 per cent of the workforce and contribute proportionally to Malta's budget. Early potatoes, cereals, potatoes, tomatoes, legumes and other vegetables are the most valuable crops; many are exported. Local limestone provides excellent building material; fuels are imported and fresh water is restricted locally. Shipbuilding and repairs are a major industry; small factories, often rural, produce plastic and metal goods, shoes, textiles, clothing and other small items. Ferries link the islands; roads and air services are adequate for the current needs of islanders and a flourishing tourist population.

Recent Developments
Centered originally on the naval dockyards, Malta's economy has diversified since independence and Britain's withdrawal; increasing emphasis is now being placed on developing light industries and expanding tourist facilities. Over half a million tourists currently visit Malta each year.

San Marino

The Country
The Republic of San Marino, a tiny kite-shaped state 13 km (8 miles) by 9 km (5.6 miles), encircles Monte Titano on the lower flanks of the Apennine Mountains in eastern Italy. Entirely surrounded by Italy, it lies on the border of

Romagna and Marches within sight of the Adriatic Sea. *Area* 61 km^2 (23.5 sq miles); *capital* San Marino; *population* 21,000 (est. 1986).

Organization
An independent sovereign state, San Marino is governed by an elected 60-member Great and General Council: the Council appoints from its members a ten-member Congress of State, and two Captains-Regent, who are heads of state and administration for six-month periods. The people are of northern Italian stock, speaking an Italian dialect; most are Roman Catholics.

Geography
Centered on the limestone ridges of Monte Titano (793 m, 2601 ft) and the valley of the Ausa River, San Marino is a country of hills and gentle slopes, villages and small medieval towns. Summers are warm, winters cool with alternating mild and cold spells: rainfall is moderate throughout the year, providing forested mountains and upland pastures.

History and Development
San Marino is named after a Christian saint who settled on Monte Titano to evade Roman persecution. Forming as an independent city-state, well defended by local fortifications, it avoided involvement with neighbours throughout the turbulent Risorgimento period (see Italy), and remained independent after the unification of Italy in the mid-19th century.

Resources and Economics
The traditional industries of San Marino – agriculture, forestry and quarrying – have declined in importance, though grapes, cereals and dairy produce still contribute much to the country's economy and appearance. More important economically are a variety of light manufacturing industries, from ceramics to footwear, based on imported materials, and commerce encouraged by free-trade agreements with Italy. Most important of all is tourism, served by good roads and efficient services.

Recent Developments
With a soundly-based economy, easy access from Italy and a well-presented endowment of scenery, climate and historic interest, San Marino continues to prosper. Despite rumbling internal politics this small, independent community remains at peace with the world, and caters for more than 2.5 million visitors (over a hundred per head of population) each year.

Vatican City State

The Vatican City State stands within the city of Rome in central Italy – a sovereign state 1 km (3300 ft) long and 750 m (2500 ft) wide. *Area* 0.44 km^2 (0.17 sq miles); *population* approx. 1000 (est. 1986). It stands on the west bank of the Tiber, almost completely ringed by walls; the unwalled southeastern corner incorporates St Peter's Square. There are a few extra-territorial enclaves, notably Castel Gandolfo, the Pope's summer residence. Vatican City is governed by the Pope, who delegates responsibility to a small appointed Papal Commission. The city includes St Peter's Basilica and several other buildings of importance to the Roman Catholic Church: it has its own railway station, telephone system, bank and post office, and is policed by a special force of a hundred Swiss Guards. Citizenship is granted to Vatican employees and cardinals in residence. A surviving remnant of the Papal States that spread across Italy during the 18th and 19th centuries, Vatican City's sovereignty and independence were guaranteed by a treaty with the Italian government in 1929. The City depends for its continuing existence entirely on the huge resources of the Roman Catholic Church.

Yugoslavia

The Country
The Socialist Federal Republic of Yugoslavia occupies the southwestern flank of the Balkan Peninsula, bordered by Italy, Austria, Hungary, Romania, Bulgaria, Greece and Albania, and with a long indented coastline bordering the Adriatic Sea. *Area* 255,804 km^2 (98,766 sq miles); *capital* Belgrade; *population* 23,351,000 (est. 1986).

Organization
A federation of six republics (Serbia, Croatia, Bosnia-Hercegovina, Macedonia, Slovenia, Montenegro), Yugoslavia is governed by a bicameral Federal Assembly, including a 220-delegate Federal Chamber and a smaller Chamber of Republics and Provinces. Delegates are elected from republican and provincial assemblies, which are themselves elected bodies made up of representatives from occupational groups and socio-political organizations. The supreme governing body is the collective Presidency, composed of one representative of each republic and one from each of the two autonomous provinces (Kosovo and Vojvodina) within Serbia. Local authority is vested in community groups, and the League of Communists is the guiding force throughout the country. There are four official languages and several local languages and dialects; Serbo-Croat is universally used. Religions include Roman Catholic, Greek Orthodox and Moslem.

Geography
The Adriatic coastline with its hundreds of inhabited offshore islands forms a narrow Mediterranean fringe. Inland the country rises steeply to the massive limestone ridges of the Dinaric Alps, with several peaks above 1600 m (5250 ft). In the northwest the mountains of Slovenia continue the Alpine ranges of Italy and Austria. In the south the crystalline rocks of the Balkan region include rich non-ferrous metal ores. Beyond the coastal mountains lie the Pannonian lowlands, drained by the Danube and Sava river systems; most of the Yugoslavian population is concentrated within this area. There is a great diversity of climates and natural vegetation, from the mild Mediterranean coast with its warm, damp winters and hot summers to the more continental and extreme climates of the interior. Forests of conifers, oak and beech are found throughout the country wherever soils, altitude and slopes permit, and wildlife (including bears, wild boar and wolves) is abundant in the less inhabited areas.

History and Development
The constituent republics of Yugoslavia each had their own colourful history, generally including settlement by wandering tribes from north or south,

development into small local communities, and inclusion in Roman, Byzantine, Ottoman and Austro-Hungarian empires. Throughout their long histories each developed a degree of independence (especially among the mountain folk) which – coupled with disparate languages and an assortment of religions – helped to retain and accentuate their separate identities. At the outbreak of World War I Serbia (which then included Macedonia) and Montenegro (including part of Albania) were independent, while Croatia, Slovenia, Bosnia and Hercegovina formed part of Austria-Hungary. In the peace settlement the Kingdom of the Serbs, Croats and Slovenes was created under Serbian King Peter I, drawing together all six units in an uneasy alliance (1918). Renaming the kingdom Yugoslavia (1929) did little to allay mutual suspicions and hostilities. Overrun by Germany and Italy in World War II, Yugoslavia was partitioned between Germany, Italy, Bulgaria and Hungary, with Croatia and Bosnia forming a separate state of Croatia. Struggles against the invaders were intermixed with a civil war between Serbian royalists (Cetniks), Croatian nationalists (Ustase) and communist-led partisans under Josip Broz Tito. With Allied support the partisans emerged victorious, setting up a People's Federal Republic in 1945. Following a break between Tito and Stalin in 1948 Yugoslavia has pursued an independent form of communism and a general policy of non-alignment.

Resources and Economics
Agriculture in Yugoslavia remains chiefly in the hands of peasant farmers who own 85 per cent of the land; about 30 per cent of the working population is involved in food production and forestry. Wheat, maize, sunflower seeds, sugar-beet and potatoes are the chief crops of the fertile lowlands; plums, wine, pigmeats and beef are also produced, mainly for export. Despite its rural emphasis Yugoslavia imports cereals, along with such luxury items as coffee and tropical fruits. There are extensive mineral resources including plentiful low-quality coal, iron, copper, lead, gold, silver and other metals; oil and natural gas are exploited, but much more is imported. Hydroelectric power provides about half the country's needs. Manufacturing industries, which have expanded rapidly in recent decades, now provide almost twice the revenue of agricultural produce and employ an increasing proportion of the workforce. Products include processed foods, chemicals and raw materials for capital and consumer goods, and a relatively small quantity of manufactured goods for home use and export. Good road, rail and air links connect the main centres, but communications are less than adequate in the mountainous interior, where poor transport facilities may inhibit mineral production. There is a flourishing tourist industry, catering for over six million visitors annually and bringing in considerable foreign currency earnings.

Recent Developments
Political instability predicted on the death of President Tito in 1980 has not materialized; the collective rotating presidency appears to work well. However, political strains within the federation continue, especially in the poorer republics and provinces; serious unrest among the Albanian minority in Kosovo in 1981 and 1982 echoed Croatian problems of a decade earlier. Economic hazards facing Yugoslavia during the 1980s include inflation, a large deficit in the balance of payments, heavy foreign debts, and the need to industrialize the more backward areas. Unemployment is high, and many Yugoslavs emigrate to find work – mostly unskilled – in other European countries.

Asia

Asia occupies the bulk of the Eurasian continent, extending by convention into Turkey, the eastern Mediterranean seaboard, the peninsulas of Arabia and India and the extensive archipelagoes of Indonesia, the Philippine Islands and Japan. Bounded mostly by shorelines, its boundaries with Europe (see introduction to Europe), Africa and Oceania are political rather than geographical. As defined here it is by far the largest continent, with an area of 50.12 million km² (19.35 million sq miles); its population of about 3000 million is also by far the world's largest, though not the fastest growing. Extending from well north of the Arctic Circle to a few degrees south of the Equator, and from 20° E to 170° W, it covers over one third of the Earth's land surface, containing the world's highest mountains and largest inland seas.

ASIA NORTH

Union of Soviet Socialist Republics (USSR)

The Country

By far the world's largest sovereign state, the USSR extends over 8000 km (5000 miles) from the Baltic to the Bering Sea, and 3000 km (1800 miles) from the Arctic coast to Asia Minor. In the west it borders Turkey, Romania, Hungary, Czechoslovakia, Poland, Finland and Norway, in the south Iran, Afghanistan, China, Mongolia and North Korea. *Area* 22,402,200 km ² (8,649,498 sq miles); *capital* Moscow; *population* 280,693,000 (est. 1986).

Organization

The USSR is a federation of fifteen Union Republics, governed by the Supreme Soviet – two legislative chambers, each of 750 members elected for five-year terms. The chambers join to elect a Presidium of 39 members and an executive council of over 100 ministers. In the Presidium the Union Republics are represented by their Presidents, in the council by their Chairmen of the Councils of Ministers. Each Union Republic has its own legislature, single-chambered but otherwise modelled on the federal plan: twenty Autonomous Republics and eight Autonomous Regions within the Union Republics also have their own legislatures. Many national minorities are recognized within the various republics. Local authority is vested in Soviets of People's Deputies, with members elected for 2½-year terms at district, city, oblast and village levels. Political authority throughout the USSR is exercised by the Communist Party, the sole political party, governed by a Congress and Central Committee. The Political Bureau of the party determines political, economic and social policies at all levels. Russian, with Cyrillic script, is the official language, and the first language of about 60 per cent of the population. Over one thousand other languages involving four alphabets are used locally. Those with religious affiliations include a majority of Russian Orthodox believers, and minorities of other Christian sects, Moslems and Jews.

Geography

The vast area of the USSR is divided geographically into western and eastern sectors by the north-south range of the Ural Mountains, which extend northward beyond the Arctic coast into Novaya Zemlya. West of the Urals spreads a broad, rolling plain, most of it below 300 m (1000 ft), drained and dissected by several major rivers – the northward-flowing Pechora, Mezen and Dvina systems, and the southward-flowing Dnestr, Dnepr, Don and Volga and their many tributaries. This plain includes much of the USSR's most fertile farmland, rich with dark 'chernozem' soils. In the north is an Arctic and sub-Arctic zone of tundra and open marshland, with poorly drained soils and permafrost. South of it lies a broad belt of forest tundra (taiga), and southward again zones of birch, coniferous and mixed forest which in turn give way to open grassland in the drier south. Among the forests are marshes rich in wildlife, though huge areas of marshland have been drained by the waterways and canals that link the major river systems. Forested hills occupy the southwestern corner of the Ukrainian SSR. In central Asia steppe yields to desert and salt-marsh. Between the Caspian and Black seas stand the lofty Caucasus Mountains, an alpine-fold range extending over 1200 km (750 miles) east and west, and rising to peaks over 5500 m (18,000 ft) high.

The Urals, extending over 2400 km (1500 miles) from the Arctic to subtropical Kazakhstan, form a narrow range in the north but broaden into a series of parallel ridges in the south. The highest peak, Narodnaya (1894 m, 6214 ft), stands close to 65° N in a zone of subpolar tundra; further south the mountains are forested, deeply incised by river valleys, and the site of heavy industries based on their minerals. East of the Urals extends the Western Siberian Lowland, a broad, marshy plain drained by the Ob, Yenisei and Irtysh rivers, desolate but well populated and growing in economic importance as agriculture and industry develop. In the north this spreads to the even more desolate and deserted Arctic shore; to the south it rises steeply to the high Kirgiz steppe and the still higher Pamirs where, in the mountainous Tadzhik SSR, stands Pik Kommunizma (7495 m, 24,590 ft), the USSR's highest peak.

Eastern Siberia is a high plateau, draining northward to the Arctic Ocean via the Lena and other great rivers, and bordered to south and east by a complex of fold mountains extending through Mongolia and north China to Asia's eastern seaboard. Forest tundra and forest extend over much of this area, thinning to alpine tundra in the mountains and polar tundra in a broad belt along the Arctic shore. Population is thin, but strenuous efforts are being made to develop the limited agricultural and more promising mining potential of the area.

The USSR has many climates. The northern coast and offlying islands are polar, invested by sea ice for much of the year with temperatures seldom rising far above freezing point except at the height of summer. Snowfall is generally light. Sea ice covers the Baltic and Sea of Okhotsk in winter, bringing subpolar conditions far south from November to March or April. In the broad belt that covers most of the land area, winters are very cold and summers warm; eastern Siberia is colder than the Arctic coast in January, with mean temperatures down to −50°C (−58°F), but much warmer in summer, and generally very dry. Central Asia is a vast area of desert and semi-desert, hot in summer and icy in winter. In the south the Black Sea and Pacific coasts have milder, damper maritime climates, but central areas are strongly continental, with extreme cold in winter. Heaviest rain and snow fall on the Caucasus and the mountains of Kamchatka. There is a huge variety of wildlife, including polar bears, reindeer and seals in the far north, mountain tigers (now very rare) in the southeast, and large populations of wading birds in the southern marshes.

History and Development

Russia's first settlers were probably Neanderthals from the southwest; more significant invaders were Scythians from Siberia about 1000 BC, Slavs, Turkic and Bulgar nomads who roamed the steppes in the 3rd to 7th centuries AD, and Scandinavians who settled the forested lands east of the Baltic Sea. The predominantly Slav community of Kiev expanded rapidly in the 8th and 9th centuries to form the Kievan Rus state, an agglomeration of widely-scattered market towns and villages under the domination of Varangian (Scandinavian) merchants, extending from the Carpathians to Lake Onega. The conversion of the overlord Vladimir I, about AD 988, established the Byzantine Christian Church over this vast area.

Tartar invaders in the 13th century took control of Kiev and brought southern Russia within the Mongol Empire of Genghis Khan (see Mongolia). The northeast meanwhile came under the control of the Grand Duchy of Lithuania, which extended through Poland and into Belorussia and the Ukraine. During the 14th century, under Ivan I and II, political power in the north shifted to Moscow: Ivan III (the Great) began the reconquest of southern lands which, under his successors, was to spread Muscovite influence to the shores of the Caspian Sea. Ivan IV (the Terrible) finally broke the power of both the southern Tartars and his rival northern lords to become Russia's first Tsar (1547).

Border warfare with western neighbours Sweden and Poland, continuing incursions from the south, and constant internal struggles for power among the widely-scattered feudal nobility kept Russia politically and economically medieval well into the 17th century. Western influences grew under Tsar Peter I (the Great), who founded St Petersburg (Leningrad) and made it his capital and a gateway to European ideas. He also created an up-to-date navy and army, and a civil service capable of administrating his huge domains. Peter and his immediate successors encouraged the colonization of neighbouring territories east and south across Asia. Under Catherine II (the Great) in the late 18th century, Russia became a major power, centered on the eastern fringe of Europe and partly Europeanized, though still governed archaically by an autocratic Tsar.

Napoleon's invasion and subsequent defeat (1812) enhanced Russia's role in European politics. Continuing expansion during the 19th century brought all the tribal lands of northeastern Asia, from the Arctic to the borders of China, under Russian economic control and exploitation. Conflict in the south with the declining Ottoman Empire extended Russian influence towards Turkey and the Balkans, precipitating an inconclusive war with France and Britain in the Crimea (1853–6). The ending of serfdom in 1861 was one of several long-overdue liberalizing reforms carried out after the war, but autocratic government persisted. The Industrial Revolution that was by this time developing the resources of western Europe failed almost completely in Russia, stifled by bureaucracy, economic limitations and official indifference.

A brief far-eastern war with Japan (1904–05) again exposed the government's ineptitude, precipitating a revolution which, though quelled, brought Russia's first constitution and parliament. Military defeat in World War I, and the resulting domestic chaos, brought a second revolution (1917) which swept the Tsar from power; during the five-year civil war that followed, the Russian Soviet Federated Socialist Republic (RSFSR), political successor to Tsarist Russia, emerged rapidly as the dominant partner in a communist-inspired Union of Soviet Socialist Republics. With peace restored the Union inaugurated vigorous socialist reform, collectivizing agriculture, intensifying and modernizing industrial development and socializing education and everyday life. Totalitarian methods brought rapid success, marred by the massive setback of World War II in which the western flank of the USSR was overrun and devastated by German forces. The peace settlement of 1945 gave new territories to the USSR both along its western border and in the Far East, and created a cordon of communist-dominated countries isolating it from former enemies and allies in western Europe.

Resources and Economics

Throughout the USSR about 40 per cent of the population lives rurally and about 25 per cent is engaged in agriculture or forestry – a figure that has decreased considerably during the past three decades. In the far north hunting, trapping, fishing and reindeer-herding are still the main pursuits of the indigenous populations, who live at low densities in scattered settlements; formerly nomadic, most are now settled, especially along the waterways that provide the main means of transport. In the forests settlements are larger, though still widely scattered, with the major ones strung out along the Trans-Siberian Railway and its branches. Prosperity depends on forestry and farming – mostly wheat-growing under marginal climatic conditions – and on growing industrial complexes, for example in the Kuzbar of western Siberia. In the central belt of the USSR settlements and populations increase dramatically, especially west of the Urals and south of 55°N, the latitude of Moscow.

Although industries attract settlers to the main towns, much of the population remains in large village communities where collective farming is the economic mainstay. About half the total area of agricultural land is devoted to grain crops, notably wheat, barley and oats, and about one third to fodder crops for the large herds of livestock. Cotton, rice, sugar-beet, sunflowers (for oil) and potatoes are important crops. Though agricultural production is high, there is still considerable potential for improving yields in most sectors; the USSR still relies on imported staple foods, especially in years when its own harvests from marginal lands are reduced by drought. Livestock, including cattle, sheep and poultry, are reared both on the large collectives and on individual smallholdings; demand for milk, meat and eggs generally exceeds supply in the large towns, problems of distribution contributing to local shortages. Fishing is an important component of food production; the USSR has large deep-sea fleets that operate in all the world's oceans, as well as important inshore and river fisheries, usually accounting for 10 to 15 per cent of the world's total catch each year.

Well endowed with minerals, the USSR has huge reserves of coal, oil and natural gas, all exploited for both home consumption and export. To the well-established coalfields of the Don and Kuznetsk basins and the southern Urals have been added new centres of mining throughout Siberia and the Arctic. Similarly oil and natural gas production, traditionally centered in the Transcaucasus, has recently been boosted by huge new discoveries in Siberia, the Ukraine, Sakhalin, western Turkmenistan and elsewhere, and the development of an extensive pipeline network. Hydroelectricity has declined in relative importance; input from nuclear power remains small and localized.

Heavy metal ores are plentiful and widely distributed; iron, manganese, nickel, cobalt and chromium are produced for home and export markets, mostly from the southern Urals and Ukraine. Copper, lead and zinc are mined and smelted from Norilsk in the Arctic to the mountains of southern Kazakhstan. Heavy industries based on these minerals have developed at many centres, including several in remote areas of Siberia; together they employ about one third of the country's workforce and generate over two thirds of its wealth. Emphasis is laid on the production of capital goods, for example building materials, heavy machinery and industrial chemicals, all of which feed virtually insatiable markets within the USSR and COMECON bloc neighbours. Production of consumer goods is growing in importance, and the goods available for both home consumption and export are improving in quality. Clothing and other essentials are generally obtainable though not always cheap; luxury items are still scarce, and more expensive in relation to incomes than in advanced capitalist countries.

Transport facilities are adequate for a widely scattered population. Railways play an important role in the general economy, transporting about two thirds of the country's freight. Sea transport is increasing in importance, especially in the Arctic; inland waterway freight networks interconnect the major western rivers; roads, pipelines and air transport are growing as the number of heavily populated centres increases. Tourism is a slowly expanding industry and a welcome source of foreign currency.

Recent Developments

The USSR's tradition of centralized economic planning gives it one of the world's most rigidly determined economic structures – one that may be working to its disadvantage in its approach to world markets. The steady economic expansion that characterized its succession of five-year plans is maintained, though at a declining rate. Industrial and agricultural production now fall consistently below planned levels, in some sectors by 50 per cent or more. In 1982 overall growth in industrial production was some 60 per cent of the planned figures, and the lowest rate of increase since the period immediately following World War II; in the same year agricultural productivity increased by only 4 per cent – one quarter of the planned figure. There is no indication that the planning authorities have any remedies for the present situation, which reflects that in capitalist countries (and indeed in other planned economies) throughout the world. Current plans provide for a sharper increase in output of consumer goods than of capital goods, for generally higher levels of investment, and for an increase of 3.3 per cent (higher than was achieved in 1982) in national income.

The Soviet invasion of Afghanistan in 1979 resulted in strained relations with many Western countries, notably the USA which embargoed sales of grain (other than those provided for in existing contracts) and discouraged the transfer of technological information to the USSR. Alternative sources of grain were quickly found – under necessity because of poor harvests, notably in 1981 – but the embargo on technical information may well have slowed down Soviet progress in computer technology, automation, and other advanced industrial processes for the present and foreseeable future.

ASIA SOUTHWEST

Bahrain

The Country
Bahrain is made up of one large and about thirty smaller islands in the Gulf, lying mostly between the northeast coast of Saudi Arabia and the Qatar peninsula. *Area* 622 km^2 (240 sq miles); *capital* Manama (on the main island of Bahrain); *population* 369,000 (est. 1986).

Organization
An independent state since 1971, Bahrain is ruled by a hereditary Amir, with a cabinet of about seventeen appointed ministers. There is provision for a democratically elected National Assembly: the first and last one was dissolved in 1975. The people are mostly of Arab and Persian origin and Moslem, with Shi'ites and Sunnis about equally represented. Arabic is the official language, with English widely spoken.

Geography
The islands are generally low-lying, with patches of fertile soil. Bahrain itself, 52 km by 16 km (32 miles by 10 miles), is the largest, with limestone uplands rising to almost 135 m (450 ft) in the centre. The surrounding seas are rich in fish and other sea foods, with corals and pearls of commercial importance. The climate is warm and sultry. Relatively cool springs are followed by hot, humid summers, with temperatures rising to 35°C (95°F) and above in summer. Rainfall is sparse, but with underground water provides enough moisture to grow vegetables, fodder crops, rice, citrus fruit, dates and pasture grasses. Semi-desert vegetation covers the uncultivated areas.

History and Development
For long an independent pastoral, trading and fishing community of Arab stock, Bahrain was dominated by the Portuguese from 1521 to 1602, then by Persians until 1783. In 1816 it came under British influence, though continuing to be ruled by Arab sheikhs of the Al Khalifah family. It was one of the first Arab states to produce oil (1934).

Resources and Economics
Agriculture flourishes in the well-watered northern plains of Bahrain, supplying much of the local market with fruit and vegetables. Traditional fisheries and boat-building have declined, but growing port facilities now make Bahrain an important staging post and trade centre. Crude oil production continues from the central oilfield, but the state now earns far more from its refineries and oil-based chemical industries, which use oil pumped by submarine pipelines from neighbouring Saudi Arabia. Aluminium-smelting, construction, banking and finance and important food and drinks industries contribute to a well-balanced economy. Good roads connect the major centres, with causeways linking the main islands.

Recent Developments
Though Bahrain's own oil production is already declining, output from wells

shared with Saudi Arabia continues to expand. Oil-processing and refining, and the processing of natural gas, play increasing roles in the economy. Prosperity is spreading through the rapidly-expanding population, which benefits also from a welfare state with free education and medical care. A causeway between Bahrain and Saudi Arabia will further enhance Bahrain's position as a centre of commercial activity among the Gulf states.

Iran

The Country
The Islamic Republic of Iran, formerly called Persia, lies between the Caspian Sea, the Gulf and the Gulf of Oman. In the north it is bordered by the USSR (Azerbaijan and Turkmenistan), in the east by Afghanistan and Pakistan, and in the west by Iraq and Turkey. *Area* 1,648,000 km^2 (636, 293 sq miles); *capital* Tehran; *population* 45,689,000 (est. 1986).

Organization
Iran is an Islamic republic, with an elected President as Head of State and an appointed Religious Leader with authority to protect the constitution (Ayatollah Khomeini will hold this position for the rest of his life). Administrative responsibility rests with an elected National Consultative Assembly (Majlis) of 270 members, and a smaller Senate including both elected and nominated members. For local government the country is divided into 33 provinces. Iranians are mostly Shi'ite Moslems with a minority of Sunnis and other sects. The official language is Persian, with local languages used among Kurds and other minorities. English is widely spoken in business circles.

Geography
Iran lies across alpine-fold mountains – part of the huge system that runs latitudinally through Europe and Asia. The Zagros Mountains extend southeast from Turkey and Armenia towards the Arabian Sea, with several peaks above 3500 m (11,500 ft). Less extensive but higher ranges form the Elburz Mountains, rising above 5500 m (18,000 ft) from a fertile plain at the southern end of the Caspian Sea. East of the Zagros Mountains lie Dasht e Kavir and Dasht e Lut, the Great Salt Desert and Great Sand Desert that together form an arid central plateau. Southwest of the Zagros lies the broad, fertile plain of Khuzestan, at the head of the Gulf. Climates vary with altitude. Only a few hundred kilometres north of the Tropic of Cancer, Iran's southern coast is hot and humid, and the uplands of the interior are intensely hot, especially in summer. Winters can be bitterly cold, especially among the mountains where snow and sub-zero temperatures prevail. Rain is sparse over much of the country, but favoured areas are well enough watered to grow natural forests, rice, wheat, vegetables and citrus fruits. Some of the mountains, and the Caspian coastal strip, are well wooded and traditionally rich in wildlife.

History and Development
Though there is good evidence that human occupation of the Iran plateau began over 100,000 years ago, its written history begins during the first millennium BC – the late Iron Age when Medes and Persians lived there and recorded their activities in cuneiform script. Strategically placed on routes between Europe

and India, Iran was invaded by the Greeks under Alexander, the Parthians and spasmodically by the Romans; from it there spread the Persian empires that lasted until the Islamic invasion of AD 640. Arab, Mongol and ultimately Ottoman domination followed. Iran's modern history began in 1925 when, following the defeat of Turkey in World War I and the dismantling of its empire, newly independent Persia acquired a new leader – Reza Khan, a former Cossack officer. Replacing the hereditary Shah, he took the title Reza Shah Pahlavi, founding a new but short-lived dynasty. Reza Shah abdicated in 1941, and his son Mohammad Reza Pahlavi ruled for thirty-eight years before revolution swept the Shahdom away. Father and son between them engineered the development of the modern state, making use of steadily growing oil revenues to build up a mixed economy, while maintaining political stability and economic growth over several decades. Political unrest throughout the late 1970s, leading to the establishment of a single-party system and an increasingly repressive regime, precipitated the Shah's downfall. Ayatollah Khomeini, a religious leader with a strong following, returned from exile to guide the nation along its post-revolutionary path.

Resources and Economics

Traditionally an agricultural society, Iran has for long been a producer of livestock and grower of cereals; rice, wheat and sugar-beet are staple crops in the north, rice, vegetables and sugar-cane in the tropical southwest. About one third of the labour force works in agriculture and forestry, the latter providing small but significant supplies of timber, mainly for local use. Oil, mostly unrefined and destined for Japan and Western Europe, is Iran's most valuable export. Petroleum products, natural gas, small quantities of coal, and iron, copper, lead, zinc and chromite ores are also extracted. There is a substantial tobacco industry, and the early and mid-1970s saw progress in the planned development of light engineering and manufacturing industries. There are serviceable air, road and railway links between the main centres of this large, sprawling country, and plans for the improvement of all three when economic conditions allow.

Recent Developments

Iran's revolution of 1979 was only one of a series of political disruptions that slowed economic development. Minority ethnic or religious groups seeking autonomy within the country caused internal dissension, and a dispute with the USA over hostages for the exiled Shah's fortune led to costly economic sanctions. In late 1980 the Gulf War with Iraq began, precipitated by a boundary dispute in the economically important southwest, destroying oil installations and halting the flow of oil from that quarter. Continuing warfare has proved disruptive to Iran's finely-balanced economy.

Iraq

The Country

The Republic of Iraq occupies a central position in the Middle East, bounded in the south by Saudi Arabia and Kuwait, in the southwest by Jordan, in the west and north by Syria and Turkey and in the east by Iran. *Area* 434,924 km^2 (167,925 sq miles); *capital* Baghdad; *population* 15,988,000 (est. 1986).

Organization

A democratic socialist republic, Iraq is currently governed under a provisional constitution. A President and nine-man Revolutionary Command Council hold power, with a Council of Ministers running day-to-day affairs: a National Assembly and a Kurdish Regional Assembly have limited powers of legislation. For local government the country is organized into governorates and autonomous regions. Iraqis are mostly Arabs and Moslems, with Arabic the national language: there are Kurdish- and Turkish-speaking minorities in the northeast.

Geography

Centered on the ancient fertile lowland of Mesopotamia – the flood plains, valleys and delta of the Tigris and Euphrates rivers – Iraq also includes a small section of the Zagros Mountains in its northeastern corner, and wide stretches of desert or semi-desert uplands in the south and west. In the southwest it tapers towards the Gulf, reached through the narrow Shatt al Arab waterway which is Iraq's only outlet to the sea. The alluvial soils of the plains, among the first to be cultivated by man, were renewed annually by floods caused by spring snow-melt in the mountains. Iraq has hot summers with high humidity, especially on the plains. Winters are cooler in the lowlands and cold in the mountains. Rain falls sparsely throughout the year, turning to snow on the highlands in the winter. Natural vegetation ranges from desert to grassland, mountain forest and reed swamp, though centuries of grazing and cultivation have left little of it unmodified.

History and Development

Homeland of the world's oldest city states, of the ancient Sumerian language and of the Assyrian and Babylonian empires, Iraq had almost four thousand years of recorded history by the start of the present millennium. Originally a centre of Semitic culture, it was for long dominated by Persia and in the 7th century came under Arab rule. Mongol invaders devastated the area in the 13th century, destroying much of the long-established civilization. From the 16th century onward it formed a group of provinces of the Ottoman Empire (see Turkey). After occupation by British forces in World War I, modern Iraq was forged from the three Ottoman provinces of Mosul, Baghdad and Basra and declared a British mandate. In 1921 it became an Arab kingdom (with Faysal I its first monarch) and a parliamentary democracy, achieving independence as a sovereign state in 1932 though remaining strongly under British influence. Oil developments near Kirkuk during the 1930s boosted Iraq's economy. Political opposition to the monarchy, and anti-British, pro-Arab sentiment, developing during and after World War II, culminated in the republican revolution of 1958; in this and subsequent events the army played a leading role. The past two decades have seen continued unrest, civil war in the north (leading to limited Kurdish autonomy from 1961), and the emergence of the socialist Ba'th party, which currently dominates Iraqi politics. Despite these upheavals Iraq has succeeded in developing its considerable natural resources, though the economy is still oil-dominated.

Resources and Economics

Iraq is predominantly an agricultural society, with over half the workforce employed in farming, stock-raising and fruit-growing. Much of the central lowland and delta area, originally marsh or desert, has been drained, irrigated and improved for intensive cultivation. Several ancient canals, cut well over one thousand years ago to control the seasonal flooding of the rivers, are still used in modern irrigation systems. Dates, cotton and rice are the main products of lowland cultivation, while the uplands produce winter crops of wheat, barley and lentils. Dry ground above the flood plains yields good pasture for cattle and sheep, especially after winter rains: the poorer hills to the south provide forage only for nomadic stock. Iraq's present prosperity continues, however, to depend mainly on oil, which has provided the bulk of the country's revenues since the 1930s. Increased income since the price rises of the 1970s has encouraged national investment in industrial development programmes, improvement of amenities and of public health programmes.

Iraq is well served with roads, railways, air links and river ports; deep-water channels are maintained in the lower Euphrates and Shatt al Arab. Tourism has been an important source of revenue, with Ur, Nineveh, Babylon and other centres of ancient civilizations the main attractions.

Recent Developments

For over a decade Iraq has benefited from the high price of oil; reserves appear to have been underestimated and production is at present determined by demand. The country is increasing its pipeline capacity through Turkey and Syria, improving the use of associated gas, and developing further refineries and associated petrochemical plant. Cement and brick manufacture, bitumen production, textiles, sugar-refining, milling and many other industries are growing to meet the increasing demands of a society that is shifting rapidly from rural poverty to urban semi-affluence, and the most recent economic development plans lay emphasis on improved housing, roads and internal communications. Long-standing border disputes led in 1980 to active hostilities with Iran and finally to a full-scale war, fought mostly among the settlements and oil installations in the south which have been much damaged.

Israel

The Country

Israel stands at the southeastern end of the Mediterranean Sea – a narrow, wasp-waisted country bounded in the southwest by Egypt, in the east by Jordan and Syria, and in the north by Lebanon. *Area* (excluding occupied territories) 20,770 km² (8019 sq miles); *capital* Jerusalem; *population* 4,489,000 (est. 1986).

Organization

A democratic republic, Israel is governed by an elected 120-member Assembly (Knesset) with a four-year term, that elects the President for five-year terms. A cabinet of about 18 ministers, presided over by a Prime Minister, is responsible to the Knesset. Local government is organized in six districts with municipal, local and regional councils. The official language is Hebrew; English, other European languages and Arabic are widely spoken. Judaism is the official religion: the large Arab minority (11%) is mostly Sunni Moslems.

Geography

Israel includes a coastal plain backed by low rolling hills; in the north are the fertile plains of Esdraelon and the hills of Galilee and Samaria, in the south the

Negev desert, tapering to a narrow coastal enclave at Elat, on the Gulf of Aqaba. The narrow strip of central Israel is currently broadened and the eastern boundary lies along the rift valley containing the Dead Sea and Sea of Galilee. Territories occupied since the war of 1967 include the West Bank and eastern sector of Jerusalem (from Jordan), the Golan Heights (from Syria), the Gaza Strip and much of Sinai (from Egypt). Summers are mainly hot and dry, winters mild and damp with most rain on the northern hills. The original desert, thornbush and forest are now mostly replaced by cultivation.

History and Development

Formerly the homeland of Semitic tribes (including the Hebrews from about 1200 BC), this corner of the southeastern Mediterranean coast and hinterland was fought over and incorporated into a succession of empires; the Old Testament outlines its early history. Falling readily to Roman legions in 63 BC it was incorporated in Syria Palaistina – part of the Roman province of Syria; conquered again by Byzantines, Arabs, Christian crusaders and Turks, it was eventually included in land which, at the end of World War I, was transferred from Ottoman ownership to British mandate under the revived name of Palestine. Hallowed by Christians as the birthplace and homeland of Christ, and by Arabs as an Islamic holy place, Palestine was for long regarded by Zionists as the potential Jewish homeland. Israel came into being in 1948 when Palestine was partitioned, on UN recommendation and by force of Jewish arms, into separate Jewish and Arab states. Despite almost constant strife with Arab neighbours (occasioned partly by its occupation of land originally designated for the Arab state of Palestine), Israel has survived and flourished. Its cosmopolitan population has risen steadily, boosted by immigration and a high birth rate.

Resources and Economics

Irrigation, capital investment, research and expertise have converted much of Israel from semi-desert to highly productive land; agriculture is its major industry, though only about 6 per cent of the workforce is involved. Important products include citrus and other fruits, wheat, potatoes, greens and sugar, grown mainly on community farms (kibbutzim), with a high proportion for export. Chemicals from the Dead Sea, copper, phosphates and gypsum are among the few minerals available. Though short of indigenous raw materials, Israel has developed heavy and light industries, producing paper, cotton, textiles, flour, chemicals, processed foods and manufactured goods, and processing imported diamonds and metals. About one third of the workforce is engaged in these industries. Little oil or natural gas are drilled locally; most of the country's fuel is imported. Rail, road and air communications are excellent, and Israel's endowment with shrines (Jewish, Christian and Moslem) and historic sites gives it special attractions for pilgrims and tourists.

Recent Developments

Israel's economic development continues; helped by capital from overseas (notably the USA), agricultural and industrial productivity have increased in recent decades far beyond those of neighbouring countries. However, tensions within the occupied territories (only partly relieved by the recent return of Sinai to Egypt), the implacable hostility of the Palestine Liberation Organization and the enmity of Arab neighbours to north and east pose constant threats to Israel's security; the need to maintain well-armed forces hampers further economic development.

Jordan

The Country
The Hashemite Kingdom of Jordan lies between Israel, Egypt, Saudi Arabia and Iraq, with Syria along its northern border. Its single port, Aqaba, lies on the narrow Gulf of Aqaba that opens into the Red Sea. *Area* 97,740 km² (37,737 sq miles); *capital* Amman; *population* 4,032,000 (est. 1986).

Organization
A democratic state with a hereditary monarch, Jordan is governed by a Parliament consisting of a 60-member House of Representatives re-elected every four years, and a Senate of 30 members appointed by the King. As Head of State the King, advised by a Council of about 20 ministers, has executive powers including those of dissolving both Senate and House of Representatives; the latter was dissolved in 1967 because Israeli occupation of the West Bank prevented elections. Parliament was reconvened in 1984. Local authority is vested in eight provinces, three of which are occupied by Israel. Jordanians are mostly Arabs, Sunni Moslems by religion, with small dissident Moslem and Christian minorities. The official language is Arabic.

Geography
Jordan is a country of rolling hills and deserts, split in the west by the huge rift of the Jordan Valley. Scarplands above the valley rise to 1754 m (5754 ft) at Jebel Ramm close to the Gulf of Aqaba. The valley floor falls more than 400 m (1300 ft) below sea level at the Dead Sea in central Jordan. Most of the agricultural land lies within or close to the Jordan Valley; the eastern hills of Ard-as-Sawwan and the broad stretch of uplands east of Amman are mainly desert. The climate is mostly dry and hot, tempered by altitude and proximity to the Mediterranean. Winter rains bring fertility, especially in the northeast where grassland, trees and scrub form the natural vegetation.

History and Development
Formerly part of the Ottoman Empire (see Turkey), Jordan (then called Transjordan) came under British mandate in 1922 and finally achieved independence in 1946. Joining the Arab war against Israel in 1948, Transjordan gained and held Palestinian territory (including part of Jerusalem) west of the Jordan River, and accordingly in 1949 changed its name to Jordan. In the war of 1967, however, Jordan lost its sector of Jerusalem and all its West Bank territory – almost 6000 km² (2300 sq miles) – which remains under Israeli occupation. Endowed with few natural resources, Jordan has been helped by Britain, the USA and Arab neighbours to approach a viable economy. The country progresses under the leadership of King Hussein, despite its front-line position in Arab–Israeli conflicts and the presence within its borders of thousands of Arab refugees who drain its meagre resources and threaten its political balance.

Resources and Economics
Agriculture, a major employer in Jordan though contributing only about 10 per cent to the national income, has improved steadily under cooperative programmes. The main products – livestock, green vegetables, olives, fruit and cereal crops – depend on seasonal rains, though damming and irrigation from artesian wells are helping to remove some of the uncertainties. Jordan has a little

oil, recently discovered, and is developing other mineral resources, notably phosphates (for fertilizers), limestone (for cement), iron, copper, feldspars, and chemicals from Dead Sea deposits. Adequate railways and good roads link the main centres of population, most of which lie in the north and west. A growing tourist trade caters for over a million visitors each year.

Recent Developments

Still dependent on foreign aid for much of its development, Jordan continues to accept help from Western and Arab countries alike, absorbing political pressures from both sides. Improvements in agriculture and mineral resource development secured economic growth of almost 10 per cent per year during the 1976–80 five-year plan; the current plan seeks to continue along similar lines and develop new areas – notably the social services. Oil-refining capacity, phosphate-handling and processing, and cement production are expanding. Remittances from Jordanians working abroad add to the flow of foreign capital from tourism, and help to reduce the heavy annual deficit on imported goods.

Kuwait

The Country

Kuwait lies at the western end of the Gulf, bounded by Iraq in the north and west and Saudi Arabia in the south: the coast is indented, with several large islands. *Area* 17,818 km² (6880 sq miles); *capital* Kuwait; *population* 1,795,000 (est. 1986).

Organization

Kuwait is a sovereign state ruled by an Amir chosen from the royal family of al-Sabah. As Head of State the Amir appoints a Prime Minister: a council of about 18 ministers, mostly appointees, holds executive responsibility. In the Constitution of 1962 provision was made for a 50-member elected National Assembly: the first was elected in 1975 and dissolved a year later – a second has recently been elected. Local government is vested in one rural and two municipal authorities. Kuwait's indigenous population – mostly Arab – is outnumbered by transient workers of many nations. The official religion is Moslem, the language Arabic, with English widely spoken.

Geography

Practically all Kuwait is stony desert, rising from sea level to over 300 m (1000 ft) inland. There is little natural vegetation beyond hardy grasses and shrubs; exceptions are small oasis areas, mostly near the coast, fed by spring water. Rainfall, sparse and unreliable, produces spring growth that dries out in the searing heat of summer. The human population relies mainly on imported or desalinated water.

History and Development

For centuries a desert sheikhdom in an impoverished corner of the Ottoman Empire (see Turkey), Kuwait was known mainly as a source of salt. It came under British political influence at the end of the 19th century as a link in the sea route between Britain and the Far East, and was declared a Protectorate in 1914. Oil, discovered shortly before World War II and exploited from 1946 onward, brought increasing wealth. Kuwait gained independence and statehood in 1961, secured with British help after a threat of annexation by Iraq.

Resources and Economics
Though Bedouin pastoralists still wander the desert inland, agriculture plays little part in the Kuwait economy. Over 90 per cent of its rapidly-growing population now lives in Kuwait City and suburbs. Fishing has always been important, and continues to employ Kuwaitis in catching, processing and exporting. But most of the country's current wealth is generated from oil and associated gas – directly by its production and sale, indirectly from oil-processing and servicing industries, and more recently through industries primed or supported by the country's oil wealth. Building and construction, involving thousands of immigrant workers, are among the main activities. The service industries are expanding rapidly; local labour costs barely justify efforts to diversify the local economy.

Recent Developments
The current recession in oil prices has reduced production of Kuwait oil, but had little effect on domestic spending or the development of the country as a whole. Kuwaitis and their employees continue to enjoy one of the world's highest standards of living, and to invest their surplus capital more profitably abroad than at home.

Lebanon

The Country
The Republic of Lebanon is a coastal state of the eastern Mediterranean, bordered by Syria in the north and east, and Israel in the south – a narrow country only 80 km (50 miles) wide at its broad northern end, and tapering to less than 40 km (25 miles) in the south. *Area* 10,400 km² (4015 sq miles); *capital* Beirut; *population* 3,033,000 (est. 1986).

Organization
Lebanon is nominally governed by a Chamber of Deputies with 99 elected members, including Christians and Moslems in a ratio of six to five; elections are normally held at four-yearly intervals. The Deputies elect a President, who as Head of State appoints a Prime Minister and small executive cabinet. Local government is administered through six Governorates. Lebanese are mainly of Arab stock, with an admixture of Greek and other eastern Mediterranean blood. There is no official religion: strong Maronite Christian and Moslem factions tend to divide the country politically. Arabic is the national language; English and French are widely spoken.

Geography
A coastal plain, mostly narrow but broader in the north, is backed by the limestone and sandstone ridge of the Lebanon Mountains, up to 3088 m (10,000 ft) high. Behind rises the parallel Anti-Lebanon range, separated by the fertile al-Biqa Valley which carries the Litani River southward. The mountains are well timbered, though less so than in biblical times, and cultivated on their lower slopes. Summers in the Lebanon are hot and tend to be humid, especially

in the lowlands. Winters are warm on the plains but much colder in the mountains, which are normally snow-capped for several months each year. Rain and snow provide adequate moisture over most of the country; much of Lebanon is former forest and grassland converted over many years of careful husbandry into productive farmland.

History and Development

Site of the ancient cities of Tyre, Sidon and Byblos (modern Sûr, Sayda and Jubayl), Lebanon shared its early history with Syria (see entry); in the first millennium BC it formed part of the coastal state of Phoenicia, gaining wealth from trading and the export of its own agricultural and forestry produce. Occupied successively by Romans, Turks, crusading Christians and Mongols, it ultimately formed part of the Ottoman Empire (see Turkey), and the Arab state of Greater Lebanon was created under French mandate at the end of World War I. From its inception the new state – a unique mixture of Christian and Arab communities – developed strong mercantile and cultural ties with Europe, becoming a commercial centre for the eastern Mediterranean. Independence from France came in 1943, and the decade after World War II brought increasing prosperity. Though Christians and Moslems cooperated well at first, fears over a shift in the balance of power, factions in both communities and the presence of militant Palestinian refugee groups have combined in recent years to produce dissension, including a year and a half of destructive civil war in 1975–6.

Resources and Economics

Agriculturally Lebanon is perhaps the best endowed of all Middle Eastern countries, with a mixed output including wheat and other cereals, beet sugar, potatoes, cotton, tobacco, green vegetables, citrus and other fruits, and livestock. Forestry products from the hills also contribute to exports: roughly one in every ten Lebanese is employed on the land. In peacetime industrial production, jewellery and precious-metal working, textiles, banking and general trading contribute substantially to Lebanon's national income, but all have been reduced during the disturbances. Communications are good; the major ports of Beirut and Tripoli are linked with the interior by good roads and a rail network; Tripoli and the southern port of Sayda are terminals for oil pipelines from Iraq and Saudi Arabia. Tourism is a major peacetime industry, with scenic beauty, relics of ancient civilizations and cosmopolitan entertainments the main attractions.

Recent Developments

Despite the intervention of Syria and other neighbours from a concerned Arab world and invasion by Israeli forces, rifts between Lebanon's rival communities – mainly-left-wing Arabs (including many Palestinians) and mainly-right-wing Christians – have refused to heal. Civil disturbances, which began in 1958, continue to take a heavy toll of life, despite efforts of a Conference of National Reconciliation and a UN peace-keeping force. Loss of production erodes the prosperity of this small, scenically beautiful and potentially wealthy Mediterranean state.

Oman

The Country
The Sultanate of Oman, occupying the southeastern corner of the Arabian peninsula, is bounded by the United Arab Emirates, Saudi Arabia, and South Yemen. The Musandam Peninsula, isolated to the north, forms part of Oman. *Area* 212,457 km^2 (82,030 sq miles); *capital* Muscat; *population* 1,074,000 (est. 1986).

Organization
Oman is an independent state ruled by a Sultan (who is both Head of State and Premier) with a cabinet of about twenty appointed ministers. The people are mostly of Arab origin, with an admixture of African negro derived from former slave trading. The religion is Moslem, the official language Arabic, with English widely spoken.

Geography
Much of Oman is made up of a low, rolling plateau, contiguous to north and west with the Rub al Khali (Empty Quarter) of Saudi Arabia. The main northern range of Jebel Akhdar rises to over 3000 m (9700 ft), overlooking a narrow coastal plain facing the Gulf of Oman. The climate is uniformly hot–humid near the coast and on the mountain slopes, and drier inland. Winter rains provide a growing season for cereals and fruit in the north, and the southern uplands of Dhofar grow pasture in the summer monsoon rains. Natural vegetation is sparse: inland the specialized desert fauna includes the recently re-introduced white oryx.

History and Development
Formerly a Persian settlement on the trade route to India and China, Oman acquired an Arab population in the 2nd to 6th centuries and became a centre of shipping and trade. Omanis resisted Portuguese colonization in the 16th century, developing trade with East Africa (notably Zanzibar), Persia and India. Internal strife divided Oman between coastal factions who supported the Sultanate and interior tribes led by Imams (religious leaders). British influence from 1871 strengthened the Sultanate and suppressed slavery, finally helping to unify the country in 1959. A rebellion starting in the southern province of Dhofar in 1963 led to a police coup that installed the present Sultan (Qaboos bin Said) in 1970.

Resources and Economics
Formerly the rural, economically backward state of Muscat and Oman (the name was changed in 1970), development of oil from 1967 onward provided the revenues that have brought Oman rapidly into the present century. Cereals, dates, pomegranates and citrus fruits continue to be grown for local use and export, and agriculture remains the main form of employment. However, construction and manufacturing industries are growing rapidly, under a development policy designed to make the best use of oil revenues. Good roads connect the main centres and link Oman with neighbouring countries.

Recent Developments
Oman continues to prosper on oil revenues, which provide more than 90 per

cent of the state's income; recent discoveries of further oil and natural gas extend known reserves for several decades. Meanwhile Oman is investing in copper-mining, oil-refining and cement manufacture as alternative industries, and trying to improve output from lagging agriculture and fisheries.

Qatar

The Country
A peninsular state on the western shore of the Gulf, Qatar has short land frontiers, only loosely defined, with the United Arab Emirates and Saudi Arabia. *Area* approx. 11,000 km² (4247 sq miles); *capital* Doha; *population* 294,000 (est. 1986).

Organization
Qatar is an independent state, ruled by a hereditary Amir who is both Head of State and Prime Minister. There is a 16-member appointed Council of Ministers, and a Consultative Council of 30 members, also appointed. The people are almost entirely Wahabi Arabs; Arabic is the national language, with English widely spoken, and most of the population is Moslem.

Geography
Qatar peninsula, 200 km by 90 km (125 miles by 55 miles), is low-lying, with a rocky or sandy surface and little water. For generations it provided only a meagre living for small, semi-nomadic tribes – the surrounding waters were richer, encouraging local fishing and pearl-diving. The present prosperity of Qatar is based on oil, discovered in 1940. The climate is hot and humid throughout the year, with little rainfall or ground water. Desert vegetation or bare ground prevail over most of the peninsula.

History and Development
Though little more than a desert, Qatar was fought over intermittently by Persian invaders from the north and Arabs from the south. During the 18th and 19th centuries it formed part of the Bahraini sheikhdom, though never at peace with its island masters. In 1862 the British, intent on settling the area, installed a political resident and a sheikh of the local Al-Thani family, starting the dynasty that rules in Qatar today. British influence survived Turkish incursions, and in 1916 Qatar became a Protected State. Oil was discovered in 1940, but remained undeveloped until 1949, when the first locally-produced crude oil was shipped from newly-built port installations. Qatar achieved independence in 1971.

Resources and Economics
Qatar's lack of water and fertility made it one of the least developed areas of the Gulf up to the time when its oil was first exploited. For two further decades it remained a backward state, but the present ruler, taking control from his uncle in 1972, used oil revenues lavishly to modernize the country and diversify its economy. Already-developed offshore fields provided further income which was brought entirely under government control. Qatar has modernized its fishing industry, invested in further port facilities, and is currently developing chemical, steel and cement industries: at the same time it is providing advanced social welfare and education facilities for its small population.

Recent Developments
After a short period of recession, Qatar's economy is again expanding, with the development of gas-liquefying plant and petrochemical industries; further port facilities, power stations, roads and water supplies are under construction, and Qatar may soon achieve self-sufficiency in food production.

Saudi Arabia

The Country
The Kingdom of Saudi Arabia lies centrally on the Arabian peninsula between the Red Sea and the Gulf; its neighbours include Egypt (across the narrow Gulf of Aqaba), Jordan, Iraq, Kuwait, Bahrain, Qatar, the United Arab Emirates, Oman, Yemen and South Yemen. *Area* approx. 2,149,690 km² (829,996 sq miles); *capital* Riyadh, *centre of administration* Jeddah; *population* 11,220,000 (est. 1986).

Organization
Saudi Arabia's hereditary King is Head of State and may also be Prime Minister. He appoints a Council of Ministers (currently about 25), including members of the royal family. Local government is vested in eighteen provinces, with municipal and district councils. The people are Arabs, mostly Sunni Moslems; Arabic is the national language.

Geography
The Arabian peninsula, of which Saudi Arabia occupies four fifths, is high in the west and southwest, falling in stages to the east. From the narrow Red Sea coastal plain a steep escarpment rises to over 2000 m (6500 ft) in the north and over 3000 m (10,000 ft) near the Yemen border. The ancient Pre-Cambrian rocks of the escarpment are overlain in the east by younger sandstones and limestones, which dip to yield the rich oilfields of the Gulf coast. In the south is the desert of Rub al Khali (the Empty Quarter). Seasonal water courses cut the mountains on both flanks, some rarely reaching the sea. Summers are generally hot and dry, with irregular monsoonal rain in the western mountains. Winters are cool, with snow likely on high ground. Most of Saudi Arabia is desert, with oases and mountain grasslands where water is available.

History and Development
Occupied for millennia by Semitic tribes, the Arabian peninsula in the 7th century became the homeland of Islamic religion and Arab culture, both of which spread far beyond its boundaries. Mostly desert, Arabia itself continued to support only small local communities, though the holy cities of Medina and Mecca and the port of Jeddah flourished under Sharifian rulers. In the 16th century it came under Ottoman control. The final years of the Ottoman Empire (see Turkey) saw the rise to power of the House of Saud in the central peninsula; after World War I the head of the family, Ibn Saud, took control by conquest and diplomacy and shaped the modern state of Saudi Arabia. Ruled by Saudis under strict Islamic law, Saudi Arabia remained pastoral until the development of the eastern oilfields shortly before World War II. Within a few years it became one of the world's leading oil-exporters, with roughly a quarter of the world's known reserves of oil under its arid eastern lowlands.

Resources and Economics

Saudi Arabia continues to be primarily a pastoral country, with over half its population still making a living by subsistence herding on mountain pastures, or agriculture in the limited oasis areas. Nomadic and semi-nomadic herdsmen raise sheep, goats, camels and horses. Agricultural produce, grown mostly under irrigation, includes dates, citrus and other fruits, wheat, maize, sorghum, millet, forage crops, and tomatoes and vegetables for the town markets. Oil and oil-handling revenues provide over nine tenths of national income. Natural gas is exploited in the northeast; copper, iron and zinc ores are present but as yet unmined. Steel, petrochemical and cement industries are developing.

Saudi Arabia has good port facilities, internal air links, rapidly-improving roads, a railway linking Riyadh and other eastern towns with the Gulf coast, and a growing network of pipelines for exporting oil and natural gas. About a million visitors – mostly pilgrims to Mecca – are catered for annually.

Recent Developments

Saudi Arabia has entered its third five-year plan of economic development, which is especially concerned to develop secondary industries based on gas- and oil-processing. Better use is to be made of gas associated with existing oilfields; there are plans for new refineries and processing plant that will yield liquefied gas and a range of petrochemical products. These developments are centered mainly on new purpose-built industrial cities. The road network elaborated during the preceding five-year plan is due for extension, and telecommunications, water and electricity networks will be expanded both in cities and in rural areas. There is a successful scheme of economic incentives to encourage light manufacturing industries, hitherto undeveloped. Now diversifying its economy in stages, Saudi Arabia remains a strongly conservative influence – economic, political and religious – in Arab affairs. Benefits from the country's wealth, notably education and social welfare schemes, are gradually extending through the predominantly rural population.

South Yemen

The Country

The People's Democratic Republic of Yemen (also called Democratic, Southern, or South Yemen) occupies the southwestern end of the Arabian peninsula from Perim to Ghubbat al Qamar, and includes the island of Socotra. Oman lies to the east, Yemen and Saudi Arabia to the north. *Area* approx. 332,968 km^2 (128,559 sq miles); *capital* Aden, *administrative capital* Madinat al Shaab; *population* 2,186,000 (est. 1986).

Organization

A Supreme People's Council of 111 members is elected from the ruling Yemen Socialist party. The Council elects a presidium whose chairman is President and Head of State. He is advised by the presidium and an appointed cabinet of about 20 members. The country is divided into six Governorates. The people are mainly Moslem Arabs; Arabic is the official language.

Geography

The indented coastline is backed by a narrow plain with a range of steep mountains of limestone, sandstone and volcanic rock rising beyond. The highest peaks, in the central block of mountains, rise to almost 2500 m (8100 ft). Behind lies a high plateau, rising to further inland peaks and ultimately falling to merge with the desert of central Arabia, Rub al Khali (the Empty Quarter). The climate is generally hot and humid near the coast, cooler and drier inland; the mountains attract rainfall that allows crops to grow in the valleys. Natural vegetation includes seasonal grasses and semi-desert shrubs in the uplands, palms and other trees along the coast.

History and Development
Occupied by Britain from 1839, the tiny fishing port of Aden was developed as a staging post between Europe and India. It grew in importance from the opening of the Suez Canal thirty years later, and with its surrounding countryside became a British colony and protectorate, administered from Bombay. Development under British rule was virtually restricted to Aden and its environs; the rest of the country to the east remained pastoral, with both nomadic and settled tribes, some of Malaysian or Indian rather than Arab origin. Britain withdrew in 1967, leaving power in the hands of the left-wing National Liberation Front. Skirmishes with North Yemen and Oman, constant internal dissension and a weak economy have hindered development.

Resources and Economics
Agriculture is possible in upland and scattered oasis areas where meagre rainfall is backed by ground-water; the main crops are millet, sorghum, wheat, dates, cotton and livestock – mostly sheep and goats. Fishing from the many small ports is a major industry: agriculture and fishing together employ almost half the country's workforce. Salted and dried fish are exported. Though minerals (probabled including oil) are present, especially in the eastern Hadhramaut, they have not so far been exploited; rock-salt and sea-salt are the main mineral products. Oil-refining and a few light industries are centered on Aden. Roads connect the main coastal towns and a few extend inland, giving way to a network of tracks; there are no railways.

Recent Developments
Aden, the main centre of population, has declined since 1967 as a port and centre of trade. The rest of this widespread, thinly-populated country remains poor and virtually undeveloped, despite financial and technical aid, notably from the USSR and China. Union with the Yemen Arab Republic (Yemen), agreed in treaties since 1972, has never been realized.

Syria

The Country
The Arab Republic of Syria lies at the eastern end of the Mediterranean Sea, bordered by Lebanon, Israel and Jordan to the south, Iraq in the east and Turkey to the north. *Area* 185,180 km² (71,498 sq miles); *capital* Damascus; *population* 11,337,000 (est. 1986).

Organization
Syria is governed by an elected People's Council of 195 members, under an

elected President; the President appoints a cabinet of about 35 ministers, led by a Prime Minister. Most Syrians are Arabs, mainly Sunni Moslems with significant Alawite, Druze and other minorities: the official language is Arabic, though Turkish, Kurdish and Armenian are heard locally in the north and east.

Geography

Behind the short coastline (180 km, 112 miles) and narrow coastal plain rise the Jebel Alawite Mountains, to peaks of 1500 m (5000 ft) in the north. Southward along the Lebanon border extend the higher Anti-Lebanon Mountains, rising to 2814 m (9232 ft) at Mt Hermon. The interior of Syria is a desert or semi-desert plain crossed by lower hills, notably the Palmyra Range in the centre and Jebel ad Duruz in the south. Surface water is rare, except in the Euphrates and Orontes river systems and a number of freshwater or saline lakes. Summers are hot and generally dry; winters are cool and moist in the west, drier and sometimes very cold in the desert areas of the east. The coastal mountains, receiving most rainfall, are forested; grass or scrub vegetation grows in all but the driest areas of the plains.

History and Development

Forming the northern edge of the fertile crescent that extends across the Middle East, Syria has been occupied – and its rich western lands have been cultivated – for over ten thousand years. Successively under Egyptian, Hittite, Assyrian, Babylonian, Persian and Greek rule, it was a Roman province in biblical times and part of the Ottoman Empire from the 16th century onward. The modern state of Syria was formed from Ottoman provinces that passed under mandate to France after World War I; two provinces, Aleppo and Damascus, were joined in 1925 and became the French-dominated Republic of Syria in 1927; Jebel ad Duruz and the coastal state of Latakia were incorporated in 1936. Syria held its first parliamentary election in 1932 and attained full independence in 1946. Joining briefly with Egypt in the short-lived United Arab Republic (1958–61), it has since returned to independence, though seldom at peace with itself or its neighbours.

Resources and Economics

Agriculture is Syria's most extensive industry, employing about half the workforce. The coastal plains, better-watered mountain slopes and river basins are the traditional areas of cultivation, now extended and improved by irrigation. Wheat and barley are the main cereal crops; lentils, maize, millet, sesame, sugar-beet, potatoes and tomatoes are grown where the climate allows. Grapes, olives, figs and citrus fruits grow on the terraced mountain slopes, dates in the drier river valleys. Syria is a major producer of cotton, and of harsh Latakia tobacco. Heavy crude oil, exploited since 1968, is blended for export with lighter oils brought in by pipeline from Iraq; the value of oil sales far exceeds that of all other exported commodities. Natural gas is also drilled; phosphates and iron ores are among the few other minerals exploited. There are good road, rail and air links, supporting a growing tourist industry.

Recent Developments

Syria's current five-year plan provides for further agricultural research, especially in livestock production and development of the oil-seed industry – both with help from the World Bank. Phosphate-mining is scheduled to double or treble during the current five-year plan. Harnessing the Euphrates has more than doubled electricity production in the past decade, and further increases are expected. With a mixed economy recently boosted by oil revenues, Syria has potential for prosperity. However, hostility with neighbours – notably Israel – and its intervention in Lebanon commit it to heavy expenditure on defence (currently about 30 per cent of the national budget); inflation and other pressing problems have combined to slow down the rate of economic growth that might otherwise be expected of a country so well endowed.

Turkey

The Country
The Republic of Turkey lies between the Black Sea and the northeastern Mediterranean Sea, spanning the Bosporus, Sea of Marmara and Dardanelles. Eastern Thrace in Europe is bounded by Bulgaria and Greece; Anatolia in Asia is bordered by Syria, Iraq, Iran and the USSR. *Area* 780,576 km^2 (301,381 sq miles); *capital* Ankara; *population* 52,314,000 (est. 1986).

Organization
Nominally a parliamentary democracy, Turkey is emerging from a period of military rule imposed in 1980, when the bicameral Grand National Assembly of elected and appointed members was dissolved. A new constitution introduced in 1982 provides for a single-chambered Grand National Assembly: the first was elected in 1983. A President and Head of State, formerly elected by its own members from the Grand National Assembly, holds office for seven years: the Prime Minister and Council of about 25 ministers are Presidential appointees. Local authority is vested in 67 provinces. Turks are of mixed racial origin, including Mediterranean, Alpine and Eastern stocks. Sunni Moslems predominate, though there is no state religion. The official language is Turkish, with minorities in the south speaking Kurdish and Arabic.

Geography
Part of the alpine-fold belt that extends across Europe and Asia, Turkey is a mountainous country with extremes of relief and climate. Eastern Thrace, generally lower than Anatolia, includes a broad rolling plateau with mountains to northeast and southwest; low escarpments overlook the waterway that isolates it from the rest of Turkey. Anatolia is fringed by a narrow coastal plain, but rises steeply inland to ranges of 3500 m (11,500 ft) and more. The western region overlooking the Aegean Sea is the most hospitable, with broad valleys and relatively low mountain ridges. Central Anatolia is high plateau, dotted with volcanic cones and salt lakes that indicate its geologically-recent origins. To the south the Taurus Mountains extend eastward in irregular folds, lining the Mediterranean coast. In eastern Anatolia, close to the Iranian border, stand Turkey's highest peaks; Mt Ararat rises to 5165 m (16,945 ft). Summers are hot in coastal regions, tending to be dry in the Mediterranean and wet along the Black Sea shore; coastal winters are warm and damp. Inland summers are warm and winters cold – bitterly cold on the heights – with sparse rain and snow. Dry areas carry scrub or semi-desert vegetation, wetter areas forest or grassland, considerably altered by grazing and agriculture.

History and Development
Osman I, 13th-century Sultan of northwestern Anatolia, and his successors

(Ottomans) in the 14th century established an empire that spread from Algeria and Spain in the west to Iraq in the east, taking in much of southeastern Europe. Reaching its zenith under Süleyman the Magnificent in the mid-16th century, the Ottoman Empire declined steadily towards modern times, finally disintegrating at the end of World War I. Modern Turkey was founded from the ruin of its homeland. Defeated in war and threatened with dissection by the victorious powers, the country rallied under the leadership of Mustafa Kemal, a former Ottoman general. Often in opposition to his government, Kemal waged a political struggle and war of independence that, between 1919 and 1923, restored order and united a demoralized country. Bringing together irregular forces, he drove Greek invaders from eastern Anatolia and compelled the withdrawal of French and Italian occupation troops from southern provinces. Treaties established borders with Greece, Bulgaria, Armenia and Syria. Rejecting altogether its Ottoman imperial past, the newly-defined state deposed its Sultan and declared itself a republic under Kemal's presidency. Kemal's policy – to modernize Turkey along European lines – was put into effect immediately and maintained under his autocratic leadership until his death in 1938. Remaining neutral for most of World War II, Turkey subsequently aligned itself with the Western powers, seeking military and financial aid from the USA. It is currently a member of NATO, with associate membership of the EEC.

Resources and Economics

Despite its mountainous interior Turkey is a mainly agricultural country. Almost two thirds of its workforce farm, mostly on smallholdings of a few hectares; about a third of the national income is derived from farming. The main field crops include wheat, barley, maize, rye, potatoes, sugar-beet and onions. Cotton and tobacco are grown extensively on the lowland soils, grapes (for drying), tea, nuts, olives and citrus fruits on the warm mountain slopes. Livestock are plentiful but often of low quality. Small-scale fishing satisfies local markets but contributes little to the national economy; forestry is relatively undeveloped. Turkey has workable deposits of coal and lignite, and a small output of petroleum covering about one fifth of its domestic needs. Other minerals include chrome, copper and iron ores, bauxite and borax. Manufacturing industries are increasing slowly. Railways, roads, domestic airlines and coastal shipping are adequate for current needs. Tourism is expanding, with almost two million visitors now catered for each year.

Recent Developments

Economically Turkey has developed slowly, hampered by lack of capital and expertise and – in recent years – by overpopulation, unemployment and political indecision. However, economic development programmes have raised its economy above the standards of its poorer Middle Eastern neighbours, although it remains well behind those of the poorer European countries. Its income (GNP) per capita is about one third that of Greece or Italy. Development continues slowly. The population, concentrated mainly in the north and northwest, is drifting steadily towards the cities, where industries are growing and diversifying. Textiles and other manufacturing industries (petroleum products, chemicals, iron, steel and non-ferrous metals, food-processing, automobiles, domestic appliances, paper) now account for about one fifth of the national income. However, lack of employment sends many of Turkey's workforce (often the most enterprising section) to poorly-paid jobs abroad; their remittances add substantially to the country's budget. Long-standing hostility with Greece over Cyprus (see entry) and territorial issues in the Aegean Sea to some extent alienate it from the European community with which it is politically and economically aligned.

United Arab Emirates

The Country
The federation of seven small emirates that form the United Arab Emirates extends along the southern shore of the Gulf and Gulf of Oman, between Qatar and Oman, spreading inland to an undefined boundary with Saudi Arabia. *Area* approx. 83,600 km^2 (32,278 sq miles); *capital* Abu Dhabi; *population* 913,000 (est. 1986).

Organization
The Supreme Council of seven ruling sheikhs select one of themselves as President for a five-year term, and appoint a Prime Minister and cabinet of about 24 ministers to be responsible for day-to-day administration. An elected 40-man Federal National Council scrutinizes and if necessary amends laws originating from the Council of Ministers. The people are mostly Shi'ite or Sunni Arabs; the language is Arabic, with English spoken in the towns.

Geography
Abu Dhabi is the largest emirate, occupying most of the coast from Qatar eastward and including many offshore islands. Five of the remaining six emirates – Dubai, Sharjah, Ajman, Umm al Qawain and Ras al Khaimah – extend along the western flank of the peninsula that separates the Gulf and the Gulf of Oman; Fujairah occupies the eastern flank. Most of the area is desert, low-lying and featureless, rising to the al-Hajar Mountains on the peninsula. Winters are warm, summers very hot, with little rain: vegetation is sparse, except in the few oases where crops are raised.

History and Development
Formerly Arab sheikhdoms, the Emirates' first European contacts were 17th-century Portuguese and British voyagers. In the early 19th century Britain suppressed piracy and slave-trading along the Gulf coast, arranging truces with local rulers. The Trucial States, with neighbouring Qatar and Bahrain, regained independence on Britain's withdrawal from the Gulf in 1971: six formed a federation in that year (the United Arab Emirates), the seventh (Ras al Khaimah) joining early in 1972. Oilfields revolutionized the economy from the 1950s onward.

Resources and Economics
Only in the hills of Ras al Khaimah and the Buraimi and Liwa Oases of Abu Dhabi is there enough water for irrigation and agriculture. Wheat, dates and green vegetables are produced, and fish are caught locally in the Gulfs, but most food is imported. Oil and natural gas, found both on land and in the Gulf, provide most of the Emirates' current wealth. Abu Dhabi and Dubai own most of the oilfields, but the federation as a whole benefits from them; they form the bases of growing petrochemical industries. There are few other mineral

resources. Locally-produced cement is widely used in the booming construction industry, and relatively cheap power is available for aluminium-smelting and water-desalination. Roads and airlines link coastal centres.

Recent Developments
Like other oil-rich Gulf states, the Emirates are planning ahead for the time – probably within a century – when the oil runs out. Research and investment in agriculture and fishing seek to provide food for rapidly growing populations. Efforts are being made to introduce both heavy and light industries, from shipbuilding to small components manufacturing, in countries which were entirely pastoral less than a generation ago.

Yemen

The Country
The Arab Republic of Yemen (also called Yemen or North Yemen) occupies the southwestern corner of the Arabian peninsula, a coastal state of the Red Sea, bordered inland by Saudi Arabia and South Yemen (the People's Democratic Republic of Yemen). *Area* approx. 195,000 km² (75,289 sq miles); *capital* Sana; *population* 6,702,000 (est. 1986).

Organization
The Republican Constitution of 1970 is suspended; government is currently the responsibility of a three-man Military Command Council, under a Chairman who is Head of State, with an appointed cabinet of about twenty ministers. A General People's Congress of 1000 members met in 1982 to provide for a new charter, involving an elected National Assembly. Local government is administered through eight provinces. The people are Arab, with an admixture of African, particularly on the coastal plain and in the south: they are predominantly Shi'ite or Sunni Moslems, with Arabic the national language.

Geography
Yemen's lowland is a broad coastal strip – the Tihama – punctuated by wadis and rising steeply inland to a serrated upland between 500 and 1500 m (1500 to 4500 ft) above sea level. Behind stand the steep Yemen Highlands, parallel to the coast, and rising to peaks of 3250 m (10,000 ft) and more. Inland from the peaks the land falls through a series of upland plateaus to about 1000 m (3250 ft), merging behind an ill-defined eastern border into Rub al Khali (the Empty Quarter), the desert heartland of Saudi Arabia. Climates range from a hot semi-desert regime along the coast to damp, cool-temperate conditions with frequent winter frosts in the highlands. The Tihama is a zone of sandy deserts and semi-arid vegetation, with seasonal grass on the damper slopes above: the mountains and high plateaus, once heavily forested, are now extensively farmed.

History and Development
The Arab Republic of Yemen forms part of a once-larger Arab region – Arabia Felix to the Romans – extending northward along the Red Sea coast and eastward across the Arabian peninsula. Turkish forces occupying from 1849 never fully subdued the region, which was ruled by Imams of the Zoydi tribe. The southern border of the present state was determined by an Anglo-Turkish

treaty before World War I, though it was disputed after the war when Turkey withdrew. The northern border was determined by treaty with Saudi Arabia in 1934. Yemen remained an independent feudal kingdom until 1962, when a revolution (opposed by Saudi Arabia but supported by Egypt, and involving a civil war) deposed the last Imam. Civil unrest continued, culminating in a military seizure of power in 1974. Since then the country has remained relatively peaceful (interrupted only by a brief war with South Yemen in 1979), with slow and uncertain economic development.

Resources and Economics

Agriculture is the mainstay of the economy, employing up to an estimated 80 per cent of the population: practically all of it is centered in the highlands, where terracing and irrigation improve the land. Crops include sorghum and millet, barley, maize, wheat, cotton, qat (a narcotic) and many kinds of fruit and vegetables. Cotton, qat, coffee (traditionally exported through Mocha) and hides are prominent among Yemen's few valuable exports. Fishing is of relatively minor importance, and there is little left of the country's formerly extensive forests. Oil and other minerals (notably iron ore) are present but relatively undeveloped; salt is one of the few natural products featuring as an export. Local handicrafts in leather, metals, jewellery and textiles are well developed, though not as yet on an industrial scale. There are no railways; a growing road network connects the main settlements, and the port of Hodeida has been modernized and extended.

Recent Developments

The Arab Republic of Yemen, for long a feudal kingdom with little involvement in events beyond its borders, remains a backward state with many potential resources undeveloped. A high proportion of national income derives from Yemeni emigrants who have left the Yemen to work elsewhere: income per capita within the country is probably amongst the lowest for any Middle Eastern state. Links with South Yemen, promised by treaties after border warfare from 1972 to 1979, remain unforged; ideological differences between the two ruling groups continue to hold the two Yemens apart.

ASIA SOUTH

Afghanistan

The Country

The Republic of Afghanistan lies sandwiched between Pakistan in the south and the USSR (Turkestan) in the north, bordered in the west by Iran and in the extreme northeast by India (Kashmir) and China. *Area* 647,497 km^2 (250,000 sq miles); *capital* Kabul; *population* 18,570,000 (est. 1986).

Organization

A democratic republic with elected National Assembly under its 1980 constitution, Afghanistan is currently ruled by a Revolutionary Council, with a Presidium of seven members, a Council of 17 appointed Ministers, and a President; the President is also General Secretary of the Central Committee of the only political party, the People's Democratic Party. The country is divided into 26 provinces. Most Afghanis are Sunni Moslems. Official languages are Pashtu and Dari, with Uzbek and Turkoman widely spoken in the north.

Geography
Land-locked and 500 km (over 300 miles) from the nearest ocean, Afghanistan is a high country centered on the Hindu Kush mountains. Most of its lowlands lie between 600 m (2000 ft) and 1200 m (4000 ft), and the highlands that fill the centre of the country have extensive ranges above 3000 m (9800 ft); the highest peaks in the centre and northeast – extending into the narrow Wakhan corridor – rise well above 5000 m (16,500 ft). North of the Hindu Kush, foothills and plains descend rapidly to the valley of the Amu Darya (Oxus River) which forms the boundary with the USSR. South and west of the mountains lie drier and more extensive uplands, descending in broad terraces to the sandy wastes of the extreme southwest. Summers are hot and dry; winters are cold – intensely so in the mountains – with snow and biting winds. Vegetation ranges from desert scrub to upland pastures and dense mountain forest capped by alpine tundra; there is a short season of spring growth before the country dries out under the summer sun.

History and Development
Afghanistan was known to ancient travellers and writers as a crossroads for trade routes between Iran and China, and from India to central Asia. The modern state extends beyond the area occupied by the original Afghans (ancestors of the Pashtuns or Pathans), taking in other peoples of the Indo-European language group, as well as northerners from central Asia with Ural–Altaic languages. Incorporated successively into Greek, Indian, Moslem, Mongol and Mughal empires, surviving devastation by Genghis Khan, Tamerlane and other unruly neighbours, Afghans first united to form a nation under a southern leader, Ahmad Shah Durrani, in 1747. Regarding Afghanistan as a bulwark between India and the Middle East, Britain attempted alternately to woo it and subdue it by force, failing in both. Mutually antagonistic, united only in hostility to outsiders, the tribes that made up Afghanistan were immune to diplomatic tactics and successfully fought off three British invasions from India, the last in 1919. Internal quarrels continued to keep the country, under its feudal monarchy, virtually undeveloped until after World War II. Then a series of five-year plans for economic development, coupled with moves toward a liberal constitution, were initiated by the reigning monarch. He was, however, deposed in 1973, and reforms have continued slowly under a republican constitution.

Resources and Economics
Traditionally pastoral and with a large nomadic population, Afghanistan employs almost three quarters of its workforce on the land, cultivating small peasant holdings or herding sheep, cattle and goats on poor pastures. Small amounts of wheat, maize, fruit, vegetables, rice and other foods are grown; the land provides over 80 per cent of the country's tiny export income but much food is imported. Afghanistan's potential mineral wealth is probably great; currently it yields only coal, natural gas, salt, and small quantities of other minerals. Hydroelectricity is produced in small but increasing amounts. Industrial products include cotton, wool and synthetic textiles and leather goods (using local and imported raw materials), fertilizers and other industrial chemicals and plastics. Afghanistan's difficult terrain and climate and chronic

poverty have made roads a luxury; a slowly-increasing network of highways is growing from the ancient tracks and military roads that have served in the past. Some of the larger rivers – notably the Amu Darya – are navigable, and there are internal and international air links.

Recent Developments
Since the republican revolution Afghanistan's governments have brought the country into closer alignment with the USSR. As Soviet aid has increased, and Soviet involvement in the country's affairs become more tangible, aid from other sources (notably the USA and China) has been cut or withdrawn, and trade with the Communist bloc has increased. Afghani tribesmen are as unyielding in their hostility to Soviet forces (present in strength since December 1979) as their ancestors were to British invaders a century ago, and still sturdily resistant to interference by the armed forces of their own government. Helped by Soviet advisers the country proceeds with its economic development programmes; considerable investment has been made in agriculture, mineral-exploitation and development (natural gas is exported to neighbouring parts of the USSR), hydroelectricity-generating capacity, and the improvement of roads and communications.

Bangladesh

The Country
The People's Republic of Bangladesh stands between the Bay of Bengal and the foothills of the eastern Himalayas, bordered by Indian states (West Bengal, Assam, Meghalaya, Tripura and Mizoram) and Burma. *Area* 143,998 km² (55,598 sq miles); *capital* Dacca; *population* 104,211,000 (est. 1986).

Organization
Bangladesh's constitution of 1973, amended in 1977, provides for an elected President, a Council of Ministers, and an elected parliament (Jaliya Sangsad) of 300 members. In a military coup of March 1982, the Commanding Officer of the Army suspended the constitution and declared martial law, suspending the President and appointing himself chief martial law administrator. Under martial law the country is divided into military districts. The people of Bangladesh are of mixed ethnic background, including Veddas, Aryans, Mongoloids, Persians, Turks and Bengalis in their pedigrees. About 80 per cent is Moslem (mostly Sunni, a few Shi'ite), the rest mainly Hindu. The common language is Bengali, with English widely spoken.

Geography
Crossed by the lower waters of the Ganga (Ganges), Brahmaputra, Meghna, Surma and other great rivers, Bangladesh is mostly low-lying and slopes almost imperceptibly towards the south. Land alternates with rivers, lakes, streams and marshes; some lies on the flood-plains of the major rivers and periodic inundation brings both problems and renewed soil fertility. Southwestern and southern Bangladesh are made up almost entirely of delta deposits, annually extending further into the Bay of Bengal. Chittagong in the east has a more stable coastal plain of sand and clay. The highest land, rising to little over 330 m (1100 ft), occurs near Sylhet in the northeast and in the hill tracts of Chittagong.

Climatically Bangladesh lies squarely in the Bengal monsoon area, with very warm, relatively dry winters, and hot summers with heavy rain almost daily from June to September. The heaviest rains – up to 500 cm (200 in) – fall on the northeastern hills. Late spring and early autumn are storm seasons in the Bay of Bengal, with gale-force winds. High winds and low pressure cause 'storm surges' in the Bay, bringing devastating floods and salinization in the delta and along the Bangladesh coast. Heat and abundant water provide lush vegetation over much of the country. Forests of bamboo and palms clothe the eastern hills, and mixed monsoon forest fills the Madhupur jungle region north of Dacca. Huge areas of the southern deltas are covered with a distinctive mangrove and hardwood forest – the Sundarbans. Many of the forested areas are infiltrated by man and felled to provide agricultural land; those with least disturbance contain Bengal tigers, leopards, buffalo, several species of deer, elephants, bears, and a range of smaller animals.

History and Development
Before the arrival of the British in northeast India (1690), Bangladesh formed the eastern half of the State of Bengal, ruled by Nawabs and with a long background of Moslem dominance. Under British rule Moslem influence in the east increased; in 1905 for administrative reasons a predominantly Moslem East Bengal was partitioned from a mainly Hindu West Bengal and linked with Assam, but the split proved politically disastrous and Bengal was re-united in 1911. At Independence in 1947, when India itself was divided and the state of Pakistan came into being, Bengal was again partitioned: West Bengal remained in India and East Bengal became East Pakistan – a remote but integral province of the new Moslem state.

By the late 1950s East Pakistan, isolated physically from the united western provinces and falling behind economically, was already seeking autonomy. During the following decade its position worsened and its sense of alienation increased, fostered by insensitive government from West Pakistan and language difficulties between Urdu-speaking officials and Bengali-speaking locals. In 1971 Sheikh Mujib, leader of the Awami League (the political party favouring autonomy), initiated the rebellion that gave East Pakistan – now Bangladesh – its independence. In the civil war that followed Pakistani troops were eventually neutralized by the Indian army, and a free Bangladesh formed its first government in 1972. The immense problems facing the new country – one of the poorest and most densely populated in the world – were intensified by political instability. Sheikh Mujib, the first President, suspended the parliamentary constitution early in 1975 and was assassinated later in the year during an army coup. Two further coups followed in 1975 and a fourth in 1977. General Ziaur Rahman, who headed the government from 1975 and became a popular President in 1977, was assassinated in 1981 after four years of authoritarian but progressive rule, and a military coup followed in 1982.

Resources and Economics
Bangladesh, one of the world's most fertile countries, has an enormous potential for even higher agricultural productivity; however, yields are seldom optimal due to uneconomically small holdings of land, archaic methods and reliance on traditional crops – often compounded by drought or flood. Up to 80 per cent of the workforce is believed to be involved in farming, providing almost half the country's annual budget and nearly all its export revenue. Rice is the major crop; although high yields are obtained in good years, rice is imported in

quantity to feed the growing human population. More wheat is being grown as an alternative to rice, and wheat and other cereals are imported. Jute is a successful crop for export, but demand both for raw fibre and for its products – carpet backings, rope and coarse fibres – is variable and if anything decreasing as synthetic substitutes are found. Tea is grown in the hills as a plantation crop, sugar-cane, potatoes, yams and vegetables for local consumption, and livestock marginally and fish importantly add to Bangladesh's larder – ill-distributed rather than meagre. Forestry provides little more than building timber and fuel for local consumption: the hill forests and Sundarbans yield small amounts of pulp for paper-manufacture and export. Hides and skins are exported raw, and provide the basis for small-scale leather industries: locally-produced wool and cotton are processed industrially and on a domestic scale in the villages.

Few workable minerals have so far been discovered. Low-quality coal is drawn with difficulty from deep mines; newly-exploited natural gas gives promise for a petrochemical industry and further products for export. Hydroelectric power is generated at Karnaphuli Reservoir, northeast of Chittagong. Cement-manufacture and steel-fabrication are among Bangladesh's few heavy industries; cars, motor cycles, fertilizers and other industrial and consumer products are appearing in larger quantities on the home market. Bangladesh has a fair network of roads, railways and air services, and an immense network of shifting but navigable waterways.

Recent Developments
Civil strife, lack of capital, and the burden of a huge, mainly illiterate and rapidly growing population continue to hamper economic development, in a country with few natural assets but its climate and soil. Growth of 13 per cent in agricultural output and 8 to 9 per cent in industrial output are balanced by a 10 per cent inflation rate and inexorable 2.5 per cent annual increase in population – over two million new citizens a year. Current economic plans seek to make Bangladesh self-sufficient in grain crops – mostly wheat and rice – by increasing the number of wells and irrigation, making flood control more reliable, using better cereal strains and better farming methods. Output of rubber, cotton, sugar-cane, tobacco and other crops of industrial significance is similarly being stimulated. There are schemes to distribute natural gas (currently available only near the Bakhrabad centre of production in the east) more generally about the country by pipeline, so that some of the smaller settlements may have it for industrial use. Basic problems of high birth rate and illiteracy are being tackled at local level. To finance even these modest development schemes Bangladesh relies heavily on foreign aid and loans, receiving help from the USA, Western European countries, OPEC and the Soviet bloc, and benefiting significantly from the remittances of Bangladeshis working abroad. The efficacy of foreign aid, especially in helping underprivileged groups, is increasingly questioned.

Bhutan

The Country
The Kingdom of Bhutan lies on the southern edge of the Himalayas, bounded by Nepal, China (Tibet) and India. *Area* approx. 47,000 km^2 (18,147 sq miles); *capital* Thimphu; *population* 1,484,000 (est. 1986).

Organization

Bhutan is a monarchy governed by the King, a nine-member Royal Advisory Council, and a six-member Council of Ministers. The Councils are responsible to a National Assembly composed of 110 elected members, 10 regional representatives of monasteries and 30 officials, including the Council members. Northern Bhutanese come of Tibetan stock, speaking Tibetan and practising Buddhism. Easterners too are Buddhists, while southerners tend to be Nepalis, speaking Nepali and practising the Hindu religion.

Geography

Southern Bhutan is the Duars plain, a narrow fringe of the Brahmaputra River plain, in places less than 16 km (10 miles) wide. Behind it rise the foothills of the Himalayas, with narrow valleys and passes leading up between the mountains. Forested ridges alternate with long, fertile, interconnected valleys, rising in steps to peaks of 2500 m (8500 ft) and more. Above soar the main peaks of the eastern Himalayas; several along the Chinese border rise above 7000 m (23,000 ft), and many are permanently ice-capped. Southern Bhutan is hot and rainy; the foothills are cooler and moderately wet, and the mountains have a dry, alpine climate. The plains and lower mountains are forested, yielding to grasslands and tundra among the peaks.

History and Development

Bhutan's history is little known. It appears to have become a kingdom in the Middle Ages, acquiring a Tibetan lama as monarch. The king and his successors, who included both spiritual and temporal leaders, seem to have brought little unity to the country: local governors and their followers fought for the privilege of ruling, causing strife between neighbouring settlements. In 1907 a particularly powerful governor (great-grandfather of the present king) declared himself hereditary monarch; in 1910 Bhutan entered into a treaty relationship with Britain that helped to stabilize both monarchy and country.

Resources and Economics

With an economy based almost entirely on agriculture and forestry, Bhutan produces practically all its own food. Rice, wheat, maize and mountain barley are the main crops, but almost anything can be grown in its fertile lowland soils, and the country exports timber, cereals, fruit, cardamom and many other products. Minerals remain mostly untapped; a little hydroelectric power is generated. Industries, mostly small and local, include woodwork, weaving, food-processing and plywood manufacture. Roads are poor but improving; there are airlinks within the country and with the outside world, and a limited tourist industry has begun.

Recent Developments

In a series of five-year development plans supported by Indian and international aid, Bhutan is gradually organizing its resources. Priorities in the current plan include extending the road network, improving education and building further hydroelectric power stations. Indian influence is now very strong from the south, as a response to Chinese claims from the north.

Burma

The Country
The Socialist Republic of the Union of Burma lies on the east flank of the Bay of Bengal and Andaman Sea, bordered by Bangladesh, India, China (Tibet, Yunnan), Laos and Thailand. *Area* 676,552 km² (261,216 sq miles); *capital* Rangoon; *population* 41,812,000 (est. 1986).

Organization
A one-party socialist republic, Burma has an elected People's Assembly (Pyithu Hluttaw) of 464 members; this elects within itself a 29-member State Council (which selects the President and Head of State), and a Prime Minister and Council of about 16 ministers responsible for governing. Local elected People's Councils work at different levels in the constituent states of the Union. Historically the Burmese blend northern stocks from Tibet with eastern stocks from Thailand; about 80 per cent are Buddhist, with Christian, Moslem and Hindu minorities. Burmese is the official language; many tribal languages are spoken locally, and English is widely understood in the cities.

Geography
Burma is made up of alternating mountain ridges and valleys, strongly oriented north and south. In the centre lies the broad valley of the Irrawaddy and Chindwin rivers, falling steeply from the high mountains that fringe the north and line the border with China. Thala La (5881 m, 19,295 ft) is the highest peak. To the west bordering India are the Chin and Arakan mountains, rising to 3053 m (10,018 ft) at Mt Victoria. To the east stands the more complex Shan plateau, split longitudinally by the Salween river valley; its folded hills stretch southward into the Tenasserim mountains and ultimately into the Malay Peninsula. Burmese territory extends along the west side of the peninsula to Kawthaung at 10° N, flanked by the many islands of the Mergui Archipelago. The climate is tropical – warm from October to February and hot for the rest of the year. Heavy monsoon rains fall along the coast between May and September; the central valley and Shan plateau are relatively dry. Burma is heavily forested with hardwoods, especially in the mountains where rainfall is heaviest. The river deltas and coasts support dense mangrove forests: bamboos, thornbush and grasses grow in the drier lowlands.

History and Development
With its long coast and accessible valleys Burma has for long been a gateway allowing immigrants and traders easy access to Asia from the west. The first settlers moved south along the Irrawaddy and Salween valleys. About 300 BC came later immigrants – the Mons from the northeast who settled lower Burma, and Pyus from the northwest who spread southward down the Irrawaddy and into Arakan. Strong cultural influences, including Buddhism, crossed the sea from India, contributing to the foundation of several peaceful and prosperous societies. From them arose in the 9th century the Burmese Kingdom and Empire of Pagan, an impressive civilization, reported on by Marco Polo and other travellers, that was destroyed by the Mongol invasion of Kublai Khan in the 13th century. Split into several kingdoms after the Mongols withdrew, Burma gradually regained its integrity, but in the 19th century lost territory to the British, who were advancing from Assam. Following a final war with Britain

97

in 1886, the kingdom was annexed and made a province – though never a contented one – of British India. In 1937 Burma became a separate colony with a degree of self-government, achieving full independence in 1948. A coup in 1962 led ultimately to the creation of the Socialist Republic in 1973.

Resources and Economics

Burma's economy depends heavily on agriculture and forestry, which between them employ about two thirds of the workforce and provide half the national budget. Agriculture is centered on rice-growing, mostly in the lower Irrawaddy; the country is self-sufficient and gains about 60 per cent of its export income from rice. Sugar-cane, ground-nuts, beans, wheat, maize, vegetables and livestock are raised for domestic consumption. Burma's forests are heavily exploited for teak and other hardwoods, mostly for export and for fuel; oil palm and rubber plantations replace them in some areas. Rivers are well endowed with fish; marine fish are plentiful but relatively under-exploited. Minerals include ores of zinc and lead, mined mainly in Shan, and tin from Tenasserim: tungsten, silver and other minerals are also mined, with promise of more to be discovered. Poor-quality coal is exploited in the north, and Burma's oilfields currently supply the country's own needs. Water is plentiful except in the driest inland areas: the rivers are widely used for irrigation but under-used for power-generation. Manufacturing industries include cement, steel, cotton yarn, textiles, soap, pharmaceuticals and fertilizers. River transport is widely used; road, rail and air links are adequate. Tourism is virtually undeveloped.

Recent Developments

Following its socialist revolution Burma became isolated from its neighbours and from international markets, as a result of policies of nationalization, rejection of foreign interference and slow development toward economic self-sufficiency. After a decade these policies were relaxed slightly, to encourage limited private enterprise and allow selected foreign aid. Since 1975 economic growth has increased, currently matching rates in neighbouring countries. Burma meanwhile has profited from its long spell of stability and calm, and now shows signs of developing its economy from a firm base, in a politically tranquil atmosphere that neighbours might envy.

India

The Country

The Union of India occupies most of the Indian subcontinent, extending north to the Himalayas, bounded to east and west by ocean, and bordered by Pakistan, China, Nepal, Bangladesh, Bhutan and Burma. The Andaman and Nicobar Islands in the Indian Ocean form a territory of the Union. *Area* 3,287,590 km² (1,269,339 sq miles); *capital* New Delhi; *population* 766,515,000 (est. 1986).

Organization

India is a federal republic of twenty-two self-governing states and nine administered territories. Power rests with a bicameral federal Parliament – a lower house (Lok Sabha – House of the People) of 542 elected members and two presidential nominees, and an upper house (Rajya Sabha – Council of States) with 232 members elected by the States' Assemblies, and 12 presidential nominees. The President and Head of State, elected by a college drawn from Parliament and the State legislatures, appoints a Prime Minister and (with the Prime Minister's advice) a Council of about 20 ministers. State governments have their own elected Parliaments (of one or two houses), Governor, Chief Minister and Council of Ministers. The territories are governed directly by the federal government through appointed administrators. The official language is Hindi but many others are spoken, including English which is widely used. Over 80 per cent of the population is Hindu, with substantial minorities of Moslems and other religions.

Geography

Kite-shaped and spanning over 3500 km (2200 miles) from north to south, India is Asia's second-largest state; with its huge and ever-growing population it is the world's second-largest nation, faced with perhaps the world's largest problems of organization in its everyday affairs. Geographers divide it into three major zones – the northern mountains, the central river plains and the plateau or peninsula that lies to the south.

The northern mountains – folded alpine ridges and valleys still being re-shaped by lateral pressures and vertical uplift – rise in steps from a few hundred metres above sea level to over 7000 m (23,000 ft). Several of the highest peaks and most extensive areas of snow and ice are found in the Karakoram and the Ladakh plateau area of Jammu and Kashmir – west and north of cease-fire lines with Pakistan and China respectively. But high peaks occur all along the Himalayan border, in Himachal Pradesh, Uttar Pradesh and Arunachal Pradesh (India's remote northeastern corner). Though the mountains are relatively bare above 5000 m (16,500 ft), the lower slopes and valleys carry forest and rich alpine pastures; cool, sunny and well-watered by monsoon rains, they support surprisingly large human populations in hundreds of small village communities. Meghalaya, an isolated plateau massif rising to 1961 m (6434 ft) in the northeast, has one of the wettest climates on Earth (see data for Cherrapunji, Section 3); adjoining north-to-south ranges of eastern Assam are also rainy and heavily forested except where they are cleared for agriculture.

South of the foothills the great plains cross India from Assam to the Punjab, continuing southward through Pakistan and the western lowlands of Rajasthan. They end in Gujarat, in partly-forested Kathiawar and the marshy Rann of Kutch bordering the Arabian Sea. Across the north the great rivers run – the Brahmaputra in the east, the Ganga (Ganges) and Jumna with their many tributaries in the centre, all converging on the huge common delta that now lies mostly in Bangladesh. In the dry northwest canals mesh with rivers, forming an irrigation network that brings fertility to millions of semi-arid hectares. In the centre and east there is less need for irrigation and more for flood control, to keep the wayward rivers in their place. This is the heartland of India – site of its oldest civilizations, now home of its biggest cities, densest populations, busiest industries, and best agricultural lands. Warm and dry in winter, hot and wet during the summer monsoon, it bustles irrepressibly with human activity from Calcutta (India's largest city) in the east to Agra, Delhi and Amritsar in the west. The plains of Rajasthan are drier, ranging from bare, year-round desert to seasonal farmland; canal-irrigated land is gradually being extended. In Gujarat, where monsoon rains are more reliable, deciduous forest grows in the south and the inland steppes are widely cultivated for cotton.

India's third region, the peninsula of the Deccan Plateau, is an area of wide plateau surfaces, high, rolling hills and broad river valleys, edged along its western flank with a range of jagged peaks – the Western Ghats. Forested on their rainier, sea-facing slopes, the Western Ghats rise from low plateaus and patches of coastal plain, once a jungle and now an important rice-growing area. Bombay, India's second-largest city, stands below the Ghats at the northern end of the coastal lowland. Facing the Indian Ocean are the Eastern Ghats, less continuous, generally lower and less spectacular than those of the west, and overlooking a broader coastal plain. In the dry centre lie the 'black cotton soils' of Maharashtra, and the less fertile red loams of Madhya Pradesh and Andhra Pradesh, cultivated for cotton, beans, millet and other staple crops that flourish under seasonal rainfall (with local irrigation). Eastern and Western Ghats meet in the hills of Karnataka and Tamil Nadu towards the southern point of the continent.

History and Development

The fertile flood-plains of the Indian subcontinent have supported human societies from the early Stone Age onward. The Indus Valley civilization (see Pakistan) that ended about 1700 BC founded the first cities. This was soon followed by the Aryan civilizations that spread from the northwest along the Ganga (Ganges) plains, bringing horses, chariots, pottery, bronze, iron and the elements of the Hindu religion. Small states with royal houses and bureaucracies, dating from the early centuries BC and identified in early religious writings, were from time to time welded into empires. The Mauryan Empire, founded under Candragupta about 320 BC, brought northern India and Afghanistan briefly under one rule, disintegrating about 185 BC: the Gupta Empire lasted a little longer (AD 320–540), falling eventually to White Hun raiders from the north. Similar empires, predominantly Hindu, formed and dispersed in the south during the early centuries AD.

The earliest Moslem influences were felt during the 7th and 8th centuries when Arab invaders conquered Kashmir, the Punjab and Sind. Permanent Moslem settlement dates from the 12th and 13th centuries, when Turkish armies swept in and established a sultanate at Delhi. From then onward rival Moslem armies squabbled over northern India, establishing petty kingdoms well into the south and west. The first well-organized Moslem empire was that of Babur (called the Mughal), a descendant of Timur the Great and Ghengis Khan, who in 1526 began to unite northern India once again under a single administration. The Mughal Empire lasted over two centuries, reaching its zenith under Babur's grandson Akbar the Great: at his death in 1605 it stretched from eastern Afghanistan to Bengal, and from the Himalayas to the Deccan. The Taj Mahal, built by Shah Jehan (Akbar's grandson) as a memorial to his wife (Mumtaz Mahal, the jewel of the palace), is one of the Mughal Empire's many splendid relics; the Moslem populations of Pakistan, Bangladesh and India are its most tangible legacy for modern times.

As Mughal power waned and fragmented during the 18th century, lesser empires arose. Most notable was the Hindu Maratha Empire, based on Maharashtra, that spread across the Deccan south of the Narmada River. There were many small, independent states, both Hindu and Moslem, and European influence was growing. The Portuguese, based since 1510 on Goa, were limited to the west coast with their influence already declining. Dutch, Danish, French and British coastal forts, established in mutual competition for trade during the 17th century, were now becoming bases for expansion. Dutch and Danish influences remained small: French competition was eliminated in 1761 after military defeat, leaving Britain free to expand. British interests were represented by the East India Company, a private trading company which, as its responsibilities in India grew, was progressively regulated and brought under control by the British government. From a handful of trading rights granted by the Mughal Emperor in 1615–18, the Company's holdings had spread by the late 18th century to include ownership of Bengal and several southern enclaves, and political influence or control over much of the rest. After the revolt of 1857–59 (the Indian Mutiny), when power was finally transferred from Company to Crown, all of India came under British domination – though many areas remained under the control of native rulers who had sworn allegiance to the Queen-Empress.

Indian politicians, both Moslem and Hindu, began to sue for independence from the late 19th century onward. Success came in 1947 when the modern federal India – British India shorn of its Moslem-majority states – achieved sovereignty as a Dominion within the Commonwealth; in 1950 it was declared a republic. Since 1949 Pakistan has held a section of Jammu and Kashmir west of a cease-fire line (redefined after further hostilities in 1965 and 1971), while India has incorporated former Portuguese enclaves of Goa, Dadra and Jagar Haveli (1961), and since 1975 the princely state of Sikkim.

Resources and Economics

Despite massive industrialization since independence, India continues to live mainly off the land; about 70 per cent of the workforce is employed n agriculture, mostly at subsistence level on small farms, bringing in over 40 per cent of the national income. The main products are rice, wheat, sorghum and other millets, maize, beans, peas and lentils, oil-seeds and sugar-cane, and livestock (especially cattle, sheep, goats and poultry). Tea, rubber, coffee, cotton and jute are grown both for export and for local use. Dairy produce is important for local consumption, though milk yields are low by Western standards. Hides, skins and wool are processed for local consumption.

In normal years India grows enough food for itself, with a little over to store or export. However, with rainfall unreliable over large areas, only one third of the land effectively irrigated, and the human population increasing rapidly, crop failure can quickly lead to famine on a scale demanding emergency relief measures. Chronic undernutrition and malnutrition are common in under-privileged groups. Much grain is lost in store. More than 20 per cent of India is forested, supporting a small forestry industry; with cow-dung the only other cheap fuel in rural areas, wood is much in demand and all but the protected forests are delining rapidly. Fish provide an important local addition to diet along the coasts and rivers: marine fisheries are expanding to meet increasing demands.

India is well endowed with minerals; among the more valuable are ores of iron, chromium, lead, zinc, manganese and aluminium, and there are large-scale workings of clay, dolomite, gypsum, and limestone for building and cement. Graphite, garnets for abrasives, gold, silver and precious stones are also mined. Coal and lignite are taken in large quantities; petroleum and natural gas are present in fields as far apart as Assam and Bombay, and more reserves are likely to be found. Surface water is abundant in the north, where there is still undeveloped potential for irrigation and hydroelectricity. Industrial production now employs about 10 per cent of the population – a small but slowly-growing proportion – and accounts for almost 20 per cent of national income. Heavy industrial products include iron and steel, heavy machinery and castings, cement, petroleum-derivatives and chemicals; lighter industries produce electronic and electrical goods, paper, cotton and textiles, processed jute, leather goods, bicycles, motor cars and motor cycles, engines, sewing machines, handicrafts, foodstuffs, and many other consumer products for the growing home market and for export. Roads and railways are plentiful though not always well maintained; there are good air links and ferries, and India has a large and economically significant tourist industry.

Recent Developments
Like its neighbours Pakistan and Bangladesh, India has a large population living mainly in rural poverty, and increasing at a rate that tends to keep it poor despite economic progress. While development since independence has been erratic but positive, the population has also increased steadily: there are twice as many Indians as there were in 1947, and at the present rate of increase there will be over one billion by the end of the century. The current five-year plan aims to reduce the birth rate significantly and to increase agricultural output by 4 per cent, industrial output by 8 to 9 per cent, and coal production by over 50 per cent. Efforts are being made to reduce imports, which currently cost almost twice as much as exports yield in revenues. Fuel imports may be reduced substantially as more local petroleum and gas come on stream, and output of coal increases. Nuclear power production is planned to double during this period, and hydroelectricity production to increase substantially. Tourists and Indians working abroad – notably in the Middle East – contribute significantly to overseas funds. Much of the current plan is to be financed by India itself, though some foreign aid will be sought, especially in developing oil resources and industry as rapidly as possible. India's twin problems of poverty and unemployment, currently producing social unrest, especially in the more densely populated states and cities, are adding to the already severe difficulties of a country still practising parliamentary democracy at federal and state level.

Nepal

The Country
The Kingdom of Nepal stands towards the southern side of the Himalayas, bordered by China (Tibet) in the north, India in the east (Sikkim), south and west. *Area* 140,797 km^2 (54,362 sq miles); *capital* Katmandu; *population* 16,382,000 (est. 1986).

Organization
Nepal is ruled by a hereditary king, advised by councils (panchayat). After a brief experiment in parliamentary government with party politics (1959–60), the King dissolved the elected parliament and cabinet, reverting to authoritarian, non-party rule. Locally-elected village and town councils send representatives to district councils, which are in turn represented on zonal councils. The National Council (Rashtriya Panchayat) includes 112 members elected from zonal councils, 28 representatives of professional organizations, and royal nominees (not more than 15 per cent of elected members): from it the King selects a council of about 16 ministers. Most Nepalis are of southern (Indo–Aryan) stock; about 20 per cent are northern (Mongoloid). Hinduism (90%) and Buddhism are the main religions. Nepali is the official language; local languages and dialects are spoken.

Geography

Predominantly mountainous, Nepal rises steeply from a narrow lowland belt – the Tarai, 25 to 38 km (15 to 20 miles) wide – fringing the Ganga (Ganges) plain. Above rise the spectacular folds of the Siwalik Hills, a series of escarpments alternating with forested valleys and narrow plains, at altitudes of 1000 to 1300 m (3300 to 4300 ft). Beyond them are further ranges of folded mountains at 2500 to 4500 m (8000 to 14,800 ft), enclosing high fertile valleys that once held glacial lakes – among them the vale of Katmandu. Above all rise the snow-covered, glaciated peaks of the Himalayas, in steps from 5000 m (16,400 ft) to over 8000 m (26,000 ft). The highest peaks stand in the northeast, Kanchenjunga (8598 m, 28,210 ft) on the Sikkim border, Makalu (8481 m, 27,825 ft) and Mount Everest (8848 m, 29,030 ft) on the boundary with Tibet. The Tarai has a warm monsoon climate with moderate-to-heavy summer rains: the higher mountains bask in sunshine but are permanently snow-covered. Vegetation ranges from deciduous forest and pasture in the foothills to alpine tundra at the snow-line: very little manages to live above 5000 m (16,400 ft).

History and Development

The high, fertile valleys, foothills and plains of Nepal have been settled by successive waves of immigrants – a minority of Buddhist Tibetan hill-folk spreading down from the north, and a majority of Indians bringing Brahminic Hindu culture up from the crowded southern plains. The mixture has usually proved a happy one, with the Hindus providing most of the government and social organization that has kept Nepal intact and virtually independent for over two thousand years. Successive dynasties can be traced from the early centuries AD. As a buffer between China and India, Nepal profited by trading with both, though most of the population – then as now – were village farmers concerned more with the struggle for survival than with international affairs. British influence was felt from 1860, when a pact with the Ranas – Nepal's then hereditary prime ministers – guaranteed Nepal's continuing independence, but accepted British control over foreign affairs and allowed Nepalis to be recruited into Gurkha units of the British Army. Nepal remained feudal and undeveloped until British withdrawal from India (1947) undermined the Ranas' control: in 1950 the Royal Family unexpectedly led a revolution, supported by India, that introduced a measure of democracy and opened Nepal to foreign influences.

Resources and Economics

Despite recent attempts to bring Nepal into the 20th century, it remains relatively undeveloped, with slow and unsteady economic growth. Over 90 per cent of the population lives rurally and works in food production or forestry. The plains and lower hillslopes are cleared of forest and terraced for rice production; the higher valleys grow maize, wheat, millet, barley, sugar-cane, jute and lesser crops. Rice, wheat and some sugar are Nepal's main exports, nearly all from the lowland Tarai, contributing substantially to income from abroad. Cropping is usually reliable but only a few areas are irrigated adequately and rain failure can lead to local starvation. Livestock and river fish provide additional protein in the generally limited diet. Forests cover over one quarter of the country, providing firewood and timber for export; increasing demands are fast destroying them locally. Kerosene and other fuels are imported; the country has immense potential for hydroelectric power but there are few power stations as yet. Few minerals are exploited commercially. Lacking raw materials, industrial development is restricted: sugar, jute, leather and cotton goods, paper and tobacco are produced so far on a small scale. There are only short lengths of railway in the lowland Tarai. Lack of motor roads isolates Nepal itself and inhibits internal movement (apart from one good link with India, one into China by Tibet, and one or two northwest–southeast highways). Air links bring in many tourists to visit the spectacular mountains.

Recent Developments
With some dissent the 'Back to the Village' campaign (1975), promoting the council (panchayat) system, has been well received, and was backed by a majority in the referendum of 1980. Committed to slow economic development, Nepal accepts aid from many countries including the USA, United Kingdom, New Zealand and West Germany, carefully balancing benefits received from its two major sources, India and China, and pursuing a policy of non-alignment with either. The current development plan emphasizes land reform, irrigation, soil-management and forestry-planning, further industrial development, and spending on health, education and transportation. There are longer-term plans for massive development of hydroelectricity that would make Nepal a major exporter of power.

Pakistan

The Country
The Islamic Republic of Pakistan lies between the Arabian Sea and the mountains of the Hindu Kush and western Himalayas, bordered by Iran and Afghanistan in the west, China (Sinkiang) in the northeast, and India in the east. *Area* 803,943 km^2 (310,402 sq miles); *capital* Islamabad; *population* 102,689,000 (est. 1986).

Organization
Pakistan's third constitution (1973) provided for an elected President and bicameral Federal Parliament. The current President (General Zia-ul-Haq), who seized power in a military coup of 1977, is advised by a three-man Military Council and a larger appointed Advisory Council: a nominated Federal Council of 288 members, inaugurated in 1982, has some parliamentary functions but no controlling powers. Provincial organization is currently suspended. Pakistanis are of mixed Indo-Aryan stock, predominantly Sunni Moslem. The official language is Urdu; English is widely spoken and there are many local languages.

Geography
Pakistan is centered on the Indus plains, with mountains to north and west, a central flood-plain, and extensive deserts in the south and southeast. The highest mountains of the north, including the Karakoram and eastern peaks of the Hindu Kush, rise well above 7500 m (25,000 ft); the highest peaks – Rakaposhi (7788 m, 25,551 ft), Nanga Parbat (8126 m, 26,661 ft), and K2 (Mt Godwin Austen) (8,611 m, 28,253 ft) – are in occupied Kashmir. Between them the Indus, a fierce mountain torrent swollen by annual snow-melt, carves a gorge for itself over 4.5 km (3 miles) deep. A road now crosses the Karakoram into China. South of the mountains the land drops rapidly in a series of steps, from high foothills to the dusty, rolling plateau of Peshawar in North-West Frontier Province. Along the Afghan border the mountains continue

southward, forming steep, almost impenetrable western ramparts that gradually fall toward Baluchistan in the southwest. The Khyber Pass, west of Peshawar, is one of the few readily-negotiable mountain passes. In the east the upland plateau falls away rapidly to the broader, lower Potowar plateau some 450 m (1500 ft) above sea level, densely populated and carrying the cities of Rawalpindi and Islamabad. The Indus, now a broad, mature river, continues southward across the plateau and through the Salt Range to enter the Punjab plain, where five major rivers join it. Central and southeastern Pakistan are mainly low-lying plains, some sandy or limestone desert, others made fertile by rich alluvium from the river itself and a network of irrigation channels.

Climate in the mountains and foothills is cool, with rain in summer and snow in winter. The plateaus, hot in summer and cool in winter, are drier throughout the year, with some rain from winter depressions. The Indus Valley is hot – sometimes extremely hot – in summer, with dry winds that carry desert sand; in winter it may be warm during the day, cooling quickly after sundown. Desert and semi-desert scrub grow in the dry regions, including the bare, harsh hills, with narrow strips of secondary forest and steppe along the waterways. Mangroves flourish in the Indus delta, and the high mountains carry some forest and alpine pastures, capped by alpine tundra.

History and Development

The uplands of Baluchistan supported pastoral settlements as long ago as 3500 BC, and the flood-plains of the Indus were one of the earliest cradles of civilization. At Mohenjo-Daro, Kalibangan, Harappa and several other sites in the Indus Valley are the remains of substantial walled cities over four thousand years old, whose populations lived by farming, manufacture and trading. The Indus civilization declined about 3500 years ago, to be replaced by waves of settlers, mainly Aryans from the north and west, who are ancestral to modern Pakistanis. Intruders of classical times who left their mark include Alexander the Great, campaigning in the Punjab in 327 BC, and Demetrius II of Bactria, a Greek who conquered the Punjab and upper Indus Valley about a hundred years later. In the centuries that followed the northwest came alternately under southern and northern influences. There was a settled period under the Hindu Gupta Empire during the 4th to 6th centuries AD, but it was later invaded by Hunas (Huns), Arabs, and ultimately rival dynasties of Turks who fought each other, as well as the local Indians, over northern India from the late 12th to the early 16th century.

Under the Mughal Empire that followed (1526–1761), the whole of northern India, including the northwestern provinces, remote Baluchistan and eastern Afghanistan, came firmly under Moslem rule. British influence, spreading from the three original centres of the East India Company, reached the northwest long after the rest of India came under its control. In 1843 Sind – the Indus plain – was annexed, and in 1849 the Punjab – home of the impressive and well-organized Sikhs now mainly in the Indian state of Punjab. The turbulent North-West Frontier Province and Baluchistan became part of British India in 1896. Half a century later, when Britain withdrew and India faced partition accompanied by tragic bloodshed, Sind, Baluchistan and the North-West Frontier Province opted – together with a partitioned Punjab and East Bengal – to form the new federal Moslem state of Pakistan. In 1949 Pakistan occupied part of neighbouring Jammu and Kashmir, fighting brief wars with India over the issue in 1965 and 1971. In 1972 East Pakistan left the federation to become an independent state (see Bangladesh).

Resources and Economics

Pakistan's chief assets are land and plentiful water, combined especially in the fertile Indus valley and Punjab plains. Agriculture employs well over half the labour force, currently accounting for about one third of the domestic income, with considerable potential for improvement. Wheat is the most important cereal, with rice, maize, millet and sorghum also significant. Pakistan is currently self-sufficient in wheat production, and rice is a major export crop that accounts for one fifth of the country's revenues from abroad. Sugar-cane and cotton are vital crops, the latter supporting considerable spinning, weaving and processing industries. Animal husbandry provides meat, eggs and dairy produce, plus the leather and wool used in handicrafts, carpet weaving and other traditional crafts. Fish, both riverine and coastal, find ready local markets and are processed for export. Minerals include plentiful low-quality coal, small yields of oil and more promising supplies of natural gas. Limestone, gypsum, rock-salt and a few other minerals are exploited.

River and ground water are plentiful; irrigation has for long been an essential element in Pakistan's agriculture, and several recently-developed management schemes involve hydroelectric-generation as well. The country now produces about two thirds of its power from local resources, one fifth as hydroelectricity. Manufacturing industries as yet contribute less than 20 per cent of national income and employ only about 10 per cent of the workforce – cotton and wool textiles lead; cement, fertilizers, sugar and chemicals are also produced from local raw materials, mostly for the domestic market. Pakistan has adequate road networks in its well-populated areas, a limited but recently modernized railway system and good internal and international air links. Tourist facilities are relatively undeveloped, though there are many visitors to its magnificent northern mountains and historic cities.

Recent Developments

Despite warfare, political upheavals, influxes of refugees and explosive population growth (almost doubling in the past twenty years), Pakistan has managed to alleviate some of its poverty and develop economically during the decades of independence. Politically non-aligned and free to seek aid from many sources, its most recent development plans have come closer to success than earlier ones, encouraging further aid from international funds. The fifth five-year plan (1978–83), stimulating transport, power supplies, agriculture and rural industrial development, provided for overall economic growth of over 7 per cent per annum, which is likely to have been realized: only one quarter of this plan required foreign aid. Though committed to socialism, the regime is encouraging private enterprise and the development of small industries. Religious influences are growing stronger in government, politics and law, and Pakistan is seeking closer links with neighbouring Islamic states in Asia and Africa.

Sri Lanka

The Country

The Democratic Socialist Republic of Sri Lanka lies southeast of India, 35 km (22 miles) from the Coromandel Coast across Palk Strait. *Area* 65,610 km^2 (25,332 sq miles); *capital* Colombo; *population* 16,755,000 (est. 1986).

Organization
Sri Lanka is governed by an elected National State Assembly of 168 members:
from it an elected President appoints a Prime Minister and Cabinet of about 22
ministers, responsible to the Assembly. Local authority is vested in twenty-four
district councils, grouped in nine provinces. Over 70 per cent of the population
are Buddhist Sinhalese, speaking the official language Sinhala; about 20 per cent
are Hindu Tamils, including many of Indian origin, and 6 per cent are Moslems
of Arab descent.

Geography
Geologically a fragment of India, and sharing its continental shelf, Sri Lanka is a
pear-shaped island 440 km (275 miles) long and 220 km (138 miles) wide. Low
rolling plains surround a central massif, slightly offset to the south; the highest
mountain, Pidurutalagala (2524 m, 8281 ft), is surrounded by lesser peaks with
striking ridges and escarpments. The mountain complex extends toward the
southwest, where the coastal plain is narrowest. Rivers drain outward from the
centre; Sri Lanka is generally well watered, though its northern limestone plains
become arid during the dry season. On the plains temperatures and humidity
are high throughout the year; the uplands are cooler and pleasant. Rainfall is
generally abundant, especially in the west and southwest during the monsoon
period (May to October). The island is well forested, with tropical monsoon
jungle in the wetter areas and more open forest in the lee of the mountains: much
of the original woodland of the plains has been cleared for agriculture.

History and Development
Sri Lanka's early history dates back to the Old Stone Age; Indian settlers who
established themselves along the coast from the 5th century BC dispossessed an
aboriginal population and drove them inland. Later the settlers too moved
inland, establishing a city and state at Anuradhapura in the northwestern
uplands. Originally Hindu, they were converted to Buddhism in the 3rd century
BC. Buildings, irrigation schemes and advanced farming marked this culture,
which lasted over a thousand years. During its decline Arab and South Indian
(Tamil) influences increased; the island was repeatedly invaded and a Tamil
kingdom was established at Jaffna in the north. Sinhalese civilization shifted
southward and into the highlands. During the 16th and early 17th centuries
Portuguese traders settled in Colombo, gradually taking possession of the whole
island except for an inland kingdom based on Kandy, which held out against
them. Later the Dutch replaced the Portuguese along the coast, in turn being
displaced by the British in 1796. Ceylon, as it was called, became a British
colony in 1802; the kingdom of Kandy finally came under its control in 1818.
Coffee, tea and other plantations brought in indentured Tamil labourers from
southern India, whose descendants form a second Tamil minority. Ceylon was
made a Dominion in 1947, and an independent republic within the
Commonwealth, with a more centralist republican constitution, under its
present name in 1972.

Resources and Economics
Agriculture in Sri Lanka includes both the huge plantations of tea, rubber and
coconuts (now largely state-owned), and the smaller holdings where rice, sugar-
cane, cassava, sweet-potatoes, cashew-nuts, spices and a host of other crops are
produced. Between them they employ more than 40 per cent of the workforce
and generate over two thirds of the country's export earnings. The plantation

crops provide most of the earnings; rice and other food crops grow well in good years, but Sri Lanka does not yet grow enough for its own needs. Many of the smaller farms run at little more than subsistence level. The forests provide for local timber needs; fishing, both marine and freshwater, is a considerable industry, adding substantially to local diets. Mining is limited – graphite, coal, ilmenite, rutile, and precious and semi-precious stones (including sapphires and rubies) are among the few products worked so far: sea-salt is also produced in quantity. Water-power provides a high and increasing proportion (now about 85 per cent) of the country's electricity. Manufacturing industries make growing use of locally-produced materials (rubber, tobacco, leather, paper, wood products), as well as imported petroleum, chemicals, steel and textiles. Good roads, railways and air links join the main centres and cater for a large and expanding tourist industry.

Recent Developments
Well endowed with natural resources and well equipped for communications, Sri Lanka is making good economic progress under a stable government, helped considerably by foreign aid and stringent planning. Its current economic plans provide for more hydroelectric power, irrigation and flood control, improved agricultural output (with special attention to the long-term plantation crops) and the development of both heavy and small industries to stimulate employment. Considerable effort is being made to expand tourist facilities for an ever-increasing market. Sri Lanka's main problems are its rapidly increasing population, which constantly absorbs and nullifies benefits from economic growth, and social unrest due to unemployment and ethnic tensions; social problems are acute between the Sinhalese majority who are prominent in government and public life, and the Tamil minority who feel at a disadvantage and seek to establish an independent state in the north and east.

ASIA SOUTHEAST

Brunei

The Country
The Sultanate of Brunei is made up of two small coastal enclaves on the north coast of Borneo, bordered and separated by Sarawak (Malaysia). *Area* 5765 km^2 (2226 sq miles); *capital* Bandar Seri Begawan; *population* 310,000 (est. 1986).

Organization
Brunei is a sovereign state ruled by a Sultan, advised by small appointed Religious, Privy and Legislative Councils and a Council of Ministers. External relations, formerly managed by Britain, reverted to Brunei responsibility in 1983 and it is now fully independent. About half the population are Malay, one quarter Chinese; the balance includes Europeans and forest aboriginals. Most are Moslem, with Confucian, Taoist and Christian minorities. Malay, English and Chinese are spoken.

Geography
Hills up to 900 m (3000 ft) occupy the interior, which is mostly forested and

inaccessible except by river: the southeastern corner is higher, rising to Buket Pagon (1850 m, 6070 ft) on the border with Malaysia. There is a narrow coastal plain, marshy and overgrown with mangroves at the river mouths. Only 4° from the Equator, Brunei is hot throughout the year, with heavy monsoon rains from November to March.

History and Development
Formerly the capital of a small empire that included most of Borneo and extended to the Philippine Islands, Brunei declined in importance during the 19th and early 20th centuries, For long supported by subsistence farming and fishing, its economic basis shifted dramatically in 1929 when oil was discovered. With British support and management it became a major producer, though remaining politically independent. It elected to remain independent in 1963 when North Borneo joined the Malaysian Federation.

Resources and Economics
Brunei's agriculture currently employs only about one tenth of its labour force; the main products are rice, cassava, sweet-potatoes, bananas and livestock, but most of the country's food is imported. Forests support aboriginal cultivators and a developing hardwood industry. The country's wealth is based on oil, natural gas and their derivatives, drilled in the west and exported through the recently expanding ports of Lumut and Muara. There are few roads, but Brunei has five sea ports and an international airport.

Recent Developments
Efforts are being made to diversify the economy, improving agriculture to increase self-sufficiency in rice and other staples, developing industries based on the country's indigenous wealth (timber, paper-making, petrochemicals), and developing an infrastructure to improve the general quality of life.

Cambodia

The Country
Cambodia (Democratic Kampuchea) lies between Thailand, Laos and Vietnam, bordering the Gulf of Thailand. *Area* 181,035 km^2 (69,898 sq miles); *capital* Phnom Penh; *population* 7,854,000 (est. 1986).

Organization
Cambodia is governed by an elected assembly of about 115 members replacing a Revolutionary Council: a Council of State under a President holds executive power. The United Nations continues to recognize the Chinese-supported Khmer Rouge government-in-exile under President Khieu Samphan. The official language is Khmer, the majority religion Buddhism.

Geography
Cambodia is centered on a low-lying basin surrounding a lake – the Tonlé Sap – and crossed in the east by the flood-plain of the Mekong River. Sandstone uplands lie along the border with Thailand in the west and north (including a striking escarpment over 320 km (200 miles) long) and with Vietnam in the east; the country's highest hills, rising to 1813 m (5948 ft), stand between the Tonlé

Sap and the sea. The climate is hot and generally moist; the heaviest monsoon rains fall with southwesterly winds between May and October, while the months of November to March are relatively dry. Monsoon floods reverse the flow of the Mekong River, filling the Tonlé Sap and depositing sediment on the surrounding plains. Monsoon forest still covers about two thirds of Cambodia, especially in the hilly regions; much of the lowland forest has been cleared for agriculture.

History and Development

The fertile lowlands of Cambodia, crossed by important trade routes between India and China, supported several early civilizations; most notable was the Khmer Empire (803–1444) that spread across much of the Indochina peninsula and left as its most tangible legacy the temples of Angkor Wat. Fragmented during the mid-15th century, the Empire fell into warring kingdoms. Cambodia in the centre was seldom free from warfare with its Thai and Vietnamese neighbours for the next four centuries. In 1863 the French, who had recently established a colony in Vietnam (Cochinchina), made Cambodia a protectorate, governing it by supporting and controlling its hereditary royal family. Cambodia achieved independence in 1953 under Prince Sihanouk, son of the reigning monarch, who served as Prime Minister and later as Head of State. Deposed in 1970, he formed a government in exile, linking up with the Communist-inspired Khmer Rouge Party. General Lon Nol who replaced him renamed Cambodia the Khmer Republic. In 1975 the Khmer Rouge took over the country, renaming it Kampuchea and renouncing all foreign aid and influence. In the civil war that followed Vietnamese troops intervened (1978–79), driving the Khmer Rouge into the hills and installing the People's Revolutionary Council that until recently (1981) ruled Cambodia.

Resources and Economics

Despite constant political upheavals and devastation, flooding caused by the monsoon brings annual fertility, especially to the rice paddies. In normal times over 80 per cent of the cultivated lowland grows rice, and the country is a net exporter. Maize, fruit, pepper, sugar and vegetables are also grown, and the uplands carry huge plantations of rubber trees – the rubber tree has in the past provided over 40 per cent of Cambodia's export income. Freshwater fish are an important item of diet, and the extensive forests provide fuel and timber for export. Over 85 per cent of the workforce is normally involved in agriculture, fisheries and forestry, though only a fraction of the country's potential for crops is currently realized. Cambodia exploits phosphate rock but few other minerals; there is no oil, gas or coal and little hydroelectric power, and industries remain undeveloped.

Recent Developments

Continuing in its unenviable role of central Indochinese buffer state, Cambodia has been devastated successively by war and civil strife for well over a decade. More than a million of its population (some estimate three million) are said to have died during the period of Khmer Rouge government and its aftermath of famine. Under current Vietnamese domination the country appears to be returning to stability, though the threat of renewed civil war continues and substantial foreign aid – mostly from Vietnam and the USSR – is needed to help its ruined economy.

Indonesia

The Country
The Republic of Indonesia includes the major islands of Sumatra, Java, Sulawesi, Halmahera, Seram, Flores and Timor, and some 13,000 lesser islands in the Java, Banda and Arafura seas; Kalimantan (southern Borneo); and Irian Jaya (western New Guinea). The eastern half of Timor (formerly Portuguese East Timor, now Loro Sae) was occupied by Indonesia in 1975 and made a province in 1976. *Area* approx. 2,042,012 km² (788,421 sq miles); *capital* Jakarta (Java); *population* 164,074,000 (est. 1986).

Organization
Indonesia is governed by a People's Consultative Assembly that includes a 460-member House of Representatives (360 elected, 100 nominated) and a further 460 appointees representing regional assemblies, political parties and other bodies. The Assembly elects an executive President for five-year terms; the President appoints a cabinet of about twenty-four ministers. Local government is based on twenty-seven elected provincial assemblies, and smaller assemblies down to village level. Indonesians include many local island stocks with some intermixture of Malay, Chinese etc., especially in coastal areas. Bahasa Indonesia (basically Malay) is the official language, but many other languages and dialects are spoken locally. Most of the population is Moslem, with Christian and (much smaller) Buddhist minorities, and relict Hindu populations (for example in Bali).

Geography
The islands that form Indonesia lie on a series of arcs formed by intense crustal pressures. Their steep mountain ranges are of geologically recent origin, and the thousands of minor islands that form stepping stones between the larger land-masses are mostly the peaks of further ranges, parallel and structurally similar, beneath the sea. This is a zone of frequent earthquakes, and Indonesia has many active or recently-active volcanoes, especially in the south. West of Kalimantan the sea is mostly shallow; deeper water lies between Sulawesi and Irian Jaya, and there are trenches over 6500 m deep (21,300 ft) south of Java and in the eastern Banda Sea. Indonesia lies across the Equator, extending from almost 6°N in the Andaman Sea to 11°S in the Timor Sea: east-to-west it spans over 5000 km (3100 miles) – considerably wider than Australia or the USA. Its administrative problems are correspondingly immense.

Kalimantan and the chain of islands to south and west of it stand on the Sunda Shelf, forming the edge of the Asian continental shelf. Kalimantan's main complex of mountains lies in the northwest, extending into Malaysia and Brunei: along its main ridge are several peaks over 2000 m (6500 ft). The mountains are mainly cloaked in dense tropical rain forest; foothills and swampy lowlands are also forested, except in the more accessible fringes where the land has been cleared for agriculture.

Sumatra, Java and the other fringing islands have spines of long, steep-sided mountain ranges, forested and dissected by swiftly-flowing torrents. Intersecting razor-backed ridges rise to peaks of over 3500 m (11,500 ft) on the two larger islands. There are several active volcanoes, over seventy in Java alone; Krakatoa, the volcano that blew up so spectacularly in 1883, is an isolated island mountain in the Sunda Strait, between Java and Sumatra. All the islands have fringing coastal plains; Sumatra alone has a broad plain on its northeastern side, low-lying and swampy but gradually being drained and converted into good agricultural land. As in most of the other volcanically-active islands, its lowland soils are enriched locally by debris washed down from the basaltic mountains: elsewhere more acid lavas yield poor soils and poor agriculture. The Lesser Sunda Islands continue eastward in a volcanic chain through Bali, Sumbawa and Flores: south of them runs an outer chain of non-volcanic islands including Sumba, Timor, Yamdena and Trangan.

Sulawesi is an island of steep, intersecting mountain ranges, mainly of hard igneous and metamorphic rocks; the long northern area alone is volcanic. The highest peaks of Sulawesi rise above 3000 m (9800 ft). The Molucca Islands to the east stand on a separate crustal plate – that which has carried Australia and New Guinea northward and seems still to be exerting pressure on the neighbouring southern edge of the Asian plate. Only in the east-to-west ranges of Irian Jaya has the resulting uplift produced spectacular mountains – the range of Pengunungan Maoke, with highest peaks above 5000 m (16,400 ft).

Uniformly hot and humid, Indonesia's equatorial climate is stabilized by the warm, shallow seas surrounding the islands. Over most of the region rainfall is plentiful throughout the year, with especially heavy monsoon rains between October and March. Only in the southeastern islands is there a relatively dry season from June to August. Rain forest is the dominant vegetation, turning to mangrove forest in the swamps and along the coasts. Much of the lowland forest has been destroyed for cultivation.

History and Development

Indonesian culture grew from many small, almost self-sufficient coastal settlements, virtually inaccessible to each other overland but trading locally by sea. Ancestral stocks may have come from the Pacific or from mainland Asia; from a common tradition each settlement evolved its own dialect and customs, giving rise to the many local languages and attitudes still to be found throughout Indonesia today. Indonesians are thought to have traded their local produce – mainly spices and resins – with Africa during the first century AD and with China by the 5th century. Buddhist and Brahmin religious influences were present in some of the settlements by the 6th and 7th centuries, when Palembang, on the southeastern plain of Sumatra, had already become a centre for international trade with India, China and other countries. Small kingdoms and later small empires rose and fell among the southern island settlements. Notable among them were the Javanese empires of the 10th to 14th centuries that flourished on the China trade and maintained peaceful relationships with many island and mainland states, and the Malaccan Empire that united southeastern Sumatra with the southern Malay peninsula during the 13th to 16th centuries.

From the late 13th century onward Indian trading settlements, founded first in northern Sumatra and later in Java, spread a growing Moslem influence throughout the islands. Aceh (Atjeh) in northern Sumatra became the centre of a Moslem empire, and many Javanese coastal states accepted Islam as strongly as the more conservative inland states rejected it. Christianity arrived with the Portuguese, who seized Malacca in 1511 but failed to establish permanent bases elsewhere. The Dutch who followed were more determined. From beachheads in Malacca, Batavia (now Jakarta) and many small coastal 'factories' throughout the islands, their commercial and political interests expanded persistently. For over a century and a half the Dutch East India Company monopolized the spice trade in the area, while its agents exerted a growing influence over the local princes and their courts.

After the defeat of the Netherlands by France in the European wars of the early 19th century, the Dutch East Indies factories came briefly under French and later British control. Returned to Dutch hands after the defeat of Napoleon, Java became the main centre of a new form of colonialism – a system of compulsory cultivation (cultuur stelsel) that increased and diversified its agricultural productivity, largely for export and for the benefit of the Netherlands, more marginally for the benefit of the local landowners and producers. During the 19th and early 20th centuries Dutch influence intensified and spread to other islands. Capital invested in a wide range of enterprises, from plantation cultivation to mining, developed resources on a large scale; by the 1930s virtually the whole area of present-day Indonesia was under Dutch colonial control, administered centrally from Batavia.

Freedom movements that developed during the 1920s and 1930s gained strength under Japanese occupation in World War II; their leaders were ready to declare independence when the occupation force surrendered in 1945. After considerable negotiation and an armed struggle, the Dutch withdrew in 1949 from all but Irian Jaya, leaving a United States of Indonesia under its first President, the revolutionary leader Sukarno. Within a year Sukarno unified the state, as a first step towards welding its disparate and widely-scattered elements. His subsequent policies as executive president earned the hostility of neighbouring Malaysia, took Indonesia out of the United Nations and brought it to the verge of bankruptcy. However, he and his successor, President Suharto (now in his fourth term of office), between them brought the new state to economic and political maturity. Irian Jaya was incorporated in 1969; East Timor's annexation in 1975 has not been recognized by the United Nations.

Resources and Economics

Year-round warmth and rainfall make much of lowland Indonesia ideal agricultural country; over 60 per cent of the workforce is engaged in agriculture, which generates one quarter of the national income. A high proportion of the output comes from peasant farms and smallholdings; many of the huge estates – particularly those taken over from Dutch ownership – were neglected after independence, but large-scale rehabilitation is bringing them back into production. The most important crop is rice, grown mainly in lowland paddies. Despite increased efficiency of production in recent years, Indonesia cannot grow enough to feed its rapidly increasing population, and is a net importer of rice. Cassava, maize, sugar, sweet-potatoes, bananas, tobacco and many other fruits and vegetables are grown for local consumption. Coffee, tea, rubber, coconuts and oil-palm nuts are produced on the estates, mostly as cash crops for export. Indonesia's lowland forests have provided huge quantities of timber for export; recent legislation, however, has reduced the rate of felling and export of logs, and increased the proportion used locally in timber-processing. Fishing is an important local industry.

Indonesia's second major source of income is minerals; already a major producer of tin and nickel ores, the country has largely untapped reserves of bauxite, copper, manganese and other minerals. Coal is mined in Sumatra; oil and natural gas are plentiful, and being exploited rapidly to generate capital. Crude oil and petroleum products, including liquid natural gas, provide over 60 per cent of the country's export income. Manufacturing industries are relatively small, providing textiles, cement, fertilizers, motor cycles, chemicals, paper and household goods, mostly for the home market. Indonesia has good inter-island boat and air links; there are railways and roads on the most heavily-populated islands of Java, Madura and Sumatra; the smaller islands have unmetalled roads and tracks. No special efforts are made to attract tourists except to Java and Bali, where scenery, temples and Hindu folk art are the main attractions.

Recent Developments
Now in its fourth decade of independence, Indonesia remains a sprawling giant that has not yet gathered its strength. Few other countries have a fraction of its problems. Its population is already enormous (Indonesia is the world's fourth-largest country) and growing at an annual rate of over 2.5 per cent. Its people are heterogeneous and polyglot, mostly poor, illiterate, unskilled in modern techniques, and distributed unevenly over an area of ocean half as big as Europe. Insular in every sense, they have little in the way of tradition or common interest to hold them together. Yet Indonesia survives as a community, even contriving slow but steady economic growth through three successive five-year development plans. The first plan, starting in 1969, emphasized agricultural development and brought Indonesia close to self-sufficiency in staple foods. The second emphasized industrial objectives, making better use of the country's own raw materials. Contemporary planning is concerned with the daunting tasks of distributing wealth more evenly and creating work – both in agriculture and in industry – for the one third or more of the labour force that is currently without work or under-employed.

Laos

The Country
The Lao People's Democratic Republic is a long, narrow state, bordered by Vietnam in the east, Thailand in the west, Burma and China (Yunnan) in the north and Cambodia in the south. *Area* 236,800 km^2 (91,429 sq miles); *capital* Vientiane; *population* 4,281,000 (est. 1986).

Organization
Laos is governed by a Supreme People's Council of about 45 members, under a President (who is also Head of State) and including a Prime Minister, four Vice-Prime Ministers and a cabinet of ministers and councillors: the Council was appointed by a National Congress of People's Representatives, formed in 1975, which required it to provide the country with a new constitution. Local government is managed through People's Committees at town and village level. The official language is Laotian; Vietnamese and French are widely spoken and there are several tribal languages. The most popular religion is Buddhism.

Geography
Laos consists of a high northern plateau of eroded limestone, rising to about 900 m (3000 ft), and a long backbone of deeply-dissected mountains – the Annamite Chain – extending southeastward along its border with Vietnam. The high central knot of mountains east of Luang Prabang rises over 2500 m (8200 ft). A narrow strip of lowland lies between the mountains and the Mekong River, which flows southward from the plateau and then turns sharply eastward to form much of the border with Thailand. The climate is warm and sultry by day,

cooler in the hills at night, with a marked monsoon that brings heavy rains from May to October. The hills are forested, with clearings for shifting agriculture; much of the original lowland forest has been replaced by rice paddies.

History and Development

Laotians originated long ago in southwestern China from whence they migrated in early medieval times: the Laotian state of Lan Xang was established under their first King, Fa Ngum, who died in 1371. After a turbulent history of wars with neighbouring Siam and Vietnam, Lan Xang was partitioned into separate states in the early 18th century, which neighbours continued to fight over. Fortified by Siam as a protective buffer zone against Vietnamese attacks, these states were finally reunited when France annexed Vietnam (Cochinchina) towards the end of the 19th century, becoming the autonomous French protectorate of Laos. After World War II Laos was established as an independent kingdom within the French Union. Caught up in the communist struggle for Indochina it became once again a buffer state between Siam (now Thailand) and Vietnam, splitting longitudinally with pro-communist Pathet Lao forces occupying the northern and eastern hills, and an anti-communist government remaining strong in Vientiane and the lowlands. Despite strong US involvement the Pathet Lao prevailed, taking Vientiane and proclaiming the People's Democratic Republic in 1975.

Resources and Economics

Like other states of the Indochinese peninsula Laos is primarily agricultural; between 80 and 90 per cent of its workforce is involved in farming, mostly producing rice in the irrigated lowland paddies or drier hill farms. Maize, fruit, vegetables and livestock are also produced for local consumption. Food crops depend heavily on rainfall, which is occasionally unreliable; bombing, defoliation and guerrilla warfare have reduced production and agricultural potential. Freshwater fisheries are an important source of food, and timber provides one of the country's few material exports. Tin is one of the few minerals currently exploited; coal and petroleum are of potential value, and the country exports a proportion of its hydroelectricity. Manufacturing industries are small and localized. River traffic is important, especially on the Mekong: there are adequate roads between the main centres.

Recent Developments

Devastated by decades of warfare with neighbours and between internal factions, Laos has never been able to develop economically beyond a stage of subsistence agriculture: even its capacity for growing rice has been seriously undermined, and Laos imports a proportion of its food. Though used for many years as a pawn in international power games, Laos lost US support at the end of the Vietnam War (see Vietnam) in 1975 and Chinese intervention became unwelcome in 1980; its development, necessarily slow, now depends mainly on funding from the Soviet bloc, Sweden and Vietnam.

Malaysia

The Country

The sovereign State of Malaysia includes two separate regions – Peninsular

Malaysia (formerly the Federation of Malaya) on the Malay peninsula, bordered by Thailand and Singapore, and Sabah (formerly North Borneo) and Sarawak, bordering the Indonesian province of Kalimantan and the Brunei enclaves. *Area* 329,749 km^2 (127,316 sq miles); *capital* Kuala Lumpur; *population* 16,205,000 (est. 1981).

Organization
Malaysia is a federation of eleven western states (Peninsular Malaysia) and two eastern states (Sabah and Sarawak). Head of State is a King, elected for five-year terms from the Conference of Rulers, a corps of nine hereditary state monarchs. The Federal Parliament includes a Senate (two elected Senators from each state and 42 appointed members) and an elected House of Representatives (114 from west Malaysia, 40 from east Malaysia). From Parliament the King appoints a Prime Minister and cabinet of about 20 ministers. The states have separate elected Legislative Assemblies. West Malaysia's population is over 50 per cent Malayan, 35 per cent Chinese and 10 per cent Indian: in east Malaysia about 25 per cent are Chinese, 12 per cent Malayan, and the majority Dayak (indigenous Borneans). Malay is the official language: Chinese, English and Tamil are spoken, and there are many local languages and dialects. Over half the population is Moslem, about a quarter Buddhist, with sizeable minorities of Hindus and Christians.

Geography
West Malaysia is a mountainous peninsula 700 km (440 miles) long and up to 320 km (200 miles) wide. Interlacing ranges of granite and limestone form the spine, with peaks rising over 2000 m (7000 ft); there is a narrow coastal plain in the east and a broader one in the west. Sabah and Sarawak occupy the north coast and northeastern corner of Borneo, a wide strip of rough mountainous country with several peaks over 2000 m (6500 ft): the highest is Kinabalu (4101 m, 13, 455 ft) in northern Sabah. The climate is equatorial – hot and humid throughout the year at sea level, cooler in the mountains, rains increasing with the northeast monsoon from September to March. The vegetation is mostly tropical rain forest, peculiarly rich and varied in species. Poorer secondary forest, grassland and scrub take over where the rain forest has been destroyed. Much of the lowland forest has been replaced by rice paddies or plantations.

History and Development
Malaysia has been inhabited from Stone Age times onward by hunters and cultivators of many origins. Western Malaysia was strongly influenced by Indian settlers from the 2nd century AD. These set up small states that combined in various ways to form empires; for example the Islamic Malaccan Empire of the 15th and 16th centuries, which extended far into the southeast (see Indonesia). Eastern Malaysia remained isolated for longer: its Dayaks – strongly localized riverine, coastal or hill-folk – were less affected by outside influences except for Chinese settlements from the north. In the 16th and 17th centuries Portuguese and Dutch traders vied with local Sumatran imperialists for control of the Malayan peninsula. British influence increased during the early 19th century, treaties in 1819 and 1824 establishing a foothold which eventually gave Britain control over the whole peninsula area. In Borneo Sarawak formed part of the Javanese and later the Brunei Empire: in 1841 an Englishman, James Brooke, was made hereditary Rajah, and the Brooke family ruled there until Sarawak became a British colony in 1946. Sabah and Labuan

Island (North Borneo) formed part of the Philippines' sphere until the mid-19th century, when they became British colonies. Achieving independence in 1957 and 1959, Malaya and Singapore united with Sarawak and North Borneo in 1963 to form Malaysia; Singapore left the federation two years later (see entry).

Resources and Economics
Throughout Malaysia agriculture is the main source of employment – between 40 and 50 per cent of the workforce is engaged in both hill and lowland paddy rice-growing, subsistence farming in smallholdings, and work in orchards and huge commercial plantations. Rice, palm oil, coconuts, rubber and tea are the main crops, together earning about a fifth of the Federation's total income; pepper, cocoa, pineapples and many other crops are grown. Forestry maintains a high output of saleable timber. Almost 750,000 tonnes of fish are caught annually, mostly from the sea. Iron, ilmenite, gold, oil, natural gas and especially tin are the most valuable of Malaysia's minerals, providing substantial export revenues. Industrial output is rising rapidly. Processed rubber and rubber products, petroleum products, textiles, electrical goods, chemicals and many small manufactured items provide both for export and for expanding home markets. Peninsular Malaysia (which leads the economy) has good road, railway and air communications; Sabah and Sarawak are less advanced. Good air and sea links join the two. There is a rapidly-growing tourist industry, especially on the peninsula.

Recent Developments
Richly endowed in many ways, Malaysia has a boom economy: recent planning has yielded an annual growth rate of 8 to 10 per cent, and further growth at similar rates can be expected if the Federation can maintain its political stability. Perennial problems include the economic backwardness of Sabah and Sarawak, and tensions between Malayan, Chinese, Indian, Dayak and other minority groups; these are accentuated by the relative prosperity of some Chinese and Indians who dominate business affairs. The Federation has from time to time excited the hostility of neighbours, both Indonesia in the south and the Philippines and mainland states in the north. Remaining alert to the possibility of communist infiltration and an active member of ASEAN, it pursues a general policy of non-alignment in the world as a whole.

Philippines

The Country
The Philippines Republic is a group of two large islands (Mindanao, Luzon) and over 7000 smaller ones extending between Taiwan and eastern Malaysia. Of the smaller islands only five (Samar, Negros, Palawan, Panay, Mindoro) have areas approaching or exceeding 10,000 km² (4000 sq miles) and only a few hundred have sizeable human populations. *Area* 300,000 km² (115,830 sq miles); *capital* Manila; *population* 57,329,000 (est. 1986).

Organization
Following eight years of martial law (to January 1981) the Philippines are now governed by an elected National Assembly, with an executive President (Head

of State) and Prime Minister (both elected from the Assembly) assisted by a cabinet of about 26 ministers. Local government is vested in thirteen regions, divided into provinces with provincial, city and municipal councils. The official language is Pilipino, a specially-formulated common language based on Malayan, designed to overcome the problem of some seventy or more local languages. English and Spanish are widely understood. About 85 per cent of Filipinos are Roman Catholic: there are small Protestant and Moslem minorities, the latter politically important on the southern islands.

Geography

The Philippines are mountainous – ranges of mostly inactive volcanoes rising steeply from the sea with narrow coastal plains and broad interior plateaus on some of the larger islands. Only a few of the cones are of recent origin, but earthquakes are frequent. Several islands have peaks of over 1500 m (5000 ft); the highest mountains, on Luzon and Mindanao, rise above 2900 m (9500 ft). Most of the ranges are oriented north-to-south; their rock debris, washed down into the valleys, provides rich, fertile soils. Many islands are ringed by coral reefs. Between 10° and 20° N, the Philippines are hot throughout the year; they are generally wet, though there may be dry spells during December to May and heavy rains in July and August. Rainfall is heaviest in the east, and typhoons frequently cross the islands between June and December. The mountains – including about half the area of the islands – are densely covered with monsoon forest; most of the lowlands have been cleared for agriculture, with rice paddies predominant in the wetter areas, grasslands and maize fields on the drier slopes.

History and Development

Filipinos probably originated from Malaya and Indonesia. Chinese immigrants joined them from the 10th century onward, the earlier ones integrating, later arrivals tending to form a separate business community that remains isolated today. The Spanish who colonized the islands from 1521 found the local people farmers and fishermen, with little political or social organization. Only in the south had a Moslem culture penetrated from Malaysia – a culture that proved (and still proves) strongly resistant to Catholicism and to European influences generally. Manila, founded in 1571, became the seat of government, and the Philippines developed as a trading centre, linking Mexico with the silks, spices and gemstones available cheaply from China. During the 19th century their farming potential grew; from the islands coffee, sugar, hemp and other plantation products were exported to Europe, especially after the opening of the Suez Canal in 1869.

Independence movements grew during the late 19th century. The Spanish yoke was thrown off – with the help of the USA who were at war with Spain – in 1898. However, the new republic immediately became an American protectorate, though with some degree of self-government: it finally acquired independent Commonwealth status in 1935. Liberated by US forces after Japanese occupation in World War II, the Philippines have retained – not always enthusiastically – close economic and military ties with the USA ever since. Political disturbances led President Marcos to rule by martial law from 1972 to 1981.

Resources and Economics

Agriculture is important throughout most of the islands; roughly half the workforce is engaged in farming, a high proportion of them on smallholdings producing rice, maize, fruit, vegetables, nuts and livestock, mainly for home consumption. Cane sugar, hemp, coconut and tobacco are grown for export: the coconut industry is especially important, providing one fifth of export earnings when prices are high. There is a substantial offshore and deep-water fishing industry, and fish-farming is widely practised. Timber is taken extensively from the remaining accessible forests, mostly for export as logs or cut lengths; a small but increasing proportion is used in local manufacture. Iron, lead, copper, manganese and chrome ores are exploited on several islands and large reserves of these and other minerals are known. Coal is mined locally; petroleum is extracted with difficulty, providing no more than a small and fluctuating proportion of the country's needs. Manufacturing industries employ only one sixth of the labour force but contribute a quarter of the national income. Products include electrical equipment, textiles, clothing and chemicals. There are adequate roads, air links and inter-island ferries; only Luzon has a railway network. Tourism is a major and growing industry.

Recent Developments
Under a stable but authoritarian government the Philippines make slow economic progress, though growth of national income is challenged by growth of population, and benefits per capita have been slight in the current planning period. Social unrest centres on the southern Moslem community, which seeks independence, and on a growing militant communist party. The five-year development plan for 1983–7 aims to improve agricultural output, especially through reforms in land ownership and marketing policies. Attempts are being made to stimulate small industries, especially those that are labour intensive and which make use of indigenous products. By 1985 the government hopes to cut expensive oil imports by almost a third, doubling geothermal and hydroelectric energy, installing nuclear power plant and increasing coal production to sixteen times its current level. Meanwhile many enterprising Filipinos leave their islands to take up poorly-paid work overseas.

Singapore

The Country
The Republic of Singapore consists of Singapore Island, off the southwestern tip of the Malay peninsula, and over fifty neighbouring islands bordering the Strait of Malacca. *Area* 581 km^2 (224 sq miles); *capital* Singapore; *population* 2,585,000 (est. 1986).

Organization
Singapore is governed by a Parliament of 75 elected members. Parliament elects a President, who is Head of State, and who in turn appoints a Prime Minister and a cabinet of about 15 members. Citizens of Singapore are of mixed Chinese (76%), Malay (15%) and Indian (7%) background; official languages include Malay, Tamil, several Chinese dialects and English; religions include Islam, Christianity, Hinduism and Buddhism.

Geography
Singapore City stands on the southwestern flank of a lozenge-shaped island 40 km (25 miles) long and 24 km (15 miles) across; behind the city stand low hills

and ridges (highest point 177 m, 580 ft) of granite and sandstones. The uplands were originally forested, the lowlands swampy, with extensive mangrove forests bordering creeks and inlets. Only a few thousand hectares of the upland rain forest remain in central areas set aside for water catchment: the rest has been cleared for farming and building, though soils are thin and liable to erosion once the forest has gone. Just over 1° from the Equator, Singapore is uniformly hot and humid throughout the year, with year-round rainfall that intensifies during the northeast monsoon season of November to January.

History and Development

Originally one of many small fishing ports of the medieval Malaccan Empire (see Malaysia), Singapore was settled and converted to a major port by Sir Stamford Raffles on behalf of the British East India Company in 1819. Growing rapidly as a trading centre it became part of the Straits Settlements, a British colony established in 1867 to include the three ports of Penang, Malacca (Melaka) and Singapore. Later connected to the mainland by road and rail, and dominated by large immigrant populations from southern China, it developed into the major commercial port of Malaya, and Britain's main naval and military base in southeastern Asia. Liberated from Japanese occupation after World War II, Singapore became a separate colony and in 1959 was granted self-government. After a short spell as part of Malaysia (1963–5), it withdrew from the Federation and became a sovereign state within the Commonwealth (see also Malaysia).

Resources and Economics

With few natural assets apart from its strategic position, harbour facilities and lively population, Singapore has traditionally depended on trade for its prosperity. Agriculture and fishing are mostly restricted to small local communities on the main and off-lying islands. There are few other local natural resources; almost everything that supplies Singapore's people and industries is imported. Out of a total labour force of over a million, about one third is employed in manufacturing, about one quarter in commerce, and one fifth in the service industries. Manufacturing contributes about one quarter of the national budget; its products range from precision instruments and textiles to oil-rigs and bulk chemicals, over two thirds of which is exported. Singapore has no oil of its own, but it refines and processes imported oil, and services local oilfields on a large scale. Banking, insurance and financial services are increasing, and Singapore's importance as a sea and air terminus continues to grow. Millions of passengers in transit use it each year, and there is a flourishing tourist trade.

Recent Developments

With its nose for business, and its lasting political stability based on a huge, hard-working Chinese majority, Singapore has outdistanced all its neighbours in economic development over the past three decades. Ten recently-promoted industrial estates, concentrating mainly on high technology products, indicate how the city-state sees its future. Services, including international banking and exchange, are growing even more rapidly than industry, and the annual flow of tourists now outnumbers the teeming population itself. Inflation remains low despite a significant spread of prosperity through the population as a whole, and Singapore seems set for further years of stability and successful economic development.

Thailand

The Country
The Kingdom of Thailand (formerly Siam) lies centrally in the Indochina peninsula, bordered by Burma in the north and west, Laos and Cambodia in the east, and Malaysia in the extreme south: it has a long coast surrounding the Gulf of Thailand, and a shorter one facing the Andaman Sea. *Area* 514,000 km^2 (198,456 sq miles); *capital* Bangkok; *population* 53,539,000 (est. 1986).

Organization
A constitutional monarchy, Thailand is governed (under its constitution of 1978) by a House of Representatives of 301 elected members and a smaller Senate appointed by the King. As Head of State the King also appoints a Prime Minister (on the advice of House and Senate) and cabinet of about 20 ministers; he is advised by a Privy Council of 15 members. Local government is vested in 72 provinces; locally-elected councils operate down to village level. Thai is the common language; English and Chinese are widely understood, especially in the cities, and several hill tribes have their own languages. Most Thais are Buddhist; about 10 per cent are Moslem, Hindu or Christian.

Geography
Central Thailand is a broad plain surrounding the main river, the Chao Phraya. Flowing southward through a wide flood basin, the river brings down alluvium from the hills and extends the country seaward in a broad, ever-growing delta. To the east lies a low escarpment bounding the rectangular plateau of the Khorat, a high forested plain that extends eastward to the Mekong River. In the north and along the Burmese border are the mountains – ranges with north–south orientation that continue the folded eastern Himalayas. Several peaks rise above 1500 m (5000 ft); the highest is Doi Inthanon, rising to 2595 m (8514 ft) in the northeastern ranges. The mountains continue spasmodically down the Malay Peninsula, with mangrove-forested islands off either coast. The climate is warm and seasonally wet, with heaviest rains from May to September: frosts occur on the northern mountains in winter. Monsoon forest originally covered most of Thailand and still forms two fifths of the cover; the lowlands and most of the accessible hill slopes are now cultivated.

History and Development
The Thai people are of southern Chinese origin; migrating southward in the 10th or 11th centuries, they settled mainly in the river valleys of Indochina where they practised their Buddhist religion and their skills of fishing and wet rice culture. Kingdoms based on Chiangmai, Sukhothai and Ayutthaya flourished in the 13th and 14th centuries, the southern kingdoms spreading to include neighbouring Cambodia and conducting trade with China, Malacca (see Malaysia), India and Ceylon during the 16th and 17th centuries. Portuguese, Dutch, English and French merchants traded with Ayutthaya, but Dutch and French attempts to control the kingdom were rebuffed; in 1688 all Western emissaries were expelled. A Burmese invasion in 1767 brought to power a new Thai dynasty, the Chakkri, which survives today. Under Chakkri kings the borders of Siam extended south to the Malay peninsula and north into Chiangmai; neighbouring states were included as vassals, and trade flourished with China, and later with Britain, France and the USA. Siam lost territory to

the colonial powers during the late 19th and early 20th centuries, but retained its independence up to 1941, when it was occupied by Japanese forces. The name Thailand was adopted in 1939. A constitutional monarchy since 1932, Thailand has suffered frequent constitutional changes, and government mainly by a succession of military power groups, often (in recent years) under martial law.

Resources and Economics
Well endowed with alluvial lowland soils and plentifully supplied with water, Thailand is primarily agricultural; about 65 per cent of its workforce is engaged in food production and forestry, or works in the huge rubber plantations of the lowland and peninsular region. The main products are rice and cassava (tapioca), maize, cane sugar, bananas, pineapple and rubber; Thailand is amply self-sufficient in crop production and a world leader in exports of rice and cassava. Fishing provides an important contribution to local diet and shrimps, prawns and other specialities are exported. Well endowed with minerals, Thailand is a major exporter of tin concentrates (the second-largest producer after Malaysia) and also mines ores of antimony, lead, tungsten, manganese, zinc and copper. Petroleum has not yet proved exploitable, but natural gas has recently been brought ashore from a large field in the Gulf of Thailand. Manufacturing industries employ about 5 per cent of the workforce and contribute 20 per cent to national income: processed and canned foods, textiles and chemicals are the main products, Thai textiles finding a ready market overseas. Road, rail and air links are currently being improved, and Thailand attracts many tourists with its splendid scenery and ancient buildings.

Recent Developments
In successive five-year economic development plans, Thailand has gradually converted itself from a mainly pastoral country to one with a diverse, forward-looking economy. The most recent plan aims to spread the country's prosperity – so far concentrated mainly in the cities – as far as possible into the agricultural sector on which much of it is based. Thailand's chief problem has been lack of indigenous fuel, necessitating imports of expensive oil. The development of natural gas, oil-refining capacity, hydroelectricity and other local sources of power should help the country to expand its small industries, hitherto held back by fuel costs. Continued economic development is expected, though perhaps not as fast as in earlier five-year periods.

Vietnam

The Country
The Socialist Republic of Vietnam occupies the eastern flank of the Indochina peninsula from the Gulf of Tonking to the South China Sea; its neighbours are China (Yunnan, Kwangsi-Chuang (Guangxi-Zhuangzu)), Laos and Cambodia. *Area* 329,556 km^2 (127,242 sq miles); *capital* Hanoi; *population* 61,204,000 (est. 1986).

Organization
Under its constitution of 1980 Vietnam (formerly North and South Vietnam) is governed by an elected National Assembly; this elects a small Council of State, representing the presidency, and a council of about 36 ministers and senior

officials under a Prime Minister, who hold executive powers. The government is dominated by the Communist Party of Vietnam. Local government is vested in elected provincial, municipal and district People's Councils. The official language is Vietnamese; there are many religions including Buddhism, Taoism, Confucianism and Catholicism.

Geography

The northern mountains of Vietnam form a series of ridges, steep-sided and pointing southeast toward the Gulf of Tonking: the highest rise to 3000 m (9800 ft) close to the Chinese border. Between the ridges run parallel valleys, broadened by rivers that flow toward the Gulf: the longest river, the Hongha, forms an extensive delta southeast of Hanoi. Central Vietnam (Trung-Phan or Annam) is a narrow coastal plain between the Annamite chain of mountains and the sea; in the south the mountains broaden to reach the coast, backed by a high limestone plateau that continues westward into Cambodia. In the far south (Nam-Phan or Cochin-China) are the alluvial plains of the Mekong River delta: on their edge stands Ho Chi Minh (formerly Saigon), the southern capital. Vietnam's summer climate is warm and sultry, with southwesterly winds bringing heavy rain to the south in April and May. Between September and January northeasterly winds bring cool dry weather: in spring and autumn typhoons are frequent on the eastern plains and foothills. Vietnam was heavily forested; much of the lowland forest and some of the hill forests have been cleared for agriculture.

History and Development

The Vietnamese people settled in northern Vietnam from China some two thousand years ago, displacing earlier cultures of Indonesian and Melanesian origin. Chinese influences remained strong; the Vietnamese, who extended to about 19°S, remained vassals of China until the end of the T'ang dynasty, early in the 10th century. During the following centuries the Vietnamese repeatedly asserted their nationhood, beating off raids by Cambodia and the Mongol armies of Kublai Khan, and driving out the Chinese after a brief period of occupation in the early 15th century. Spreading continually southward, Vietnam came to occupy its present boundaries by the early 19th century. From the mid-19th century it gradually fell under French influence; occupied in sections, the whole country became a colony by 1883, forming (with Laos and Cambodia) the French Indochinese Union. Under Japanese occupation in 1945 it was declared independent by the communist leader Ho Chi Minh, but by 1954, after nine years of warfare, the communists had secured only the northern half of the country (to 17°S) while the French retained South Vietnam. On French withdrawal after further fighting and defeat at Dien Bien Phu, the communist Viet Cong movement, helped by North Vietnam, led resistances against successive governments in the south. US forces intervened in support of the south and Communist China helped the north, in a destructive war that ended with northern victory in 1975. Vietnam was re-unified under communist control in 1976.

Resources and Economics

Vietnam's economy is based mainly on agriculture, over 70 per cent of the workforce being occupied in food production. Climate and soils are normally excellent for wet rice production, especially in the south, but typhoons and flooding occasionally inflict serious damage; Vietnam cannot yet rely on feeding itself. Maize, cane sugar, sweet-potatoes, sorghum and beans are other important food crops; tea, coffee, ground-nuts, tobacco and rubber are also grown for local use and as cash crops for export. Forestry is developing; marine and river fisheries add substantially to the diet, and shrimps and other crustaceans are exported.

Minerals, found mostly in the north, include coal, limestone, iron ore, phosphatic rock, chromite, bauxite and a little gold; exploitable oil and natural gas have been discovered. Industries include fertilizers and cement manufacture, and Vietnam makes glass, paper, steel, synthetic yarns and fabrics and many other domestic products for local consumption. Road, rail and air links are being restored after wartime devastation, and tourism is growing.

Recent Developments
More than three decades of war, including the heaviest aerial bombardments experienced by any country, left Vietnam semi-derelict; not only were buildings and roads damaged, but huge areas of once fertile countryside were depopulated, forests destroyed and towns packed with refugees. Many in the south still feel threatened by northern domination and communist rule, and refugees still leave the country in large numbers. The million-strong army (part of it currently deployed in Cambodia) is a constant drain on resources. After a breach with China, foreign aid comes mainly from the USSR, and Vietnam is making measurable economic progress. Current plans include resettlement of small farmers, development of industries to absorb surplus labour, flood control measures, and reshaping of the economy to include limited private enterprise.

ASIA EAST

China

The Country
The People's Republic of China covers a huge expanse of southeastern Asia from high central plateau to eastern seaboard. Its neighbours are the USSR and Mongolia in the north, Afghanistan (a narrow corridor), Pakistan, India and Nepal in the southwest, Bhutan, eastern India (Sikkim and Arunachal Pradesh), Burma, Laos and Vietnam in the south, and North Korea, Macau and Hong Kong in the east. *Area* 9,596,961 km^2 (3,705,390 sq miles); *capital* Peking (Beijing); *population* 1,064,000,000 (est. 1986).

Organization
Under the 1978 constitution China is governed by an elected Congress of about 3000 deputies; the Standing Committee of Congress takes the role of Head of State. Responsible to it is an executive State Council of over 50 Vice-Premiers and ministers, led by the Prime Minister. Local government is vested in elected People's Congresses in twenty-one provinces, three municipalities and five autonomous regions; lesser congresses, with executive revolutionary committees, are elected down to town and rural commune levels. Both national and local affairs are dominated by the Communist Party of China. The state language is Modern Standard Chinese, a simplified form of northern (Mandarin) dialect; there are many local languages and dialects, especially in the

autonomous regions. The Pinyin system of transliterating ideographs phonetically into Roman script is now universal. Buddhist, Taoist, Moslem and Christian faiths are practised.

Geography

China includes a complex of high plateaus and folded mountain ranges in the west and north, and an equally complex system of lower ranges, plateaus and water-logged plains in the south and east; most of the fertile soils and a high proportion of the population are concentrated in the eastern lowlands.

Highest and least hospitable to man is the Tibet (Xizang) plateau, of mean elevation 4500 m (14,800 ft) – higher than many of Europe's Alpine peaks. From its southern edge rise most of China's highest mountains, including several over 7500 m (24,600 ft). On the high plateau climatic conditions are harsh, soils are thin and dry, and vegetation is restricted to tundra or coarse grasses. Lower sheltered areas (for example, the valleys around Lhasa) provide marginally better living conditions with possibilities for farming. Similarly, throughout much of northwestern China (including Inner Mongolia and Sinkiang (Xinjiang)) summer heat, winter cold, strong winds and year-round aridity bring desert or semi-desert conditions. Cultivation is impossible except in a few favoured oasis areas, and nomadic grazing is the traditional way of life.

Northeastern China is centered on the broad, dry plains of Manchuria, surrounded on three sides by uplands and divided into basins by low hills. Here soils are deep and rich; though the growing season is short, the grasslands that formerly covered the plains have in many areas been ploughed for cereal crops. The Changpai Shan highlands bordering North Korea are heavily forested. The plain of northern China, crossed by the Hwang-ho (Yellow) River and built up for centuries from its alluvium, is now one of the most intensively cultivated areas. Though cold in winter, dominated by air-masses from Siberia, the plain warms up quickly in spring and has a long growing season. To the west lies a high, loess-covered plateau, from which the Hwang-ho derives its load of yellow sediment. The Shantung (Shandong) hills form an ancient, weathered bloc to the east of the Hwang-ho plain.

In southwestern China lies the Szechwan (Sichuan) basin, backed by high mountains that protect it from cold northerly winds. With its warm climate and fertile soils, Szechwan is a rich province; its western bamboo forests, bordering on Tibet, are the home of the giant panda. From the Szechwan basin drains the huge Yangtze Kiang (Chang Jiang) River, that runs eastward across the plains of southern China; other rivers joining it, together with a network of lakes and canals, criss-cross the fertile and heavily populated plains. In the southeast stand the Wuyi Shan ranges, in the southwest the higher Himalayan foothills of Yunnan, which between them isolate the Si Kiang (Xi Jiang or Pearl River) basin of the far south. Southern China is tropical, dominated for much of the year by warm, moist air from the South China Sea and Pacific Ocean. Summers are hot and steamy, winters warm and damp. The lush forest that formerly draped the south is now largely replaced by cultivated land. This is China's most productive region; two and even three rice crops a year can be grown in the extreme south.

History and Development

Home of Peking Man, one of our earliest-known human ancestors, the plains of China have seen human and pre-human occupation for at least half a million years. The Hwang-ho plains supported farming settlements well over four thousand years ago, and similar cultures are reported in Szechwan, Shantung (Shandong) and elsewhere. The origins of the Chinese people are doubtful; they may have drifted eastward from central Asia or spread from focal areas in China itself. The Shang dynasty of northern China (c. 1600 to 1100 BC), rich in bronze artifacts, provided the earliest widespread culture, unmatched until the Ch'in dynasty of 220 to 206 BC. The chief surviving Ch'in monument is the Great Wall, built across northwestern China to keep out the mountain barbarians.

Chinese civilization spread slowly southward, accelerated from time to time by northern invaders. During the Han (c. 200 BC–AD 220) and T'ang (618–907) dynasties, warlike emperors had made their presence felt far afield, in Turkestan, Tibet, Manchuria, Korea, Mongolia and Indochina. This pattern was to continue for another thousand years. So massive was the empire that foreign domination altered its character only slightly. A Mongol invasion of the 13th century under Ghengis Khan and his successors provided a new dynasty (the Yüan), but the bureaucracy and social order that maintained cohesion within the empire gradually reasserted themselves, and Mongol influence quickly waned. Longer-lasting was the Manchu (Ch'ing) domination, that began in 1644 when an invading army captured Peking. The Ch'ing period, which lasted until 1912, saw China's borders stabilized and brought contacts with Western powers, though the country's domestic economy changed little.

Portuguese traders first appeared on the China coast in 1514, and soon established their settlement at Macau. Jesuits propagated Christianity from the late 16th century onward, and by the end of the century several Catholic missions were established. Tea was among China's first direct exports to European countries. Chinese attempts to suppress a contraband trade in opium, imported from India, led to war with Britain in 1839, and ultimately to concessions that allowed Britain, France, the USA and other Western countries both trading and territorial rights. Though anti-foreign feeling remained strong, the Chinese began to adopt Western ways, especially in warfare. However, many further trading and territorial concessions were forced from them, often at gunpoint, in deals with German, Russian and Japanese governments. Impoverished and broken by internal factions, imperial power declined; in 1912 the last Ch'ing Emperor abdicated, leaving China a republic.

Then followed a long period of anarchy, with wars between provinces and rival armies, from which two powers emerged – the Communist Party under Mao Tse-tung, and the Nationalist Party (Kuomintang) under Sun Yat-sen and his successor Chiang Kai-shek. The Japanese invasion of Manchuria in 1931 and China's later involvement in World War II brought the Communists to prominence; after the defeat of the Japanese in 1945 the Red Army fought its way into power, driving the Kuomintang government into exile in Taiwan. The People's Republic of China came into being in October 1949, and Marxist philosophy was faced with its greatest-ever challenge – bringing order to a poor, underdeveloped, war-devastated country of over 500 million people – most of them semi-literate and many at the point of starvation. Despite major setbacks, errors and continuing problems, the philosophy appears to have succeeded; within little more than a generation China has become an ordered state, and a power in world politics strong enough to rival the USA and USSR.

Resources and Economics

Roughly 10 per cent of China's vast area is cultivable; organized into over 50,000 communes, farmers produced between 25 and 50 per cent of the national income – a proportion generally thought to be in rapid decline as industry increases. In good years China produces nearly all the food it needs, though bad weather, flooding and distribution problems can still produce local dearth; three to four million tonnes of wheat are imported each year to make up current deficits. Rice, wheat and other cereals are the mainstay; beans, potatoes and green vegetables, sugar, tea, cotton, oil seeds, tobacco, and a range of other food and industrial crops are raised, together with livestock – notably pigs and poultry. These are mostly for home consumption, with a little over for export. By Western standards agriculture is currently undercapitalized and capable of further development. There is some evidence of recent increases in productivity following a partial return to smallholdings and family farming. China's extensive forests provide timber (including teak and other tropical hardwoods), resins and oil mainly for local use; devastated by war and over-exploitation, many of the lowland forests have been replanted. River fishing and fish-farming provide important additional protein, and China supports a substantial deep-water fishing fleet.

China is rich in minerals, with enormous potential for further exploitation. Mining of the commoner ores is at present mostly for domestic consumption, but there are valuable reserves of copper, tungsten, molybdenum, titanium and other metal ores, currently being developed, that are likely to find increasing value in world markets. Coal, the main source of domestic energy, supplies about 70 per cent of the country's current needs and is also a reliable export. Production increased rapidly during the 1970s, testifying to increasing industrial demand and a successful drive to export more to North Korea and other energy-hungry countries. Petroleum and natural gas are now on stream, with some of the early fields already nearing exhaustion and new ones – both on land and offshore – still being discovered. Petrol and crude oil, made available with the help of foreign capital and technology, are valuable sources of foreign currency. Hydroelectric power currently provides about one twentieth of China's needs; more power stations are being built in the western mountains where the potential for development is greatest.

In the early years after World War II China concentrated on developing its heavy industries – notably coal, iron and steel production, chemicals and the provision of tractors and heavy equipment for agriculture, civil engineering and other major works. Recently emphasis has been changing to lighter industries – the production of household and luxury goods, processed foods and other consumables both for domestic consumption and for export. China's vast population, growing rapidly after World War II, was brought under control by rigorous family planning policies; annual increase has been reduced to possibly as little as 1 per cent, which is currently in balance with its economic growth.

Rivers remain an important component of China's huge transport system; there are indications that road and rail freight-transport facilities are proving inadequate for the country's rapidly-growing needs. There is a small, rigorously controlled tourist industry.

Recent Developments

Recent political developments, including the adoption of a new (fourth) constitution late in 1982, suggest still further evolution of policy for this massive Marxist state. While dramatic economic progress has been made over a thirty-year period, recent years have seen a slowing-down of growth in every economic sector.

In agriculture, hitherto organized into politically oriented communes with policies dominated by central planners, there is a marked shift away from political control and a strengthening of family smallholdings. The communes, effectively responsible for local government within their areas, have retained a management function but have lost their political significance; the farmers, given greater freedom and choice of action, now stand a better chance of farming effectively. Plans to increase productivity include provision of more fertilizers and capital for development.

Industrial reorientation has included the re-shaping and modernization of the coal and steel industries, and increasing support for light industry. Washing machines, sewing machines, refrigerators, television sets and other domestic appliances are now receiving priority, together with watches, cameras and personal goods formerly regarded as inessential. This policy aims to absorb raw materials that were previously exported at unimproved value, stimulates light industries (plastics, non-ferrous metals, etc.) previously undeveloped, and provides opportunities for small factories to create employment locally. This is probably the country's most rapidly-growing sector at present, stimulated by recently-permitted development loans from international funding. Further economic growth, at a faster rate than is currently being managed, may depend on the country's willingness to invest more in schemes of this kind.

Hong Kong

The Country
The Crown Colony of Hong Kong stands in an enclave of the southeastern coast of China, 32 km (20 miles) east of the Zhu Jiang (Pearl River estuary). Its only frontier is with China (Kwangtung (Guangdong) province). *Area* 1045 km^2 (403 sq miles); *capital* Hong Kong; *population* 5,820,000 (est. 1986).

Organization
Hong Kong's Governor (representing the British Crown) is advised by an Executive Council of four *ex officio* senior military and civil officers and about twelve other nominated members. The Governor presides also over a Legislative Council of 15 nominated officials, 29 appointed unofficial and three *ex officio* members. Most citizens are of Chinese descent, about 60 per cent of them born in the colony. English and Chinese are the official languages. Religions include Taoism, Buddhism and several forms of Christianity.

Geography
Hong Kong Island, 13 km (8 miles) long and 76 km^2 (296 sq miles) in area, lies across a channel $1\frac{1}{2}$ km (1 mile) from the peninsula of Kowloon (10.5 km^2, 41 sq miles) among a cluster of larger and smaller islands; Victoria Peak, near its western end, rises to 554 m (1817 ft). The colony also includes the New Territories, about 970 km^2 (379 sq miles) of mainland coast and islands with steep hills rising to 958 m (3143 ft). Summers are hot, rainy and humid, winters warm and relatively dry. Little of the original forest vegetation remains except in patches on the mainland. Soils are fertile when watered but arid in winter. Fresh water is sometimes scarce; rainfall stored in reservoirs is augmented with piped supplies from mainland China.

History and Development
Punitive raids into China by the British Royal Navy in 1840 resulted in the

Treaty of Nanking (1842), by which Hong Kong – a barely inhabited offshore island – was ceded to Britain in perpetuity. Intended as a trading post down-river from Canton (now Kwangchow (Guangzhou)), the excellent harbour encouraged Hong Kong's development as a port and naval base. Kowloon peninsula and nearby Stonecutters Island were added by a Convention of 1860, and in 1898 the New Territories were leased to Britain by the Chinese for a period of ninety-nine years. Under Japanese occupation in World War II, Hong Kong has since grown remarkably in population and prosperity.

Resources and Economics

Agriculture and fisheries account for less than 2 per cent of the national income. About 30 per cent of the fresh vegetables consumed and 85 per cent of the fish are local produce; all the rest of the colony's food is imported, mostly from China. Hong Kong's prosperity is based mainly on manufacturing and trading. Heavy industries include iron and steel processing, and shipbuilding and repairs. Light industries now employ almost one sixth of the colony's population (two fifths of the workforce) and provide one quarter of the annual income. The main products are textiles, clothing, electric and electronic goods, clocks and watches (about one third of the world's supply), cameras, footwear and plastic goods. Hong Kong is a trading centre and rapidly becoming a centre of banking and finance, important especially as a gateway to China. Ferries, roads and a modernized railway system provide good internal transport and, with a modern airport, link Hong Kong with China, Macau and the rest of the world. Over two million tourists are catered for annually.

Recent Developments

Virtually autonomous despite its colonial status, Hong Kong's lively economy has managed to keep pace with its population; currently it is eastern Asia's third most prosperous community after Japan and Singapore, and possibly its most rapidly growing one. Hong Kong and Kowloon together hold four fifths of the population, housed in one of the world's most densely-packed urban areas; overspill population has spread to six growing satellite towns on the mainland. With an economy based mainly on the export of goods and services, depending heavily on imported food and fuel, Hong Kong's prosperity is peculiarly vulnerable to world market fluctuations. Over recent years, however, it has managed to maintain annual economic growth of about 10 per cent, low unemployment and the continuing confidence of overseas investors. Joint business ventures across the border enhance its usefulness to mainland China. However, the lease on the New Territories expires in 1997, and an Anglo–Chinese agreement of 1984 commits Britain to the return of Hong Kong to mainland control after that date.

Japan

The Country

Japan is a group of four large islands (Hokkaido, Honshu, Shikoku, Kyushu) and many small ones in the northwestern Pacific Ocean, extending between 26° and 45°N. The nearest point of mainland Asia is Pusan, South Korea, 176 km (110 miles) northwest of Kyushu. The tip of Sakhalin and the Kuril Islands, both Soviet territory, lie within 40 km (25 miles) of Hokkaido. *Area* 372,313 km² (143,750 sq miles); *capital* Tokyo; *population* 120,835,000 (est. 1986).

Organization

Under its constitution of 1947 Japan is a parliamentary democracy: the Emperor is titular Head of State but plays only a symbolic role in government. The Diet (parliament) consists of two elected Houses, a 511-member House of Representatives (which has pre-eminence) and an upper, 252-member House of Councillors. There is an executive cabinet of about thirteen ministers under a Prime Minister. Local government is vested in 47 prefectures, each with an elected governor and representative assembly. The official language is Japanese. Shintoism and Buddhism are the most widely practised faiths: there are small Christian minorities, both Protestant and Catholic.

Geography

Japan's islands have developed along intersecting arcs of intensive mountain building; they are the largest of a series of island chains that rim the northwestern Pacific Ocean. Much of their land surface is steep mountains and hills, with many coalescent volcanic cones and lava domes. Unstable slopes and rapid erosion testify to the youth of the landscape in many areas. Several of the volcanoes have formed or erupted within living memory. Others are cones of relatively recent origin, only slightly eroded and in many cases topped with crater lakes. Earthquakes happen often, some causing severe damage. The Sea of Japan to the west is shelving and relatively shallow. The Pacific Ocean to the east drops away rapidly to great depths; there is an abyssal trench over 8000 m deep (26,000 ft) only 240 km (150 miles) off eastern Honshu.

Hokkaido in the north has a central range of mountains aligned along a north-to-south ridge; the highest rise above 2000 m (6500 ft), falling in steps to coastal uplands and plains. Honshu, the largest island, has a curved backbone formed from parallel arcs of mountains, some of older, more resistant rocks, ringed by narrow coastal plains. Its central complex consists of high ridges, often snow-capped, intersected by steep-sided valleys. To the south of this complex stands Fujiyama, Japan's highest and most famous mountain – an elegant, almost symmetrical cone rising to 3776 m (12,389 ft). To the east lies the Kanto plain, the heavily populated lowland basin part-covered by Tokyo's sprawl.

Southwestern Honshu and neighbouring Shikoku and Kyushu islands are built on older granites and schists, faulted, down-warped and flooded by the shallow Inland Sea that separates them. The crystalline rocks are in part overlain with the lava and ash of recent volcanoes, forming clusters of low cones and rolling hills, mostly between 1000 and 2000 m (3000 and 6500 ft) high. Southward again Japan tails off into the Ryukyu chain of volcanic islands, extending south in a gentle arc that curves toward Taiwan. Okinawa, almost on the 26th parallel, is the largest island of the archipelago.

Spanning a considerable latitudinal range, Japan has a wide range of climates from subtropical southern to cool-temperate northern. In winter cold Siberian air, warmed and moistened in passage over the Sea of Japan, brings rain and snow to the western mountains; in Hokkaido, average temperatures are below freezing for four months of the year. In summer warm southeasterly winds from the Pacific prevail; cold sea currents keep the northern islands cool, while the southern islands bask in subtropical warmth. Typhoons with strong winds and heavy rainfall affect southern and central Japan in late summer.

Japan was originally forested, with subtropical rain forests prevailing in the south, broad-leafed deciduous forests in the centre and pines in the uplands and north. Most of the original lowland stands have been cleared for cultivation, but the mountains are well-wooded with a blend of native and exotic species.

History and Development

Japan's earliest (Palaeolithic) inhabitants probably entered from Korea or the north during the last glacial period, perhaps 20,000 years ago, when sea level was low. They left few remains: the earliest signs of widespread culture are pottery shards dating from 10,000 to 2000 years ago. The modern Japanese are thought to be descended in part from Siberian stocks that spread eastward about this time. Crossing in waves from China via Korea, they brought with them Iron Age and later Bronze Age cultures, including techniques of wet rice cultivation, and developed a group of loosely-linked communities that coalesced into embryonic states during the 4th century AD. The most important of these states, Yamato, came to dominate Japan by the end of the 5th century. Buddhism appeared early in the 6th century. By the mid-7th century Japan was a well-founded constitutional state, controlled by the dynastic Yamato clan from a capital near Kyoto, with sovereignty fully recognized by China and Korea.

Japanese culture developed strongly under Chinese influence during the 8th to 12th centuries. The distinctive Japanese kana script was supplemented by Chinese ideographs, and philosophy, literature and art flourished under aristocratic civil government, linked strongly with Buddhist religion. In the 12th century a struggle for power among leading families led to civil unrest and the evolution of a new caste of military leaders – the shoguns. Although the imperial court at Kyoto and successive civil administrations continued, shoguns effectively dominated the country for long periods of its history. Their strength was behind the resistance that in the 13th century kept Kublai Khan's and other invading armies out of Japan, but it was also responsible for imposing a succession of oppressive feudal systems and a social hierarchy – aristocrats, samurai (warriors), peasants, artisans and merchants – that lasted with only slight variation for over six hundred years.

Western emissaries, initially Portuguese traders and missionaries, appeared on Japanese shores from the mid-16th century onward. Dutch and other nations followed, but in 1612 Christianity was proscribed throughout Japan, and by 1639 foreign trading was severely curtailed. Only Chinese and Dutch merchants could visit, and the latter were restricted to an island near Nagasaki. This embargo, and Japan's voluntary isolation, were finally broken in 1853; where attempts by other Western nations had failed, the USA used naval strength to open the country to trade and international commerce. After a period of political uncertainty and struggle, the power of the shoguns was finally broken in 1868. The rule of the imperial family was restored and the country began its long-overdue social revolution; under a young emperor and a relatively young, radical government, Japan started to remodel itself along Western lines.

Colonial expansion for space and raw materials was the first lesson learned from the West. Japan absorbed the Ryukyu Islands (1879), warred with China over Korea, gaining territory and trade concessions (1895), and fought Russia successfully for rights in southern Manchuria and Sakhalin (1904–5). Korea was annexed in 1910, and parts of eastern Siberia and China were occupied temporarily after World War I. In 1932 Manchuria became a Japanese puppet state (Manchukuo), used as a springboard for invading northern China in 1937. Japan's involvement in Indochina (1940) resulted in a US embargo on oil shipments. Japan's attack on the US fleet at Pearl Harbour and occupation of British and Dutch possessions in southeast Asia finally brought massive retaliation; Japan was defeated in 1945, ultimately by the first two atomic bombs used in warfare. Vigorous rehabilitation programmes under US guidance set the country along the economic and political paths it pursues today.

Resources and Economics

Chronically short of good agricultural land, Japan has only about 15 per cent of its surface available for cultivation and stock-rearing. Some 10 per cent of its workforce is employed in primary food production, currently providing less than 6 per cent of the national income. Farms are generally small family units; about half the area cultivated is devoted to wet rice production. Potatoes, vegetables, fruit, beans, tobacco, sugar and livestock are also raised; reflecting dietary changes, there is a trend away from rice toward fruit, vegetables and livestock. Silkworms, tea, and many other small, traditional crops are raised, but Japan grows only a small proportion – about 10 per cent – of the cereals and fodder crops that it consumes. Forests are extensive – over 65 per cent of the land is wooded – and a small but flourishing industry supplies home markets with timber and wood products.

Fishing contributes substantially both to the national larder and to exports. Japanese fishermen range widely across the north and central Pacific, taking pollack, pilchards, cod, salmon, mackerel and many other species, and Japan is second only to the USSR in whaling. There are important inshore fisheries for squid, clams, crustaceans, shallow-water fish and dolphins, and several kinds of fish-farming and culture are practised.

Minerals are scarce and generally of low value; Japan mines coal, chromite, copper, lead, titanium, iron and other ores, but still has to import most of its industrial and domestic needs. Petroleum and natural gas are exploited; so far only a fraction of the country's annual consumption is produced domestically, mostly from small onshore fields in northern Honshu.

Though largely dependent on imported raw materials, Japan's industry is the mainstay of the economy. Manufacturing industries currently employ one quarter of the workforce, and their products provide about one third of the national income. Diversification of industry began long before World War II, giving Japan an advantage over its post-war rivals. Traditional heavy industries still important in the economy include steel and cement manufacture, shipbuilding, refining of lead and other non-ferrous metals, engineering, motor cycle and automobile manufacture; large-scale spinning, weaving and garment industries handle both synthetic and natural materials. Industrial chemicals, produced mostly from imported feedstocks, include petroleum products, synthetic rubber, plastics, fertilizers, pharmaceuticals, yarns and dyes. In light industry Japan's reputation is firmly based on precision engineering and electronics, including cameras, watches, scientific instruments, and radio, television, robotic machinery, computing and telecommunications equipment. Construction and building have boomed during the years of re-emergence and economic development, and the service industries play an increasing role in organizing this bustling, developing community. Japan's mainland islands are well served by road, rail and ferry links, and well over a million tourists are catered for each year.

Recent Developments

Japan's determined policy of industrialization from 1945 onward, involving modern plant, innovation, organization of labour, quality control and vigorous export marketing, carried the country from post-war ruin to comparative affluence in little more than a generation. For over a decade in the 1960s and early 1970s national income rose at over 10 per cent per annum, boosted mainly by aggressive overseas marketing. Heavily committed to buying petroleum from overseas, both for fuel and for its refining and chemical industries, Japan managed to remain economically buoyant throughout the oil crisis of the 1970s, though its rate of economic growth fell. Currently, annual growth rests at 4 to 5 per cent, still based mainly on exports but sustained by a strong domestic market for its own manufactured goods. Stable government, trouble-free labour relations and consistently low rates of inflation have contributed much to the country's economic success; unemployment has remained low even during the less expansive years. Japan's self-sufficiency in manufactured goods, and its success in selling overseas, have made it unpopular among the international trading community: several countries are now seeking to restrict import of Japanese goods until Japan itself imports more.

Macau

The Country
The Portuguese Overseas Province of Macau occupies a peninsula and two nearby islands (Taipa, Colôane) on the south China coast. The only border is with China (Kwangtung (Guangdong) province). *Area* 16 km² (6 sq miles); *capital* Macau; *population* 320,000 (est. 1986).

Organization
Macau is governed by a legislative council consisting of a Governor (appointed from Portugal), six elected members and eleven other members (of whom six represent local business interests and five are appointed by the Governor). It is officially designated Chinese territory under Portuguese administration. Macau City holds over 97 per cent of the population, the islands forming a separate municipality. The people are mostly Chinese; languages include Portuguese, Cantonese and some English. The main religions are Buddhism and Taoism, with a small Catholic minority.

Geography
Macau peninsula, a low, granite foreland 4 km (2½ miles) long, lies at the western entrance to the Zhu Jiang (Pearl River estuary) and some 65 km (40 miles) from Hong Kong. The islands, Taipa and Colôane, are of similar length but slightly higher, with granite hills rising above 160 m (525 ft): a causeway and bridge link them with the mainland. Small alluvial plains surround the hills and fringe the islands, providing pockets of farmland and building sites. Summers are warm with monsoon rainfall, winters cool and dry. Little original forest remains.

History and Development
First visited by Portuguese adventurers in 1497 and settled sixty years later, Macau was for centuries a trading post dealing mainly with Canton (Kwangchow (Guangzhou)) – leased from China but under Portuguese rule: it was also the centre of a Catholic diocese covering the whole Far Eastern area. Portugal declared it independent from China in 1849: it was, however, already in decline, because of the silting of the harbour and the rise of a more dynamic neighbour – Hong Kong – which gradually eclipsed it. Its present status in relation to Portugal was defined in 1976.

Resources and Economics
Macau has few natural resources. Soils are generally meagre and there is little

agricultural production. Fish, prawns and other sea foods are trawled for local consumption and export. Most other foods and much of the territory's water are imported. Manufacturing industries depend mainly on imported raw materials; products include fabrics, clothing, footwear, enamel and porcelain goods, wines, fire-crackers and electronic equipment. Tourism is an important industry, attracting visitors mainly from Hong Kong and Japan; gambling dues are a major source of government revenue.

Recent Developments
Regarded by China as Chinese territory only temporarily (though quite acceptably) under Portuguese influence, Macau continues as a trading centre and tourist resort. Refugees from the mainland swell its population, providing cheap labour for its flourishing industries. Its main economic links are now with Hong Kong rather than Portugal.

Mongolia

The Country
The Mongolian People's Republic lies in eastern Asia, bordered in the north by the USSR and in the east, south and west by China. *Area* 1,565,000 km² (604,247 sq miles); *capital* Ulan Bator; *population* 1,962,000 (est. 1986).

Organization
The Great People's Khural (parliament) of about 350 deputies is elected for five-year terms; from it are elected a nine-member Presidium and executive council of ministers. The chairman of the Presidium is Head of State. Local authority is vested in three city and eighteen provincial khurals. The communist Mongolian People's Revolutionary Party retains political power at all levels. Mongolian is the official language; Kazakh is spoken in the northwest. Buddhists and Shamanists are minority religious sects.

Geography
A country of high plateau and mountains, Mongolia's lowlands average 1500 m (4900 ft) above sea level. The highlands, mainly in the north and west, are of strongly folded mountains with northeast to southwest trend; the highest ranges of the Altai Mountains (Aerht'ai Shan) rise over 4000 m (13,000 ft) in the extreme west. There are several large lakes in the northwest. The main rivers of the eastern plateau flow northward into Lake Baykal, beyond the Soviet border. Summers are hot and arid, winters extremely cold, though with little snow. The western mountains are forested and many of the valleys are farmed; the plains are mostly arid grasslands, falling away to desert (the Gobi) in the southeast.

History and Development
Peopled by a variety of nomadic tribes, Mongolia (formerly Outer Mongolia) was for long the homeland of enterprising nomadic tribesmen who, on horseback, spread widely across Asia; from a united Mongolia in the 13th century Genghis Khan's hordes spread from China to western Russia. Gradually overcome by China, Mongolia was divided into inner and outer provinces; while Inner Mongolia was comparatively easy to manage (and remains today a Chinese province), Outer Mongolia's remoteness across the Gobi desert gave its feudal chiefs greater autonomy. On the fall of the Manchu

dynasty in 1911–12, Outer Mongolia, supported by Tsarist Russia, declared itself an independent monarchy. Chinese and White Russian forces struggled spasmodically for control until 1921, when a communist-inspired revolution restored autonomy; the People's Republic was declared in 1924, and Mongolia has since remained independent under Soviet protection.

Resources and Economics
Predominantly pastoral for most of its history, Mongolia has developed huge stock-raising collective farms producing cattle, sheep, horses and camels. Cereal cultivation is increasing with wheat, barley and oats predominant; other crops include potatoes and fodder, notably hay. The mountain forests provide timber. Coal, fluorspar and other minerals are mined, the latter mainly for export to the USSR: other minerals including petroleum are being developed. Industries centered on the capital and other main settlements are mainly agriculture-based; products include wool, woollen cloth and felt, hides, leather, footwear and processed meat, mostly for sale to the USSR and other Communist-bloc countries. Except around the cities roads are mostly unpaved; air and rail links are limited but adequate, and tourism is slow to develop.

Recent Developments
Mongolia appears to be developing its resources gradually under a succession of five-year plans; the current seventh plan concentrates, like earlier ones, on intensifying agricultural production in the state and collective farms, and increasing mining and electricity production. The country's role as a Soviet buffer state and economic satellite remains assured.

North Korea

The Country
The People's Democratic Republic of Korea (North Korea) occupies the northern half of the Korean peninsula in the Sea of Japan, bounded in the north by China (Liaoning, Kirin (Jilin)), in the extreme northeast by the USSR, and in the south by the demilitarized zone separating it from South Korea. *Area* 120,538 km² (46,540 sq miles); *capital* Pyongyang; *population* 20,543,000 (est. 1986).

Organization
An elected Supreme People's Assembly of about 600 members in turn elects a President (Head of State), Prime Minister and about 14 other delegates who together form an executive Central People's Committee. The Committee appoints and directs the work of an Administration Council of about 40 Vice-Premiers, ministers and Chairmen of Commissions. Local government is vested in the elected People's Assemblies of nine provinces and two municipalities. The communist Korean Workers' Party dominates government at all levels. The language is Korean, with Chinese widely spoken. Religions still extant include Buddhism, Taoism and Shamanism, with small Christian minorities.

Geography
Much of North Korea lies on a high plateau averaging over 1000 m (3300 ft) above sea level. In the northwest the plateau falls to the valley of the Yalu River, which for much of its length forms the border with China. In the northeast and

east it rises to merge with a complex of high volcanic mountains; there are several peaks above 2000 m (6600 ft), the highest – Paektu-san just inside China – rising to 2744 m (9003 ft). South of the plateau run herringbone ridges of lower mountains and foothills, descending to narrow coastal plains on either flank of the peninsula. The climate is generally dry, with continental extremes of temperature. Winters are cold, especially in the mountains, with frosts and a little snow. Summers are warm and humid, especially along the eastern seaboard, with monsoon rainfall. Coniferous and broadleaf forests, once universal, still cover about two thirds of the country; most of the plains and foothills have been cleared for rice-growing.

History and Development
For most of their history North and South Korea were a single country; their current division dates from the end of World War II. Koreans form a distinct stock with both Chinese and Japanese affinities. Protected by sea on three sides and inhospitable mountains to the north, their culture evolved in partial isolation; however, Koreans have seldom been free from intrusions, and were often dominated by one or other of their larger neighbours. Developing first as three kingdoms, the country was for long a feudal monarchy, governed from Seoul, its capital city, by the Yi dynasty which seized power in 1392 and held it for over five hundred years. Trading, missionary and diplomatic relationships with Western countries were discouraged, remaining minimal until the late 19th century when aggression by China and Japan caused Korea's rulers to seek alliances with the USA and Europe.

In 1895 Japanese forces defeated Chinese invaders and effectively assumed control of Korea, formally annexing it and deposing the last Yi monarch in 1910. Although modernized and to some degree developed economically under Japanese rule, Korea resented its colonial status; a freedom movement, operating mainly from China, sought to liberate the country from colonial domination up to and during World War II. Following the downfall of Japan in 1945, Korea was occupied by Soviet troops from the north and US troops from the south, the armies meeting along latitude 38°N. Though guaranteed independence, Korea remained divided when governments of opposing ideologies were set up in the two zones, each claiming to represent the whole country but failing to agree on policies for unification. Invading the south in 1950, North Korean troops were opposed by a UN force which eventually drove them back. Southern forces were then opposed and swept southward by a Chinese army: the armistice line established in 1953, now a demilitarized zone, remains the official boundary between North and South Korea. Though given only observer status in the UN, North Korea is now widely regarded as a country in its own right.

Resources and Economics
Traditionally agricultural (though with some industrial development under Japanese rule), the population is concentrated in the narrow coastal plains and lowlands. North Korea employs about 45 per cent of its workforce on the land, almost entirely on large-scale collective and state farms. Rice, maize and potatoes are the main crops and livestock (especially pigs) are important: wheat, barley, rape, sugar, millet, sorghum, beans, tobacco and many other crops are raised, providing a surplus for export. Timber is exploited mainly for domestic use; inshore and offshore fishing add substantially to the national budget. North Korea is well endowed with minerals, notably coal, refractory clays, phosphates

and ores of iron, magnesium, tungsten, copper, lead and zinc, many of which are exported: there is little oil or natural gas, but hydroelectric power is well developed. Under recent development programmes North Korea has diversified its manufacturing industries, increasing output of steel, iron, non-ferrous metals, fertilizers and cement. Railways, roads and docks are improving, though many areas of the interior remain difficult to reach; rivers, canals and sea transport provide important internal links.

Recent Developments
Impoverished and physically devastated by the war of 1950–53, North Korea effected recovery through a series of economic development plans. Increasing heavy industrial output and energy production were among the first priorities, coupled with self-sufficiency in food and industrial raw materials. For much of the time since then North Korea claims an average annual growth rate of 12 per cent; this is at present slowing-down, and current planning recognizes more modest targets of 7 to 10 per cent. Trading with other countries and borrowing developed late: North Korea still has little to export apart from primary materials – metals and ores, coal, cement and refractory-clay products – for which world demand is currently low. There is now an effort to develop more diverse industries with the help of foreign capital, a trend that involves the country in increasing debt, notably to Japan and the USSR.

South Korea

The Country
The Republic of Korea (South Korea) occupies the southern end of the Korean peninsula between the Yellow Sea and the Sea of Japan: its only land boundary is the demilitarized zone that separates it from North Korea. *Area* 98,484 km^2 (38,025 sq miles); *capital* Seoul; *population* 42,444,000 (est. 1986).

Organization
Under the constitution of 1980 legislative power rests in an elected National Assembly of 276 members; the executive consists of a President (Head of State) and a cabinet of about 20 ministers led by a Prime Minister. The President is elected by a separate body, an electoral college, made up of over 5000 delegates who are themselves elected by universal suffrage. Local authority is vested in nine provinces and four municipalities. The language is Korean, with Chinese, Japanese and English widely spoken. Religions include Buddhism, Christianity, Taoism and indigenous faiths.

Geography
South Korea is built about a massif of ancient highlands – the Taebaek Mountains – that extends southward along its eastern flank. From these mountains run a succession of lower ridges and valleys, extending southwestward to a broad, undulating lowland and coastal plain. The eastern shore is steep, with only a narrow plain and few settlements; the west has a deeply indented coastline, with many islands and sheltered harbours. The large volcanic island of Cheju, 70 km (43 miles) off the southwestern tip, includes South Korea's highest peak (1950 m, 6398 ft). The climate is continental. Cold northwesterly winds bring frost and snow to the mountains in winter; only the

coastal regions remain comparatively mild. Summers are hot and humid, with monsoon rains, tropical storms and occasional typhoons from June to September. Much of South Korea's lowland forest has been cleared to provide fuel and space for agriculture; removal of upland forest has left soils exposed to leaching and erosion.

History and Development

For the early history of Korea, see North Korea. When a joint US–USSR commission failed to unite Korea in 1946 the United Nations established a commission briefed to hold a nationwide election. The north did not respond, and the UN recognized the southern-elected National Assembly as Korea's only lawful government. After the Korean War (see North Korea), massive economic aid, mostly from the USA, supported South Korea through the succession of political upheavals and coups that followed. Constitutional changes were made affecting the balance of power between President and National Assembly. The first President, Syngman Rhee, was deposed in 1960. The army has from time to time imposed martial law – most recently on the assassination of the second President, Park Chung Hee, in 1979. Under a new President and constitution and with continuing US support, some political stability has now been achieved. Meanwhile, re-unification talks with the government of North Korea continue desultorily.

Resources and Economics

Agriculture plays an important role in the economy, employing some 30 per cent of the workforce and contributing about one fifth of the national income. The main crops are rice, sweet-potatoes, barley, potatoes and a wide range of fruit and vegetables, grown mostly on smallholdings; livestock production – especially pigs, cattle and poultry – is increasing. In good seasons South Korea is self-sufficient in many foodstuffs. Forestry is an expanding industry, providing plywood, newsprint and other products for export. Inshore and deep-sea fishing industries too have grown, providing additional protein for the home market and high-quality frozen fish for export. South Korea mines small quantities of coal, graphite, gold and silver and ores of iron, tungsten, lead, zinc and copper. Hydroelectric power is important, though most electricity is generated from coal (some of it imported) and imported oil. Manufacturing industries, expanding and diversifying rapidly, employ only one fifth of the workforce but contribute almost a third of the country's income, mostly from exports. The main products include fertilizers and other industrial chemicals, ships, steel, motor vehicles, petrochemicals, rubber, synthetic and natural textiles, garments, footwear, processed foods and a wide range of electric and electronic equipment. Heavy construction work overseas, notably in the Middle East, is a South Korean speciality. There are good internal road and rail links, mostly rebuilt after the Korean War. Tourism is an important and growing industry.

Recent Developments

Helped by the USA and other Western nations, South Korea was successful in maintaining economic growth in the period following the Korean War. Annual growth, then averaging over 9 per cent, is now down to about 6 per cent. The country, still very poor by Western standards, can ill afford its massive spending on defence, which alone swallows over one third of the total national income. The current five-year economic plan provides for slight growth in industry, mostly in the manufacturing industries (textiles, electronics) that help to boost exports. More mines are being sunk, and more hydroelectricity produced, in an attempt to reduce dependence on imported oil and coal. Service industries and social welfare, hitherto neglected, will be encouraged to grow, and efforts to spread the new prosperity through the population are promised.

Taiwan (Republic of China)

The Country
Taiwan, effectively a self-governing province of China, lies 140 km (87 miles) off the mainland coast in the China Sea. Included in its territory are the Penghu Archipelago and the islands of Mazu, Changshu and Quemoy close to the mainland. *Area* 35,961 km^2 (13,885 sq miles); *capital* Taipei; *population* 8,025,000 (est. 1986).

Organization
The National Assembly includes about 1000 life-members elected in 1947 (representing the post-war Government of China) and about 150 members elected in 1980. The Assembly elects a President (Head of State) who governs through a Legislative Yuan (assembly) of about 370 members, aided by an Executive Yuan (council) of 15 ministers under a Prime Minister. Technically a province of China, Taiwan vests control of its domestic affairs in a 77-member Provincial Assembly; local government is vested in county and municipal authorities. The official language is Mandarin Chinese, though other dialects are spoken; Buddhism and Taoism are the popular religions, with Moslem and Christian minorities.

Geography
An isolated bloc standing at the edge of the continental shelf, Taiwan appears to have separated from the mainland and tilted westward. Its main mountain ranges, aligned with the island itself, run almost north and south; the highest mountains – the Chungyang Shanmo – form a steep ridge to the east, reaching the coast in high cliffs or a narrow coastal plain. There are many peaks above 3000 m (10,000 ft), the highest rising to 3997 m (13,113 ft). The western flank descends more gently toward the Strait of Formosa. A tilted, dissected tableland rimmed by a broad coastal plain, it carries most of the island's settlements and teeming human population.

Crossed by the Tropic of Cancer, Taiwan has long, hot summers and mild winters. Rainfall is plentiful – heaviest in summer, when tropical storms cross the island, and heaviest of all in the eastern mountains. Much of the island is forested, with lush growth that defies man's efforts to destroy it.

History and Development
Chinese settlers from southern mainland provinces occupied Taiwan from the 7th century onward, making it an integral part of China and driving an aboriginal population into the mountains, where their descendants are still found. Portuguese explorers discovered it in 1590, calling it Formosa; Dutch and Spanish colonists established trading posts in the early 17th century, but were expelled by a Chinese warlord who established his own kingdom there in 1662. He in turn was ousted twenty-one years later by the Manchus, who

followed him from the mainland. In 1895 the province was seized by Japan and developed as a colony. Returned to China after World War II, Taiwan and its neighbouring islands became the final refuge of General Chiang Kai-shek's Nationalist Government, which was driven from the mainland by Communist forces in 1949. US intervention protected this last remnant of Nationalist China from invasion by the People's Republic, and US aid helped it towards economic independence. In the UN, US support maintained the Nationalists' claim to represent the whole of China for over twenty years. By 1971 other nations' recognition of the People's Republic was overwhelming, and Taiwan lost its seat in the Assembly. US aid was withdrawn in 1979, but an economically sound Taiwan continues on its independent way.

Resources and Economics
Warm and well watered, Taiwan grows most of its own food; about one quarter of its workforce is engaged in agriculture. The main crops are rice (double-cropped, and occupying over half the cultivated area), sugar-cane and sweet-potatoes; tea, wheat and a wide range of fruit and vegetables are grown, mostly in peasant smallholdings. Industrial crops include cotton, hemp and jute. Agriculture currently contributes about 10 per cent of the national income. Forestry products include sawn timber, plywood and paper, and fuel for local use. There is a large and expanding deep-water fishing industry. Taiwan has few exploitable minerals: coal, dolomite, marble, salt and as yet relatively small amounts of petroleum and natural gas are among its more valuable products. Most electricity comes from coal-fired and oil-fired generators.

Manufacturing industries, boosted in recent economic development plans, now employ over 30 per cent of the workforce and generate a quarter of national income. Iron and steel, cement, petrochemicals and shipbuilding are the traditional heavy industries; garments, plastic goods and synthetic yarns, fabrics, motor spares, plywood, processed foods, radio and television equipment and – most recently – computers and microprocessors are among Taiwan's many successful light industrial products. Road, rail and air links have spread to cover most of the island, and there is a flourishing tourist industry.

Recent Developments
American capital and know-how have been conspicuously successful in marshalling the human resources of Taiwan since World War II. In little more than a generation it has become, in economic terms, one of the most advanced of all Third-World countries. Alertness to new products, vigorous marketing and a lively labour force have kept its economy buoyant even through a decade of world depression; economic expansion approached 10 per cent each year throughout the 1970s, only recently falling with continued increases in the costs of imported oil and raw materials. Mean income per head now exceeds that of mainland China by a factor of ten, a circumstance making rapprochement between mother country and errant province unlikely. Taiwan's further development, projected in the current four-year plan, will be financed largely from its own resources, though foreign capital and expertise are still welcome: if successful, it will almost quadruple Taiwan's standard of living by 1990.

Oceania

Oceania is a portmanteau name for the many islands and communities of the Pacific Ocean, but by no means a precise one. It includes Australia (which alone accounts for 90 per cent of the total land area), New Zealand, the eastern half of New Guinea, and many island groups scattered across the length and breadth of the Pacific. The islands are grouped according to the ethnic origins of their populations, though boundaries are blurred by the proclivities of all the islanders, especially the Polynesians, for ocean travel. Melanesia includes New Guinea and islands of the Torres Strait, the Bismarck Archipelago and Solomon Islands, Vanuatu (formerly New Hebrides), New Caledonia and Fiji. Micronesia forms an arc of small islands to north and east of these, including Kiribati and the Caroline, Mariana and Marshall islands. Polynesia includes many islands of the central and eastern Pacific, including Tonga, Samoa, Tuvalu (formerly Ellice Islands) and the Cook, Society, Tubuai, Marquesas and Tuamotu islands – also Pitcairn, Ducie, Easter Island and Sala-y-Gomez in the far southeast. The total land area is about 8.5 million km² (3.28 million sq miles), the total population about 25 million.

OCEANIA SOUTHWEST

Australia

The Country
The Commonwealth of Australia occupies a continental bloc lying southeast of Indonesia between the eastern Indian and southwestern Pacific oceans; it includes the island of Tasmania. *Area* 7,686,848 km² (2,967,895 sq miles); *capital* Canberra, *largest city* Sydney; *population* 15,512,000 (est. 1986).

Organization
A parliamentary democracy and member of the Commonwealth, Australia is governed by a House of Representatives of 125 members elected every third year and a Senate of 64 members elected for six-year terms. Head of State is an appointed Governor-General representing the British Crown, who presides over an Executive Council; a cabinet of about 14 senior ministers under a Prime Minister holds day-to-day executive responsibility. Five of the six states have bicameral parliaments (Legislative Council and House of Assembly); Queensland (and Northern Territory, self-governing since 1978) has only a Legislative Assembly, while the Australian Capital Territory has a legislative body responsible to a federal minister. Local areas within the states are administered by city, town, shire or municipal councils. Christianity is the dominant religion, English the official language.

Geography
Geologically Australia consists of a broad western shield of ancient granites and gneisses, worn down to a series of plateaus and plains, occupying over half the

continent; the eastern and some southern parts of this shield are covered by sandy sediments with patches of limestone. Further east, the contorted rocks of the eastern highlands are mostly plateaus, but with some ranges aligned north-south; the highest peak, Kosciusko (2230 m, 7317 ft), is in the Snowy Mountains in the southeast. Much of the interior is arid with extensive areas of stony desert and dunes. Mean annual rainfall ranges from over 200 cm (80 in) in the northeast to less than 10 cm (4 in) in the southern centre, but is highly variable from one year to the next. The best agricultural soils lie where rainfall exceeds 75 cm (30 in), in patches of the eastern uplands and adjacent coast, in the southwest and in Tasmania. About half the continent is without rivers; most of the existing rivers are seasonal and virtually useless for transportation.

Vegetation ranges from perennial dry desert scrub to seasonal grasslands, with temperate, subtropical or tropical rain forest in the wettest areas. Australia's flora and fauna are distinctive and markedly different from that of the Asian mainland; eucalypts are the dominant trees, birds and insects are plentiful, and the indigenous mammal fauna is restricted to marsupials, seals and bats.

History and Development

Australia's aboriginal inhabitants entered the continent about 40,000 years ago, spreading to Tasmania by 30,000 years ago and developing a culture and life style well adapted to the extremes of the Australian environment. Dutch explorers first mapped the north, west and south coasts in the early 17th century, but found the country too inhospitable to settle. The discovery of the fertile, densely-vegetated southeast by James Cook in 1770 led to the establishment of the first British settlement, a penal colony, near Botany Bay in 1788. From there the interior was explored with difficulty, and further coastal settlements were established at Hobart (Tasmania) in 1804 and at Port Phillip (later Melbourne) in 1835. From such settlements arose the separate colonies of Van Diemen's land (later Tasmania) in 1825, South Australia (1837), Victoria (1851) and Queensland (1859), all except Tasmania being taken from the original colony of New South Wales. In the west the separate Swan River settlement, established in 1827, did not become the self-governing colony of Western Australia until 1890. Australia's colonies federated into a self-governing Commonwealth in 1901.

Sheep introduced early in the 19th century increased the value of grazing land; cattle-raising and arable farming followed, and minerals – notably copper and gold – were discovered in the interior. Gold was the primary stimulus to the growth of European settlement from the mid-19th century onwards, leading to the emergence of Melbourne as the great commercial centre. Australia's population swelled to six million by the end of World War I and seven million by 1945, more than doubling during the country's huge industrial expansion after World War II when immigration policies encouraged much greater ethnic diversity and greatly reduced the dominance of the British among the European population. Australia remains, however, a thinly-populated continent, with 65 per cent of its people concentrated in a few cities of over 100,000 population.

Resources and Economics

Current prosperity is based on agriculture and minerals. Farming employs only 6 per cent of the workforce but provides about one quarter of the export income. Beef, wool, wheat and other cereals and fruit are the main crops; meat and cereal output especially are subject to periodic droughts, which can still significantly affect the country's prosperity. Timber, pulp and paper products are significant in the economy of Queensland and Tasmania. Minerals are of prime importance; coal and iron ore alone exceed agricultural produce in export value, most being exported to Japan for steel manufacture. Bauxite, copper, rutile and ilmenite (the titanium oxides used in paint manufacture) are now the main ores exported, gold and other precious metals being less important than they were.

About 15 per cent of the country's energy needs are met by hydroelectricity, mostly from the Snowy Mountains (New South Wales and Victoria) and Tasmania. Some 70 per cent of petroleum needs are provided locally, mostly from the Bass Strait. A wide range of manufacturing industries, centered mostly in Sydney, Melbourne and Perth, include food-processing, textiles, chemicals, motor vehicles and machinery; they provide for local needs and are a major source of employment. Iron and steel manufacture occurs at three coastal sites, Newcastle and Wollongong (New South Wales) and Whyalla (South Australia). Despite the huge distances involved, excellent air services link all the towns, with good roads between the main centres and a recently improved transcontinental railway. Tourism and leisure activities are taken seriously by Australians and good facilities are found in all but the most remote parts of the continent.

Recent Developments
Although hampered by vastness, the relative inhospitability of its huge interior, a highly variable and often arid climate and remoteness from markets in both Europe and North America, Australia has been a lucky country and has immense resources. Much of its potential agricultural land has been exploited, and now supplies a wide range of markets, not only in Europe but also in the Middle East, North America and Japan. Being dependent on world commodity prices and the victim of fluctuating demands, the development of Australian mineral resources has been slow, but large investments have made great iron-mining enterprises possible in the remote northwest and encouraged much exploration. The huge natural gas discovery on the northwest shelf of Western Australia will provide a further boost to Australia's wealth. More than self-sufficient in food and with strong local manufacturing industries protected by government tariffs, Australia's continuing prosperity seems assured. The smallest continent now houses one of the world's wealthiest nations, with egalitarianism ensuring a high standard of living for almost every Australian.

Nauru

The island state of Nauru lies in the southwest Pacific Ocean, west of Kiribati, north of the Solomon Islands and just south of the Equator. *Area* 21 km^2 (8.1 sq miles); *population* 8000 (est. 1986). An oval-shaped coral island with fringing reef, Nauru rises inland to a low plateau. Agricultural land is confined to a fertile section 100 to 300 m (330 to 1000 ft) wide between the beach and a cliff. Above the cliff the plateau has been mined for almost a century for its rich deposits of phosphatic rock.

The island was discovered in 1798, and left almost untouched until 1888 when it came under German rule. Australian forces occupied it in World War I, and it was subsequently mandated to Australia by the League of Nations. Australia and New Zealand provided the main market for its phosphate. After occupation by Japanese forces in World War II, the Australian mandate was renewed. Nauru gained its own Legislative Council in 1966 and independence two years later: it is currently self-governing with an elected parliament of 18 members. Phosphate is still its only significant export, now providing its tiny population with a high income per capita, much of which has been invested in property overseas by the government to provide an income when the phosphate deposits are exhausted.

New Caledonia

The Country
The island of New Caledonia, some 1100 km (700 miles) east of Australia, forms the administrative centre of an extensive South Pacific island territory of the same name, governed as an Overseas Territory of France. *Area (of territory)* 19,058 km² (7358 sq miles); *capital* Noumea; *population* 148,000 (est. 1986).

Organization
The territory is administered by an appointed High Commissioner (Chef du Territoire) and a 7-member Council of Government elected from the 36-member Territorial Assembly. New Caledonia returns two deputies to the French National Assembly and one senator to the Senate. Local authority is administered through communes. Just under half the population are Melanesian, about 30 per cent European, the rest Polynesian, Asian and mixed; Christianity is the dominant religion, French the official language with many local dialects.

Geography
New Caledonia (area 16,627 km², 6419 sq miles), the largest island, is long, narrow and mountainous, with the highest peaks rising about 1500 m (5000 ft). Other islands in the territory (Île des Pins, Walpole, the Loyalty, Chesterfield, Huon and Bélep groups) are much smaller, some high and volcanic with seasonal rainfall, others drier limestone platforms. All have fringing coral reefs. Rain is heaviest from December to March, especially on the eastern flanks; the uplands of New Caledonia Island and other mountainous islands support dense pine forests.

History and Development
The island of New Caledonia was discovered and named by James Cook in 1774, but left to its Melanesian population for a further two decades. French interest began with explorer Bruni d'Entrecasteaux, who visited it in 1792; settlers and missionaries from France colonized several of the islands in the territory during the early 19th century, and New Caledonia Island was annexed by France as a penal settlement in 1853. Formerly a colony, the island of New Caledonia and most of its former dependencies became an Overseas Territory in 1958 and in 1976 achieved a degree of autonomy.

Resources and Economics
Though soils on the volcanic islands are fertile and climates benign, less than 10 per cent of the land area is cultivable. Large estates raise coffee and field crops (notably maize); farms and smallholdings provide meat, especially beef and pork, vegetables, fruit and subsistence crops. The Loyalty Islands and several

smaller islands raise coconuts for copra. Mineral ores, the territory's chief asset, include nickel, chrome, iron, gold, silver, cobalt and copper; most of the nickel, the main export, is processed before leaving the islands. New Caledonia is well provided with roads; air and shipping services link it with neighbouring islands and with the outside world, providing for a flourishing tourist industry.

Recent Developments
New Caledonia's main wealth lies in its minerals, though these employ only a small proportion of the workforce. The subsistence agriculture and fishing that occupy most New Caledonians are slowly being replaced by small industries, services etc (notably tourism) that offer a higher standard of living. About one third of the revenues come from French subsidies which help protect the economy against world fluctuations in metal prices; nevertheless political unrest is endemic, fanned by unemployment, and many in the Melanesian population seek complete independence from France.

New Zealand

The Country
The state of New Zealand consists of three large and many smaller islands in the southwestern Pacific Ocean, 1600 km (1000 miles) east of Australia. *Area* 268,676 km^2 (103,736 sq miles); *capital* Wellington, *largest city* Auckland; *population* 3,495,000 (est. 1986).

Organization
An independent parliamentary democracy and dominion of the Commonwealth, New Zealand has an elected House of Representatives; Head of State is a Governor-General representing the British Crown. Local authority is vested in county, district, borough and town councils. Many Christian denominations are represented; the official language is English, the Maori population (10 per cent) speaks its own language.

Geography
Mountainous and volcanic, New Zealand has about 75 per cent of its land above 200 m (650 ft). The North Island is made up of folded ridges and fertile valleys, with a central plateau dominated by three volcanic cones: the highest, Ruapehu, rises to 2796 m (9174 ft). Earthquakes are frequent; geothermal energy is harnessed at Wairakei. The South Island's spine of alpine mountains includes the Southern Alps, clustered about Mt Cook (3764 m, 12,349 ft), with glaciers on either flank. The Canterbury, Southland and less extensive Westland plains are formed from the outwash fans of montane rivers. The temperate oceanic climate is windy, with plentiful rain from the southwest; the far north is virtually frost-free, while a few places in the lee of the Southern Alps have semi-arid climates. Dense rain forest in the wetter areas grades to grassland in dry areas and uplands; exotic forests and pastures now dominate many parts of the country. New Zealand has no native land mammals except bats and seals; many alien species have been introduced with devastating effects on native flora and fauna.

History and Development
The first human settlements by Polynesian voyagers occurred around AD 300,

with the major migration from eastern Polynesia in 1350. By the time Tasman sailed round New Zealand (1642), the Maoris were hunting and farming throughout the two islands, but with the main settlements in the North. Seals, whales and timber were exploited by the first European contacts before the pastoral settlements began in 1839. Much of the settlement was an eastward move from Australia. Britain took possession in 1840 under the Treaty of Waitangi, which gave equal status to all. Merino sheep, introduced from Australia in 1844, provided the basis of a predominantly agricultural economy that persists to the present day. By the mid-19th century Europeans (mostly British) made up one third of the population of 90,000, but the Maori component declined sharply to 5.5 per cent of the population in 1936; since then it has risen to 10 per cent and Maori birth rates remain higher than those of the European population.

Resources and Economics
Pastoral production provides 75 per cent of New Zealand's export earnings; the high productivity of exotic pastures is maintained by improvement of grasses and applications of lime and superphosphate. Forestry, using both native and exotic timbers, is expanding and its products are being diversified. Iron sands, coal and gold are staple minerals; newly developed natural-gas fields provide a welcome substitute for imported fuel oil. Hydroelectricity meets 87 per cent of demand for this form of power, which is also produced geothermally at Wairakei. Manufacturing industries are developing slowly, currently providing about 20 per cent of export earnings and balancing imported fuel bills. Tourism is expanding slowly. New Zealand has for long been a welfare state with a high standard of living and well-developed health, education and social services. There are good internal rail, road and air transport networks and Auckland, Wellington and Christchurch have international airports.

Recent Developments
New Zealand's export trade continues to grow, despite the impact of EEC regulations on the traditional sales of agricultural produce in Britain. Efforts to diversify produce and markets have been partly successful, but the rising price of oil (New Zealand's most costly import) and other raw materials has hampered development of manufacturing industries. Generating foreign exchange for imports, on which New Zealand's high standard of living depends, is currently taxing the country's resources to the full.

Papua New Guinea

The Country
The state of Papua New Guinea occupies the eastern half of the island of New Guinea, and includes the Bismarck and Louisiade Archipelagos, the Trobriand and D'Entrecasteaux islands and other off-lying groups. *Area* 461,691 km² (178,259 sq miles); *capital* Port Moresby; *population* 3,708,000 (est. 1986).

Organization
Head of State is an appointed Governor-General, representing the British Crown. A unicameral National Parliament of 109 members is elected for five-year terms; a Prime Minister leads an executive cabinet, the National Executive

Council, of about 20 ministers. The 19 provinces and the capital city have small provincial legislatures and local authority covering the settlements. Local religions predominate, with Christianity represented in various denominations. English and Pidgin English are used in government, and there are many hundreds of local languages and dialects.

Geography
Papua New Guinea is dominated by a complex series of mountain ridges thrust up relatively recently by pressure between adjacent crustal plates, trending east–southeast from the border with Irian Jaya. The main chain, from Victor Emanuel Range in the west to Owen Stanley Range in the east, is dissected by deep river gorges. The highest snow-covered peaks rise above 4000 m (13,100 ft); highest of all is Mt Wilhelm (4508 m, 14,790 ft). North of the main ranges a broad valley is crossed by the Sepik and Ramu rivers; the north coast and islands beyond are further volcanic ranges arising from deep water. New Guinea's southern plain, traversed by the meandering Fly River, rises gently at first through inhospitable marshes and forest to steep limestone foothills. The archipelago islands are steep-flanked and mostly volcanic, fringed with coral reefs. Papua New Guinea's climate is hot and wet, especially on the windward (southern) side. Coastal mangroves give way to lowland forest extending up to 1000 m (3300 ft) and mountain forest or grassland above. A rich endemic fauna includes marsupials and abundant insects and birds.

History and Development
Dutch explorers knew of New Guinea and its neighbouring islands from early 16th-century voyages. British settlers farming on the western (Irian Jaya) end of the mainland from 1793 were displaced by Dutch colonists, but those on the southeastern shore persisted. Later German traders and settlers established themselves in the northeast. These spheres of influence were backed by formal claims in the late 19th century; in 1884 Britain annexed the territory of Papua along the southeastern coast, and in 1899 German New Guinea was established in the northeast. During World War I Australia annexed the German colony, in the post-war years governing both British and German areas as separate territories. Occupied by Japanese troops in World War II and subsequently recovered, the two were combined in 1949 under Australian mandate as the United Nations Trust Territory of Papua and New Guinea. This evolved in stages toward self-government, and independence was granted in 1975.

Resources and Economics
The dense rain forests that cover much of Papua New Guinea restrict access and limit agriculture to coastal sites and upland plateau areas. On the most accessible ground subsistence farming for yams, sago, cassava, bananas and vegetables competes for space with plantation-grown cash crops of coconuts, coffee, cocoa, palm oil, rubber and tea. Over two thirds of the workforce is engaged in farming, fishing and forestry, which together provide the main exports and source of overseas revenues. Minerals are present but generally difficult and costly to extract. Copper ore is mined on Bougainville Island and by the Ok Tedi company on the mainland, providing over one third of the country's export income. Natural gas is present in the Sepik valley. Hydroelectric power has immense potential, but is at present generated on a large scale only on the Ramu River. There are few manufactures other than food-processing and brewing for local consumption. Apart from the Highlands Highway, linking the port of Lae

with the central highlands, road links are poor. Air, sea and river transport remain important in the local and national economy. There is a small tourist industry.

Recent Developments
Geographical difficulties combine to ensure that Papua New Guinea's economic development will be a slow and gradual process. Much of the population has moved from a subsistence to a cash economy, sometimes with little improvement in well-being, but many tribal groups remain dispersed, difficult to reach and remote from government. Bougainville's bid (1976) for independence reflects a lasting problem of scale and distance. The urban centres of Port Moresby, Lae, Madang and Rabaul attract many migrants from the forests and villages, but offer little employment and few facilities for those seeking wages and a higher standard of living. Copper and coffee, the two most significant exports, are subject to wide fluctuations in market prices, and as yet few alternatives are available. Development is helped by financial and other aid from Australia and the international community.

Solomon Islands

The Country
The state of the Solomon Islands occupies the southern islands of the Solomons group, east of Papua New Guinea in the equatorial Pacific Ocean. The twenty-one large and many smaller islands include Guadalcanal, San Cristobal, New Georgia, Malaita, the Russell and Florida groups, Ontong Java (Lord Howe Island) and remote Santa Cruz. *Area* 28,446 km^2 (10,983 sq miles); *capital* Honiara (Guadalcanal); *population* 271,000 (est. 1986).

Organization
Head of State is a Governor-General, representing the British Crown. A single-chambered Parliament (Legislative Assembly) of 38 members is elected for four-year terms; from it is elected a Prime Minister, who leads an executive council (cabinet) of about 15 ministers. Local administration is vested in eight elected regional councils, which are of growing importance. Christianity is the dominant religion, English the official language, with many local languages and dialects spoken.

Geography
The main islands are volcanic and steep, forming a double chain oriented northwest–southeast. Several are ringed by coral reefs and have coral platforms indicating recent uplift. The climate is tropical maritime, wet throughout the year and intensely hot December to March. Most of the islands are heavily covered with seasonal rain forest, which is replaced by grassland in the drier areas.

History and Development
When discovered by Spanish explorers in the mid-16th century, the islands were thinly populated by Melanesians who fished and raised crops. Few Europeans chose to live there until the late 19th century, when German annexation of Bougainville and Buka islands (now in Papua New Guinea)

stimulated the British to annex the rest of the Solomons group. The southern islands formed a British protectorate until 1942, when Japanese forces occupied them; returned to British control after World War II, they evolved in stages towards independence which was granted in 1978.

Resources and Economics
Most Solomon islanders live in small villages at subsistence level, fishing and producing cassava, yams, vegetables, rice and other crops on smallholdings for their own consumption. A small proportion in the more accessible areas are involved in plantation agriculture, commercial fishing and forestry. Timber and processed fish provide two thirds of export revenues; copra, palm oil, cocoa and tobacco are also exported. Minerals including copper ore, bauxite, gold, phosphatic rock and asbestos are present, but currently under-exploited; industries are virtually limited to food- and timber-processing. Roads are poor; sea and air links connect scattered population centres with the capital.

Recent Developments
Despite many decades of European contact the islands remain at a primitive stage of development. Because of the distances involved, government from Honiara is difficult and ineffective. Regional councils are playing increasing roles in economic planning and development, which stress the importance of the regions, the improvement of transport and the promotion of local industries.

Vanuatu

The Country
The Republic of Vanuatu occupies a chain of islands in the south central Pacific Ocean, southeast of the Solomon Islands, northeast of New Caledonia, some 1800 km (1100 miles) from the Australian coast. *Area* 14,763 km² (5700 sq miles); *capital* Vila; *population* 138,000 (est. 1986).

Organization
Vanuatu is governed by a Representative Assembly of 42 members, elected for four-year terms; the Assembly elects the President, who as Head of State appoints an executive Prime Minister and cabinet. Local authority is vested in island councils. Christianity is the dominant religion; Bislama, English and French are the official languages, with Pidgin English widely spoken.

Geography
A dozen large islands and many smaller ones make up the Vanuatu chain; most are volcanic (some active) and rugged, with raised coral beaches and fringing reefs; the highest and largest island, Espiritu Santo, rises to 1888 m (6195 ft). Warm and well-watered throughout the year, the mountains are forested and the lowlands intensively cultivated.

History and Development
Discovered by Portuguese seamen in 1606, the islands were for long left to their hostile Melanesian population. French and English navigators charted them in the late 18th century, James Cook calling them the New Hebrides. French and British settlers followed, and slavers raided the islands to provide labour for

Australia. When European interest in Pacific colonies quickened during the 1880s, the New Hebrides became a joint French and British responsibility, formalized as a condominium in 1906. This lasted until 1980, when the islands achieved independence as Vanuatu.

Resources and Economics

Most of the islanders are farmers and fishermen; subsistence farming provides manioc, taro, yams and fruit, and plantations yield sugar, cocoa, coffee and copra for export. Stock-raising, forestry and deep-water fishing are growing industries: other industries include food-processing, and handicrafts for a steadily increasing tourist market. A major manganese mine on Efate provides export income. Roads are adequate for dry weather, sea and air links between the islands generally good: Vila and Santo have well-developed port and airport facilities.

Recent Developments

Among the more favoured groups of Pacific islands, Vanuatu benefits from stable government, and a limited economy capable of further development as funds become available. Post-independence problems, including the attempted secession of Espiritu Santo, appear to have been settled, and land reform measures may remove another threatening source of internal friction.

OCEANIA NORTH

Guam

The island of Guam is the most southerly of the Mariana Islands chain, lying 2200 km (1375 miles) southeast of Japan and 2000 km (1250 miles) east of the Philippine Islands. *Area* 549 km² (212 sq miles); *capital* Agaña; *population* 115,000 (est. 1986). An unincorporated territory of the USA, Guam is virtually self-governing. A legislature of 21 members is elected for two-year terms; to it is responsible a Governor, elected for four-year terms, who heads an executive cabinet of 15 appointed ministers. An elected non-voting delegate represents Guam in the US House of Representatives. Catholicism is the dominant religion, English the official language.

Low volcanic mountains rising to 400 m (1310 ft) are fringed in the north by a limestone plateau; the island is ringed by a reef. The climate is warm and damp, with heaviest rains from July to September; vegetation includes both scrub mountain forest and dry grassland. Discovered by Magellan in 1521, Guam was claimed by Spain, together with the rest of the Marianas chain, in 1668. There was little development until 1898 when the USA acquired it after the Spanish-American War. Under US management it became a mid-ocean naval base and air staging post. After Japanese occupation in 1941–4 its population opted to remain under US government, evolving in stages towards its present semi-autonomy.

Guam's economy is mainly agricultural; staple foods are grown on smallholdings, and copra, palm oil and processed fish are exported to ready markets in Japan, Australia and the USA. Under US patronage small industries have been encouraged, and the military bases provide additional employment.

Tourism is a flourishing industry, bringing further prosperity to this small but strategically important island.

Northern Mariana Islands

The Commonwealth of the Northern Mariana Islands includes all the Marianas except Guam; over a dozen volcanic islands form a chain some 650 km (400 miles) long in the northwestern Pacific Ocean, south of Japan and some 2500 km (1560 miles) east of the Philippines. *Area* 480 km^2 (185 sq miles); *capital* Saipan; *population* 19,500 (est. 1986).

In 1975 the Northern Mariana Islands became a Commonwealth in Union with the USA. A self-governing territory of the USA, the islands have a 9-member Senate, a 14-member House of Representatives and an executive Governor; senators and Governor are elected for terms of four years, representatives for two. The dominant religion is Catholicism, the official language English.

The Marianas are mostly volcanic (three are still active) with coral limestone and lava shores; several islands have peaks over 450 m (1500 ft), the highest, Agrihan, rising to 963 m (3160 ft). A hot and damp climate supports forest and scrub; rich valley soils are cultivated. Discovered by Magellan in 1521, the islands were inhabited by Chamorros, probably of Malaysian ancestry, whom Spanish settlers displaced or enslaved. In 1899 Spain sold the Marianas to Germany. Captured by Japanese troops in World War I, they were developed by Japan under a League of Nations mandate. US troops occupied them in World War II, depopulating some of the islands for defence purposes. After the war the USA held them under UN mandate as part of the US Trust Territory of the Pacific (see entry). They were awarded separate status in 1975 and self-government in 1978, though part of the Trust Territory until its dissolution.

Marianians, now a blend of Chamorro, Japanese and mixed European stock, are concentrated mainly in the southernmost islands of Saipan, Tinian and Rota; most are subsistence farmers and fishermen. On some of the islands commercial crops and stock are raised, providing vegetables and meat for export. There is little industry apart from food-processing. US bases provide work and cash, and there is a small but flourishing tourist trade. Roads are good on the main islands; air and sea links are maintained between the islands and with the outside world. The islanders' everyday standard of living benefits considerably from their voluntary association with the USA.

US Trust Territory of the Pacific Islands

The US Trust Territory of the Pacific Islands includes two major groups, the Caroline Islands (the Federated States of Micronesia and Republic of Belau) and the Marshall Islands, north of Papua New Guinea in the western Pacific Ocean (see also Northern Mariana Islands). *Area* 1779 km^2 (687 sq miles); *population* 137,000 (est. 1986). The islands are in process of forming three self-governing divisions, which will retain voluntary association with the USA.

Mostly of volcanic origin, the islands vary from coral-fringed mountains (many of the Carolines) to almost completely submerged atolls (most of the Marshalls); few rise above 120 m (400 ft). Climates are warm and damp throughout the year, enlivened by hurricanes; vegetation varies from thin scrub on the low, dry atolls to forest on the wetter hillsides. Native peoples are mostly Micronesian with some Polynesian infiltration. Spanish, Dutch, Russian, British and French explorers mapped the area from the 16th century onward, Spain exercising the most persistent claims and colonizing the more promising islands. German interest developed during the late 19th century, the Marshalls and later the Carolines becoming German colonies between 1885 and 1899. Japanese forces took them over in World War I, and the islands were mandated to Japan in the inter-war years. US troops ejected the Japanese during World War II, holding the islands first under military occupation and later as a Trust Territory. Several islands, including Bikini and Eniwetok, have been used for nuclear testing.

Subsistence farming is the main occupation throughout the islands, though commercial farming is practised on the larger ones where climate and soils are favourable. Crops include coconuts, cane sugar, cassava and yams: livestock, notably pigs and poultry, are also raised for local consumption, and fishermen work from most of the islands. Copra and locally-processed fish products are major exports. Tourism flourishes, bringing much-needed revenue to many of the larger islands. US administration and military services provide wages for many island employees.

Each of the island groups (the Federated States of Micronesia, the Republic of Belau and the Marshall Islands) will shortly gain independence, the USA retaining responsibility for defence and allowing a substantial grant-in-aid extending over several years.

OCEANIA CENTRAL

American Samoa

American Samoa lies in the central southern Pacific Ocean, the easternmost islands of an east–west chain some 3500 km (2200 miles) north–northwest of New Zealand. *Area* 197 km² (76 sq miles); *main settlement* Pago Pago, *seat of government* Fagatogo; *population* 35,000 (est. 1986). The islands form an external territory of the USA, with an elected legislature of 18 senators and 20 representatives (plus 1 non-voting member), and an elected executive Governor. Christianity is the dominant religion, English the official language.

The five main islands (Tutuila, Ta'u, Olosega, Ofu and Aunu'u) are volcanic and hilly; Tutuila, the westernmost, rises to 653 m (2142 ft), Ta'u in the eastern group to 970 m (3182 ft). Swain's and Rose islands are distant, low-lying atolls. All have wet tropical climates, the mountains attracting heavy rainfall of up to 750 cm (300 in). When first visited by Europeans in the 18th and 19th centuries the Samoan islands formed part of a Polynesian kingdom. American whalers were frequent visitors, and in 1878 the US Navy negotiated with the King for a mid-Pacific base in the natural harbour of Pago Pago. In 1904 all islands east of 171° W were ceded to the USA, though the offer was not officially accepted until 1929. Administered since then by the US Department of the Interior, American

Samoa received its first elected Governor in 1978.

Many of the islanders are smallholding farmers, growing bananas, breadfruit, cassava, yams, pineapples, vegetables and other produce mainly for local consumption. Fishing is a major industry, the bulk of the catch being canned for export. Tourism too is an important dollar-earner, and US military and civil administrations help to support a flourishing wage economy on the main islands. Many wage-earners go overseas to find temporary work in the USA and elsewhere.

Cook Islands

The Cook Islands form a widely scattered group of volcanic and coral islands centered some 3200 km (2000 miles) northeast of New Zealand. *Area* 236 km^2 (91 sq miles); *administrative centre* Avarua (Rarotonga); *population* 21,500 (est. 1986). The islands are fully self-governing with an elected Legislative Assembly, Prime Minister and cabinet of ministers. They are linked to New Zealand by a common Head of State, the British Sovereign, and a common citizenship; an appointed High Commissioner represents the British Sovereign and New Zealand interests. Christianity is the dominant religion, English the official language with local languages widely spoken.

The northern group of islands are mostly low-lying atolls, the southern (or 'lower') group mainly volcanic with fringing coral reefs; the highest island, Rarotonga, rises to 650 m (2130 ft). The climate is damp and tropical, with rainfall heavy on the forested volcanic slopes of the southern islands. 16th-century Spanish and Portuguese explorers were probably the first Europeans to see many of the islands; James Cook made several visits in 1773–7, and the British missionary John Williams converted the Polynesian inhabitants, paving the way for colonization in the 19th century. The islands became a British protectorate in 1888 and a New Zealand dependency in 1901. Self-government was granted in 1965.

Most Cook islanders are subsistence farmers and fishermen. The main crops are vegetables and fish for local consumption, and citrus fruit, pawpaws, capsicums, beans, pineapples, aubergines and other luxury vegetables for New Zealand. Rising freight costs and almost total dependence on a small, fluctuating New Zealand market precipitate recurring crises in the economy which affect all the islands. There is a marked migration of population from the outer islands to Rarotonga, and many Cook islanders have settled temporarily or permanently in New Zealand.

Fiji

The Country

The state of Fiji occupies two large islands, Viti Levu and Vanua Levu, together with some 300 lesser islands, many of them uninhabited, in the southern Pacific Ocean 2000 km (1250 miles) north of New Zealand. *Area* 18,274 km^2 (7056 sq miles); *capital* Suva (Viti Levu); *population* 694,000 (est. 1986).

Organization

Head of State is a Governor-General appointed by and representing the British Crown. Parliament includes a House of Representatives of 52 elected members

153

(22 Fijian, 22 Indian and 8 general) serving five-year terms, and an appointed Senate of 22 members serving six-year appointments. An executive Prime Minister heads a cabinet of about ten ministers. Local authority is vested in thirteen provinces, each with an elected council. A Fijian Council of Chiefs advises on affairs affecting the Fijian sector of the population. The indigenous people are Melanesian; there are also large Hindu and smaller Chinese, Polynesian and European communities. Christianity is the dominant religion, English the official language, with Hindi and Fijian in general use.

Geography
The larger islands are mountainous and made up of ancient volcanic and sedimentary rocks, the lesser ones mainly low-lying coral atolls. The climate is hot and damp, with heavy rainfall on the mountains. Forests cover the uplands and wetter plains, and mangrove forests line much of the coast where rainfall is high; in the drier areas of the west and north trees give way to savanna and thorn scrub.

History and Development
Abel Tasman in 1643 and James Cook in 1774 were the first Europeans to visit the Fijian islands. 19th-century whalers and traders called in on trans-Pacific voyages; settlers and missionaries found the flourishing, aggressive Melanesian population difficult to deal with, and introduced indentured Indian labour to work the plantations. At the request of warring local chiefs Britain took control of the group in 1874; Fiji remained a colony for almost a century, gaining independence in 1970.

Resources and Economics
About one third of Fijians work in agriculture, both as subsistence farmers growing cassava, rice and yams, and in the sugar and coconut plantations on which community income depends. There is a growing livestock industry. Sugar dominates the export trade, with coconut oil and gold of lesser significance. Apart from sugar mills and coconut-oil processing, cement manufacture and gold-mining are the main industries. Roads are adequate on the main islands; Suva is the major international port while Nadi on the western side of Viti Levu is a major international airport. Inter-island boat and air services support a growing tourist industry and local commerce.

Recent Developments
Fiji's main assets are its rich soils and benign climate; efforts are being made to develop and improve efficiency in agriculture and forestry. Few other potential assets have been developed during or since colonial times. Racial problems between Hindu and Fijian, which once threatened political stability, have now receded, and the islands seem set for slow, steady progress towards prosperity.

Kiribati

The Country
The republic of Kiribati occupies over thirty islands, most of them coral atolls, just north of the Equator in the central Pacific Ocean. *Area* 728 km^2 (281 sq miles); *capital* Tarawa; *population* 68,000 (est. 1986).

Organization
The House of Assembly is made up of 35 elected members and 1 nominee representing Banaba; all serve four-year terms. Head of State is an executive President, normally elected, who heads a small cabinet drawn from the House of Assembly. Christianity is the dominant religion, English and Gilbertese (Kiribati) are the main languages.

Geography
Kiribati includes the former Gilbert Islands, the Phoenix Islands, Banaba (Ocean Island) and eight of the Line Islands; most are low-lying coral atolls. Banaba was extensively covered with phosphatic ores which have now been worked out. Soils are generally poor but responsive to cultivation. The climate is hot and humid, tempered by trade winds and well watered; vegetation ranges from scrub to thin forest.

History and Development
The islands were discovered by Spanish, British and other survey expeditions mainly during the 18th and early 19th centuries, and later visited by traders and whalers. Unpromising for colonization, they came under formal British control only during the international scramble for Pacific colonies in the late 19th century. The Gilbert Islands and Ellice Islands (now Tuvalu) were claimed in 1892 and linked with Ocean Island as a Crown Colony in 1915. Ocean Island was mined for its phosphate rocks; there was little other development. Independence was granted in 1979, the new state of Kiribati becoming a republic within the Commonwealth.

Resources and Economics
Currently most islanders fish within a few kilometres of the islands, grow their own food (coconuts, breadfruit, pandanus and vegetables), and rear livestock, mainly pigs and poultry. Since the decline of the phosphate industry in the late 1970s, copra and fish have been the main exports, providing most of the overseas revenues; the islanders have few other sources of income except mother-of-pearl, shells and handicrafts. Living standards are simple. There are few roads, and most links with the outside world are through the ports of Banaba and Betio (Tarawa). Tarawa has an international airport; there are frequent inter-island flights.

Recent Developments
A small but rapidly growing community, spread over a wide area, Kiribati has many indigenous problems. Since the end of the phosphate industry living standards have declined, and no alternative resources have appeared to boost the economy. The islanders face a bleak future subsidized by grants-in-aid from Britain, and loans from international sources for modest development programmes.

Niue

The island of Niue lies south of the Cook Islands in the south central Pacific Ocean, 2140 km (1340 miles) east of New Zealand, of which it is a self-governing dependency. *Area* 259 km² (100 sq miles); *main settlement* Alofi; *population* 3000 (est. 1986). The island is governed by an elected assembly, under a High Commissioner representing the British Crown and New Zealand government. Christianity is the dominant religion, English the official language with a Polynesian dialect widely used.

Niue is mainly coralline with a flat, rolling interior and porous soils; rising centrally to about 75 m (250 ft). The climate is subtropical and damp, supporting woodland in the central uplands. Called 'Savage Island' by James Cook, who visited it in 1774 and found the natives hostile, Niue was little touched by Europeans until the mid-19th century, when missionaries converted the population to Christianity. The islanders petitioned for and accepted British sovereignty, Niue becoming a protectorate in 1900. Administered by New Zealand, it achieved internal self-government in 1974.

The economy is mainly agricultural; most islanders earn subsistence wages on government relief work, and raise vegetables, fruit, pigs and poultry for home consumption. Copra and fruit, mostly for New Zealand, are the main exports, and the island receives an annual grant-in-aid from New Zealand to help balance its budget.

Tokelau Islands

The Tokelau (Union) Islands include three atolls, Atafu, Nukunonu and Fakaofo, lying in the central Pacific Ocean about 3500 km (2200 miles) north–northeast of New Zealand. *Area* 10 km² (3.9 sq miles); *main settlement* Nukunonu; *population* 1800 (est. 1986). External territories of New Zealand, they are governed by local village councils under a New Zealand administration. Christianity is the dominant religion, English and Polynesian are the spoken languages.

The atolls are low-lying complexes of islands and coral reefs rising only a few metres above sea level; their climate is hot and generally humid, tempered by trade winds, and all carry dense scrub modified by cultivation. Discovered by 18th-century British navigators, the Tokelaus were of little interest as colonies, but came under British protection in the mid-19th century when threatened with depopulation by slave raiders from Australia and elsewhere. Administered as part of the Gilbert and Ellice Islands, later with Western Samoa, they have from 1948 been regarded as New Zealand territory. Efforts to encourage their small populations to shift permanently to New Zealand have had limited success; the remaining islanders continue to fish, raise subsistence crops of yams, taro, bananas, coconuts and pandanus, and export a little copra, helped by substantial grants from the New Zealand government.

Tonga

The Country
The Kingdom of Tonga occupies a group of about 150 islands in the tropical southwest Pacific Ocean, 2250 km (1400 miles) northeast of New Zealand. *Area* 699 km² (270 sq miles); *capital* Nuku'alofa (Tongatapu Island); *population* 107,000 (est. 1986).

Organization
Tonga is governed by a hereditary monarch, whose privy council includes an executive Prime Minister and small cabinet: a Legislative Council, part-appointed and part-elected, meets annually. Christianity is the dominant religion, English the official language with Polynesian dialects widely spoken.

Geography
The islands form a double chain running north–south. The western islands are mainly volcanic, with low cones (some still active) between 500 and 1000 m (1650 to 3280 ft) high; the eastern islands are mostly low atolls. The climate is hot and damp, hurricanes often striking during the summer months. Originally forested or scrub-covered, many of the islands are now intensively cultivated.

History and Development
Dutch seamen discovered the group in the early 17th century; James Cook, who visited in 1773, called them the Friendly Islands, though internecine warfare was common. The Kingdom of Tonga was unified under Taufa'ahau Tupou in 1845, and became Wesleyan Christian in 1860. Declared a neutral zone in 1886, Tonga became a British protectorate in 1899, though still under its own monarchy. This arrangement ceased by agreement in 1970, when Tonga returned to complete autonomy.

Resources and Economics
The land of Tonga is held by the Crown and every youth receives a smallholding; Tongan families therefore raise their own livestock and subsistence crops of manioc, yams, breadfruit and fruit. Copra, vanilla and bananas are produced for export. One of the most successful agricultural economies in the Pacific, Tonga nevertheless suffers from occasional devastation by hurricanes. Fishing provides additional food and export revenues, and tourism is a small but growing industry. Communications within and between the main islands are good, and Tonga has two international and several smaller airports.

Recent Developments
Sensible planning has helped Tonga's economy to grow steadily, despite climatic setbacks and world market depressions. The rapidly growing population threatens to create a land shortage, despite migration both within the islands and overseas. Tourism may help to preserve the balance, at least for a few years.

Tuvalu

The Country
The state of Tuvalu occupies a chain of islands in the central Pacific Ocean, some 4000 km (2500 miles) northeast of Australia. *Area* 26 km² (10 sq miles); *capital* Funafuti; *population* 8400 (est. 1986).

Organization
Tuvalu is governed by an elected parliament of 12 members, serving four-year terms. An elected Prime Minister and small cabinet hold executive powers;

Head of State is the British Sovereign, represented by a Tuvaluan Governor-General. Local administration is organized through elected island councils. Most islanders are Christian; the official language is English with Tuvalu Samoan widely spoken.

Geography
Tuvalu's nine atolls are coralline and low-lying. The climate is hot and humid throughout the year, and subject to occasional hurricanes. Formerly covered with forest and scrub, many of the islands now grow coconut palms and are cultivated. The surrounding reefs are largely unspoilt and rich in marine life.

History and Development
Discovered in 1764 by the British navigator John Byron, Tuvalu was for long known as the Ellice Islands. Subject to slave raiding during the 19th century, the group was brought under British protection in 1892 and administered as a colony jointly with the Gilbert Islands (now Kiribati) from 1915. On the basis of a referendum in 1974, Tuvalu became independent in 1978.

Resources and Economics
Most Tuvaluans are family smallholders, raising subsistence crops of yams and other vegetables, bananas and coconuts, and fishing in the lagoons. Copra is the only export of any consequence: it is the islands' only marketable resource except manpower. Many Tuvaluans work overseas, particularly in the Nauru phosphate industry, supporting their families by remittances. Funafuti has the only considerable port and commercial airstrip: a limited floatplane service linking the islands began in 1980.

Recent Developments
Tuvalu has few resources to support its growing population, and faces a difficult future unless new assets (tourism, deep-water fishing) can be exploited. Its annual budget is currently balanced by grants-in-aid from Britain, leaving very little over for economic development.

Wallis Archipelago

The island territory of Wallis Archipelago (Wallis and Futuna) is made up of the Wallis and Horn islands, the latter including Futuna Island. These lie 200 km (125 miles) apart, northeast of Fiji in the south central Pacific Ocean. *Area* 200 km^2 (77 sq miles); *capital* Mata-Utu; *population* 10,000 (est. 1986). The islands are an Overseas Territory of France, governed by an appointed Administrator and represented in the French Parliament by a deputy and senator. Island councils manage local affairs.

Wallis has a central island, Uvea, rising to 150 m (492 ft), ringed by low-lying coral reefs. The Horn Islands are volcanic, Futuna rising to a forested peak 789 m (2590 ft) high. All are warm and damp, mainly scrub-covered but cultivated wherever soils and local conditions allow. The islands were discovered by European seamen during the 18th century, and occupied by French settlers for plantation development in 1842. They became an Overseas Territory of France in 1959. Subsistence farming and fishing are the main activities, copra the only significant export. Wallis Island has roads connecting the main settlements, and a serviceable port and airport.

Western Samoa

The Country
The state of Western Samoa includes two large islands, Savai 'i and Upolu, and seven smaller islands, forming the western end of the Samoan chain, 2880 km (1800 miles) north-northeast of New Zealand. *Area* 2842 km^2 (1097 sq miles); *main settlement* Apia (Upolu); *population* 180,000 (est. 1986).

Organization
The islands are governed by a Parliament which includes a Head of State (currently hereditary, though future Heads will be elected) and a Legislative Assembly of 45 representatives; the Head of State appoints an executive Prime Minister and small cabinet. The dominant religion is Christianity; official languages are English and Samoan.

Geography
Western Samoa's islands are volcanic and mountainous, fringed with coral reefs; the highest peaks are on Savai 'i, rising above 1800 m (6000 ft) and surrounded by relatively recent lava flows (the last eruption ended in 1911). The climate is humid tropical, wet throughout the year, but with the heaviest rains from November to May, when hurricanes are likely. From June to November the southeast trade winds blow constantly. Uplands are mainly forested, lowlands covered in grass or dense thicket except where they are cultivated.

History and Development
Discovered by Jacob Roggeveeen in 1722, the Samoan islands were found to have a friendly Polynesian population, socially organized and prosperous under hereditary monarchs. The islands provided ports of call for whalers and traders throughout the 18th and 19th centuries, and were readily Christianized. In the colonial carve-up of Pacific islands during the late 19th century Samoa was jointly protected by Britain, Germany and the USA. By an agreement of 1899 Britain withdrew, the USA confined its interests to islands east of 171° W (see American Samoa), and the western islands became an exclusively German protectorate. After World War I Western Samoa passed to New Zealand under a League of Nations mandate; the UN renewed the mandate after World War II, and the islands gained their independence in 1962.

Resources and Economics
Western Samoa is primarily agricultural, most of the islanders farming smallholdings or working in the plantations and forests. Subsistence crops include yams, taro, maize and vegetables; plantation crops for export include copra, cocoa and bananas, and timber is also exported in quantity. Few other resources have been developed. The main islands have adequate roads and sea links; Apia is an important international air staging-post and focal point for Pacific routes. There is a small but growing tourist industry.

Recent Developments
With few developed resources and a large population, Western Samoa tends to live beyond its limited means, precipitating financial problems which are resolved by periods of cutback and restriction. Over one thousand Western Samoans leave each year to join their compatriots in New Zealand.

159

OCEANIA SOUTHEAST

Easter Island

Easter Island (also known as Rapanui) lies some 3500 km (2200 miles) west of Chile in the southeastern Pacific Ocean. *Area* 120 km² (46 sq miles); *settlement* Hanga-Roa; *population* 1300 (est. 1986). Administered as a district of Chile, the island has a governor and locally elected council. The dominant religion is Catholicism, the official language Spanish.

A triangular island of three linked volcanoes, Easter Island has a rolling upland edged by steep cliffs; it rises to about 600 m (2000 ft). The climate is subtropical, cooled by constant winds. Discovered by Dutch navigator Jacob Roggeveen in 1722, Easter Island was the easternmost outlier of Polynesia, supporting a population of about 4000. The island is noted for its possession of over 600 stylized stone figures up to 20 m (66 ft) tall, carved from basalt and tufa, set on stone platforms and used in sun-worship. Recent research suggests that land degradation, following forest clearance to provide the timber needed to erect the huge monuments, led to agricultural decline and the reduction of the original population. In 1864 Spanish missionaries recorded fewer than 200 inhabitants, and by 1888, when Chile annexed the island, there were only about 100.

Easter Islanders today raise yams, maize, fruit, cattle and sheep on dry but fertile soils; there is currently an international airport and considerable exchange of population with Chile.

French Polynesia

The Country
The island territory of French Polynesia occupies five scattered island groups in the southeastern tropical Pacific Ocean; the main island, Tahiti, lies almost midway between Australia and South America. They include the Society Archipelago (Windward and Leeward groups), Tuamotu and Gambier islands, Austral (Tubuai) Islands and Marquesas Islands; Clipperton Island, a distant uninhabited atoll some 3000 km (1875 miles) west of Panama, is administered by the High Commissioner but is not part of the territory. *Area* 4000 km² (1544 sq miles); *capital* Papeete (Tahiti); *population* 167,000 (est. 1986).

Organization
The islands form an Overseas Territory of France, administered by an appointed High Commissioner and Council of Government, who are advised by a Territorial Assembly of 30 members elected for five-year terms; two deputies and a senator represent French Polynesia in Paris. The people are mostly Polynesian, with European and Chinese admixtures; the dominant religion is Christianity (rather more Protestants than Catholics), the official language French but local languages are widely spoken.

Geography
Most of the islands are volcanic, mountainous and ringed with coral reefs,

standing on submarine reefs aligned northeast–southwest; the Tuamotu and Gambier groups are mainly low-lying atolls. Tahiti, formed of two volcanic cones linked by an isthmus, is the loftiest, rising to 2237 m (7339 ft). The climate is tropical and humid. Rain forest covers the uplands, grassland and dry scrub the lowlands and atolls; palms have been widely planted on the plains.

History and Development

When discovered by Spanish, Dutch and British navigators during the late 16th and 17th centuries, the islands had well-developed Polynesian societies ruled by local chiefs and hereditary monarchs. European traders and whalers were the main visitors until the mid-19th century, when French missions began operating in Tahiti and other islands. France declared protectorates progressively from 1842, ultimately colonizing the whole area by the end of the century. 'French Oceania' became an Overseas Territory in 1958.

Resources and Economics

The economy is based on smallholdings growing vegetables and fruit, and plantations providing coconut oil and copra for export. Stock-rearing and fishing add to the diet but staple foods are imported. Few other resources are developed and living standards are generally low. Roads are adequate on Tahiti, which is linked by sea and air to other islands and to the outside world; there are more limited sea and air links between the islands, stimulated by a flourishing tourist traffic which provides most of the community's overseas earnings.

Recent Developments

Lack of employment and poverty on the outer islands encourage islanders to move towards the main centres, notably Tahiti, or emigrate further away, even to France.

Pitcairn Islands

Pitcairn Island, with its uninhabited satellites Ducie, Henderson and Oeno, lies in the southeastern Pacific Ocean east of French Polynesia. *Area* 27 km^2 (10 sq miles); *settlement* Adamstown (Pitcairn); *population* 60 (est. 1986). A British Crown Colony, the islands are governed by the British High Commissioner in New Zealand, who is advised by a local council of 10 elected and nominated members, headed by an elected magistrate. The dominant faith is Seventh Day Adventism, the official language a dialect of English.

The islands are volcanic, with high lava cliffs and rugged hills; Pitcairn itself, with an area of 4.6 km^2 (1.7 sq miles), rises to about 330 m (1080 ft). The climate is subtropical. Discovered in 1767 by a British navigator, Pitcairn remained unoccupied until 1790 when a group of British naval mutineers and Tahitians arrived in HMS *Bounty*. Scuttling the ship, they lived there undetected until 1808. Later outgrowing their resources, the community moved in 1856 to Norfolk Island (southwest Pacific), but 43 people returned a few years later. Most of the islanders farm, raising livestock and vegetables and fishing for their own consumption and trading fresh food and handicrafts with passing ships. The island has few resources beyond its fertile soils; there is no anchorage and landing is restricted to a single bay. The population has recently declined due to emigration.

The Americas

North, Central and South America, together with the Caribbean islands, make up a huge linear continent with total area exceeding 40 million km^2 (15 million sq miles). North America, the largest component, covers 19.34 million km^2 (7.47 million sq miles), spanning 116° of longitude (almost one third of the way round the world) and extending from a point within 7° of the North Pole almost to the Tropic of Cancer. Among other superlatives, it affords many of its large population the highest material standard of living the world has ever seen. Central America and the widely-scattered Caribbean islands lie mostly within the northern tropical zone, their peoples linked by a common heritage of colonial rule, mostly disastrous, from which they are slowly recovering. South America's 17.81 million km^2 (6.88 million sq miles) extend from well north of the Equator to cold latitudes below 50°S, encompassing a wide range of climates and scenery from the rain forests of the Amazon basin to the high ice-fields of the Andes. Its population of over 270 million, formerly Amerindian with Hispanic and Negro admixtures and now a remarkable blend of all the world's races and cultures, is growing faster than that of any other continent.

NORTH AMERICA AND BERMUDA

Bermuda

The Country
The Crown Colony of Bermuda, an isolated island group, stands 912 km (570 miles) east–southeast of Cape Hatteras (USA) in the western Atlantic Ocean. *Area* 53 km^2 (20 sq miles); *capital* Hamilton; *population* 60,000 (est. 1986).

Organization
A colony of the British Commonwealth, Bermuda is largely self-governing. The British Crown is represented by an appointed Governor, who appoints an 11-member Senate to include members of both government and opposition parties. A 40-member House of Assembly is elected for a five-year term; executive power rests with a Prime Minister and cabinet of about 10 ministers. Many Christian faiths are represented; English is the official language.

Geography
Formerly the Somers Islands, Bermuda (or the Bermudas) is a group of over one hundred coral-ringed islands capping a submarine volcanic cone; the largest, Great Bermuda (or Main Island), is about 16 km (10 miles) long and supports most of the population. The highest point, Town Hill, rises to 79 m (260 ft). Lying between 32° and 33°N, the islands are scenically beautiful with white beaches and subtropical vegetation; the climate is warm and moist throughout the year, but subject to frequent gales.

History and Development
Discovered by Juan de Bermúdez in 1515, the islands remained uninhabited until Sir George Somers, bound for New England, was wrecked there in 1609. Farmed by plantation owners with imported slaves, Bermuda was at first of only minor economic importance, though its harbours provided a victualling point for naval, merchant and pirate ships. Becoming a colony in 1684, it acquired increasing significance as a mid-ocean staging-post during successive wars in the 19th and 20th centuries, and today has a strategically and commercially important air base as well.

Resources and Economics
Thin but fertile soils are found on about twenty of the islands; crops include potatoes, green vegetables, citrus fruits, bananas, meat and dairy produce, mostly for local use, and flowers for perfumery and export. Less than 2 per cent of the workforce is engaged in farming and fishing. Tourism is the most important industry and source of revenue; each year over half a million tourists, mostly from the USA, provide more than half the national income and catering for them employs three quarters of the workforce. Bermuda is also an offshore financial centre and tax haven for many British and US companies.

Recent Developments
Firmly geared to tourism and finance, though with little else to sustain it, Bermuda's economy has remained enviably buoyant despite world recession. Inflation was high in 1980–2 but has since declined; unemployment is low, and the political issue of independence currently appears to be shelved.

Canada

The Country
The Dominion of Canada occupies most of the northern half of the North American continent, bounded by the United States of America in the south and northwest and with the tiny French islands of St Pierre and Miquelon in the east. In the northeast Nares Strait, Baffin Bay and Davis Strait separate it from Greenland. *Area* 9,976,139 km² (3,851,791 sq miles); *capital* Ottawa, *largest city* Montreal; *population* 26,726,000 (est. 1986).

Organization
Canada is governed by a bicameral federal Parliament, including a Senate of 104 nominated members and House of Commons of about 280 elected members. The British monarch is Head of State, represented locally by an appointed Governor-General who in turn appoints a Prime Minister and cabinet of about 30 members. Each of the ten provinces has its own elected legislature with Prime Minister, ministers and Lieutenant-Governor. Official languages are English and French; Roman Catholicism is the majority religion, with many Protestant denominations well represented.

Geography
The northeastern two thirds of Canada is underlain by the eroded and glacially-polished rocks of the Pre-Cambrian Canadian Shield, of which the raised eastern flank forms the highlands of Quebec, Labrador, and Baffin and Ellesmere

islands. In the south and west the Shield forms the featureless plains of northern Ontario, reaching its lowest point in the Hudson Bay basin; it also underlies the tundra-covered uplands of northern Manitoba and Saskatchewan, and much of the Northwest Territories. The Shield is flanked on south and west by fertile upland plains – the prairies – and the rolling country bordering the Great Lakes. In the southeast are the deep faulted valley of the St Lawrence River and the mountains of New Brunswick and Nova Scotia, which are the northernmost extensions of the Appalachian system. The western third of Canada is crossed by the Western Cordillera, including the Rocky Mountains and their northern outliers, the Cassiar and Mackenzie mountains. The seaward ranges form a rugged coastline of islands, fjords and drowned river valleys. On the Alaskan border stands Mt Logan (6050 m, 19,850 ft), Canada's highest peak.

Western coastal Canada has a mild, damp climate, with heavy snow in the mountains, and warm, humid summers. East of the Rockies winters are cold and dry; summers are hot on the prairies and warm even in the far north as well as being the wetter season. Eastern Canada has cold snowy winters and warm humid summers. Apart from the prairies, much of the country was originally forested up to the tree line, with tundra and polar desert beyond. Wildlife includes a polar fauna (bears, caribou, seals and migrants) and a rich forest and prairie fauna of deer and wildfowl.

History and Development

Following Jacques Cartier's discovery of the Gaspé Peninsula (Quebec) in 1534, eastern Canada was initially opened up by French explorers and settlers (for the early history of occupation, see United States of America). While small French trading posts were established in Nova Scotia (from 1606) and Quebec (from 1608), Britons pressed in from New England and the south, establishing larger farming settlements and fur-trading posts inland from the Great Lakes to Hudson Bay. Much of this land was allocated to the Hudson's Bay Company, which maintained scattered stores and trading posts along navigable rivers. French and British rivalries broke into open warfare, in which local Indian tribes were often involved. Under the Treaty of Utrecht (1713), Britain acquired Acadia (Nova Scotia), Newfoundland and the Hudson Bay area; sixty years later, after James Wolfe's victory over the Marquis de Montcalm at Quebec, almost all French possessions in eastern North America came under British rule.

'Lower Canada' (an extended, predominantly French-speaking Quebec) and 'Upper Canada' (now Ontario) were united in 1841, later to be joined by Nova Scotia and New Brunswick (1867), the Red River settlement (Manitoba, 1870) and Prince Edward Island (1873). The separate colonies of Vancouver Island and British Columbia, originally explored by Captain Cook and part of the vast Hudson's Bay Company territories, were united in 1866 and joined the eastern confederation in 1871. Saskatchewan and Alberta joined in 1905. Populated largely by British immigrants, Canada was given self-governing status under the British Crown from 1867, and dominion status when the Empire became a Commonwealth in 1931. Newfoundland – Britain's oldest colony – received dominion status at the same time, keeping its independence until 1949.

Resources and Economics

The early settlers who cleared the eastern forests farmed glacial and alluvial soils; later settlers found more open ground far inland, grazing the prairies and growing cereals for European and US markets. Predominantly rural until well into the 20th century, Canada still obtains about one tenth of its income from farm produce, though currently employing less than 5 per cent of its labour force on the land. Wheat, oats, barley, maize, apples, peaches, livestock and dairy products are the main crops. Timber, wood pulp and paper are produced from the huge areas of native forest and there are well-established and up-to-date fisheries along both east and west coasts. Farm, forest and fish products together provide about one quarter of the value of Canada's exports.

Mineral wealth includes iron ore, asbestos, zinc, copper, silver, nickel, molybdenum, potash and uranium; several of these minerals are mined in areas far from civilization, though few mines recently developed in the Arctic have paid their way. Petroleum and natural gas are abundant, chiefly in the Prairie Provinces – although enormous Arctic resources have also been proven, they are beset by costly development problems. Manufacturing industries, based mainly in the towns and cities of the southeastern population belt, currently occupy one quarter of the workforce and provide about half of Canada's wealth. The most valuable commodities are processed foods, automobiles and other machinery, timber, metal and petroleum products, and chemicals; the USA provides by far the largest market for Canada's industries. Despite the vast distances involved, road, rail and air communications are excellent. The St Lawrence Seaway provides a canal system for deep-water ships, linking the Great Lakes directly with the Atlantic Ocean. Tourism is an important industry, the rich variety of scenery and outdoor activities attracting many Americans, Japanese and Britons.

Recent Developments

Canada's perennial problem is its size. With much of its population concentrated in a narrow southern band of settlements, there is a tendency for east, centre and west to segregate, and for each to look south toward the USA for markets, raw materials, culture and ideas. Unity is especially fragile in Quebec, where the ruling political party – strongly supported by the French-speaking majority – opposed the new Canadian constitution recently introduced (1982) by the Federal Government, and a vocal separatist movement seeks a wide measure of self-government. The rapidly-developing western provinces, although supporting the new constitution, also often find themselves at odds with Ottawa and seek more independence. Yet Canada remains one of the world's most stable and wealthy democracies, well endowed with everything that its relatively small population needs to maintain its high level of prosperity.

St Pierre and Miquelon

The Country

Forming an Overseas Department of France, these two groups of small islands (eight in total) lie 25 km (15 miles) west of the southernmost tip of Newfoundland. *Total area* 241 km² (93 sq miles); *main settlement* St Pierre; *population* 6300 (est. 1986).

Organization

Government is administered by a Prefect, appointed by the French government, who presides over a 14-member elected General Council. In Paris the islands are represented in both the House of Representatives and the Senate.

Geography

Granitic islands, once heavily glaciated but now bare and exposed to tumultuous weather, St Pierre and Miquelon are low-lying and windswept with a thin soil covering and meagre vegetation. Miquelon, some 32 km (20 miles) long, is the largest island. Their main geographical assets are their harbours, which provide accommodation for fishing fleets, and their proximity to the Newfoundland Grand Banks; fishing is the islanders' main source of revenue.

History and Development

Discovered and probably settled by Basque or French fishermen in the 16th century, the islands were claimed as part of France's North American possessions in 1604 and garrisoned in 1700. Britain captured them in 1702 and claimed them in the Treaty of Utrecht (1713), but restored them to France under the Treaty of Paris fifty years later. Recaptured in 1778 and again during the Napoleonic Wars, they were returned to French possession in 1814 (Treaty of Paris) on the condition that they remained ungarrisoned. In 1935 France granted them local autonomy, and in 1976 they acquired Departmental status.

Resources and Economics

Cloudy, wet and often fogbound, the islands support limited crops of vegetables and livestock for local consumption. Fishing is the main industry, occupying both local fishermen and boats visiting seasonally from Channel and Atlantic ports of France; dried salted, smoked and frozen fish are the chief exports. Virtually all other food and consumable goods are imported with the help of French subsidies. Roads are adequate for the islanders' needs; there are good sea and air links with Nova Scotia and Newfoundland. Tourism is a flourishing industry. The only remnant of France's former North American territories, these tiny communities continue to survive as a historic anomaly, viable and ebullient though costly to the taxpayers of their distant homeland.

United States of America

The Country

The United States of America (USA) dominates the North American continent and is bordered by Canada in the north and Mexico in the south. Its territory includes Alaska, forming the northwestern extremity of the continent, and the isolated Pacific island chain of Hawaii. *Area* 9,363,123 km^2 (3,615,105 sq miles); *capital* Washington DC, *largest city* New York; *population* 236,809,000 (est. 1986).

Organization

A federal republic of fifty states, the USA is governed by a bicameral Congress. The 100-member Senate includes two senators for each state, elected for six-year terms; one third are elected every second year. The 435 members of the House of Representatives are elected for two-year terms, each state being represented in proportion to its population. The President, who is elected for four-year terms by a college of state representatives, appoints an executive cabinet responsible to Congress. Each state has its own bicameral legislature and governor; local authority is vested in city, town and rural councils. The national language is English; Christianity is the most widely-accepted religion.

Geography

The eastern coastal plain, narrow in the north, broad and often swampy in the south, is backed by the rugged Appalachain Mountains. These extend from Alabama in the south to New England in the northeast in a complex of plateaus and folded ridges, mostly of ancient sedimentary rocks. They rise to 2000 m (6500 ft) and more in the Blue Ridge Mountains of Kentucky and Virginia. West of the ridge lies the coal-rich Allegheny plateau which extends westward to merge with the rolling uplands of Kentucky, Ohio and Pennsylvania. The Adirondack Mountains, an outlier of the much older and more heavily eroded Canadian Shield, form a compact block in northeastern New York State. South of the Appalachians the coastal plain broadens toward the Gulf of Mexico, spreading westward through Mississippi, Louisiana and Texas and southeastward into the low limestone plateau of Florida.

The western Appalachians descend to the central lowlands of the Mid-West, which form a half-saucer tilted toward the Gulf of Mexico and are drained south by many rivers, notably the vast Mississippi–Missouri–Ohio system. At the northern rim stand the Great Lakes. Gradients toward the Gulf of Mexico are broken by ancient dissected uplands, the Ouachita and Ozark plateaus, which rise some 600 m (2000 ft) above the plains. West of the Ozarks the saucer rim rises to form the Great Plains extending from the Dakotas in the north to Texas in the south, a wide belt of grassland rising to 1500 m (5000 ft) and more, from which the foothills of the Rocky Mountains rise abruptly.

The western half of the USA is dominated by the Western Cordillera, a complex of mountain ranges and high plateaus with a predominantly northwest to southeast trend. The Rocky Mountains form the high eastern flank. In the southern states of Colorado and New Mexico they rise to a knot of ancient granitic peaks over 4000 m (13,000 ft) high. The central Rockies of Wyoming, Idaho and Montana stand as high, in a series of deeply-incised, permanently snow-capped ranges. Between these massive blocks lie the high intermontane plateaus of the Wyoming Basin, flanked in the southwest by the Uinta and Wasatch mountains of northern Utah.

West of the southern Rockies lie the semi-deserts of the sandstone Colorado Plateau, deeply incised by the canyon of the Colorado River, and beyond them the dry uplands of Arizona. West of the central Rockies lie the broader plateaus and mountains of Nevada's Great Basin in the south, and the forested uplands of Oregon and Washington, drained by the Columbia and Snake rivers, in the north. Along the Pacific coast runs a double fold of mountains, separated intermittently by steep-sided valleys. The inner fold rises to the Sierra Nevada of California and the Cascade Ranges of Oregon and Washington; the outer fold forms a semi-continuous coastal range which starts in the Olympic Mountains south of Juan de Fuca Strait, and ends in the long arm of Baja California below the Mexican border.

The Western Cordillera continues northwestward through Canada and into Alaska, where it turns westward through a wide arc and extends southwest into the Alaska Peninsula and Aleutian Islands. Central to the arc stands Mount McKinley (6194 m, 20,322 ft), North America's highest peak; beyond it to the north lies the snow-covered Brooks Range, separated from the Arctic Ocean by the oil-rich North Slope.

The United States has many climates, ranging from warm, damp subtropical conditions on the Gulf of Mexico coast to intense cold and aridity in Arctic Alaska. The western seaboard becomes drier from north to south with the coastal mountains capturing most of the rain and giving rise to the desert areas of the central Cordillera. Coastal California has a Mediterranean climate. New England's cool maritime regime contrasts with the extreme continental conditions of the humid central plains and the arid western plateaus.

Vegetation ranges from the coastal mangroves of the south to tundra and polar desert in the far north; between these lie a wide variety of deciduous and evergreen forests, grasslands and hot deserts, with a rich variety of wildlife.

History and Development

North America's first human settlers came from Siberia across the Bering land-bridge some 25,000 years ago, dispersing eastward through the Arctic basin and south into the more promising lushness of the central continent. From them arose the many stocks of 'Indians' – mostly brown-skinned, with a Mongolian cast of countenance – who are the aboriginal North Americans. Many remained nomadic or semi-nomadic hunters of forest and plain. Some settled to establish villages or small towns, growing crops and trading in raw materials with the nomads. Notable among them were the Hopewell tribes of the central plains, who flourished up to AD 500, and the Pueblo Indians who later developed irrigation and other farming techniques in the southwest.

The first Europeans to investigate North America were Norsemen from Iceland, who made several landfalls about AD 900 and may have founded temporary coastal settlements in the northeast. Explorations by Columbus and his contemporaries in the Caribbean Sea in the late 15th and early 16th centuries led to Spanish settlements in Mexico and Florida; Cabot's discovery of Newfoundland (1497), Verrazano's demarcation of the eastern seaboard (1524) and Cartier's exploration of the St Lawrence River (1534–5) were followed in the 17th century by a rash of British, Swedish, Dutch and French settlements along the east coast. By the early 18th century the Swedish settlements of Delaware and Dutch settlements of New York and New Jersey had passed into British hands, and Britain alone remained in possession of colonies from New England to South Carolina. French settlers occupied the St Lawrence valley, the southern shores of Lake Ontario, and Louisiana, a huge inland territory represented by a string of forts and fur-trading posts extending along the Mississippi River, south to Fort Maurepas on the Gulf of Mexico.

During the early to mid-18th century Spanish influence spread northward from New Spain (Mexico) into present-day California, Nevada, Utah, Arizona and New Mexico. Northward beyond the mission of San Francisco lay territory claimed by both Spain and France, but occupied only by Indians and itinerant fur traders. The latter included Russians penetrating southward from the Alaskan coast which, discovered during the voyages of Vitus Bering in 1741, had come to be regarded as Russian territory. Under the Treaty of Utrecht (1713), Newfoundland and Nova Scotia passed to Britain; under the Treaty of Paris (1763), Canada, Florida and eastern Louisiana joined the British colonies, while Louisiana west of the Mississippi became part of New Spain.

The successful revolt of Britain's American colonies in the War of Independence (1775–83) created an English-speaking United States of America, bordered by the Great Lakes in the north, the Mississippi in the west, and Florida (which Britain returned to Spain in 1783) in the south. Louisiana reverted to France in 1800 and was sold by Napoleon Bonaparte to the USA in 1803, opening a new western frontier which Americans quickly exploited. The westward movement of white settlers displaced many indigenous communities; Indians were destroyed or forced into reservations, many of which were in turn overrun by the advancing tide. Florida was ceded by Spain in 1819, Texas,

California and other former Spanish possessions were added between 1821 and 1853 (see Mexico). Apart from a brief war with Britain in 1812–14, Canadian border problems were in general settled amicably, leaving the USA free to expand northwestward to the 49th parallel. The Civil War (1861–5), precipitated by a confederacy of southern states on issues of slave-owning and self-determination, ultimately strengthened the federal ties that held the states and territories of the Union together. In the following decades the USA bought Alaska from Russia (1867), consolidated its southern boundary and emerged as a leading industrial and political power, its wealth being rapidly mobilized under a system of aggressive free enterprise, its population expanding rapidly through both natural increase and massive immigration from Europe.

During the present century, and especially since 1939, the USA has graduated from its former isolationism in world affairs to a position of full participation, aligning itself politically with Western Europe, opposing the spread of communism, and generally exercising its powers as a large, rich and highly organized nation.

Resources and Economics

With its huge areas of ploughed grasslands and temperate forests, the USA has a long tradition of self-sufficiency in food and timber production. Stimulated by research in state universities and the ready availability of cheap farm machinery, highly-capitalized farming techniques have evolved rapidly to keep pace with the needs of an expanding population and the demands of export markets; however, the broad zonal patterns of agriculture, which evolved in response to climate and soils, remain intact. In the northeastern states from New England to the Great Lakes small farms predominate, their output of dairy produce, potatoes, fruit, vegetables and poultry destined for ready markets in the cities. Many of the 160-acre (65-hectare) farms carved by the settlers from virgin forest have reverted to bush, their thin glacial soils no longer justifying efforts to keep them productive; yields are higher from smaller, more fertile farms further south. West and southwest of the Great Lakes former grasslands produce spring wheat and barley on a massive scale; further south from Nebraska to Ohio is the warmer corn belt, where maize, oats, soya beans and other feed crops are grown for an enormous pig and cattle population. The central plains through Kansas, Missouri and Kentucky support mixed arable farming, with winter wheat, barley, maize and fodder grasses predominant.

The southern and southeastern states grow cotton, tobacco, peanuts and other high-yielding crops; subtropical Florida grows both citrus fruits and sugar-cane, and rice is produced along the coast of the Gulf of Mexico. In the drier southwest wheat fields and pastures extend high into the uplands of Texas, Arizona and New Mexico. Cattle and sheep are still raised extensively on range-lands throughout the central and western states; elsewhere intensive stock-raising on feed-lots competes with open grazing, especially where water is scarce or good pasture at a premium. On the Pacific coast, Oregon and Washington are renowned for their apples, berry fruits and nuts. California's Great Valley, between Sierra Nevada and the coastal ranges, is intensively cultivated for vines, apples, citrus fruits, peaches, tomatoes and olives; field crops include cotton and rice.

Forestry is widespread throughout the USA. With the westward advance of population the focus of exploitation shifted quickly from New England and the Great Lakes into the southern states, and ultimately to the west coast. Currently about half the country's timber needs are met by Oregon and Washington, though the southeast produces increasing quantities of softwoods for pulp. Fish are plentiful and form the basis of important industries on both Pacific and Atlantic coasts.

Industrial development has been spectacular: fed by abundant resources and stimulated by the needs of a prosperous, ever-expanding home market, the USA has evolved from a rural to a mainly-urban industrial society within the present century. Basic raw materials include abundant coal and lignite, and ores of iron, copper, nickel and many other essential metals. Petroleum, natural gas, hydroelectric power and uranium have provided energy for a range of manufacturing industries, although in spite of constant efforts to increase home production, the USA currently relies heavily on imported petroleum to sustain its industrial momentum and transport needs. Besides catering for its huge home market, the USA exports machinery and electrical goods, transport equipment, chemicals and foods, especially cereals. Rail, road, river, canal and air transport links are excellent, and the natural beauty of many parts of the country provides for flourishing year-round tourism.

Recent Developments

Like every other industrial nation that relies heavily on imported oil, the USA suffered in the recession of the 1970s and early 1980s. Unemployment in 1982 reached an unprecedented level of almost 11 per cent of the workforce, especially in the heavy manufacturing and distributing industries on which many of the major northern cities were founded. Black communities, both urban and rural, were hit especially hard. One result has been a substantial reorientation of industry; this has involved major shifts of the mobile workforce from the northeast to the south and Pacific west, where high-technology industries are located, communities are growing and living tends to be cheaper. Coupled with a marked migration of retired folk to the warmer south, this has left many northern cities in decline. However, still ahead of the world in industrial and social innovation, the USA is currently pioneering the 'post-industrial age', characterized by increasing industrial efficiency based on automation and more positive use of the leisure which widespread prosperity affords. The USA remains overall the most prosperous community the world has ever seen.

CENTRAL AMERICA

Belize

The Country

Belize lies on the Caribbean coast of Central America, bordered by Mexico in the north and Guatemala in the west and south. *Area* 22,965 km² (8867 sq miles); *capital* Belmopan, *largest city* Belize City; *population* 161,000 (est. 1986).

Organization

Formerly British Honduras, Belize was granted independence in 1981. Head of State is the British Sovereign, represented by an appointed Governor-General. The National Assembly includes a Senate of 8 appointed members and an 18-member House of Representatives, elected every five years. A Prime Minister and cabinet of about eight ministers hold executive powers. The people of Belize are mostly of Indian, Negro and European extraction; Indians are mostly found in the back-country villages. About half the population is Roman Catholic, a quarter Anglican, with many minor religions; the national language is English.

Geography

From its low-lying Caribbean coastline of mangrove swamps, fringed with coral islets, cays and a spectacular barrief reef, southern Belize rises fairly sharply to a broad plateau, backed by the Maya Mountains, a succession of serrated ranges with peaks of up to 1100 m (3600 ft). The northern half of the country is mainly low-lying and swampy. Belize has a warm, humid climate, with cooling breezes from the sea; rain is heaviest from October to December, followed by a relatively dry season from February to May. Hurricanes are a hazard in late summer. Dense tropical forest occupies the wetter plains and uplands, yielding to savanna in the drier areas.

History and Development

Populated originally by Mayans, Belize was among the territories claimed by Spain in the 16th century, but settled during the 17th and 18th centuries by pirates and by British woodcutters from Jamaica, the latter attracted by the stands of mahogany and other valuable timbers. Disputes with Spanish settlers from neighbouring provinces were resolved by the Convention of London in 1786, and British sovereignty was later reinforced by treaties and settlements with Mexico and Guatemala; however, Guatemala periodically reaffirms a claim to sovereignty. In 1862 British Honduras became a colony linked with Jamaica, and an independent colony in 1884. It attained self-government in 1964, adopting in 1973 the name of its most prominent river and city.

Resources and Economics

Mainly agricultural, with about one third of the workforce employed on the land, Belize grows most of its own food on smallholdings and exports cane sugar, citrus fruits and juices, coconuts, bananas and meat. Forestry provides important revenues from the sale of hardwoods, notably mahogany, logwood, lignum-vitae (Guaiacum) and cedar; though forestry has for long been the colony's prime industry, there is scope for modern development. Chicle, the original chewing gum, used to be tapped but has been largely superseded by artificial gums. A growing fishing industry provides shrimps and lobsters for export. There is no mining, and industries are under-developed and limited mainly to food-processing. Several of the major rivers are navigable by shallow-draft boats and the port facilities at Belize City have recently been improved. Roads are poor but adequate; there are no railways.

Recent Developments

Economic progress is hampered by loss of revenue due to depression in the world sugar market; production of cacao, coconuts, peanuts and other crops is being increased in an effort to diversify exports, and more food is being produced for home consumption to reduce import bills. The longstanding dispute with Guatemala over sovereignty has necessitated the presence of British army and air force units in Belize since 1977.

Costa Rica

The Country
The Republic of Costa Rica straddles the isthmus of Panama in Central America, bordered by Nicaragua in the north and Panama in the south. *Area* 50,700 km² (19,575 sq miles); *capital* San José; *population* 2,541,000 (est. 1986).

Organization
Costa Rica is governed by an Assembly of 57 deputies, elected for four-year terms; executive power is vested in a President, who is also elected for four-year terms, and a cabinet of about 13 appointed ministers. Local government is administered through seven provinces, each under an appointed governor, divided into cantons and districts. The population is mainly of Spanish descent with some Indian and Negro admixtures; along the Caribbean coast English-speaking West Indians predominate. The most widely practised faith is Roman Catholicism; the national language is Spanish.

Geography
The high central massif consists of three volcanic ridges, rising in stages to the southwestern Cordillera de Talamanca and the country's highest mountain, Chirripo Grande (3837 m, 12,590 ft). The line of volcanic cones (at least four of them active in recent decades) continues northwestward into the Cordillera de Guanacaste, which bisects the northern half of the country. The Pacific coastal plain is more limited than that bordering the Caribbean. The capital and the economic core of the country are in the Valle Centrale, a highland basin. The climate is warm and humid, driest in the northwest where extensive savanna alternates with lowland forest.

History and Development
Formerly part of the captaincy-general of Guatemala, Costa Rica was thinly settled after the Spanish conquest of the 16th century. It remained relatively undeveloped, lack of local labour preventing the establishment of large-scale estates. Independent after 1821, it formed part of the Central American Federation until 1838. Coffee and banana plantations were developed, largely with US capital, during the 19th century and the country evolved slowly and relatively peacefully. Recent movements have been towards greater economic independence and diversification. A democratic political system and social restructuring have given Costa Rica a reputation for stability in the unsettled world of Central American politics. Its abolition of armed forces in 1948 has apparently been entirely beneficial.

Resources and Economics
Agriculture is the main support of the country's economy, employing almost 30 per cent of the workforce, many as peasant farmers. About two thirds of Costa Rica's export earnings come from coffee, bananas, meat and sugar: cocoa and palm oil are increasing in importance, timber and fishing also contribute. Minerals and manufacturing industries remain undeveloped. With few indigenous raw materials Costa Rica imports what it can afford.

Recent Developments
Vulnerable to shifts in world prices for its few export commodities, Costa Rica

has been hard hit by the recent depression. Inflation and unemployment run high and standards of living are declining, bringing severe pressures to bear on a harassed but persistently democratic government. A recovery programme begun in 1982, aimed at increasing revenues and cutting public spending, seems to be taking effect, but a long spell of austerity is forecast.

El Salvador

The Country
The Republic of El Salvador lies on the Pacific coast of Central America, bordered by Honduras to north and east, and Guatemala in the west. *Area* 21,041 km² (8124 sq miles); *capital* San Salvador; *population* 5,725,000 (est. 1986).

Organization
Legislative power is vested in a 52-member Assembly, elected for three-year terms, with effective political power in the hands of an executive consisting of a President, elected for five-year terms, and an appointed cabinet of about 12 ministers. Local government is administered through 14 departments, divided into cantons and districts, each with a provincial governor. Less than 10 per cent of the population is white; the majority is mestizo or Indian. The dominant religion is Roman Catholicism, the national language Spanish.

Geography
El Salvador is crossed from east to west by two chains of volcanic mountains. Between them lies the high valley of the Lempa River, which flows across the northwestern corner of the country and cuts south through the mountains, effectively dividing the country into eastern and western halves. The seaward ranges, rising from a narrow coastal plain, form clusters of volcanic cones; Santa Ana in the west rises above 2500 m (8200 ft) and many others reach heights of over 1500 m (4900 ft). Several are active; others have spectacular crater lakes. Behind these stand further clusters of volcanoes marking the rim of the main cordillera. The climate is warm and humid in the plains, cool and temperate in the highlands where most of the main settlements occur; there is a dry season from November to April over most of the country. Formerly forested, much of the country is now under cultivation.

History and Development
El Salvador was seized by Spanish conquistadors in 1524–5, and formed part of the captaincy-general of Guatemala. The Spaniards did little to develop its resources, concentrating almost entirely on mining for precious metals and dye-plants; the Indian communities were reorganized into villages to serve the haciendas. Gaining independence from Spain in 1821, El Salvador formed part of the Federation of Central America until 1839. Genuine independence brought little advance in its fortunes, wars with neighbours and frequent revolutions absorbing the surplus energies of the towns while the peasants and estate-owners continued to farm as best they could. Coffee, cotton and sugar joined maize as the main crops, and processing industries arose to serve them. Increasingly violent guerrilla warfare since 1981 inhibits any further investment towards industrial or social progress.

Resources and Economics
Agriculture employs about half the workforce and generates one quarter of the national income; the main products are coffee and cotton (which together bring in half the country's foreign exchange), sugar, beef and rubber. Agrarian reforms since 1980, involving the breaking-up of large estates and their disbursement among cooperatives, have resulted in a temporary decrease in production. Many smallholdings produce maize, rice and other foods for local consumption; wheat-flour is imported. Timber is a minor export, and a small fishing fleet provides shrimps for the export market. There is little mining; processed foods, cigarettes, cement, fertilizers and textiles are among the main manufactured products. El Salvador has no indigenous mineral fuels but some potential for hydroelectric power, which is being developed as rapidly as possible in an effort to reduce fuel-oil imports. Roads (many unmetalled) and railways are adequate for current needs, but are subject to dislocations arising from the current civil war.

Recent Developments
Almost every enterprise in El Salvador, from agriculture to manufacturing industries, has suffered because of the continuing civil war. Investment capital and foreign exchange have disappeared, farms and industries damaged in the fighting remain unproductive, bankruptcies and unemployment increase; inflation is high, and in real terms both national and personal incomes decline annually. There seems little likelihood of improvement while the strife continues.

Guatemala

The Country
The Republic of Guatemala lies at the northern end of the isthmus of Panama, bounded by Mexico in the north and west, Honduras and El Salvador in the southeast and Belize in the east; it has a long Pacific coast and a short Caribbean one. *Area* 108,889 km² (42,042 sq miles); *capital* Guatemala City; *population* 8,646,000 (est. 1986).

Organization
Guatemala is constitutionally governed by a national Congress of 61 deputies elected for four-year terms. Executive power is vested in a President, also elected for four-year terms, and an appointed cabinet of about 10 ministers. In 1982 the constitution was indefinitely suspended following a military coup. For local government purposes the country is divided into twenty-two departments, each subdivided into municipalities. The population is mostly Indian or Mestizo. Roman Catholicism is the majority religion, Spanish the national language, with many Indian dialects spoken in country districts.

Geography
The Pacific coastal plain, 320 km (200 miles) long and formerly forested, is now largely cultivated. Behind it rise the steep slopes of the Sierra Madre Occidental, formed by a chain of volcanic cones, several over 3000 m (13,000 ft). North of the Sierra extends the Altos, a highland dissected by streams which have cut deep ravines and eventually flow out into the Caribbean. North of the Altos are

rolling uplands formed from a series of low parallel ranges; these descend to Petén, a limestone plain dotted with freshwater lakes. Rainfall is heavy on both coasts, especially in the wet season (May to October) along the Caribbean. The coastal lowlands are hot and humid, the interior is relatively dry and much cooler.

History and Development
Between 1524 and 1821 Guatemala was a captaincy-general in the Spanish Empire and included the whole of Central America. Before the arrival of the Europeans, Guatemala had been a centre of Mayan civilization, evident today in many remarkable archaeological remains. The dense Indian population attracted the interest of the Church in colonial days, but the absence of gold and the distance from Mexico City and metropolitan Spain helped preserve the Indian culture and much of this has survived to the present day. The old captaincy-general shifted allegiance from Spain to newly-independent Mexico in 1821, but two years later split into five states united in the Federation of Central America. Guatemala ultimately detached itself from its neighbours (Honduras, El Salvador, Nicaragua and Costa Rica) in 1839. Moves to re-form the Union were made many times in different guises during the next half century.

Internally Guatemala, like most of its neighbours, remained politically unstable – the cockpit of constant battles between rival 'liberal' and 'conservative' elements. Never properly resolved, these disputes have more recently turned into a virtual civil war between 'left' and 'right', supported respectively by communist regimes and the USA.

Resources and Economics
The Guatemalan economy depends heavily on agriculture, which employs half its workforce and provides more than a quarter of the country's revenues. Smallholdings grow maize and vegetables for local consumption, large estates grow the coffee, cotton, sugar, bananas and beef that provide the main export earnings. Timber and fishing make smaller contributions to the economy. Nickel, zinc, lead and other metal ores are mined; petroleum output is increasing slowly, though Guatemala still imports four fifths of its energy needs from other Caribbean countries. Hydroelectric power is growing in importance. Manufacturing industries are increasing, hampered by such natural hazards as earthquakes, which periodically destroy the plant, and by lack of capital; processed foods, textiles and tyres are the main products exported. Tourism has declined with the chronic civil unrest. Road and rail links meet current needs, though many of the roads are unpaved and liable to wash away in heavy rains.

Recent Developments
With its main income dependent on climatic vagaries and the world price of coffee, its energies and resources dissipated by civil strife, its industries starved for development capital and raw materials and its political future uncertain, Guatemala still manages to survive economically. Potentially a wealthy country, it requires only stability and peace to bring prosperity, but continuing struggles for political power keep resources undeveloped and the population trapped in rural poverty.

Honduras

The Country
The Republic of Honduras lies in Central America, bordered in the northwest by Guatemala, in the southwest by El Salvador, and in the south by Nicaragua. *Area* 112,088 km² (43,277 sq miles); *capital* Tegucigalpa; *population* 4,514,000 (est. 1986).

Organization
Nominally a presidential democracy, Honduras was ruled by the military between 1972 and 1981. A new constitution was promulgated in 1982 following the election to a National Constituent Assembly of 82 representatives in 1981; in the same year, 1981, a President was elected to hold office for four years. Local government is vested in eighteen departments. The population is mostly mestizo, with a significant Indian minority. Spanish is the official language with a number of local languages spoken by the native populations. The dominant religion is Roman Catholicism.

Geography
Apart from lowland plains on the short Pacific and longer Caribbean coasts, Honduras is mainly hilly, much of it over 1000 m (3300 ft) high. The northern half includes a high dissected plateau, traversed by rivers flowing northeastward into the Caribbean across a narrow coastal plain. The highest peaks are in the southern ranges, forming the watershed and main backbone of the country, and rising in the southwest to over 2800 m (9000 ft) near the Guatemalan border. A high valley, the Comayagua, crosses centrally, carrying the Humuya River north to the Caribbean and the Goascoran south to the Pacific Ocean. Several of Honduras's larger rivers are navigable, providing useful waterways. The climate is hot and humid on the coasts, pleasantly temperate in the interior, with a wet season from May to November and the rest of the year relatively dry. There is a lasting territorial dispute with Nicaragua over Mosquitia, a strip of low-lying coast and interior valley along the southern border.

History and Development
Christopher Columbus landed on the Caribbean shore of Honduras in 1502 and claimed the continent that lay behind it. The territory, valued for its silver and gold mines, became a province of the captaincy-general of Guatemala. Except for its mines it remained relatively undeveloped, its Indian population (who lived mostly in the hills) largely undisturbed. Gaining independence from Spain in 1821, Honduras formed part of the Federation of Central America, and was among the first to break away from the dominance of Guatemala in 1838. Its economic development began with an influx of US capital in the late 19th century and the establishment of banana plantations. Mining continued to play a small but significant role in the economy. Since 1975 agrarian reform has encouraged more small farmers onto the land and helped to bridge the wide gap between peasants and large landowners.

Resources and Economics
Honduras is primarily agricultural; crop production, mainly on the fertile lowlands, occupies about 60 per cent of the workforce. The main crops, coffee, bananas, cotton, beef, sugar and tobacco, generate well over half the country's

overseas earnings. Subsistence farming provides maize, rice, beans and other staple foods; wheat is imported. Timber yields useful export earnings; over 40 per cent of Honduras is covered with hardwood and pine forests, which have yet to be systematically exploited. Gold, silver, copper, zinc and lead are mined in the mountains. Few industries have been developed but food-processing, tobacco and chemicals currently contribute about one sixth of the country's wealth. Tourism is relatively under-developed, despite the potential attraction of Mayan relics, coastal resorts and fishing. Roads are generally poor and railways are used mainly for transporting bananas from plantations to ports.

Recent Developments
War with El Salvador over illegal immigrants (which caused Honduras to leave the Central American Common Market in 1969), and a continuing border dispute with Nicaragua, have to some degree helped to isolate this country from its neighbours. The dominance of foreign capital and heavy dependence for its income on a few agricultural products make it economically vulnerable. However, land reforms, a degree of internal stability and some prospect of a planned, more diversified economy give Honduras reason to hope for a brighter future.

Mexico

The Country
The United Mexican States occupy the southernmost triangle of North America, bordered in the north by the USA and in the southeast by Guatemala and Belize. *Area* 1,972,547 km² (761,601 sq miles); *capital* Mexico City; *population* 82,734,000 (est. 1986).

Organization
Mexico's thirty-one constituent states and single Federal District (Mexico City) are governed by a bicameral Congress of 64 senators and 400 deputies, elected respectively for six-year and three-year terms. Executive power is vested in a President, elected every six years, and an appointed cabinet of about 20 ministers. Each state has a governor and elected Chamber of Deputies. Over half the population is Mestizo, the rest of European origin or Amerindian. The national language is Spanish, with local dialects spoken in rural areas; Roman Catholicism is the predominant religion.

Geography
Mainly mountainous, Mexico occupies the southern end of North America's Western Cordillera, which tapers sharply south and east towards the isthmus of Panama. Bordered by a narrow coastal plain, the heartland rises steeply to a high plateau, bounded in the east by the Sierra Madre Oriental and in the west by the Sierra Madre Occidental; the plateau reaches 2000 m (6500 ft) in the south, declining to 1000 m (3280 ft) or less along the northeastern border. Both sierras have several peaks above 3500 m (11,500 ft), but Mexico's highest mountains occur in a complex of volcanic peaks at the southern end of the plateau. Here stand snow-capped Orizaba (5700 m, 18,700 ft) and Popocatepetl (5452 m, 17,888 ft), the latter overlooking Mexico City which itself stands on the high Anahuac plateau at an elevation of over 2300 m (7500 ft).

South of the mountain complex rises a lower coastal range, Sierra Madre del Sur, which extends eastward along the isthmus to Guatemala. The southeastern extremity of Mexico is the low-lying limestone peninsula of Yucatan; the northwestern extremity is the narrow mountain peninsula of Baja California, separated from the mainland by the Gulf of California, 1000 km (625 miles) long. Standing on an unusually active sector of the Earth's crust, virtually all Mexico is subject to earthquakes. The Tropic of Cancer bisects the country. Temperatures depend on altitude as much as latitude: coastal lowlands are hot throughout the year. Annual rainfall inland varies from a few cm in the arid north to 75 cm (30 in) in the capital; southern coasts are generally wetter, with 140 cm (55 in) in Acapulco, 170 cm (67 in) at Veracruz and over 200 cm (79 in) on the heavily forested slopes of the southern coastal mountains.

History and Development

Long before the arrival of the Spanish conquistadors Mexico was the centre of successive Indian civilizations. Notable among them were those of the Mayas of Yucatan, and the Teotihuacans and their successors in the central uplands, including the Aztecs who swept in from the north during the 13th century to dominate the whole area. From their island stronghold of Tenochtitlán, in Lake Texcoco, the Aztecs subdued most of their neighbours. Mexico had a long history of advanced agricultural techniques, pottery, textile manufacture and metal-work before the arrival of the Spaniards. Hernández de Cordoba, who visited Yucatan in 1516, was the first European to report on Mayan culture. In 1519 the Spaniard Hernán Cortés landed with his small army at Veracruz; two years later, with the help of Indians previously subjugated by the Aztecs, he captured and destroyed the citadel of Tenochtitlán, replacing Aztec oppression with that of imperial Spain.

Declared the Viceroyalty of New Spain in 1528, Mexico's large Indian population attracted missionaries looking for converts, while adventurers came looking for minerals and land. Rich silver mines were worked by the natives, who were also employed on the land and kept in subjugation by their Spanish overlords, though within a century the Indian population had been decimated by European diseases. During the following three centuries the export of precious metals and certain plantation products allowed limited economic development to take place. Independence was won in 1821, and the new state was generally successful in maintaining the federation on which it was based. It is true that, under President Santa Anna, Mexico lost first Texas (1836) and subsequently the remaining border provinces of California, Utah and New Mexico (1846–8) to the USA, but the core area remained united.

Civil war (1858–61), and a brief period of monarchy under the Habsburg Maximilian (1864–7), were followed by further anarchy. The virtual dictatorship of Porfirio Diaz (1876–80, 1884–1910) brought a long period of political stability and economic development, though control of many of Mexico's resources passed into foreign hands. The Revolution of 1910–17 resulted in a new constitution, new political alliances and the beginnings of badly-needed agrarian reform. Expropriation of land and its redistribution to the peasantry started in the 1920s and gathered momentum in the 1930s. In 1938 Mexico startled the world by nationalizing its oilfields and set a pattern many other countries have since followed. The last twenty years have seen unprecedented growth, both in population and in economic production, to the point where Mexico City is now the largest city in the world, Mexico the largest Spanish-speaking country in the world, and its economy a major force.

Resources and Economics
Agriculture, unlike that of most Latin American countries, is based mainly on small uneconomic subsistence farms; over one third of the workforce are farmers, although they generate only about one twelfth of the country's wealth. Irrigation is a valuable aid in the dry lands of the north and centre. Well-watered plots produce high yields of sugar-cane, maize, wheat, sorghum, tomatoes, bananas, citrus fruits, beans, rice, coffee and many other tropical and subtropical crops, some of which are exported. In the drier areas agricultural production from the unimproved lands fluctuates, but in good seasons Mexico produces a surplus of many staple foods, as well as cash crops for export. Forests yield both hardwoods and softwoods for timber and pulp. Fish are plentiful; fishing and fish-processing remain of minor significance.

Fluorite, phosphates, sulphur and graphite are among Mexico's many important non-metallic minerals; silver, gold, copper, antimony, zinc, lead, iron and many other useful metals are mined and processed. Mexico has a long-established oil industry: in the early 1970s it was second only to the USA as a world producer. Huge new discoveries of both petroleum and natural gas since 1972 have transformed the economy, and currently provide over two thirds by value of Mexico's exports. Ranking fourth in world production, Mexico sells mainly to the USA and also supports a growing petrochemical industry of its own. Other industries include iron, steel and aluminium production, also cement manufacture and the assembly of automobiles and other consumer goods, mostly from imported raw materials. Among light industries are the manufacture of textiles, pottery and handicrafts. Manufactured goods account for some 17 per cent of exports. Despite difficult terrain and lack of capital, road, rail and air links are good and help to support a flourishing tourist industry.

Recent Developments
Within the past few decades Mexico has grown enormously in stature. Land reforms and redistribution have continued: there is a slow but significant modernization of agriculture, and a wide range of new industries have been introduced, but these are still insufficient to absorb the rapidly increasing workforce. Oil development provided an enormous boost to the economy, and the euphoria of the 1970s has now given way to a more realistic view of the contribution of oil to the economy in the 1980s. In 1982 Mexico nationalized the banks in an effort to control runaway inflation encouraged by growing overseas indebtedness. Financial problems continue to hamper development and austerity measures pose a threat to political and social stability, but long-term prospects for this potentially wealthy country are promising.

Nicaragua

The Country
The Republic of Nicaragua lies in the southern half of the Central American isthmus, bounded in the north by Honduras and in the south by Costa Rica. *Area* 130,000 km^2 (50,193 sq miles); *capital* Managua; *population* 3,342,000 (est. 1986).

Organization
From 1938 to 1979 Nicaragua was a dictatorship, initially under Anastasio

Somoza, and then under his two sons. In 1979 the Sandinist National Liberation Front seized power and established a 5-member Junta of National Reconstruction; a 51-member nominated Council of State advises the Junta. Elections are promised in 1985. For local government the country is divided into sixteen departments. Over 70 per cent of the population is of mixed Indian, Spanish and Negro blood, the rest mainly of Spanish descent. Roman Catholicism is the dominant religion, Spanish the official language, though English is widely understood.

Geography
The western half of Nicaragua is mountainous, with a triangle of volcanic ranges and deep river valleys in the northwest and a chain of volcanic peaks, some active, lining the Pacific coast. The highest mountains in the north rise to over 2000 m (6500 ft). A broad depression, once filled by the sea, crosses the country southeast from the Gulf of Fonseca and contains two large lakes (Managua and Nicaragua) and several smaller ones. To the east are rolling uplands and broad forested plains, descending in steps to the Caribbean shore. The climate is warm and moist; rainfall is seasonal with longer and heavier rains on the eastern flank. Tropical forest covers the uplands and fills the eastern valleys; drier savanna occurs mainly in the west where most of the population lives. Earthquakes are frequent and sometimes devastating.

History and Development
Nicaragua was sparsely settled by Indians when Spanish colonists first arrived in the early 16th century. Founding settlements mainly in the west, they ignored the eastern plains, which from the 17th to mid-19th centuries remained a (largely undeveloped) British protectorate, the Meskito or Mosquito Coast. Administered as part of the captaincy-general of Guatemala, Nicaragua gained independence from Spain in 1821 and left the Federation of Central America in 1838. US intervention in Nicaraguan affairs dates from the mid-19th century when plans were developed to cut an inter-ocean canal across its lowlands. The canal never materialized, but US interest was maintained. This included prolonged military occupation between 1912–33 and support for favourably disposed candidates in elections, including President Anastasio Somoza and his sons.

Resources and Economics
Agriculture is the main industry, occupying almost half the workforce. Much of the produce is for home consumption but Nicaragua exports coffee, cotton, sugar, timber and beef, its main sources of foreign exchange. Fishing, especially for shrimps and lobsters, is important on both coasts. Gold, silver and copper ore are mined, mainly for export. Nicaragua depends heavily on imported oil. There are few manufacturing industries of consequence. Roads and railways are adequate for present needs; tourism remains undeveloped.

Recent Developments
Throughout its unsettled history Nicaragua has suffered ruthless exploitation by dictators and foreign interests, few of whom have attempted to develop its resources rationally. Agricultural output and industrial capacity are slowly growing, hampered by lack of indigenous raw materials, fuels, skills or capital, and civil unrest, currently at the level of civil war. Long-overdue social reforms imposed by the Junta, including redistribution of land and nationalization of

mining, exporting and other enterprises, have intensified US hostility and reduced financial aid from that source; aid is now being sought from Mexico, West Germany, South American neighbours and communist countries.

Panama

The Country
The Republic of Panama occupies the southern end of the Central American isthmus, bordered by Colombia in the east and Costa Rica in the west. *Area* 77,082 km^2 (29,761 sq miles); *capital* Panama City; *population* 2,162,000 (est. 1986).

Organization
Panama is governed by a President, who is elected for four-year terms, and an executive cabinet of about 13 ministers; the President is elected by and responsible to the 505 members of a National Assembly of Community Representatives, who are elected by popular vote for six-year terms. The country is divided into nine provinces, each subdivided into municipal districts and headed by an appointed governor. Panamanians are a mixture of Indian, European and Negro stocks; many Americans work on contract in the Canal Zone. Roman Catholicism is the dominant religion, Spanish the official language though English is widely spoken.

Geography
Long and narrow, with an S-shaped curve, Panama has a high western mountain region (Serrania de Tabasará), dotted with jagged volcanic peaks. Toward its western end stands Chiriqui (3374 m, 11,070 ft), the country's highest mountain, and from the southern coast juts the mountainous Azuero Peninsula. The eastern half of the country is made up of lower mountain arcs, generally highest along the northern seaboard and backed by broad valleys. The famous canal is cut through the lake-studded lowland that runs centrally across Panama. The climate is hot and damp; dense forests clothe most of the mountains, opening to savanna along the drier Pacific coast.

History and Development
Peopled originally by forest Indians, Panama formed part of Spain's huge colonial empire during the 16th century; its importance as a crossing place between Caribbean and Pacific was realized early, though the unhealthy climate inhibited lowland development. At the dissolution of the Spanish Empire in 1821 Panama formed part of the independent state of Colombia. US capital promoted the building of a railway across the isthmus in 1848–55. Canal construction, begun in 1881, proved less successful; however, in 1903 US interest underwrote a revolution that secured Panama's independence from Colombia and the canal was re-started under US supervision in 1906, ultimately opening for traffic in 1914. The Canal Zone, a strip 8 km (5 miles) wide on either side of the canal, was administered by the USA until 1979, when sovereignty passed to Panama.

Resources and Economics
Outside the Canal Zone Panama's fertile river valleys and lowlands produce bananas, coffee, cacao and cane sugar, and the drier savannas provide good

range for cattle; these are the country's main exports. Rice, maize and beans are grown for local consumption. Timber provides another valuable export, though large pockets of indigenous forest remain untouched except by the native Indians. Panama is rich in copper ores and well provided with hydroelectric power. Petroleum is present but as yet unexploited; oil is bought at favourable rates from Mexico and Venezuela and processed for export, and Alaskan oil flows by pipeline from the Pacific to the Caribbean port of Chiriqui Grande, helping to reduce tanker congestion in the canal. The country's economy is centered mainly upon the canal and the ports (Colón, Panama) at either end of it. Four fifths of Panama's wealth is generated within 20 km (12 miles) of the Canal Zone, from transit royalties, flag-of-convenience shipping registration fees and other benefits accruing from free trading and liberal tax laws. Road and rail links are poor over much of the country, except close to the canal.

Recent Developments
After more than a decade of political instability, Panama appears to have settled into a period of slow, steady and relatively peaceful development. Away from the prosperous Canal Zone the country as a whole has hitherto given an impression of poverty no less intense than that of every other Central American state. Integrating the Zone more closely with the country's general economy may help to spread its benefits more widely; Panama now plans, and has the means, to diversify and improve its industries, power output and agriculture.

GREATER ANTILLES AND BAHAMAS

Bahamas

The Country
The Commonwealth of the Bahamas occupies a widely-scattered group of 700 islands and more cays in the western Atlantic Ocean, extending from 100 km (62 miles) off southeastern Florida, USA, east-southeast in a broad arc toward Cuba and Hispaniola in the Greater Antilles. *Area* 13,935 km² (5380 sq miles); *capital* Nassau (New Providence); *population* 231,000 (est. 1986).

Organization
The Bahamas are a parliamentary democracy within the British Commonwealth. Their Head of State is a Governor-General appointed by and representing the British Sovereign. Legislative power is vested in a 43-member elected House of Assembly and a 16-member Senate; senators are appointed by the Governor-General with the advice of the Prime Minister and Leader of the Opposition. Parliament extends over five-year terms. The population is mostly of mixed European and Negro stock, with some Spanish and Indian blood. Many forms of Christian faith are represented; the language is English.

Geography
Forming an arc more than 800 km (500 miles) long and covering a huge area of ocean, the Bahamas are the visible portions of two massive reefs of coralline

limestone, the Great and Little Bahama Banks; they include over a dozen large islands with substantial settlements and eight others which are inhabited, plus some 700 smaller islands and over 2000 reefs and islets. The highest point, on Cat Island in the centre of the group, is 120 m (400 ft) above sea level. The islands have a warm temperate climate, generally dry but with a rainy season between May and October. Hurricanes are likely in the second half of the year. Soils on the larger islands are fertile; several islands are forested, others heavily cultivated.

History and Development
The Bahamas were the first land in the Americas discovered by Christopher Columbus, who landed on Watling Island in 1492. Spanish settlers took Indians from the islands to work as slaves in the Greater Antilles, but made no claims or settlements on the Bahamas; the first permanent settlers were Britons who from 1649 established plantations on Eleuthera and New Providence islands. After an uncertain start, bedevilled by pirates and French and Spanish privateers, the community became a British protectorate under a Royal Governor from 1718, and began to thrive. The population was augmented by further settlers, including American loyalists after the War of Independence, and by Negro slaves brought in to work the plantations. Prosperity increased during the American Civil War, when the islands were used by blockade-runners. Trade and social links with the USA increased; the Bahamas became an offshore holiday and business centre for wealthy Americans, a role that has greatly expanded in the present century. Independence was granted in 1973.

Resources and Economics
While Bahamians on the smaller islands continue their traditional small-scale agriculture and fishing, those on the larger islands are now occupied mainly in catering for tourists. About half the total workforce of the Bahamas serves over 1.5 million long-stay holiday makers and cruise-ship visitors each year, generating two thirds of the islands' annual income. Building too is a major source of employment, providing tourist hotels and offices for expanding financial and banking enterprises, which low taxation and other concessions attract to the islands. Oil-refining and chemical and other manufacturing industries are developing, mainly on Grand Bahama. Roads on the main islands and boat services between the islands are adequate, and there are good air links with the USA and elsewhere.

Recent Developments
Despite high unemployment, especially among unskilled school-leavers, many Bahamians currently enjoy a prosperity never before seen on the islands. Efforts to diversify the economy and spread benefits through the community include the development of new tourist centres, general encouragement of service industries, improvements in communications, and research and capital investment to increase agricultural efficiency on the outlying islands.

Cayman Islands

The Cayman Islands are a British dependent territory of three islands (Grand Cayman, Little Cayman, Cayman Brac) in the Caribbean Sea; Grand Cayman, the largest and most westerly, lies 290 km (180 miles) south of Cuba and a similar distance west-northwest of Jamaica. *Area* 259 km^2 (100 sq miles); *capital* Georgetown (Grand Cayman); *population* 20,000 (est. 1986). Administration is vested in a Governor (appointed by and representing the British Sovereign) who is chairman of a small Executive Council of elected and appointed members; the Governor also presides over a Legislative Assembly of three *ex officio* and twelve elected members.

Grand Cayman, 32 km (20 miles) long and 12 km (8 miles) across, lies 100 km (63 miles) west of the other two islands, all of which are low-lying and ringed by coral reefs. Their climate is warm and equable all through the year. Formerly known as Las Tortugas, the islands were discovered by Christopher Columbus and named after the marine turtles that visited their beaches to breed. They remained unoccupied for many years, finally attracting settlers from Jamaica, their nearest British neighbour. The settlers, mostly poor white or coloured smallholders, planted palms, grew food crops, and exported fish, turtles, sponges, coconuts, sisal and other local products, mainly to Jamaica. Later a phosphate and guano export industry developed. The Caymans became a dependency of Jamaica, but chose to revert to the status of a dependent of the UK in 1962 when Jamaica achieved independence. In recent years they have developed flourishing tourist, banking and insurance industries, and Little Cayman offers oil trans-shipment and refinery facilities. Tourism currently provides 70 per cent of the islands' income, the financial sector contributes a growing proportion, and building has replaced agriculture and fishing as the main area of employment.

Cuba

The Country
The Republic of Cuba includes two large islands (Cuba, Isle of Youth) and over a thousand small coral cays and reefs in the north Caribbean Sea, 144 km (90 miles) off the southern tip of Florida, USA. *Area* 114,524 km^2 (44,218 sq miles); *capital* Havana; *population* 10,121,000 (est. 1986).

Organization
Cuba is governed by a 481-member National Assembly of People's Power, elected by municipal groups for five-year terms. From its members the Assembly elects a 31-member Council of State, the President of which is Head of State. The country is administered by the President in consultation with an appointed council of about 45 Ministers of State and Vice-Presidents. Only one political party, the Cuban Communist Party, is permitted. The population is mostly of mixed European (mainly Spanish) and Indian extraction. Many Cubans are Roman Catholics; the national language is Spanish.

Geography
Cuba is the least mountainous of the larger Caribbean islands. Plains extend the length of the island broken by occasional uplands and mountain ridges. The highest mountains are in the central range of Sierra de Trinidad, rising to over 1000 m (3300 ft), and in the even higher Sierra Maestra in the southeast which includes a single peak, Pico Turquino, rising to 2000 m (6562 ft). There is a deeply-indented coastline of cliffs, bays and coral strands. The climate is

tropical, cooled by year-round sea breezes: May to October are wet months, November to April dry. Formerly forested, the islands are now intensely cultivated.

History and Development
When first visited by Spanish explorers in the late 15th century, Cuba was heavily populated by Arawak and other Indian tribes who lived mainly as hunters and gatherers of food, or in small agricultural settlements. Slow to develop the land, the Spanish colonists divided the country into large estates, at first growing a variety of crops but later bringing in Negro slaves and concentrating on sugar-cane; by 1850 sugar dominated the island's economy. Prolonged civil unrest and hostility to Spanish colonial rule during the second half of the 19th century led to a war of independence (1895–8) in which US intervention and occupation helped to secure Spain's defeat. Ceded briefly to the USA, Cuba became independent in 1902, with the USA retaining naval bases and a strong interest in the country's internal affairs.

The early 20th century saw a succession of corrupt regimes in power, some backed and others opposed by the USA. Despite successful sugar crops and Cuba's role as a popular haven for US tourists, the country as a whole remained poor. Between 1953 and 1959 a small group of Cuban nationalists led by Fidel Castro and Ernesto (Che) Guevara conducted a campaign which finally dislodged the right-wing dictatorship of Fulgencio Batista and established an authoritarian Marxist regime, from which has gradually emerged the present socialist democracy. US hostility, including support for the Bay of Pigs invasion attempt in 1961 and long-term economic sanctions, helped push Cuba to the left. By 1961 Cuba had joined the Soviet bloc and embarked on a Marxist–Leninist approach to running the life of the country. Cuba has subsequently been a source of support for left-wing groups elsewhere in the Caribbean, in Latin America and Africa.

Resources and Economics
Cuba is still a mainly agricultural country with almost a quarter of its workforce employed on the land. Key crops are cane sugar, rice, citrus fruits and tobacco, with sugar and sugar products far exceeding all other exports in bulk and value. Most other crops are grown for home consumption. Fishing is an important and rapidly-expanding industry. Nickel, chrome and other metal ores are mined, mainly for export; short of fuel, Cuba imports most of its petroleum needs from Soviet bloc countries but is actively seeking to expand its own production. Cement, fertilizers, chemicals, textiles and steel are manufactured, and there are plans for increasing power output with both conventional and nuclear power stations. Roads and railways are adequate; the tourist industry is expanding slowly.

Recent Developments
Despite loss of income due to depressed world sugar prices, crop diseases and the long-standing embargo on trade with the USA, Cuba continues to develop and diversify its economy. Its main trading partner, the USSR, heavily subsidizes its agricultural and industrial growth, but Cuba is seeking both trade and aid in other parts of the world too. Its well-trained troops fight for the communist cause in Africa and elsewhere, to the further detriment of relations with the USA.

Dominican Republic

The Country
The Dominican Republic occupies the eastern two thirds of the island of Hispaniola, which it shares with Haiti. Its nearest large island neighbour, Puerto Rico, lies 100 km (63 miles) to the east. *Area* 48,734 km^2 (18,816 sq miles); *capital* Santo Domingo; *population* 6,874,000 (est. 1986).

Organization
A 27-member Senate and 120-member Chamber of Deputies make up the National Congress, all members of which are elected for four-year terms, as is the President. The President governs with the assistance of a cabinet, which includes about 17 Secretaries of State and the chiefs of the armed forces. Local authority is administered through 26 provinces and a National District (capital), each with an elected council and appointed governor. The people are mostly of Spanish or mixed Spanish and Indian extraction. Roman Catholicism is the dominant religion, Spanish the official language.

Geography
The country is traversed by the Cordillera Central, a heavily-wooded complex of mountains and valleys with many peaks rising over 3000 m (10,000 ft); the highest mountain is Pico Trujillo (3175 m, 10,417 ft). In the north, beyond Santiago, deep valleys separate this massif from a lower coastal range; in the southwest a broader valley cuts east–west through the mountains, accommodating Lake Enriquillo. The eastern third of the country opens to a wide coastal plain, backed in the north by low hills, with the port of Santo Domingo (formerly Ciudad Trujillo) at its western end. The climate is tropical, cooled by sea breezes which bring heavy rainfall to northern flanks of the mountains but leave the southern half of the country relatively dry. The mountains remain forested; the plains are now mainly under cultivation.

History and Development
Discovered by Christopher Columbus, the island of Hispaniola became a prominent Spanish colony in the 16th and 17th centuries. Following the Treaty of Ryswick (1697) Hispaniola was partitioned, the eastern province of Santo Domingo remaining Spanish and the western third, Haiti, passing into French possession. In 1803 Santo Domingo was taken over by Haiti which, better developed and more prosperous, had gained its independence from France. Briefly reclaimed by Spain, Santo Domingo fought for its own independence in 1821, only to be taken over again by Haiti in the following year. A further revolution in 1844 restored independence, but under its new name of Dominican Republic the country suffered a succession of weak administrations which did little to develop its potential or establish law. Spain reoccupied it in 1861, to be driven out four years later. Further weak governments ensued; the USA, which from time to time intervened in a peacekeeping role, eventually occupied the country between 1916 and 1924. A revolution in 1930 brought to power the dictator General Rafael Trujillo, who dominated the Dominican Republic for three decades until his assassination in 1961. US troops returned to maintain order in 1965–6. Since then three Presidents have been elected to power and the country has been governed in a constitutional manner.

Resources and Economics

Agriculture currently employs about 40 per cent of the workforce, mainly on subsistence farms and smallholdings, and generates about one fifth of the national income. Sugar-cane, mangoes, rice, avocadoes, tomatoes, oranges and tobacco are the major crops, with raw sugar and sugar products the most valuable agricultural exports. Coffee and cocoa, introduced experimentally and grown under irrigation, represent an attempt to diversify output. Bauxite is a significant export, though subject to fluctuations in world demand; silver and a little gold are more reliable assets. Petroleum has recently been discovered, though reserves may be small and current yields leave no surplus for export. Manufacturing industries employ only about 20 per cent of the workforce and generate a further fifth of the national income; manufactures are mainly confined to processed food and tobacco. The tourist industry is relatively small. There are adequate road networks, backed by limited internal airways, and good air and sea links with the USA and neighbouring islands.

Recent Developments

The Dominican Republic's long-neglected natural assets are slowly being developed against a background of chronic political instability. Producing mainly cash crops, bauxite and ferro-nickel ores at fluctuating prices for overseas markets, the country is strongly affected by world depression. Lack of indigenous capital inhibits industrial development and the purchase of raw materials; political uncertainty makes the republic a weak candidate for foreign investment. Briefly prosperous during the early 1970s, its economic growth has since slipped toward stagnation, despite efforts to diversify agriculture into more profitable crops. Foreign debt repayments have been reorganized and an IMF-sponsored programme of national austerity is currently helping to reshape the economy.

Haiti

The Country

The Republic of Haiti occupies the western end of Hispaniola, in the Caribbean Sea; it shares the island with the Dominican Republic, and its nearest island neighbour is Cuba, some 80 km (50 miles) to the west. *Area* 27,750 km^2 (10,714 sq miles); *capital* Port-au-Prince; *population* 6,758,000 (est. 1986).

Organization

Haiti is ruled by a Life President who holds complete executive authority. The President is assisted by an appointed council of about 15 Secretaries of State, and there is an elected National Assembly of 58 members. Local authority is administered through nine departments. Haitians are mostly descendants of Negro slaves and mulattos. Roman Catholicism and voodoo are the main religions; French is the official language, with a creole patois widely spoken.

Geography

Shaped like a double claw, Haiti consists mainly of two mountainous peninsulas separated by a deep bay. The northern peninsula emerges from a triangular bloc of mountains, Massif du Nord, that extends across the border into the Dominican Republic; several of its ridges rise above 1500 m (5000 ft). The southern peninsula consists of a narrow mountain range, Massif de la Hotte, that extends eastward to a higher bloc of coastal mountains including Haiti's highest peak, Mont La Selle (2280 m, 7480 ft). Between the claws lies Île de la Gonâve. A deeply indented coastline is backed by narrow plains, broadening in the north to a fertile valley. The climate is warm and mainly humid at sea level, pleasantly cool in the hills. Much of the country was forested but the lowlands are now heavily cultivated.

History and Development

The island of Hispaniola, discovered by Columbus in 1492, was occupied initially by Spanish settlers who introduced slave labour and grew sugar-cane. English and French settlers arriving about 1630 developed the unoccupied western lowlands; Haiti was created when, under the Treaty of Ryswick (1697), the western third of the island was allocated to France. The French colony prospered, growing sugar-cane, coffee and indigo. Toward the end of the 18th century landowning mulattos were granted political rights, provoking tensions between white and coloured communities. English and Spanish forces sent to intervene were driven out by local troops commanded by the Haitian leader General Toussaint-Louverture, who later became Governor. His replacement by a French governor led to a revolt and ultimately, in 1804, to the independence of the new state of Haiti. From 1822 Haiti and Santo Domingo, the eastern two thirds of Hispaniola, were a single state, but Santo Domingo gained its own independence in 1844 (see Dominican Republic).

Throughout the 19th century Haiti, politically corrupt and never far from violent revolution, made little economic progress. After prolonged disorder in 1915 US troops landed and a US administration, working mainly through the Haitian government, tried to develop the country along rational lines. US forces finally left in 1934. Further corruption and political unrest led to the assumption of power in 1957 by dictator François Duvalier (also known as Papa Doc), who made himself President for Life. His notoriously repressive regime alienated the country from the rest of the world, including many possible sources of foreign aid. His son Jean-Claude Duvalier, also President for Life, appears to be maintaining many of the family traditions.

Resources and Economics

Haiti's main industry is subsistence agriculture, occupying about 70 per cent of the workforce on half a million tiny, uneconomical plots scattered over the hills and plains. Maize, cassava, green vegetables, mangoes, plantains, beans and sorghum are the main produce, almost entirely for local consumption; rice is also grown but more is imported, rice being one of the staple foods. Coffee, cotton, cocoa and sisal are among the few significant cash crops; sugar-cane appears to be decreasing in importance. Bauxite is the only mineral produced in significant quantities; light manufacturing industries, mostly funded by foreigners taking advantage of cheap labour, are concentrated around the capital. There is a small but important tourist industry, catering mainly for American visitors. Roads are adequate for the country's present needs; Port-au-Prince has modern port facilities, and there are adequate air links with the USA and elsewhere.

Recent Developments

After centuries of mismanagement Haiti is among the most backward of the Caribbean countries. Income per capita, amounting to a few hundred dollars per annum, is the lowest in the Caribbean and among the lowest in the world. Overseas earnings, heavily dependent on the fluctuating prices of a few commodities, provide little revenue to help the country develop and are especially vulnerable to natural disasters; hurricanes of 1979 and 1980, for example, destroyed much of the coffee crop and substantially reduced the national income. Overseas aid pays for the development of roads, hydroelectric-power schemes and other much-needed modernizations.

Jamaica

The Country
An island state in the Caribbean Sea, Jamaica lies south of the main arc of the Greater Antilles, 150 km (94 miles) south of Cuba and about the same distance west of southern Haiti. *Area* 10,991 km² (4244 sq miles); *capital* Kingston; *population* 2,394,000 (est. 1986).

Organization
Jamaica is a parliamentary democracy within the British Commonwealth. Head of State is the Governor-General, appointed by and representing the British Sovereign. A Senate of 20 members, appointed by the Governor-General in consultation with the Prime Minister, and a House of Representatives of 60 elected members, make up the island's Parliament. Executive power is vested in the Prime Minister and a cabinet of about 20 ministers. Local authority is centered in fourteen parishes. Many Christian faiths are represented; English is the official language.

Geography
A mountainous island with fine cliffs and beaches along its coasts, Jamaica is crossed by a range of hills and high plateaus, mostly of limestones overlying older crystalline rocks. Many of the ridges rise above 500 m (1640 ft); the highest peak, Blue Mountain (2256 m, 7402 ft), lies behind the port of Kingston at the eastern end of the island. Deep valleys dissect the mountains, spilling their alluvium onto wide coastal plains. Dominated by northeast trade winds, Jamaica's climate is warm and damp for nine months of the year; in winter northerly winds bring colder weather from the American continent. Rains are heavy from May to October, especially on the northern sides of the mountains. The southern plains are drier, even arid except for summer showers. Lowlands were once heavily forested but have largely been cleared; rich subtropical forest remains in the wetter mountain areas.

History and Development
When first seen by Christopher Columbus in 1494 Jamaica was heavily populated by Arawak and Carib Indians. Spanish settlers cleared both them and the forests, introducing Negro slaves and opening up the land for ranching and agriculture. Britain annexed the island in 1655. Bringing in more slaves, British planters created a huge sugar-cane industry which flourished for over a century and a half, declining ultimately with the emancipation of slaves in 1838. A period of relative poverty followed and in 1866 Jamaica, which had been largely self-governing, became a Crown Colony. It retained this status until the end of World War II. Its gradual return to agricultural prosperity and economic self-

sufficiency was accompanied by a series of steps towards greater autonomy. Self-government was introduced in 1944 and gradually extended until in 1962 Jamaica was granted independence. Most Jamaicans are descendants of Negro slaves, with some admixture of European blood.

Resources and Economics

Agriculture currently employs about one third of the island's workforce, mainly in sugar, coffee, cocoa and fruit plantations and on subsistence farms and smallholdings. Sugar, sugar products and bananas are major exports; citrus fruit, coffee, cocoa and other crops also contribute significantly to export earnings. Many of the island's staple foods are produced locally; there is a substantial local and deep-water fishing industry. Mining employs fewer Jamaicans than agriculture but generates a far higher proportion of the country's wealth; bauxite is the main product, exported raw or processed locally into alumina. Manufacturing industries are poorly developed, limited by the cost of energy and raw materials, both of which have to be imported. Tourism is a major employer of labour and generator of income for the island; almost a million tourists are catered for each year. However, unemployment levels are high, and many Jamaicans find it necessary to emigrate temporarily or permanently.

Recent Developments

Jamaica has survived a long period of economic recession and inflation. Some growth in the economy is now apparent, though the country's products and services remain very much at the mercy of fluctuating world prices. Political stability and a sound record of achievement ensure that foreign and international capital flow readily into the country. Both the USA and IMF give substantial support, allowing Jamaica to continue to diversify its sources of revenue, increase employment, and make some improvements in the social infrastructure and the lot of its poorest families.

Puerto Rico

The Country

The Commonwealth of Puerto Rico is the easternmost island of the Greater Antilles group, lying between the western Atlantic Ocean and the Caribbean Sea, and between the Virgin Islands (US) to the east and the Dominican Republic to the west. *Area* 8897 km^2 (3435 sq miles); *capital* San Juan; *population* 4,448,000 (est. 1986).

Organization

A semi-autonomous territory of the USA, Puerto Rico is governed by an elected Senate of 27 members and an elected House of Representatives of 51 members with full power over local government: the executive is formed by a Governor, elected for four-year terms, and a 14-member advisory Council of Secretaries. Puerto Rico is represented in the US Congress by an elected Resident Commissioner, who sits in the House of Representatives. The population is mainly of mixed Spanish and Negro blood, with contributions from Indian and non-Spanish European stocks. Roman Catholicism is the major religion; Spanish and English are the official languages, the former more widely spoken.

Geography

Puerto Rico is a rectangular island with two outliers, Culebra and Vieques, off its eastern end. Rising steeply from the sea, it has a broad coastal plain in the north and a narrower one in the south; the northern plain rises in steps to a high plateau and ultimately to the Cordillera Centrale, a range of rugged mountains over 1000 m (3300 ft) high. The highest peak, Cerro de Punta, rises to 1338 m (4390 ft). The southern flanks of the mountains fall more steeply, crossed by deep gullies that carry torrents during the rainy season. Temperatures are mainly warm but seldom extreme. Atlantic winds bring heavy rain to the northern plains, especially in winter; the southern flanks are drier with occasional seasonal downpours. Formerly forested, the island is now heavily cultivated.

History and Development

Visited by Christopher Columbus in 1493, Puerto Rico was originally the home of Carib and Arawak Indians who cultivated the lowlands, fished and hunted in the forests. Spanish occupation dates from 1508: although gold was mined and sugar-cane planted, for long the colony's main value to Spain was its strategically-placed harbours, for which it suffered constant French, Dutch and British attacks. During the late 18th and early 19th centuries it developed as a sugar-producing colony; it remained Spanish during the revolution that gave most other Latin-American countries their independence, and provided sanctuary for displaced Spanish settlers who helped it prosper. A separatist movement that developed during the late 19th century won self-government for Puerto Rico in 1897. Shortly afterwards the Spanish–American War brought a US army of occupation, and the island was ceded in 1898, becoming an unincorporated territory of the USA. Its current status was granted in 1952.

Resources and Economics

Agriculture currently employs about 6 per cent of the workforce, a dramatic decrease in recent decades due mainly to industrialization. The most important crops are sugar, tobacco, pineapples and other tropical produce; dairy products and livestock are also significant. Minerals are undeveloped; the most promising candidate for future development is copper ore. Fuels are lacking and have to be imported; offshore oil deposits are currently being investigated.

Much of the economy hinges on free access to the US market and on heavy investments of US capital in manufacturing; the earlier advantage of low wages has weakened, but the benefit of assured US markets remains. The island is densely populated and unemployment is high; many Puerto Ricans move to the USA where lack of skills and education often confine them to low-paid jobs. Tourism is well developed, catering particularly for Americans. Roads and internal air services are good; there are strong air and shipping links with the USA and other areas of the Caribbean.

Recent Developments

The Puerto Rican economy is strongly influenced by the prices obtainable for its few export commodities. Of these almost 90 per cent are destined for the USA, which also provides about 40 per cent of its imports; thus in every respect the prosperity of the country is tightly enmeshed with that of its larger neighbour and trading partner. Puerto Rico also depends substantially on US support to balance its budget, and Federal spending cuts affect it seriously. While its close association with the USA brings many benefits (notably citizenship and welfare payments), there are moves within the country either towards statehood, or alternatively towards a greater degree of economic independence; this is a live issue debated hotly by politicians and public alike. The USA is committed to granting absolute independence to the island when the legislature requires it.

Turks and Caicos Islands

The Turks and Caicos Islands, a semi-autonomous British dependency, form a group of about thirty islands (six of them inhabited) off the southeastern end of the Bahamas in the western Atlantic Ocean. *Area* 430 km² (166 sq miles); *capital* Cockburn Town (Grand Turk); *population* 8300 (est. 1986). Administration is the responsibility of a Governor, appointed by and representing the British Sovereign, who presides over an Executive Council of eight appointed and *ex officio* members; a Legislative Council of 17 members, including 11 elected, 3 *ex officio* and 2 nominated, is presided over by a Speaker. Several Christian faiths are represented; the official language is English.

These low-lying islands stand on an eastern extension of the Great Bahama Bank, separated from the Bahamas by the deep Caicos Passage. The largest island, Grand Caicos, is 48 km (30 miles) long and 4 km (2.5 miles) wide; Grand Turk, the most populated island and seat of government, is only one third as big. The climate is subtropical, cooled by trade winds, and generally dry. Discovered by Ponce de Leon in the early 16th century, the islands remained unoccupied and undeveloped, except by salt workers who raked and collected sea-salt from the lagoons. Disputes between Britain, France and Spain over their sovereignty were resolved in 1765 when they were linked formally to the Bahamas. In 1848 responsibility for the Turks and Caicos Islands was transferred to Jamaica. They gained their present status when Jamaica became independent in 1962, being granted more local control of affairs in 1976. Smallholdings provide some food for local consumption. Fishing and catering for tourists are the main sources of income today; development aid is helping to expand the tourist industry.

British Virgin Islands

The colony of the British Virgin Islands consists of four large islands (Tortola, Virgin Gorda, Anegada, Jost Van Dyke) and some thirty smaller ones in the north and east of the Virgin group of the West Indies. *Area* 153 km² (59 sq miles); *capital* Road Town (Tortola); *population* 13,500 (est. 1986). The colony is administered by a Governor, appointed by and representing the British Sovereign, who presides over a five-member Executive Council; a Legislative Council of ten or eleven members, several of whom are elected, is presided over by a Speaker. The population is mainly of Negro or mixed Negro and European stock. The dominant religion is Protestant Christianity, the official language English, which many islanders speak in a creole patois.

The Virgin Islands, split between US and British administrations, are a group of about a hundred islands, cays and reefs lying east of Puerto Rico between the western Atlantic Ocean and the Caribbean Sea. They mark the peaks of a submarine mountain range, the eastern extremity of the Greater

Antilles chain. Mount Sage (543 m, 1780 ft) on Tortola is the highest peak in the British islands. The subtropical climate is cooled by trade winds, with a limited rainy season from September to December. The lowlands are generally dry; only the hills are damp enough to support forest.

The Virgin islands were visited by Christopher Columbus in 1493, but remained unoccupied by Europeans until Dutch pirates settled on Tortola in the mid-17th century. British planters colonized Tortola in 1666, spreading to nearby islands and bringing the eastern group under the administration and protection of the Leeward Islands. Negro slaves imported to work the plantations soon formed the bulk of the population. The British Virgins became a Crown Colony in 1956–60 when the Leeward Islands federation broke up, receiving their present constitution in 1967. The small scattered population is concerned mainly with fishing, growing food (much of it for export to the neighbouring Virgin Islands of the USA), and catering for a small but growing tourist industry. Development aid programmes support and seek to diversify the economy.

Virgin Islands of the United States of America

Three large islands (St Croix, St Thomas and St John) and about fifty smaller ones in the south and west of the Virgins group form an unincorporated territory of the USA. *Area* 344 km^2 (133 sq miles); *capital* Charlotte Amalie; *population* 107,000 (est. 1986). Administered by the US Department of the Interior, their constitution provides for an elected Governor and an elected Senate of 15 members with limited local functions. The islanders are US citizens with a representative in the US Congress. Protestant Christianity is the most widely-represented faith, and English is the official language.

St Croix, the largest island, lies 65 km (40 miles) south of the main group, separated by a deep channel. Many of the islands are coral-fringed and rugged, with steep cliffs and valleys; Crown Mountain (474 m, 1555 ft) on St Thomas is the highest peak in the American group. Danish planters settled on St Thomas in 1666, importing slaves to tend their sugar-cane and cotton crops. Later St John and St Croix came under the same rule, amalgamating as a Danish Crown Colony in 1754. Britain took over the islands periodically during the Napoleonic Wars, returning them finally to Denmark in 1815. They remained Danish until 1917, when the USA bought them to provide a protective base for the approaches to the newly-opened Panama Canal. Control passed from the Navy Department to the Department of the Interior in 1931; since then successive Acts of Congress have increased the islanders' autonomy.

Tourism is the main industry, currently providing over a quarter of the annual income. Small-scale farming flourishes, though plantation agriculture has almost ceased. On St Croix, the most heavily populated island, there are several small manufacturing industries; heavier industry is represented by an aluminium-ore processing plant and an oil-refinery. Many islanders work in the USA, where there are better prospects for their unskilled labour.

LEEWARD ISLANDS

Anguilla

Northernmost of the Leeward Islands, Anguilla lies 8 km (5 miles) north of the Dutch and French island of St Martin, between the western Atlantic Ocean and the Caribbean Sea. *Area* 150 km^2 (58 sq miles); *capital* The Valley; *population* 8500 (est. 1986). A British dependency since 1980, Anguilla's Governor (appointed by and representing the British Sovereign) presides over a six-member appointed Executive Council and a Legislative Assembly of eleven members presided over by a Speaker. Christianity is represented by many denominations; the official language is English.

A low-lying island of rolling limestone plains and hills, Anguilla is 26 km (16 miles) long and 5 km (3 miles) wide. Its climate is tropical and generally dry, with cooling trade winds. Discovered by Christopher Columbus in 1493, it was colonized by Britain in 1650 but remained relatively undeveloped; many Anguillans today are descendants of Negroes who worked smallholdings and salt-flats through the colonial period. Administered jointly with St Kitts and Nevis for many years, in February 1967 Anguilla was united with them in a formal association; this broke up three months later, and British police were brought in to restore orderly government. For a time the island was administered directly by Britain, and in 1980 its separate status from St Kitts-Nevis was confirmed. Anguillans raise crops and livestock, notably pigs and cattle, mainly for their own use, and export lobsters, fish and salt. Roads are adequate for the islanders' needs; sea and air ferries provide frequent links with neighbouring islands. There is a small, slowly-developing tourist trade.

Antigua and Barbuda

The independent state of Antigua and Barbuda lies centrally to the Leeward Islands arc on the northeastern (Atlantic) side. Antigua, the main island, is almost equidistant from Montserrat, Nevis, Guadeloupe, and its own dependencies of Barbuda to the north and Redonda to the west. *Area* 442 km^2 (171 sq miles); *capital* St John's; *population* (including dependencies) 83,000 (est. 1986). Until 1981 Antigua was one of several West Indian islands in formal association with each other and with Britain. Head of State is the Governor-General, appointed by and representing the British Sovereign; there is a Senate of 17 appointed members and a House of Representatives. Many Christian denominations are represented on the islands; the official language is English.

Mainly low-lying, with an indented coastline of headlands and sandy bays, including several good harbours, Antigua rises along its western flank to 405 m (1330 ft). The climate is tropical, cooled by trade winds. Discovered by Christopher Columbus in 1493, it was colonized in the mid-17th century by British settlers, who introduced Negro slaves and grew tobacco and sugar-cane. English Harbour, now a yacht basin, was for long an important Royal Naval dockyard for the West Indies fleet. A member of the Federation of the West Indies until 1962, Antigua became an Associated State of the United Kingdom in 1967, and obtained independence in 1981.

The islanders, most of whom are descendants of freed slaves, grow much of their own food; sea-island cotton and molasses are currently their most lucrative exports. Arrowroot, once a famous product, is no longer grown commercially. There is a developing tourist industry, operating mainly through Coolidge, the island's international airport, and through the important cruise liners that call at St John's. Barbuda, 50 km (31 miles) to the north, is also a tourist attraction; smaller, and with a much smaller population centered on the single settlement of Codrington, it has fine beaches, lagoons and undisturbed wildlife.

Guadeloupe

The Country
A cluster of former French colonies in the central Lesser Antilles, Guadeloupe includes seven islands and many islets, mostly in the Windwards arc. *Area* 1779 km² (687 sq miles); *capital* Basse-Terre (Basse-Terre), *largest town* Pointe-à-Pitre (Grande-Terre); *population* 335,000 (est. 1986).

Organization
With the status of an Overseas Department of France, Guadeloupe is administered by an appointed Commissioner, who is advised by a General Council of 36 elected members and a Regional Council of 41 elected members. In France the islands are represented by two senators and three deputies. Local affairs are administered through three arrondissements, divided into thirty-four communes. The dominant religion is Roman Catholicism, the official language French, spoken mainly in creole dialect.

Geography
Basse-Terre and Grande-Terre, the two main islands, are separated only by an easily-bridged, narrow channel; together they make up 85 per cent of the land area and accommodate over 90 per cent of the population. Basse-Terre is mountainous, with several volcanic peaks rising to over 1200 m (4000 ft): Grande-Terre is smaller and lower, rising only to 150 m (490 ft). Marie-Galante, Îles des Saintes and La Désirade lie close to the main islands; St Martin (an island shared administratively with the Netherlands) and St Barthélemy lie 250 km (156 miles) to the northwest in the Leeward Islands. The climate is warm and humid, tempered by trade winds. Rainfall is heaviest in the mountains, and there is a dry season from December to April. The uplands are forested, the lowlands grass-covered or cultivated.

History and Development
Inhabited by Carib Indians when discovered by Columbus in 1493, the main islands were colonized sporadically by Spanish settlers; after 1635, when Guadeloupe became a French colony, more determined French planters moved in, introducing Negro slaves and sugar-cane and thus helping to found the colony's prosperity. Occupied twice by British forces during the 18th century, fought over by French royalists and revolutionaries, slave-owners and abolitionists, Guadeloupe remained prosperous throughout its chequered colonial history. In 1946 it received departmental status. Most of the islanders are descendants of black slaves, with varying admixtures of European blood; Îles des Saintes and St Barthélemy have a high proportion of whites, descended from 17th-century French settlers.

Resources and Economics

Guadeloupe's economy has for long been based on bananas and sugar-cane, vanilla, cocoa and a small range of other tropical produce. Manufacturing industries remain undeveloped, limited by lack of cheap power and indigenous raw materials, and unemployment throughout the islands is high. Tourism is well developed, but Guadeloupe's budget is balanced annually by subsidies from metropolitan France. Roads are generally good on the larger islands; Grande-Terre has a busy international airport, and the smaller islands are adequately linked by ferries.

Recent Developments

The islands' main problem is a relatively dense and unskilled population, subsisting mainly on overburdened land resources, with few alternative means of employment; migration to metropolitan France is an option taken by many of the more enterprising young people.

Montserrat

On the western or Caribbean flank of the Leeward Islands, the island of Montserrat lies between Antigua, St Kitts-Nevis and Guadeloupe, north of the Guadeloupe Passage. *Area* 98 km² (38 sq miles); *capital* Plymouth; *population* 13,000 (est. 1986). A British Crown Colony, Montserrat is administered by a Governor (appointed by and representing the British Sovereign), who presides over an appointed Executive Council of six ministers; there is also a Legislative Council of seven elected, two nominated and two appointed members. Many Christian faiths are represented; the official language is English.

Though only about 18 km (11 miles) long and 11 km (7 miles) wide, Montserrat includes a range of volcanic mountains rising to 900 m (3000 ft); hot springs are signs of current volcanic activity. The climate is warm and moist, tempered by trade winds. Forests formerly covered much of the island, but the rich, well-watered lowland soils are now intensively cultivated. Discovered by Columbus in 1493, Montserrat was formally occupied in 1632 by a group of Irish settlers, who introduced a plantation economy with slave labour. Prospering through the turbulence of the 18th and early 19th centuries, it became a British Crown Colony in 1871. In 1958 the colony joined the West Indies Federation, reverting to colonial status when the Federation disbanded in 1962.

Most of the islanders are farmers of mixed Negro and European stock; their main products are cotton, citrus fruits, tomatoes, spices and cattle for export, and fruit, vegetables and livestock for local consumption. Increasing numbers of islanders now have their own smallholdings. Light industries are developing, mostly with capital from overseas. There are good roads and inter-island air and sea links. Tourism, already the mainstay of the economy, continues to grow in importance.

St Kitts-Nevis

The Country

The islands of St Christopher (better known as St Kitts) and Nevis jointly form an independent state in the central Leeward Islands. Their nearest neighbours are St Eustatius, some 24 km (15 miles) to the northwest, and Redonda, Montserrat and Antigua in the southeast and east. *Area* 258 km² (100 sq miles); *capital* Basseterre (St Kitts); *population* 50,000 (est. 1986).

Organization

Lying only 5 km (3 miles) apart, St Kitts and Nevis became independent in 1983 but remain in close association with Britain. The Head of State is the British Sovereign represented by a Governor-General. Legislative power is vested in a Parliament of 12 elected and nominated members; the executive is formed by a Prime Minister who presides over a small cabinet. Many Christian faiths are represented; English is the official language.

Geography

Both islands are volcanic; St Kitts has a range of rugged, forested peaks rising to central Mt Misery (1156 m, 3792 ft); Nevis is almost entirely a single cone rising to 985 m (3232 ft). The coasts are generally steep, with a few beaches of dark volcanic sand. The climate is warm, tempered by trade winds, with a summer rainy season from May to November.

History and Development

Discovered by Columbus in 1493, St Kitts and Nevis remained relatively undeveloped until 1623, when St Kitts was colonized by British settlers. Following this first British settlement in the Caribbean, the neighbouring island of Nevis was occupied five years later. Meanwhile French settlers had also claimed parts of St Kitts; friction between the two nations continued until 1783, when the two islands were declared British under the Treaty of Versailles. Many fortified sites are reminders of the islands' turbulent history. From 1816 St Kitts and Nevis were linked administratively with Anguilla and the British Virgin Islands; St Kitts and Nevis retained their links with Anguilla until 1967, when Anguilla broke away unilaterally.

Resources and Economics

Agriculture provides most of the employment on both islands. Smallholdings now replace many of the former plantations; the crops are mostly vegetables and livestock for local consumption, with cotton and coconuts for export. Sugar, still grown mainly on plantations on St Kitts, remains the country's major export and precarious source of income. Light industries, including food-processing, electronics and clothing manufacture, are supported by overseas funding in an effort to diversify the economy and provide employment for the small workforce. Roads are adequate on both islands; both have airfields (that on St Kitts large enough for international traffic), and a fast boat service plies between the islands.

Recent Developments

St Kitts and Nevis have the characteristic problem of supporting large, predominantly unskilled populations on meagre resources. Efforts to improve and diversify their agriculture, boost industrial development and encourage the tourist industry are hampered by lack of capital. Disagreements between the two island communities weaken their union, and may lead ultimately to political separation.

WINDWARD ISLANDS

Barbados

The Country
Lying 160 km (100 miles) east of St Vincent in the western Atlantic Ocean, Barbados is the most isolated of the West Indian islands. *Area* 431 km^2 (166 sq miles); *capital* Bridgetown; *population* 280,000 (est. 1986).

Organization
An independent state within the British Commonwealth, Barbados is governed by an appointed 21-member Senate and an elected 27-member House of Assembly. Head of State is the Governor-General, appointed by and representing the British Sovereign; the Prime Minister has executive powers, heading a small cabinet. The population is mostly Negro with a small British admixture; there are small but dominant European and Asian minorities. Protestant Christianity is the dominant religion, English the official language with a local dialect widely spoken.

Geography
Barbados is made up of sandstones, clays and mudstones capped by coralline limestone, which rise in ridges to a central range of low rolling hills; the central peak, Mt Hillaby, is just over 330 m (1100 ft) high. About 34 km (21 miles) long, 22 km (14 miles) broad and pear-shaped, the island is ringed by a coral reef, with a single natural harbour in the southwest. The climate is tropical, tempered by sea breezes and occasionally blasted by hurricanes; most of the rain falls between May and December. Formerly forested, Barbados is now densely cultivated.

History and Development
Originally occupied by Carib Indians, the island was probably depopulated by Spanish slavers; first mentioned by Portuguese explorers in the late 16th century, it was claimed for Britain in 1605 and first settled by British colonists in 1627. Sugar plantations, worked by imported slave labour, made it a highly prosperous colony throughout the late 17th and early 18th centuries; later its community suffered attacks from French and American privateers. Emancipation of the slaves in 1834 and a free-trade policy by Britain in the 19th century weakened the economy but the inherent fertility of its lowland soils and a well-organized sugar industry carried it forward into the 20th century. A Crown Colony for almost three centuries, Barbados was given self-government in 1961 and independence in 1966.

Resources and Economics
Agriculture is the mainstay of the economy, occupying about 10 per cent of the workforce. There is still strong emphasis on sugar production and processing, though many of the plantations have been broken up into smallholdings where subsistence and market crops are grown. However, Barbados continues to import much of its food from neighbouring islands. Fishing is a growing industry, helped by grants from overseas. Petroleum, discovered offshore, may contribute to the economy in the future. Light manufacturing industries, including glass, ceramics and assembly of electric and electronics components,

provide a steady proportion of the national income, and Barbados is developing as a financial centre. Tourism is well developed, catering annually for almost half a million visitors and providing almost half the country's overseas earnings. Roads are adequate for the island's needs; there are good air and sea links with the USA and with other Caribbean islands.

Recent Developments
Democratically governed, politically stable and relatively prosperous, Barbados has the potential for steady development at a modest rate, though inequitable incomes and large numbers of landless unemployed continue to give cause for concern.

Dominica

The Country
The Commonwealth of Dominica lies at the northern end of the Windward Island chain, between the French island groups of Guadeloupe and Martinique, in the eastern Caribbean Sea. *Area* 751 km² (290 sq miles); *capital* Roseau; *population* 88,000 (est. 1986).

Organization
An independent republic within the British Commonwealth, Dominica is governed by a House of Assembly of 30 members (21 elected), to which is responsible a small executive cabinet headed by a Prime Minister. An elected President is Head of State. Christianity, predominantly Roman Catholicism, is the main religion; English is the official language, with French widely spoken.

Geography
About 50 km (30 miles) long, lofty, rectangular and with a deeply-indented coastline, Dominica is forested and rises steeply from the sea. The interior is dominated by mountains and deeply-incised valleys; Morne Diablotin, the highest peak, rises to 1447 m (4747 ft). Fumaroles and a steaming lake are reminders of latent volcanic activity. The climate is warm and humid, tempered by trade winds; rainfall is heavy on the mountains and windward coasts, lighter in the lowlands, with a marked dry season only on the western flank. Dominica lies in the path of hurricanes, which occur frequently. Tropical rain forests cover about 80 per cent of the islands.

History and Development
Dominica was discovered by Christopher Columbus in 1493, but left to its aggressive Carib Indian inhabitants. French settlers attempted colonization in the late 17th century, but in 1748 it was returned to the Caribs by Anglo–French agreement. British planters settled in the southwest in 1763, introducing Negro slaves; plantations and later small farms spread, restricted mainly to river flats and lowlands, and leaving the mountain forests untouched. Dominica became a Crown Colony in 1805. From 1958 to 1962 it formed part of the Federation of the West Indies, gaining full independence in 1978. Most Dominicans are of mixed Negro and European stock; a small community of Carib Indians is still to be found in a forest reserve.

Resources and Economics

With most of the interior inaccessible from the coast and densely forested, Dominica remains largely undeveloped. Much of its cultivated land is in smallholdings, producing vegetables and livestock for local consumption. Plantations produce citrus fruits, notably limes, which were for many years Dominica's major export; bananas and coconuts have now overtaken them in importance. Pumice is quarried for export. Roads connect the two main centres and some of the coastal settlements. There are two small airfields; port facilities at Roseau are used mainly by inshore fishing boats, small cargo boats and inter-island transport.

Recent Developments

Rivalry between the two main political parties, resulting in unrest 1979–83, and a succession of hurricanes that damaged the plantations in 1980, combined to set back Dominica's slowly developing economy. Forestry and tourism are hopeful possibilities for the future; meanwhile the island relies heavily on IMF and other international support to balance its annual budget.

Grenada

The Country

Grenada is the southernmost of the Windward Islands, 160 km (100 miles) north of Trinidad in the eastern Caribbean Sea. Included with it are Ronde and Carriacou, southernmost of the Grenadines, a chain of islets extending north toward St Vincent. *Area* 344 km² (133 sq miles); *capital* St George's; *population* 120,400 (est. 1986).

Organization

Independent since 1974, Grenada has dominion status within the British Commonwealth, governed by an appointed 13-member Senate and an elected 15-member House of Representatives; the Governor represents the British Sovereign, who is Head of State. An executive cabinet of about 15 ministers is headed by the Prime Minister. (See also Recent Developments below.) Roman Catholicism is the dominant religion, with many other denominations represented; English is the official language, with a French patois widely spoken.

Geography

From a mountainous central spine, Grenada descends in steep slopes and valleys to a broad coastal plain; the highest peak is Mt St Catherine (840 m, 2756 ft). Most of the island is made up of schists, sandstones and volcanic rocks; there are two extensive crater lakes, and several fumaroles and hot springs. In the north, marine limestones overlie the older rocks. The climate is warm and humid, with a rainy season from May to December. Winds are generally moderate, but hurricanes of destructive force occasionally hit the island. Formerly forested, Grenada is now extensively cultivated.

History and Development

Although discovered in 1498 by Columbus, Grenada remained virtually uncolonized until 1650, when French settlers from Martinique established themselves. Destroying the Carib Indian population, they imported slaves to raise cocoa, coffee and cotton. The island passed into British possession in 1763, was recaptured by France in 1779, and returned to Britain four years later. During the 19th century East Indian indentured labour replaced slaves; modern Grenadans are mostly of mixed Negro, East Indian and European descent. The island became a self-governing colony in 1967 and independent in 1974.

Resources and Economics
The mainstay of the economy is still agriculture; Grenada grows bananas, cocoa, nutmegs (about one third of the world's supply) and other spices, citrus fruits (notably limes), sugar and other produce for export, and many Grenadans grow food for local consumption on their smallholdings. The fishing industry is developing, and tourism is increasing with great potential for the future. Roads are adequate for local needs, and the island is well served by air and shipping lines; the main airport runway has recently been extended. Unemployment, chronically high, has recently declined as more land has become available for smallholdings.

Recent Developments
Political factions in Grenada are strong. The left-wing People's Revolutionary Government that took over power in 1979, dedicated to ending corruption and to agricultural and social reforms, faced strong opposition from extremist parties on both left and right. Following the murder of the Prime Minister and members of his cabinet, US troops invaded in November 1983 to restore government and order. Elections were held in the autumn of 1984.

Martinique

The Country
Among the northernmost of the Windward Islands, Martinique lies between St Lucia and Dominica in the eastern Caribbean Sea. *Area* 1102 km² (425 sq miles); *capital* Fort-de-France; *population* 329,000 (est. 1986).

Organization
Martinique is an Overseas Department of France, administered by a Prefect (appointed by and representing the French Government) and an elected council of 36 members. The island returns three deputies and two senators to the National Assembly in Paris. Roman Catholicism is the dominant religion, French the official language, with creole dialect widely spoken.

Geography
About 61 km (38 miles) long and 24 km (15 miles) wide, Martinique rises steeply from the sea, especially on northern coasts where high cliffs are capped by a narrow dissected plain that rises to the steep volcanic massif of Mt Pelée (1397 m, 4583 ft). The southern half of the island is lower, with a rugged but less spectacular coast. The climate is warm to hot, tempered by trade winds. Rain is abundant, especially in summer (June to November); only the southern end of the island is dry. Lush tropical vegetation once covered Martinique, ranging from coastal mangroves to mountain forest; most available lowland is now intensively cultivated.

History and Development

Discovered by Christopher Columbus on his voyage of 1493, Martinique was first colonized in 1635 by French planters from St Kitts, who grew cotton and tobacco. Later settlers included Jews displaced from Brazil and both English and French colonists. First quelling and destroying the native Carib Indians, the new wave of planters introduced sugar-cane, cocoa and coffee to the island; slave labour was brought in from West Africa (later replaced by indentured labour from China and India) to run the plantations. Attacked frequently by British, Dutch and other naval forces during the 17th century, the island changed hands several times, finally reverting to France in 1814. For long administered as a colony, it became an Overseas Department of France in 1946. In 1902 the eruption of Mt Pelée destroyed the northwestern town of St Pierre, killing all but one of its inhabitants. Most islanders are of mixed Negro and European stock; a European minority dominates commerce and the administration.

Resources and Economics

With its year-round warmth and humidity and rich volcanic soils, Martinique has a mainly agricultural economy. Its peasant farmers grow food crops on higher ground, while the best land is given over to commercial crops of sugar-cane and bananas; exports include sugar and rum. Oil-refining and fertilizer manufacture provide the main industrial resource. A flourishing tourist industry is based on the island's natural beauty and its French flavour and connections. A busy international airport caters mainly for visitors from Western Europe and the USA. There are few other indigenous sources of income to be developed. Roads are good; the many small ports provide for fishing and both local and inter-island shipping.

Recent Developments

Among the most densely populated of the Caribbean islands, Martinique makes the best of its considerable natural resources but relies heavily on France and the European community for financial aid, both to balance its budget and to develop new industries. Dogged by unemployment, many of its young folk emigrate to France in search of work.

The Netherlands Antilles

The Country

Administered as part of the Kingdom of the Netherlands, the Netherlands Antilles are made up of two island groups – the small islands of St Eustatius, Saba and St Maarten (of which the northern half is administered by France) in the northern Leewards group, and the larger islands of Aruba, Bonaire and Curaçao in the southern Caribbean Sea. *Area* 961 km^2 (371 sq miles); *capital* Willemstad (Curaçao); *population* 290,000 (est. 1986).

Organization

A Governor, appointed by and representing the Dutch Sovereign, presides over a council of about seven ministers, who are responsible under a Prime Minister to a parliament (Staten) of 22 elected members. The three southern islands singly, and the northern islands jointly, are administered by local executive councils, and the Antilles are represented in the Netherlands government. Roman Catholicism is the dominant religion; Dutch is the official language, with English and a local patois called Papiamento widely spoken.

Geography
Saba and St Eustatius are volcanic islands; Saba, the smallest, is little more than an extinct volcanic cone, though it is also the highest of the group, rising to 860 m (2821 ft). St Maarten is of coralline limestone fringing an igneous core. So too are the three southern islands: Curaçao, the largest (444 km², 171 sq miles), Bonaire (288 km², 111 sq miles), and Aruba, the smallest (193 km², 75 sq miles). These three between them carry over 90 per cent of the total population. All the islands have warm tropical climates; the northern ones are well watered and covered with vegetation, the southern group are dry and semi-desert.

History and Development
Discovered by Columbus or his immediate successors and claimed initially for Spain, all the Netherlands Antilles islands were occupied by Dutch planters, traders or privateers during the 17th-century rivalry between the European powers; several were subsequently held by Britain or France before finally reverting to Dutch ownership. Their populations are mostly of European or mixed European/Negro descent, with admixtures of Asian and Indian blood. A small population of Arawak Indians remains in the hinterland of Aruba.

Resources and Economics
The northern group, damp and fertile, grow much of their own food as well as cotton, sugar and potatoes for export and inter-island trading. St Maarten is also a tourist resort. The drier southern islands export aloes for medicinal use; Curaçao grows a few oranges for the manufacture of its famous liqueur. Aruba and Curaçao have good port facilities and large oil-refineries, which process crude oil (mainly from nearby Venezuela) and hold the refined products available for bunkering or transport. Both cater also for tourists, mainly from Venezuela and the USA. Bonaire is less developed, with small textile and tourist industries; much of its male population finds work on neighbouring islands.

Recent Developments
Relying heavily on oil and tourism, the Netherlands Antilles have been hard hit by world recession, though they remain among the more prosperous of the Caribbean islands. Their main alternative sources of funds, the Netherlands government and European Development Fund, provide substantial development aid each year. Aruba has begun a slow transition towards separate status and ultimate independence.

St Lucia

The Country
Central to the Windward Islands, St Lucia lies 140 km (87 miles) west–northwest of Barbados and 30 km (19 miles) south of Martinique. *Area* 616 km² (238 sq miles); *capital* Castries; *population* 130,000 (est. 1986).

Organization
An independent democracy within the British Commonwealth, St Lucia is

governed by a Governor-General (appointed by and representing the British Sovereign), an 11-member appointed Senate and a 17-member elected House of Representatives. Executive powers are held by a cabinet of nine ministers, headed by a Prime Minister. Roman Catholicism is the dominant religion, English the official language, with a French–English patois widely spoken.

Geography
Volcanic in origin, St Lucia is made up of craters and high lava ridges, deeply incised by fast-flowing streams. Mt Gimie (959 m, 3145 ft) is the highest of several small but spectacular peaks. Fumaroles and warm springs enliven the southern end of the island. The climate is warm, with constant trade winds and abundant rainfall, especially in the mountains. The uplands and ravines remain well wooded, the lowland flats are mostly under cultivation.

History and Development
Discovered during the late-15th-century Spanish exploration of the Caribbean, St Lucia was stoutly defended against European incursions by its Carib Indian inhabitants. Where British settlers tried and failed, French planters gained a foothold, starting a colony in 1650. St Lucia suffered depredations at British hands during the wars of the 18th century, and was finally ceded to Britain in 1814. Throughout the 19th and early 20th centuries its fortunes rose and fell with those of its single product, cane sugar. It was a member of the Federation of the West Indies 1958–62 and of the West Indies Associated States between 1967 and 1979, when it achieved full self-government.

Resources and Economics
With rich soils and year-round rainfall, St Lucia's is a strongly agricultural economy. Bananas, coconuts and other plantation crops have displaced cane sugar as the principal export, though the plantations have not yet fully recovered from damage inflicted by hurricanes in 1980. Smallholders raise food crops, and fishing contributes to the islanders' diet. Helped by foreign investment, food-processing and other light manufacturing industries are growing in importance and providing much-needed employment. The tourist industry is expanding rapidly; the island has adequate roads, good air links through its international airport, and improving port facilities.

Recent Developments
St Lucia maintains political stability and a democratic government, and enjoys the confidence of Commonwealth, European and other funding agencies that are helping to develop its economic potential.

St Vincent and the Grenadines

The Country
St Vincent lies centrally in the Windward Islands, 160 km (100 miles) west of Barbados and 48 km (30 miles) south of St Lucia. Administratively it is linked with Bequia, Canouan, Mustique, Union and other small islands of the northern Grenadines group, which lie to the south. *Area* 388 km² (150 sq miles); *capital* Kingstown; *population* 138,000 (est. 1986).

Organization

A 'special member' of the British Commonwealth, St Vincent and the Grenadines is a parliamentary democracy. Head of State is the Governor-General, appointed by and representing the British Sovereign. There is a House of Assembly of 6 appointed senators and a lower house of 4 elected representatives; an executive cabinet of about 8 ministers is headed by the Prime Minister. Protestant Christianity is the dominant religion, English the official language.

Geography

St Vincent, some 29 km (18 miles) long and 16 km (10 miles) across, rises in a series of forested ranges to the Soufrière, a central peak 1234 m (4048 ft) high. The rocks are mainly volcanic; Soufrière erupted with devastating effect in 1821, 1902–3, and most recently in 1979. The climate is warm and moist, with high rainfall on the uplands. Much of the available lowland, formerly forested, is now cultivated.

History and Development

Discovered in 1498 by Columbus, St Vincent was claimed by Britain in the early 17th century. It remained uncolonized by Europeans until 1773, when British colonists planted sugar-cane using imported slave labour. The indigenous Carib Indians, confined to reserves at the northern end of the island, were incited by French interests in 1795 to revolt against the planters; their revolt was suppressed and many were killed or deported. Despite continuing French hostility and a succession of damaging hurricanes, the colony prospered on exports of sugar; after the emancipation of the slaves in 1834 the plantations continued to flourish using indentured East Indian labour, and most of the islanders today are of mixed European, East Indian and Negro descent. From 1958 to 1962 St Vincent and its neighbours formed part of the West Indies Federation. It became a self-governing Associated State of the UK in 1969 and achieved full independence in 1979.

Resources and Economics

St Vincent is predominantly agricultural, producing much of its own food on smallholdings; bananas, arrowroot, coconuts and spices are grown for export. The volcanic upheavals of 1979 and the hurricanes of the following year partly destroyed the banana plantations. Small manufacturing industries, helped by financial aid from overseas, produce cement, furniture, flour and other consumable goods, mostly for local use. Roads are adequate for the islanders' needs; inter-island shipping and air links are improving slowly, stimulated by a small but expanding tourist industry.

Recent Developments

St Vincent and the Grenadines is hampered by lack of capital with which to diversify its agriculture and industries, and dogged by more than its fair share of natural misfortunes. Nevertheless, it retains political stability and the confidence of overseas investors, including the IMF whose all-important contributions help to keep it financially stable.

SOUTH AMERICA

Argentina

The Country

The Argentine Republic (Argentina) occupies much of the southeastern flank of South America from the Tropic of Capricorn to Tierra del Fuego. In the north it borders Bolivia and Paraguay, in the northeast Brazil and Uruguay, and in the west Chile. Tierra del Fuego is divided between Chile and Argentina, with islands in the Beagle Channel disputed; Argentina also claims the Falkland Islands (Islas Malvinas). *Area* 2,766,889 km² (1,068,297 sq miles); *capital* Buenos Aires; *population* 29,013,000 (est. 1986).

Organization

Argentina is governed by an elected National Congress consisting of a 46-member Senate and a 192-member House of Deputies; senators are elected for terms of nine years, representatives for four years. An executive President is elected for six-year terms. The country's twenty-two provinces are governed by their own elected legislatures under elected governors. Between 1966–73 and 1976–1982 Argentina was at all levels under military rule; elections in October 1983 restored constitutional government under a civilian president. The population is mostly of European origin. Roman Catholicism is the dominant religion, Spanish the official language.

Geography

South America's second largest country, Argentina occupies the southeast sector of the continent from the Chaco (22°S) to its southern tip (55°S). Its northern boundary follows the Pilcomayo River through subtropical forests and grasslands; in the northeast the boundary with Uruguay follows the Uruguay River south, through the damper, richer grasslands of Entre Rios. West of the Paraná River lie the pampas, the fertile plains on which much of Argentina's prosperity has been built; these continue south of the La Plata estuary into Patagonia. The long western frontier follows the Andean watershed from the dry northern heights of Puna de Atacama to the lower, heavily-glaciated mountains and valleys of the far south. The Uspallata Pass (3800 m, 12,470 ft), the most important of several trans-Andean passes, links Mendoza with the Pacific at Valparaiso in Chile by road and railway. Above it tower Argentina's highest peaks, including ice-capped Aconcagua, at 6960 m (22,835 ft) the highest in the southern hemisphere. In the north the Andes overshadow the high, semi-desert plains of the Gran Chaco; in the south they merge more gently with Patagonia's dry uplands. Argentina's climates range from dry and windswept on the central plains to frigid and storm-bound in the far south. Flora and fauna are diverse; there is a distinctive variety of wildlife including mountain guanacos, llamas, rheas, penguins, parrots, armadillos, chinchillas and sea-lions.

History and Development

Originally the home of a variety of Indian peoples, Argentina was settled by Spanish adventurers who moved into the north across the Andes during the early 16th century, simultaneously opening the La Plata area from the sea.

Buenos Aires, founded originally in 1536, was destroyed by Indians; re-settled in 1580, it became the capital of a Spanish viceroyalty covering present-day Uruguay, Paraguay, southern Bolivia and Argentina. In 1810, following Napoleon's occupation of Spain, the La Plata viceroyalty set up its own government, declaring independence six years later as the United Provinces of the Rio de la Plata. Unsettled years followed: what are now Paraguay, Bolivia and Uruguay broke away, royalists in the north fought against the new republican authority in Buenos Aires, federalists fought unionists over the division of power between central and provincial governments, and Indians fought for life and lands. But with the arrival of the first regular steampacket service between Buenos Aires and England in 1851, the first railway in 1857, the opening up of the pampas after the ending of the Indian Wars in 1879, and the final move towards the establishment of a federal republic in 1880, Argentina attracted large numbers of settlers and foreign capital for development. Exports of beef and wheat reached enormous quantities and confirmed Buenos Aires as the country's main port and largest city. Argentina grew quickly into South America's most populous and most prosperous Spanish-speaking country. Though constitutionally democratic, political tensions have kept it unstable and subject to alternating military and civilian dictatorships.

Resources and Economics
Argentina's prime wealth is its agriculture, which employs 15 per cent of the workforce and generates about 70 per cent of the country's overseas earnings. Cereals (notably wheat, maize, sorghum and barley) and meat are the main products exported; other farm produce includes linseed and sunflower oil, olives, grapes, ground-nuts, potatoes, rice, soya, cane and beet sugar, cotton and tobacco. Argentina is almost self-sufficient in timber and timber products. A quarter of a million tonnes of fish are caught annually offshore. Coal is one of the country's few commercially exploited minerals. More significant are oil and natural gas, found mainly offshore in southern Patagonia; Argentina aims toward fuel self-sufficiency in the 1980s. Hydroelectricity, currently providing 10 per cent of power needs, is capable of considerable expansion; nuclear power is also being developed to make use of large indigenous uranium deposits.

Manufacturing industries generate about one third of the country's wealth; products include cement, steel, chemicals, fertilizers, plastics, paper and wood-pulp. Argentina also produces automobiles, cotton goods and other consumables. Roads are plentiful though largely unpaved; river, rail and air links are adequate. Many tourists visit Argentina each year, and there is potential for a much larger tourist industry.

Recent Developments
Both military and civilian extravagances in recent decades have left Argentina heavily in debt to foreign banks and credit agencies. Scarred by the repressions of the Galtieri military regime (1981–2), and by its inefficiency in the 1982 Falkland Islands War, Argentinians have rejected both military dictatorship and its predecessor in government, the Peronist Party, electing instead a Radical-Party President. With good soils and climates, an energetic immigrant population, latent democratic traditions and strong national spirit, Argentina needs only political stability to develop its potential as South America's leading industrial power.

Bolivia

The Country
The Republic of Bolivia is a land-bound central state of South America, bordered by Peru and Chile in the west, Argentina and Paraguay in the south, and Brazil in the north and east. *Area* 1,098,581 km² (424,163 sq miles); *political capital, largest city and seat of government* La Paz, *legal capital and seat of the judiciary* Sucre (less than one tenth of the population of La Paz); *population* 6,547,000 (est. 1986).

Organization
Constitutionally democratic, with provision for an elected President and bicameral Congress, Bolivia suffers chronic political unrest. Elections of 1980 were set aside by a military junta; precarious democracy was restored in October 1982 with the re-opening of Congress and election of a civilian President. Local government is vested in nine departments, each divided into provinces and cantons. The people are mostly of indigenous Andean stock, with an admixture of Spanish. Roman Catholicism is the dominant religion; Spanish, Quechua and Aymará are all official languages.

Geography
Bolivia's western frontier runs along the high Cordillera Occidental of the Andes. Sajama, its highest peak (6520 m, 21,400 ft), is one of many ice-fringed volcanic mountains. To the east stands the Cordillera Real, a range of similar though slightly lower peaks. Between these ranges lies the Altiplano, a high plateau 3600 m (12,000 ft) above sea level and 400 km (250 miles) long, on which over half the country's population lives. East of the Andes broad foothill ranges give way to rolling plains, thinly-inhabited and underdeveloped; northward-flowing rivers converge to join the Guaporé, a southern tributary of the Amazon. Though well within the tropics the Andes and Altiplano have an alpine climate, supporting grassland and tundra vegetation. The northern foothills, hot and densely forested, grade southward into the cooler, drier semi-desert of the scrub-covered Chaco.

History and Development
The Altiplano, in particular Lake Titicaca, was a centre of early Indian culture; the region was already heavily populated by Aymará-speaking peoples in the 7th to 10th centuries. Quechua-speaking people from Cuzco in Peru brought Inca civilization into the area around 1200; the two societies lived uneasily together until 1538, when both fell to Spanish conquistadors. Spain's interest quickly focused on the mineral wealth of 'Upper Peru'. The huge silver reserves of Potosi were exploited, and most of the cities of the Altiplano, including Chuquisaca (now Sucre) and La Paz, were founded during the early years of Spanish settlement. 19th-century independence movements began in these cities, and General Sucre finally liberated Bolivia from imperial Spain in 1825. Underpopulated, undeveloped and politically unstable, Bolivia lost its seaboard province of Atacama to Chile in the War of the Pacific (1879–84), valuable rubber forests along its northern frontier to Brazil in 1903, and a section of southern frontier lands to Paraguay in 1935.

Resources and Economics
Some 40 per cent of Bolivians are involved in farming, producing one fifth of the national income. Land reforms in the Altiplano from 1953 divided most of the larger estates, and productivity increased on these unrewarding lands. Though potatoes, cane sugar, cereals, coffee and livestock are the main produce, Bolivia imports much of its food. Cotton is also grown; illegally-produced cocaine is far and away the country's most valuable agricultural product.

Although the silver that attracted the Spaniards is largely exhausted, it has been replaced by other metals this century, during which Bolivia has provided one fifth of the world's tin. Tin, together with other metals (notably tungsten, antimony, lead and gold), continue to provide 70 per cent of Bolivia's legitimate foreign exchange. Self-supporting in petroleum, Bolivia is developing natural gas for export; manufacturing industries remain small and serve only a local market. The road and railway system is fragmentary, and poor communications between the Altiplano and the Amazon lowlands hinder development.

Recent Developments
Hard hit by world depression, Bolivia's metal-based economy is virtually stagnant. Domestic inflation and foreign debts rise, with fiscal remedies introduced by the new government bringing little improvement. Unemployment runs high in cities and countryside alike, and political stability is again severely strained. Bolivians remain among South America's poorest citizens with no immediate hope of relief.

Brazil

The Country
The Federative Republic of Brazil occupies a huge eastern and central block of the continent. It shares boundaries with every other South American state except Ecuador and Chile, and includes the Atlantic islands of Fernando de Noronha and Trindade. *Area* 8,511,965 km² (3,286,473 sq miles); *capital* Brasilia, *largest city* São Paulo; *population* 140,344,000 (est. 1986).

Organization
Brazil's constitution provides for a 69-member Senate and a 479-member Chamber of Deputies; senators are elected for terms of eight years, deputies for four years. An executive President is elected through national and state legislatures for a six-year term, governing with the advice of a council of ministers. Brazil's armed forces currently safeguard the constitution. The twenty-three federated states, three federal territories and capital federal district each have elected governors and legislatures. Brazilians include a wide range of stocks – European, Asian, Negro and Indian, in every combination of colour and background. Roman Catholicism is the dominant religion, Portuguese the official language, with many local dialects spoken.

Geography
Occupying almost half continental South America, Brazil falls into two regions – basin and upland. The low-lying Amazon basin is dominated by the river systems of the Amazon and its many tributaries. The Amazon rises in the eastern Andes less than 200 km (125 miles) from the Pacific Ocean, collecting

South America

tributaries from the western basin and other major river systems, notably the Negro from the north and the Madeira and Tapajós from the south. Their combined waters make up about one fifth of the world's total river flow, carrying an enormous weight of sediment to the Amazon delta and beyond. All are navigable, allowing sea-going ships far into the country's heartland. The eastern uplands form a high tableland of ancient crystalline rocks, deeply dissected and worn. These fill the eastern bulge of the continent, ending in a spectacular escarpment overlooking the narrow lagoon-strung coast. In the south the uplands extend almost to the Uruguayan border, in the west to the Andean foothills. A comparable but much smaller tableland, the Guiana Highlands, occurs north of the Amazon.

Brazil's climate is tropical, hot and wet in the lowlands, cooler and drier on the uplands. The northern highlands are subject to drought. Dense forest with a rich tropical fauna covers most of the lowlands, grading to deciduous forest and savanna on high ground. There are extensive areas of wooded grassland and semi-deciduous forest to the south of the Amazon basin; in the far south, where there are winter frosts, prairie grasses and pine forests grow. Brazilian habitats are rich in insects (notably butterflies and beetles), tree-frogs, snakes, colourful birds, jaguars and other cats, monkeys, sloths, armadillos, ant-eaters and tapirs.

History and Development
First sighted by Vasco da Gama in 1498, Brazil was claimed by Portugal and penetrated mainly from the north and east coasts. Settlers brought cattle, sugar-cane and Negro slaves to Pernambuco (now Recife); Jesuits established missions far up the Amazon, while mining prospectors and slavers headed inland through the Bahia and Minas Gerais uplands. The nomadic Indians of the interior were abducted for farm work or killed. By the mid-18th century Portuguese-speaking communities were scattered throughout most of modern Brazil, and several of the river and coastal settlements, notably Rio de Janeiro, were already sizeable towns.

In 1808 the Portuguese court, driven from its homeland by Napoleon's invasion, moved to Rio de Janeiro. In 1822, shortly after the King had returned to Lisbon, his son Dom Pedro proclaimed Brazilian independence and was crowned Emperor in São Paulo. Under Dom Pedro and his son Dom Pedro II, who succeeded to the throne in 1840, Brazil developed as a federation. Political power was held by the wealthy landowners whose mines and plantations generated most of the country's income. Abolition of slavery in 1888 turned many against the Emperor; in 1889 the army also grew hostile to the Crown, and Dom Pedro II was deposed.

As a republic Brazil became more democratic, acquiring a constitution similar to that of the USA, attracting immigrants from Europe and advancing socially and economically, though its economy remained mainly rural. The dictatorships of Getúlio Vargas (1930–45, 1951–4) redistributed power in favour of the central government and diversified the economy, encouraging both agricultural and industrial development. In the decades following World War II, Brazil's economy boomed, the middle class grew and the industrial regions of the south became more prosperous. The gap between the wealthy and poorer regions was magnified under the military governments after 1964.

Resources and Economics
Agriculture employs one third of Brazil's workforce and generates about 40 per cent of its overseas earnings. Key exports include coffee, sugar, livestock, cocoa

beans and butter, vegetable oils, fruit-juice and tobacco; Brazilians also grow nuts, bananas, citrus fruit and many other tropical foods on smallholdings, and all the maize, beans, rice and cassava needed to meet internal demand. A campaign is under way to grow more wheat under irrigation. Hardwoods from the rain forests are being felled in quantities that dismay conservationists; all forests are exploited heavily, for wood is an important fuel over much of the countryside. A large fishing fleet takes almost a million tonnes of fish annually.

A major exporter of high-quality iron and manganese ores, Brazil also produces mica, high-grade quartz, chrome, lead, bauxite, tin, precious metals, coal, phosphate and many other useful minerals; huge reserves have been proved but remain undeveloped. Petroleum and natural gas, much of it from the continental shelf, supply one quarter of current needs. In a drive to reduce imports the country is developing a technology based on ethyl-alcohol, distilled from home-grown sugar and cassava. Hydroelectricity meets much of Brazil's electricity demands; output is growing from large-scale international projects on the Paraná River. Nuclear power is adding to the annual output. Manufacturing industries provide almost two thirds of Brazil's export earnings. Steel and other building materials, rubber, machinery (including automobiles), wood-pulp and paper are among the many goods produced. Road, rail and air routes link the main centres, and the major river systems carry up to 15 per cent of all cargoes. Over 1.2 million tourists visit Brazil each year, mainly from the Americas.

Recent Developments
Optimistic and ebullient, potentially one of the world's wealthiest countries, Brazil currently has huge debts. The buying power of the enormous population has grown more slowly than expected, especially in the rural areas of the north; Brazilians generally are still too poor to buy the goods their industries are producing, and the country has too little of value to sell beyond its borders. Although efforts are being made to diversify exports, two commodities, coffee and iron ore, control Brazil's economy. Despite rigorous domestic economies, including cuts in public spending, wage index reductions, currency devaluation and severe import restrictions, annual inflation continues to be in excess of 100 per cent. The long-standing external debt, incurred to build Brasilia and finance other grandiose schemes in the 1960s and 1970s, continues to grow. In the short term prospects are hard for all but the richest Brazilians. Only in the long term may its poorer citizens realize their share of this vast country's potential wealth.

Chile

The Country
The Republic of Chile occupies a narrow strip of western South America from latitude 17°S, sharing borders with Argentina, Bolivia and Peru. Included also are the Archipelago de Juan Fernández, San Félix, San Ambrosio, Sala-y-Gomez and Easter Island (see entry) in the southeastern Pacific Ocean. *Area* 756,945 km² (292,256 sq miles); *capital* Santiago; *population* 12,272,000 (est 1986).

Organization
Chile's most recent constitution provides for a directly-elected executive

President, who is responsible to an elected Senate and Chamber of Deputies. Currently, however, the country is ruled by a junta which took over from the last democratically-elected government in September 1973; elections are suspended for several years. Roman Catholicism is the dominant religion, Spanish the official language.

Geography

Coastal ranges form a long, narrow belt. In the north these rise above 3000 m (9800 ft); in the centre and south they are lower, in the far south breaking into isolated blocs separated or surrounded by sea channels. Behind the coastal mountains lies a central depression, 40 to 60 km (25 to 40 miles) wide, and rising to over 1200 m (4000 ft). Crossed by fast-flowing rivers, the alluvial soils in this central valley provide some of Chile's most fertile farmlands. Inland stand the cordilleras of the Andes, rising to a high central section that includes Ojos del Salado (6863 m, 22,517 ft) in Argentina and Llullaillaco (6723 m, 2058 ft). South of 40°S the mountains fall away, becoming heavily ice-capped and glaciated and curving eastward into Tierra del Fuego. Climatically the country includes the hot, dry Atacama desert in the north, a temperate central zone with a Mediterranean climate, and a cold, windy and wet southern zone. Plant cover ranges from nothing in the arid desert of the north to dense coastal rain forest on the southern islands. There is a small but interesting mammal fauna including llamas, guanacos, vicuna, alpacas and chinchillas; sea-lions and dense colonies of penguins and other sea-birds haunt the southwestern coast.

History and Development

Occupied originally by Amerindian tribes, Chile became a loosely-knit Spanish colony during the early 16th century, forming part of the Viceroyalty of Peru. Its breakaway from Spain began in 1810 with the establishment of a local government; Spanish forces were finally defeated in 1817 by a combined Chilean and Argentine force, leaving Chile independent under its first head of state, General Bernardo O'Higgins. Chile was ruled by a small oligarchy of landowners for most of the next hundred years. Rich nitrate deposits were exploited and added to in the War of the Pacific (1879–84) with the annexation of additional reserves beyond Chile's northern frontiers in Peru and Bolivia; the ports of Antofagasta and Iquique were developed to serve a rich trade which grew up with Europe. Central Chile's wealth accrued mainly from agricultural produce, exported to newly-developing California and Australia through Valparaiso. Basque, German and Italian immigrants in turn helped to diversify Chilean culture, producing by the early 20th century a stable and wealthy society, of mixed European and Indian background, living mainly in the central sector of the country.

Resources and Economics

The Chilean economy continues to centre on agriculture and mining. Agriculture has expanded and diversified following a programme of agrarian reform begun in 1967. Wheat and livestock, potatoes, sugar-beet, corn, fruit and wines are produced for both home consumption and export. Fishing has recently become an important industry in the north. Timber products, mainly from the southern forests, now account for some 10 per cent by value of Chilean exports. Copper, mined and smelted in the north, provides half the country's export earnings and one third of government revenues; silver, gold, molybdenum, nitrates and coal are also mined. Magellan's Strait has recently been tapped for large quantities of petroleum and natural gas, which currently meet about half the country's needs; hydroelectric power is being developed in an effort to meet all Chile's energy needs internally as soon as possible. Manufacturing industries, based mainly on metals, timber, leather, petrochemicals and other indigenous resources, have declined in consequence of the world recession; building especially has declined with the general loss of buoyancy in the economy. Road and rail networks are adequate as far south as Puerto Montt on the mainland and Quellóna on Chiloé Island; trans-Andean routes provide links with neighbouring countries. There are several international airports and a well-developed internal air transport network.

Recent Developments
Following a brief spell of government by an elected left-wing coalition under Marxist leadership, Chile was subject to a brutal military coup in 1973. A new constitution of 1980 provided for the return of democracy with free congressional and presidential elections in 1989. Up to 1981 the country enjoyed economic stability and considerable economic growth, but world economic conditions have since deteriorated, and resulted in devaluation, inflation and a rise in unemployment. However, Chile remains stable under a stern regime, its basic wealth of minerals and agriculture keeping it viable.

Colombia

The Country
The Republic of Colombia occupies the northwestern corner of South America, bounded by Panama to the north, Venezuela to the east, Brazil to the southeast, Peru and Ecuador to the south. It has both Caribbean and Pacific coasts. *Area* 1,138,914 km² (439,735 sq miles); *capital* Bogotá; *population* 29,325,000 (est. 1986).

Organization
A Senate of 112 members and House of Representatives of 199 members (both elected for four-year terms) are responsible for legislation; an executive President, also elected four-yearly, governs with the advice of a 14-member cabinet. Local government is vested in twenty-two departments and the Distrito Especial of Bogotá, each with an appointed governor. The population is mostly mixed Amerindian and European, with a wealthy white minority. Most Colombians are Roman Catholic; the official language is Spanish.

Geography
Three diverging fingers of the Andes subdivide western Colombia. From the hot Pacific coastal plain the forested Cordillerra Occidental rises steeply to heights of over 2000 m (6600 ft). Behind this, separated by the long valley of the Cauca River, tower the much higher volcanic peaks of the Cordillera Central; Huila, highest of all, rises to a snow-capped 5750 m (18,865 ft). Eastward again lies the Magdalena river valley, beyond it the longer and broader Cordillera Oriental, which spreads centrally in a series of high plateaus and basins; here on a lofty shelf at 2610 m (8563 ft) stands the capital city. Northwest of the mountains the two valleys open onto a rolling plain, crossed by several rivers that drain into the Caribbean. The eastern half of the country falls gently away

from the Andes toward the Orinoco river basin in the northeast and the Negro and Amazon basins in the east and south. Colombia's lowlands are hot and sultry especially along the coasts; its uplands, where most of the population lives, are drier and cooler. Tropical forests clothe most of the lowlands. The drier upland forests and meadows have been partly cleared for cultivation, though much wild country remains.

History and Development

When Spanish conquistadors arrived in the early 16th century Colombia was settled by Amerindians. As Spanish influence and settlements spread, many thousands of Indians were displaced: Negro slaves were brought in to work the plantations and Indians became peasant workers on the ranches. Colombia formed the centre of the Viceroyalty of New Granada, administered from Santa Fe de Bogatá. During three centuries of Spanish rule local power shifted gradually to creoles (locally-born whites), who by the early 19th century came to resent the bureaucratic control of the Spanish homeland. The breakaway began when Napoleon I occupied Spain and contact with the colonies was lost; independence came in 1819 when Venezuelan liberator Simón Bolívar crossed the northern Andes from the Orinoco River, defeating Spanish imperial forces at Boyacá, close to Bogotá. Gran Colombia (present-day Colombia, Ecuador, Panama and Venezuela), the successor to New Granada, soon split up; Venezuela separated in 1829 and Ecuador the following year (Panama in 1903). Colombia's subsequent history has been characterized by violence between rival political parties, with frequent revolutions and civil wars.

Resources and Economics

Predominantly agricultural, Colombia employs about one third of its workforce on the land, generating between one fifth and one quarter of its national income. Coffee and bananas are the main exports, between them accounting for almost two thirds of Colombia's overseas earnings. Cotton, sugar and cut flowers are also exported; rice, beans, maize, wheat, potatoes, tobacco and many other crops are produced for local consumption; the country is virtually self-supporting for food. Minerals are plentiful but undeveloped; Colombia produces increasing amounts of nickel, iron, gold, silver and platinum, and is an important source of emeralds. There are enormous reserves of coal, more modest, proven reserves of oil and natural gas; hydroelectric power has enormous potential for expansion. At the present time domestic coal meets a little under one quarter of Colombia's energy requirements, local oil a little under one half, natural gas one fifth, and hydroelectricity the rest. Manufacturing industries are limited, mostly supplying local consumer markets. Roads and railways are barely adequate; internal air transport is well developed. The Magdalena River is an important waterway navigable for 1400 km (900 miles) up-country.

Recent Developments

Potentially wealthy, Colombia's development is hampered by a remarkably high birth rate and lack of indigenous capital. Economically it remains overdependent on a single crop – coffee – and is seeking to diversify, notably by developing virtually untapped mineral resources. Politically unstable due to chronic inter-party rivalries, it currently appears to be enjoying an unusual spell of domestic harmony and cooperation, from which its citizens must all ultimately benefit. Despite setbacks it retains the confidence of international investors and sources of funding, and may expect a brighter future.

Ecuador

The Country
The Republic of Ecuador lies across the Equator on the Pacific flank of South America, bordered by Colombia in the north and Peru in the east and south; it includes the Galapagos Islands. *Area* 283,561 km² (109,483 sq miles); *capital* Quito, *largest city* Guayaquil; *population* 9,677,000 (est. 1986).

Organization
An executive President is responsible to a legislative 69-member Chamber of Representatives, both being elected by universal suffrage for five-year terms. There are twenty provinces, each under an appointed Governor. Ecuadoreans are mostly mixed European/Amerindian, with a wealthy white minority. Roman Catholicism is the dominant religion, Spanish the official language with Indian dialects widely spoken.

Geography
Ecuador is crossed centrally by the main cordillera of the northern Andes. To the west spreads the Costa, a broad cultivated plain on which about half the country's population lives. High and rolling in the north, it descends in the south to a lowland basin which broadens into the wide Gulf of Guayaquil. From the Costa the Andes rise steeply in serried, irregular chains to high peaks, many volcanic and some snow-capped. Chimborazo reaches 6267 m (20,562 ft) in the south; Cotopaxi (5896 m, 19,344 ft) overlooks the capital city, itself at over 2800 m (9000 ft). East of the mountains Ecuador falls away to the Oriente, a heavily-forested and little-developed region dissected by rivers that flow eastward into the Amazon. Hot and humid in the lowlands, Ecuador has a bracing mountain climate.

History and Development
Part of the Inca Empire, with a long history of pre-Inca settlement, Ecuador fell to Spanish invaders in the mid-16th century. Except for the port of Guayaquil, the hot, unhealthy Costa remained empty; colonial settlements arose mainly in the Andes where Spanish landlords built up large estates worked by Indians under peonage (serfdom). Within the Viceroyalty of New Granada, Ecuador remained Spanish for over three hundred years. Ruling creoles (locally-born whites) began a breakaway movement early in the 19th century, attaining freedom in 1822 as a result of the campaigning of Simón Bolívar and Antonio José de Sucre. Linked initially with Colombia, Venezuela and Panama, Ecuador separated in 1830. Strong political factions, based mainly on rivalry between the mountain communities and Guayaquil, kept the new state divided for well over a century and still dominate Ecuadorean politics.

Resources and Economics
Agriculture employs about half the workforce and generates over a fifth of national income. Bananas, coffee, cocoa, vegetable oils, cane sugar, rice, maize and cotton, grown on the Costa, are exported through Guayaquil; potatoes, cereals, beans and livestock from the sierras provide staple foods. There is a growing fishing industry. Forestry and mining are underdeveloped and capable of expansion. Oil from Oriente province, exploited since 1972, has revolutionized the country's economy. Shifted by trans-montane pipeline to the

port and refinery centre of Esmeraldas, it has for several years provided almost half Ecuador's export earnings. Less is now sold, but it still reduces Ecuador's import bill and provides new capital for development. Hydroelectric power contributes a growing proportion of the country's energy needs. Manufacturing industries, developing slowly, include textiles, food-processing and a few domestic consumer items. Road, rail and internal air links barely cope with the increased demands of Ecuador's growing economy.

Recent Developments
After long stagnation, Ecuador's economy has begun to develop, stimulated mainly by oil revenues. These have provided the capital that has helped to reduce the country's dependence on agriculture, and promoted a more rewarding mixture of industrial output and export products. The current five-year plan for economic development includes provision for more hydroelectric energy, the development of promising natural-gas fields in the Gulf of Guayaquil and the Oriente, and major petrochemical and steel works, all of which will reduce dependence on imports. The new prosperity seems to have moderated political differences between highland and lowland communities, helping to maintain stability.

French Guiana

The Country
One of South America's smallest countries, French Guiana lies centrally on the north coast, bounded in the west by Suriname and in the south and east by Brazil. *Area* 91,000 km² (35,135 sq miles); *capital* Cayenne; *population* 77,000 (est. 1986).

Organization
An Overseas Department of France, French Guiana is governed by a French-appointed Commissioner who is advised by a locally-elected Council-General of 16 members. It is represented in the French National Assembly by a senator and a deputy. Local authority is administered through two arrondissements. Most of the population are creoles, with European, Amerind and Negro minorities. Roman Catholicism is the dominant religion, French the official language, with creole patois and Indian languages widely spoken outside the towns.

Geography
A broad expanse of heavily-forested rolling country between the Oyapock and Maroni rivers, French Guiana rises almost imperceptibly from coastal mangrove swamps to a range of uplands at 200 to 500 m (650 to 1600 ft) in the south. The highest point, Mitaraka (690 m, 2263 ft), stands in Sierra Tumucumaque in the southwestern corner on the Suriname border. Deep river gorges dissect the ancient quartzites and sandstones that underlie the forest. The climate is hot and humid, cooled intermittently by trade winds.

History and Development
Part of a coast discovered by Columbus in 1493, French Guiana was first colonized by French traders who settled in 1626 on the Sinnamary River and in

1635 on the offshore island of Cayenne. Several attempts during the 18th century to bring more settlers to this difficult, fever-ridden coast ended in disaster; the interior, occupied by Inini Indians, remained relatively untouched. Sugar plantations thrived in the early 19th century but failed when slavery ended in 1848. In 1852 the colony was made a penal settlement for hardened criminals from France. Several prison settlements were established on the mainland and the Îles du Salut, including the notorious Île du Diable (Devil's Island). The prisons were closed in 1945; in the following year French Guiana became an Overseas Department.

Resources and Economics
French Guiana produces manioc, maize, rice, sugar-cane and many vegetables, mostly for local consumption. Locally-caught and processed shrimps are the most valuable export. The extensive forests yield a little timber; mining is desultory, mainly for gold. Roads are limited to the coast and mostly primitive: rivers allow access for a few kilometres inland, and there are adequate air and sea links with the outside world.

Recent Developments
Bolstered by metropolitan France, French Guiana has developed little since its colonial days, and seems to have little ambition to develop further.

Guyana

The Country
The Cooperative Republic of Guyana lies centrally on the northern coast of South America, bounded by Venezuela in the west, Brazil in the south and Suriname in the east. *Area* 214,969 km^2 (83,000 sq miles); *capital* Georgetown; *population* 998,000 (est. 1986).

Organization
A legislative National Assembly includes 53 elected and 12 other members; the leader of the majority party becomes the President, who is advised by an appointed cabinet of 5 Vice-Presidents (one of whom is Prime Minister) and about 25 ministers. Various Christian denominations are well represented; the official language is English, with Hindi, Urdu and local dialects widely spoken.

Geography
Behind Guyana's mangrove coast lies swampy ground, backed by forested plains and upland savanna. In the far south the Rupununi savannas mark the watershed with the Amazon basin and rise to almost 500 m (1640 ft). The highlands of the west rise more steeply in sandstone escarpments to the Pakaraima Mountains; Mt Roraima, at the boundary of Brazil, Venezuela and Guyana, stands 2810 m (9220 ft) above sea level. The major rivers, navigable in the lowlands, cascade from the mountains in spectacular waterfalls. Coastlands are humid, with heaviest rains from April to August; highlands are cooler with occasional droughts.

History and Development
Discovered by Columbus in 1498, the Guyanese coast and the banks of

navigable rivers were settled by French, British and Dutch traders. The Dutch West Indian Company first settled Guyana in the early 17th century, growing sugar-cane in coastal plantations. Three of their colonies, Demerara, Essequibo and Berbice were twice taken over by British forces in 1781 and 1796 and twice returned. Finally ceded to Britain in 1814, they became the colony of British Guiana. Though gold and diamonds were mined in the interior, sugar, molasses and rum provided the main revenues. Independence within the Commonwealth came in 1966. The townspeople are mostly Negro, the labourers on the sugar estates and in the rice paddy-fields of East Indian descent; half the population is indigenous Amerindian.

Resources and Economics
Over 80 per cent of Guyana's workforce is employed in farming, mainly on the rich, well-watered lowlands. They generate about one quarter of the country's wealth, growing cane sugar, rice, coffee, coconuts, tropical fruit and vegetables. Rivers and coastal waters provide good fishing. Over 80 per cent of the country is forested, though only a small proportion is economically exploitable. Gold and diamonds are still extracted, but bauxite has become the most important single mineral – converted to alumina it contributes almost as much as agriculture towards the national income. Most roads and railways are coastal; river transport and airstrips are important for communications with the interior, and there is an international airport near Georgetown.

Recent Developments
Long famous for sugar and rum, Guyana still depends heavily on sugar and only a few other products (notably rice and bauxite) for its overseas earnings. Well endowed with forests, water-power and possibly oil, shortage of capital currently inhibits its development. The province of Essequibo is claimed by Venezuela and a joint commission is seeking to resolve this long-standing dispute.

Paraguay

The Country
The land-locked Republic of Paraguay lies in the southern half of South America, between Brazil in the east, Argentina in the southwest and Bolivia in the north. *Area* 406,752 km² (157,047 sq miles); *capital* Asuncion; *population* 3,789,000 (est. 1986).

Organization
Nominally a democracy, Paraguay has a bicameral National Congress including a 30-member Senate and 60-member Chamber of Deputies, both elected for five-year terms. It is effectively ruled by its executive President, who is also elected for five-year terms. He appoints the cabinet and can govern by decree through the Council of State when the National Congress is in recess. For local administration the country is divided into an Occidental and an Oriental province, each subdivided into departments. Most of the population is of native Guaraní descent. The dominant religion is Roman Catholicism, Spanish is the official language, with Guaraní widely spoken.

Geography

Paraguay lies on either side of the Paraguay River, roughly two thirds to the west (Occidental) and one third to the east (Oriental). Rivers mark most of its borders – the Paraguay itself to north and south, the Apa in the northeast, the Paraná in the southeast and the Pilcomayo in the southwest. The eastern highlands are a plateau of old, worn-down crystalline rocks 350 to 600 m high (1100 to 2000 ft), forested and separated from the Brazilian uplands by the Paraná river valley. The western plains rise gently from a wide marshy basin to the savanna of the Chaco Boreal, some 500 m (1600 ft) high at the Bolivian border. Paraguay is generally warm and dry, with poorly-defined seasons; the Chaco is semi-arid and subject to drought.

History and Development

Paraguay was thinly settled by Amerindians when exploring Spaniards found it in the early 16th century. Establishing Asunción in 1537, the conquerors spread across the uplands, enrolling the Indians as peons (serfs) on their estates. Part of the Viceroyalty of Rio de la Plata, Paraguay gained independence from Spain in 1811 and from Buenos Aires two years later, falling almost immediately under a rigid dictatorship which isolated the country from its neighbours. Re-emerging in 1852, Paraguay developed rapidly towards industrialization under a liberal regime. However, a disastrous territorial war with Argentina, Brazil and Uruguay (1865–70) resulted in the loss of tens of thousands of men and substantial slices of borderland. There followed some eighty years of political anarchy, which ended in 1954 with the assumption of dictatorial power by General Alfredo Stroessner. In 1932–5 Paraguay fought the Chaco War against her neighbour Bolivia, gaining territory but suffering heavy losses.

Resources and Economics

Agriculture is Paraguay's mainstay, occupying over half the workforce and providing a third of the country's income. Cotton, soya beans, vegetable oils, tobacco and livestock products are exported, and Paraguay produces most of its own food. Timber also brings in overseas funds. Mining contributes comparatively little to the exchequer. Oil and gas are exploited on a small scale. The main industries are construction, food-processing and small-scale manufacturing for domestic markets. Hydroelectric energy is Paraguay's principal asset, realized by the recent opening of a complex of power stations (the world's largest) developed in cooperation with Brazil at Itaipú, on the Paraná River. Further stations are being built at Yacireta on the Argentinian border. Road, rail and air links, coupled with river transport, are adequate for the country's current needs.

Recent Developments

After generations of stagnation, Paraguay's economy seems about to take off, stimulated by growing revenues from sales of hydroelectric energy to neighbouring countries. Though in terms of income per capita Paraguay is still one of South America's poorest countries, the agricultural potential of the Chaco and the minerals of the highlands provide promise for future development; much will depend on whether political stability ensues when Stroessner's authority declines.

Peru

The Country
The Republic of Peru extends along the central west coast of South America and across the Andes into the Amazon basin, bounded in the south by Chile, in the east by Bolivia and Brazil and in the north by Colombia and Ecuador. *Area* 1,285,216 km² (496,222 sq miles); *capital* Lima; *population* 20,855,000 (est. 1986).

Organization
Peru's current constitution provides for a 60-member Senate, 180-member Chamber of Deputies and an executive President, all elected simultaneously for five-year terms; the President is aided by a council of about 16 ministers. For local government the country is divided into 24 departments. Peruvians are mostly mestizo (European/Indian) with admixtures of Negro, Asian and other races. Roman Catholicism is the dominant religion, Spanish the official language with many Indian languages spoken.

Geography
The narrow western seaboard, normally dry but subject to torrential downpours, is crossed by the ravines of many fast-flowing rivers. Behind stand foothills of the Andes, hot, damp and heavily forested, rising from 500 to 2500 m (1650 to 8200 ft) and higher to form the Cordillera Occidental. The Cordillera is narrowest in the north and widens southwards. It includes the Sierra – a wide upland belt of grassy hills and plains. Once the centre of Inca and earlier civilizations, it remains Peru's most densely-populated region. Higher still is the wind-blasted Altiplano, at 4000 to 5000 m (13,100 to 16,400 ft) among the world's highest farmland. The peaks of the Peruvian Andes are mostly volcanic and permanently snow-capped; Huascaran, in a central bloc only 80 km (50 miles) from the coast, rises to 6768 m (22,206 ft). East of the Andes Peru falls away rapidly to forested uplands in the south and the jungles of the Amazon basin in the north. Climates range from scorching desert along the coast to glacial in the mountains, from warm and moist in the cloud-forest to the dry chill of the Altiplano. Earthquakes are frequent in the mountains.

History and Development
Tribal Amerindians of the Peruvian region developed distinctive cultures for mountains, forests and plains. Following the arrival of the Spanish under Pizarro in 1532, many Indians were slaughtered or enslaved, their cities and mines looted of precious metals and their lands sequestered. Under Spanish domination until 1824, Peru's ruling creoles welcomed the liberating armies of Antonio José de Sucre and Simón Bolívar. Independence brought a succession of dictatorships, military and civilian, that continued through the mid-to-late 19th century. Joint loser with Bolivia in the War of the Pacific (1879–84), Peru forfeited its southern coastal provinces with their valuable nitrate deposits to Chile; Lima was sacked, and bankruptcy staved off only when valuable assets were handed over to international creditors. Chronically poor, Peru fell behind its neighbours in the race to industrialize and modernize its economy. The early 20th century brought little improvement, feudalism, political instability and lack of capital obstructing progress. Overseas investment helped change the scene from the 1960s onward.

Resources and Economics

Although almost half the workforce are farmers, productivity is low; agriculture yields only about 10 per cent of the national income and Peru imports much of its food. Sugar, coffee and cotton are exported from the lowlands, wool (including alpaca and vicuña) from the highlands. The anchovy bonanza of the early 1970s, making Peru the world's leading producer of fish-meal, collapsed in 1977 from overfishing; current output is less than 8 per cent of peak value. When demand is high, mining yields 8 to 10 per cent of national income and over 40 per cent of export income: copper, zinc, lead and iron provide the greatest bulk; silver, gold and many other metals are mined in smaller quantities. Petroleum from the eastern uplands, crossing the Andes by pipeline to coastal ports and refineries, is exported. Manufacturing industries grew in the 1970s but have since stagnated; Peru produces cement, steel, refined metals, paper, industrial chemicals, textiles, leather and a small range of consumer goods, including automobiles. Road, rail and air links are adequate for the present needs of the widely-dispersed population.

Recent Developments

Peru's long-stagnant economy, enlivened briefly by revenues from fish-meal and petroleum, is currently in recession. Overdependence on a small range of goods (notably metal ores and petroleum) in depressed world markets may be a basic cause, but Peru has long been plagued by social inequalities, feudal management of land, inept dictatorships and a burgeoning population for which little provision has been made. With massive foreign debts, high unemployment and inflation, and an economy currently demanding austerity, social unrest is apparent. Economic relief in the near future seems unlikely, and the political stability of an uncertain democracy is once again at risk.

Suriname

The Country

The Republic of Suriname lies centrally on South America's northern coast, sharing boundaries with Guyana in the west, French Guiana in the east and Brazil to the south. *Area* 163,265 km^2 (63,037 sq miles); *capital* Paramaribo; *population* 460,000 (est. 1986).

Organization

Since 1980 Suriname has been governed by a National Military Council, advised by a small council of ministers, which was replaced in 1984 with a civilian interim government. Local affairs are administered through nine districts. Christianity, Hinduism and Islam are well represented. Most of the population are creoles, Asians or Indonesians, with smaller numbers of Negroes and Amerindians. The official language is Dutch, but Hindustani, Javanese, Chinese, Spanish and local languages are widely spoken.

Geography

Between the Corentyne and Maroni rivers, Suriname rises gently from a low marshy coast to a dissected plateau of crystalline rocks; finger-like ridges of grassland and savanna alternate with forested river valleys. Higher ranges in the south rise above 1000 m (3300 ft); Julianatop in the southwest stands at 1280 m

(4200 ft). Suriname is hot, but trade winds cool the coast and high interior. The coast is wet, especially in December, May and June; the interior is drier, especially in February and March.

History and Development
Part of the Caribbean coast discovered in 1498 by Columbus, Suriname was originally occupied by hostile forest Indians. British, Dutch and French traders settled in the mid-17th century, the British planting sugar-cane. In 1667 the Dutch accepted the colony from Britain in exchange for relinquishing North American possessions (including New York), and characteristically proceeded to drain and farm the coastal marshes. Captured by Britain and France during the late 18th century, Dutch Guiana was returned to the Netherlands in 1815. The colony became self-governing in 1954 and independent in 1975.

Resources and Economics
Agriculture thrives; Suriname grows most of its own food including rice, cane sugar, bananas, maize, oranges, palm oil and coffee. Tropical hardwoods, and locally caught and processed shrimps, contribute slightly to overseas earnings. Iron, nickel, manganese, copper and other ores are mined; the most important mineral is bauxite, some of which is converted to alumina and aluminium using local hydroelectric power. Bauxite and its derivatives provide 80 per cent of Suriname's export earnings. Hydroelectric power is being developed. Roads or river transport link the main settlements, and there is an international airport.

Recent Developments
Endowed by the Netherlands with a substantial fund to aid development, Suriname is currently expanding agriculture, forestry, fishing and hydroelectric power, and seeking to reduce its dependence on bauxite. Shortage of manpower hampers development; roughly half the Suriname population, including most of its skilled workers, has migrated to the Netherlands. Political power rests with a left-wing military group, though successive coups weaken its control and maintain chronic instability.

Trinidad and Tobago

The Country
The Republic of Trinidad and Tobago consists of the island of Trinidad, off the coast of Venezuela, and its smaller neighbour Tobago to the northeast. *Areas* Trinidad 4830 km^2 (1865 sq miles), Tobago 300 km^2 (116 sq miles); *capital* Port of Spain (Trinidad); *population* 1,269,000 (est. 1986).

Organization
Parliament includes a Senate, a House of Representatives and a President. The 36 representatives are elected for five-year terms. The 31 senators are partly appointed by the President, partly with the advice of government and opposition leaders; the President is elected by representatives of both houses. A Prime Minister and small cabinet are responsible to Parliament. Tobago has its own 15-member House of Assembly. Most inhabitants are of Negro, Indian or European stock. Roman Catholicism is the dominant religion, English the official language; large Moslem and Hindu minorities maintain their own cultures and languages.

Geography

Roughly rectangular, Trinidad lies 14 km (9 miles) from the Venezuelan coast, separated by narrow channels. A high, forested range extends along the northern coast; Aripo, in the northwest, rises to 940 m (3084 ft). A lower range marks the south coast. Between them lies a fertile plain, crossed by a ridge rising a little over 330 m (1000 ft). Tobago, lying 29 km (18 miles) from Trinidad's northeast point, is a mountainous ridge some 42 km (26 miles) long, densely forested and rising to about 550 m (1800 ft) at its midpoint. Both islands are warm, with a humid wet season from June to December.

History and Development

Both islands were discovered by Columbus during his voyage of 1498. Spanish settlers occupied Trinidad in the 16th century, developing plantations with Negro slave labour. Attacked periodically by French, British and Dutch forces, Trinidad remained Spanish and attracted displaced settlers of several nations from other Caribbean colonies. In 1802 it was ceded to Britain under the Treaty of Amiens. Tobago was colonized by Dutch, English and French settlers, finally becoming British in 1814. It was linked administratively with the colony of Trinidad in 1899. Trinidad and Tobago became independent within the Commonwealth in 1962, and a separate republic in 1976.

Resources and Economics

Agriculture employs about 10 per cent of the workforce but contributes only about 3 per cent to the national income; once almost self-sufficient, the republic now imports three quarters of its food. Sugar was, and to some extent remains, an important export crop. Fishing and forestry provide mainly for local needs. Petroleum products, including natural gas, account for almost 90 per cent of exports. Steel, cement, industrial chemicals and some consumer goods are manufactured locally. Good roads link the main centres; Trinidad has deep-water port and international airport facilities. Tourism contributes significantly to employment and overseas earnings.

Recent Developments

Trinidad and Tobago have survived and modernized their economy on the strength of petroleum royalties; their high-grade product continues to be in demand despite world recession, and there are sound reserves of lower-grade petroleum as yet untapped. Economic growth is currently slow and unemployment remains a problem, but Trinidad and Tobago appear to have a sound base for a prosperous future.

Uruguay

The Country

The Eastern Republic of Uruguay lies north of the La Plata estuary on the Atlantic seaboard of South America, bounded in the west by Argentina and in the northeast by Brazil. *Area* 176,215 km^2 (68,037 sq miles); *capital* Montevideo; *population* 3,061,000 (est. 1986).

Organization

Uruguay's long record of democracy was broken in 1973 when, after civil unrest, the elected Congress was replaced by a military-dominated regime.

Government is currently upheld by a Council of State of 25 appointed members; together with 20 military officers these make up a Council of the Nation, which appoints the executive President. Parliamentary elections are promised for the near future. Most Uruguayans are descendants of European immigrants. Roman Catholicism is the dominant religion, Spanish the official language.

Geography

Southern Uruguay is a rolling plain, grass-covered and punctuated by ridges of ancient weathered rocks. Rising steadily towards the north, this merges into a higher sandy plateau, crossed by two north-to-south ridges – Cuchilla Grande in the east and Cuchilla de Haedo in the northwest – separated by the wide basin of the Negro River and its tributaries. Western plains drain towards the Uruguay River, which forms the country's western boundary. The eastern coastal plains are low-lying and sandy, ringed by saline lakes. Pleasantly subtropical in climate, Uruguay is warm and dry in summer, cool and moist in winter, with heavy rains only in autumn and early winter (April to June).

History and Development

When first sighted by Spanish maritime explorers in 1513 the north bank of the La Plata estuary was inhabited by warlike Charrúas Amerindians. Europeans avoided it until 1726, when Montevideo was founded by Spanish settlers from Buenos Aires to counter the Portuguese settlement of Colonia to the west. Possession of 'Banda Oriental del Uruguay' (land east of the Uruguay River) was disputed sporadically between Spain and Portugal. When the Spanish colonies achieved independence in the early 19th century Banda Oriental became an Argentine province; after struggles with both Brazil and Argentina, Uruguay's existence as an independent republic was confirmed in 1828 with the help of British mediation. Though hostility between rival Colorado and Blanco parties bedevilled politics well into the present century, Uruguay has achieved social reforms and until recently a level of democracy rare in South America.

Resources and Economics

Uruguay is mainly agricultural, employing about 15 per cent of its workforce on the land to generate about 15 per cent of national income. Livestock products, wheat, maize, sorghum, vegetable oils, rice and potatoes are the main crops, figuring large among its exports. Fishing is a growing industry, aimed mainly at export markets. Steel is produced for local use; food-processing and hide- and leather-processing are major industries. Poorly endowed with oil, coal or forest, Uruguay depends increasingly on indigenous hydroelectricity for power. Road and rail links are adequate for the country's needs; the Uruguay River carries a considerable volume of traffic, and Uruguay has excellent port and airport facilities. Tourism is a small but growing industry.

Recent Developments

With little more than agricultural produce to sell, Uruguay has difficulty in meeting payments for fuel and other necessities from overseas. Hydroelectric schemes developed internationally with Brazil and Argentina are expected to provide surplus power for export in the near future. Meanwhile the annual budget remains unbalanced, unemployment and inflation continue to run high, and this hitherto well-ordered, successful country is forced into borrowing to tide it over a difficult period.

Venezuela

The Country

The Republic of Venezuela is one of South America's two northernmost countries, bounded in the east by Guyana, in the south by Brazil and in the west by Colombia. Several offshore Caribbean islands are included. *Area* 912,050 km² (352,143 sq miles); *capital* Caracas; *population* 18,959,000 (est. 1986).

Organization

Venezuela is governed by an executive President and a bicameral National Congress made up of a Senate (49 members) and Chamber of Deputies (199 members), all elected for five-year terms; ex-Presidents also sit in the Senate. The President is advised by a council of about 26 ministers. The twenty constituent states each have an elected legislature and an executive governor appointed by the President; two thinly-populated territories and the capital are under federal management. Most of the population are mestizos, with European and Amerindian minorities. Roman Catholicism is the dominant religion, Spanish the official language with many Indian dialects spoken.

Geography

Western Venezuela includes an extension of Colombia's Cordillera Oriental which splits around Lake Maracaibo, the main cordillera turning eastward to form the north coast. Coastal ranges rise to over 2500 m (8200 ft); the inland Cordillera de Mérida rises twice as high to Pico Bolívar (5007 m, 16,428 ft) southeast of Maracaibo. Between the mountains and the Orinoco River spread the dry grassy plains and wooded lowlands of the Apure river basin; at a mean elevation of 350 m (1150 ft) they cover over a quarter of the country. The Orinoco delta is heavily forested, mangroves lining its maze of waterways. East of the Orinoco the land rises gently to the Guiana Highlands, a weathered granitic massif covered with thin soils and pasture. In the far south and along the Guyana border this rises over 2000 m (6500 ft). The climate is hot and generally humid. Along the coast trade winds exert a cooling and drying influence. Seasonal rains flood the plains from April to November; uplands and mountain areas are watered more evenly through the year.

History and Development

Columbus first saw Venezuela in 1498. Spanish settlers followed quickly, displacing the Amerindians to establish themselves at coastal settlements by the mid-16th century, and spreading inland to the healthier Andean uplands. Using Negroes and Indians as slaves and serfs, the Spanish raised food crops for themselves and sugar, tobacco and hides for export. Dutch, English, French and Portuguese traders settled during the 17th century, making Venezuela a Caribbean commercial centre. Locally-born whites (creoles) in 1810 took over government from the Spanish colonial masters, declaring independence a year later. Prolonged warfare ended with the defeat of imperial forces in 1821 at the hands of Simón Bolívar's creole army. For over a century successive caudillos from rival political parties ruled and prospered while the country as a whole remained underdeveloped. Exploitation of petroleum from Maracaibo in the early 20th century brought increased wealth, but mainly to the ruling families; only recently have moves towards democracy and a more general distribution of wealth begun.

Resources and Economics

About 20 per cent of the labour force is agricultural, bringing in about 6 per cent of the country's revenue; the cultivated area has recently increased but Venezuela still imports half its food. Coffee, wheat, maize, cocoa, tobacco and sugar are the main crops; horses, cattle and sheep range on the cool uplands, and the tropical forests yield timber, rubber and other crops. Minerals include gold, nickel, iron, manganese, copper and bauxite; coal, diamonds, phosphate, asbestos and sulphur are important non-metals. Petroleum and its products provide most of the country's income, including over 90 per cent of export earnings; reserves offshore and in the Orinoco valley promise a continuous flow well into the 21st century. Natural gas is tapped for domestic use, and hydroelectric power is drawn from the Caroni River. Venezuela produces cement, steel, aluminium, chemicals and processed foods; shipbuilding is a growing industry and many consumable goods (notably automobiles) are now manufactured. Road, river and air links provide excellent communications.

Recent Developments

Relying heavily on sales of oil, Venezuela's economy is currently depressed by the world recession. Attempts to diversify and improve farm output have had mixed success but should bring long-term benefits. Industrial development and diversification include increasing hydroelectric power output from the Caroni River and enhancement of an industrial complex at Ciudad Guayana, a growing centre on the Orinoco downstream from Ciudad Bolivar. Though the steady growth of earlier decades has halted, Venezuela remains one of South America's wealthiest countries, now with a more equable distribution of wealth and higher standard of living than most of its neighbours. Politically stable, with a growing middle class and proven record in economic planning, it has every chance of increasing prosperity when the recession passes.

Africa

Traversed by the Equator and both tropics, Africa covers an area of 29.73 million km^2 (11.48 million sq miles) and houses a population of 500 million. Across the north runs the Sahara desert, an arid waste crossed by the elongate oasis of the Nile valley, home of some of the world's earliest civilizations. South of the Sahara and the fringing semi-desert Sahel, increasing altitude and rainfall bring a variety of scenery, habitats and human cultures. In the west year-round tropical rains cover hills and plains impartially with a blanket of forest. In the east rises the cloud-capped tableland of Ethiopia, source of the Nile and home of an early Christian culture. To east and south, almost to the Cape of Good Hope, extends a broad, rolling plateau, generally drier but with seasonal rains that support a covering of grass and savanna. The home of wandering game and nomadic herdsmen, this parched land may also be the area in which *Homo sapiens* originated. Across the east runs a complex tension fracture, the still-widening Great Rift Valley, with its string of lakes and menacing volcanic peaks.

AFRICA NORTHWEST

Algeria

The Country
The Democratic and Popular Republic of Algeria lies on the western Mediterranean coast of north Africa, bounded in the east by Tunisia and Libya, in the south by Mali and Niger, and in the west by Mauritania, Morocco and a narrow sector of Western Sahara. *Area* 2,381,741 km^2 (919,591 sq miles); *capital* Algiers; *population* 23,403,000 (est. 1986).

Organization
A legislative 261-member National People's Assembly and an executive President are elected by popular vote for five-year terms. The President appoints a cabinet of about 26 ministers; a High Security Council is responsible for matters of state security. The Front de Libération Nationale (FLN) is the sole political party, dedicated to socialism. Local authority is vested in districts, subdivided into communes. The state religion is Islam; the official language is Arabic with French widely spoken in the cities, Berber in the villages.

Geography
Fold mountains extend from Morocco into northern Algeria, forming a high, inhospitable coast with cliffs and headlands. A few stretches of coastal plain occur where valleys meet the sea, some extending inland behind the coastal ridges. The mountains rise in a series of high ridges and plateaus to the peaks of the Saharan Atlas; Djebel Chelia (2328 m, 7638 ft) in the northeast forms the highest point. South of Chelia the land falls steeply to Chott Melrhir, the easternmost and largest of a series of depressions. To west and south spreads the central plateau, a high, undulating sandstone plain crossed by dry valleys and

ribbed with dunes. In the far south rises the isolated mountain massif of Ahaggar, capped by volcanic peaks; the highest bloc includes Mt Tahat (2918 m, 9574 ft). Hot dry summers and warm, moister winters characterize the coast and mountains; where moisture is sufficient there are forested hills and grassy plains. Inland the climate is more extreme, with hot days and cold nights, little rain, and patchy desert vegetation.

History and Development

For long the Algerian interior supported wandering pastoral tribes whose way of life remained basically unchanged for centuries; the coast and coastal mountains by contrast were overrun by successive invaders from the Phoenicians of the 12th century BC to the 19th-century French. Phoenician villages, the earliest settlements, fell in turn under Carthaginian and Roman domination. Rome developed northern Africa as a granary, making coastal Algeria a prosperous agricultural settlement. Vandal and Byzantine invasions followed when Rome fell, and Arab incursions gradually established a number of minor Islamic states. Spain captured Algiers and other ports in 1510, to be displaced twenty years later by corsairs who made Algeria a Turkish province and its Barbary Coast a haven for pirates. In 1830 French forces invaded and gradually subdued the hinterland. Most of Algeria became a Department of France in 1897. Nationalist movements developing before and during World War II, violently opposed by the settlers, precipitated an eight-year struggle leading to Algeria's independence in 1962.

Resources and Economics

About one third of the Algerian workforce is employed in agriculture, generating less than one tenth of the country's income. The main crops are wheat, barley, potatoes, grapes, citrus fruits, melons and other semi-tropical produce, grown on a relatively small area of the north; the huge arid area of the south produces little more than dates and livestock for local consumption, and much of the country's food is imported. Iron ore and phosphatic rock are mined for local treatment and export; natural gas and petroleum together account for 90 per cent of export earnings. Heavy industries recently developed include cement, steel and fertilizer manufacture and a petrochemical industry producing plastics and industrial chemicals; light industries are in comparison poorly developed, but Algeria assembles electrical goods and tractors and other motor vehicles. There are good roads and railways in the northern third of the country, substantial port facilities, and good internal and external air services.

Recent Developments

Heavy reliance on petroleum sales leaves Algeria vulnerable to world market fluctuations, though diversity of products from a versatile petrochemical industry have helped it to maintain output during the depression. Natural gas should ultimately overtake petroleum as Algeria's main export; one of the world's largest reserves underlies the country, and markets are already established with France, Italy and other European countries. Though Algeria remains firmly socialist in principles, large, unwieldy national corporations are being split up and streamlined, and private enterprise encouraged in light industries, farming and commerce. The rate of economic development has slowed in recent years, but few African countries can have brighter prospects when international markets recover.

Burkina Faso

The Country

The Republic of Burkina Faso (formerly Upper Volta) is a land-locked state in the south of the west African bulge, ringed by Niger and Benin in the east, Togo, Ghana and Ivory Coast in the south, and Mali in the northwest. *Area* 274,200 km² (105,869 sq miles); *capital* Ouagadougou; *population* 8,119,000 (est. 1986).

Organization

Constitutionally provided with an elected National Assembly, Burkina Faso has since 1966 been ruled by a succession of authoritarian governments under executive Presidents, mostly military. The current government is headed by a 12-member People's Salvation Council, with an executive President who is advised by an appointed cabinet. Local religions dominate, with small Moslem and Christian minorities; the official language is French, with Moré, Diula and a dozen or more local languages and dialects spoken.

Geography

Burkina Faso is a platform of ancient crystalline rocks, overlain in the south by sandstones, with upland blocks rising from a mean elevation of 300–400 m (1000–1300 ft); a central massif forms a setting for the capital, and Bobo-Dioulasso, the second city, stands on higher ground in the southwest. The country's highest point is at about 750 m (2460 ft), close to the southwestern border. Tilted southward, the platform drains mainly into tributaries of the Volta River, or towards the Niger in the east. Rivers tend to be seasonal, some drying completely between rains. Except along the major waterways, soils are thin and leached of nutrients. The climate is hot and dry. In the south, where savanna and thin woodland cover the country, rains are fairly reliable between June and September. In the north sporadic and unreliable rainfall produces meagre desert scrub, which springs into leaf after showers.

History and Development

Part of the vast, dry savanna that extends between the northern desert and southern forests of west Africa, Upper Volta was created in 1920 as a convenience for French colonial government. Traditionally occupied by several tribal groups of farmers, in the late 18th and 19th centuries it formed the homeland of a dominant tribe, the Mossi, who controlled an extensive empire from their capital Ouagadougou. French penetration began in the second half of the 19th century, military units from Senegal moving eastward to pacify and settle the huge area that became French West Africa. Opposition was strong, the Mossi resisting until the last decade of the century. Upper Volta was carved from adjacent tracts of Niger, Ivory Coast and Mali (then the colony of Upper Senegal and Niger). Dissolved in 1932, it was resurrected fifteen years later, to become self-governing within the French community in 1958 and fully independent in 1960. It changed its name to Burkina Faso in 1984.

Resources and Economics

Subsistence agriculture employs over 90 per cent of the population and accounts for almost half the national income. The main products are sorghum, millet, beans and maize; smaller crops of cassava, nuts, yams and vegetables are also grown on smallholdings, rice, cotton, cane sugar and fruit on cooperative plantations. Cotton, ground-nuts and livestock are the main exports. All crops are subject to drought, and have several times been devastated in the decades since independence. Manganese and phosphate ores are present but mining is underdeveloped, only small amounts of gold being available for export. Burkina Faso has no exploited coal or petroleum, and little timber or hydroelectric power. Manufacturing is limited to cotton, processed foods, cigarettes from local tobacco, shoes and bicycle assembly. Roads are mostly tracks; a single railway from Ouagadougou links Burkina Faso through Ivory Coast with Abidjan.

Recent Developments

One of the world's poorest and in places most densely populated countries, Burkina Faso has little to sell to raise its standards of living. Agriculture sometimes yields small surpluses for export, but all too often droughts bring crop failure, decimation of flocks and herds, and starvation. A UN-backed scheme aims to clear the southwestern river beds of endemic 'river-blindness' parasites; its success may bring much-needed new land under production and encourage migration from the overcrowded uplands. The country's high birth rate is partly offset by emigration. Thousands of workers have moved to richer neighbouring countries, their remittances adding significantly to national income. The strongly left-wing government, chronically beset by tribal differences, does not encourage overseas investors, but Burkina Faso is aided economically by France and by international agencies.

Mali

The Country

The Republic of Mali lies centrally in the bulge of Africa, ringed by Algeria in the northeast, Niger and Burkina Faso in the southeast, Ivory Coast, Guinea and Senegal in the southwest and Mauritania in the west. *Area* 1,240,000 km^2 (478, 764 sq miles); *capital* Bamako; *population* 8,233,000 (est. 1986).

Organization

A legislative 82-member National Assembly and an executive President are elected, for three-year and six-year terms respectively; there is a single political party, the Union démocratique du peuple malien (UDPM). Local authority is vested in seven regions and the capital district. Islam is the dominant religion, with Christianity well represented; French is the official language, but local languages are widely used.

Geography

Southern Mali lies on a high dissected plateau, continuous in the south with the uplands of Ivory Coast and Guinea and in the north with the Ahaggar massif of southern Algeria. Its arid plains lie between 300 and 500 m (1000 to 1600 ft) above sea level. In the southwest the Senegal river system drains westward. Within Mali the Niger flows northeastward from the Guinea boundary through the inland Niger delta, turning east at Timbuktu and then southeast to enter Niger. Both river systems cut deeply into the plains, flowing through gorges with cliffs up to 1000 m (3300 ft) high. Northern Mali is a rolling, featureless desert, lacking surface water and scattered with shifting sand dunes. Mali as a whole is hot and dry. The heaviest rains fall in the south between June and

October. The northern desert, which is part of the Sahel, receives irregular seasonal rains; frequent failures cause great hardship among the nomads and their herds.

History and Development
The southern half of Mali formed part of an empire that controlled the upper Niger valley in the 14th to 16th centuries, Mandingos dominating several neighbouring tribes – Borribora, Soninka, Songhai Dogon and many others – all of which retain their identity today. Their territories were taken over in stages by French forces advancing eastward from Senegal between 1879 and 1883, and linked with Sahel lands to form the colony of French Sudan. Bamako, the capital, was ultimately linked by rail with Dakar, but the colony remained poor and relatively undeveloped. Joining briefly with Senegal in 1959 to form the Federation of Mali, it gained independence from France in June 1960; Senegal broke its ties almost immediately and Mali was recognized as a separate republic in the same year.

Resources and Economics
Though less than 2 per cent of its land is suitable for cultivation, Mali depends on agriculture for its livelihood and export revenues. About 90 per cent of its workforce scratches a living by herding or cultivation. Cotton grown in the south is one of the few exports, alone providing about half the country's overseas income. Sugar-cane and ground-nuts are less successful crops. River fish are dried for export, and add variety to the home-grown diet of millet, cassava, pulses and other vegetables. Mali is close to being self-supporting in food, but must buy in when crops fail due to drought: irrigation using Niger water will help to stabilize and improve output. There are few manufacturing industries beyond food-processing. Salt, phosphates, gold and uranium ores are mined in small amounts for export. Rivers are important means of transport, though seasonal and liable to flooding. Roads are poor but adequate; the railway from Dakar in Senegal to Bamako continues only as far as Koulikoro.

Recent Developments
Chronically short of development capital and deeply in debt, Mali is still obliged to buy in fuels and other essentials (even food in years of drought) to maintain its meagre standards of living. It draws heavily on overseas aid funds (including those of the EEC) to balance its annual budget; even remittances from expatriates working in more prosperous countries to the south help to keep the economy afloat. Few state-run enterprises are profitable; unemployment and inflation run high, and the country's per capita income remains among the world's lowest. With water shortage a constant hindrance to development, Mali's main hopes for the future depend on mobilization of water supplies for agriculture, and sales of minerals for investment capital.

Mauritania

The Country
The Islamic Republic of Mauritania lies on the Atlantic coast of western Africa, bordered by Mali in the east and southeast, Senegal in the southwest and Western Sahara in the northwest. *Area* 1,030,700 km^2 (397,953 sq miles); *capital* Nouakchott; *population* 1,948,000 (est. 1986).

Africa Northwest

Organization
The constitution adopted at independence, providing for an elected National Assembly, was supplanted in 1978 by one temporarily recognizing a military government under an executive President, who rules with the advice of a council of about sixteen appointed ministers led by a Prime Minister. For local government the country is divided into twelve regions. Islam is the state religion; Arabic and French are the official languages, with Arabic widely spoken in the north and French in the south.

Geography
Forming the western end of the Sahara belt, Mauritania is a desert of dry plains, rising gradually from coastal dunes to an undulating plateau at 200–250 m (650–800 ft), and a high point, Kediet Ijill (915 m, 3002 ft), in the northwest. Palaeozoic crystalline rocks in the north and sandstones in the centre and south are weathered to coarse sandy soils; except for a few fertile oasis areas, drifting sand dunes up to 100 m (330 ft) high cover much of the country. The coastline, over 580 km (360 miles) long, has several sheltered harbours in the north, notably the Bay of Lévrier. The climate is uniformly hot; rainfall is reliable between June and October in the south, sparser and less reliable in the north.

History and Development
Mauritanians are traditionally nomadic Moors of mixed Arab, Berber and Negro descent, thinly scattered over inhospitable country. In the 11th century Mauritanian Berbers briefly led the Almoravides Islamic crusade, which swept northwestern Africa and southern Spain. Mauritanian oases have in the past been important as trading centres on major trans-Saharan routes. However, most Moors remained simple nomads; colonial domination from the late 19th century onward, when Mauritania became part of French West Africa, barely altered their way of life. Mauritania gained independence in late 1968, seeking links with other Arab countries. In 1976 it annexed part of Western Sahara, relinquishing it in 1979 after losing the war with the guerrilla independence movement Frenta Polisario.

Resources and Economics
About 80 per cent of Mauritanians are still nomadic or semi-nomadic, raising cattle, sheep, goats, donkeys, camels and horses on sparse grasslands and thorn-scrub, mostly in the south. Oases grow dates, cereals and vegetables; millet, maize, yams and cotton are raised in the Senegal river valley, where rains are more reliable and soils more fertile. Offshore waters provide excellent fishing for a fleet based mostly on northern ports. Iron ore is mined at Zouérate and moved by rail to Nouadhibou (formerly Port Étienne); rich copper deposits are mined at Akjoujt and shipped from the newly-built capital city. There are few all-weather roads; air links join the main centres.

Recent Developments
Mauritania's export earnings from copper and iron ores are currently low due to depressed markets; the newly-developed fishing industry helps to fill the gap, but revenue losses have slowed economic expansion. The country's main hope for further development seems to lie in its as yet barely exploited mineral resources. Drought in the Sahel (southern zone) has dried out watercourses and devastated the wandering herds. Forcing nomads into the settlements, this may possibly encourage more settled and efficient methods of agriculture.

Morocco

The Country
The Kingdom of Morocco occupies the northwest corner of Africa, fronting both the Mediterranean and the Atlantic. It shares a long southeastern border with Algeria and a shorter southern border with Western Sahara, which Morocco currently occupies (see Western Sahara). Two small enclaves (Ceuta, Melilla) and three offshore islands (Alhucemas, Chafarinas, Peñón de Vélez) remain under Spanish sovereignty. *Area* 446,550 km^2 (172,413 sq miles); *capital* Rabat, *largest city* Casablanca; *population* 24,636,000 (est. 1986).

Organization
A legislative 267-member Chamber of Representatives (two thirds elected by popular vote, one third by towns, regions and institutions) is elected for six-year terms. An executive Prime Minister heads a cabinet of about 23 ministers; all are appointed by the Monarch as Head of State. Islam is the state religion, and there are large Christian and Jewish minorities. Arabic is the official language, with French, Spanish and Berber widely spoken.

Geography
Northern Morocco is centered on the Rif Atlas, a range of tightly folded mountain ridges (mostly limestone and sandstone) separated by deep ravines; they form the steep Mediterranean coast from Tangier to Melilla and extend inland to high peaks rising over 2400 m (7870 ft). Immediately south lies the Middle Atlas, a high limestone plateau cut by ravines and deep river gorges. Central and southern Morocco include broad coastal plains which rise in stages to a high forested tableland; beyond lie the three complex chains of the main Atlas Mountains. Along the central ridge of the High Atlas are many peaks rising above 3500 m (11,500 ft); highest of all is Toubkal (4165 m, 13,665 ft). The southeastern flank descends through arid foothills to the Saharan plain. In the far south lies the smaller Anti-Atlas range of arid mountains separated by green valleys. Northern Morocco and the western coastal plains have hot dry summers, sometimes with severe drought, and warm moist winters. Southern and eastern Morocco are hot and dry, with uncertain winter rains.

History and Development
Phoenicians, Carthaginians and Romans built settlements along the coast of Morocco, but the interior tribes of pastoral nomads remained untouched until Arabs invaded from the 7th century onward. In the 11th and early 12th centuries Morocco formed the heartland of the Almoravid movement, which carried a unified Islamic faith across the western Maghreb (Moslem northwest Africa) and into southern Spain. Thereafter Moslem alliances created a state which in the early 20th century fell gradually under European control. In 1904 Spain claimed influence along the northern coast and the Atlantic coastal enclave of Ifni; from 1912 the rest of Morocco became a French protectorate (promoting a long war of subjugation), and in 1923 Tangier was made an international city. Independence movements emerged after World War II; with little struggle Morocco freed itself in 1956, though Spain held Ifni until 1970 and still retains its northern enclaves and islands. In 1976 Morocco annexed the northern sector of Western Sahara (see entry), and in 1979 took over the southern sector when Mauritania withdrew.

233

Resources and Economics

Morocco is still mainly agricultural; farming employs over half the workforce and provides about one third of export income. The main crops are wheat, barley, maize, citrus fruits and vegetables; Morocco imports many of its staple foods. Fish are plentiful off the long Atlantic coast, but Morocco itself takes only a small catch. Minerals include phosphatic rocks (the country's single most important export), coal, and a range of metal ores including copper, lead, cobalt and manganese. There are small reserves of petroleum, but Morocco currently imports most of its fuels. Hydroelectric power output is small but being expanded. Heavy industries produce cement and steel, processed foods, textiles, paper and timber products, metals and chemicals; automobiles and other consumer goods are assembled. The main towns are linked by road, rail and air; local road networks are barely adequate for a rapidly developing country. Tourism is an important and expanding industry.

Recent Developments

Morocco's agricultural policy is to improve and diversify crops with the aim of greater self-sufficiency. Though the dry climate limits productivity over much of the country, attempts are being made to grow such staple crops as cane sugar and tea, using irrigation where possible. Processing of phosphatic rock forms the basis of a growing fertilizer and chemical industry. Mineral development is being encouraged and oil exploration has high priority, especially along the Atlantic coast. The take-over of Western Sahara produced national unity at a difficult period for the government; Morocco controls output of phosphatic rock, but maintaining garrisons against guerrillas is proving costly.

Niger

The Country

The Republic of Niger lies centrally in the African bulge, ringed by Chad in the east, Nigeria in the south, Benin and Burkina Faso in the southwest, Mali in the west, and Algeria and Libya in the north. *Area* 1,267,000 km² (489,189 sq miles); *capital* Niamey; *population* 6,392,000 (est. 1986).

Organization

Though constitutionally provided with an elected National Assembly, since 1974 Niger has been ruled by a military President and Supreme Military Council, advised by a council of 20 ministers. Islam is the dominant religion; French is the official language, with Hausa and local languages widely spoken.

Geography

On the southern flank of the Sahara, Niger occupies a high plateau of old, weather-worn rocks. In the centre stands the Air massif, crossed from north to south by a line of peaks; the highest point, Mont Gréboun, rises to about 2000 m (6600 ft). To the north stands the high, arid Plateau de Manguéni; to east and west are extensive areas of shifting sand where little grows. Only in the south is cultivation possible; notably around the Niger River in the southwest and the shores of Lake Chad in the southeast. Niger is hot throughout the year, with a summer rainy season of varying length; rain falls longest and most reliably in the south, sparsely and fitfully in the north.

History and Development

Modern Niger includes both northern desert homelands of Fulani and Tuareg nomads, and southern 'Sudan' regions of Negro farmers whose culture links them firmly with countries to the south. Created in the late 19th century, Niger was occupied in stages by French forces advancing eastward from Senegal and French Sudan; its boundaries express the political expediency of European administrators rather than African nationhood. Colonial Niger developed little under French rule, the northern nomads continuing to pasture their herds of sheep, goats and cattle, and the southern farmers raising ground-nuts and other cash crops in addition to their traditional subsistence crops. Niger sued for and was granted independence in 1960. For over a decade its policies remained closely linked with those of France, but the coup of 1974, triggered off by drought and acute economic difficulties, set it on the more independent course it pursues today.

Resources and Economics

Economically Niger depends on agriculture and mining. About 90 per cent of its workforce are herders or farmers. The country is almost self-sufficient for food, millet, sorghum, rice, cassava and beans being the principal crops. Cash crops include ground-nuts, cotton and livestock; although affected by a varying rainfall and market fluctuations, in good years they yield over 80 per cent of Niger's overseas earnings. Processed uranium concentrate is a growing export; other minerals, including salt, coal and ores of iron and tin, are present in workable quantities, and oil has been discovered near Lake Chad. Manufacturing industries cover the country's most immediate needs (building materials, textiles, food-processing). Roads are poorly developed and maintained except in the south; external and internal air links are adequate for present needs.

Recent Developments

A decade of prosperity followed the development and exploitation of Niger's uranium ores. Competition from other sources and slackening in world demand have now restricted output; overseas income has fallen and economic growth has slowed considerably. At the same time the country has been faced with widespread drought and crop failure, requiring food to be bought in from outside; coupled with additional domestic expenses, this has further reduced the capital available for economic investment and expansion. Plans to improve standards of living still depend heavily on mining revenues; efforts are being made to develop coal, petroleum and other products that will at least help to reduce the annual imports bill. Meanwhile Niger depends heavily on overseas aid in balancing its budget.

Tunisia

The Country

The Republic of Tunisia lies centrally on the Mediterranean coast of Africa, bordered by Libya in the east and Algeria in the west. *Area* 163,610 km^2 (63,170 sq miles); *capital* Tunis; *population* 7,322,000 (est. 1986).

Organization

A 136-member legislative National Assembly is elected by popular vote for five-year terms. An executive President is also elected for five-year terms, though the current incumbent is President for Life. He appoints an executive Prime Minister and cabinet of about 22 ministers. Local authority is vested in eighteen departments, each under an appointed governor. The state faith is Islam; there are substantial Christian and Jewish minorities. Arabic is the official language, with French widely spoken.

Geography
Northern Tunisia is mountainous, its Dorsale Mountains forming the eastern extremity of the Moroccan and Algerian Atlas. Sandstones in the northwest and limestones elsewhere create the rugged northern coastline which includes Cap Blanc, Africa's northernmost point. Inland they create spectacular scenery; the highest peak is Djebel Chambi (1544 m, 5066 ft) close to the Algerian border. Immediately south of the mountains, thinly-forested ridges and grass-covered plateaus descend steeply to an east-west trough that crosses inland from the Gulf of Gabes, containing a series of saline lakes. To the south lies a dry, sandy upland. Northern Tunisia has a Mediterranean climate of hot dry summers and warm moist winters; only rarely are its forested slopes and well-farmed valleys affected by serious drought. The southern uplands are hotter, drier and covered with semi-desert scrub vegetation.

History and Development
Forming the eastern flank of the Maghreb (Moslem northwest Africa), Tunisia stands at the crossroads of Mediterranean traffic. Its northeastern cities of Tunis and Carthage may have begun as Stone-Age settlements; Carthage, on the Gulf of Tunis, was in turn Libyan and Phoenician. In pre-Roman times it formed the centre of an empire that filled the western Mediterranean from Spain to Sicily and extended north to Sardinia and Corsica. Falling to Romans, Byzantines, Vandals and Arabs, Tunisia became a province of the Ottoman Empire (see Turkey). To its already cosmopolitan population was added a huge influx of Spanish Moslems in the 17th century. In 1883 it was adopted as a protectorate by France. Under both Turkish and French influence Tunisia maintained its distinctive Arab culture; this re-emerged strongly when in 1956 it became an independent republic.

Resources and Economics
With a predominantly agricultural economy, Tunisia grows wheat, barley, maize and oats together with grapes, olives and citrus fruits in the Mediterranean north; dates and livestock are the main products of the more Saharan south. Olive oil is an economically significant export. Fishing is important in inshore waters, yielding shrimps and several kinds of fresh fish for local consumption and export. Tunisia's most important mineral exports are petroleum (both its own and Algeria's), and chemical products derived from its extensive deposits of phosphatic rocks. Ores of iron, zinc and other metals are also mined extensively. Textiles are made mainly from imported materials; other manufacturing industries remain relatively undeveloped. Roads are good between the main centres in the north, indifferent or poor in the south; railways connect northern centres and there are good internal and external air links.

Recent Developments
In good years Tunisia produces most of its own food, with a substantial surplus of fruit, olive oil and wine for export; when rains fail and yields are down,

cereals, sugar and other staples have to be imported in bulk. Self-sufficiency is a major objective of the current development plan, which aims also to build up manufacturing industries and provide work for the many thousands of urban unemployed. Tourism is increasingly important; well over a million visitors each year enjoy the scenery, splendid coastline and antiquarian sites.

Western Sahara

The Country
On the Atlantic coast of northwest Africa, Western Sahara is bounded in the north by Morocco, in the northeast by a narrow sector of Algeria, and in the south by Mauritania. *Area* 266,000 km² (102,703 sq miles); *capital* El Aaiún; *population* c. 80,000 (est. 1986).

Organization
Western Sahara is disputed territory; formerly the province of Spanish Sahara, it is currently occupied and administered by Morocco and without a government of its own. The religion of most of its people is Islam; Spanish and Arabic are the national languages, Berber the most widely-spoken language.

Geography
A bare dune coast rises almost immediately to a broad, bare tableland 100–200 m (330–660 ft) high, crossed by seasonal (mainly dry) river beds and scattered with sand dunes and desert vegetation. Inland in the centre and north there is a steady, almost imperceptible rise to about 1200 m (4000 ft), with little change in general appearance. The climate is hot and dry.

History and Development
Río de Oro peninsula was first visited and named by Portuguese navigators in the mid-15th century. Spanish interest in this inhospitable coast was stimulated because of its proximity to the Canary Islands; small Spanish forts and settlements were established, and in 1885 Spain gazetted the protectorate of Río de Oro, between Cape Blanco and Cape Bojador. Spanish control was extended northward to Cape Yubi in 1904 and to the present Moroccan border in 1912; eastern boundaries were defined, but Spain exerted little influence beyond the few, mainly coastal settlements. In 1958 Spanish Sahara became a province of Spain. In 1975 Spain initiated tripartite control with Morocco and Mauritania, despite strong United Nations' and World Court recommendations, based on plebiscites, that Western Sahara be given independence. Spain withdrew from the arrangement in 1976, and Mauritania in 1979, encouraged in their departure by Frente Polisario, a militant liberation movement supported by Algeria.

Resources and Economics
Western Sahara's pastoral nomads and farmers maintain themselves but have little to offer the outside world. The territory's most important asset so far discovered is phosphatic ore, mined since 1972 at Bu Craa and transported by conveyor belt to the coast. Shipments have been intermittent because of guerrilla activity by Polisario supporters. Roads are generally tracks; there are several airstrips and port facilities at the main coastal settlements.

Recent Developments
Morocco's occupation of Western Sahara, illegal by United Nations standards and strongly opposed by Algeria, appears to have US support. Polisario guerrilla activities, under the banner of the Democratic Saharwi Arab Republic, require Moroccan forces to maintain substantial garrisons.

AFRICA WEST

Benin

The Country
The People's Republic of Benin lies on the southern coast of west Africa, bounded by Nigeria in the east, Togo in the west, Burkina Faso in the northwest and Niger in the north. *Area* 112,622 km^2 (43,483 sq miles); *capital* Porto Novo; *population* 4,263,000 (est. 1986).

Organization
Benin is governed by an executive President, who is elected by a National Revolutionary Assembly of 336 elected People's Commissioners. The President is advised by an Executive Council of about 22 ministers. Local government is administered through six provinces, each with an appointed Prefect and Provincial Revolutionary Council. The Parti de la Revolution Populaire du Bénin exerts considerable influence at all levels of government. The official language is French; several local languages are spoken. Traditional religions are widely practised; Christianity and Islam are minority faiths.

Geography
From a narrow stretch of sand-bar coast some 100 km (60 miles) long, backed by brackish lagoons, Benin rises gently to a fertile lowland plain. Once forested but now intensively farmed, this is crossed by south-flowing rivers with marshes in the east. Inland the ground rises in steps to a savanna plateau at about 400 m (1300 ft), with higher mountains above 500 m (1640 ft) in the Atakora chain to the northwest. In the northeast the plateau falls towards the Alibori river valley and the broader valley of the Niger River, which forms the border for part of its length. The climate is hot and humid on the coast, tempered by sea breezes, with heavy rains from March to July and September to November. Inland there is a single wet season from June to October, with drought possible in the far north.

History and Development
Formerly Dahomey, Benin formed the centre of a group of Negro kingdoms that extended far beyond its present borders. The earliest Europeans to make contact were slavers; forts established on the sand-bars of the lagoon coast during the 17th and 18th centuries attracted rival tribes who sold each other into Portuguese, Dutch, British or French slavery. Notable among local soldiery were the Amazon regiments of women, who guarded and fought for the rulers. French influence grew during the late 19th century. Following an agreement with Britain in 1889 a French force captured Cotonou and Porto Novo, declaring a protectorate and pensioning the Dahomey King. After further fighting up-country (1894), boundaries were defined with British and German

neighbours and Dahomey was developed as a colony. Dahomey was granted self-government within the French Community in 1958 and independence in 1960; in 1975 the name was changed to Benin.

Resources and Economics
About half the workforce is employed in agriculture, generating two fifths of the national income and rather more of the export income. Crops include cassava, yams and other edible roots, maize, sorghum and beans, grown mostly on smallholdings which are gradually being merged as cooperatives. Benin is currently almost self-supporting for staple foods. Cash crops include palm oil, cotton, coffee, cocoa and ground-nuts, grown mainly on cooperative and government farms. Fish from rivers, lagoons and the sea add variety to the diet. Limestone is quarried for cement manufacture; other minerals are present but unexploited. Petroleum has recently been discovered offshore. Roads and a northern railway bring traffic from the interior and from surrounding countries to the coast at Cotonou, which is a major port.

Recent Developments
Though potentially as wealthy as many of its neighbours, Benin has remained relatively undeveloped. The 1972 coup that swept away its French-inspired constitution alienated it from several actual and possible sources of aid. Since then it has pursued independent Marxist–Leninist policies that have resulted in solid but unspectacular economic progress. The discovery of oil 16 km (10 miles) offshore in the Bight of Benin and its growing exploitation should bring the country much-needed capital for development.

Cameroon

The Country
The United Republic of Cameroon lies in the northeastern corner of the Gulf of Guinea, sharing boundaries with Central African Republic in the east, Congo, Gabon and Equatorial Guinea in the south and Nigeria in the northwest. *Area* 475,442 km^2 (183,568 sq miles); *capital* Yaoundé; *population* 9,796,000 (est. 1986).

Organization
Cameroon has a National Assembly of 120 members and a President who is Head of State; both are elected for five-year terms. The President appoints an executive Prime Minister and a cabinet of about 30 ministers and vice-ministers. Local government is administered through seven provinces, each with an appointed governor. Official languages are French and English, the latter commonest in the western provinces; several local languages are spoken. Christianity, Islam and traditional religions are well represented.

Geography
Behind the 320-km (200-mile) coastline extends a broad, jungle-covered plain, rising to a forested plateau at about 300 m (1000 ft) cut by large river valleys; the Sanaga river system occupies a central basin. Along the Nigerian border the plateau rises to the Adamawa Highlands, a savanna-covered ridge with peaks over 2000 m (6500 ft) high, extending west to east across the country. Dry

northern plains fall in stages toward Lake Chad, 280 m (918 ft) above sea level. Southwest from Adamawa runs a tectonic rift marked by volcanic peaks, some over 2400 m (7800 ft) high; highest of all is Mt Cameroon (4070 m, 13,354 ft), some 50 km (30 miles) from the coast. Coastal Cameroon is hot with rains from April to November; Mt Cameroon receives over 10 m (33 ft) of rain annually. The interior is generally drier, tailing to near-desert in the far north.

History and Development
Cameroon's mixed population, including pygmy hunter-gatherers in the southern forests, Bantu farmers in the centre and Sudanic Fulani herdsmen in the north, reflects a varied but mainly unrecorded pre-European history. Portuguese mariners investigated the coast from 1472, and several European nations were involved in the slave trading that followed, especially during the 17th to 19th centuries. German interest dates from the Berlin West African Conference of 1884, following which its imperial forces occupied the coast and explored inland. Defeat in World War I lost Germany the colony to Britain and France, who gained mandates from the League of Nations to administer it. In 1960 France gave independence to the French sector; in the following year the southern half of the British mandate elected to join the newly-constituted Republic of Cameroon, the northern half joining Nigeria.

Resources and Economics
Cameroon's economy is based soundly on agriculture; about 70 per cent of its workforce have smallholdings or are wage-earners on larger farms and plantations. The country grows most of its own staple foods including cassava, maize, rice, sugar and livestock. It is also a major exporter of food crops, including cocoa, coffee, bananas, vegetable oils, cotton, tobacco, rubber and timber, which together provide one third of its annual income and export earnings. Offshore petroleum provides a further half of its export earnings; natural gas and other minerals (especially bauxite and iron ore) are potentially valuable. Manufacturing industries include food-processing, aluminium-smelting (mostly from imported ores) and cement, tyre and wood-pulp manufacture. Cheap hydroelectricity is supplanting output from thermal power stations. Growing rail, road and air networks reflect the increasing needs of the community; Douala has been developed as a major international port.

Recent Developments
Despite its widely-scattered and polyglot populations, Cameroon has developed since independence into one of the most stable and successful of all African countries, enjoying good relations with neighbours and former colonial masters and remaining politically neutral and economically sound. Cameroon's economy was well-founded on progressive agriculture even before the exploitation of its petroleum resources. Increasing revenues from oil, sensibly applied towards the diversification of resources, have helped to maintain steady economic expansion during the world recession, and have provided Cameroon with a sound platform for further development in the future.

The Gambia

The Country
The Republic of the Gambia occupies a narrow strip on either side of the Gambia River, close to the westernmost point of Africa; it has a short Atlantic coastline and is ringed on all other sides by Senegal. *Area* 11,295 km² (4361 sq miles); *capital* Banjul; *population* 705,000 (est. 1986).

Organization
The Gambia is governed by a 43-member House of Representatives; of these 35 are elected by popular vote, four represent the tribal Chiefs and four (including the Attorney-General) are nominated. The leader of the majority party becomes President and Head of State; he appoints a Vice-President and cabinet of about 12 ministers. The official language is English, with several local languages spoken; Islam and Christianity are the main faiths.

Geography
Some 470 km (294 miles) long, the Gambia for much of its length is only 45 km (28 miles) wide, virtually limited to the Gambia River and its immediate hinterland. From the Senegal border the river cuts through a low sandstone plateau, broadening and deepening to a tidal estuary 11 km (7 miles) wide; it is navigable by ocean-going ships over 200 km (125 miles) inland, forming the country's main arterial route. Hot throughout the year, the Gambia has a rainy season from June to October.

History and Development
An important route for Africans long before Europeans arrived, the banks of the Gambia River were populated by many tribes, notably the Mandingo who are still prominent today. Portuguese adventurers discovered the river in the mid-15th century but did little to exploit it. British traders settled on St Mary's Island at the estuary mouth, developing Bathurst (now Banjul) in the early 19th century as a naval station important in suppressing illegal slaving. The Gambia became independent in 1965, and a republic in 1970.

Resources and Economics
About 80 per cent of the population are farmers, growing rice and vegetables for food, ground-nuts and cotton for export. Crops are from time to time seriously affected by drought. There are no known minerals of economic importance and few manufacturing industries to buffer the economy. Goods passing between northern and southern Senegal bring valuable revenues to the country. There are few roads and no railways. Banjul is a deep-water port and has recently acquired an international airport that caters for a growing tourist trade.

Recent Developments
Recent droughts have exposed the Gambia's economic vulnerability, requiring food to be imported and reducing funds available from exports. The current five-year plan includes plans to increase the area under irrigation, and to improve methods of growing cotton and raising stock. Long-term plans include a joint programme with Senegal and Guinea to develop the Gambia river basin, involving a bridge, barrage, and hydroelectric power schemes. Closer links with Senegal are envisaged through the Senegambia Confederation.

Ghana

The Country
The Republic of Ghana lies centrally on the southern coast of west Africa, bounded by Togo in the east, Ivory Coast in the west and Burkina Faso in the northwest and north. *Area* 238,537 km² (92,099 sq miles); *capital* Accra; *population* 14,216,000 (est. 1986).

Organization
A Parliament of 140 members is elected for five-year terms, an executive President every four years. As Head of State the President appoints (subject to parliamentary approval) a Vice-President and cabinet of about 20 ministers, and a Council of State including former presidents and other prominent citizens. The constitution is currently suspended, a provisional National Defence Council assuming responsibility for government since 1981. Regional government is administered through nine regions, each in the charge of an appointed minister. The official language is English; Christianity and local religions are about equally represented.

Geography
Roughly rectangular, Ghana has a coastline of sand-bars and lagoons some 500 km (310 miles) long. Behind lie low rolling plains, savanna-covered in the east and forested in the west, and now intensively cultivated. The plains rise in steps to the mainly-forested Ashanti plateau. In the east sprawls the huge basin of the Volta River; now dammed 80 km (50 miles) from the sea, the basin has been flooded to form Lake Volta, converting fever-ridden swamps to a water store and useful waterway. East of the lake, along the Togo border, stands Ghana's highest mountain range; Mt Afadjato in the south rises to 885 m (2904 ft). North of the Ashanti plateau lies the Black Volta valley; beyond rise savanna uplands that form the border with Burkina Faso. The coastal climate is hot and humid, with wet monsoon seasons from April to July and September to November. Inland the climate is cooler and drier, with unreliable rains in the north.

History and Development
West Africa's southern forests and savannas were for long occupied by Negro farmers, whose slash-and-burn agriculture kept them constantly on the move and often at war with neighbouring tribes. From the 17th century the Ashanti dominated, their influence spreading far to the north among the Moslem herdsmen of the savanna. Europeans settled on the coast from the 16th century, trading for gold and slaves from the interior. British influence increased during the 19th century; a successful war with the Ashanti and border negotiations with France, Germany and other European powers gave Britain its large and wealthy Gold Coast colony in 1874. World War I brought Britain a mandate over the neighbouring sector of Togoland, the former German colony. The Gold Coast sued for and was granted independence within the British Commonwealth in 1957, incorporating western Togoland and changing its name to Ghana; in 1960 it became a republic.

Resources and Economics
Predominantly agricultural, Ghana has both smallholdings and plantations occupying over half the workforce. In good years it produces much of its own

food, including cassava and other tubers, maize, millet, sorghum, rice, sugar-cane, vegetables and livestock, and cocoa, its only important cash crop, which alone brings in 60 per cent of the country's foreign exchange. However, recent droughts and management problems have reduced yields, requiring Ghana to import staple foods and significantly cutting its cocoa revenues. Gold, manganese ore, bauxite and diamonds are mined, and offshore petroleum is being exploited, as yet on a small scale. The few manufacturing industries are limited to goods for local consumption. Road and rail links are adequate for current needs, though poorly maintained and overdue for rehabilitation; there are good international ports and airports.

Recent Developments
First of the African colonies to achieve independence, and for some time a model to those that followed, Ghana is passing through a phase of political and economic difficulty. Drought, the ageing of its cocoa plantations, overdependence on a single crop, chronic mismanagement of the economy at all levels, and long-standing corruption have all been blamed for its problems. Whatever the root causes, the expulsion of Ghanaians from Nigerian employment early in 1983 added an estimated one million unemployed to the country's already high tally. Development of Tema as a deep-water port and metal-smelting centre may help to alleviate unemployment. Political stability and economic austerity are the main objectives of the present authoritarian government, which is urgently seeking financial aid from overseas sources.

Guinea

The Country
The Popular and Revolutionary Republic of Guinea lies on the southwestern coast of west Africa, bounded by Ivory Coast in the east, Liberia and Sierra Leone in the south, Guinea-Bissau, Senegal and Mali in the north. *Area* 245,857 km² (94,925 sq miles); *capital* Conakry; *population* 5,897,000 (est. 1986).

Organization
A legislative National Assembly of 210 members is elected for seven-year terms; an elected commission acts for it between its biannual meetings. An executive President, also elected for seven-year terms, appoints a Prime Minister and cabinet of about 30 ministers. Local authorities have limited responsibilities within 33 administrative districts. The Parti démocratique de Guinée (PDG) is powerful in all aspects of government. French is the official language, but Susu, Malinké, Fulani and other local languages are widely spoken. Islam is the dominant faith; there are many local religions and small Christian communities.

Geography
From a muddy, mangrove-forested coast Guinea rises to a coastal plain 50–60 km (30–40 miles) wide, forested and widely cultivated. Behind rise the escarpments of the Fouta Djalon highlands, edging a sandstone plateau some 900 m (3000 ft) above the plain. Above the plateau's deeply dissected surface rise higher massifs; Mt Loura (1515 m, 4970 ft) and Mt Tangue (1537 m, 5042 ft) near the Senegal border are among the highest. In the east grassy plains crossed

by deep river valleys fall away to the upper basin of the Niger River. In the south are the forested Guinea Highlands, generally over 1000 m (3300 ft) and rising in the extreme south to Mt Nimba (1752 m, 5748 ft). Guinea is hot, with monsoon rains from April to October. Rainfall is heaviest in the south (where the wet season lasts longest) and on the coast; the north and east are comparatively dry.

History and Development
Guinea's lowland forests and upland savannas attracted African settlers of varying origins; the many small communities that developed lived in near-isolation for centuries, speaking a variety of languages and dialects. This was the pattern discovered by European adventurers of the 15th and 16th centuries who first explored the difficult, unhealthy Guinea coast. Slavers set up forts and traded inland through the 18th century; French interest dates from the early 19th century when the coast was charted and inland routes explored to Senegal and beyond. Working south from Senegal, France made treaties with coastal and inland tribes, finally making 'Rivières du Sud' (later Guinée Francaise) a colony. Independence was granted in 1958, Guinea immediately breaking all ties with France and pursuing an independent left-wing course.

Resources and Economics
Predominantly agricultural, Guinea has almost 80 per cent of its workforce on the land, mostly on small farms linked as cooperatives. Staple food crops include rice, cassava, maize, sorghum, manioc and vegetables; crops grown for export include coffee, bananas, ground-nuts and palm kernels. Productivity has generally been low, because of drought and other natural causes, and possibly also because of unpopular changes in distribution and marketing methods. Minerals include high-grade bauxite, which is already a major export and source of foreign earnings; exploitation of other ores, including iron, manganese, copper and uranium, is limited by poor transport facilities. Offshore petroleum is available for development, and many of Guinea's rivers are suitable for hydroelectric power generation. Road and rail links are less than adequate; Conakry has good port and international airport facilities, and a new port has been developed at Kamsar.

Recent Developments
Potentially a wealthy state, Guinea's rejection of continuing links with France exposed its immediate poverty and lack of skills; the decades of development since independence have left it economically far behind other former colonies. Rigid socialist control of the economy is now being replaced selectively by opportunities for private enterprise, and trade links with France and other countries are developing. The current development plan promises increasing public investment in agriculture and food-processing industries, more mining and mineral-processing, increasing power-generation, other industrial expansion and improved road and rail transport.

Guinea-Bissau

The Country
The Republic of Guinea-Bissau lies on the southwestern coast of west Africa, with Guinea to the east and south and Senegal to the north. *Area* 36,125 km^2 (13,948 sq miles); *capital* Bissau; *population* 640,000 (est. 1986).

Organization

Guinea-Bissau's constitution provides for an elected National People's Assembly, but a coup in 1980 installed a military Revolutionary Council with a President and cabinet of some 16 appointed ministers. The Partido Africano da Independencia da Guiné e Cabo Verde (PAIGC) is the single ruling party. Local government operates through nine regional administrations. Portuguese is the official language, but a creole dialect and several local languages are in general use; Islam and local religions are the main faiths, with Christians a small minority.

Geography

A deeply-indented coast of islands and mangrove-lined estuaries is backed by forested coastal plains. Rivers wind through the forests, allowing shallow-draught coastal shipping far into the interior. Higher savanna-covered plateaus rise in the south and east; the highest point, on the Guinea border, is a little over 150 m (500 ft) above sea level. Off the coast lie the forested islands of the Bijagos Archipelago, with many small ports and inlets. The coast is hot and humid, with heavy monsoonal rains between May and October. Inland the rainy season is shorter and rainfall more sporadic.

History and Development

Guinea-Bissau is the homeland of many indigenous peoples including Negro farmers, Sudanic herdsmen and island fisher-folk. Though Portuguese mariners explored the coast in the mid-15th century, Portugal paid little heed to its Guinea coast until the late 19th century. Long campaigns of pacification yielded a colony which virtually stagnated for want of development capital. Liberation movements during the 1960s resulted in a further decade of guerrilla warfare, which indirectly helped to topple Portugal's dictatorship and in 1974 brought independence to Portuguese Guinea.

Resources and Economics

Guinea-Bissau's economy is based on agriculture; about 90 per cent of the workforce are smallholders raising rice in the lowlands and maize, sorghum, cassava, beans, yams, and cattle and sheep on the drier uplands. Palm oil and ground-nuts are important cash crops, providing over half the country's export earnings in good years; fish and shrimps trawled off the Bijagos Archipelago provide much of the balance. Timber is exported from time to time. There are few industries apart from construction and food-processing. Roads are only good in the northeast; Bissau has international port and airport facilities.

Recent Developments

The long war of liberation left Guinea-Bissau with a sense of unity and a network of military roads in the north, but little else of value; its struggle to develop has been hampered by poverty, lack of trained administrators and many other problems due to years of colonial neglect. With current resources its climb to economic efficiency and reasonable standards of living is likely to be slow.

Ivory Coast

The Country

The Republic of the Ivory Coast lies on the southern coast of the west African bulge, bordered by Ghana in the east, Liberia and Guinea in the west, and Mali and Burkina Faso in the north. *Area* 322,463 km^2 (124,503 sq miles); *capital* Abidjan (planned to move to Yamoussoukro); *population* 9,712,000 (est. 1986).

Organization
A legislative National Assembly of 147 members and an executive President are elected for five-year terms; the President appoints a council of about 22 ministers who are responsible to him. There is a single ruling party, the Parti Démocratique de la Côte d'Ivoire. The official language is French, with many local languages spoken; local religions are dominant, with sizeable Roman Catholic and Moslem minorities.

Geography
A surf and sand-dune coast borders the Gulf of Guinea for 500 km (300 miles), backed in the east by lagoons, which provide sheltered waterways with access to the rivers; the port of Abidjan is reached by a canal. Inland lies a broad coastal plain, crossed at intervals by southward-flowing rivers; here forests have been partly replaced by plantations and farms, scattered with villages and larger settlements. Inland again the country rises to a savanna-covered upland generally 300 to 350 m (over 1000 ft) high, dissected by the rivers into long north–south ridges. Higher ridges in the west and northwest rise above 1000 m (3300 ft); the highest point is the Mt Nimba massif (1752 m, 5748 ft) on the border with Guinea and Liberia. The climate is hot and wet along the coast with rain for most of the year; the north is drier, with little rain from November to July.

History and Development
Ivory Coast's southern negroid farmers and northern pastoralists both have stronger cultural and language affinities with neighbours to east and west than with each other. European explorers from the 15th century onward traded with the southerners for slaves, gold, ivory and palm oil. French trading posts were established during the 18th and 19th centuries, those at Assini and Grand Bassam being formally occupied by France and used as centres for exploration from the mid-19th century onward. French colonial penetration and settlement in the centre and north was strongly opposed by the natives, sporadic guerrilla warfare continuing well into this century. Ivory Coast became independent in 1960, retaining strong cultural and economic links with France.

Resources and Economics
Agriculture employs about 80 per cent of the workforce and generates about one quarter of the national income. Smallholdings and family farms grow maize, millet, sorghum and manioc, though not enough for local needs. Cotton, oilseeds, sugar-cane, bananas and pineapples are among other important crops; key cash crops are coffee and cocoa, which together generate almost half the country's export revenues. Tropical hardwoods are exported in quantity. There are few minerals, but offshore petroleum provides most of Ivory Coast's needs, and huge reserves of natural gas have been capped for future use. Hydroelectric power meets most domestic needs, though drought currently restricts output. Manufacturing industries provide processed foods, textiles, shoes, electrical equipment and other consumables mainly for local use, and there is an expanding petrochemical industry. Road and rail links, including a line to Ouagadougou in Burkina Faso, are adequate and well maintained; Abidjan has

deep-water port and international airport facilities, and there are several large regional airports.

Recent Developments

Ivory Coast's political stability and continuing links with France have ensured it the investment capital, expertise and long-term security needed for the continuing development of its resources. Current prosperity, in which it is far ahead of most other African states, seems soundly based and attracts immigrant labour from neighbouring states; its spectacular economic progress since independence is likely to resume once the world recession is past. The current five-year plan seeks to provide for further investment in agriculture and export industries, and enhance hydroelectric energy output so that more petroleum is available for export.

Liberia

The Country

The Republic of Liberia occupies the southwestern corner of the west African bulge, bounded by Ivory Coast in the east, Sierra Leone in the northwest and Guinea in the north. *Area* 111,369 km² (43,000 sq miles); *capital* Monrovia; *population* 2,442,000 (est. 1986).

Organization

Liberia's constitution (based on that of the USA) was suspended in April 1980 with the assassination of the President and establishment of military government. The country is currently ruled by a People's Redemption Council, mainly military, of between 20 and 30 members. The Council chairman, who heads both state and government, appoints a cabinet of about 20 ministers. The official language is English; Christianity is the dominant religion with a substantial minority of Moslems.

Geography

A narrow littoral zone is backed in the north and south by broad coastal plains, which rise inland to a plateau 200 to 300 m (650 to 1000 ft) high; in the central province the plateau rises steeply out of the sea, extending inland as a high rolling upland. The highest ground is in the northeast, rising to over 1000 m (3300 ft) on the border with Guinea and Ivory Coast. Swiftly-flowing rivers cross the plateau and plains, studded with rapids and blocked at the mouth by sand-bars. The climate is hot and wet, with over 380 cm (150 in) of rain per annum in the west, about 250 cm (100 in) in the east. Much of Liberia is forested, though parts of the coastal plains have been cleared for farming or plantations.

History and Development

Mapped by Portuguese explorers in the 15th century, this coast was harbourless and inhospitable, inhabited by Negro farming and hunter-gathering communities with a well-established social hierarchy and trade network. It was visited by Dutch, British and other European traders for slaves, spices and gold. In 1822 Cape Mesurado (site of the present capital) became a settlement, funded by the American Colonization Society, for repatriated slaves from the American plantations. Other coastal settlements followed, to be united in 1847 as the independent Negro state of Liberia. Hostility from native populations and neighbouring colonies, and lack of development capital, dogged the early days of the republic, although it was helped intermittently by the USA.

Resources and Economics
About 75 per cent of Liberians farm, generating over half the country's wealth. Food crops include rice, cassava, palm oil, yams, fruit, vegetables and livestock, but many staples are imported. Rubber, cocoa and coffee are grown for cash; rubber plantations employ a third of Liberia's paid workers and provide some 15 per cent of export revenues. Fish and timber are exploited but much valuable timber is lost in slash-and-burn agriculture. Iron ore in the past yielded 60 per cent of export earnings but world depression has cut demand; diamonds, gold and other minerals are less important. Food-processing and construction are the main industries, with hydroelectric power providing 70 per cent of energy needs. Liberia's 'flag of convenience' merchant fleet brings small revenues. Roads and railways are improving to carry increasing traffic. Monrovia has a deep-water port and international airport.

Recent Developments
Overdependent on iron ore and rubber, Liberia relies heavily on foreign aid and investment to service its debts and provide development capital. The initial excesses of the revolutionary government proved discouraging to foreign investors, and confidence has been slow to return. With inflation, budget deficits and unemployment running high, economic recovery is unlikely to be rapid.

Nigeria

The Country
The Federal Republic of Nigeria lies in the eastern corner of the Gulf of Guinea, bordered by Chad in the extreme northeast, Cameroon in the east, Benin in the west and Niger in the north. *Area* 923,768 km² (356,667 sq miles); *present capital and largest city* Lagos, *future capital* Abuja; *population* 94,316,000 (est. 1986).

Organization
Nigeria is a federation of nineteen constituent states. The federal National Assembly consists of a Senate of 95 members (five for each state) and a 449-member House of Representatives; both are elected for four-year terms. The executive President, who is also elected by popular vote for four years, appoints a Federal Executive Council of about 24 ministers. Each state has an elected House of Assembly and Governor. Following the 1984 coup, Nigeria is currently governed by a Supreme Military Council. English is the official language. Hausa is widely spoken in the north, where Islam is the dominant religion. In the south Ibo and Yoruba are the most important local languages, and both Christianity and local religions prevail.

Geography
Nigeria's coastline is mostly sand dunes backed by brackish lagoons, but the centre is occupied by the Niger delta, 350 km (220 miles) long and covering over

10,000 km^2 (3900 sq miles). Lagoons and delta waterways are lined with mangroves and coastal forest. Inland a coastal plain rises gently to about 150 m (500 ft), backed in the west by low forested hills up to 300–400 m (1000–1300 ft) high, and in the east by a steeper rise to a plateau at 600 m (2000 ft) along the Cameroon border. In the southeast stand Nigeria's highest peaks, on the flank of Cameroon's Adamawa Highlands. Highest of all is Mt Dimlang (2042 m, 6699 ft). Half the lowland forest has been cut or clear-felled for farms and plantations; some has reverted to a mixture of forest and grassland.

Through central Nigeria roll two great rivers, the Niger from the northwest and the Benue from the northeast, in broad, savanna-clad valleys that meet near Lokoja; both rivers are strongly influenced by seasonal rains. Beyond them rises the high Jos Plateau, a central massif of eroded volcanic rocks, woodland-covered and capped by Sara Peak (1780 m, 5840 ft). In the north the plateau falls gently toward the Niger border, and to the Lake Chad basin in the northeast corner, the vegetation deteriorating from savanna to steppe and desert scrub.

The coast is generally hot and humid, with annual rainfall exceeding 300 cm (120 in); the heaviest rains are monsoonal, falling in June–July and September–October. Across central and northern Nigeria temperatures remain high but rainfall decreases, especially between November and March; in the far north these are virtually rainless months, and annual precipitation is less than 50 cm (20 in).

History and Development

Nigeria's savanna and southern forests have been occupied at least since the early Stone Age, the traditions of savanna stock-raising and forest cultivation dating from early days of settlement. Iron tools allowed cultivators to slash-and-burn their way more deeply into the forest; fine copper and bronze artifacts came later, in the city states that flourished from about AD 900 onward. By the 13th century there were well-founded dynastic kingdoms in the north, later to be unified in the Moslem caliphate of Sokoto which continued into the early years of the present century. In the south were many smaller communities, some of which gave rise to the tribal groupings which are still in evidence today.

Coastal city states of the Niger delta were the first to encounter Europeans, who from the 15th century (possibly earlier) came to trade in gold, slaves and other products of the interior. By the early 19th century Britons predominated in the coastal factories and were penetrating far inland toward the sources of trade goods. With the decline of slaving, palm oil became the major attraction. In 1861 Lagos Island was adopted formally as a British colony, providing a base for anti-slavery patrols. By 1885 Britain had acquired, through treaties with local chiefs, almost exclusive trading rights along the lower Niger; in that year the Oil River Protectorate was established along the coast, later to be extended by conquest into Yorubaland, and later still to incorporate Lagos and become the southern province of Nigeria. The north, more thinly populated but better organized under its Moslem rulers, resisted traders and treaty-makers alike, but became a protectorate in 1900.

By 1914 both protectorates, more or less pacified, were combined as the colony of Nigeria. Despite amalgamation they retained their identities, reflected in differing forms of local administration under colonial rule. One of the most prosperous African colonies, Nigeria gained self-government within the Commonwealth in 1960, adding the northern part of former British Togoland to its eastern border. Three years later it became a republic within the Commonwealth. After a military coup in 1967 federal authority was challenged by the eastern province ('Biafra') which feared domination by the north and sought independence. A costly civil war lasting $2\frac{1}{2}$ years ended Biafran aspirations. Although civil government was restored in 1979, military rule was again enforced in 1984.

Resources and Economics

Though in some ways an advanced African state, Nigeria retains a strong agricultural bias. Some 60 per cent of the workforce is involved in farming, many still at subsistence level, generating only about 20 per cent of the national wealth. Crops grown for local consumption include yams, cassava, maize, rice, millet, vegetables and livestock; formerly almost self-sufficient for food, Nigeria currently imports several of its staples. Crops for export include rubber, cocoa, ground-nuts, and hides and skins. Fish are caught in Lake Chad and off the Gulf of Guinea coast, but most of the fish eaten in Nigeria are imported. Timber and timber products are exported from the southern forests.

Nigeria has substantial mineral resources, mostly underdeveloped; it produces tin from its own ores, columbite and coal, and is developing iron ore and bauxite deposits for smelting locally. Petroleum is currently the most valuable mineral, accounting for over 90 per cent of export earnings; a proportion is refined locally. Natural gas accompanying the oil is at present wasted, and there are huge reserves available for future use. Limited hydroelectric power is produced from the Niger River; gas-operated power stations are also in production.

Industry is responsible for about 10 per cent of the national income. Processed foods, building materials, plywood, textiles, electrical equipment and locally-assembled motor vehicles are the main products, mostly for local use. Roads and railways are less than adequate for the country's needs, and the rivers are important though limited seasonal routes for heavy traffic. Nigeria has substantial port facilities at Calabar, Lagos, Warri and Port Harcourt, and good internal and external air links.

Recent Developments

Nigeria's most pressing economic problem is its heavy dependence on petroleum. Oil revenues rolling in during the early years of independence encouraged ambitious development projects; current income, still coming mainly from this single source, is depressed by poor prices on the world market and cannot maintain the momentum. Planning deficiencies and extravagances are apparent, while hopes of improving standards of living for Nigerians are in general receding. The gap between rich and poor is great, leading readily to suspicions that one tribal group benefits at another's expense, and bedevilling internal relations. The large standing army, though a drain on the economy, is maintained mainly because there is little alternative employment. Import restrictions and scaling-down of public spending help to reduce overseas debts, but the resulting shortages, unemployment and internal discontent are unwelcome in a country so readily divided against itself.

Senegal

The Country

The Republic of Senegal occupies the most westerly point of the west African bulge, bordered by Mauritania in the north, Mali in the east, Guinea in the southeast and Guinea-Bissau in the southwest; it entirely surrounds the Gambia. *Area* 196,192 km^2 (75,750 sq miles); *capital* Dakar; *population* 6,654,000 (est. 1986).

Organization

A legislative National Assembly of 120 members and an executive President are elected by popular vote for five-year terms. The President appoints a Prime Minister and cabinet of about 28 ministers, who are responsible to the Assembly. The official language is French, with several local languages widely spoken; Islam is the dominant religion, with minority Christian and local religions.

Geography

Cape Vert, a volcanic peninsula 100 m (330 ft) high, forms the westernmost point of Africa and protects the city and port of Dakar. To the north lies a long, featureless dune coast beaten by Atlantic surf; to the south dunes give way to mudbanks, estuaries and mangrove forests. Northern Senegal is an extensive basin, thinly covered with grass and Sahelian semi-desert vegetation, bounded in the north by the Senegal River and drained mainly by seasonal streams. The southern half of the country is also low-lying, rising gently in the southeast to about 500 m (1600 ft) on the Guinea border. The climate is hot and arid in the north, with rain likely from July to October. Rainfall increases toward the south, the vegetation changing from savanna north of the Gambia River to forest along the Guinea-Bissau border.

History and Development

Senegal stands at the western end of the Sahel, spanning northern deserts and southern forests; its northern peoples are Berber farmers and stock-raisers, its southern majority negroid, mostly Mandingos. Portuguese explorers in the 15th century based themselves in the southern estuaries and penetrated eastward in search of gold. French traders founded St Louis in 1626, in the following century edging out Dutch and other settlers from the coast, and in turn being expelled by the British. Restored to France after the Napoleonic Wars, the territory between the Senegal and Casamance rivers remained virtually unexploited until 1854, when it was colonized and made the base for French colonial sorties throughout western Africa. Senegal achieved independence within the French Community in 1960.

Resources and Economics

Agriculture employs 75 per cent of Senegal's workforce and generates 30 per cent of the national income. Rice, sugar, sorghum, millet, maize and livestock are the main food crops; many small farmers grow cotton as a cash crop. Wheat, rice and sugar are imported, especially in years of drought. Ground-nuts grow on roughly half the country's productive land, yielding most of Senegal's export earnings in good cropping years. Fishing is a major industry; in some years fresh and processed fish contribute more than ground-nuts to national income. Phosphate rock is the only significant mineral; natural gas and petroleum are being developed, and hydroelectric power generation is increasing rapidly. Timber is an important fuel. Textile-manufacture, food-processing and shipbuilding and repairing are important industries. Road and rail networks improve as the economy develops. Dakar has major port facilities and an international airport.

Recent Developments

After a slow and difficult start, Senegal's economy burgeoned during the first two decades of independence. Though still reliant on a few marketable products (notably ground-nuts, fish and phosphates) for its main income, Senegal has built up infrastructures in agriculture, transport and industry which are strong enough to see it successfully through several years of world recession. Its economy continues to expand slowly from firm foundations, and closer links with the Gambia are envisaged through the Senegambia Confederation. Irrigation (in which Senegal has long been a pioneer) to increase and stabilize crop production, hydroelectric developments, and expansion of the mining and consumer industries feature in the current development plan, which will also encourage foreign investors and tourists.

Sierra Leone

The Country

The Republic of Sierra Leone lies on the southwest coast of the west African bulge, bordered by Liberia in the southeast and Guinea in the north and northeast. *Area* 71,740 km² (27,699 sq miles); *capital* Freetown; *population* 4,112,000 (est. 1986).

Organization

Of 104 representatives in the Parliament, 85 are elected for five-year terms, 7 hold presidential appointments and 12 are Paramount Chiefs. The executive President and Head of State, who is elected by the single political party, the All People's Congress (APC), appoints a cabinet of about 20 ministers. Local government is administered through three provinces, each divided into Chiefdoms, and the Western Area which includes Freetown. English is the official language with local languages widely spoken. Local religions are dominant, Christians and Moslems forming minority groups.

Geography

Sierra Leone's name ('Lion Mountains') derives from the isolated range of intrusive volcanic rocks on Freetown peninsula, forming a prominent landfall on an otherwise low-lying mangrove-and-mud coast. A broad plain extends inland, flat and savanna-covered in the north, rolling and forested in the south, rising in steps to a dissected plateau of weathered granite at about 120 m (400 ft) above sea level. The western half of the country rises higher to a mean level of 500 m (1650 ft); the highest peak, Loma Mansa (1948 m, 6391 ft), stands with others almost as high near the western border. The climate is generally hot and humid with rains from May to October. The east receives up to 380 cm (150 in) of rain annually, almost twice as much as the inland mountains.

History and Development

Discovered by Portuguese navigators in 1462, Sierra Leone was thinly populated by small Negro farming and trading communities. In 1787 British abolitionists bought land on the peninsula to settle slaves freed from the North American plantations. Freetown settlement grew as more freed slaves arrived. In 1807 its harbour became a naval base for anti-slaving operations, and a year later the peninsular area, isolated by swamps from the hinterland, was declared a

British Crown Colony. As the century progressed Freetown became the administrative centre for the Gambia, Gold Coast and Lagos, later to be made separate colonies; in 1896 it acquired the hinterland as a protectorate. Descendants of the slaves, called creoles, mixed little with mainland Negroes, most of whom are Mende and Temne; the distinction is still apparent. Sierra Leone became self-governing within the Commonwealth in 1961 and a republic ten years later.

Resources and Economics

Almost two thirds of Sierra Leone's workforce are smallholders; rice, maize and cassava are the staple crops produced, but rice is also imported. Cash crops include cocoa, coffee, ginger, palm nuts and kola nuts; ground-nuts and sugar are being encouraged as potential crops for export. Timber is important as a fuel, though increasingly hard to come by in the densely inhabited areas. Fish are plentiful; a newly-developed fishing industry adds substantially to the diet. Minerals are relatively undeveloped; diamonds alone contribute about half the country's import earnings, and iron ore, bauxite and rutile add varying proportions according to their market value. Apart from food-processing, industries are mostly at a cottage level. Roads are being improved as finances permit; railways no longer exist. Freetown has fine deep-water port facilities and an international airport.

Recent Developments

Sierra Leone's heavy reliance on coffee, cocoa and diamonds for its living is misplaced. Neither food crops nor cash crops can by present methods be produced reliably, and government marketing policies seemingly make the key cash crops unrewarding to producers. Output of diamonds from alluvial sources has fallen, there is a slump in world demand, and smuggling is difficult and expensive to control. In consequence foreign earnings fluctuate widely and the economy remains static. Help from the IMF is conditional on improvements being made in agriculture, extension of mining to include bauxite and iron ores, increases in hydroelectric power capacity, and fiscal tightening – changes designed to diversify the economy and cut unnecessary spending.

Togo

The Country

The Republic of Togo lies on the Guinea coast of west Africa, bordered by Benin in the east, Ghana in the west and Burkina Faso in the north. *Area* 56,785 km^2 (21,925 sq miles); *capital* Lomé; *population* 3,158,000 (est. 1986).

Organization

The Togolese elect a National Assembly of 67 representatives for five-year terms from nominees of the dominant political party, the Rassemblement du peuple togolais, which controls affairs of state. A President and Head of State, elected for seven-year terms, governs with a cabinet of about 20 members. Local government is effected through five regions, subdivided into prefectures headed by chiefs and elected councils. Local religions predominate, with about one third of the population Catholic or Moslem. French is the official language; local languages are widely used.

Geography

From a narrow lagoon coast and low-lying plain Togo rises to an upland some 450 m (1500 ft) above sea level. The centre is crossed from northeast to southwest by the Togo and Atakora mountains, dominated by Pic Baumann (986 m, 3235 ft). Beyond lies a northern lowland extending into Ghana, which rises to north and west to form the high Oti Plateau. The climate is hot and humid on the coast, cooler and drier in the north; forest and scrub characterize the lowlands, thinning to grassland and dry savanna on high ground.

History and Development

Formerly part of the Kingdom of Togoland, Togo stood at the crossroads of many migration routes, acquiring a heterogeneous population of farming and pastoral settlers from east, north and west, and losing many of them during the 18th and 19th centuries to slave raiders from the south. German missions and trading factories established during the mid-19th century led to the definition in 1885 of a German Togoland protectorate, sandwiched between Britain and French claims. After World War I the area was divided between Britain and France, present-day Togo arising in 1960 from the former mandated, later trusteeship territory of French Togo.

Resources and Economics

About 80 per cent of the workforce are farmers and smallholders, generating less than half the national income; the main subsistence crops are maize, rice, cassava, yams and ground-nuts, the main export crops coffee, cocoa, copra, palm oil and cotton. Phosphate ores, exported through Kpémé, provide the main source of overseas earnings; other minerals, including bauxite and iron-bearing limestones, are present but under-exploited. Industries include cement manufacture, oil-refining, steel-milling and food-processing. Roads and railways are limiting development; there are good port and airport facilities.

Recent Developments

Political stability since 1967 has encouraged French and other European investment, advancing Togo's economy and placing it on a sound footing for development. To good agriculture, efficient mineral production and growing industries may be added promise of indigenous oil and hydroelectricity from the Mono River, all indicating a prosperous future for this small country.

AFRICA NORTHEAST

Chad

The Country

The Republic of Chad lies centrally in north Africa, bounded by Sudan in the east, Central African Republic in the south, Cameroon, Nigeria and Niger in the west and Libya in the north. *Area* 1,284,000 km² (495,752 sq miles); *capital* Ndjamena; *population* 5,066,000 (est. 1986).

Organization

Constitutionally provided with an elected National Assembly, Chad was under military rule from 1975 and involved in civil war from 1978 to 1982. Under a new constitution of 1982 an executive President heads an executive council of 31 ministers, most of whom are Moslem. For local government the country is divided into fourteen prefectures. The official language is French, with Arabic widely spoken in the centre and north; many local languages are in use. The north is mainly Moslem; local religions and Christianity prevail in the south.

Geography
Land-locked Chad is mainly a semi-desert plateau 200 to 500 m (660 to 1650 ft) above sea level, with a high rim in the north, east and south. In the southwest lies Lake Chad, 281 m (922 ft) above sea level, in a wide basin to which the southern Chari and Logone rivers drain. Most other rivers are seasonal, flowing only after rains. To east and south rise parched uplands, highest along the Sudan border where isolated massifs reach 1500 m (4900 ft). In the north tower the dramatic escarpments of the Tibesti mountains, an ancient volcanic bloc rising above 3200 m (10,500 ft); the highest peak is Emi Koussi (3415 m, 11,204 ft). The climate is generally hot and dry, the vegetation desert scrub or steppe. The south is moderately wet beween May and October but dry for the rest of the year, supporting savanna and thin forest.

History and Development
Northern Chad is the home of desert nomads with strong Arab affinities, southern Chad part of the forest and savanna zone occupied by Negro farmers and herdsmen. Trade routes crossed in all directions, travellers making use of oases in the drier central and northern areas. Europeans explored this area during the mid-19th century, and the colonial carve-up of the late century left the country east of Lake Chad under French influence. As part of French Equatorial Africa, Chad province proved difficult to pacify and was for long under military rule, becoming a colony in 1920. Granted autonomy within the French Community in 1959 and independence in 1960 it soon fell into disharmony. In 1965 the Moslem north rebelled against the dominant and non-Moslem south, starting a civil war in which Libyan forces supported the north and French troops the south. This ended in 1982 with the defeat of southern forces by the Forces Armées du Nord.

Resources and Economics
Chad's economy is based on agriculture; about 90 per cent of the people are subsistence farmers or herdsmen. Rice, millet, wheat, maize, ground-nuts and cassava are grown in the south and in the fertile Chad basin, where underground water supports irrigation. Elsewhere sheep and cattle provide the main living, sometimes in association with crops. The main cash crop is cotton, grown chiefly in the south and ginned locally; meat is also exported, and fish, abundant in Lake Chad, are eaten locally and dried for export. Chad has no exploited minerals apart from lake salts, and no industries of more than local interest. There are many tracks but few paved roads; the capital (formerly Fort Lamy) has an international airport.

Recent Developments
The fierce tribal independence that held generations of French colonial troops at bay continues to thwart national unity. Among the world's poorest countries, with few resources to command, Chad can ill-afford modern warfare; to the rural population whose everyday enemies are drought, disease and hunger, the

antics of armed forces fighting across their parched grazing lands must seem strangely inept. Economic progress may now become possible if the long-standing struggle for power has been settled, and a government established that can accept whatever help the world community can give.

Djibouti

The Country
The Republic of Djibouti occupies the western shore of the Gulf of Aden on Bab el Mandeb, the entrance to the Red Sea, bounded in the east by the Somali Democratic Republic and in the south and west by Ethiopia. *Area* 22,000 km^2 (8494 sq miles); *capital* Djibouti; *population* 481,000 (est. 1986).

Organization
From a legislative chamber of 65 deputies, elected by universal suffrage, is selected an executive Prime Minister and council of about 15 ministers. The Head of State is an elected President. The official language is Cushitic Arabic, with French and other European languages common currency in the capital; the dominant faith is Islam.

Geography
Centered around the Gulf of Tadjoura, Djibouti presents a dry, volcanic landscape. In the south is a low rolling plateau, parts of it below sea level, and some depressions containing shallow lakes. North of the Gulf of Tadjoura the partly-forested Mabla and Gouda mountains form a spectacular backdrop, Mt Gouda rising to 1783 m (5850 ft); towards the northern border are higher ranges, Moussa Ali rising to 2063 m (6768 ft). Hot and dry, with less than 50 cm (20 in) of rain annually, most of the country is semi-desert.

History and Development
The Djibouti area traditionally supports two nomadic groups, the Afars of Ethiopian affinity and the Issas (currently about half the total population) of Somali origin. French interest developed in the late 19th century, when a treaty with Abyssinia (Ethiopia) allowed the port of Djibouti to be expanded into a naval base commanding the Gulf of Aden and Red Sea. A rail link with Addis Ababa, completed in 1917, made it a port of entry for Abyssinia. French Somaliland became a French Overseas Territory (Afars and Issas) in 1967, gaining its independence and current name ten years later.

Resources and Economics
About half the population is in the capital city; the remainder lives as wandering herdsmen, passing freely into neighbouring countries. Dates and vegetables are grown for local use; cattle, sheep, goats and fish add to the diet. Minerals and industries are of purely local importance. The country's main revenues come from the port, which in normal times is a transit point for Ethiopian commerce, and has ship-refuelling and repair facilities.

Recent Developments
The urban half of Djibouti's population live precariously on transit trade, which has recently been depressed by warfare in the 'horn' of Africa and the closure of

e railway to Ethiopia. The rural population carries on the timeless traditions
nomadic life, only marginally affected by government schemes to provide
atering points and encourage fodder crops. Both Ethiopia and Somalia claim
e country.

gypt

he Country

he Arab Republic of Egypt occupies the northeastern corner of Africa with
oth Mediterranean and Red Sea coasts, bounded in the south by Sudan and in
e west by Libya. *Area* 1,001,449 km^2 (386,659 sq miles); *capital* Cairo;
pulation 48,318,000 (est. 1986).

rganization

legislative People's Assembly of 392 elected members (and up to ten more
esidential nominees) nominates a President who is elected for terms of six
ars; the President appoints a Vice-President, Prime Minister and council of
out 28 ministers. There is also a Consultative Council of 140 elected and 70
ominated members. For local government the two major divisions of Lower
d Upper Egypt are subdivided into 26 governorates. The official language is
rabic, with English and French widely spoken; most Egyptians are Moslem,
ith a Christian minority.

eography.

gypt's western desert is a limestone plateau covered with dunes and parched
aharan vegetation, rising from a narrow coastal plain on the Mediterranean to
tween 100 and 300 m (300 and 1000 ft). To the southwest stands Gebel
weinat (1893 m, 6210 ft) on the Libyan and Sudan borders. In the east the Nile
ver valley runs the full length of Egypt from man-made Lake Nasser in the
uth to a coastal delta in the north. Beyond the valley an eastern desert plain is
dged by volcanic mountains, which in turn border the Red Sea. Their highest
ak, Gebel Shayib el Banat, rises to 2187 m (7175 ft). At the head of the Red
a, between the Gulfs of Suez and Aqaba, the Sinai triangle of desert and
ountain includes Gebel Katherina (2637 m, 8652 ft), Egypt's highest peak.
he Suez Canal crosses at sea level from the Gulf of Suez to the Mediterranean
a. Summers are hot and dry, winters cold and slightly moister; the highest
midity is along the coast (especially in the delta), in the Nile valley and a few
ses, and in the eastern mountains.

istory and Development

ccupied by nomads at least from Neolithic times, Egypt's Nile valley became
early centre of civilization, annual floods providing a dependable cycle of
rtility. For over five thousand years these have supported a series of
vilizations of which the pyramids and temples form the most lasting
onuments. Egyptians paid heavily for their prosperity, Libyans, Persians,
reeks, Romans, Syrians and Turks in turn coveting and conquering the Nile
lley and delta; Egypt was for over four centuries (1517–1914) a province of the
ttoman Empire (see Turkey). Increasing involvement by France and Britain
ring the late 19th century led to British occupation in 1882 and the gradual
tablishment of a British protectorate over the kingdom of Egypt. At

257

independence in 1922 Britain continued to exercise control over defence and some other matters. British forces occupied Egypt in World War II, withdrawing shortly after the war. A military coup in 1952 ousted the King, and in 1953 Egypt became a republic. Israeli, British and French troops invaded briefly in 1956 but withdrew leaving Egypt in possession of the Suez Canal. Attempts at federation with Syria, Libya and Iraq proved unsuccessful, and open war with Israel in 1948, 1967 and 1973 resulted in the loss and ultimate recovery of Sinai.

Resources and Economics

Agriculture, restricted mainly to the Nile valley, occupies about 40 per cent of the workforce. The opening of the Aswân High Dam in 1970 improved control of flood waters (a benefit shared with Sudan by an agreement of 1959) and increased the irrigated area. Food crops include maize, millet, rice, wheat and sugar-cane; potatoes, rice, fruit and cotton are grown for export, raw cotton and textiles alone yielding over a third of export income. The Nile provides fish for local consumption. Iron, lead, zinc and manganese ores, salt and phosphate rock are mined in small amounts. Petroleum resources meet local needs and yield a further third of the country's export earnings. Egypt has abundant hydroelectric power; large manufacturing industries include food-processing, textiles, petrochemicals, iron and steel, motor vehicles and electrical goods, and there are many smaller industries. Road, railway, river and air transport networks are well developed in the populated areas, and the Suez Canal adds considerably to the national income. Egypt's antiquities support a flourishing tourist industry.

Recent Developments

Israeli–Egyptian accord since the peace treaty of 1979 reduced the dangers of war over Sinai and other disputed territories but left neighbouring Arab countries hostile to Egypt. As these rifts slowly mend, the country benefits from peace, economic recovery and expansion. Oil, cotton, canal dues, tourism, and remittances from many Egyptians working in other countries all contribute to a flourishing national economy, which has recently expanded at over 8 per cent per annum. Substantial aid flows in from the USA, OECD and other sources; though growth has now slowed and inflation runs high, the country prospers as never before. Current five-year plans aim to stimulate industry, mining and agriculture, and to improve transport, housing and other services. Port facilities are to be extended, and the highly profitable Suez Canal improved.

Ethiopia

The Country

The Republic of Ethiopia occupies much of the eastern end of north Africa with a coastline on the Red Sea; it shares boundaries with Djibouti and the Somali Democratic Republic in the east, Kenya in the south and Sudan in the west. *Area* 1,221,900 km² (471,776 sq miles); *capital* Addis Ababa; *population* 36,651,000 (est. 1986).

Organization

A de facto republic, Ethiopia has not replaced its former monarchic constitution, which was abolished by decree in 1974. The country is governed by a

Provisional Military Administration Council (Derg) of about 80 appointees, with an inner central committee and smaller standing committee. These are all chaired by the Head of State, who also presides over a council of about 27 appointed ministers. Local government is administered through Kebeles or local cooperatives. The official language is Amharic; English, Arabic and many local languages are also spoken. Coptic Christianity is well represented in the north and in the mountains; Islam is widespread elsewhere.

Geography

A towering bloc of volcanic mountains fills three quarters of the country in the west and south, split by an arm of the great African Rift Valley that opens to the northeast in a plain bordering the Red Sea. The western mountains form a plateau at 1500 to 2000 m (4900 to 6500 ft), deeply cut by river valleys and edged in the east by the high (4000 m, 13,000 ft) Rift Valley escarpment. Ras Dashen, Ethiopia's highest peak, overlooks the Rift Valley at 4620 m (15,154 ft) in the north. The southeastern mountains are generally lower, falling away to the Ogaden and Somali plateaus in the east. The northeastern plain slopes toward the Red Sea, crossed centrally by the arid Danakil Depression. Ethiopia's mountains and uplands are mostly forested, especially in the west where the climate is most consistently warm and humid. The east is drier with less reliable rains, forests giving way to savanna and desert in the lowlands.

History and Development

Ethiopia's heartland has for long been the home of pastoral and farming tribes, many of them Christian from the 6th century onward. The peripheral lowlands have generally been dominated by Moslems, invading from Somalia, the Sudan or the Red Sea. In the 16th century Portuguese troops helped Christian Ethiopians to expel Somali invaders. After the opening of the Suez Canal in 1869, Italy attempted to dominate the flourishing empire of Menelik II, but Italy's defeat in battle guaranteed Ethiopia freedom from further European meddling, establishing the country as an independent feudal power. In 1935 Italy invaded again, this time successfully. The Emperor was exiled and Ethiopia (then Abyssinia) was incorporated with Eritrea and Italian Somaliland into Italian East Africa. Liberated in World War II, Abyssinia again became a feudal empire, absorbing Eritrea in 1962 after a decade of close attachment and fighting Somalia sporadically over southern territories. A revolution in 1974 deposed the Emperor, the military government which replaced him attracting military and economic aid from Cuba and the USSR.

Resources and Economics

Ethiopia is one of Africa's poorest countries. About 95 per cent of the workforce raises crops or livestock, some in cooperatives. Maize, wheat, sorghum and other cereals, potatoes, beans, vegetables and cane sugar are the main food crops. Coffee is the most important cash crop, providing about 70 per cent of the country's export earnings; fruit, vegetables and hides make up the balance. Crop-raising is precarious; even in good years Ethiopia is not self-sufficient for food and droughts and floods all too frequently necessitate famine relief. Gold is mined in the mountains; other minerals including platinum, copper and other metal ores remain virtually unexploited. Timber is plentiful but used mainly for fuel. Industries are limited mainly to food-processing, textiles and building materials; Ethiopia has few manufactured products and imports almost all its consumer goods. Some roads have recently been improved with foreign aid;

most others are poor. Railways connect Addis Ababa with Djibouti, and Massawa with Keren and Akordat in Eritrea. Aseb is a large and growing Red Sea port; Addis Ababa and two other centres have international airports.

Recent Developments

Ethiopia's aspirations to be a leading African power fell with its feudal emperor, Haile Selassie, in 1974. Socialist principles now replace feudalism but poverty continues. Eritrean independence movements in the north and Somali claims to the Ogaden in the east have involved the country in costly wars; though resolved after a fashion with Soviet and Cuban help, their legacy of debt (paid mainly in agricultural produce) will cripple the economy for years to come, leaving little over for development. Accepting Soviet aid for long isolated Ethiopia from Western sources, but aid is currently flowing in from all sides to relieve famine, to help the development of mining, geothermal and hydroelectric power and roads, and increase the efficiency of cotton and livestock production.

Libya

The Country

The Socialist People's Libyan Arab Jamahiriya lies centrally on the north African coast, bounded by Egypt in the east, Sudan in the southeast, Chad and Niger in the south, and Algeria and Tunisia in the west. *Area* 1,759,540 km^2 (679,359 sq miles); *capital* Tripoli; *population* 3,748,000 (est. 1986).

Organization

Libya is governed by a General People's Committee of about 20 appointed Secretaries, who are responsible to a General People's Congress of over 1100 appointees. De facto Head of State is the Revolutionary Leader Col. Muammar Qadhafi, although he holds no formal post in the administration; the sole political party is the Arab Socialist Union. Local authority is vested in 186 Basic and 25 Municipal People's Congresses which govern through appointed Popular Committees. The official language is Arabic, with Italian and English widely spoken in the cities. Most Libyans are Moslem.

Geography

Much of Libya's long Mediterranean coast is backed by desert, mainly of limestone ridges, sandflats and dry river beds. Important exceptions are the eastern and western uplands, Jebel Akhdar and Jebel Nafusah, which rise to over 850 m (2800 ft) within sight of the coast, attracting winter rains and providing the country's most fertile soils. The interior, from the Cyrenaica desert in the east to the uplands of Fezzan and Tripolitania in the west, is a desolate landscape of arid ridges and dunes, rising steadily toward the south. Libya's highest land lies in the far south beyond the Tropic of Cancer, in the Uweinat massif (1893 m, 6210 ft) on the Egypt and Sudan borders, and the Tibesti massif (over 2000 m, 6600 ft) bordering Chad. The climate is generally hot and dry, with damp winters along the Mediterranean coast.

History and Development

Libya's coastal plains were farmed by Greek and Roman settlers, who developed the ports of Tripoli and Benghazi. The dry interior remained virtually empty, crossed only by trading routes linking oases to the south and west. The coastal towns fell to the Vandals and Arabs; by the late 16th century the whole coastal strip formed part of the Ottoman Empire (see Turkey), governed locally from Tripoli and haunted by pirates. Italy invaded in 1911–12, ousting Turkish rule from the coast but failing to subdue the nomads of the interior. The provinces of Tripolitania and Cyrenaica were united in 1934 as the colony of Libya. Fought over in World War II, Libya came first under combined Anglo–French government (1943–9) and then under the UN, achieving independence as a Moslem kingdom in 1951. A socialist military revolution in 1969 installed the present republican regime.

Resources and Economics

Desperately poor up to 1960, Libya became wealthy within a decade of discovering and exploiting its petroleum resources. Agriculture remains an important industry, occupying about 20 per cent of the workforce, but currently generating only about 2 per cent of national income. Wheat, barley, citrus fruits, olives, vegetables and livestock are the main products, now boosted by large-scale irrigation; however, over half the country's food is currently imported. Few minerals are exploited apart from oil and natural gas, which now employ a tenth of the workforce. Their export provides over half the national income. Industrial development is limited by lack of skilled workers and, over much of the country, by shortage of water, but iron-, steel- and aluminium-processing, petrochemicals, fertilizers, construction and other industries are slowly expanding. Benghazi and Tripoli are major ports, and Tripoli has an international airport. Good roads and tracks connect the main coastal centres and inland villages.

Recent Developments

A dramatic increase in wealth, a popular revolutionary movement combining Moslem theocracy with intense nationalism and socialism, and strong but idiosyncratic leadership, have left Libya breathless. Oil wealth continues to flow, and socialism ensures that most Libyans benefit directly from it; however, world overproduction and fluctuating world prices keep the country's economy unstable, requiring import restrictions and cutbacks in the planned expansion of industry, agriculture, transport and social services. Nationalism and socialist convictions have prompted Libya to interfere in the affairs of most of its neighbours, causing diplomatic friction. Meanwhile a chronic lack of skilled management and shop-floor workers holds up the economic progress that the new wealth should provide.

Somali Democratic Republic

The Country

The Somali Democratic Republic, known as Somalia, occupies the easternmost 'horn' of Africa, with shores along the Gulf of Aden and Indian Ocean; it shares borders with Kenya, Ethiopia and Djibouti in the west. *Area* 637,657 km^2 (246,199 sq miles); *capital* Mogadishu; *population* 5,694,000 (est. 1986).

Organization

Somalia is governed by a President nominated by the sole political party, the Somali Revolutionary Socialist Party, which has considerable authority at all levels. There is an executive council of about 28 ministers and a single legislative chamber (People's Assembly) of 121 elected and 6 appointed deputies. The official language is Somali; Arabic, Italian and English are widely spoken. Islam is the state religion.

Geography

From a parched coastal plain, narrow in the north but wider in the south, Somalia rises in steps to an interior plateau almost 1000 m (3300 ft) high. Mountains along the Gulf of Aden coast, geologically an extension of Ethiopia's southern highlands, rise over 2400 m (7800 ft) in spectacular forested ranges. Much of the plateau is grassland or thin scrub, suitable only for nomadic grazing. Somalia is hot and generally arid. Rain is most likely from March to June and September to December, but may fail altogether; only the uplands receive more than about 50 cm (20 in) of rain annually.

History and Development

Sailing dhows visiting the Somali coasts stimulated the development of small settlements, where Arab and other immigrant traders provided water and victualling. The interior gave a scant living to Somali nomads. Arabs, Ottoman Turks and pirates from time to time dominated the area without benefiting greatly from it. Its strategic value increased with the opening of the Suez Canal in 1869, and French, British and Italian protectorates were established from the mid-19th century onward, mainly to provide bases for naval and other forces protecting the Red Sea route. After World War II most of British and Italian Somaliland were combined into Somalia, which achieved independence as the Somali Republic in 1960. Somalia's efforts to include other Somali-speaking areas in its boundaries led to war with Ethiopia (1964–7) and other expensive quarrels with neighbours. An army-led coup in 1969 established the Somali Democratic Republic and present regime.

Resources and Economics

Most Somalis are pastoral nomads, raising sheep, cattle and goats, or farmers growing maize, sorghum, sugar-cane, cassava and vegetables for local use. Others are employed in plantations in the Shebeli and Juba river regions where crops of sugar and bananas are grown under irrigation. Livestock and meat are the country's main exports. Bananas, timber and cork are also exported, and offshore fisheries have recently been expanded – initially under Soviet guidance – with a view to exporting processed seafoods. Minerals, including valuable uranium and iron ores, remain largely undeveloped; petroleum is present in the south and under active investigation. Industries are few and of local interest only. A network of poor but adequate roads and tracks links the main centres of population. Mogadishu is the main Indian Ocean port and has an international airport; Kisimayu and Berbera are growing ports on the Gulf of Aden.

Recent Developments

Concocted from former British and Italian colonies, awkwardly shaped and intrinsically poor, Somalia is nevertheless a viable homeland for Somali-speaking peoples – independent folk whose path to nationhood is proving erratic. Their attempts to form a Greater Somalia were a costly failure and hindrance to economic development. Under socialist military government since 1969, they have achieved a measure of national unity but little forward momentum. The country's annual income has fallen considerably since 1978, and current plans to develop irrigation and hydroelectric power in the Juba valley, to improve plateau grazing and provide more watering points, to develop fisheries and provide country-wide basic services and education, all depend heavily on foreign aid.

Sudan

The Country
The Democratic Republic of the Sudan lies centrally in northeastern Africa, with a Red Sea coastline; its neighbours are Ethiopia in the east, Kenya, Uganda and Zaïre in the south, Central African Republic, Chad and Libya in the west and Egypt in the north. *Area* 2,505,813 km² (967,495 sq miles); *capital* Khartoum; *population* 21,832,000 (est. 1986).

Organization
Sudan is ruled by an authoritarian President who is also Prime Minister and heads the ruling Sudanese Socialist Union party. He governs with the advice of a partly-elected legislative National Assembly of 151 members, and an executive cabinet of about 28 appointed ministers. An elected regional assembly and appointed executive council, based on Juba, are responsible for government in the southern region. Arabic is the official language, with English widely spoken. Most northern Sudanese are Moslems, most southerners support local faiths or (a small minority) Christianity.

Geography
Sudan is a saucer-shaped plateau, much of it above 400 m (1300 ft), drained by the Nile and its many tributaries. The eastern rim is formed by the Nubian uplands and a higher escarpment fringing the Red Sea, with peaks rising over 2000 m (6500 ft). In the southeast stand the foothills of Ethiopia's western highlands, the source of the Blue Nile, and in the south those of the Imatong Mountains on the Kenya and Uganda borders, dominated by Mt Kinyeti (3187 m, 10,456 ft), Sudan's highest peak. The White Nile flows south from this direction. In the west the Darfur massif rises from a high plateau at 1500 m (5000 ft) to the volcanic peaks of Jebel Marra (3088 m, 10,131 ft). The central plain includes the huge marshy Sudd in the far south, the fertile clays of Gezira below Khartoum, and Saharan rocks and dunes in the north. Through all of these winds the Nile, descending in a series of cataracts to man-made Lake Nasser on the Egyptian border. The climate is hot; rainfall is scarce over the northern desert but plentiful for most of the year in the savanna-covered southern hills.

History and Development
Sparsely populated by negroid farmers and pastoralists, the lands of the southern Nile formed a crossroads linking black southern Africa with the north and the southern Sahara with the Red Sea. Nubia, now northeastern Sudan, was colonized by Egypt about 2000 BC, yielding talented slaves and soldiers, gold, ivory and precious stones. In 750 BC Nubians controlled Egypt briefly before being driven south by the Assyrians. Nubia continued to dominate the middle Nile until AD 350, when it was colonized by the Ethiopia-based empire of Aksum. With Ethiopia Nubia accepted Christianity in the 6th century, remaining in the faith until recolonized by Moslems in the 15th century. Egypt

formally reoccupied Nubia in 1821, founding Khartoum as an administrativ centre. From the mid-19th century Egyptian influence extended southward meeting opposition from fanatical Moslems whose power was destroyed onl with British help in 1899. Sudan then became an Anglo–Egyptiai condominium, remaining so until 1956 when it achieved independence Parliamentary government lasted only two years; civil war between south ani north led to military coups in 1958 and 1969 and the establishment of th present pattern of authoritarian government.

Resources and Economics

Sudan is primarily agricultural, with 75 per cent of its workforce farmers o herders. The main food crops are sorghum, sugar-cane, wheat, millet, cassav and other tubers, vegetables and livestock. Cotton, ground-nuts, gum arabic sesame seeds and sorghum are exported, and wheat is a major import Agriculture accounts for about 40 per cent of national income; cotton and it products alone can supply up to half the country's export earnings, thoug growing and marketing problems often depress revenues. Attempts to grov wheat and rice on a large scale have not proved viable; new sugar plantation have been more successful. Chromium ores are exploited commercially; iror manganese and other ores are present but largely inaccessible. Oil has recentl been discovered in the south. Manufacturing industries are limited mainly t food and vegetable-oil processing, building materials and textiles; furthe development is restricted by shortages of fuel, power and raw materials, ani poor transport facilities. Road, river and rail networks are inadequate fo present needs and inhibit further development. Port Sudan is the main seapor Suakin immediately to the south is being extended. There is a small touris industry with considerable potential.

Recent Developments

Sudan's chances of development are hampered by political unrest arising fror its religious and ethnic diversity; the north is predominantly and aggressivel Moslem, the south non-Moslem, racially distinct and fearful of norther domination. Devolution of some powers to the southern People's Assembly an ultimately to sub-regions may help to solve this problem. Economic difficultie too are pressing. Sudan is deeply in debt to foreign governments and agencie and may find difficulty in raising further loans to carry out such essentia developments as oil exploration and agricultural improvements. Economi progress is therefore likely to be slow, though the potential wealth of this vas country – Africa's largest by area – is enormous.

AFRICA CENTRAL

Angola

The Country

The People's Republic of Angola is a coastal state of western Africa, bordere by Zambia in the east, Namibia in the south and Zaïre in the north. Cabinda, detached province, lies to the north between Congo and Zaïre. *Area* 1,246,70 km^2 (481,351 sq miles); *capital* Luanda; *population* 8,298,000 (est. 1986).

Organization
Government is dominated by the Movimento Popular de Libertaçao de Angola – Partido do Trabalho (MPLA-PT). The president of the party is President and Head of State of the country, who governs through an executive council of about 20 appointed ministers; there is a National People's Assembly of 203 elected members and a further 20 appointed by the Central Committee of the MPLA-PT. Each of the eighteen provinces has an elected assembly. The official language is Portuguese, with many local languages spoken; religions are mostly local, with a substantial Roman Catholic minority.

Geography
The coastal plain is narrow in the south, broadening in the north to a wider lowland ending at the Congo River delta. Inland lies a high plateau, which rolls eastward into central Africa at a mean elevation of 1200 m (4000 ft). In the south peaks of over 1500 m (5000 ft) crowd the edge of the plateau within sight of the coast: in the centre and north gradients are gentler and the main uplands lie further inland. Angola's highest peaks stand on a central massif, the Bié Plateau, capped by Serro Môco (2619 m, 8593 ft). The climate is tropical, tempered inland by elevation. Most rain falls between October and May, heaviest in the north (notably in the forested Cabinda enclave) and lightest over the southern savanna and semi-desert coast.

History and Development
Discovered by Portuguese navigators in the late 15th century, Angola was thinly populated by Negro farming communities. Luanda was founded in 1575 as one of several ports through which thousands of slaves were channelled for shipment to the plantations of Portugal's New World possession, Brazil. Otherwise colonial exploitation was slow, the depopulated country remaining relatively undeveloped until the present century. For long a colony, it became a province of Portugal in 1951. During the 1950s and 1960s three rival militant movements sought independence; this was gained in 1975 after a long guerrilla struggle, but fighting between the factions continued with Cuban, Soviet and South African interventions. With communist help MPLA (now MPLA-PT) gradually gained control, though guerrilla fighting continues, especially with UNITA (União Nacional pela Independência Total de Angola).

Resources and Economics
Angola's agriculture is normally strong, employing almost one third of the workforce. Subsistence crops include maize, beans, millet, sugar-cane, fruit, vegetables and livestock; the country is currently far from self-sufficient. Cash crops, severely depleted through war, depopulation and drought, include cotton, coffee, sisal, rice, sugar-cane, palm oil, tobacco and cocoa. Forestry is an important industry in Cabinda and the north; coastal fishing provides food and fish-meal for export. Diamonds and iron ore are significant exports, second in value only to petroleum, mostly from Cabinda, which currently earns over two thirds of Angola's export revenues. Industries are mainly restricted to food-processing, textiles, cement, soap, oil-refining and other essentials. Roads and railways suffered damage during the war but are now being improved and extended; Angola has several good ports and airports for international traffic.

Recent Developments
Every aspect of Angolan life suffered during the war for independence and the

civil war that followed; industries and plantations were destroyed, thousands of workers displaced and many Portuguese and other knowledgeable expatriates exiled. Remnants of UNITA, MPLA-PT's main rival, maintain ferment in the south and require continuing military expenditure; otherwise Angola is now gradually reverting to peace. Oil revenues are a timely aid to economic reconstruction, and many outside sources of aid show interest in supporting this large, attractive and potentially very wealthy country.

Central African Republic

The Country
Central African Republic is a land-locked state of central Africa, bounded in the east by Sudan, in the south by Zaïre and Congo, in the west by Cameroon and in the north by Chad. *Area* 622,984 km^2 (240,534 sq miles); *capital* Bangui; *population* 2,593,000 (est. 1986).

Organization
A Military Committee for National Recovery rules the country, headed by a Chairman who is also Head of State. He is advised by a council of about 20 appointed ministers. There is a single ruling party, the Mouvement pour l'évolution sociale de l'Afrique noire (MESAN). The official language is French; Sango is the most widely-spoken local language. There are many local faiths and a minority of Roman Catholics.

Geography
Central African Republic occupies a high, rolling plateau which forms a watershed between the Chad and Congo basins, with a mean elevation of 600 m (2000 ft). Most northern rivers drain toward Lake Chad, across thinly forested or savanna country; those of the south drain through deeply cut, forested valleys into the Ubangi River, which forms the Republic's southern border and ultimately joins the Congo. The highest mountains rise above 1300 m (4300 ft) in the northeast and northwest. The climate is tropical tempered by altitude, with a rainy season from March to November. Most rain falls in the south.

History and Development
Once a forested inland refuge where peripheral tribes could hide from slavers, the area now occupied by Central African Republic was thinly populated in the 19th century. French colonial influences began in 1887 with treaties and trade agreements; called Oubangui-Chari, the territory ultimately became one of four making up French Equatorial Africa. Self-government came in 1958 and independence two years later. In 1965 the Republic fell under the military dictatorship of Jean-Bédel Bokassa, who suspended the constitution and governed by decree; in 1976 he was made Emperor, but a coup of 1979 deposed him and restored the republican constitution.

Resources and Economics
Central African Republic's economy is mainly agricultural, employing almost all the population and generating a third of national income. Subsistence crops, including cassava, maize, rice and ground-nuts, make the Republic virtually self-supporting for food; cash crops include cotton, coffee, cocoa, rubber, palm oil and timber, produced mainly in the south where rivers can be used for

transport. Diamonds yield over half the total export revenues; uranium ore is one of the few other minerals available. There are few industries. Roads are being improved; river and air transport are widely used, and Bangui has an international airport.

Recent Developments
Freed from the extravagances of the Bokassa regime, Central African Republic is on a difficult road to economic recovery, aided substantially by France and international funding. Development plans include better roads, railways and improved river navigation to help the Republic export its products.

Congo

The Country
The People's Republic of the Congo lies on the Equator in western Africa, with a short coastline on the Atlantic Ocean; it is bounded in the east and south by Zaïre, in the west by the Cabinda enclave of Angola and Gabon, and in the north by Cameroon and Central African Republic. *Area* 342,000 km² (132,046 sq miles); *capital* Brazzaville; *population* 1,810,000 (est. 1986).

Organization
Congo has a legislative People's National Assembly of 153 elected members, all nominees of a single political party, the Parti congolais du travail (PCT). Chairman of the Party's Central Committee is President and Head of State; he is also chairman of an executive council of about 22 ministers. Local administration is exercised by nine regional councils under the direction of Party representatives, with a separate capital district. The official language is French; local religions and Roman Catholicism are prevalent.

Geography
The short coastline (160 km, 100 miles) is backed by a wide mangrove-covered plain. Inland lies a transverse ridge of mountains up to 900 m (3000 ft) high, and behind it the deep Niari valley. From the valley terraced hills climb steeply to Monts de la Lékéti (1040 m, 3411 ft) on the Gabon border. To the north lies a high tilted basin, drained by rivers flowing east and south toward the Congo River, which forms the country's southern boundary. The climate is equatorial, with heavy rainfall and high humidity. Much of the country is covered with forest or dense grassland and forest.

History and Development
Congo's original populations included pigmy hunter-gatherers and Negro subsistence farmers. The Portuguese discovered the coast in the late 14th century; Europeans set up trading posts but did not penetrate far inland until the 19th century, when French traders set up a collecting network for ivory, rubber and other products. In 1908 the territory became a colonial province of French Equatorial Africa. Gaining autonomy in 1958 and independence in 1960, Congo became Africa's first Marxist state. Military government was imposed from 1968, but the democratic constitution was restored in 1979.

Resources and Economics
Agriculture and forestry employ over a third of the workforce and generate one

eighth of national income. Cassava, maize, rice, yams, ground-nuts and banana are the staple crops; cash crops of sugar-cane, tobacco, coffee, cocoa and palm oil are produced in state plantations. Accessible stands of valuable hardwood timber are now mostly used up. Minerals remain undeveloped except for offshore petroleum, which currently yields 90 per cent of Congo's export income. Road, rail, river and air links are adequate for present needs; Pointe Noire is the main port, Brazzaville the main airport.

Recent Developments
Oil revenues seem to have solved many of Congo's long-standing problems, including the tribal squabbles that dogged post-independence politics. The current regime maintains internal order and (despite a strong Marxist bias) good relations with France and other Western sources of aid. Economic growth is strong; the current five-year plan aims to invest in basic facilities, including roads, ports, railways, agriculture, rural industries and electricity.

Equatorial Guinea

The Country
The Republic of Equatorial Guinea includes coastal Rio Muni, sandwiched between Cameroon and Gabon on Africa's western coast, with the three small off-lying islands of Corisco, Elobey Grande and Elobey Chico, and the two larger and more distant islands of Bioko (formerly Fernando Póo and most recently Macías Nguema Biyoga), and Pagalu (formerly Annobon) in the Gulf of Guinea. *Area* 28,051 km^2 (10,830 sq miles); *capital* Malabo (Bioko); *population* 421,000 (est. 1986).

Organization
Equatorial Guinea is currently ruled by a Supreme Military Council of about 10 ministers under a President who is Head of State. Provision has been made for a new constitution (1982), allowing an elected House of Representatives and a small State Council. The official language is Spanish; different local languages are spoken on the mainland and islands. Roman Catholicism is the dominant religion.

Geography
Rio Muni, a rectangular enclave, rises steeply eastward from a narrow strip of mangrove coast to a range of forested mountains over 1100 m (3600 ft) high. Inland extends the main African plateau, jungle-covered and deeply incised by rivers. The Benito River bisects the country, reaching the sea in a long muddy estuary. Bioko, a rectangular island 160 km (100 miles) to northwest, has spectacular volcanic peaks; the highest, Santa Isabel, rises to 3008 m (9869 ft). Pagalu, much smaller, lies in isolation 560 km (350 miles) southwest of Rio Muni. The climate is hot and humid.

History and Development
The Portuguese discovered Bioko and Pagalu in the 15th century but ceded them to Spain in 1778. Bioko's aboriginal Bubi population was ousted by planters, slaves, convicts and wanderers; Pagalu too was planted, its current population, descended from slaves, continuing to speak Portuguese. Fang tribes

of Rio Muni were little troubled by settlers, though the enclave was allocated to Spain in 1885. Gaining independence in 1968, for over a decade Equatorial Guinea suffered a harsh dictatorial regime which drove out most Europeans and many locals. A coup in 1979 brought military government and restored peace.

Resources and Economics
Equatorial Guinea lives mainly by agriculture, importing most of its staple foods but exporting plantation-grown coffee, palm oil, bananas and tropical hardwoods. Minerals and industries remain undeveloped. Road, sea and air links are adequate for the country's needs; Bata (Rio Muni) and Malabo (Bioko) have port facilities and international airports.

Recent Developments
The corrupt and unsavoury regime that took over at independence left Equatorial Guinea undeveloped and heavily in debt; its precarious economy lay devastated, few expatriates remained, and a quarter of its population were refugees in other countries. Potentially a producer of valuable cash crops, the country's return to a semblance of prosperity is likely to take a long time, despite development aid and expert help from Spain, China and other sources.

Gabon

The Country
The Gabon Republic lies on the Atlantic seaboard of Africa, bounded to east and south by Congo and to north by Equatorial Guinea and Cameroon. *Area* 267,667 km^2 (103,346 sq miles); *capital* Libreville; *population* 600,000 (est. 1986).

Organization
A legislative National Assembly of 84 elected and 9 appointed members stands for five-year terms. An executive President and Head of State, elected for seven years, is advised by an appointed council of about 28 ministers. The Parti démocratique gabonais (PDG) is the sole legal political party. French is the official language; several local languages are spoken. About one third of the population is Christian; others follow local faiths.

Geography
From a broad, low-lying coastal plain punctuated by lagoons and estuaries the country rises in steps; easiest access to the interior is along the many forested river valleys that wind inland towards the great African plateau. Much of Gabon lies within the basin of the Ogooué River and its tributaries, which enter the Atlantic near Cape Lopez. The plateau rolls east at 1000 to 1200 m (3300 to 4000 ft), forests thinning to savanna parkland as rainfall decreases inland. The climate is hot and wet, with heaviest rains near the coast April and October.

History and Development
Sparsely inhabited by subsistence farmers, the Congo basin was of little interest to Europeans until 1843, when French traders built a factory on the site of modern Libreville. Named for the liberated slaves that helped to build it, the township became an administration centre from which French naval

Africa Central

expeditions explored inland, and later the headquarters of French Equatorial Africa (Gabon, Chad, Oubangui-Chari (now Central African Republic) and Congo). Gabon became autonomous in 1958 and independent in 1960. A military coup of 1963 was suppressed with French help.

Resources and Economics
About half the Gabon workforce is agricultural, producing maize, cassava and other tubers, vegetables, bananas and livestock mainly from smallholdings, and cash crops of cocoa, coffee and palm oil. Meat, cereals and other foods are imported to make up deficiencies. Timber, for long Gabon's main export, now takes second place to petroleum, which has been produced since 1957. Manufactures include cellulose, textiles and petrochemicals. Road, rail and river transport are inadequate; there are three international airports.

Recent Developments
Gabon's economy has boomed with the help of oil revenues; further developments depend largely on improving transport within the country. Planned improvements include the new Trans-Gabon railway, as yet incomplete, which will provide new outlets for existing products and open up new areas of forest and mineral exploitation (especially iron).

São Tomé e Principe

The Country
The Democratic Republic of São Tomé e Principe includes two main islands and several smaller ones in the Gulf of Guinea. *Area* 964 km^2 (372 sq miles); *capital* São Tomé; *population* 106,000 (est. 1986).

Organization
A People's Assembly of 40 members is elected for four-year terms. The Assembly elects a President and Head of State, also for four-year terms, who governs with the advice of a small cabinet. All candidates for election must be approved by the ruling political party, Movimento de Libertação de São Tomé e Principe (MLSTP). The official language is Portuguese; Roman Catholicism is the dominant faith.

Geography
These are volcanic islands with small outliers some 200 km (125 miles) from the Gabon coast. São Tomé, the larger, lies almost on the Equator. From broad lowland plains its main peaks rise centrally to 2024 m (6640 ft). Principe, about 145 km (90 miles) to the northeast, has a lower central massif. Both are hot and humid, with least rain from June to September. Dense forest has been partly cleared for agriculture.

History and Development
Discovered in 1470 and 1471 by Portuguese navigators, the islands were settled originally by convicts, Jew and other outcasts from Portuguese society. The settlers cleared huge tracts of forest to establish sugar plantations, importing slaves from the mainland. Mainly prosperous, the islands suffered French and Dutch depredations in the 17th and 18th centuries. Coffee and later cocoa replaced sugar as the main crop, and indentured labourers replaced slaves. For

long a province of Portugal, the islands gained their independence in 1975.

Resources and Economics

São Tomé and Principe are mainly agricultural islands, with almost all the workforce employed in raising crops for export; subsistence crops are also grown, but the islands import most of their food. The plantations, now mostly government-owned, grow cocoa (yielding 90 per cent of foreign revenues), copra, palm kernels, coconuts and bananas. Local fishing is good; there are no minerals or industries of importance. Roads are adequate, and São Tomé has an international airport.

Recent Developments

Heavily dependent on the cocoa market for its annual income, this tiny state has a slender and unstable economy. Grants from the EEC and African sources help balance the budget, modernize production methods and improve transport.

Zaïre

The Country

The Republic of Zaïre lies mostly inland but has a short Atlantic coast. It is bounded in the east by Uganda, Rwanda, Burundi and Tanzania, in the south by Zambia and Angola, in the west by Congo and Cabinda, and in the north by Central African Republic and Sudan; the Congo River provides its outlet to the ocean. *Area* 2,345,409 km^2 (905,563 sq miles); *capital* Kinshasa; *population* 33,601,000 (est. 1986).

Organization

Zaïre is governed by an executive President, elected for seven-year terms, who appoints and is advised by a National Executive Council of about 27 Commissioners. A National Legislative Council of about 300 members is elected by universal suffrage for five-year terms. Only one party, the Mouvement Populaire de la Révolution (MPR) is permitted. The official language is French, with many local languages and dialects spoken. Christianity (mostly Roman Catholicism) and local religions are well represented.

Geography

From a short coastline some 40 km (25 miles) long, Zaïre extends inland along the flood-plain of the Congo River (locally called the Zaïre), which for over 650 km (400 miles) forms the international boundary. East and south of the river extends a wide, low-lying basin, in the centre of which lie Lakes Mai-Ndombe and Tumba, some 350 m (1100 ft) above sea level. From these the land rises east to a plateau at 500 to 1000 m (1650 to 3300 ft), densely forested and crossed by parallel rivers draining north to the Congo. In the east the plateau is rimmed by a chain of volcanic mountains marking the western escarpment of the Rift Valley. Many peaks rise above 2500 m (8200 ft); the highest form the Ruwenzori massif, towering to 5109 m (16,763 ft) on the Uganda border. Zaïre's eastern boundary lies along a chain of lakes within the Rift Valley. In the southeast the rolling Shaba plateau rises to 1500 m (4900 ft). Crossed by the Equator, Zaïre is generally hot and damp. Trade winds bring dry seasons to the north and south. The Congo lowlands are heavily forested; the uplands have a mixed vegetation of forest and savanna.

History and Development

The Congo basin, sparsely populated by riverside farming communities of several tribes, was frequently raided for slaves. Hot and generally unhealthy to outsiders, it was otherwise left relatively undisturbed until explored by Europeans, notably Henry Morton Stanley, in 1876–7. Stanley's discoveries stimulated Belgian King Leopold II to open trading posts along the Congo River, from which rubber and other products were collected. Exploitative methods of collection used by concessionaires and their agents created a scandal which resulted in the adoption of the territory by Belgium in 1908. The Belgian Congo remained a colony for just over half a century, achieving independence in 1960 as Congo. Almost immediately an army mutiny and the attempted secession of mineral-rich Katanga (now Shaba) province caused strife, which continued intermittently until 1971, when the country's name was changed to Zaïre. In 1977 and 1978 Angolan rebels invaded Shaba but were ultimately repulsed. Constitutional changes and reforms since 1960 have tended to confirm the control of the President as sole power in a one-party state.

Resources and Economics

Agriculture plays a relatively minor role in Zaïre's export economy, though over 70 per cent of the workforce is involved in raising crops and livestock. The main subsistence foods are cassava, yams, maize, rice, beans and other vegetables, bananas and other fruits, and livestock. Once self-supporting, Zaïre now imports many of its staple foods. Important cash crops are coffee and palm oil; many others, including rubber, tea, cocoa, cotton and pyrethrum, are currently grown only in small amounts. Minerals include copper, cobalt, tin, cadmium, gold and diamonds, which together earn about 80 per cent of the country's export income; world prices of copper and cobalt effectively determine prosperity from year to year. There are small reserves of petroleum offshore. There are many small local industries, based mainly in Kinshasa, Shaba and a few other centres. Hydroelectric schemes on the rivers provide practically all the country's power; the rivers are also important waterways, especially as roads and railways are in poor repair. There are international airports.

Recent Developments

Zaïre's intrinsic wealth, demonstrated and partly developed by Belgian colonial enterprise, has virtually disappeared in the decades following independence. Internal power struggles, chronic maladministration, corruption, attempts at secession and tribal nepotism – a combination known locally as 'mal zaïrais' – have all played their part. The practical result is a fertile country no longer able to feed itself, staggering under a load of international debts, mineral-rich though virtually devoid of economic credibility, and rapidly decaying in the hands of a self-sustaining oligarchy.

Zambia

The Country

The Republic of Zambia lies centrally in southern Africa, bounded by Tanzania and Malawi in the northeast, Mozambique, Zimbabwe, Botswana and Namibia in the south, Angola in the west and Zaïre in the north. *Area* 752,614 km^2 (290,584 sq miles); *capital* Lusaka; *population* 7,054,000 (est. 1986).

Organization

A National Assembly of 125 elected and 10 nominated members holds office for five-year terms. An executive President and Head of State, who is also the President of the ruling United National Independence Party (UNIP), governs with the advice of a council of about 20 ministers, led by a Prime Minister. The official language is English; several local languages are widely spoken. Most Zambians are Christian, though many in remote areas follow local religions.

Geography

Zambia lies on a high plateau of ancient, weathered rocks, much of it between 1200 and 1500 m (3900 to 5000 ft) above sea level. The highest mountains are in the north and east; mountains bordering Zaïre and extending across the east of the country rise to 1700 m (5500 ft), and higher ranges line the eastern border where several peaks stand above 2000 m (6500 ft). Most rivers drain south, ultimately into the Zambezi river system. There are several extensive swamps, including the huge area of marshland surrounding Lake Bangweulu in the northeast. The tropical climate is tempered by altitude; warm throughout the year, there is a marked dry season from August to October and a rainy season from November to April. Vegetation ranges from open forest to savanna, grading to semi-desert steppe and evergreen thickets in the dry southwest.

History and Development

Zambia's open spaces first attracted European interest as a possible source of minerals. In 1890 Cecil Rhodes' British South Africa Company (BSA) spread its mineral-exploration operations northward into Southern Rhodesia (Zimbabwe) and beyond. First results in Northern Rhodesia were unpromising, but European settlers farmed and grew tobacco; from the 1930s onward increasing demand for copper stimulated mining, using British engineering skills and local labour, centered on Broken Hill (Kabwe) and the northern Copper Belt. In 1953 Northern Rhodesia federated with Southern Rhodesia and Nyasaland (Malawi); the federation was dissolved ten years later when Africans attained a majority in the legislature, and in the following year (1964) Zambia came into being as an independent state.

Resources and Economics

About 65 per cent of Zambia's workforce is involved in farming. The main products are maize, millet, wheat, sugar, cassava, ground-nuts and sorghum, grown mainly on smallholdings. Zambia imports much of its food, especially in years of drought when crops may fail completely. Cotton, tobacco and maize are cash crops. Minerals, especially copper and cobalt, provide over 95 per cent of the country's export revenues, though the income fluctuates with world prices. Other minerals include coal, lead, manganese, gold and recently-discovered phosphatic rocks. Industries are of no more than local significance. Some 60 per cent of energy needs are met by hydroelectric power from Kariba and Kafue Gorge, and surplus power is exported. Zambia has good road and rail links with neighbouring countries; Lusaka has an international airport, and there is a developing tourist industry.

Recent Developments

Zambia's one-sided economy is sensitive to world prices of copper, which have been depressed for over a decade; after a brief post-independence boom this has forced the country into economic stagnation and unwelcome austerity, with import cuts, reductions in living standards, and high unemployment and inflation. The government is seeking to improve the efficiency of its copper-mining operations, but long-term debts leave little surplus for this or any other development that involves capital expenditure. Overseas aid is of major importance in balancing annual budgets and servicing debts.

AFRICA EAST

Burundi

The Country
The Republic of Burundi lies centrally in eastern Africa, bounded to east and south by Tanzania, to the west by Lake Tanganyika and Zaïre and to the north by Rwanda. *Area* 27,834 km² (10,747 sq miles); *capital* Bujumbura; *population* 4,954,000 (est. 1986).

Organization
A National Assembly of 52 elected and 13 appointed members, with five-year term of office, holds legislative power. All members are nominated by the Unité et Progrès National Party (UPRONA), the sole authorized political party; leader of the party is the executive President and Head of State, who appoints and leads an Executive Council of about 20 ministers. There are 8 provinces with military governors. Official languages are French and Kirundi; Swahili and English are also spoken. Roman Catholicism is the main faith.

Geography
A small, densely populated country, Burundi occupies a flank of Africa's western Rift Valley, lying partly within the valley along the eastern shore of Lake Tanganyika, 772 m (2533 ft) above sea level. Bujumbura, the capital, is a lakeside port. From the valley wooded slopes rise to a north–south ridge that runs the length of the country, with peaks above 2600 m (8500 ft). To the east lies an extensive plateau at about 1500 m (500 ft), covered with mixed forest and grassland, dotted with smallholdings and crossed by small rivers that drain northward to the Nile basin. The climate is tropical tempered by altitude. Rainfall averages over 125 cm (50 in) per annum on the mountains, 100 cm (40 in) or less on the plateau, with a dry season from May to September.

History and Development
Burundi's population includes pygmy hunter-gatherers of the forests, Hutu farmers of Bantu stock whose ancestors invaded in the 13th century, and Nilotic Tutsi cattle-herders who established neighbouring kingdoms in Rwanda and Urundi during the 17th century. Both kingdoms fell under German colonial rule in the last decade of the 19th century. The Germans were displaced by Belgians during World War I, and Belgian control was confirmed in 1919 by mandate from the League of Nations. In 1946 the kingdoms were united as a UN Trust Territory, both gaining independence in 1962. In Burundi civil war between Hutu majority and ruling Tutsi minority raged intermittently for over a decade; the country became a republic in 1966, and came under military rule in 1976. Civil government was restored in 1982.

Resources and Economics

About 85 per cent of Burundi's workforce are smallholders, producing yams, sorghum, cassava, millet, maize and beans, and livestock; the country is virtually self-sufficient in these staple foods. The main cash crop, coffee, provides 80 per cent of government revenues and 90 per cent of export revenues; tea, cotton and animal hides are also exported. Lake and river fish are caught for local consumption. Minerals are present but only small amounts of gold and metallic ores are extracted. Timber and peat are the main fuels; some hydro-electric energy is produced locally but more is bought from neighbouring countries. Industries are mostly small and local. Roads are adequate for local needs, though lack of trunk road or rail outlets is one of Burundi's main economic problems. Bujumbura has port and international airport facilities, and is the centre of a small tourist industry.

Recent Developments

A small country with a crowded and still-growing population, Burundi can no longer support its population by subsistence agriculture. Nor can it currently afford to develop its mineral or industrial resources; present hopes centre on foreign aid to improve farming methods, diversify cash crops, and develop local resources (for example hydroelectric power and phosphates) that will replace expensive imports. Inter-tribal hostilities smoulder, but the country is currently pacific enough to attract the foreign aid it so badly needs.

Kenya

The Country

The Republic of Kenya lies on the east coast of Africa, bordered by the Somali Democratic Republic in the east, Tanzania in the south, Uganda in the west, Sudan in the northwest and Ethiopia to the north. *Area* 582,646 km² (224,960 sq miles); *capital* Nairobi; *population* 21,061,000 (est. 1986).

Organization

A legislative national Assembly of 158 elected, 12 appointed and 2 *ex officio* members is convened for five-year terms. Head of State is an executive President, also elected for five-year terms, who appoints a cabinet of about 25 ministers. There is a single political party, the Kenya African National Union (KANU). Local government is administered through seven provincial councils and the Nairobi local authority. The official language is Kiswahili; English and several local languages are widely spoken. Local religions predominate, with a large Christian and smaller Moslem and Hindu minorities.

Geography

From a reef-fringed coast 400 km (250 miles) long, Kenya rises in steps to a plateau at 350 to 1000 m (1100 to 3300 ft). Narrow in the south but broadening in the north, it covers the eastern half of the country; thin scrub is the typical vegetation, though parts support subsistence farming. Inland volcanic massifs mark the flanks of the eastern Rift Valley; they include the fertile Aberdare Range, almost 4000 m (13,000 ft) high, and the snow-capped massif of Mt Kenya (5199 m, 17,058 ft). Across the Rift the western highlands include the spectacular Mau Escarpment (2700 m, 9000 ft), backed by Mt Elgon (4321 m,

14,177 ft) on the Uganda border. The Rift itself is marked by a series of lakes from Turkana in the north to Natron on the southern border. In the southwest lies Lake Victoria, just over 1000 m (3300 ft) above sea level. Crossed by the Equator, Kenya has a tropical climate tempered by altitude. Rains are heaviest from March to May, the rainy season lasting longest in the south and west. The plains are famous for their vast herds of game, including several species of migrating antelopes, elephants, warthogs, lions, cheetahs, zebras and giraffes, now protected in extensive game parks.

History and Development

The Kenya uplands, farmed for at least three thousand years, may well have been occupied over a million years ago by earliest man. The coast was known to Arabs two thousand years ago, and Arabs settled near Lamu in the 9th century AD. Arab and Portuguese traders clashed over ivory, gold and coral during the 16th to 18th centuries, Mombasa becoming an important Portuguese market and garrison. By the early 19th century the Sultanate of Zanzibar owned most of the coast, and Arabs were conducting a flourishing trade in goods (including slaves) from the interior. British and German missionaries and traders entered the area in the late 19th century. In 1887 the British East Africa Association began exploration north of an agreed boundary (the present Kenya–Tanzania border), surrendering responsibilities to the British East Africa Protectorate government in 1895–7. The Mombasa–Lake Victoria railway, built at this time, facilitated trade between coast and interior and opened the uplands to British settlement. Many Indians also arrived, becoming traders and small-scale businessmen. The black population, always a large majority, revolted against continuing British rule in 1952–6. Kenya became independent in 1963 and a republic in the following year.

Resources and Economics

Agriculture employs almost 80 per cent of Kenyans and yields 35 per cent of the country's income, including half its export revenues. Maize, wheat, barley, sorghum, fruit, vegetables, cassava, sugar and livestock are the main products; in drought-free years Kenya is close to self-sufficiency in all but cereals. Cash crops include coffee, tea, sugar, pyrethrum, sisal, pineapples and meat, raised largely on smallholdings and cooperatives. Fish are plentiful in the lakes and rivers. Soda ash, fluorspar and limestone are important minerals; no exploitable petroleum has been found. Hydroelectric and geothermal power provide 25 per cent of the country's needs; wood and charcoal are important local fuels. Small industries cater mostly for local needs; processed foods, tobacco, cement, textiles, clothing, building materials, paper, petrochemicals from imported stock (an important source of foreign exchange) and fertilizers are the main products. Road, rail and air links are generally adequate. Nairobi has an international airport, Mombasa has good port facilities, and there is a substantial tourist industry based on splendid game parks and scenery.

Recent Developments

For a country whose capital was an obscure railway junction less than a century ago, Kenya has made enormous economic progress, especially since independence. Current economic problems arise from a high rate of population increase (among the world's highest) and heavy reliance on coffee and tea for overseas earnings. Fluctuations in income due to drought and uncertain markets have required severe import restrictions, slowing industrial development, raising costs of consumer goods and feeding inflation and unemployment. Current development plans provide for modest continuing growth under a predominantly free-enterprise regime, with emphasis on local production and substantial help from overseas funds. Kenya's record of self-help, political stability and the pulling-together of its diverse ethnic groups, are of major importance for future progress.

Malawi

The Country
The Republic of Malawi lies in southeastern Africa, land-locked and bounded by Lake Malawi in the east, Mozambique in the south and southeast, Zambia to the west and Tanzania in the north and northeast. *Area* 118,484 km² (45,747 sq miles); *capital* Lilongwe, *largest city* Blantyre; *population* 7,541,000 (est. 1986).

Organization
A legislative Parliament of 101 members is elected for five-year terms; all candidates represent the sole authorized political party, the Malawi Congress Party (MCP). Up to 15 additional members are appointed by the executive President, who is Head of State and president of MCP; he also appoints a cabinet of about 12 ministers. Local authority is vested in three regions, each with a minister in charge, and twenty-four districts. The official language is English; local religions predominate with Christian, Moslem and Hindu minorities.

Geography
Malawi nestles in the western arm of the Rift Valley system along the western and southern shores of Lake Malawi, 473 m (1550 ft) above sea level. South from the lake runs the Shire river valley, overlooked by mountains which rise to 3000 m (10,000 ft). The Shire drops in stages toward the Zambezi River, with spectacular waterfalls and broad marshlands in the south. In central Malawi a high, savanna-clad plateau rises 700 m (2300 ft) and more above the lake, grading in the north to a steep valley wall that towers to peaks of 2500 m (8200 ft) or more. Malawi's forests and grasslands have been modified by grazing and agriculture. The climate is hot, with heaviest rains in the mountains; a marked dry season from May to October may extend into drought.

History and Development
Occupied originally by forest hunters, the Malawi area was infiltrated about AD 1500 by Bantu farmers and warriors, who established a powerful kingdom in the Shire river valley. From there they conquered the land to west and south, but were themselves overcome during the mid-19th century by neighbouring tribes who sold them into slavery. European travellers first entered during the 17th and 18th centuries. British missionaries (notably David Livingstone) explored and founded settlements during the mid-19th century, attempting to stop the Arab slave trade, and in 1892 Britain took over the area as the British Central Africa Protectorate. A British colony from 1907, Nyasaland gained independence as Malawi in 1964 and became a republic in 1966.

Resources and Economics
About half Malawi's workforce is in agriculture, generating half the country's

income and up to 90 per cent of its export revenues. Maize, millet, sorghum, beans, fruit, cassava and potatoes are the main subsistence crops, in which the country is usually self-sufficient. Cash crops include tobacco, cane sugar, tea and ground-nuts. Tea, tobacco and sugar are grown on plantations; most other crops are raised on smallholdings and sold through marketing cooperatives. Fish are plentiful in Lake Malawi; timber is used mainly for fuel. Few minerals are extracted. Industries are generally small, but food-processing, ethanol production from sugar-cane, cement and fertilizer manufacture are growing in importance. Hydroelectric energy is produced along the Shire River. Roads are adequate for the country's needs; a railway network links with Mozambique, giving direct access to sea ports. Lilongwe and Blantyre have international airports, servicing a small but growing tourist industry.

Recent Developments

Malawi's economic dependence on agriculture is justified by its good soils and generally genial climate, and backed by sound research, marketing and investment policies. Together these have assured good farming, with high yields in a range of profitable crops, and sensible marketing procedures within the country. Markets outside Malawi remain less certain; the recent slackening in the rate of economic growth reflected fluctuations in world prices of its main export commodities (tobacco, tea and sugar), against which Malawi remains unbuffered. Overseas aid is being used to maintain high standards of farming and marketing, to promote small industries, and to generate regional development planning – all made possible by the down-to-earth pragmatism of a stable government.

Mozambique

The Country

The Republic of Mozambique lies on the east coast of southern Africa, bordered in the south by South Africa and Swaziland, in the west by Zimbabwe, Zambia and Malawi, and in the north by Tanzania. *Area* 801,590 km² (309,494 sq miles); *capital* Maputo; *population* 12,362,000 (est. 1986).

Organization

Mozambique is ruled by a political party, Frente de Libertação de Moçambique (FRELIMO). The Party leader, who is President and Head of State, appoints a council of about 20 ministers, and presides over a 210-member legislative People's Assembly made up of ministers, Party officials and other representatives. Local authority is vested in provincial and district governments. The official language is Portuguese; local languages are widely spoken. Local religions dominate, with Christian and Moslem minorities.

Geography

A long, wasp-waisted country bordering the Indian Ocean, Mozambique is split by the Zambezi River. In the south the coast is low-lying and sandy, fringed with mangroves and palms. Inland lies rolling grassland, backed in the south by low volcanic hills and in the north by the high edge of the Zimbabwe plateau, with elevations up to 1500 m (5000 ft). North of the Zambezi the coast is rugged and the coastal plain narrower; the interior is a savanna-covered plateau 800 to

1000 m (2600 to 3300 ft) above sea level. The highest ridges and peaks are forested, rising to 2000 m (6600 ft) along the southern Malawi border. Mozambique includes part of Lake Malawi's eastern shore and a large man-made lake occupying the upper Zambezi valley. The climate is hot and generally dry, with most rain falling between October and March.

History and Development
Mozambique was thinly settled by Bantu farmers from the northwest some two thousand years ago; the coast was known to Arabs, who set up trading networks for ivory and gold from the interior. Vasco da Gama's explorations of 1498 led the way for Portuguese settlements; many trading posts developed into extensive plantations, which dispossessed Africans of their land and on which they were used as indentured or slave labour. The Portuguese laissez-faire policy was replaced in 1890 by more vigorous colonization, Portuguese East Africa coming into existence as a colony in 1910. Development was haphazard, however, meeting vigorous opposition from local Africans. In 1951, when the colony became an Overseas Province of Portugal, resistance to white settlers increased; in 1964 it boiled over into guerrilla warfare, and Mozambique gained its independence in 1975.

Resources and Economics
Nine tenths of the workforce is in agriculture, generating half the national income and almost all export revenues. Subsistence foods, grown on smallholdings and collective farms, include maize, cassava, beans, bananas, potatoes, rice, ground-nuts and livestock. Mozambique usually has to import maize and other staples, especially in years of drought. The most important cash crops are cashew nuts, tea and sugar-cane; others include cotton, copra, sisal and tropical hardwoods. Prawns and other seafoods are caught and some exported. Minerals are present but barely exploited. Industries include sugar-refining, cotton-processing and other basic manufacturing; refined oils (from imported stock) and railway rolling stock are also produced. The Cabora Bassa Dam on the Zambezi River provides hydroelectric power for local use and export to South Africa. Roads are adequate; railways serve local needs patchily, and also transport goods for South Africa and land-locked Swaziland, Zimbabwe and Malawi. There are modern port facilities at Beira and Maputo, which also have international airports.

Recent Developments
Mozambique is developing its none-too-generous resources only with difficulty. Skills, equipment and capital that fled with the white population in 1975 have proved difficult to replace. Civil war in neighbouring Zimbabwe cut transit revenues severely; droughts and floods have limited agricultural production, and poor prices on world markets have further reduced income, affecting every aspect of development that involves foreign capital or goods. Dissident guerrilla activities are a costly nuisance, increasing government spending and slowing down development. Mozambique is currently investing in agricultural development and improvement of road and rail facilities to increase transit revenues. It relies heavily on aid, mostly from the West.

Rwanda

The Country
The Republic of Rwanda lies centrally in east Africa with Tanzania in the east Burundi in the south, Zaïre in the west and Uganda in the north. *Area* 26,33 km^2 (10,169 sq miles); *capital* Kigali; *population* 5,821,000 (est. 1986).

Organization
A legislative National Development Council of 70 members is elected for five year terms. An executive President, also elected for five-year terms, govern through a council of appointed ministers. There is a single political party, th Mouvement Révolutionnaire National pour le Développement (MRND) Local government is vested in ten prefectures. Official languages are French an Kinyarwanda; local religions predominate, with large Christian and smalle Moslem minorities.

Geography
Rwanda flanks the eastern shore of Lake Kivu, 1460 m (4790 ft) above sea leve in the western Rift Valley. From the lake an escarpment rises steeply, forming forested ridge that runs the length of the country from north to south. To th east extends a high, savanna-covered plateau at about 1700 m (5600 ft), dotte with plantations and smallholdings and cut by deep river valleys. In the southeast the plateau falls to a marshy, lake-studded plain, drained b southward-flowing rivers. In the northwest stands a high volcanic massif, th Virunga Mountains, forested and rising to over 4000 m (13,000 ft) – home of th rare mountain gorilla. Rwanda's highest mountain is Karisimbi (4507 m, 14,78 ft). The tropical climate is cooled by altitude, rainy from October to Decembe and again from March to May.

History and Development
The forest pygmies and Hutu (Bantu) farmers who first inhabited the area wer overrun in the 16th century by Tutsis from the northeast, who set up th kingdom of Rwanda. In 1890 the kingdom became a German colony linked wit neighbouring Urundi (Burundi) and Tanganyika (Tanzania) in German Eas Africa. Belgians from the Congo (Zaïre) invaded in 1916, and the 1919 peac settlement following World War I gave Rwanda and southern neighbou Urundi to Belgium under a League of Nations mandate. From 1946 contro passed to the UN. Power struggles between Hutu majority and Tutsi rulin, minority increased during the 1950s. In 1961 the Tutsi King was deposed. Th first decade of independence (1962–72) was marked by inter-tribal fighting After further violence in 1973 a military government took over, civil rul returning ten years later.

Resources and Economics
Agriculture and stock-raising occupy 90 per cent of Rwandans, generating ha the national income and 70 per cent of export revenues. Smallholdings gro subsistence crops of yams, cassava, bananas, potatoes, beans and sorghum livestock are also reared, adding to the diet and economy. The main cash crop are coffee and tea; livestock, meat, cotton, and pyrethrum also contribute. Lak Kivu and the rivers provide fish for local consumption; dwindling forest provide fuel, building timbers and new ground for farming. Potentially rich i

minerals, Rwanda currently exports tin concentrates and wolfram; small industries cater for local needs. Hydroelectric power is available, and natural gas is an untapped asset in the floor of Lake Kivu. Roads are barely adequate: Kigali has an international airport, providing for a small but growing tourist industry.

Recent Developments

With one of the world's most densely-packed populations, Rwanda can barely support itself on the farmland available. Serious inroads into its mountain rain forest (a valuable tourist attraction) are to some degree being countered by more efficient farming methods, but the threat of insufficient farmland remains. Many Rwandans work outside the country. The economy is restricted by the difficulty of moving goods into and out of the country; Rwanda suffered severely when its frontiers with Uganda and Tanzania closed during recent troubles. Hopes for the future, expressed in the current five-year plan, are pinned on self-sufficiency in food and consolidation of the country's basic industries.

Tanzania

The Country

The United Republic of Tanzania, including the Indian Ocean islands of Zanzibar and Pemba, lies on the east coast of southern Africa. Its neighbours are Mozambique, Malawi and Zambia in the south, Zaïre, Burundi, Rwanda and Zambia in the west, and Uganda and Kenya in the north. *Area* 945,087 km² (364,898 sq miles); *capital* Dodoma, *largest city* Dar es Salaam; *population* 21,752,000 (est. 1986).

Organization

The legislative National Assembly includes 127 nominated or *ex-officio* members and 111 elected for five-year terms. An executive President, also elected for five-year terms, governs with the aid of an appointed cabinet of about 28 members. The single political party, Chama cha Mapinduzi, nominates all candidates for election. Local government is vested in twenty-two regions. Although Zanzibar is constitutionally autonomous in many respects, it is currently ruled by decree. Official languages are Swahili and English; local religions predominate with Christian, Moslem and Hindu minorities.

Geography

From a coastline of almost 800 km (500 miles), Tanzania extends inland to the western Rift Valley, including parts of Lakes Tanganyika and Malawi and the southern half of Lake Victoria. Behind a narrow coastal strip, mostly of dunes, coral reefs and mangroves, rises a rolling savanna-covered plateau. The southern third rises 1000 m (3300 ft) above sea level, bordered in the west by the Kipengere Range (almost 3000 m (10,000 ft) high) and the less impressive Southern Highlands. The northwestern two thirds of the country rises to between 1200 and 1500 m (4000 to 5000 ft), dotted with rolling uplands and volcanic mountains. In the northeast on the Kenya border stands Kilimanjaro (5895 m, 19,341 ft), Africa's highest peak. Also in the north lies Lake Victoria, in a wide basin 1134 m (3720 ft) above sea level. Zanzibar and Pemba islands are low-lying and fringed with coral reefs. The climate is tropical tempered by height; rain is heaviest in the mountains, lightest and least reliable on the southern plains. The driest season is usually from May to November. The country is rich in wildlife and well provided with reserves.

History and Development
The Tanzania area, occupied originally by Negro farming settlements, was for long crossed by trade routes from Zanzibar to the Rift Valley, carrying coastal Arab influences and Swahili far inland. German influences began in the late 19th century with the German East Africa Company, developed to exploit the area; riots involving both Arabs and Africans were subdued by German troops, and the country became a reluctant and turbulent colony. Meanwhile Zanzibar, under Arab domination, became a British protectorate. German East Africa was taken by British forces in World War I, and Britain was then granted a League of Nations mandate over Tanganyika. A UN Trust Territory in 1946, it gained its independence in 1961. Under the guidance of a strongly left-wing ruling party it has since developed as a socialist republic. Zanzibar and Pemba, with mixed Arab, Indian and African populations, remained under British control until 1963. The Arab-controlled government was toppled by a radical group in the following year and the islands united with Tanganyika to form Tanzania. The country has since taken many leads in the politics of southern Africa.

Resources and Economics
Tanzania employs 90 per cent of its workforce in agriculture, raising subsistence crops of maize, millet, sorghum, wheat, rice, cassava and bananas, mostly in village cooperatives. Cash crops, virtually the only exports, include coffee, tea, cotton, sisal, tobacco, sugar, cashew nuts, cloves (mostly from Zanzibar), coconuts and pyrethrum. Drought, pests and poor management combine to reduce output; Tanzania cannot feed itself and its annual income remains painfully low. Deposits of coal, iron ore, gold and phosphates are known, but only diamonds are currently exported in quantity. Industries include cotton-processing and textiles, food- and tobacco-processing, and cement, glass, motor tyre and paper manufacture, mostly for local use. Hydroelectric power provides two thirds of the country's modest needs, but only in years of adequate rainfall. Roads are generally poor; railways cross the country in three directions (including an important line going to Zambia) from the main port of Dar es Salaam; goods are also carried by sea and lake shipping. There are three international airports. A growing tourist traffic is attracted by splendid wildlife.

Recent Developments
With its resources underdeveloped, a widely-scattered rural population, poor agriculture and an unreliable climate, Tanzania makes slow, halting progress: a dedicated socialist regime is attempting to build on 'ujamaa', or family-based concepts of collectivism. Price controls, import restrictions and austerity encourage a strong black market and alternative economy; inept bureaucracies stifle initiative and absorb profits. However, illiteracy has dropped and corruption is being dealt with; despite crippling debts the country advances steadily, its basic stability attracting aid from both East and West.

Uganda

The Country
The Republic of Uganda is a land-locked state of central east Africa, bordered

by Kenya in the east, Tanzania and Rwanda in the south, Zaïre in the west and Sudan in the north. *Area* 236,036 km^2 (91,133 sq miles); *capital* Kampala; *population* 15,994,000 (est. 1986).

Organization

A legislative Parliament of 124 members is elected for five-year terms. The leader of the majority party becomes President, and governs with an appointed cabinet of about 30 ministers. Local authority is vested in ten provincial governments. The official language is English with Kiswahili generally understood; many local languages are also spoken. Christianity is the majority religion, with local faiths widely practised.

Geography

Uganda stands on a high plateau between the eastern and western arms of the Rift Valley system. The southern half of the country lies in the basin of Lake Victoria. From the lake shore, 1134 m (3720 ft) above sea level, the basin extends west and north at about 1200 m (4000 ft), rising to 2000 m (6500 ft) and more along the Rift Valley escarpment in the northeast. The spectacular Ruwenzori range marks the Zaïre border in the far west; Ruwenzori itself (5109 m, 16,763 ft) rises from dark forest to ice-rimmed crater, and the lesser peaks nearby are glaciated. The Victoria Nile runs through central Uganda, leaving Lake Victoria and tumbling northward to Lake Kioga, ultimately joining the Nile itself. Northern Uganda is a high and mainly dry plateau of rough grassland and semi-desert. In the east stands Mt Elgon (4321 m, 14,177 ft), towering over a vast area on the Kenya border. Uganda is hot and generally damp, with over 250 cm (100 in) of rain per annum in the mountains, much less on the plains.

History and Development

The Lake Victoria basin was infiltrated over three thousand years ago by northern tribes whose agriculture provided the prosperity to support several small kingdoms. Remoteness virtually isolated them until the mid-19th century, when explorers J.H. Speke (1858–63) and H.M. Stanley (1874–7) made contacts that allowed Christian missions into the area. Simultaneously Moslem influences from Zanzibar reached Buganda and neighbouring kingdoms, and Anglican, Catholic and Moslem factions vied for ascendancy over the ruling monarchs. The Anglo–German agreement of 1890 confirmed British influence; in that year the British East Africa Company established itself in Kampala. A protectorate was declared in 1894 and Uganda settled eventually to peaceful development. Independence returned in 1962, and in the following year Uganda became a republic. A coup in 1966 installed the former Prime Minister (Dr Milton Obote) as President; a military coup in 1971 brought General Idi Amin, whose reign of escalating terror ended in 1979 after armed intervention by Tanzania. Though constitutional government has been restored under President Obote, civil unrest, much of it tribal in origin, continues to cripple the country.

Resources and Economics

Uganda has an agricultural economy; in normal times farming employs 80 to 90 per cent of its workforce and generates virtually all export revenues. Most of the produce comes from small farms. Subsistence crops include millet, maize, bananas, sorghum, yams, cassava and livestock; Uganda is usually self-sufficient in staple foods. Cash crops include coffee, tea, cotton, tobacco and cane sugar. Output has declined seriously in the past decade and is only now showing signs of recovery. Fish are plentiful in Lake Victoria. Uganda was major exporter of copper, but production has been low since the civil war. Ti and tungsten ores, apatite and other minerals are also mined, but poorl represented in recent returns. Food-processing, textiles, and cement an copper manufacture are the main industries; others include motor assembly metal-processing, tanning and small local enterprises. Hydroelectricity generated at Owen Falls on the Victoria Nile; surplus power is exported Tanzania and Kenya. Roads and railways, in disarray after the fighting, a slowly being rehabilitated. Entebbe is Kampala's international airport.

Recent Developments
Uganda is a potentially prosperous country, unusually favoured with soil water and climate, with many resources waiting to be developed. Its mai misfortunes since independence stem largely from tribal problems, released b the powerful and dangerous personality of former President Idi Amin. H expulsion of the large Asian community in 1972 divested the country of some its best businessmen, organizers and professionals, a trauma from which it ha yet to recover. The tribal purges that followed in the army, public service an political arena have continued long after his departure; tribalism remains muc to the fore, exemplified by armed maurauders settling old scores, disruptin order and making the country virtually ungovernable. Uganda's return t prosperity can only be a slow process, depending much on the goodwill neighbours and the international community.

AFRICA SOUTH

Botswana

The Country
The Republic of Botswana is a land-locked state of southern Africa, bordered b Zimbabwe in the east, South Africa in the southeast and south, and Namibia the west and north. *Area* 600,372 km^2 (231,804 sq miles); *capital* Gaboron *population* 978,000 (est. 1986).

Organization
A legislative National Assembly of 32 elected members, four nominated and tw *ex officio*, holds office for a five-year term; the Assembly elects an executiv President, who appoints a cabinet of about 15 ministers. Local authority vested in town and district councils. The official languages are Setswana an English; Christianity is the dominant religion.

Geography
Much of Botswana is an arid plateau of red sand 1000 m (3300 ft) above sea leve generally undulating and covered with grass, acacia scrub and thin fores Extensive pans or hollows accumulate surface water to form swamps, many which spread during the rainy season and then dry out to salt pans under the h sun; the Okavango Swamp in the north is famous for its wildlife. The climate hot in summer and cool in winter, with most rains December to April.

History and Development

Botswana was thinly populated by nomadic herdsmen and Bechuana (Bantu) farmers, dominated during the early 19th century by the Matabele, a warrior tribe based in the north. British explorers and missionaries explored from the south, followed in mid-century by Boer farmers who set up 'republics' and tried to annex the land to the Transvaal. In 1885 Bechuanaland instead came under British rule, a southern area being added to Cape Colony and the north forming Bechuanaland Protectorate, under the control of its own chiefs. The Protectorate gained independence as Botswana in 1966.

Resources and Economics

Botswanans graze cattle on their thin grasslands, losing many in times of drought; livestock and meat provide 20 per cent of the country's income. Crop-growing is relatively unimportant; most food is imported, often as famine relief when drought strikes the smallholdings. About 15 per cent of the workforce is employed in South Africa. Mining is the country's mainstay. Botswana is high in the world list of diamond producers; copper, nickel and coal are also important. Except for meat-canning, industries are small and local. Roads are generally adequate; a single railway crosses the country in the east from Zimbabwe to South Africa.

Recent Developments

With a small population and underdeveloped, Botswana is emerging only gradually from pastoralism to an industrially-oriented society. Relying for its income on diamonds and beef, it is vulnerable to drought and world market vagaries, and dependent on outside aid for development capital. Current planning seeks to develop rail and road networks, diversify agriculture and encourage small industries.

Lesotho

The Country

The land-locked Kingdom of Lesotho, one of Africa's smallest independent countries, lies in the southeast ringed entirely by South African territory. *Area* 30,355 km² (11,720 sq miles); *capital* Maseru; *population* 1,559,000 (est. 1986).

Organization

The hereditary monarch is Head of State but has few direct powers in government. Parliament consists of a National Assembly of 60 elected members, and a Senate of 22 Chiefs and 11 others appointed by the King. The Prime Minister governs with an appointed cabinet of about 14 ministers. An interim nominated assembly, dominated by the National Party, currently replaces the elected assembly. There are ten local administrations. Official languages are English and Sesotho; Christianity is the dominant religion.

Geography

Lesotho is a high volcanic plateau, deeply incised by rivers. Over half the country lies above 2000 m (6500 ft); the highest massifs of the north and east rise above 3000 m (10,000 ft), notably in the spectacular Drakensberg escarpment. Thabana Ntlenyana (3482 m, 11,424 ft) is the highest point in southern Africa;

285

from its flanks flow the Orange and Tugela rivers. Lesotho is hot and rainy in summer, cool and dry in winter; savanna and wooded valleys cover most of the country.

History and Development
The Sotho people who first settled the area joined forces against Zulu incursions in the early 19th century under a paramount chief. Strongly united under purposeful leadership, they resisted Boer incursions and avoided engulfment by South Africa later in the century. Basutoland first became a British protectorate in 1868, remaining under its indigenous chiefs. It regained independence in 1966. The Prime Minister suspended the constitution in 1970 and has since governed with a nominated assembly.

Resources and Economics
About 40 per cent of Lesotho's workforce are labourers in South Africa, their remittances adding substantially to home income. Most of the rest are smallholders, raising subsistence crops of maize, sorghum, wheat, peas, beans and barley. Wool, mohair and other animal products are the main exports. Diamonds are mined, the main mine closing in 1982; industries are small and local. Roads are adequate for present needs; just over a kilometre of railway links Maseru with South African railways. The small tourist industry is growing.

Recent Developments
Lesotho's National Development Corporation tries to attract labour-intensive industry; its Highlands Water Scheme plans to sell hydroelectric power and diverted water to South Africa. Both are potentially profitable, but meanwhile Lesotho remains poor. Its problems are increased by economic dependence on South Africa, and its refusal to recognize the 'independence' of neighbouring Transkei, a South African 'native state', through which runs its main import/export route.

Namibia

The Country
Namibia lies on the Atlantic coast of southern Africa, bordered by Botswana in the east, South Africa in the southeast and south, and Angola and Zambia in the north. *Area* 824,292 km^2 (318,259 sq miles); *capital* Windhoek; *population* 1,206,000 (est. 1986).

Organization
Namibia is governed by a Legislative Assembly of 18 elected representatives, which appoints an executive 12-member Ministerial Council; an advisory Administrator-General is appointed by the South African Government, which retains strong control over government. Local government is vested in 22 districts. Official languages are Afrikaans and English; German and local languages are widely used. The dominant religion is Protestant Christianity.

Geography
Dunes and bare rock of the Namib desert face the Atlantic, rising inland to a dissected escarpment over 1000 m (3300 ft) high; isolated massifs stand above

the general level, including granitic Brandberg (2606 m, 8550 ft), Namibia's highest peak. Tableland at 1500 to 2000 m (5000 to 6500 ft) occupies the centre and extends southward behind the escarpment; to east and south spread the dunes and thin grasslands of the Kalahari desert. Only the Orange, Kunene and Okavango rivers are permanent. A dry tropical climate is tempered along the coast by the cool Benguela current and inland by altitude; rainfall is highest and most reliable in the north.

History and Development
Peopled originally by Bushmen and Bantus, the area was annexed by Europeans in the late 19th century, Britain claiming Walvis Bay as a naval base in 1878 and Germany occupying the rest in 1884. South Africa drove out the German colonists in World War I, administering South West Africa after 1921 by mandate from the League of Nations. Since 1946 the territory has been in dispute. As successors to the League, the United Nations ended the mandate in 1966, assuming direct responsibility for the territory, renaming it in 1968, and arranging for its early independence; however, South Africa continues to occupy and administer it.

Resources and Economics
Agriculture employs most rural blacks, contributing one fifth of national income; maize, millet, sorghum and other cereals, beans and livestock are the main subsistence crops; sheepskins and hides are exported. Fishing is important offshore, with much of the produce canned for export. Some timber is cut in the north. Mining is the main economic activity, generating most of the export income; diamonds, and uranium, copper, lead and other metal ores are plentiful. Industries include food- and ore-processing and local manufacturing; there is a large hydroelectric scheme on the Kunene River. Roads and railways are adequate and well maintained; Walvis Bay (technically in South African territory) is the main port.

Recent Developments
South Africa's continuing occupation and its full application of apartheid law generates unrest, particularly among the black Africans who form a 90 per cent majority. The South West Africa People's Organization (SWAPO), recognized by the UN as representing the Namibian people, is one of several opposition groups dedicated to removing South African influence. Guerrilla activity is rife, especially in the north near the Angola border. Meanwhile the country's economy develops, bringing prosperity especially to the white minority.

South Africa

The Country
The Republic of South Africa lies at the southern end of Africa, bordered in the northeast by Mozambique and Swaziland, in the northwest and north by Namibia, Botswana and Zimbabwe, and enclosing Lesotho; Walvis Bay and a surrounding enclave on the Namibian coast are also South African territory (see also Namibia). *Area* 1,221,037 km^2 (471,443 sq miles); *administrative capital* Pretoria, *legislative capital* Cape Town, *judicial capital* Bloemfontein, *largest city* Johannesburg; *population* 34,799,000 (est. 1986).

Africa South

Organization

Under the constitution initiated in 1984 a tricameral Parliament includes a House of Assembly of about 170 elected members, for which only white citizens may vote or be elected, and separate smaller houses for coloured and Indian electoral rolls. An electoral college drawn from all three houses but with a white majority elects the President for a seven-year term. The President appoints a cabinet of about 20 ministers from all three houses, including a Prime Minister, and is helped by a 60-member President's Council. The four provinces each have an appointed Administrator and elected council, holding office for five years. Official languages are English and Afrikaans; several African languages are widely spoken. Christianity forms the dominant religion.

Geography

South Africa's coastal plain is rarely more than a few kilometres wide. In the west it rises gently to the dry hills of Namaqualand, in the southwest and south to a complex of fold mountains lining the coast. Behind rises a spectacular escarpment that sweeps eastward through Cape Province to Natal, Swaziland and the Transvaal. The Great Escarpment reaches its highest peaks of over 3000 m (10,000 ft) in the Natal Drakensberg along the Lesotho border; elsewhere it ranges between 1500 and 2500 m (5000 to 8200 ft). Central South Africa is a high basin, dominated by the rolling high plateau of the Orange Free State and Transvaal in the northeast and tilted westward to the Orange river basin and Great Karroo plateau at about 1200 m (4000 ft). The climate is subtropical, warm and generally dry. The Cape Town area has a Mediterranean climate with winter rains; elsewhere most rain falls in summer, heaviest in the east over the forests and grasslands of Natal, lightest in the west where desert prevails.

History and Development

Southern Africa was thinly populated by Bushmen and Hottentot farmers when Portuguese navigators explored the coast in 1488. About the same time Bantus from central Africa were searching southward for new lands to farm and raise cattle. In 1652 the Dutch East India Company established Cape Town as a victualling station. From it Dutch settlers spread inland, farming with imported slaves. Dutch and native Africans clashed in the late 18th century over land and cattle. Following the Napoleonic Wars the Cape became British in 1814; disgruntled Boer (Dutch) settlers migrated to the interior in the Great Trek, establishing the Orange Free State and Transvaal as independent republics. Further influxes of white settlers followed the discovery of gold and diamonds, and indentured Asians were introduced to work the Natal sugar plantations. War between the republics and Britain (1899–1902) led to a Boer defeat and, in 1910, the establishment of the Union of South Africa as a British dominion. Under increasing Afrikaans influence the Union became a republic in 1961, adopting apartheid racial policies that gave inferior status to black, Indian and coloured populations and establishing black 'homelands' or 'bantustans' in eastern South Africa, with a degree of self-government but still part of and dominated by the Republic.

Resources and Economics

Agriculture employs about one third of the workforce. Many South Africans, particularly those in the 'homelands', are smallholders producing maize, sorghum, potatoes, livestock and other subsistence crops. Elsewhere large-scale agriculture grows sugar-cane, cereals, grapes, citrus fruits, cotton and a wide range of other produce for local consumption and export. Fishing is also an important industry, adding to South Africa's substantial tally of exported foods. But the most important sections of the economy are mining and industry. Coal and phosphates, gold, silver and diamonds, chrome, vanadium and many other metal ores generate about one third of the country's income and over two thirds of its export revenues; gold alone accounts for a high proportion of the total value. Highly industrialized, South Africa employs about 12 per cent of its workforce in manufacturing, processing foods and metals, and producing a range of consumer goods for its own use. Good road, rail and air networks connect the main centres and link South Africa with the outside world.

Recent Developments
South Africa is unusual among African states in being a prosperous country with political stability and a varied economy. Although its stability is maintained by the determined policies of a minority, and its prosperity (like many other desiderata) is inequitably distributed among its heterogeneous population, these are features it shares with many other countries. South Africa's racial attitudes, and its self-defending policies in Namibia and Angola, make it repugnant to most of the rest of Africa, to the UN, and to many other states throughout the world. However, neighbouring countries depend on it economically and benefit from the market and employment opportunities it affords. South Africa is fostering relations with Angola and Mozambique in an attempt to find common ground. Its current prosperity is firmly based on well-developed natural resources, and although social and political policies offend liberal thought elsewhere, the South African government's determination to maintain the internal status quo is unswerving.

Swaziland

The Country
The Kingdom of Swaziland, southern Africa's smallest country, lies in a land-locked position in the southeast, bounded in the east by Mozambique and on all other sides by South Africa. *Area* 17,363 km^2 (6704 sq miles); *administrative capital* Mbabane, *legislative capital* Lobamba; *population* 667,000 (est. 1986).

Organization
The advisory Parliament consists of a 50-member House of Assembly and 20-member Senate. Tribal Chieftaincies elect 40 representatives and 10 senators; the hereditary monarch appoints the rest. A National Council that includes all adult male Swazis advises on law, customs and traditions. Four District Commissioners are responsible for local administration, working through rural and urban councils. Official languages are English and Siswati; Christianity and local religions are well represented.

Geography
Swaziland occupies the eastern flank of the South African plateau. In the west is the Highveld, rising to over 1400 m (4500 ft). In the east the Middleveld and Lowveld descend from 1000 m (3300 ft) to about 250 m (800 ft). These zones, mainly savanna-covered, are crossed by deep-cut, forested river valleys. In the northeast stand the Lebombo Mountains, an escarpment 600 m (2000 ft) high

overlooking the Mozambique coastal plain. The warm climate is tempered in the west by altitude; rainfall is plentiful on the uplands, especially during the wet season in October to March.

History and Development
Swazi migrants of Bantu stock first settled the country from the southwest in the 18th and early 19th centuries, establishing a kingdom which successfully resisted mid-19th-century Zulu and Boer incursions. Britain guaranteed independence in 1881, and in 1903 it became a British protectorate; white settlers farmed but interfered little in native affairs. Swaziland became self-governing in 1967 and independent in 1968. Four years later the King, with parliamentary approval, reassumed all ruling powers.

Resources and Economics
Over 80 per cent of Swazis are farmers, generating 40 per cent of the country's income and over 65 per cent of export revenues. Subsistence crops include maize, yams, sorghum, potatoes, fruit and livestock; plantations yield sugar, tobacco and cotton. Natural forests and plantations provide fuel, timber and wood-pulp. Coal, asbestos, diamonds and gold are mined. Industries include sugar-refining, cotton-ginning, pulp and fertilizer manufacture and tourism. Roads are adequate for present needs; railways link mining centres in western Swaziland with the ports of Maputo (Mozambique) and Durban (South Africa).

Recent Developments
With good soils and climate (though currently affected by drought), plentiful minerals and a reasonably balanced economy, Swaziland is well favoured. A customs union with South Africa brings benefits free of economic and political domination; a new hydroelectric scheme should reduce costly power imports. Domestic stability encourages foreign investment and aid, allowing slow but steady economic growth.

Zimbabwe

The Country
The Republic of Zimbabwe lies centrally in southern Africa, land-locked and bounded in the east by Mozambique, in the south by South Africa, in the southwest by Botswana and in the north by Zambia. *Area* 390,580 km^2 (150,803 sq miles); *capital* Harare; *population* 9,119,000 (est. 1986).

Organization
A 100-member House of Assembly is elected by universal suffrage, one fifth from 'white roll' constituencies; a 40-member Senate includes 'white roll' and 'common-roll' electees and nominated members. Both houses run for five-year terms. The President, elected by parliament for six-year terms, appoints an executive Prime Minister and cabinet of about 25 ministers. English is the official language; Shona and Ndebele are widely spoken. Local religions and Christianity are the main faiths.

Geography
Occupying a high plateau, Zimbabwe's upland veld forms a broad east-to-west

ridge across the country at 1200 m (4000 ft) and more, falling on north and south flanks to a lower veld at 500 to 1000 m (1600 to 3300 ft). The Eastern Highlands, lining the Mozambique border, include Inyangani (2593 m, 8507 ft), Zimbabwe's highest mountain. Northern rivers flow mainly into the Zambezi, southern rivers into the Limpopo and Sabi. The climate is tropical tempered by altitude, with a rainy season from October (the hottest month) to March. Dry savanna covers much of the country, with forests in the eastern mountains.

History and Development

Bantu settlers arriving about AD 300 found an area already occupied by Bushmen, farmers and miners. A complex culture developed, including farming, metal-working and building; the ruined city of Zimbabwe, from which the modern country takes its name, is one of many decorated forts and settlements of the first millenium AD. Shona skills of mining, metal-work and pottery survived 16th-century incursions by Portuguese traders and 19th-century devastation by Ndebele invaders, who eventually settled. Christian missionaries brought a measure of peace in the 1860s. From 1889 Cecil Rhodes' British South Africa Company gained concessions that allowed British settlers to farm, mine and trade. From 1923 Southern Rhodesia was a self-governing colony, from 1965 unilaterally independent under white-dominated government. Full independence was gained in 1980.

Resources and Economics

Agriculture employs 70 per cent of the workforce in growing and processing crops, and generates an eighth of the country's income. A wide range of foods is produced including maize, wheat, sorghum, millet, rice, cassava, vegetables and livestock; Zimbabwe is self-supporting and an exporter of food in good years. Cash crops include tobacco, sugar, cotton, fruit and beef, which are mostly processed before export. Minerals include gold, silver, asbestos, copper, chrome and nickel. Zimbabwe has small but well-developed industries, processing its own agricultural crops and metals, and manufacturing steel, cement and consumer goods for local use. Hydroelectric power output is backed by coal-fired stations. There are good rail and road networks; Harare has an international airport.

Recent Developments

Independence was for long delayed by guerrilla war and since then inter-tribal rivalries, notably between Shona and Ndebele, have taken their toll; despite this unpromising start, Zimbabwe's economy expanded well in the first few years of independence, and subsequent cutbacks have been due more to drought and world recession than to internal problems. Naturally well endowed with soils, climate and minerals, favoured by outside investors, Zimbabwe needs only sensible management and domestic peace to ensure its prosperity.

Islands of the Atlantic and Indian Oceans

The Mid-Atlantic Ridge, an active cleft in the ocean floor, and similar cracks to right and left are responsible for many of the Atlantic islands, from Iceland and Jan Mayen in the north to isolated Bouvetøya in the far south. Madeira and the Azores, the Canary and Cape Verde Islands, Fernando de Noronha, St Paul Rocks, Ascension Island, St Helena, Tristan da Cunha, Trindade and Martin Vaz are all volcanic islands of geologically recent origin, many showing convincing cones, some still active enough to unsettle their inhabitants from time to time. The Falkland Islands by contrast are a granitic remnant of Gondwanaland (the supercontinent which split up to form our present continents), with strong South African affinities. In the Indian Ocean Madagascar, the Seychelles, and the Maldive and Laccadive islands are continental fragments, the smaller islands built up into coral banks. Most of the others, including the Mascarenes, Comoros, Cocos (Keeling) of warm seas, and the Antarctic Marion and Prince Edward islands, Kerguelen, Crozet, St Paul and Amsterdam Islands, are volcanic, rising from deep-water platforms.

ATLANTIC OCEAN ISLANDS

Ascension Island

Ascension Island is an isolated volcanic island on an arm of the Mid-Atlantic Ridge, some 1100 km (700 miles) northwest of St Helena, of which it is politically a dependency. *Area* 88 km^2 (34 sq miles); *capital* Georgetown; *population* approx. 2000 (est. 1986). The floating community of technicians, manual workers and their families, mostly from Britain, St Helena and the USA, is under the administration of a resident magistrate.

An inactive volcanic cone, Ascension rises from a coastal plain to a single peak, Green Mountain (875 m, 2870 ft). The climate is tropical, tempered by trade winds throughout the year. The plain is arid; the mountain is capped by thickets of exotic trees introduced by the Royal Navy during the 19th century. Ascension was discovered in the late 15th century by Portuguese navigators. It remained unoccupied until 1815, when a British naval garrison was installed to prevent its use as a rescue base for Napoleon. A coaling and revictualling point in the 19th century, it later gained importance as a cable station, and in World War II as a mid-ocean airfield for US aircraft in transit to Europe. In recent years it has accommodated a US missile tracking station and BBC relay station, and is currently a staging post for aircraft plying between Britain and the Falkland Islands.

Azores and Madeira

The Azores archipelago (Arquipélago dos Açores) includes ten major and several smaller islands in the central North Atlantic Ocean, in the latitude of southern Portugal. The islands form three groups (eastern group Formigas, Santa Maria, São Miguel; central group Faial, Graciosa, Pico, São Jorge, Terceira; western group Corvo, Flores). *Area* 2335 km^2 (902 sq miles); *capitals of three administrative districts* Ponta Delgada São Miguel), Horta (Faial), Angra (Terceira); *population* 280,000 (est. 1986). Madeira is an isolated archipelago of two large and several small islands, 800 km (500 miles) southwest of Cape St Vincent, southern Portugal. *Area* 797 km^2 (308 sq miles); *capital* Funchal; *population* 285,000 (est. 1986). The islands are administered as districts of Portugal, with considerable autonomy, returning representatives to the Portuguese parliament. Catholicism is the main faith, Portuguese the official language.

All the islands are volcanic, with steep cliffs and rolling uplands, often with cones and lava or ash plains representing recent vulcanism. Several have peaks above 500 m (1650 ft). The main volcanic cone of Ponto do Pico in the central Azores soars in isolation to 2351 m (7713 ft); Madeira's highest mountain, Ruivo de Santana, rises to 1861 m (6106 ft) from a complex of steep hills and gorges. The Azores have a warm oceanic climate, subtropical in summer but damp and often tempestuous in winter; originally forested, they are now heavily cultivated. Madeira, subtropical throughout the year, has lost most of its original forest, and all lowlands are under cultivation. None of the islands had indigenous human populations. They were discovered by Portuguese adventurers early in the 15th century (though Madeira may well have been known to earlier explorers) and have remained Portuguese colonies throughout their history.

Azoreans and Madeirans rely mainly on agriculture for their living, using their islands' rich soils and generally benign climates to grow cereals, vegetables and fruit, and raise cattle, sheep and goats mainly for local consumption. Both Madeira and the Azores produce wines, and Madeira grows and exports cane sugar and tropical fruits, notably pineapples and bananas. Both groups have long traditions of fishing and whaling, and of providing crews, water and victuals for visiting ships. Open-boat whaling for migrating sperm whales is still practised off the Azores, deep-water fishing with long lines off Madeira, though modern fishing and processing are gradually replacing traditional methods. The islands are well provided with roads; inter-island shipping links the main ports, and Pico, Santa Maria and Madeira have international airports. Tourism has for long flourished on Madeira and is a growing industry on the Azores. Dense populations and underemployment drive many islanders temporarily or permanently to emigration, mainly to Portugal and the USA.

Canary Islands

The Canary Islands (Islas Canarias) are an archipelago of seven large and many small islands lying in tropical waters of the eastern Atlantic Ocean off the coast of Morocco. In the west are Hierro, Gomera, Gran Canaria, La Palma and Tenerife, in the east Fuerteventura and Lanzarote. *Area* 7273 km^2 (2808 sq miles); *provincial capitals* Las Palmas (Gran Canaria) and Santa Cruz (Tenerife); *population* 1,400,000 (est. 1986). The islands form two provinces of Spain under provincial governors, and are subdivided into municipalities for local government. Catholicism is the dominant religion, Spanish the official language.

The islands are mainly volcanic, steep-sided, dotted with extinct cones and fumaroles, and cliffs, hummocks and plains of lava and ash. The western group is highest, with peaks rising above 1000 m (3300 ft); the high peak of Pico de Teide, capped with permanent snow, forms a prominent landmark on Tenerife. The climate is hot and dry at sea level, milder and damper on the uplands; the lower plains are arid, the uplands were forested and are now heavily cultivated wherever conditions allow. Discovered originally by Arabs and settled by nomadic pastoralists from mainland Africa, the Canaries were visited and fought over by French, Spanish, and Portuguese forces: Spanish sovereignty was recognized by treaty in 1479, and the islands have remained under Spanish rule since then.

Rich soils, year-round warmth and reliable rains make many parts of the islands cultivable; agriculture is the main industry, producing cereals, sugar cane, wines, and both tropical and temperate fruit and vegetables. The main cities of Las Palmas and Tenerife have long been important ports-of-call and trading points for international shipping. Fishing is a traditional industry now modernizing for export; ferries link the coastal settlements. International and local airports provide a network of communications for the main islands, most of which cater for a large and steadily-growing tourist industry.

Cape Verde

The Country
The Republic of Cape Verde occupies a group of ten large and many small islands 560 km (350 miles) off the coast of west Africa, in the eastern Atlantic Ocean. *Area* 4033 km^2 (1557 sq miles); *capital* Praia (São Tiago); *population* 356,000 (est. 1986).

Organization
Cape Verde is governed by an elected National People's Assembly of 56 members, who in turn elect an executive President and Head of State; there is a single political party, the Partido Africano da Independencia da Guiné e Cabo Verde (PAIGC). Catholicism is the dominant religion, Portuguese the official language with a creole dialect widely spoken.

Geography
The islands are volcanic and mountainous; the highest peak, Fogo, is an active cone rising to 2829 m (9281 ft). A tropical climate is tempered by northeast winds; the islands are hot and dry at sea level, cooler and damp in the uplands where the best soils are found. Coastal plains are semi-desert, mountains covered with savanna or thin forest. About half the population live on São Tiago, with most of the rest on Santo Antão (14%), Fogo (11%) and São Vicente (14%).

History and Development
Discovered by Portuguese navigators in the mid-15th century, the Cape Verde islands were colonized by Portuguese settlers who quickly disposed of a small aboriginal population. The islands became a Portuguese colony and victualling point for transatlantic shipping, providing water, fresh food, and later bunkering coal and oil; islanders include a mixture of European, African and

Asiatic races who settled from time to time. Eventually forming an Overseas Province of Portugal, Cape Verde achieved independence in 1975.

Resources and Economics
About 70 per cent of the workforce are farmers or smallholders, mostly raising subsistence crops of maize, beans, potatoes, cane sugar, yams, bananas and livestock; plantation crops of cane sugar, coffee and bananas are exported when available, together with meat and hides. Fishing has gained in importance since independence. Few minerals are exploited except salt, limestone and pozzolana (volcanic silica ash); manufactures include cement, canned foods and clothing.

Recent Developments
Poorly endowed and underdeveloped, Cape Verde has to struggle to support its large island populations. Prolonged drought necessitates substantial food imports; most trading is with Portugal, and foreign aid and expatriate remittances help to balance the meagre annual budget. Deep-water fishing and improved agriculture (based on more efficient water management) are the islands' brightest hopes for the future.

Falkland Islands

The Country
The Falkland Islands are an archipelago of two main islands and over two hundred smaller ones in the southwestern Atlantic Ocean, 480 km (300 miles) east of central Argentina (see also South Georgia). *Area* 15,800 km² (6100 sq miles); *capital and only town* Stanley (Port Stanley); *population* 3000 (est 1986).

Organization
The islands form a British Crown Colony, administered by a Civil Commissioner assisted by a part-nominated and part-elected Executive Council. The population is largely of British descent; the main faiths are Christian, and English is the official language. Since the Argentinian occupation of 1982 a large military garrison is maintained.

Geography
The islands are mostly ancient crystalline rocks, with smooth round profiles producing a rolling landscape; the highest points on the main islands of East and West Falkland (respectively Mt Usborne and Mt Adam) rise to about 700 m (2300 ft). The smaller islands are mainly hilly, many with spectacular cliffs and crags. The Falklands have a cool, windy climate with frequent cloud and drizzle. Peaty soils support moorland vegetation and grassland; indigenous grasses are now mostly replaced by forage species for introduced sheep and cattle. Trees grow only in sheltered hollows. Indigenous land birds are plentiful, and spectacular congregations of sea birds and fur seals, feeding in the rich surface waters, come ashore to breed in large colonies.

History and Development
Discovered in 1592, the Falklands were first occupied by British and French colonists in 1764–5. French interests, bought by Spain in 1770, passed to Buenos Aires (ultimately to Argentina), which retained settlements in East

Falkland. The British withdrew in 1774 without relinquishing their claim, returning in 1833 and dispossessing a small Argentine settlement. Scattered farming communities formed mainly on coastal inlets where peat was available for fuel. The colonists ranched cattle and introduced sheep for wool and tallow production. The islands became a Crown Colony in 1892. Long-standing Argentine claims to sovereignty reached a climax in April 1982 when the Argentine army invaded the islands, to be defeated by a British task force three months later.

Resources and Economics

Sheep-farming for wool production provides the main occupation and income of the islanders, and the economy is boosted by grants-in-aid from Britain. There is little industrial development or exploitation of natural resources; most requirements (except peat, the main domestic fuel) are imported. About half the population lives in Stanley, the rest in isolated settlements on the 'camp'. Good radio and telephone networks cover the main settlements, which are linked also by a floatplane service; roads and sea links are poor. Charter vessels call periodically from Britain and a few tourist ships call in summer. Military air services now form a direct link with the UK.

Recent Developments

Hampered by a small population, low investment, limited development of resources and almost total economic dependence on wool, the Falklands show a reasonable standard of living but a static or declining economy and long-term depopulation. Potential resources include abundant marine fish and kelp, while there is also scope for tourism and improved and diversified farming. Argentine claims to the islands persist, but local feeling strongly favours continuing association with Britain.

St Helena

The island of St Helena stands in the southeastern Atlantic Ocean 1900 km (1200 miles) from the coast of Angola (see also Ascension Island and Tristan da Cunha). *Area* 122 km^2 (47 sq miles); *capital* Jamestown; *population* 5000 (est. 1986). A British Crown Colony, the island is governed by an appointed Governor who presides over a part-appointed, part-elected Legislative Council.

A steep-sided volcanic island with rolling top, St Helena rises to 822 m (2697 ft); the formidable cliffs are cut by steep ravines, of which the widest contains the capital, facing a small anchorage. The climate is subtropical and damp; originally wooded, the uplands are now mostly grazed or cultivated. Discovered by Portuguese navigators in 1502, St Helena became a port of call and victualling point for Portuguese ships. Later Dutch and British mariners called in, the Dutch claiming it in 1633 and the British East India Company establishing the first settlement in 1659. The island acquired a population of mainly Asian and European origin. Fortified in 1815 to receive the exiled Napoleon, it became a Crown Colony in 1834. St Helena was for long a coaling and victualling station on the route from Europe to Cape Town, but declined in importance with the opening of the Suez Canal in 1869.

Most of the population are smallholding farmers on the fertile uplands, producing vegetables and fruit for local consumption; flax production, once the island's main source of overseas earnings, has now ceased. About one third of the population lives in Jamestown, where many people are employed on government relief work. There are few industries beyond handicrafts. Roads are adequate, mostly legacies from St Helena's military past; shipping links with the outside world are few. The island's budget is balanced annually by a grant-in-aid from Britain and other overseas funds, but the community gains little from membership of a Commonwealth that seems to have overlooked and neglected it for many decades.

South Georgia and South Sandwich Islands

South Georgia and the South Sandwich Islands lie east–southeast of the Falkland Islands (of which they are politically dependencies) in the Antarctic waters of the Southern Ocean. South Georgia, a mountainous island with an area of 3755 km^2 (1450 sq miles), is ice-capped with peaks rising to 2934 m (9626 ft) and glaciers down to sea level. The South Sandwich Islands form a north–south arc some 386 km (240 miles) long, of eleven large and several small islands with a total area of about 600 km^2 (230 sq miles); most are ice-capped, and the tallest peak, on Montagu Island, rises to 1370 m (4500 ft). The climate is cold, with frequent snow and strong winds. South Georgia's lowlands are covered with tussock grass and heath vegetation; the South Sandwich Islands, which are surrounded by sea ice for most of the winter, have little vegetation.

South Georgia was first sighted in 1675, and first landed on by Captain James Cook in 1775; in the same year he discovered the South Sandwich Islands. Both are claimed by Britain and Argentina, and were the scene of hostilities in 1982. South Georgia, formerly an important whaling centre, carries a permanent British scientific station; Thule, in the South Sandwich group, was temporarily occupied by an Argentinian station 1981–2.

Tristan da Cunha

The Tristan da Cunha group lies in the southern Atlantic Ocean some 3200 km (2000 miles) west of Cape Town. *Areas*: Tristan da Cunha 98 km^2 (38 sq miles), Inaccessible Island 11 km^2 (4 sq miles), Nightingale Island less than 2 km^2 (0.75 sq miles), Gough Island, 360 km (225 miles) to south–southeast, 91 km^2 (35 sq miles); *main settlement* Edinburgh; *population* (Tristan plus South African government weather station on Gough) 300 (est. 1986). The islands are dependencies of St Helena, under a resident administrator.

All are volcanic and steep sided, ringed with cliffs or narrow beaches. Tristan has a single cone rising to 2060 m (6760 ft) and a narrow northwestern coastal plain which carries the settlement. Warm-temperate, damp and windy, all the islands support forest and scrub, the haunt of a few indigenous land birds and huge colonies of burrowing or surface-living sea birds. Tristan was discovered by Portuguese navigators in 1506. Only castaways and possibly sealers inhabited the islands until 1810, when Tristan was settled by three American seamen. Britain laid claim in 1816, establishing a garrison to keep the islands out of French hands. When the troops left in the following year, six (including a wife and two children) elected to remain. Other settlers arrived from Britain, St Helena and elsewhere, the community growing to eighty-five by the mid-century with a livelihood based on whaling, sealing, and barter with passing ships. They became a colony in 1876 and a dependency of St Helena in 1938.

Commercial fishing began in 1948; fishing and fish-processing, together with farming, are currently the main occupations. A volcanic eruption close to Edinburgh led to the evacuation of the community in 1961, but most returned in 1963. Currently the Tristan community remains small and viable, enjoying a limited but clearly tolerable standard of living remote from the rest of the world.

INDIAN OCEAN ISLANDS

British Indian Ocean Territory

This territory, established in 1965, isolated four island groups in the western Indian Ocean and retained them for strategic purposes under British sovereignty. Aldabra, Farquhar and Desroches were sequestered from Seychelles, and have since (1976) been returned. Chagos Archipelago, detached from Mauritius, remains under British control despite protests from the Mauritian government. The archipelago of low-lying coral atolls has few remaining inhabitants (three thousand were removed to Mauritius and subsequently compensated) but accommodates military staff responsible for US air and naval facilities in Diego Garcia island. *Area* 78 km² (30 sq miles).

Cocos (Keeling) Islands

Comprising two isolated atolls in the eastern Indian Ocean, the Cocos or Keeling Islands lie some 2000 km (1250 miles) southeast of Sri Lanka. *Area* 14 km² (5.5 sq miles); *settlement* West Island; *population* 600 (est. 1986). The islands are Australian territory, governed by an Administrator who is advised by an elected council. Transient Europeans occupy West Island; a permanent Cocos Malay population lives on Home Island. The climate is warm and equable; coconut palms are the main vegetation.

Discovered by a British mariner (Captain Keeling) in 1609, the islands remained unoccupied until the early 19th century, when British settlers with Malay labourers began coconut cultivation. Under formal British rule from 1857, the Cocos (Keeling) group became the property of the Clunies-Ross family (heirs of one of the early settlers), whose representatives were responsible to successive colonial governments. In 1955 the islands came under Australian authority and the family rights were bought out by the Australian government in 1978. Copra is the main product.

Comoros

The Country
Occupying the three northwestern Comoro Islands, the Federal and Islamic

Republic of Comoros lies in Mozambique Channel between northern Madagascar and the African coast. Mayotte Island (see entry) is claimed as part of the republic, though currently under French administration. *Area* 1862 km² (719 sq miles); *capital* Moroni; *population* 336,000 (est. 1986).

Organization
The islands are governed by a Federal Assembly of 39 elected members, with an executive President; much of the administration devolves on individual island councils. The dominant faith is Islam, the main language Swahili with French and Arabic widely spoken.

Geography
The three main islands (Njazidja, Mwali and Nzwami) are volcanic; the highest (Njazidja, formerly Grande Comore) rises to a central range 2361 m (7746 ft) high. The climate is hot and damp, with a wet season in January, the hottest month. Formerly forested, the islands are now intensively cultivated, with substantial remnant rain forests on the mountains and mangroves along the coast.

History and Development
Known to Arab traders and travellers during the 15th and 16th centuries, the Comoro Islands were first recorded by Europeans in the early 16th century. Having declared a protectorate over Mayotte in 1843, France took over the remaining three islands in 1886, administering the group as a dependency of Madagascar. In a referendum of 1974 which offered the group independence, only Mayotte voted to remain in the French Community. The remaining three islands declared independence on behalf of all four, seeking then and since to include Mayotte.

Resources and Economics
Mainly agricultural, the islanders raise subsistence crops of vegetables, cassava, rice and yams. Plantations and smallholdings grow sugar, coffee, cacao, coconuts, perfumes and spices for export, and timber is cut on Njazidja, mainly for local use. The islands have few other developed resources or industries. Roads are generally inadequate: Njazidja has an international airport.

Recent Developments
Poor in resources, with a large and rapidly-expanding population split unevenly between three islands, Comoros as it stands is barely viable. Even the inclusion of Mayotte (recommended by the UN but opposed by a majority of the island's population and by France) would make little difference to the moribund economy, which is likely to continue at subsistence level into the forseeable future.

Madagascar

The Country
The Democratic Republic of Madagascar lies off the southeastern coast of Africa, separated by the Mozambique Channel. *Area* 587,041 km² (226,657 sq miles); *capital* Antananarivo; *population* 10,322,000 (est. 1986).

Organization
Since 1975 Madagascar has been governed by a military dictatorship. A Supreme Revolutionary Council of about 20 members is appointed by the President, who as Head of State also selects the executive Prime Minister and a small cabinet of ministers. Local government is administered through six provinces, divided into prefectures and smaller units. The dominant faith is Roman Catholicism; the official language is Malagasy, with French and English widely spoken.

Geography
A longitudinal spine of mountains rises in stages from coastal plains bordering the Mozambique Channel to a rolling, dissected plateau, dominated by three mountain massifs. Tsaratanana (2876 m, 9436 ft) in the north and Tsiafajavona (2643 m, 8671 ft) in the centre are volcanic, Pic Boby (2658 m, 8720 ft) in the south is an exposed granitic massif. Towards the eastern seaboard the mountains fall more steeply, in a series of stepped faults that produce spectacular cliffs and escarpments. Northern and eastern Madagascar are hot and humid, with heavy rainfall supporting dense rain forests. The west and southwest are drier; grasslands, scrub and secondary forest are characteristic, giving way to desert in the south. Long separated from Africa, the island has many endemic species of trees and shrubs, and a remarkable fauna including chameleons and lemurs.

History and Development
Malagasques are descendants of African and Indonesian colonists who began to arrive over two thousand years ago. Portuguese and other European visitors in the 16th century found Arab coastal settlements guarding a difficult and inaccessible hinterland. French traders of the 17th century established fortified posts to secure slaves from the interior, and British intervention in the early 19th century helped to establish a native kingdom that eventually controlled much of the island. French influences remained strong; when disputes arose over land concessions in the north, French troops invaded, and in 1895–6 the Madagascan royal family accepted the inevitability of French rule. Intensive colonial development brought a measure of order and prosperity, coupled with a massive increase in population. During World War II Madagascar sided with the Vichy government and was invaded by British troops. In 1946 it became an Overseas Territory of France, and in 1958 gained independence.

Resources and Economics
Agriculture employs most of the workforce and produces over half the national income. Rice, maize, ground-nuts and cassava are grown, mainly on smallholdings; grazing lands, formerly forested, now support sheep, cattle, pigs and goats. Coffee, vanilla, cloves, sugar, tea, cotton and soya beans are grown for local consumption and export, coffee alone accounting for over one third of overseas earnings. Chromite, graphite, gemstones and mica are also exported. Manufacturing industries process agricultural produce, including food and cotton; there are a few assembly plants and oil-refineries, and most industrial fuel has to be imported. Roads and railways are barely adequate, especially in the wet season. Ports are plentiful but tend to be isolated from their hinterlands by distance and bad roads. Major airfields provide good internal and external air links.

Recent Developments
A country of subcontinental size with difficult terrain, poor communications and a rapidly-growing population, Madagascar still depends heavily on relatively few resources and has managed only halting steps toward economic progress in the decade since independence. Tight budgets leave little to spare for development, and Madagascar's unsettled politics have discouraged financial aid and development loans.

Maldives

The Country
The Republic of Maldives occupies a chain of over a thousand coral atolls 3200 km (2000 miles) from southern India in the northwestern Indian Ocean. *Area* 298 km² (115 sq miles); *capital* Malé; *population* 177,000 (est. 1986).

Organization
The Maldives are governed by an executive President, elected for five-year terms, who is assisted by an appointed cabinet; the legislative body is a House of Representatives of 48 elected and appointed members serving five-year terms, including two from each of the nineteen major settlements. Islam is the dominant faith, Divehi (based on Sinhalese) the main language.

Geography
The islands, clustered on an elongate submarine ridge, are low-lying and coral-fringed, with a hot and damp tropical climate throughout the year. Over two hundred are inhabited; the islanders, whose ancestors came mainly from Ceylon (now Sri Lanka) and the Arab coasts, have a strong maritime tradition. Much of the land was originally forested and scrub-covered, but the best soils are now under cultivation as plantations and smallholdings.

History and Development
The Maldives were well known to Arab and Portuguese explorers in the 16th and 17th centuries. Malé was founded as a 16th-century Portuguese staging post, but the thinly-populated islands were left very much to themselves. A sultanate linked ethnically with Ceylon, they remained mainly under local rule while Ceylon was colonized successively by the Dutch and British. Under their own sultan they became a British protectorate in 1887. The Maldives achieved independence in 1965 and declared themselves a republic three years later.

Resources and Economics
Well-watered, and fertile in patches, the Maldive islands grow coconut palms, millet, breadfruit and tropical fruits and vegetables, some of which are exported. The main commercial wealth is based on a modern fishing fleet, which cans and freezes locally-caught tuna and bonito, mainly for export to Japan. There are currently few other resources or developments.

Recent Developments
Although communications are difficult among the main atolls, the Maldives seem to have achieved unity and common purpose under an enterprising government. The economy is flourishing, though heavily committed to agriculture and fishing. Tourism may well provide the needed diversification;

several of the islands have airfields, and tourist facilities are expanding rapidly with ready financial help from outside sources.

Mauritius

The Country
The independent state of Mauritius includes the island of Mauritius, 2500 km (1600 miles) east of Madagascar in the southwestern Indian Ocean, and the smaller island of Rodriguez 560 km (350 miles) to the east. *Area* 2045 km^2 (790 sq miles); *capital* Port Louis; *population* 1,057,000 (est. 1986).

Organization
Head of State is the British Sovereign, represented by a Governor-General who appoints an executive Prime Minister and cabinet. There is an elected Legislative Assembly of 71 members, who serve five-year terms. Hinduism and Christianity are the leading faiths; English is the official language with Hindi, Urdu and creole French widely spoken.

Geography
Mauritius is a rugged volcanic island, dominated in the south by a lava plateau that rises to a massif 826 m (2710 ft) high; a fringing coral reef gives protection from heavy seas. Rodriguez is smaller but similar in structure. The climate is hot and rainy in summer, cooler and drier in winter when the trade winds blow. Both islands have forested uplands and heavily cultivated valleys and plains.

History and Development
The islands were discovered originally by Arabs and later (in the early 16th century) by Portuguese voyagers. Mauritius was occupied towards the end of the 16th century by Dutch planters, but they abandoned it about a hundred years later. From 1722 French settlers moved in, planting the islands with sugar-cane and importing slave labour to manage it. Britain captured both islands during the Napoleonic Wars and retained them as colonies, introducing indentured labour from India when slavery was abolished. They were granted independence in 1968.

Resources and Economics
Sugar-cane dominates the economics of both islands; on Mauritius it covers over four fifths of the cultivable land, occupies a quarter of the workforce and accounts for over half the export earnings. Tea, tobacco and subsistence crops of fruit, maize, rice and vegetables are also grown, but most food is imported. Food-processing, textiles, fishing and tourism are growing in importance. Roads and port facilities are adequate, and Mauritius has an international airport.

Recent Developments
Sugar has for long brought prosperity to these two communities, but overdependence on a single crop leads Mauritius into serious economic problems when hurricanes strike or world prices fluctuate. Poverty and high unemployment create further problems among the teeming, heterogeneous population, occasionally promoting racial tensions. Many Mauritians work overseas, their remittances proving a welcome addition to the islands' budgets.

Mayotte

An Overseas Territory of France, Mayotte is the most southeasterly of the Comoro Islands, west of Madagascar in the Mozambique Channel. *Area* 374 km² (144 sq miles); *capital* Dzaoudzi; *population* 72,000 (est. 1986). The island is administered by a Commissioner assisted by an elected council, returning a deputy and senator to the French Parliament. Islam is the dominant faith, French the official language with Swahili widely spoken. Mayotte is volcanic, rising to a rugged plateau at about 660 m (2200 ft), and fringed by a coral reef. The climate is hot and humid with monsoon rainfall in summer, warm and dry in winter. Dry heath covers the high ground, grassland and mangrove forest the lowlands, though these are now largely cultivated.

Like the rest of the Comoros, Mayotte was known to and colonized by Arab voyagers long before Europeans rounded the Cape of Good Hope. Occupied by French settlers from 1843, its lowland forests were gradually replaced by plantations. From 1914 it was administered with the other Comoro islands from Madagascar. When the Comoros achieved independence in 1974, Mayotte elected to remain French, maintaining a special status within the French Community. Most of its population are subsistence farmers or fishermen; vanilla, coffee, copra and shellfish are produced for export, but the island is heavily subsidized by France.

Réunion

An Overseas Department of France, Réunion is one of the Mascarene islands, lying in the western Indian Ocean some 900 km (570 miles) east of Madagascar. *Area* 2510 km² (969 sq miles); *capital* Saint-Denis; *population* 571,000 (est. 1986). An appointed Commission presides over elected general and regional councils; the community is represented in the French Parliament by three deputies and two senators. Local government is administered through four arrondissements and 24 communes. The dominant faith is Roman Catholicism, the official language French.

Réunion is volcanic and mountainous, the high central peak (Piton des Neiges) rising steeply to 3071 m (10,076 ft); one area in the east is intermittently active. The climate is hot and humid in summer, cooler in winter when trade winds blow; the mountains are forested and the lowlands heavily cultivated. Long known to Arab and Portuguese voyagers, the island was first settled by French planters in the mid-17th century, who imported African slave labour to grow coffee and cane sugar. In the 19th century indentured labour from India and southeast Asia replaced the Africans, giving rise to a cosmopolitan population.

Agriculture remains the mainstay of Réunion's economy, with sugar and rum predominant; maize, potatoes, vegetables, vanilla, fruit and livestock are raised on smallholdings and farms, but staple foods have to be imported. There are few industries apart from sugar-processing. Roads are good; there are several small ports and the island has an international airport. Réunion's main problems are its massive population (from which many thousands emigrate each year to France, Madagascar and elsewhere), and its almost complete dependence on a single commodity, cane sugar, to balance its annual budget.

Seychelles

The Country
The island state of Seychelles lies in the northwestern Indian Ocean, some 1200 km (750 miles) northeast of Madagascar. *Area* 280 km² (108 sq miles); *capital* Victoria (Mahé); *population* 69,000 (est. 1986).

Organization
The islands are governed by an executive President, who is responsible to a People's Assembly of 23 elected and 2 nominated members; there is currently only one political party, the Seychelles People's Progressive Front. The dominant religion is Christianity, the official language English, with French and a local patois widely spoken.

Geography
Four main islands (Mahé, Praslin, Silhouette and La Digue, which hold about 98 per cent of the population) and twenty-eight smaller ones form a central granitic group. These are rugged, Mahé's central peak rising to 906 m (2972 ft). To south and east lie a scattering of smaller, low-lying coralline islands including the Amirante, Cosmoledo and Farquhar groups, Coetivy and Aldabra. The climate is tropical and humid; forests grow on the damp uplands, giving way to grass and dense scrub on lower ground.

History and Development
The Seychelles were known to many early voyagers including Arabs, Portuguese and British, but remained unoccupied until colonized by French settlers from Mauritius in 1768. After the Napoleonic Wars they passed with Mauritius to Britain; gaining population from Africa, India and the East Indies as well as Europe, the community grew and prospered throughout the 19th century, in 1903 becoming a separate colony. The Seychelles gained independence as a republic within the Commonwealth in 1976.

Resources and Economics
The larger islands are well watered and fertile, growing subsistence crops of vegetables and fruit and supporting livestock. Copra and cinnamon from plantations have for long provided the main exports. Fish and guano are also economically important, but the current mainstay of the economy is tourism, stimulated during the past decade by Mahé's international airport. The main islands have adequate roads and good inter-island shipping services; the outer islands tend to be isolated and are losing population.

Recent Developments
Troubled by political coups and attempted counter-coups, and hard-hit by a recession in tourism, their greatest single source of revenue, the Seychelles have developed only slowly since independence. Plans to improve agriculture towards self-sufficiency in food production, expand the deep-sea fishing industry, diversify their small industries and stimulate tourism are among the main economic objectives, and the Seychelles are seeking closer cooperation with neighbours Mauritius and Madagascar in an Indian Ocean Commission.

Antarctica and Subantarctic Islands

Antarctica

Antarctica is an ice-covered continent of 13.9 million km² (5.4 million sq miles), surrounding the South Pole and isolated from the rest of the continents by the Southern Ocean. The ice cap, with an estimated volume of 24 million km³ (5.9 million cubic miles), has a mean thickness of 1880 m (6170 ft), and in places reaches depths of 4000 m (13,00 ft) or more. The ice cap overspreads most of the continental shore, flowing out to sea as slow-moving ice shelves and glaciers.

Only about 5 per cent of Antarctica's rocks are exposed. Beneath the ice lies a continent of about 8 million km² (3 million sq miles), formed of two blocs separated by a deep channel. East Antarctica includes a massive bloc of ancient rocks similar to those of Australia and South Africa; some of these are exposed at the surface in the Transantarctic Mountains of Victoria Land. Beneath the ice West Antarctica is an archipelago of steep mountainous islands. High peaks are exposed in the partly-buried Vinson Massif (5139 m, 16,861 ft), Antarctica's highest mountain; much of West Antarctica is exposed in Antarctic Peninsula and its fringing islands, which stretch towards the tip of South America.

The climate is cold near the coast, where the sea is frozen or covered with pack ice for much of the year: inland it is extremely cold, with annual mean temperatures about −50° C (−58° F) at the South Pole and below −55° C (−67° F) on the highest parts of the ice cap. Winds are generally strong; ice needles and snow, rather than rain, are the main form of precipitation. Vegetation is restricted by cold, dryness, wind and lack of soil. Small patches of lichen and moss are characteristic of the colder regions; mosses flourish more widely in the peninsular area, where summers are warmer and Antarctica's two species of flowering plants may be found. The terrestrial fauna is limited to minute insects and mites which crawl among the mosses and lichens. The more spectacular animals of Antarctica are marine birds (notably penguins and petrels) and seals, which feed at sea and breed on the land or sea ice, but seldom venture inland.

Antarctica has a transient human population amounting to hundreds in winter and thousands in summer, living in widely-scattered bases along the coast; there are a few bases also on the ice cap, maintained generally by air-lifts. Scientific exploration is the main industry; climatic, geophysical, biological and other data collected in Antarctica, both practically and theoretically important, are deemed well worth the trouble, danger and enormous expense of collecting them. Petroleum, coal and many other minerals are present, though none has yet proved economically worth exploiting.

Sectors of Antarctica are claimed by Britain, Argentina, Chile, Norway, France, Australia and New Zealand. Claims are currently shelved in favour of international cooperation under the Antarctic Treaty of 1959, to which all nations working on the continent are signatories. The treaty, which provides a forum for discussion on all matters scientific, technical, logistic and administrative, is subject to review in 1989.

Subantarctic Islands

The southern Indian Ocean has several groups of islands, uninhabited except by scientists and technicians but claimed on grounds of discovery, occupancy or use by France, Australia and South Africa. Almost all were discovered by explorers, sealers or whalers during the 18th and 19th centuries, and were visited periodically by sealers in search of oil and skins. They are generally rugged, with formidable cliffs of lava or volcanic detritus, and rolling uplands covered with tussock grass and low shrubs. Climates are cold, overcast and rainy, with strong, persistent westerly winds. The southernmost are snow-covered for several months each year, and some have glaciated mountains. All are the haunt of sea birds (notably penguins and petrels) and seals; almost all have been severely modified by introductions of exotic animals from mice to pigs, rabbits and reindeer.

Australian Islands
Heard Island and the McDonald Islands lie 500 km (300 miles) southeast of the Kerguelen Islands, washed by cold Antarctic waters and with a uniformly colder climate. Heard Island is a complex of volcanoes of which the central cone, Big Ben, is still mildly active; rising to over 2700 m (8800 ft), it is heavily glaciated down to sea level. The McDonald Islands form a compact group 48 km (30 miles) west and slightly north of Heard Island. Lower-lying, they are relatively ice-free, though difficult of access because of steep cliffs. Macquarie Island lies across the Antarctic Convergence (boundary of cold Antarctic water) southeast of Tasmania and southwest of New Zealand, a long narrow island with a rolling plateau, and the only Australian island with a permanent scientific base.

French Islands
The Crozet Islands form a scattered archipelago in latitude 46° S, 2300 km (1430 miles) south–southeast of Madagascar. The main islands, Île de la Possession and Île de l'Est, lie 16 km (10 miles) apart in the east; the smaller Île aux Cochons, Île des Pingouins and Îles des Apôtres form a widespread group 100 km (60 miles) to the west. The Kerguelen Islands lie 1500 km (940 miles) east–southeast of the Crozets, closer to the Antarctic Convergence and in a slightly harsher climate. A deeply-dissected volcanic massif, the main island (Grande Terre) rises to an inactive crater 1960 m (6429 ft) high, from which a large glacier descends almost to sea level. St Paul and Amsterdam islands are warmer islands standing in subtropical waters to the northwest. All three groups carry permanent scientific bases.

South African Islands
South Africa is responsible for the Prince Edward islands, a pair of islands some 2000 km (1250 miles) southeast of Cape Town, in similar latitude to the Crozet but about 1000 km (625 miles) further west. Marion, the larger island, has a lava plateau rising to just over 1000 m (3280 ft), capped by cones rising to 1230 m (4000 ft); Prince Edward Island rises to 670 m (2200 ft), with sheer cliffs up to 500 m (1640 ft) high. A permanent station is maintained on Marion Island.

Section 2
World Statistics

World Statistics

This section gives statistics on area, population and GNP for all the entries in Section 1, Countries of the World, with the exception of some minor islands and the Antarctic regions. Most values of GNP refer to 1981, most growth rates to the period 1970–80.

Urb = Urban   Bths = Births   LE = Life Expectancy   AI = Annual Increase

EUROPE

	AREA		POPULATION						GNP
	Km²	Sq mls	1986 Estimate ('000)	1990	Urb %	0–14 %	Bths per 1000	LE per 1000	US($) per head
Europe West									
Belgium	30,513	11,781	9,873	9,905	74	19	12	73	11,920
France	547,026	211,207	54,426	54,970	80	21	14	74	12,190
Ireland	70,283	27,136	3,536	3,694	61	31	21	73	5,230
Luxembourg	2,586	998	356	355	82	17	11	72	15,910
Monaco	(1.5)	(0.6)	26	27	95	—	—	—	—
Netherlands	40,844	15,769	14,458	14,682	76	19	12	75	11,790
United Kingdom	244,046	94,226	55,600	55,479	92	19	12	73	9,110
Europe North									
Denmark	43,069	16,629	5,170	5,195	86	19	12	75	13,120
Faroe Islands	1,399	540	47	49	—	—	—	—	11,100
Finland	337,032	130,128	4,979	5,020	67	19	13	73	10,680
Greenland	2,175,600	840,000	52	53	—	—	—	—	10,850
Iceland	103,000	39,768	245	254	90	25	17	76	12,860
Norway	324,219	125,182	4,155	4,203	57	20	13	75	14,060
Svalbard, Jan Mayen	62,422	24,101	—	—	—	—	—	—	—
Sweden	449,964	173,731	8,258	8,199	89	18	11	75	14,870
Europe Central									
Austria	83,849	32,374	7,448	7,441	56	18	12	72	10,210
Czechoslovakia	127,869	49,370	15,808	16,078	66	25	17	71	—
East Germany (GDR)	108,178	41,767	16,885	16,913	78	19	13	72	—
Hungary	93,030	35,919	10,890	10,912	59	22	14	71	2,100
Liechtenstein	157	61	27	28	—	—	—	—	—
Poland	312,677	120,725	37,869	38,967	59	25	19	72	—
Romania	237,500	91,699	23,322	29,994	52	25	17	71	2,540
Switzerland	41,288	15,941	6,490	6,693	60	18	11	75	17,430
West Germany (FRG)	248,577	95,976	59,992	59,622	86	16	10	73	13,450
Europe Southwest									
Andorra	453	175	36	39	—	—	—	—	—
Gibraltar	(6.5)	(2.5)	31	31	—	—	—	—	4,690
Portugal	92,082	35,552	10,266	10,531	33	25	18	71	2,520
Spain	504,782	194,896	39,313	40,541	77	24	17	73	5,640

	AREA		POPULATION						GNP	
	Km²	Sq mls	1986 Estimate ('000)	1990 ('000)	Urb %	0–14 %	Bths per 1000	LE per 1000	US($) per head	AI per head
ope Southeast										
nia	28,748	11,099	3,108	3,350	39	35	28	70	—	—
aria	110,912	42,823	9,276	9,413	69	22	15	73	—	—
rus	9,251	3,572	641	654	49	25	20	73	3,740	—
ece	131,944	50,944	9,665	9,886	66	22	15	73	4,420	3.7
	301,225	116,303	57,942	58,427	72	20	13	73	6,960	2.5
ta	316	122	360	370	85	23	17	72	3,600	10.4
Marino	61	23	21	22	—	—	—	—	—	—
can City te	(0.44)	(0.17)	c.1,000	c.1,000	—	—	—	—	—	—
oslavia	255,804	98,766	23,351	23,739	46	23	16	71	2,790	5.0
A										
a North										
on of Soviet ialist ublics	22,402,200	8,649,498	280,693	290,155	66	25	19	70	—	—
a Southwest										
rain	622	240	369	410	79	38	33	68	8,960	5.7
	1,648,000	636,293	45,689	51,033	54	45	42	56	—	—
	434,924	167,925	15,988	18,136	76	46	45	57	—	—
el	20,770	8,019	4,489	4,828	91	33	25	73	5,160	1.3
an	97,740	37,737	4,032	4,657	60	47	45	62	1,620	5.8
ait	17,818	6,880	1,795	2,101	91	46	41	70	20,900	2.7
non	10,400	4,015	3,033	3,301	80	36	30	67	—	—
an	212,457	82,030	1,074	1,218	9	46	48	50	5,920	2.8
ar	11,000	4,247	294	330	88	33	31	59	27,720	−0.2
di Arabia	2,149,690	829,996	11,220	12,908	73	44	44	55	12,600	9.0
h Yemen OR)	332,968	128,559	2,186	2,459	40	45	48	47	460	10.7
a	185,180	71,498	11,337	13,227	53	48	46	66	1,570	6.0
key	780,576	301,381	52,314	57,336	52	38	34	63	1,540	3.0
ed Arab irates	83,600	32,278	913	1,025	77	32	29	63	24,660	0.2
en (AR)	195,000	75,289	6,702	7,447	13	45	49	44	460	6.1
a South										
anistan	647,497	250,000	18,570	20,618	18	45	48	41	—	—
gladesh	143,998	55,598	104,211	116,164	13	45	45	47	140	1.4
tan	47,000	18,147	1,484	1,628	5	41	41	45	80	0.0
ma	676,552	261,216	41,812	44,738	30	41	37	55	190	2.3
a	3,287,590	1,269,339	766,515	820,860	24	38	33	51	260	1.5
al	140,797	54,362	16,382	17,986	6	42	42	45	150	−0.3
istan	803,943	310,402	102,689	113,376	31	44	42	53	350	1.9
Lanka	65,610	25,332	16,755	18,066	29	34	28	66	300	2.8

	AREA		POPULATION						GNP
	Km²	Sq mls	1986 Estimate ('000)	1990	Urb %	0–14 %	Bths per 1000	LE per 1000	US($) per head

Asia Southeast

Brunei	5,765	2,226	310	360	—	—	—	—	17,380
Cambodia	181,035	69,898	7,854	8,713	16	34	38	43	—
Indonesia	2,042,012	788,421	164,074	174,473	22	37	31	50	530
Laos	236,800	91,429	4,281	4,682	16	42	41	46	80
Malaysia	329,749	127,316	16,205	17,689	31	38	31	65	1,840
Philippines	300,000	115,830	57,329	62,830	39	40	34	63	790
Singapore	581	224	2,585	2,713	74	25	19	72	5,240
Thailand	514,000	198,456	53,539	57,890	16	38	30	62	770
Vietnam	329,556	127,242	61,204	66,214	21	41	34	55	—

Asia East

China	9,596,961	3,705,390	1,064,000	1,119,152	28	30	19	70	300
Hong Kong	1,045	403	5,820	6,250	91	25	20	76	5,100
Japan	372,313	143,750	120,835	123,185	81	22	13	76	10,080
Macau	16	6	320	340	—	—	—	—	2,630
Mongolia	1,565,000	604,247	1,962	2,170	54	41	34	65	—
North Korea	120,538	46,540	20,543	22,443	64	38	31	65	—
South Korea	98,484	38,025	42,444	45,022	61	32	24	65	1,700
Taiwan	35,961	13,885	8,025	8,484	—	—	—	—	—

OCEANIA

Oceania Southwest

Australia	7,686,848	2,967,895	15,512	16,170	90	24	16	74	11,080
Nauru	21	8	8	8	—	—	—	—	—
New Caledonia	19,058	7,358	148	160	—	—	—	—	7,100
New Zealand	268,676	103,736	3,495	3,650	86	25	18	73	7,700
Papua New Guinea	461,691	178,259	3,708	4,113	39	43	41	53	840
Solomon Islands	28,446	10,983	271	293	—	—	—	—	640
Vanuatu	14,763	5,700	138	150	—	—	—	—	350

Oceania North

Guam	549	212	115	124	—	—	—	—	6,840
Northern Marianas	480	185	19	21	—	—	—	—	—
US Trust Territory of the Pacific	1,779	687	137	151	—	—	—	—	1,000

Oceania Central

American Samoa	197	76	35	39	—	—	—	—	4,170
Cook Islands	236	91	21	24	—	—	—	—	1,170
Fiji	18,274	7,056	694	736	46	35	27	72	2,000
Kiribati	728	281	68	70	—	—	—	—	420
Niue	259	100	3	3	—	—	—	—	1,080

	AREA		POPULATION						GNP	
	Km²	Sq mls	1986 Estimate ('000)	1990	Urb %	0–14 %	Bths per 1000	LE per 1000	US($) per head	AI per head
elau Islands	10	4	2	1	—	—	—	—	670	—
ıga	699	270	107	116	—	—	—	—	530	0.8
⁻alu	26	10	8	9	—	—	—	—	680	—
⁻lis ⁻chipelago	200	77	10	10	—	—	—	—	1,020	—
⁻stern Samoa	2,842	1,097	180	195	—	—	—	—	—	—

eania Southeast

⁻ter Island	120	46	1	1	—	—	—	—	—	—
⁻nch ⁻lynesia	4,000	1,544	167	180	—	—	—	—	6,980	2.3
⁻cairn ⁻ands	27	10	(60)	(60)	—	—	—	—	—	—

⁻E AMERICAS

rth America and Bermuda

⁻muda	53	20	60	61	—	—	—	—	12,910	2.2
⁻ada	9,976,139	3,851,791	26,726	28,178	76	22	16	74	11,400	2.6
⁻Pierre and ⁻quelon	241	93	6	7	—	—	—	—	—	—
⁻ted States ⁻ America	9,363,123	3,615,105	236,809	245,472	79	23	17	73	12,820	2.1

ntral America

⁻ize	22,965	8,867	161	174	—	—	—	—	1,080	4.8
⁻sta Rica	50,700	19,575	2,541	2,776	46	35	28	71	1,430	2.6
⁻Salvador	21,041	8,124	5,725	6,484	43	45	40	65	650	1.3
⁻atemala	108,889	42,042	8,646	9,676	41	43	38	61	1,140	2.8
⁻nduras	112,088	43,277	4,514	5,105	40	47	44	60	600	0.5
⁻xico	1,972,547	761,601	82,734	91,976	70	43	36	66	2,250	3.1
⁻aragua	130,000	50,193	3,342	3,778	56	48	45	58	860	−2.9
⁻nama	77,082	29,761	2,162	2,346	58	37	28	71	1,910	1.2

eater Antilles and Bahamas

⁻hamas	13,935	5,380	231	250	—	—	—	—	3,620	−2.9
⁻yman Islands	259	100	20	21	—	—	—	—	—	—
⁻ba	114,524	44,218	10,121	10,540	68	26	17	73	—	—
⁻minican ⁻public	48,734	18,816	6,874	7,534	56	41	34	63	1,260	3.3
⁻ıti	27,750	10,714	6,758	7,509	28	44	41	53	300	1.8
⁻naica	10,991	4,244	2,394	2,535	44	36	26	71	1,180	−2.8
⁻erto Rico	8,897	3,435	4,448	4,747	74	30	21	73	3,350	0.0
⁻rks and ⁻icos Islands	430	166	8	9	—	—	—	—	—	—
⁻gin Islands ⁻ritish)	153	59	13	15	—	—	—	—	—	—
⁻gin Islands (US)	344	133	107	116	—	—	—	—	7,010	−2.3

	AREA		POPULATION						GNP
	Km²	Sq mls	1986 Estimate ('000)	1990	Urb %	0–14 %	Bths per 1000	LE per 1000	US($) per head
Leeward Islands									
Anguilla	150	58	8	9	—	—	—	—	—
Antigua and Barbuda	442	171	83	90	—	—	—	—	1,550 —
Guadeloupe	1,779	687	335	339	46	28	20	70	4,340
Montserrat	98	38	13	16	—	—	—	—	1,640
St Kitts-Nevis	258	100	50	54	—	—	—	—	1,040
Windward Islands									
Barbados	431	166	280	292	41	27	19	71	3,500
Dominica	751	290	88	95	—	—	—	—	750 —
Grenada	344	133	120	130	—	—	—	—	850 —
Martinique	1,102	425	329	337	71	28	19	70	4,820
Netherlands Antilles	961	371	290	300	—	—	—	—	4,540
St Lucia	616	238	130	140	—	—	—	—	970
St Vincent and the Grenadines	388	150	138	150	—	—	—	—	630 —
South America									
Argentina	2,766,889	1,068,297	29,013	30,277	84	28	21	70	2,560
Bolivia	1,098,581	424,163	6,547	7,314	36	44	44	51	600
Brazil	8,511,965	3,286,473	140,344	153,171	37	71	31	63	2,220
Chile	756,945	292,256	12,272	13,061	83	31	25	67	2,560 —
Colombia	1,138,914	439,735	29,325	31,820	74	37	31	64	1,380
Ecuador	283,561	109,483	9,677	10,949	47	44	41	63	1,180
French Guiana	91,000	35,135	77	82	—	—	—	—	3,430 —
Guyana	214,969	83,000	998	1,069	22	37	28	71	720
Paraguay	406,752	157,047	3,789	4,231	42	42	36	65	1,630
Peru	1,285,216	496,222	20,855	23,355	71	41	38	59	1,170
Suriname	163,265	63,037	460	527	46	48	41	69	3,030
Trinidad and Tobago	5,130	1,981	1,269	1,337	23	29	21	70	5,670
Uruguay	176,215	68,037	3,061	3,166	85	27	20	70	2,820
Venezuela	912,050	352,143	18,959	21,284	85	41	35	68	4,220
AFRICA									
Africa Northwest									
Algeria	2,381,741	919,591	23,403	26,946	67	47	48	58	2,140
Burkina Faso	274,200	105,869	8,119	9,067	10	45	48	43	240
Mali	1,240,000	478,764	8,233	9,290	23	46	49	43	190
Mauritania	1,030,700	397,953	1,948	2,207	48	47	50	43	460 —
Morocco	446,550	172,413	24,636	27,840	44	45	44	58	860
Niger	1,267,000	489,189	6,392	7,278	15	47	52	43	330 —
Tunisia	163,610	63,170	7,322	7,989	56	39	34	59	1,420
Western Sahara	266,000	102,703	80	80	—	—	—	—	—

	AREA		POPULATION						GNP	
	Km²	Sq mls	1986 Estimate ('000)	1990	Urb %	0–16 %	Bths per 1000	LE per 1000	US($) per head	AI per head
ca West										
n	112,622	43,483	4,263	4,861	39	47	49	48	320	1.2
eroon	475,442	183,568	9,796	10,838	42	42	42	49	880	3.3
bia	11,295	4,361	705	788	21	45	47	43	370	3.1
a	238,537	92,099	14,216	16,214	40	47	48	51	400	−2.6
ea	245,857	94,925	5,897	6,609	22	44	46	46	300	0.4
ea-Bissau	36,125	13,948	640	693	27	39	39	43	190	—
Coast	322,463	124,503	9,712	10,964	43	45	46	49	1,200	1.5
ria	111,369	43,000	2,442	2,821	37	48	48	55	520	−0.1
ria	923,768	356,667	94,316	107,954	23	48	49	50	870	3.0
gal	196,192	75,750	6,654	7,430	27	45	48	43	430	−0.4
a Leone	71,740	27,699	4,112	4,606	28	45	45	48	320	−1.1
	56,785	21,925	3,158	3,577	20	46	48	49	380	0.9
ca Northeast										
	1,284,000	495,752	5,066	5,558	22	42	45	41	110	−3.6
uti	22,000	8,494	481	645	50	—	—	—	480	—
t	1,001,449	386,650	48,318	52,709	48	39	35	57	650	5.6
pia	1,221,900	471,776	36,651	41,259	18	45	50	41	140	0.6
a	1,759,540	679,359	3,748	4,337	60	46	46	58	8,450	−0.9
ali nocratic ublic	637,657	246,199	5,694	5,938	34	44	46	43	280	1.1
n	2,505,813	967,495	21,832	24,491	29	45	45	49	380	0.9
ca Central										
la	1,246,700	481,351	8,298	9,285	25	45	47	43	—	—
ral African ublic	622,984	240,534	2,593	2,965	46	43	45	45	320	−0.2
o	342,000	132,046	1,810	2,030	39	44	44	49	1,110	0.5
torial nea	28,051	10,830	421	468	60	42	42	49	180	—
n	267,667	103,346	600	640	41	35	35	46	3,810	3.2
Tomé e ncipe	964	372	106	112	—	—	—	—	370	−0.2
	2,345,409	905,563	33,601	37,693	44	45	45	49	210	−2.8
bia	752,614	290,584	7,054	8,079	42	48	49	51	600	−2.3
ca East										
ndi	27,834	10,747	4,954	5,516	3	43	47	43	230	1.5
a	582,646	224,960	21,061	24,831	17	52	53	56	420	2.4
wi	118,484	45,747	7,541	8,634	48	48	51	49	200	2.8
mbique	801,590	309,494	12,362	13,895	11	44	45	49	—	—
nda	26,338	10,169	5,821	6,660	5	47	49	48	250	1.7
ania	945,087	364,898	21,752	24,774	15	46	46	53	280	1.1
da	236,036	91,133	15,994	18,262	14	46	45	55	220	−4.1

World Statistics

	AREA		POPULATION						GNP
	Km²	Sq mls	1986 Estimate ('000)	1990	Urb %	0–14 %	Bths per 1000	LE per 1000	US($) per head
Africa South									
Botswana	600,372	231,804	978	1,123	42	50	51	51	1,010
Lesotho	30,355	11,720	1,559	1,726	6	41	40	53	540
Namibia	824,292	318,259	1,206	1,360	51	44	43	54	1,960
South Africa	1,221,037	471,443	34,799	39,018	52	42	38	63	2,770
Swaziland	17,363	6,704	667	754	10	46	47	48	760
Zimbabwe	390,580	150,803	9,119	10,489	27	48	47	55	870
Atlantic Ocean Islands									
Azores	2,335	902	280	309	—	—	—	—	—
Canaries	7,273	2,808	1,400	1,545	—	—	—	—	—
Cape Verde Islands	4,033	1,557	356	378	6	32	24	62	340
Falkland Islands	15,800	6,100	3	3	—	—	—	—	—
Madeira	797	308	285	314	—	—	—	—	—
St Helena	122	47	5	5	—	—	—	—	—
Indian Ocean Islands									
British Indian Ocean Territory	78	30	—	—	—	—	—	—	—
Cocos (Keeling) Islands	14	5	(600)	(600)	—	—	—	—	—
Comoro Islands	2,236	863	408	476	14	45	46	48	320
Madagascar	587,041	226,657	10,322	11,545	21	44	45	49	330
Maldives	298	115	177	195	—	—	—	—	—
Mauritius	2,045	790	1,057	1,117	57	33	26	66	1,270
Réunion	2,510	969	571	604	60	30	21	66	3,840
Seychelles	280	108	69	76	—	—	—	—	1,800

Section 3

World
Climates

EUROPE

Europe West

Britain, northwestern France, Belgium and the Netherlands have temperate maritime climates dominated by southwesterly winds. Crossed and re-crossed by the polar front, they are subject to rapid alternations of maritime, polar and continental air masses, producing changeable weather with characteristic sudden shifts between warm and cold spells. Mainland countries have intensely cold periods in winter, often with 70 to 80 days of frost and several weeks' persistent snow, especially on high ground. Summers tend to be subtropical, with plentiful rain-showers, especially in the south where Mediterranean and even African influences are strong. Britain and Ireland are cooler than mainland countries in summer and milder in winter, though subject to cold spells at any time; they are generally damp, especially in the west.

Belgium

		J	F	M	A	M	J	J	A	S	O	N	D
Brussels	°C	1.5	3.5	6.3	9.7	13.1	16.3	17.4	17.3	15.5	11.3	6.0	2.9
100 m	mm	66	61	53	60	55	76	95	80	63	83	75	88
Gerdingen	°C	0.6	2.2	4.3	7.8	11.3	14.9	15.7	15.6	13.5	9.5	4.8	2.1
63 m	mm	71	58	51	62	61	68	89	84	69	72	76	91
Ostend	°C	2.7	4.1	5.9	8.5	12.3	14.9	16.3	16.6	15.4	11.7	7.35	4.1
10 m	mm	41	38	31	38	34	38	62	58	56	68	74	60
Virton	°C	0.4	2.5	4.7	8.7	11.7	15.6	16.5	16.5	14.1	9.5	5.1	1.7
242 m	mm	75	72	61	66	61	62	74	88	74	67	85	103

France

		J	F	M	A	M	J	J	A	S	O	N	D
Ajaccio (Corsica)	°C	7.7	8.7	10.5	12.6	15.9	19.8	22.0	22.2	20.3	16.3	11.8	8.7
5 m	mm	76	65	53	48	50	21	10	16	50	88	97	98
Bordeaux	°C	5.4	6.3	9.5	11.7	14.7	17.9	19.5	19.7	17.5	13.1	8.7	5.9
46 m	mm	90	75	63	48	61	65	56	70	84	83	96	109
Brest	°C	6.1	6.1	8.1	9.3	11.7	14.3	15.7	16.1	14.7	11.9	8.9	6.9
98 m	mm	133	96	83	69	68	56	62	80	90	104	138	150
Caen	°C	4.3	4.6	6.9	9.2	12.3	15.0	16.9	17.0	15.2	11.5	7.5	5.1
66 m	mm	68	55	44	47	54	43	50	57	65	72	75	60
Clermont-Ferrand	°C	2.8	4.5	7.5	10.2	13.6	17.2	19.1	18.9	16.4	11.4	6.9	3.6
329 m	mm	25	25	29	43	67	72	51	68	61	49	40	33
Dijon	°C	1.4	2.8	7.1	10.5	14.3	17.5	19.5	19.1	16.1	10.9	5.9	2.3
220 m	mm	64	42	42	46	64	81	58	77	72	60	76	57
Grenoble	°C	1.5	3.2	7.7	10.7	14.5	17.8	20.1	19.5	16.7	11.5	6.5	2.3
223 m	mm	80	75	60	65	80	90	70	95	100	95	95	80
Marseilles	°C	5.7	6.8	10.1	12.7	16.5	20.4	23.0	22.7	19.9	15.1	10.3	6.9
4 m	mm	43	32	43	42	46	24	11	34	60	76	69	66
Paris	°C	3.1	3.8	7.2	10.3	14.0	17.1	19.0	18.5	15.9	11.1	6.8	4.1
53 m	mm	54	43	32	38	52	50	55	62	51	49	50	49
Toulouse	°C	4.5	5.4	9.0	11.4	14.8	18.6	20.8	20.7	18.0	13.0	8.3	5.3
151 m	mm	49	46	53	50	75	61	44	54	64	45	51	67

land

		J	F	M	A	M	J	J	A	S	O	N	D	Year
k	°C	5.5	5.8	7.5	9.3	11.8	14.5	15.9	15.9	13.9	10.7	7.7	6.3	10.4
15 m	mm	119	79	94	57	71	57	70	71	94	99	115	122	1048
lin	°C	4.5	4.9	6.5	8.2	10.7	13.7	15.3	15.0	13.1	10.1	7.1	5.5	9.5
47 m	mm	67	55	51	45	60	57	70	74	72	70	67	74	762
nnon	°C	5.1	5.5	7.4	9.1	11.5	14.3	15.5	15.6	13.7	10.7	7.6	6.1	10.2
2 m	mm	95	65	55	53	62	60	84	77	88	90	93	108	930
ntia	°C	7.0	6.8	8.3	9.4	11.5	13.8	15.0	15.4	14.0	11.6	9.1	7.8	10.8
9 m	mm	164	107	103	74	86	81	107	95	122	140	151	168	1398

xembourg

		J	F	M	A	M	J	J	A	S	O	N	D	Year
vaux	°C	−0.1	0.6	4.3	6.8	11.3	14.2	16.1	15.3	13.1	8.5	3.9	1.3	7.9
454 m	mm	72	73	51	53	68	81	83	108	71	62	77	86	885
embourg	°C	0.3	1.0	4.9	8.5	12.8	15.7	17.4	16.7	13.8	9.0	4.6	1.3	8.8
330 m	mm	73	57	43	54	60	64	66	74	63	55	64	68	740

naco

		J	F	M	A	M	J	J	A	S	O	N	D	Year
aco	°C	10.3	10.5	11.9	14.0	17.1	20.8	23.5	23.7	21.6	17.9	14.1	11.6	16.4
55 m	mm	61	58	71	65	64	33	21	22	66	113	123	99	796

herlands

		J	F	M	A	M	J	J	A	S	O	N	D	Year
ert	°C	1.8	2.3	5.9	9.2	13.1	16.2	17.9	17.7	15.1	10.4	6.1	3.0	9.9
16 m	mm	63	53	42	43	54	57	70	72	62	56	63	58	693
rn	°C	2.7	2.0	4.3	7.4	11.0	14.5	16.5	16.7	14.9	10.9	6.8	4.3	9.3
2 m	mm	67	50	41	25	39	43	73	90	67	95	66	71	727
	°C	1.4	1.3	4.6	8.5	12.5	15.6	17.4	17.2	15.2	10.7	6.2	3.3	9.5
2 m	mm	63	52	42	42	51	49	87	97	76	59	69	60	747
singen	°C	3.0	2.9	5.5	8.7	12.3	15.5	17.3	17.7	15.7	11.5	7.3	4.3	10.1
1 m	mm	62	45	40	41	42	50	71	65	73	70	72	58	689

ited Kingdom

gland

		J	F	M	A	M	J	J	A	S	O	N	D	Year
ningham	°C	3.5	3.7	5.9	8.5	11.5	14.6	16.3	16.1	13.7	10.1	6.7	4.7	9.6
163 m	mm	74	54	50	53	64	50	69	69	61	69	84	67	764
dford	°C	2.9	3.1	5.1	7.7	10.7	13.7	15.5	15.2	13.1	9.5	6.2	4.3	8.9
134 m	mm	90	72	49	54	58	53	68	77	67	80	91	81	840
ton	°C	1.9	2.1	4.0	6.5	9.5	12.5	14.3	14.0	11.9	8.4	5.3	3.3	7.8
307 m	mm	142	102	78	81	71	85	109	96	102	124	132	133	1255
bridge	°C	3.5	3.9	6.1	8.7	11.9	15.1	17.0	16.7	14.3	10.3	6.7	4.5	9.9
12 m	mm	49	35	36	37	45	45	58	55	51	51	54	42	558
ton	°C	3.7	3.7	5.7	8.2	11.4	14.9	17.1	17.0	15.0	11.1	7.5	5.0	10.0
16 m	mm	55	38	37	35	40	41	47	48	50	58	58	48	555
glas (e of Man)	°C	4.7	4.7	5.9	7.8	10.4	13.1	14.5	14.7	13.1	10.5	7.8	6.1	9.4
87 m	mm	125	81	72	63	69	72	81	91	111	122	124	128	1139
don	°C	4.2	4.4	6.6	9.3	12.4	15.8	17.6	17.2	14.8	10.8	7.2	5.2	10.5
5 m	mm	53	40	37	38	46	46	56	59	50	57	64	48	594
ecambe	°C	3.7	3.9	5.9	8.3	11.6	14.4	16.0	15.9	13.9	10.5	7.1	5.0	9.7
7 m	mm	90	62	51	53	64	70	85	87	100	104	99	98	963
rd	°C	3.7	4.2	6.4	9.1	12.1	15.3	17.1	16.9	14.5	10.5	7.0	4.9	10.1
63 m	mm	61	44	43	41	55	52	55	60	59	64	69	57	660
nouth	°C	6.1	5.8	7.3	9.2	11.7	14.5	16.0	16.1	14.7	11.9	8.9	7.1	10.7
27 m	mm	99	74	69	53	63	53	70	77	78	91	113	110	950

EUROPE

Location of Climatic Stations

		J	F	M	A	M	J	J	A	S	O	N	D
St Helier (Channel Is)	°C	6.7	6.2	8.2	10.1	13.1	16.0	17.6	18.1	16.6	13.3	10.0	7.7
9 m	mm	89	68	57	43	44	39	48	67	69	77	101	99
St Mary's (Scilly Is)	°C	7.7	7.3	8.5	9.7	11.7	14.3	16.1	16.5	15.2	12.7	10.3	8.6
50 m	mm	91	71	69	46	56	49	61	64	67	80	96	94
Scarborough	°C	4.1	4.5	6.1	8.5	10.7	13.9	16.1	15.9	14.1	10.9	7.4	5.3
36 m	mm	65	50	38	41	47	47	58	61	52	63	66	59
Skegness	°C	3.5	3.7	5.5	8.1	10.7	13.9	16.2	16.0	14.2	10.6	6.9	4.7
5 m	mm	57	42	36	38	44	44	57	58	51	50	59	47
Tynemouth	°C	4.1	4.4	5.7	7.7	9.7	12.9	15.1	14.9	13.3	10.4	7.3	5.4
33 m	mm	62	45	39	38	48	47	64	74	55	61	64	53
Worthing	°C	4.5	4.5	6.5	9.0	12.1	15.3	16.9	17.1	15.3	11.8	8.1	5.8
8 m	mm	74	51	44	37	44	39	55	59	64	72	88	73

Northern Ireland

		J	F	M	A	M	J	J	A	S	O	N	D
Armagh	°C	4.1	4.6	6.3	8.3	10.9	13.7	15.1	14.9	12.9	9.9	6.7	5.1
62 m	mm	79	54	51	51	56	69	92	80	75	81	72	89
Ballykelly	°C	4.4	4.1	6.4	8.3	10.9	13.4	14.7	14.6	13.3	10.5	7.2	5.4
1 m	mm	90	54	49	57	50	60	93	70	82	85	71	104
Belfast	°C	3.7	4.1	5.9	7.9	10.5	13.4	14.7	14.5	12.7	9.7	6.6	4.9
67 m	mm	80	52	50	48	52	68	94	77	80	83	72	90

Scotland

		J	F	M	A	M	J	J	A	S	O	N	D
Braemar	°C	0.6	0.9	2.8	5.3	8.3	11.4	13.1	12.6	10.3	7.1	3.8	2.0
339 m	mm	96	66	52	55	62	50	73	75	72	101	96	101
Dalwhinnie	°C	0.3	0.7	2.7	5.1	7.9	10.9	12.5	12.2	9.9	6.8	3.7	1.9
359 m	mm	133	97	70	78	69	66	90	85	103	143	125	158
Edinburgh	°C	3.3	3.5	5.1	7.4	9.9	12.9	14.8	14.5	12.5	9.4	6.4	4.6
134 m	mm	57	39	39	39	54	47	83	77	57	65	62	57
Kirkwall (Orkney)	°C	3.7	3.7	4.8	6.3	8.7	10.9	12.9	12.9	11.4	8.9	6.5	4.9
26 m	mm	105	79	65	51	46	48	71	75	78	113	107	112
Lerwick (Shetland)	°C	3.1	2.9	3.9	5.5	7.8	10.0	12.1	12.1	10.7	8.1	5.9	4.5
82 m	mm	109	87	69	68	52	55	72	71	87	104	111	118
Nairn	°C	3.1	3.6	5.3	7.3	9.8	12.7	14.3	14.1	12.3	9.3	6.0	4.2
6 m	mm	49	37	33	41	45	47	74	71	50	64	50	51
Oban	°C	3.9	4.1	5.7	7.6	10.5	12.7	13.9	14.1	12.4	9.5	6.9	5.1
69 m	mm	146	109	83	90	72	87	120	116	141	169	146	172
Perth	°C	2.4	3.1	5.1	7.7	10.5	13.7	15.3	14.5	12.5	9.1	5.5	3.7
23 m	mm	70	53	47	44	57	53	84	71	67	78	71	80
Renfrew	°C	3.1	3.9	5.7	7.9	10.7	13.5	15.1	14.8	12.6	9.5	6.1	4.4
6 m	mm	111	85	69	67	63	70	97	93	102	119	106	127
Wick	°C	3.3	3.5	4.7	6.3	8.4	10.9	12.9	12.7	11.5	9.0	6.4	4.7
36 m	mm	85	58	50	47	44	47	72	68	64	78	80	78

Wales

		J	F	M	A	M	J	J	A	S	O	N	D
Aberystwyth	°C	4.5	4.3	6.2	8.1	10.9	13.5	14.9	15.1	13.5	10.7	7.6	5.8
138 m	mm	97	72	60	56	65	76	99	93	108	118	111	96
Cardiff	°C	4.4	4.6	6.6	9.1	11.9	15.0	16.3	16.5	14.3	10.9	7.6	5.5
62 m	mm	108	72	63	65	76	63	89	97	99	109	116	108
Colwyn Bay	°C	5.2	5.2	6.9	8.7	11.3	14.2	15.9	15.9	14.3	11.2	8.3	6.5
36 m	mm	79	57	46	43	49	51	55	64	72	78	78	73

		J	F	M	A	M	J	J	A	S	O	N	D	Year
rfordwest	°C	5.2	5.1	6.5	8.6	11.2	13.9	15.5	15.6	13.8	10.7	8.0	6.3	10.0
₁o m	mm	129	84	74	63	71	67	91	88	104	118	143	128	1160
drin-														
Wells	°C	2.8	2.9	5.4	7.6	10.7	13.5	15.1	15.1	12.7	9.3	6.1	3.9	8.8
₃35 m	mm	115	82	70	60	57	71	79	73	97	91	117	110	1022
₁sea	°C	5.3	5.3	7.1	9.5	12.4	15.4	16.7	17.0	15.0	11.8	8.6	6.5	10.9
₃ m	mm	124	82	70	68	72	69	94	96	103	117	134	121	1150

Europe North

Though subpolar in latitude the Scandinavian countries have relatively mild climates, warmed throughout the year by the dominant North Atlantic Drift. In winter maritime influences are strongest along a narrow coastal strip, giving mild, rainy weather with little snow. Inland stronger polar and continental influences prevail, giving persistent frosts and snow for several months, especially on high ground. Summers are mild and damp, sometimes with clear, hot spells dominated by dry air from the southeast; southern Sweden and Finland may at times be as warm as central France and Germany. Even Iceland has a much milder climate in summer than its latitude warrants, though subject to intense cold in winter, especially along its northern coast.

₁mark

		J	F	M	A	M	J	J	A	S	O	N	D	Year
₁	°C	0.0	−0.3	2.0	6.5	11.3	15.2	17.5	17.3	14.2	9.6 '	5.2	4.8	8.6
₂5 m	mm	47	38	29	34	40	48	66	69	58	54	46	49	580
₁nhagen	°C	0.0	−0.2	2.1	6.7	11.8	15.3	17.7	17.3	14.0	9.4	5.3	2.5	8.5
₃ m	mm	49	39	32	38	43	47	71	66	62	59	48	49	603
₁	°C	0.5	0.1	2.5	6.7	11.4	14.7	17.1	16.9	14.1	9.6	5.5	2.8	8.5
₃ m	mm	60	45	38	39	43	43	74	85	88	82	68	64	729
₁bogård	°C	−0.3	−0.6	1.0	5.4	10.1	14.3	16.8	15.9	12.5	8.8	4.9	1.7	7.5
₃ m	mm	48	31	35	34	35	50	62	71	63	82	57	41	609
₁se	°C	−0.2	−0.5	1.9	6.4	11.0	14.3	16.5	16.2	13.3	8.7	4.9	2.5	7.9
₅ m	mm	49	35	30	37	42	47	63	79	56	63	49	45	595
₁vig	°C	0.5	−0.1	1.5	5.4	9.5	14.5	17.5	17.3	14.3	9.8	5.7	2.9	8.2
₁ m	mm	49	37	29	31	32	42	58	58	55	59	50	53	553
₁rvig	°C	0.1	−0.3	1.7	5.9	10.5	13.7	16.2	16.1	13.5	9.1	5.2	2.7	7.9
₉ m	mm	69	45	38	39	36	46	71	84	81	89	82	71	751

₁e Islands

		J	F	M	A	M	J	J	A	S	O	N	D	Year
₁ik	°C	3.9	3.5	4.4	5.3	7.3	9.3	11.1	11.4	9.9	7.6	6.0	4.7	7.1
₁o m	mm	149	136	114	106	67	74	79	96	132	157	156	167	1433

₁and

		J	F	M	A	M	J	J	A	S	O	N	D	Year
₁nki	°C	−5.9	−9.6	−3.3	2.7	8.9	13.9	17.1	15.9	11.3	5.4	0.9	−2.2	4.6
₁6 m	mm	56	42	36	44	41	57	68	72	71	73	68	66	688
₁ani	°C	−10.8	−10.8	−6.9	0.3	6.7	12.7	16.1	14.1	8.4	2.1	−2.2	−8.3	1.8
₁34 m	mm	34	27	24	35	38	67	72	72	63	53	43	36	564
₁sjärvi	°C	−12.9	−12.9	−8.7	−2.9	3.5	10.3	13.7	11.5	6.1	−0.5	−6.3	−9.9	−0.7
₁78 m	mm	29	26	24	24	26	48	63	63	56	34	38	36	467
₁u	°C	−6.0	−6.6	−3.6	2.2	8.7	13.9	17.1	15.7	10.6	5.2	0.9	−2.7	4.6
₉ m	mm	44	28	24	35	31	46	64	78	65	64	58	81	588

World Climates

Greenland

		J	F	M	A	M	J	J	A	S	O	N	D
Angmagssalik 35 m	°C	−7.5	−7.8	−6.4	−3.5	1.4	4.9	6.6	6.6	4.1	0.3	−2.8	−5.7
Egedesminde 47 m	°C	−14.2	−15.8	−15.7	−9.3	−0.7	3.7	6.4	6.1	2.7	−1.8	−5.9	−10.8
Nord 35 m	°C	−28.7	−30.4	−31.0	−24.0	−11.2	−0.4	3.9	1.4	−8.5	−18.3	−23.8	−27.3
Prins Christian Sund 76 m	°C	−4.4	−3.8	−2.8	−0.5	2.3	4.8	7.0	7.4	5.4	2.4	−0.5	−3.4

Iceland

		J	F	M	A	M	J	J	A	S	O	N	D
Akureyri 5 m	°C	−1.5	−1.6	−0.3	1.7	6.3	9.3	10.9	10.3	7.8	3.6	1.3	−0.5
	mm	45	42	42	32	15	22	35	39	46	57	45	54
Reykjavik 16 m	°C	−0.4	−0.1	1.5	3.1	6.9	9.5	11.2	10.8	8.6	4.9	2.6	0.9
	mm	90	65	65	53	42	41	48	66	72	97	85	81

Norway

		J	F	M	A	M	J	J	A	S	O	N	D
Alvdal 485 m	°C	−11.6	−10.7	−4.7	0.9	6.1	10.8	13.5	12.2	8.0	1.9	−3.6	−8.5
	mm	24	17	16	22	32	79	88	81	59	41	37	33
Bergen 43 m	°C	1.5	1.3	3.1	5.8	10.2	12.6	15.0	14.7	12.0	8.3	5.5	3.3
	mm	179	139	109	140	83	126	141	167	228	236	207	203
Kristiansand 23 m	°C	−1.9	−1.5	1.3	5.7	10.5	14.1	16.5	15.5	12.3	8.0	3.9	1.2
	mm	128	100	62	73	58	75	104	143	156	153	176	173
Lillehammer 226 m	°C	−9.1	−8.7	−3.1	2.7	8.9	13.7	15.7	14.3	9.5	3.7	−1.4	−5.5
	mm	44	31	25	39	42	77	96	87	70	61	61	58
Oslo 94 m	°C	−4.9	−4.1	−0.1	5.3	10.9	15.0	17.7	16.4	11.7	6.1	1.2	−2.0
	mm	49	35	26	43	44	70	82	95	81	74	63	63
Tromsø 102 m	°C	−2.7	−3.3	−2.0	1.0	4.6	8.7	12.0	11.1	7.7	3.7	0.5	−1.3
	mm	118	94	113	75	65	57	56	83	115	131	97	115
Vardø 10 m	°C	−4.3	−5.2	−4.0	−0.8	2.6	6.2	9.1	9.7	6.8	2.5	−0.5	−2.7
	mm	32	23	28	23	31	33	40	49	52	52	38	31

Svalbard and Jan Mayen

		J	F	M	A	M	J	J	A	S	O	N	D
Bjørnøya 29 m	°C	−5.3	−6.2	−7.0	−5.2	−0.8	2.4	4.5	5.2	3.0	0.6	−1.6	−3.6
	mm	32	27	30	22	21	28	25	39	47	39	28	27
Isfjord Radio 9 m	°C	−10.3	−9.9	−11.9	−8.2	−2.7	2.1	5.0	4.5	1.3	−2.4	−5.3	−7.9
	mm	22	31	31	16	21	26	32	36	36	44	23	36
Jan Mayen 9 m	°C	−4.0	−5.2	−4.8	−3.4	−0.5	2.4	5.2	5.5	3.8	0.9	−1.2	−2.9
	mm	79	54	63	58	23	28	36	61	83	93	82	75

Sweden

		J	F	M	A	M	J	J	A	S	O	N	D
Falun 122 m	°C	−7.1	−6.0	−2.2	3.7	9.6	13.9	16.7	15.1	10.5	5.0	0.3	−3.4
	mm	36	24	20	31	40	59	73	83	59	45	50	41
Göteborg 41 m	°C	−1.1	−1.2	1.0	5.6	11.0	14.5	17.0	16.3	12.9	8.8	4.2	1.6
	mm	51	34	29	39	34	54	86	84	75	65	62	57
Härnösand 8 m	°C	−6.4	−5.8	−2.9	2.1	7.7	12.8	16.4	15.1	10.4	5.0	0.7	−2.8
	mm	62	37	32	46	34	52	58	78	68	63	87	80
Jokkmokk 257 m	°C	−14.4	−13.3	−7.9	−1.5	5.0	11.3	14.7	12.3	6.7	−0.5	−7.1	−11.1
	mm	29	27	21	29	30	57	77	63	49	40	36	35
Kalmar 12 m	°C	−1.3	−1.6	0.2	4.7	9.5	14.5	17.3	16.7	13.2	8.6	4.3	1.4
	mm	37	27	25	28	36	36	56	55	47	43	43	38
Stockholm 44 m	°C	−2.9	−3.1	−0.7	4.4	10.1	14.9	17.8	16.6	12.2	7.1	2.8	0.1
	mm	43	30	26	31	34	45	61	76	60	48	53	48

		J	F	M	A	M	J	J	A	S	O	N	D	Year
y	°C	−0.9	−1.4	−0.2	4.3	8.9	14.0	17.0	16.6	12.9	8.3	4.2	1.7	7.1
8 m	mm	53	42	29	31	30	32	52	56	51	52	48	53	529

Europe Central

Europe's central lowlands are the meeting ground of several air masses of widely-differing qualities. Moist maritime air from the west provides mild, damp conditions at any time of the year; continental air from the east is intensely cold in winter, very hot in summer and generally dry, while polar air masses are always chilly and dry. Interactions between these masses provide for constant change, except in anticyclonic conditions when days or weeks of stable weather – warm or cold – may prevail. Winters are generally cold, with frost expected nightly for two or three months, conditions intensified by the arrival of extremely cold Siberian air. Summers are hot, though often punctuated by cooling showers, especially in the south. The Alpine regions are cooler, especially in winter, and generally wetter than the plains.

tria

		J	F	M	A	M	J	J	A	S	O	N	D	Year
77 m	°C	−3.8	−1.5	3.4	9.0	13.7	17.1	19.0	18.0	14.3	8.6	3.3	−1.3	8.3
	mm	31	35	34	52	93	126	114	91	80	79	57	48	840
oruck	°C	−2.8	−0.5	4.8	9.3	13.8	16.7	18.1	17.4	14.6	9.0	3.4	−1.1	8.6
82 m	mm	57	52	43	55	77	114	140	113	84	71	57	48	911
enfurt	°C	−5.3	−2.6	3.1	8.7	13.3	17.0	18.6	17.7	14.1	8.1	2.3	−2.5	7.7
48 m	mm	39	42	39	69	88	124	122	102	87	87	73	54	926
ourg	°C	−2.5	−1.1	3.7	8.3	13.2	16.0	17.8	17.1	14.0	8.4	3.3	−0.9	8.1
35 m	mm	73	70	70	89	127	167	191	163	111	82	70	65	1278
blick	°C	−13.2	−13.0	−11.2	−8.2	−3.8	−0.6	1.6	1.4	−0.5	−4.3	−8.3	−11.4	−6.0
107 m	mm	115	108	112	153	136	142	154	134	104	118	108	111	1495
na	°C	−1.4	0.4	4.7	10.3	14.8	18.1	19.9	19.3	15.6	9.8	4.8	1.0	9.8
03 m	mm	40	43	45	45	70	67	83	72	41	56	53	45	660

choslovakia

		J	F	M	A	M	J	J	A	S	O	N	D	Year
islava	°C	−0.7	0.7	5.3	11.3	15.9	19.1	21.1	20.6	17.1	10.8	5.5	1.9	10.7
53 m	mm	43	47	42	42	61	64	73	69	40	54	55	59	649
	°C	−2.7	−1.0	3.7	8.7	14.2	17.8	19.3	18.5	14.8	9.1	4.0	−0.2	8.8
23 m	mm	26	24	21	33	55	81	73	67	37	41	39	30	527
ue	°C	−2.6	−1.6	2.7	7.8	12.9	16.2	17.9	17.4	13.9	8.2	3.1	−0.8	7.9
62 m	mm	23	24	23	32	61	67	82	66	36	42	26	26	508

t Germany

		J	F	M	A	M	J	J	A	S	O	N	D	Year
den	°C	−0.9	−0.2	3.9	8.7	13.1	16.8	18.5	18.1	14.7	9.3	4.8	0.8	9.0
29 m	mm	42	40	42	48	66	69	120	67	49	53	41	43	680
fswald	°C	−1.0	−0.6	2.4	7.1	12.3	16.1	18.1	17.7	14.4	9.2	4.5	1.0	8.3
m	mm	40	33	30	39	45	55	69	55	59	51	36	41	553
zig	°C	−0.8	−0.3	3.4	8.3	13.0	16.3	18.1	17.6	14.3	9.1	4.5	0.9	8.7
41 m	mm	37	36	34	38	47	67	73	59	38	46	39	45	549
trelitz	°C	−1.0	−1.3	2.7	7.3	12.3	15.7	17.3	17.0	13.7	8.8	4.1	1.1	8.1
4 m	mm	41	34	28	42	52	62	65	63	48	37	39	42	553

World Climates

Hungary

		J	F	M	A	M	J	J	A	S	O	N	D
Budapest	°C	−1.1	1.0	5.8	11.8	16.8	20.2	22.2	21.4	17.4	11.3	5.8	1.5
130 m	mm	42	44	39	45	72	76	54	51	34	56	69	48
Keszthely	°C	−1.1	0.9	5.7	11.3	15.9	19.3	21.4	20.9	17.3	11.4	5.7	1.2
128 m	mm	40	41	36	42	74	79	76	70	57	59	62	50
Miskolc	°C	−3.2	−0.9	4.4	10.3	15.4	18.8	20.7	20.1	16.3	9.9	4.4	0.0
118 m	mm	31	32	28	39	70	84	66	66	40	49	56	40
Pécs	°C	−0.7	1.3	6.1	11.9	16.9	20.4	22.6	21.9	17.9	11.8	6.2	1.8
124 m	mm	41	46	41	58	66	69	64	55	47	64	71	45
Szeged	°C	−1.4	0.7	5.8	11.9	17.3	20.8	23.0	22.2	18.2	12.0	6.1	1.5
97 m	mm	34	38	35	41	63	63	51	47	42	46	59	39

Poland

		J	F	M	A	M	J	J	A	S	O	N	D
Gdańsk	°C	−1.1	−1.9	0.9	5.8	10.6	15.4	17.7	17.3	13.3	8.9	4.0	1.3
5 m	mm	31	24	19	32	33	58	73	70	53	38	29	39
Kraków	°C	−2.6	−2.8	1.3	7.4	12.6	16.6	18.3	17.5	13.0	8.2	3.2	0.6
209 m	mm	33	30	31	45	62	80	95	78	46	34	34	35
Lublinek	°C	−3.0	−3.1	2.1	6.9	13.0	16.6	18.1	17.3	13.6	8.7	3.3	0.3
184 m	mm	21	32	26	36	34	67	103	58	50	39	26	41
Poznań	°C	−1.7	−2.5	1.6	7.2	12.8	17.1	18.5	17.6	13.3	8.5	3.4	0.8
83 m	mm	29	27	29	34	38	62	85	55	40	29	27	37
Warsaw	°C	−2.4	−3.3	0.6	7.3	12.9	17.3	18.7	17.8	13.1	8.2	3.0	0.4
110 m	mm	25	28	20	32	40	60	79	47	41	31	31	37
Wroclaw	°C	−1.3	−2.1	2.3	7.6	12.9	17.0	18.5	17.5	13.5	8.8	4.0	1.4
116 m	mm	24	23	27	42	50	61	100	57	41	33	28	33

Romania

		J	F	M	A	M	J	J	A	S	O	N	D
Arad	°C	−1.9	0.5	5.8	11.3	16.1	19.5	21.3	21.1	17.5	11.6	6.3	1.7
116 m	mm	36	34	35	46	64	68	54	43	41	44	52	41
Bucharest	°C	−2.7	−0.6	4.6	11.7	17.0	20.9	23.3	22.7	18.3	12.0	5.5	0.4
92 m	mm	43	36	35	47	69	87	55	49	30	44	43	41
Constanta	°C	−0.3	0.9	4.3	9.5	14.9	19.7	22.3	21.9	18.2	13.3	7.5	2.7
32 m	mm	29	23	21	28	35	41	35	31	24	38	40	34
Sibiu	°C	−3.5	−1.3	3.2	8.5	12.4	15.2	16.7	16.5	13.2	8.3	3.7	−0.4
407 m	mm	29	30	28	59	77	11	82	73	46	46	33	30

Switzerland

		J	F	M	A	M	J	J	A	S	O	N	D
Bern	°C	−1.0	0.7	4.9	9.0	12.9	16.3	18.1	17.6	14.5	8.9	3.9	0.1
572 m	mm	61	54	59	68	93	123	119	116	101	70	68	54
Geneva	°C	1.1	2.2	6.1	10.0	14.1	17.8	19.9	19.1	15.8	10.3	5.7	2.1
405 m	mm	63	56	55	51	67	89	64	94	99	72	83	59
Interlaken	°C	−0.8	0.7	5.5	10.2	14.3	17.5	18.9	18.6	14.7	9.4	4.9	0.4
595 m	mm	90	85	73	81	102	139	154	146	112	89	92	72
Lugano	°C	1.9	3.6	7.5	11.7	15.4	19.3	21.4	20.5	17.4	12.1	6.9	3.1
276 m	mm	63	67	98	148	215	198	185	196	159	173	147	95
St Moritz	°C	−7.1	−5.5	−2.7	2.2	6.8	11.1	12.8	12.4	9.2	3.8	−1.9	−6.3
1833 m	mm	40	42	36	45	71	89	105	101	83	77	67	48
Zürich	°C	−1.1	0.3	4.5	8.6	12.7	15.9	17.6	17.0	14.0	8.6	3.7	0.1
469 m	mm	75	70	66	80	107	136	143	131	108	80	76	65

West Germany

		J	F	M	A	M	J	J	A	S	O	N	D
Bremen	°C	0.6	0.7	4.1	8.3	12.5	15.7	17.5	17.3	14.3	9.6	5.3	2.1
4 m	mm	57	45	42	48	54	60	90	78	61	58	60	53

		J	F	M	A	M	J	J	A	S	O	N	D	Year
rg	°C	-1.1	-0.7	3.9	8.1	12.9	16.1	17.7	17.2	13.9	8.5	3.7	-0.1	8.3
36 m	mm	58	49	37	43	59	75	72	72	55	49	46	57	672
gne	°C	1.9	2.7	5.9	9.7	13.5	17.0	18.7	18.7	15.3	10.4	6.3	2.5	10.2
5 m	mm	60	44	42	60	51	75	69	73	55	53	65	52	699
kfurt	°C	0.9	1.9	6.3	10.7	14.8	17.9	19.7	19.1	15.8	10.5	5.7	1.9	10.4
03 m	mm	58	44	38	44	55	73	70	76	57	52	55	54	676
burg	°C	0.0	0.4	3.3	7.6	12.2	15.6	17.3	16.8	13.6	9.1	4.9	1.8	8.6
2 m	mm	57	48	39	52	53	64	84	83	63	59	59	59	720
el	°C	0.0	0.8	4.6	8.8	13.2	16.4	17.8	17.3	14.0	9.1	4.8	1.3	9.0
98 m	mm	46	43	32	47	58	66	72	66	52	53	49	46	630
ch	°C	-2.2	-1.0	3.3	7.9	12.5	15.9	17.7	16.9	13.7	8.2	3.1	-0.7	7.9
24 m	mm	59	55	51	62	107	125	140	104	87	67	57	50	964
gart	°C	0.2	1.1	5.3	9.6	13.6	16.9	18.6	18.0	14.7	9.6	4.8	1.2	9.5
o1 m	mm	48	42	38	51	74	94	79	79	62	48	48	40	703

Europe Southwest

Lapped by the Atlantic Ocean in warm-temperate latitudes, Portugal and northern Spain have warm maritime climates. Air and sea are slightly chilled by a cool coastal current from the north, though plentiful sunshine provides summer heat, and warmth even in the depths of winter. These influences spread well inland, giving mild, damp winters with most of the precipitation between November and March, and warm or hot summers. Over the rest of the peninsula conditions are more variable. The interior plateau and peripheral highlands are hot and intensely dry in summer, cold and often wet in winter, with gentler conditions in the many valleys and basins. The southern and eastern coasts are under strong Mediterranean and African influences, with hot summers and warm moist winters.

orra

		J	F	M	A	M	J	J	A	S	O	N	D	Year
scaldes	°C	2.3	3.1	7.0	9.0	11.4	16.3	19.2	18.0	15.7	10.7	6.1	2.5	10.1
o8o m	mm	34	37	46	63	105	69	65	98	81	73	68	69	808
iguel agolastérs	°C	0.8	0.5	3.5	5.9	8.1	14.1	16.1	15.2	12.8	8.4	4.5	0.6	7.5
611 m	mm	33	45	45	72	97	78	60	101	90	80	55	49	805

raltar

		J	F	M	A	M	J	J	A	S	O	N	D	Year
altar n	°C	12.5	12.4	14.4	16.1	18.7	21.7	23.8	24.4	22.6	19.1	15.1	13.0	17.8
m	mm	109	92	125	99	30	5	<1	<1	18	85	149	151	863

tugal

		J	F	M	A	M	J	J	A	S	O	N	D	Year
ança	°C	3.8	5.6	7.9	10.2	12.8	17.3	20.2	20.3	16.8	12.0	7.6	4.4	23.3
20 m	mm	149	104	133	73	69	42	15	16	39	79	110	144	973
bra	°C	9.7	10.8	13.2	15.1	16.8	19.8	21.9	22.2	20.6	17.4	13.2	10.2	15.9
41 m	mm	132	95	132	76	76	38	12	18	48	87	105	142	961
n	°C	10.8	11.6	13.6	15.6	17.2	20.1	22.2	22.5	21.2	18.2	14.4	11.5	16.6
7 m	mm	111	76	109	54	44	16	3	4	33	62	93	103	708
a	°C	9.6	10.8	13.3	15.7	18.5	23.0	25.8	25.7	23.2	18.6	13.8	9.9	17.3
58 m	mm	49	32	72	46	34	17	2	2	18	48	53	55	428

		J	F	M	A	M	J	J	A	S	O	N	D
Oporto	°C	9.0	9.6	11.9	13.6	15.2	18.0	19.6	19.8	18.6	15.8	12.2	9.6
95 m	mm	159	112	147	86	87	41	20	26	51	105	148	168
Sagres	°C	12.7	12.9	14.1	15.1	16.5	18.1	18.9	19.1	19.2	18.2	15.7	13.5
41 m	mm	63	47	61	38	24	5	2	1	14	46	60	56

Azores and Madeira

		J	F	M	A	M	J	J	A	S	O	N	D
Horta (Azores)	°C	14.4	14.2	14.4	15.1	16.5	18.8	20.8	22.0	21.0	19.0	16.8	15.3
60 m	mm	120	100	105	67	62	42	27	29	81	103	120	102
Ponta Delgada (Azores)	°C	14.4	14.2	14.4	15.1	16.5	18.8	20.8	22.0	21.0	19.0	16.8	15.3
35 m	mm	120	100	105	67	62	42	27	29	81	103	120	102
Funchal (Madeira)	°C	15.8	15.6	16.0	16.7	17.7	19.6	21.0	21.9	21.8	20.7	18.6	16.7
56 m	mm	84	85	71	44	21	5	2	2	29	82	97	94

Spain

		J	F	M	A	M	J	J	A	S	O	N	D
Alicante	°C	11.0	11.7	13.9	15.2	18.2	22.6	25.2	25.8	23.6	19.2	15.1	11.5
82 m	mm	28	21	20	39	29	14	5	12	47	48	35	30
Almeria	°C	11.8	12.3	14.2	16.2	18.6	22.1	24.7	25.4	23.5	19.4	15.7	12.9
6 m	mm	28	19	21	28	15	5	0	5	16	26	28	35
Badajoz	°C	8.6	9.9	12.7	15.2	18.0	22.8	25.8	25.5	22.6	17.8	12.6	9.1
203 m	mm	61	47	68	42	37	18	3	4	25	48	61	60
Barcelona	°C	9.5	10.3	12.4	14.6	17.7	21.5	24.3	24.3	21.8	17.6	13.5	10.3
93 m	mm	30	40	53	45	54	40	30	47	79	77	54	49
Coruña, La	°C	9.9	9.8	11.5	12.4	14.0	16.5	18.2	18.9	17.8	15.3	12.4	10.2
58 m	mm	121	80	95	70	60	46	29	47	71	92	125	139
Granada	°C	7.1	8.5	10.9	13.5	16.3	22.1	25.7	25.2	21.7	16.3	11.7	7.8
689 m	mm	54	49	62	53	44	8	3	8	25	49	48	70
Madrid	°C	4.9	6.5	10.0	12.7	15.7	20.6	24.2	23.7	19.8	14.0	8.9	5.6
660 m	mm	38	34	45	44	44	27	11	14	31	53	47	48
Seville	°C	10.3	11.6	14.1	16.4	19.2	23.4	26.3	26.3	23.7	19.2	14.5	11.0
13 m	mm	73	59	90	51	36	9	1	5	25	66	68	76
Valladolid	°C	3.8	5.2	8.6	10.9	14.0	18.5	21.4	20.9	18.3	12.8	7.6	4.2
695 m	mm	36	28	46	36	43	34	14	14	30	38	44	46
Zaragoza	°C	6.1	7.6	11.3	13.7	17.0	21.2	23.9	23.7	20.6	15.4	10.2	6.7
237 m	mm	16	16	30	31	48	37	17	19	31	34	28	32

Balearic Islands

		J	F	M	A	M	J	J	A	S	O	N	D
Ibiza	°C	10.7	10.7	12.6	14.7	18.1	21.7	24.5	25.1	23.3	19.0	15.1	12.3
7 m	mm	42	35	25	22	13	22	5	12	34	85	102	47
Mahon (Minorca)	°C	10.3	10.5	12.2	14.2	15.4	21.3	24.1	24.4	22.4	18.2	14.4	11.9
47 m	mm	60	44	48	34	30	21	4	22	72	133	92	77
Palma (Majorca)	°C	10.1	10.5	12.2	14.5	17.4	21.4	24.1	24.5	22.6	18.4	14.3	11.6
10 m	mm	39	33	36	28	14	19	5	26	61	74	60	52

Canary Islands

		J	F	M	A	M	J	J	A	S	O	N	D
Las Palmas	°C	16.8	17.9	17.7	18.5	19.6	21.2	22.9	23.6	23.3	22.3	20.2	17.8
25 m	mm	22	21	12	8	3	1	1	0	4	15	47	36
Santa Cruz de Tenerife	°C	17.4	17.5	18.2	19.2	20.4	22.2	24.2	24.7	24.1	22.7	20.5	18.4
46 m	mm	36	39	27	13	6	1	0	0	3	31	45	51

Europe Southeast

Though moderated by the Mediterranean, southeastern European climates are subject to strong and often contradictory influences from the Atlantic Ocean, Africa, northern Europe and Asia, producing immense seasonal contrasts in temperature. Depressions from the Atlantic bring winter rains to northern Italy and the Adriatic, which cold air from the north may chill to heavy snowfalls; Alpine regions are intensely cold, and only the southern tip of Italy remains warm in January and February. Further east cold air flows southward across the steppes to chill the Balkans, bringing winter frosts and snow to Romania, Bulgaria and northern Greece. Summers by contrast are generally hot and dry over the whole of southeastern Europe, with rain in the mountains north of the Adriatic.

		J	F	M	A	M	J	J	A	S	O	N	D	Year
ania														
okostër	°C	5.5	6.4	9.7	13.0	17.1	21.1	23.7	24.1	20.2	15.2	11.2	7.6	14.6
193 m	mm	274	269	186	136	69	45	19	24	69	173	422	376	2062
çe	°C	0.8	1.3	4.9	9.4	13.7	17.6	20.3	20.9	17.2	11.6	7.7	3.3	10.7
899 m	mm	70	81	56	60	79	43	25	24	41	81	147	99	806
ës	°C	0.4	1.9	6.1	11.7	16.0	19.7	22.1	22.4	17.9	12.7	8.9	3.7	12.0
354 m	mm	103	96	104	99	85	51	41	35	61	86	138	133	1032
anë	°C	7.3	8.3	10.6	14.4	18.4	22.4	25.0	24.9	21.8	17.4	12.9	9.2	16.0
89 m	mm	132	120	100	87	99	60	28	39	73	157	152	142	1189
lgaria														
ven	°C	−1.9	0.4	6.2	11.9	17.3	20.9	23.3	22.3	18.4	13.7	6.1	0.4	11.6
109 m	mm	35	31	33	65	76	81	82	37	32	49	38	36	595
a	°C	−1.7	0.6	4.6	10.6	15.4	19.0	21.3	20.7	16.7	11.1	5.5	0.6	10.4
550 m	mm	42	31	37	55	71	90	59	43	42	55	52	44	622
na	°C	2.3	2.5	6.5	11.3	16.7	21.0	24.1	23.6	19.9	15.7	9.5	4.1	13.1
35 m	mm	28	30	26	37	26	64	45	37	27	58	35	63	476
in	°C	−2.1	0.3	5.9	11.7	17.5	21.4	23.7	22.5	17.9	12.7	5.9	0.5	11.5
35 m	mm	42	38	43	52	67	49	45	49	33	60	50	53	581
eece														
kand-apolis	°C	5.5	6.7	8.5	12.8	17.3	21.5	24.8	24.7	20.9	16.3	11.3	7.9	14.9
7 m	mm	81	45	46	30	32	36	18	15	25	47	86	97	558
ens	°C	9.3	9.9	11.3	15.3	20.0	24.6	27.6	27.4	23.5	19.0	14.7	11.0	17.8
107 m	mm	62	36	38	23	23	16	6	7	15	51	56	57	402
lion rete)	°C	12.2	12.8	13.5	16.6	20.4	24.4	26.2	26.5	23.6	20.2	16.9	13.8	18.9
48 m	mm	92	33	45	25	11	3	1	1	17	56	56	86	426
kira orfu)	°C	9.8	10.3	11.9	15.0	19.4	24.3	26.8	26.8	22.8	18.2	14.4	11.5	17.6
2 m	mm	221	140	102	59	48	11	8	12	109	177	228	204	1319
issa	°C	5.8	7.4	9.2	13.7	19.7	25.4	28.0	27.8	22.4	16.2	11.4	7.4	16.2
75 m	mm	51	40	49	35	45	30	15	13	31	88	64	61	522
os	°C	12.2	12.1	13.4	16.4	19.5	22.7	24.8	25.0	22.9	20.9	17.3	14.3	18.5
3 m	mm	91	73	69	19	12	11	2	1	11	45	48	93	475
rai	°C	9.7	10.4	11.9	15.6	19.7	23.8	26.3	26.4	23.1	18.7	14.4	10.9	17.6
3 m	mm	123	87	72	50	27	13	1	6	27	82	113	148	749

World Climates

		J	F	M	A	M	J	J	A	S	O	N	D
Thessaloniki	°C	5.5	7.1	9.6	14.5	19.6	24.7	27.3	26.8	22.5	17.1	12.0	7.5
7 m	mm	44	34	35	36	40	33	20	14	28	55	56	54
Trikkala	°C	4.5	7.2	10.2	14.7	18.7	23.5	26.9	26.5	22.5	18.4	11.9	7.1
149 m	mm	84	69	59	80	61	51	19	12	27	80	10	125

Italy

		J	F	M	A	M	J	J	A	S	O	N	D
Alghero (Sardinia)	°C	9.8	9.6	11.3	13.4	16.5	20.6	23.0	23.5	21.3	17.5	13.6	10.9
40 m	mm	60	42	45	41	27	17	2	9	42	77	81	86
Ancona	°C	5.7	6.6	9.2	13.6	17.1	21.4	24.3	24.1	21.0	15.8	11.2	7.8
105 m	mm	77	52	54	42	48	50	34	34	69	64	71	79
Bologna	°C	2.3	4.9	9.5	13.9	18.5	22.3	24.9	24.5	21.3	15.7	12.5	4.6
50 m	mm	47	46	65	90	73	69	49	52	53	76	101	83
Brindisi	°C	9.3	9.5	10.9	13.8	17.4	21.5	23.9	24.4	21.5	17.8	14.3	11.0
22 m	mm	79	62	43	35	36	13	13	24	38	76	88	74
Coltanissetta	°C	7.3	8.1	9.7	12.6	17.1	21.9	24.8	24.7	21.5	16.9	12.3	8.9
570 m	mm	78	47	52	47	38	16	15	8	42	60	73	74
Foggia	°C	6.7	7.9	10.3	13.8	18.3	22.6	25.7	25.7	22.3	17.1	12.3	9.1
74 m	mm	55	35	31	39	38	29	15	23	27	64	60	49
Messina	°C	11.2	11.4	12.6	14.9	18.3	22.8	25.6	25.9	23.2	19.7	16.0	12.9
54 m	mm	146	100	92	52	51	15	19	18	69	144	148	120
Milan	°C	0.6	3.1	8.1	12.5	16.8	20.8	23.0	22.3	18.6	12.7	6.9	1.9
103 m	mm	52	49	65	70	85	89	55	71	72	114	101	80
Naples	°C	8.5	8.9	10.8	13.8	17.4	21.4	23.6	23.8	21.0	16.9	13.0	9.9
68 m	mm	122	88	63	59	51	21	16	27	92	118	129	136
Palermo	°C	11.9	12.3	13.1	15.5	18.9	22.4	25.1	25.5	23.5	20.4	16.9	13.7
31 m	mm	48	58	38	34	14	10	0	30	21	51	42	69
Pantelleria	°C	11.2	11.3	12.9	14.5	17.9	21.1	24.3	24.8	22.9	19.7	16.5	12.7
254 m	mm	48	58	38	34	14	10	0	30	21	51	42	69
Pisa	°C	6.8	7.8	10.3	13.1	16.9	20.9	23.5	23.3	20.6	15.9	11.5	8.1
11 m	mm	83	81	67	66	74	50	24	33	81	148	119	109
Rome	°C	8.0	9.0	10.9	13.7	17.5	21.6	24.4	24.2	21.5	17.2	12.7	9.5
5 m	mm	83	73	52	50	48	18	9	18	70	110	113	105
Turin	°C	1.1	3.5	8.7	13.3	18.0	21.5	24.1	22.9	19.3	13.1	6.8	2.8
238 m	mm	23	40	57	109	76	112	72	45	62	93	96	60
Venice	°C	2.2	3.8	7.7	12.2	17.1	20.7	23.4	22.6	18.9	13.3	8.1	3.8
2 m	mm	50	54	62	70	82	84	67	67	66	95	90	67

Malta

		J	F	M	A	M	J	J	A	S	O	N	D
Valletta	°C	12.3	12.5	13.7	15.7	18.7	22.7	25.5	26.1	24.3	21.3	17.7	14.1
70 m	mm	90	60	39	15	12	2	0	8	29	63	91	110

Yugoslavia

		J	F	M	A	M	J	J	A	S	O	N	D
Banja Luca	°C	0.1	1.6	5.7	11.1	15.4	19.1	21.1	20.7	17.1	11.6	6.6	3.4
153 m	mm	70	70	73	91	101	120	74	66	69	105	104	115
Belgrade	°C	−0.2	1.6	6.2	12.2	17.1	20.5	22.6	22.0	18.3	12.5	6.8	2.5
132 m	mm	48	46	46	54	75	96	60	55	50	55	61	55
Dubrovnik	°C	8.7	9.4	11.1	14.2	17.8	21.9	24.7	24.3	21.5	17.4	13.5	10.6
49 m	mm	139	125	104	104	75	48	26	38	101	162	198	178
Ljubljana	°C	−0.8	0.5	5.0	9.9	14.3	17.9	20.3	19.7	16.1	10.6	5.1	1.3
299 m	mm	88	89	76	98	121	133	113	127	142	151	131	114

		J	F	M	A	M	J	J	A	S	O	N	D	Year
ievo	°C	-1.4	0.7	4.9	9.8	14.3	17.4	19.5	19.7	16.0	10.2	5.4	1.7	9.8
37 m	mm	71	69	50	59	84	86	68	62	71	84	98	87	889
je	°C	1.1	2.9	6.5	12.1	17.0	21.6	23.8	23.7	18.6	11.9	7.2	2.9	12.4
41 m	mm	46	41	38	34	52	49	35	37	42	58	71	43	546
	°C	7.8	8.1	10.3	14.0	18.6	22.9	25.6	25.4	21.6	16.8	12.3	10.1	16.1
28 m	mm	76	74	53	62	60	53	40	32	55	71	110	130	816
eb	°C	0.2	2.2	6.8	12.0	16.4	19.9	22.0	21.3	17.7	11.8	6.6	2.4	11.6
63 m	mm	56	54	47	59	86	95	79	74	70	88	89	67	864

ASIA

Asia North

Western USSR has a complex continental climate, moderated by marine influences in the south around the Black and Caspian seas. Winters are long, dominated by cold air from the north and east. Five to six months of sub-zero temperatures are normal, though the warm North Atlantic Drift keeps the port of Murmansk relatively ice-free throughout the year. Depressions from the west bring heavy winter snowfall and spring rains. Summer anticyclones bring continuous warm weather, especially in the centre and south, whilst Arctic air from the north is transformed into continental tropical air associated with hot, dry weather. Eastern USSR has an even more extreme continental climate. Winter isotherms encircle the cold pole of Verkhoyansk, where temperatures fall to $-60°C$ ($-76°F$) and lower; even the eastern seaboard is intensely cold. Mean summer temperatures vary latitudinally from freezing point in the north to 20°C (68°F) or more in the south and dry conditions prevail.

R		J	F	M	A	M	J	J	A	S	O	N	D	Year
ibinsk	°C	-14.3	-13.9	-5.3	6.3	15.5	19.9	22.5	20.1	14.0	4.7	-2.1	-11.1	4.7
26 m	mm	18	14	22	15	27	29	33	24	22	29	19	17	269
Ata	°C	-6.7	-5.1	1.6	10.8	16.0	20.4	23.3	22.3	17.4	10.0	-0.1	-5.4	8.7
47 m	mm	26	32	64	89	99	59	35	23	25	46	48	35	581
yr	°C	-21.5	-22.0	-19.9	-12.2	-3.2	5.4	10.8	9.6	4.0	-5.2	-14.2	-20.1	-7.4
2 m	mm	21	14	16	13	9	13	39	46	26	27	17	19	260
angelsk	°C	-11.7	-11.7	-8.1	-0.1	5.9	13.0	16.3	14.5	8.3	1.9	-3.4	-8.6	1.4
3 m	mm	33	28	28	28	39	59	63	57	66	55	44	39	539
habad	°C	2.1	4.7	8.8	16.3	23.3	28.6	31.2	29.3	23.5	15.9	7.7	2.8	16.2
30 m	mm	22	21	44	38	28	6	2	1	3	11	15	19	210
khan	°C	-5.7	-4.9	1.7	10.5	18.6	22.4	24.9	23.4	17.7	10.1	4.0	-2.1	10.1
8 m	mm	16	11	14	14	16	19	10	25	22	16	16	17	196
bay	°C	-6.2	-4.1	2.0	12.0	19.6	24.2	26.2	24.0	17.5	9.7	0.9	-4.7	10.1
6 m	mm	7	14	13	12	10	6	2	2	3	7	5	8	89
sk	°C	-20.8	-17.8	-9.3	1.6	8.8	15.4	17.9	15.1	8.2	1.1	-10.8	-18.5	-0.8
85 m	mm	12	8	9	15	29	83	102	99	49	20	17	15	458
as	°C	-5.1	-4.7	-1.3	6.1	12.8	16.2	18.1	17.1	12.6	7.0	1.9	-2.1	6.0
5 m	mm	33	35	29	40	49	69	98	92	57	48	39	36	625
n	°C	-13.1	-13.2	-7.2	3.8	12.0	17.6	19.4	17.7	11.1	3.5	-4.6	-10.3	3.1
4 m	mm	16	17	18	25	46	50	66	63	45	45	21	23	435

ASIA

Location of Climatic Stations

Ostrov Dikson

Naryan-Mar

For European USSR
see the European locator map.

Omsk

Semipalatinsk

Istanbul
Sinop
Izmir
Ankara
Antalya
Adana
Chimbay
Krasnovodsk
Tashkent
Alma
Aleppo
Tripoli
Dayr az Zawr *Mosul* *Tabriz*
Ashkhabad
Beirut
Damascus *Kirkuk*
Kash
Tel Aviv
Rutbah
Mazar i Sharif
Jerusalem
Baghdad *Tehran*
Mashhad
Amman
Al Diwaniya
Kabul
Srinagar
Eilat
Nasiriya *Abadan*
Murree
Shiráz
Peshawar
Lahore
Kerman *Kandahar*
Shuwaikh
Medina
Kalat
New
Jacobabad
Riyadh
Bahrain
Pasni
Jodhpur
Jeddah
Sharjah
Hyderabad
Karachi
Veraval
Riyan *Salalah*
Bombay
Poona
Vis
Aden

Bangalore

Minicoy *Trivandrum*

Colombo

Mahé

Diego Garcia

World Climates

		J	F	M	A	M	J	J	A	S	O	N	D
Kharkov	°C	−7.1	−6.5	−1.6	7.8	15.0	18.9	21.1	19.9	14.1	7.3	0.7	−4.0
152 m	mm	36	33	32	33	50	60	75	48	34	42	39	37
Kiev	°C	−6.1	−5.2	−0.5	7.6	14.7	18.6	20.4	19.3	14.2	7.5	1.4	−2.9
179 m	mm	43	39	35	46	56	66	70	72	47	47	53	41
Kirov	°C	−13.5	−13.3	−7.2	2.4	9.9	16.3	18.1	15.8	9.3	1.7	−5.8	−11.5
164 m	mm	33	24	26	28	45	58	72	69	54	56	38	35
Krasnovodsk	°C	2.1	3.0	6.0	12.6	19.3	24.1	27.6	27.5	22.3	15.3	8.2	4.1
89 m	mm	11	13	15	12	7	2	2	3	3	6	9	11
Krasnoyarsk	°C	−19.5	−17.3	−10.5	−1.9	6.3	12.9	15.9	13.7	7.4	−1.1	−11.3	−17.9
149 m	mm	3	5	3	5	25	36	31	53	43	23	13	10
Leningrad	°C	−7.6	−7.9	−4.3	3.3	9.9	15.4	18.4	16.8	11.2	5.1	−0.2	−4.4
4 m	mm	36	32	25	34	41	54	69	77	58	52	45	36
Lvov	°C	−5.3	−4.0	0.0	6.8	12.9	16.1	18.2	17.1	13.4	7.5	2.6	−1.7
325 m	mm	33	33	30	47	66	77	96	91	47	52	46	37
Minsk	°C	−7.5	−6.6	−2.8	5.0	12.3	16.0	18.1	16.4	11.6	5.5	0.1	−4.8
234 m	mm	34	30	26	42	59	72	83	81	62	47	40	30
Moscow	°C	−9.9	−9.5	−4.2	4.7	11.9	16.8	19.0	17.1	11.2	4.5	−1.9	−6.8
156 m	mm	31	28	33	35	52	67	74	74	58	51	36	36
Murmansk	°C	−10.9	−11.4	−8.1	−1.4	3.9	10.0	13.4	11.1	6.9	0.9	−3.8	−7.9
46 m	mm	19	16	18	19	25	40	54	60	44	30	28	23
Naryan Mar	°C	−15.6	−17.2	−15.1	−5.8	0.6	7.9	12.2	11.3	5.6	−0.8	−7.6	−13.4
7 m	mm	20	14	17	21	24	38	41	59	52	39	31	22
Odessa	°C	−2.2	−1.9	1.7	8.4	14.9	19.7	22.4	21.6	17.0	11.1	5.4	0.4
64 m	mm	28	26	20	27	34	45	34	37	29	35	43	31
Okhotsk	°C	−22.4	−19.2	−14.2	−5.4	1.4	6.4	11.9	13.1	8.7	−2.1	−13.5	−20.1
6 m	mm	11	6	14	17	38	44	65	55	54	39	25	10
Omsk	°C	−19.2	−17.7	−11.4	2.3	11.3	17.2	18.8	16.2	10.4	2.2	−9.3	−16.5
94 m	mm	8	6	9	18	30	53	72	46	33	23	15	12
Orenburg	°C	−14.7	−14.2	−8.0	5.5	15.0	20.2	22.1	20.5	13.6	4.7	−4.9	−11.5
109 m	mm	21	20	26	22	38	37	43	30	30	41	25	25
Ostrov Beringa	°C	−3.5	−3.9	−3.2	−0.1	2.0	5.1	8.7	10.6	9.1	4.6	0.3	−2.4
6 m	mm	38	23	30	24	31	28	48	59	53	72	64	46
Ostrov Dikson	°C	−24.1	−24.3	−25.0	−16.4	−7.0	0.7	4.9	5.4	1.9	−6.6	−17.0	−21.4
20 m	mm	20	13	17	9	11	23	32	46	42	21	14	18
Ostrov Kotelnyy	°C	−29.5	−29.9	−27.0	−20.6	−9.1	−0.2	2.5	2.0	−1.5	−10.5	−21.9	−26.4
10 m	mm	8	8	6	9	10	11	20	19	11	11	10	8
Oymyakon	°C	−47.2	−42.9	−34.2	−15.4	1.4	11.6	14.8	10.9	1.6	−16.2	−35.9	−44.0
726 m	mm	7	6	5	4	10	32	40	37	20	12	11	9
Perm	°C	−16.6	−13.5	−6.7	3.6	10.9	14.4	18.3	15.1	9.9	1.5	−4.8	−12.5
161 m	mm	40	28	29	26	62	73	89	67	52	60	51	43
Riga	°C	−6.9	−6.3	−2.5	5.6	10.9	15.1	16.5	16.1	12.7	7.7	1.5	−4.1
3 m	mm	31	29	27	33	44	45	53	70	64	62	62	47
Rostov	°C	−5.3	−4.9	−0.1	9.4	16.8	20.9	23.5	22.3	16.4	9.0	2.4	−2.7
77 m	mm	38	41	32	39	36	58	49	37	32	44	40	37
Semipalatinsk	°C	−16.8	−15.8	−8.1	5.5	14.3	20.3	22.2	19.6	12.8	5.0	−7.0	−13.8
206 m	mm	14	15	17	19	22	30	32	23	21	22	27	22
Simferopol	°C	−0.4	0.0	2.7	9.1	15.0	19.0	21.6	20.7	15.5	10.5	5.7	1.8
205 m	mm	44	40	35	36	49	75	58	34	31	41	44	41
Simusir	°C	−4.8	−5.2	−3.2	0.5	3.2	5.0	9.3	10.6	10.1	7.0	2.2	−2.1
26 m	mm	102	63	90	117	119	70	112	162	198	175	123	130

		J	F	M	A	M	J	J	A	S	O	N	D	Year
lensk	°C	−11.5	−9.7	−5.0	4.9	12.6	15.1	16.9	16.1	11.3	5.9	−0.8	−7.1	4.1
241 m	mm	35	33	45	40	54	69	81	92	38	55	60	51	653
inn	°C	−5.0	−5.9	−2.9	2.9	8.7	13.6	17.1	16.4	11.8	6.6	1.2	−1.9	5.2
44 m	mm	33	26	24	32	41	49	71	68	75	65	45	39	568
hkent	°C	−0.2	2.7	7.3	14.5	20.1	24.8	27.1	24.8	19.1	12.6	5.4	0.9	13.3
428 m	mm	49	51	81	58	32	12	4	3	3	23	44	57	417
lisi	°C	1.3	3.1	6.0	12.1	17.5	21.4	24.6	24.4	19.8	13.7	7.8	2.9	12.9
490 m	mm	20	21	36	43	87	69	50	37	42	46	37	20	508
ickij Priisk	°C	−28.8	−26.0	−18.2	−7.2	2.3	10.5	13.4	10.4	3.2	−6.4	−19.6	−26.8	−7.8
1310 m	mm	2	2	4	10	19	48	118	104	48	9	6	4	374
kiye Luki	°C	−8.2	−8.2	−4.1	4.4	11.5	15.8	19.2	16.2	10.7	5.1	−0.5	−5.0	3.8
98 m	mm	22	19	15	30	37	47	60	67	50	44	27	22	440
khoyansk	°C	−46.8	−43.1	−30.2	−13.5	2.7	12.9	15.7	11.4	2.7	−14.3	−35.7	−44.5	−15.2
137 m	mm	7	5	5	4	5	25	33	30	13	11	10	7	155
divostok	°C	−14.0	−9.9	−3.3	4.4	9.3	14.0	18.4	20.6	16.2	8.8	−1.1	−2.2	5.1
282 m	mm	8	10	18	31	53	74	84	119	109	48	31	15	600
utsk	°C	−44.5	−36.0	−23.1	−8.5	4.4	14.0	17.3	14.0	5.5	−8.3	−28.3	−41.0	−11.2
161 m	mm	8	5	3	8	10	28	41	33	25	13	10	8	192
evan	°C	−3.1	−0.8	6.7	12.3	17.9	21.7	25.1	25.3	20.5	14.1	7.9	2.1	12.5
907 m	mm	26	27	34	49	52	26	8	11	15	22	23	29	322

Asia Southwest

Turkey's coasts are rainy but warm throughout the year, with only occasional winter frosts. The high interior is drier, with a more extreme climate of hot summers and bitingly cold winters. Iran has cool-to-very-cold winters controlled by air masses from the uplands of central Asia, and hot summers, dry in all but the northern and southern coastal regions. Iraq has hot, uniformly dry summers, and cool winters dampened in the north by rain and snow. The Saudi Arabia peninsula is intensely hot and dry for most of the year, with summer temperatures often exceeding 30°C (86°F) and strong winds. Winters are cooler and may be damper, especially in the north and in the southwestern mountains where frosts and snow may occur.

		J	F	M	A	M	J	J	A	S	O	N	D	Year
hrain														
rain	°C	17.4	18.3	21.2	25.6	29.6	32.0	33.8	34.3	32.5	29.0	24.5	19.2	26.4
2 m	mm	16	15	11	6	1	0	0	0	0	0	9	18	76
n														
dan	°C	12.9	15.0	18.7	24.9	30.0	34.7	36.1	35.9	32.7	26.9	19.5	13.7	25.1
3 m	mm	20	15	19	15	4	0	0	0	0	1	32	41	144
man	°C	5.8	8.3	12.0	16.7	20.8	25.3	26.8	25.1	22.2	16.5	10.5	6.5	16.4
1749 m	mm	36	22	46	22	20	2	7	0	4	3	8	32	202
hhad	°C	2.3	3.7	7.2	13.6	18.5	23.0	25.8	24.1	20.0	13.7	7.0	3.2	13.5
985 m	mm	32	31	61	51	25	4	0	0	0	6	17	20	248
ráz	°C	6.5	8.2	11.7	16.2	21.5	26.0	28.5	27.4	24.4	18.5	12.1	7.5	17.4
1491 m	mm	77	47	63	24	13	0	1	0	0	0	65	93	383
riz	°C	0.6	0.8	4.9	11.3	16.0	20.8	24.3	24.6	20.6	14.0	6.0	0.3	12.0
1362 m	mm	15	32	45	47	43	23	11	1	9	14	29	16	285

		J	F	M	A	M	J	J	A	S	O	N	D
Tehran	°C	3.5	5.2	10.2	15.4	21.2	26.1	29.5	28.4	24.6	18.3	10.6	4.9
1590 m	mm	37	23	36	31	14	2	1	1	1	5	29	27

Iraq

		J	F	M	A	M	J	J	A	S	O	N	D
Al Díwaniya	°C	10.4	12.7	16.5	22.8	29.8	31.8	33.9	33.6	31.8	26.0	17.6	12.3
20 m	mm	17	15	19	19	9	0	0	0	0	1	15	25
Baghdad	°C	9.9	12.2	15.8	22.2	28.4	32.9	34.8	34.5	30.7	24.7	17.2	11.2
34 m	mm	25	25	29	16	7	0	0	0	0	3	22	26
Kirkuk	°C	8.6	10.2	13.3	19.4	26.4	32.3	35.1	34.8	30.4	24.2	16.5	10.6
331 m	mm	58	66	85	47	17	0	0	0	0	3	42	62
Mosul	°C	6.5	8.6	12.0	17.3	23.9	30.2	33.7	32.7	26.9	20.1	13.1	7.9
222 m	mm	70	67	65	55	20	1	0	0	0	7	43	62
Nasiriya	°C	11.8	13.7	16.9	23.7	29.6	32.7	34.1	34.2	31.6	25.9	18.8	12.6
3 m	mm	17	15	19	21	5	0	0	0	0	3	21	25
Rutbah	°C	6.8	8.8	12.5	18.2	23.8	26.9	30.3	30.1	26.6	21.1	13.8	8.3
615 m	mm	16	13	20	20	10	1	0	0	1	5	16	21

Israel

		J	F	M	A	M	J	J	A	S	O	N	D
Eilat	°C	15.8	17.5	20.3	24.5	28.9	32.0	33.5	33.7	30.7	27.4	21.6	17.0
11 m	mm	2	5	5	3	0	0	0	0	0	0	2	9
Jerusalem	°C	8.6	9.4	11.8	15.9	20.2	21.9	23.3	23.5	21.8	20.0	15.4	10.8
810 m	mm	128	106	85	17	4	0	0	0	1	8	61	82
Tel Aviv	°C	12.3	12.7	14.3	17.4	21.1	23.9	25.1	26.2	24.6	22.0	18.0	14.3
49 m	mm	131	93	58	15	4	0	0	0	2	18	79	129

Jordan

		J	F	M	A	M	J	J	A	S	O	N	D
Amman	°C	8.2	9.3	11.7	16.2	20.9	23.6	25.2	25.6	23.4	20.7	15.3	10.1
771 m	mm	68	59	44	13	5	0	0	0	1	4	31	48

Kuwait

		J	F	M	A	M	J	J	A	S	O	N	D
Shuwaikh	°C	13.9	15.6	20.0	25.6	30.6	35.0	36.7	36.7	33.3	27.2	20.6	15.0
11 m	mm	15	7	8	11	3	0	0	0	0	0	25	41

Lebanon

		J	F	M	A	M	J	J	A	S	O	N	D
Beirut	°C	13.9	14.1	15.3	18.1	21.0	24.1	26.2	27.1	25.7	23.0	18.0	15.5
16 m	mm	113	80	77	26	10	1	0	0	7	20	78	105
Rayack	°C	5.1	6.2	9.0	12.9	17.5	21.3	23.8	24.2	21.5	17.4	11.9	6.9
921 m	mm	159	123	78	34	16	0	0	0	1	16	66	113
Tripoli	°C	12.0	12.9	14.1	17.2	20.3	24.0	23.4	26.0	25.5	22.3	17.8	13.6
10 m	mm	190	110	104	44	16	1	0	0	12	23	101	144

Oman

		J	F	M	A	M	J	J	A	S	O	N	D
Salalam	°C	22.3	23.1	25.0	26.7	28.3	28.6	25.5	25.0	25.9	25.3	24.7	23.7
17 m	mm	2	2	2	2	2	5	28	25	3	13	2	8

Saudi Arabia

		J	F	M	A	M	J	J	A	S	O	N	D
Jeddah	°C	23.0	23.3	24.3	26.9	30.0	30.6	31.5	31.1	30.5	29.0	27.1	25.7
12 m	mm	3	1	0	0	1	0	0	0	0	0	12	8
Medina	°C	17.3	19.9	23.5	28.0	31.6	34.8	35.1	35.8	33.7	29.2	23.2	19.4
672 m	mm	0	3	10	4	1	0	0	0	0	0	9	10
Riyadh	°C	16.1	16.5	20.8	25.6	30.0	33.6	40.1	36.1	31.7	25.4	20.4	16.0
609 m	mm	24	6	6	11	15	0	0	2	0	0	11	7

th Yemen		J	F	M	A	M	J	J	A	S	O	N	D	Year
n	°C	25.5	25.6	27.2	28.7	30.7	32.8	32.2	31.6	31.7	28.9	26.6	26.0	28.9
3 m	mm	7	3	6	0	1	0	3	2	7	1	3	6	39
n	°C	22.8	23.9	25.0	26.9	28.6	30.3	28.9	28.3	28.6	26.4	25.0	23.9	26.5
o m	mm	8	3	15	5	2	3	3	3	2	2	18	8	72
ia														
po	°C	6.3	7.0	10.5	15.7	21.1	25.4	28.1	28.7	24.5	19.2	12.5	7.5	17.2
392 m	mm	63	46	36	35	14	4	0	2	0	18	27	74	319
ascus	°C	7.7	9.1	11.9	16.6	21.4	25.1	27.2	27.6	24.4	20.6	13.5	8.7	17.8
729 m	mm	54	39	29	15	6	0	0	0	0	5	26	60	234
r az Zawr	°C	7.6	10.4	13.0	19.1	24.2	29.5	32.4	32.4	27.5	21.2	13.7	8.4	19.9
203 m	mm	35	33	32	20	7	2	0	0	0	3	12	33	177
key														
na	°C	9.1	10.2	12.7	16.9	21.2	25.0	27.6	28.0	25.2	20.8	15.5	10.9	18.6
66 m	mm	111	93	66	45	47	18	4	5	17	42	62	102	612
ara	°C	−0.2	1.1	4.9	11.0	16.0	20.0	23.3	23.3	18.4	12.9	7.3	2.1	11.7
894 m	mm	37	36	36	37	49	30	14	9	17	24	30	43	362
alya	°C	10.0	10.6	12.6	16.2	20.5	25.0	28.2	28.1	24.9	20.3	15.5	11.6	18.6
43 m	mm	255	143	86	41	26	10	2	3	10	53	115	284	1028
bul	°C	4.6	4.3	5.3	9.7	14.9	19.6	22.2	22.0	17.9	13.8	10.3	6.9	12.6
34 m	mm	88	80	61	37	32	28	27	22	49	62	87	96	669
ir	°C	8.6	9.2	11.0	15.3	20.2	24.8	27.6	27.3	23.2	18.5	14.0	10.2	17.5
25 m	mm	141	100	72	43	39	8	3	3	11	41	93	141	695
p	°C	5.8	6.3	6.3	9.6	14.3	18.7	22.0	22.3	19.5	15.9	12.1	8.5	13.4
32 m	mm	84	56	48	48	38	41	31	43	71	69	104	109	742
ted Arab Emirates														
jah	°C	17.6	18.7	20.9	23.9	27.8	30.3	32.5	33.3	30.8	27.2	23.9	19.8	25.6
5 m	mm	23	23	10	5	0	0	0	0	0	0	10	36	107

Asia South

Afghanistan has cool-to-very-cold winters dominated by air masses from central Asia, and hot, dry summers. Peninsular India and Bangladesh lie in the path of the northeast trade winds, which blow cool and mainly dry from November to February or March. Between January and April or May, as the sun approaches the Tropic of Cancer, air temperatures rise while trade winds weaken and reverse, pulling in heavy monsoonal rains from the sea. Most heavily affected are the western coasts and eastern uplands of India, and the hills of Bangladesh; Cherrapunji, in northeastern India, has one of the world's heaviest rainfalls, exceeding 11 m (33 ft) annually. Pakistan and the central peninsula remain generally dry throughout the year. Southern India and Sri Lanka have uniformly hot and humid lowlands and cool, pleasant highlands, with little seasonal variation. While coastal Burma also receives heavy monsoon rains, the interior is relatively dry; temperatures are warm in winter, hot for the rest of the year.

Afghanistan

		J	F	M	A	M	J	J	A	S	O	N	D
Kabul	°C	−2.3	0.2	6.5	11.7	16.5	22.4	24.8	23.9	19.8	13.1	5.2	−0.3
1803 m	mm	28	61	72	117	33	1	7	1	0	1	37	14
Kandahar	°C	5.3	9.5	13.8	19.1	25.1	29.9	31.5	29.3	24.8	17.6	10.1	6.5
1010 m	mm	22	21	58	46	13	0	0	0	0	0	14	51
Mazar-i-Sharif	°C	3.9	6.7	10.8	17.2	23.1	28.8	31.6	28.9	23.4	16.3	7.2	3.6
378 m	mm	28	32	43	45	16	0	0	0	0	2	21	27

Bangladesh

		J	F	M	A	M	J	J	A	S	O	N	D
Chittagong	°C	19.9	23.6	25.6	27.7	28.3	27.8	27.5	27.6	27.8	27.3	24.1	20.7
14 m	mm	10	23	58	116	285	507	642	572	344	228	56	17
Narayanjanj	°C	19.8	22.2	26.6	28.7	29.1	29.0	28.7	28.8	29.2	28.2	24.5	20.9
8 m	mm	14	27	46	161	245	346	348	364	242	171	29	19

Burma

		J	F	M	A	M	J	J	A	S	O	N	D
Akyab	°C	21.1	22.8	25.9	28.4	29.2	27.7	27.0	27.0	27.9	27.7	25.4	22.2
5 m	mm	2	4	10	50	391	1151	1400	1134	577	286	130	19
Mandalay	°C	21.4	24.2	28.4	32.0	31.8	30.4	30.3	30.0	29.4	28.5	25.3	21.9
76 m	mm	1	5	5	36	149	151	72	102	148	127	64	11
Myitkyina	°C	17.0	19.2	22.7	25.2	27.6	27.5	27.5	27.5	27.4	25.0	21.3	17.3
147 m	mm	10	23	23	46	160	481	476	433	256	183	39	12
Rangoon	°C	24.8	26.3	28.9	30.5	29.2	27.4	26.6	26.5	27.1	27.5	26.8	25.4
23 m	mm	3	6	8	50	308	481	580	529	393	181	68	11
Victoria Point	°C	26.6	27.5	28.3	28.8	27.4	26.5	26.1	25.9	25.5	25.8	26.3	26.0
47 m	mm	10	17	55	130	503	720	731	663	711	447	161	58

India

		J	F	M	A	M	J	J	A	S	O	N	D
Bangalore	°C	20.9	23.1	25.7	27.3	26.9	24.3	23.2	23.3	23.3	23.3	21.7	20.5
921 m	mm	3	10	6	46	117	80	117	147	143	185	54	16
Bombay	°C	24.3	24.9	26.9	28.7	29.9	29.1	27.5	27.1	27.4	28.3	27.5	25.9
11 m	mm	2	1	0	3	16	520	709	419	297	88	21	2
Calcutta	°C	20.2	23.0	27.9	30.1	31.1	30.4	29.1	29.1	29.2	27.9	24.0	20.6
6 m	mm	13	24	27	43	121	259	301	306	290	160	35	3
Cherrapunji	°C	11.7	13.3	16.7	18.6	19.2	20.0	20.3	20.5	20.5	19.1	15.9	12.9
1313 m	mm	20	41	179	605	1705	2875	2855	1827	1231	447	47	5
Darjeeling	°C	6.4	7.7	11.2	14.3	15.7	17.0	17.5	17.5	17.2	15.1	11.3	8.1
2127 m	mm	22	27	53	109	187	522	713	573	419	116	14	5
Jodhpur	°C	17.1	19.9	25.2	30.3	34.4	34.3	31.3	29.2	29.4	27.7	22.7	18.7
224 m	mm	8	5	2	2	6	31	122	146	47	7	3	1
Madras	°C	24.5	25.8	27.5	30.5	32.7	32.5	30.7	30.1	29.7	28.1	25.9	24.6
16 m	mm	24	7	15	25	52	53	83	124	118	267	308	157
Minicoy (Laccadive Is)	°C	26.1	26.7	27.7	28.7	28.8	27.7	27.3	27.3	27.3	27.1	26.6	26.5
2 m	mm	35	25	16	52	200	293	212	200	144	185	141	76
Nagpur	°C	20.7	23.8	27.7	31.8	35.6	32.5	27.6	27.1	27.3	25.9	22.0	20.4
310 m	mm	14	19	22	20	13	210	407	288	173	65	17	3
New Dehli	°C	14.3	17.3	22.9	29.1	33.5	34.5	31.2	29.9	29.3	25.9	20.2	15.7
216 m	mm	25	22	17	7	8	65	211	173	150	31	1	5
Poona	°C	20.7	22.7	26.1	28.9	29.7	27.5	25.1	24.5	24.9	25.1	22.3	20.5
559 m	mm	2	0	3	18	35	103	187	106	127	92	37	5

		J	F	M	A	M	J	J	A	S	O	N	D	Year
·t Blair														
ndaman Is)	°C	26.6	26.4	27.5	28.6	28.0	26.9	26.5	26.6	26.5	26.6	26.9	25.7	26.9
79 m	mm	40	22	16	65	396	596	472	448	439	360	217	104	3176
nagar	°C	1.4	3.0	8.5	12.9	17.6	21.7	24.5	23.9	19.8	13.5	7.4	3.3	13.1
1586 m	mm	74	71	91	94	61	36	58	61	38	31	10	33	658
vandrum	°C	26.9	27.3	28.3	28.3	28.3	26.5	26.1	26.3	26.7	26.7	26.6	26.8	27.1
64 m	mm	19	21	44	122	249	331	211	164	123	271	207	73	1835
aval	°C	21.5	22.3	24.7	26.7	28.5	29.5	27.9	27.1	27.1	27.5	25.9	23.1	26.0
8 m	mm	1	1	0	5	5	135	305	146	65	28	7	1	699
hak-patnam	°C	23.4	25.3	28.1	30.6	31.9	31.3	29.3	29.5	29.0	28.1	25.7	23.7	28.0
3 m	mm	7	·15	9	13	53	88	125	99	167	261	90	17	944
·pal														
tmandu	°C	9.9	11.5	15.9	19.8	22.8	24.2	24.2	23.9	23.4	19.8	15.1	11.0	18.5
1316 m	mm	15	41	23	58	122	246	373	345	155	38	8	3	1427
·kistan														
derabad	°C	17.2	20.6	26.0	30.8	34.1	34.3	32.5	31.3	30.9	29.3	24.3	19.1	27.5
29 m	mm	4	5	1	2	4	6	69	44	15	3	1	3	157
obabad	°C	14.7	18.3	23.9	29.9	34.9	36.8	35.2	33.6	32.2	28.1	22.0	16.6	27.2
56 m	mm	8	8	7	2	4	6	37	22	1	0	1	3	99
lat	°C	2.8	5.2	9.2	13.9	18.3	22.3	24.4	23.2	18.9	13.3	8.3	4.6	13.7
2017 m	mm	54	46	38	15	6	3	30	14	2	0	3	19	230
rachi	°C	18.9	21.2	24.3	26.9	29.2	30.4	29.3	28.2	27.6	27.1	24.9	21.3	25.8
22 m	mm	7	11	6	2	0	7	96	50	15	2	2	6	204
hore	°C	12.2	15.3	20.5	26.6	31.8	33.9	32.1	31.2	29.9	25.4	18.8	13.8	24.3
214 m	mm	31	23	24	16	12	38	122	123	80	9	3	11	492
rree	°C	2.8	4.3	8.2	13.3	18.4	21.2	19.8	18.7	17.5	14.3	10.1	5.7	12.9
2168 m	mm	116	108	155	103	61	106	360	348	133	53	21	54	1618
sni	°C	18.6	20.0	23.3	26.7	29.5	30.5	29.7	28.4	27.5	26.6	23.5	20.3	25.4
9 m	mm	43	32	8	6	2	6	12	3	1	0	2	12	127
shawar	°C	10.7	13.2	17.4	22.9	29.1	33.1	32.6	30.9	28.9	23.7	17.5	12.5	27.2
359 m	mm	39	41	65	42	40	7	39	41	14	10	10	15	363
i Lanka														
lombo	°C	26.2	26.4	27.2	27.7	28.0	27.4	27.1	27.2	27.2	26.6	26.2	26.1	26.9
6 m	mm	88	96	118	260	353	212	140	124	153	354	324	175	2397
ncomalee	°C	25.6	26.2	27.3	28.7	29.8	29.9	29.7	29.4	29.3	27.8	26.3	25.7	28.0
7 m	mm	211	95	48	77	68	18	54	103	89	235	355	374	1727

Asia Southeast

The peninsula of southeastern Asia lies in the northeast trade winds, which in winter blow cool and generally dry from the continental heartland of China. March and April are transitional months of increasing heat; late April and May bring monsoon rains from the southwest, which continue almost daily until October or November. The southern peninsula and the widely-scattered southern islands that span the Equator have a similar system of alternating winds but are generally hot and wet throughout the year, with heaviest rains from October to March. The eastern islands usually have a dry season, the Philippines from February/March to May/June and the southeastern islands from June to August.

Cambodia		J	F	M	A	M	J	J	A	S	O	N	D
Kampot	°C	26.0	26.8	27.9	28.5	28.1	27.4	27.1	26.9	26.8	26.8	26.3	26.0
5 m	mm	15	33	89	141	168	226	248	390	267	280	164	45
Kompong Cham	°C	25.6	27.0	28.6	29.3	28.1	27.6	27.1	27.0	26.9	26.7	26.0	25.1
16 m	mm	2	6	29	77	246	228	219	274	253	246	112	6
Stung-Treng	°C	24.3	26.5	28.9	29.8	28.3	27.5	26.8	26.6	26.3	26.2	25.2	23.9
54 m	mm	1	11	18	73	213	259	254	344	299	183	68	6

Indonesia

		J	F	M	A	M	J	J	A	S	O	N	D
Balikpapan (Kalimantan)	°C	26.1	26.4	26.4	26.1	26.4	26.1	25.6	26.1	26.1	26.4	26.1	26.1
7 m	mm	201	175	231	208	231	193	180	163	140	132	168	206
Biak (Irian Jaya)	°C	26.7	26.6	26.7	27.1	27.1	26.8	26.5	26.7	26.8	27.3	27.4	26.9
11 m	mm	216	215	203	157	237	222	329	261	188	154	190	280
Dili (Loro Sae)	°C	26.6	26.4	26.4	26.2	26.1	25.0	24.3	23.6	23.8	25.3	26.8	27.1
4 m	mm	159	163	113	79	35	114	60	27	14	16	38	157
Jakarta (Java)	°C	26.2	26.3	27.1	27.2	27.3	27.0	26.7	27.0	27.4	27.4	26.9	26.6
8 m	mm	335	241	201	141	116	97	61	50	78	91	151	193
Manokwari (Irian Jaya)	°C	26.1	26.0	26.2	26.2	26.5	26.3	26.0	26.2	26.2	26.7	26.6	26.4
3 m	mm	295	255	268	334	259	163	216	128	144	84	185	266
Merauke (Irian Jaya)	°C	26.8	26.5	26.6	26.5	26.2	25.2	24.6	24.6	25.1	26.3	27.2	27.2
3 m	mm	204	352	202	186	83	53	37	16	8	27	62	226
Padang (Sumatra)	°C	26.9	26.9	26.9	27.2	27.5	26.9	26.9	26.9	26.6	26.6	26.6	26.6
7 m	mm	351	259	307	363	315	307	277	348	152	495	518	480
Ujung Pandang (Sulawesi)	°C	26.1	26.4	26.4	26.7	26.9	26.1	25.6	25.6	25.8	26.4	26.7	26.1
14 m	mm	686	536	424	150	89	74	36	10	15	43	178	610

Laos

		J	F	M	A	M	J	J	A	S	O	N	D
Luang Prabang	°C	20.5	22.6	25.6	27.9	28.4	27.9	27.4	27.2	26.9	25.7	23.4	20.1
304 m	mm	17	20	37	78	128	157	204	261	146	63	16	10
Pakse	°C	24.6	26.7	28.6	29.9	28.7	28.1	27.2	27.0	26.9	26.6	25.9	24.2
93 m	mm	2	8	32	38	140	264	246	418	296	84	13	1
Vientiane	°C	21.5	23.8	26.7	28.8	28.4	28.1	27.7	27.4	27.1	26.4	24.4	21.4
170 m	mm	15	14	25	78	225	261	260	354	385	49	16	1

Malaysia

		J	F	M	A	M	J	J	A	S	O	N	D
Kota Baharu	°C	25.9	26.5	27.3	28.1	28.1	27.9	27.4	27.3	27.1	26.8	26.0	25.8
9 m	mm	211	73	112	87	142	145	155	150	191	326	617	546
Kuala Lumpur	°C	26.8	27.2	27.4	27.3	27.7	27.1	27.1	27.1	27.0	26.8	26.7	26.6
38 m	mm	157	209	277	285	207	121	117	157	206	251	289	223
Kuching	°C	25.8	26.1	26.9	27.5	27.5	27.8	27.2	27.5	26.9	27.2	26.7	26.4
26 m	mm	610	511	328	279	262	180	196	234	218	267	358	462

		J	F	M	A	M	J	J	A	S	O	N	D	Year
uan	°C	27.2	27.2	27.5	28.1	28.1	27.8	28.1	27.8	27.5	27.5	27.5	27.2	27.6
18 m	mm	112	117	150	297	345	351	317	297	417	465	419	284	2571

ilippines

		J	F	M	A	M	J	J	A	S	O	N	D	Year
rri	°C	23.7	24.5	26.3	28.0	29.3	29.4	29.2	28.7	28.0	27.2	25.7	24.3	27.0
4 m	mm	146	108	51	35	106	157	165	224	307	390	386	237	2312
o	°C	25.9	26.2	26.8	28.0	28.4	27.8	27.4	27.1	27.2	27.2	26.9	26.2	27.1
14 m	mm	53	28	37	48	146	263	302	360	290	255	209	131	2120
ıila	°C	25.4	26.1	27.2	28.9	29.4	28.5	27.9	27.4	27.4	27.2	26.4	25.4	27.3
15 m	mm	18	7	6	24	110	236	253	480	271	201	129	56	1791
igao	°C	25.7	25.7	26.2	26.9	27.4	27.6	27.4	27.8	27.7	27.3	26.7	25.9	26.9
22 m	mm	589	405	398	258	184	112	195	149	197	308	415	653	3863
ıboanga	°C	26.6	26.8	27.2	27.5	27.5	27.1	26.6	26.9	26.8	26.9	26.9	26.6	26.9
6 m	mm	51	49	44	54	96	131	120	138	139	173	135	96	1226

ıgapore

		J	F	M	A	M	J	J	A	S	O	N	D	Year
gapore	°C	26.1	26.7	27.2	27.6	27.8	28.0	27.4	27.3	27.3	27.2	26.7	26.3	27.1
10 m	mm	285	164	154	160	131	177	163	200	122	184	236	306	2282

ailand

		J	F	M	A	M	J	J	A	S	O	N	D	Year
gkok	°C	26.1	27.6	29.2	30.3	29.8	28.9	28.4	28.2	27.9	27.6	26.7	25.5	28.0
12 m	mm	9	29	34	89	166	171	178	191	306	255	57	7	1492
angmai	°C	21.3	23.1	23.4	29.0	28.8	27.9	27.4	27.0	26.8	26.2	24.4	21.5	25.6
313 m	mm	7	12	15	49	144	146	188	231	289	126	39	10	1254
hon														
tchasima	°C	23.4	26.5	28.8	30.0	29.5	28.7	28.2	27.9	27.4	26.2	24.3	22.5	27.0
181 m	mm	7	33	45	83	157	111	132	139	244	171	37	3	1162

ɩtnam

		J	F	M	A	M	J	J	A	S	O	N	D	Year
Nang	°C	21.2	22.6	24.4	26.3	28.3	29.3	29.1	28.8	27.4	25.6	23.9	21.7	25.7
7 m	mm	91	42	39	43	38	130	60	87	283	533	417	206	1970
ıoi	°C	16.8	17.6	20.4	24.4	28.0	29.7	29.4	29.1	28.0	25.5	21.8	18.7	24.4
16 m	mm	18	28	38	81	196	239	323	343	254	99	43	20	1682
Chi														
nh City	°C	25.8	26.3	27.8	28.8	28.2	27.4	27.1	27.1	26.7	26.5	26.1	25.7	27.0
10 m	mm	6	13	12	65	196	285	242	277	292	259	122	37	1808
Trang	°C	24.0	24.5	25.9	27.3	28.1	28.5	28.1	28.1	27.4	26.3	25.4	24.4	26.5
6 m	mm	28	12	16	33	53	49	50	52	127	259	269	148	1095

Asia East

Northern and central China, Mongolia and Tibet are chilled in winter by cold, dry air from Siberia, and warmed in summer by moist Pacific air from the south, which brings heavy rain to the lowlands and light summer showers to the high plateaus. Southern China lies under Pacific influences for most of the year, providing cool, rainy weather in winter and warm humid conditions in summer. Japan and the neighbouring mainland have cool maritime climates, with a marked temperature gradient from north to south. In winter they are dominated by cold air masses from north and west, northern Japan especially enduring cold rain and snow for several months. In summer southern and easterly winds from the Pacific bring warmth and moisture, making the northern islands temperate and the southern subtropical.

China

		J	F	M	A	M	J	J	A	S	O	N	D
Beihai	°C	15.7	14.8	18.5	23.8	27.7	28.0	29.1	28.6	28.0	25.5	21.0	16.8
4.3 m	mm	30	41	69	89	180	269	500	483	254	91	43	41
Changsha	°C	4.5	5.9	11.5	17.4	23.2	26.6	30.2	30.2	25.8	19.6	13.7	7.3
61 m	mm	48	94	135	145	208	221	112	109	69	76	69	38
Chengtu	°C	5.9	8.1	11.8	17.1	21.8	24.9	26.6	26.1	22.1	17.6	12.3	8.1
491 m	mm	5	10	15	48	61	114	221	292	160	53	13	5
Chungking	°C	7.3	10.1	14.8	19.3	23.2	26.1	29.4	30.2	24.9	19.0	14.0	10.6
230 m	mm	15	20	38	99	142	180	143	122	150	112	48	20
Harbin	°C	-18.5	-14.8	-4.8	5.9	13.4	19.3	22.4	21.3	14.5	4.5	-5.9	-15.7
160 m	mm	5	5	10	23	43	94	112	104	46	33	8	5
Kashgar	°C	-5.3	-0.6	7.6	15.4	21.0	24.9	26.7	25.8	21.3	14.0	5.3	-2.5
1310 m	mm	15	3	13	5	8	5	10	8	3	3	5	8
Kunming	°C	9.5	10.9	11.2	17.6	19.9	21.0	20.4	20.4	19.6	16.5	12.9	10.1
1894 m	mm	10	13	18	20	109	160	224	218	127	76	43	10
Lanchow	°C	-6.7	-0.8	5.0	11.5	17.4	20.7	22.6	21.8	16.5	10.3	1.7	-3.6
1557 m	mm	5	5	5	13	20	18	84	130	56	15	2	8
Lhasa	°C	-1.7	1.1	4.7	8.1	12.3	16.8	16.5	15.7	14.3	9.0	4.0	0.0
3687 m	mm	2	13	8	5	26	63	122	89	66	13	3	1
Shanghai	°C	4.3	4.7	8.7	14.5	20.1	23.8	28.0	28.0	23.5	18.7	12.3	7.6
7 m	mm	48	58	84	94	94	180	147	142	130	71	51	36
Sian	°C	-0.3	3.1	10.6	17.1	23.2	28.3	30.0	28.9	22.6	16.5	8.4	2.2
365 m	mm	8	8	18	46	48	46	99	99	58	41	13	8
Wulumuchi	°C	-16.2	-14.0	-5.9	9.0	15.4	19.0	21.3	20.1	14.5	4.7	-5.9	-10.9
906 m	mm	15	8	13	38	28	38	18	26	15	43	41	10
Yatung	°C	0.0	1.4	4.5	8.1	11.2	13.7	15.1	14.5	13.2	9.0	4.3	1.1
2989 m	mm	15	48	63	99	107	119	130	117	102	53	18	5

Hong Kong

		J	F	M	A	M	J	J	A	S	O	N	D
Hong Kong	°C	15.4	15.8	18.2	21.8	25.6	27.5	28.4	27.9	27.3	24.7	21.2	17.4
33 m	mm	30	60	70	133	332	479	286	415	364	33	46	17

Japan

		J	F	M	A	M	J	J	A	S	O	N	D
Akita	°C	-1.1	-0.8	2.2	8.1	13.4	18.3	22.5	24.2	19.3	13.0	7.1	1.7
10 m	mm	123	102	107	128	119	138	190	164	205	176	179	158
Asahigawa	°C	-8.9	-7.9	-3.3	4.1	10.9	16.0	20.3	21.1	15.4	8.6	1.3	-5.1
113 m	mm	82	61	56	61	78	75	125	144	136	109	118	101
Fukuoka	°C	5.1	5.7	8.7	13.5	17.8	21.7	26.3	26.8	22.8	16.9	12.2	7.6
4 m	mm	69	83	98	129	127	270	253	171	244	102	80	78
Hiroshima	°C	4.2	4.7	7.6	12.7	17.1	21.0	25.4	26.6	22.7	16.7	11.5	6.6
30 m	mm	45	70	106	158	154	249	250	116	216	115	67	51
Kagoshima	°C	6.6	7.7	10.8	15.1	19.0	22.6	26.8	27.1	24.4	18.9	14.0	9.0
5 m	mm	75	116	149	228	249	454	343	220	213	120	90	79
Kochi	°C	5.2	6.3	9.6	14.4	18.5	21.8	25.7	26.3	23.5	18.0	12.9	7.8
2 m	mm	55	97	177	261	279	344	369	344	350	184	108	80
Maebashi	°C	2.4	2.9	6.1	11.6	16.4	20.4	24.4	25.3	21.2	15.3	10.1	5.1
113 m	mm	21	33	49	77	99	166	198	199	196	138	48	24
Matsumoto	°C	-1.1	-1.0	3.1	9.4	14.7	19.1	23.4	24.0	19.4	12.5	6.5	1.7
611 m	mm	35	49	65	84	87	142	132	116	138	118	58	39
Myakojima	°C	17.7	18.0	19.6	21.8	24.8	26.7	28.1	27.6	27.1	24.7	22.3	19.4
40 m	mm	152	151	137	178	247	298	219	296	167	154	146	114
Nagoya	°C	2.9	3.6	7.1	12.7	17.5	21.5	25.7	26.6	22.7	16.5	10.9	5.6
56 m	mm	49	64	100	137	145	204	178	155	212	160	86	57

		J	F	M	A	M	J	J	A	S	O	N	D	Year
ata	°C	1.7	1.8	4.8	10.2	15.3	19.9	24.1	25.8	21.4	15.5	9.8	4.7	12.9
4 m	mm	194	126	121	104	95	127	193	107	177	165	171	264	1841
ka	°C	4.5	4.9	8.0	13.6	18.3	22.3	26.6	27.8	23.7	17.4	11.9	7.0	15.5
8 m	mm	43	58	96	127	122	193	178	118	171	122	81	52	1359
dai	°C	0.1	0.6	3.5	9.0	13.9	17.8	22.0	23.8	19.8	13.8	8.2	2.9	11.3
40 m	mm	37	44	62	95	100	155	167	136	191	133	61	50	1232
yo	°C	3.7	4.3	7.6	13.1	17.6	21.1	25.1	26.4	22.8	16.7	11.3	6.1	14.7
6 m	mm	48	73	101	135	131	182	146	147	217	220	101	61	1563
ishima	°C	14.6	14.4	15.7	18.1	20.2	23.2	26.5	27.1	26.9	23.8	20.3	17.0	20.6
83 m	mm	100	110	92	159	261	249	108	114	155	286	191	131	1954
kanai	°C	−5.9	−5.6	−1.8	4.0	8.4	12.2	16.7	19.6	16.6	10.7	3.0	−2.9	6.2
3 m	mm	94	62	65	63	78	70	112	105	152	129	120	112	1161

cau

		J	F	M	A	M	J	J	A	S	O	N	D	Year
au	°C	15.1	15.4	18.2	21.8	26.0	27.8	28.5	28.2	27.5	24.5	20.8	16.5	22.5
55 m	mm	26	54	83	156	263	346	292	293	205	57	43	28	1846

ngolia

		J	F	M	A	M	J	J	A	S	O	N	D	Year
n Bator	°C	−25.8	−21.3	−12.9	−0.8	5.6	13.7	16.2	14.3	8.1	−0.8	−12.9	−22.4	−3.2
1326 m	mm	2	2	3	5	10	28	76	51	23	5	5	3	213

rth Korea

		J	F	M	A	M	J	J	A	S	O	N	D	Year
isan	°C	−3.6	−2.2	2.8	9.8	15.4	19.6	23.2	23.8	19.0	13.4	5.9	−0.8	10.6
o m	mm	38	36	48	71	89	124	274	317	178	76	66	30	1339

ith Korea

		J	F	M	A	M	J	J	A	S	O	N	D	Year
ion	°C	−4.0	−1.6	3.4	9.7	15.3	19.6	23.9	25.1	20.6	14.2	7.2	−0.4	11.1
70 m	mm	16	18	50	66	73	139	304	180	137	45	35	50	1093
po	°C	1.0	2.1	5.9	11.5	16.5	20.6	24.8	26.1	21.7	16.1	10.3	4.3	13.4
33 m	mm	37	40	58	83	102	136	183	188	156	55	44	43	1126
an	°C	1.8	3.5	7.3	12.5	16.7	19.8	23.7	25.4	21.6	16.6	11.1	5.0	13.8
71 m	mm	25	44	89	114	139	198	248	165	205	73	44	39	1982

wan

		J	F	M	A	M	J	J	A	S	O	N	D	Year
gchun	°C	20.6	21.2	22.8	25.0	27.1	27.7	27.8	27.6	27.1	25.7	23.9	21.6	24.8
24 m	mm	17	26	21	53	151	466	584	538	357	137	87	25	2462
ghu (scadores)	°C	16.4	16.3	19.0	22.5	25.7	27.5	28.4	28.2	27.6	25.0	22.1	18.5	23.1
11 m	mm	23	44	65	76	98	189	195	178	128	47	19	28	1090
ei	°C	15.2	15.4	17.5	20.9	24.5	26.8	28.4	28.3	26.9	23.3	20.5	17.2	22.1
9 m	mm	91	147	164	182	205	322	269	266	189	117	71	77	2100

OCEANIA

Oceania Southwest

Most of the western, central and eastern interior of Australia is hot and chronically dry, with meagre and unreliable rainfall. The southwest has a Mediterranean climate with reliable winter rains; the southeast receives intermittent rain from easterly-moving depressions, and the east coast is dampened year-round by rain from the southeast trade winds, especially in summer. The far north and Papua New Guinea share a tropical climate with heaviest rains in summer. Much of New Zealand lies in the Roaring Forties, squarely in the path of the westerlies that bring heavy rain to the southwest coast and southern mountains. The east is drier and often cooler, Antarctic and subtropical air masses bringing alternating extremes of temperature in rapid succession.

Australia

		J	F	M	A	M	J	J	A	S	O	N	D
Adelaide	°C	22.6	21.0	20.9	17.2	14.6	12.1	11.2	12.0	13.4	16.0	18.5	20.7
44 m	mm	23	23	21	50	66	61	61	59	49	47	36	27
Alice Springs	°C	28.2	27.4	24.7	20.2	15.5	12.4	11.9	14.1	18.2	22.6	25.4	27.6
548 m	mm	27	45	18	10	18	15	14	10	6	25	23	39
Brisbane	°C	25.0	24.7	23.6	21.2	18.2	15.8	15.0	16.1	18.1	20.7	22.5	24.3
41 m	mm	143	183	147	78	57	56	49	30	45	77	92	136
Broome	°C	29.9	29.6	29.8	28.7	24.9	22.2	21.1	22.8	25.2	27.4	29.1	30.2
12 m	mm	121	148	75	32	38	22	8	2	2	1	10	34
Canberra	°C	20.2	19.4	17.5	12.9	8.9	6.4	5.5	6.7	9.3	12.1	15.2	18.4
560 m	mm	63	59	60	47	59	47	43	40	43	72	63	55
Carnarvon	°C	24.4	25.3	24.2	21.8	18.5	15.8	14.9	15.3	17.6	18.8	20.8	22.4
5 m	mm	5	22	23	7	49	50	52	16	5	4	1	1
Cloncurry	°C	30.7	29.5	28.5	25.4	21.2	17.9	17.6	19.4	23.3	27.4	29.9	31.1
188 m	mm	112	130	78	16	26	9	9	6	8	18	26	68
Darwin	°C	28.2	27.9	28.3	28.2	26.8	25.4	25.1	25.8	27.7	29.1	29.2	28.7
27 m	mm	341	338	271	121	9	1	2	5	17	66	156	233
Hobart	°C	16.3	16.1	15.1	12.4	10.5	8.3	7.8	8.8	10.6	11.8	13.6	15.1
54 m	mm	42	47	52	63	51	66	47	53	53	72	58	64
Lord Howe Island	°C	22.6	22.9	22.2	20.4	18.5	16.8	15.9	15.7	16.6	17.9	19.6	21.3
11 m	mm	105	124	119	153	177	183	166	149	141	131	125	120
Melbourne	°C	19.9	19.7	18.4	15.1	12.5	10.2	9.6	10.5	12.4	14.3	16.2	18.4
28 m	mm	45	59	50	69	54	52	54	50	58	74	70	58
Mildura	°C	24.7	23.3	21.5	16.6	12.9	10.7	9.5	11.1	13.6	16.3	19.2	21.9
50 m	mm	21	19	16	17	35	28	30	33	28	38	31	13
Norfolk Island	°C	21.7	22.3	21.6	20.2	18.4	16.8	15.6	15.6	16.2	17.3	19.1	20.6
110 m	mm	132	92	96	99	158	164	147	128	105	104	61	94
Perth	°C	23.4	23.9	22.2	19.2	16.1	13.7	13.1	13.5	14.7	16.3	19.2	21.5
60 m	mm	7	12	22	52	125	192	183	135	69	54	23	15
Port Hedland	°C	30.4	30.6	30.5	28.4	23.4	20.3	19.2	20.6	23.7	25.7	28.9	29.7
8 m	mm	56	86	36	15	45	21	15	4	1	1	1	19
Sydney	°C	21.9	21.9	21.2	18.3	15.7	13.1	12.3	13.4	15.3	17.6	19.4	21.0
42 m	mm	104	125	129	101	115	141	94	83	72	80	77	86
Thursday Island	°C	27.7	27.5	27.2	27.5	27.2	26.2	25.5	25.7	26.3	27.5	28.4	28.5
61 m	mm	385	335	350	201	64	22	10	11	3	11	39	175
Townsville	°C	27.3	27.0	26.3	24.6	22.1	19.6	19.2	20.0	21.9	24.6	26.5	27.4
4 m	mm	332	364	275	83	34	26	22	10	10	21	55	102

Coral Sea Islands Territory (Australia)

		J	F	M	A	M	J	J	A	S	O	N	D
Willis Island	°C	27.8	27.5	27.2	26.4	25.3	23.9	23.4	23.7	24.5	25.5	26.7	27.5
0 m	mm	168	282	175	178	66	71	48	18	23	18	36	91

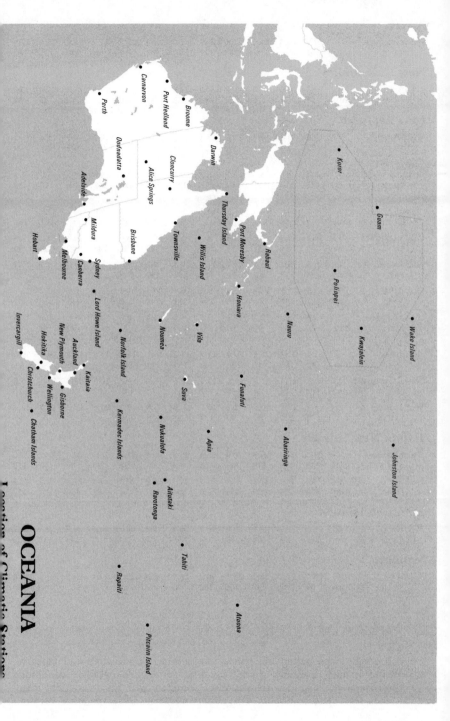

OCEANIA

Location of Climatic Stations

Nauru

		J	F	M	A	M	J	J	A	S	O	N	D
Nauru	°C	27.5	27.4	27.4	27.5	27.5	27.6	27.4	27.5	27.7	27.8	27.9	27.6
37 m	mm	331	253	192	200	172	117	151	158	96	130	131	305

New Caledonia

		J	F	M	A	M	J	J	A	S	O	N	D
Nouméa	°C	25.6	26.0	25.0	23.4	22.0	20.5	19.4	19.9	20.6	22.1	24.0	25.3
75 m	mm	117	94	174	124	93	89	84	70	53	52	47	85

New Zealand

		J	F	M	A	M	J	J	A	S	O	N	D
Auckland	°C	19.0	19.0	18.1	16.2	13.5	11.5	10.5	11.0	12.4	14.0	15.4	17.3
38 m	mm	79	94	81	97	127	137	145	117	102	102	89	79
Campbell Island	°C	9.4	9.1	8.7	7.4	6.3	5.1	4.6	5.6	5.9	6.5	7.2	7.9
19 m	mm	123	113	135	115	141	132	109	116	107	116	112	122
Chatham Islands	°C	14.0	14.0	13.5	11.8	10.2	8.1	7.4	7.7	8.8	10.2	11.3	12.9
48 m	mm	63	63	74	66	89	89	97	79	63	53	61	56
Christchurch	°C	16.4	16.7	14.6	12.3	8.7	6.3	5.0	6.9	9.3	10.8	13.8	16.5
34 m	mm	47	51	52	51	81	52	53	51	48	49	42	56
Gisborne	°C	18.1	18.5	16.7	14.4	11.9	9.8	9.1	9.7	11.2	13.3	15.4	17.2
8 m	mm	66	78	86	99	114	91	130	109	81	71	61	53
Hokitika	°C	14.8	15.1	14.1	11.9	9.4	6.8	6.4	7.7	9.1	10.7	12.2	13.7
40 m	mm	244	246	203	226	244	211	221	218	190	246	241	231
Invercargill	°C	13.3	13.5	12.4	10.2	7.5	5.5	4.8	6.2	8.2	9.8	11.1	12.3
1 m	mm	99	94	96	98	98	104	75	71	72	80	88	88
Kermadec Islands	°C	21.4	22.1	21.4	20.4	18.7	17.2	16.1	15.9	15.8	17.4	18.7	20.6
49 m	mm	82	166	137	126	162	155	170	143	112	83	77	91
New Plymouth	°C	16.5	17.3	16.2	14.1	11.9	10.1	9.1	9.7	10.8	12.3	13.8	15.2
48 m	mm	112	114	86	130	152	165	152	147	107	140	114	127
Wellington	°C	15.4	15.7	14.6	13.2	10.7	8.8	7.8	8.4	9.5	11.0	12.6	14.4
119 m	mm	74	104	80	90	127	123	128	116	92	116	79	95

Papua New Guinea

		J	F	M	A	M	J	J	A	S	O	N	D
Port Moresby	°C	27.6	27.3	27.3	26.9	25.4	26.2	25.8	26.1	26.5	27.2	27.5	27.7
43 m	mm	178	193	170	107	63	33	28	18	25	36	48	112
Rabaul	°C	27.3	27.3	27.1	27.2	27.4	27.3	26.9	27.2	27.6	27.6	27.5	27.3
6 m	mm	376	264	259	254	132	84	137	94	89	130	180	257

Solomon Islands

		J	F	M	A	M	J	J	A	S	O	N	D
Honiara	°C	26.8	26.7	26.5	26.6	26.7	26.4	26.2	26.3	26.5	26.7	26.8	26.7
58 m	mm	245	276	404	219	118	95	80	74	93	139	131	222

Vanuatu

		J	F	M	A	M	J	J	A	S	O	N	D
Vila	°C	26.7	27.2	26.4	25.5	24.2	23.4	22.3	22.3	23.1	24.5	25.0	26.4
56 m	mm	259	285	297	244	142	125	97	89	97	122	168	180

Oceania North, Central and Southeast

A generally stable pattern of northeast and southeast trade winds dominates the Pacific islands, bringing warm, equable, very stable weather conditions throughout the year. Sea temperatures dominate with little variation; many islands show less than 5°C (9°F) difference in mean temperature between summer and winter, and even diurnal variations are slight. Rains are generally plentiful, often heavier in summer than winter. Typhoons are fairly common, especially in the northwestern Pacific in late summer and autumn. Southern and northern islands that lie outside the trade wind zones for part of the year may experience easterly-moving depressions in winter, with strong cold winds and even flurries of snow.

EANIA NORTH

m		J	F	M	A	M	J	J	A	S	O	N	D	Year
m	°C	25.6	25.7	25.9	26.6	26.8	26.8	26.4	26.3	26.3	26.2	26.3	25.9	26.2
62 m	mm	118	89	67	77	106	149	228	326	339	333	261	155	2249

ston Island (US)

		J	F	M	A	M	J	J	A	S	O	N	D	Year
ston Island	°C	25.0	24.9	25.1	25.5	26.2	26.8	27.2	27.5	27.6	27.2	26.4	25.6	26.3
m	mm	99	39	59	58	25	21	33	57	60	83	52	76	663

Trust Territory of the Pacific Islands

		J	F	M	A	M	J	J	A	S	O	N	D	Year
r (Belau)	°C	26.8	26.8	27.1	27.4	27.4	27.3	27.1	27.2	27.2	27.3	27.3	27.2	27.2
3 m	mm	298	181	194	264	372	330	385	400	364	332	328	298	3746
jalein														
rshall Is)	°C	26.7	26.7	26.9	27.1	27.3	27.4	27.6	27.7	27.7	27.7	27.4	27.1	27.3
m	mm	92	55	164	128	208	220	226	242	259	276	308	228	2407
pei														
roline Is)	°C	26.9	26.9	26.9	26.9	26.9	26.7	26.5	26.3	26.4	26.4	26.6	26.7	26.7
6 m	mm	281	247	370	509	516	424	412	415	402	406	428	466	4875

e Island (US)

		J	F	M	A	M	J	J	A	S	O	N	D	Year
Island	°C	25.2	25.1	25.4	25.8	26.5	27.4	27.8	28.0	28.1	27.6	26.9	26.1	26.7
m	mm	29	34	37	47	52	48	117	180	133	134	78	46	936

EANIA CENTRAL

k Islands

		J	F	M	A	M	J	J	A	S	O	N	D	Year
taki	°C	27.4	27.4	27.4	26.6	25.8	24.4	24.6	24.1	24.9	25.2	26.3	26.6	25.8
m	mm	236	279	257	175	130	107	76	81	81	145	183	224	1974
tonga	°C	26.1	26.1	25.8	24.6	23.5	22.1	21.8	21.8	22.1	23.2	23.8	25.2	74.5
m	mm	234	257	284	196	150	122	112	119	127	135	163	206	2105
	°C	26.9	26.9	26.9	26.1	24.9	23.8	23.2	23.2	23.8	24.4	25.2	26.3	25.2
m	mm	290	271	368	310	257	170	124	211	196	211	249	317	2974

bati

		J	F	M	A	M	J	J	A	S	O	N	D	Year
iringa	°C	28.4	28.3	28.4	28.7	28.8	28.8	28.7	28.6	28.7	28.7	28.7	28.4	28.6
m	mm	66	54	63	92	110	67	66	64	31	28	41	65	748

ga

		J	F	M	A	M	J	J	A	S	O	N	D	Year
alofa	°C	25.8	26.3	26.1	24.9	23.2	21.8	21.5	21.5	21.5	22.6	24.1	24.4	23.5
m	mm	135	191	218	130	140	109	109	137	112	99	104	127	1611

alu

		J	F	M	A	M	J	J	A	S	O	N	D	Year
futi	°C	29.1	28.9	29.1	28.9	28.9	28.3	27.7	28.3	28.6	29.1	29.7	29.1	28.6
m	mm	406	450	404	279	185	274	259	292	345	358	312	437	4001

345

Western Samoa		J	F	M	A	M	J	J	A	S	O	N	D
Apia	°C	28.4	28.3	28.4	28.7	28.8	28.8	28.7	28.6	28.7	28.7	28.7	28.4
2 m	mm	424	364	352	214	186	130	115	111	147	221	279	385

OCEANIA SOUTHEAST

French Polynesia

Atuona	°C	26.3	26.4	27.0	26.8	26.3	25.7	25.2	24.9	25.2	25.4	25.4	25.8
52 m	mm	88	92	106	97	98	183	118	95	102	68	53	68
Rapaiti	°C	23.1	23.7	23.2	21.8	20.2	18.7	18.1	17.4	17.5	18.9	20.3	22.1
7 m	mm	311	219	257	254	203	149	279	225	193	202	171	193
Tahiti	°C	26.0	26.2	26.5	26.3	25.5	24.6	24.1	23.9	24.3	24.8	25.6	26.0
2 m	mm	423	240	122	92	144	60	70	47	103	81	166	252

Pitcairn Islands

Pitcairn Island	°C	24.9	26.1	25.5	23.5	22.6	21.3	20.1	20.1	20.4	21.3	22.6	24.1
0 m	mm	91	114	84	208	178	130	271	185	69	107	69	193

THE AMERICAS

North America and Bermuda

Arctic air dominates eastern and central Canada for much of the year, and spreads far south into the US in winter, bringing long, very cold winters to the eastern seaboard and north central states. Western Canada and the northwestern US share a damp maritime climate, mild and rainy in winter, cool-to-warm and still moist in summer. Further south, the west coast and mountains receive warm, moist but stable air from the Pacific, while the eastern and southern Rocky Mountains, eastern foothills and central plains remain relatively dry. The south central and eastern states have short cool winters and long, hot humid summers, dominated by warm tropical air. Hurricanes are common along the south and eastern coasts in late summer and fall. Bermuda has a subtropical maritime climate, warm but with occasional boisterous winds.

Bermuda		J	F	M	A	M	J	J	A	S	O	N	D
Hamilton	°C	17.0	16.9	16.9	18.3	21.1	23.9	26.1	26.7	25.5	23.3	20.0	18.3
46 m	mm	112	119	122	104	117	112	114	137	132	147	127	119

Canada

Churchill (Man)	°C	−27.6	−25.6	−19.5	−10.1	−2.2	6.2	12.2	11.7	5.6	−1.4	−11.9	−21.6
35 m	mm	17	17	21	36	40	48	39	60	52	42	46	25
Coppermine (NWT)	°C	−28.6	−30.1	−25.8	−17.2	−5.6	3.4	9.3	8.4	2.6	−6.9	−19.9	−26.3
0 m	mm	13	8	15	14	12	20	34	44	29	27	17	13
Edmonton (Alta)	°C	−14.1	−11.6	−5.5	4.2	11.2	14.3	17.3	15.6	10.8	5.1	−4.2	−10.4
676 m	mm	24	20	21	28	47	80	85	65	34	23	22	25

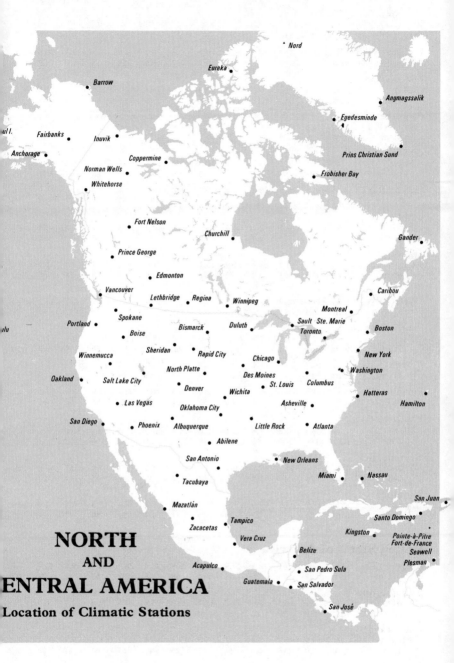

NORTH
AND
ENTRAL AMERICA
Location of Climatic Stations

347

World Climates

		J	F	M	A	M	J	J	A	S	O	N	D
Eureka (NWT)	°C	−35.9	−37.3	−37.6	−26.8	−9.7	2.7	5.7	3.8	−6.7	−21.6	−30.6	−35.2
11 m	mm	3	2	2	2	3	3	16	14	11	9	2	2
Fort Nelson (BC)	°C	−22.4	−17.2	−8.8	1.2	10.0	14.4	16.8	14.7	9.1	1.2	−11.7	−20.6
375 m	mm	25	27	28	20	38	68	70	55	36	24	30	30
Frobisher Bay (NWT)	°C	−26.6	−24.8	−21.2	−13.2	−2.2	3.9	8.1	7.0	2.7	−5.0	−13.8	−21.7
21 m	mm	32	35	24	26	21	42	30	58	38	43	40	28
Gander (Newf)	°C	−6.1	−6.1	−3.7	1.1	6.5	11.5	16.8	16.1	12.1	6.3	1.7	−3.7
147 m	mm	83	88	81	69	59	76	84	101	86	97	107	87
Inuvik (NWT)	°C	−28.8	−27.6	−22.6	−12.7	−0.7	9.4	13.6	10.4	3.4	−7.0	−19.9	−27.0
61 m	mm	14	11	10	12	9	19	32	33	27	27	19	13
Lethbridge (Alta)	°C	−8.2	−7.1	−2.4	5.4	11.2	14.7	18.9	17.4	12.7	7.4	−0.4	−4.6
0 m	mm	21	23	29	35	52	74	39	40	35	29	26	21
Montreal (Que)	°C	−9.6	−8.3	−2.2	5.9	13.1	18.6	21.4	20.3	15.4	9.4	2.5	−6.4
30 m	mm	83	81	78	72	72	85	89	77	82	78	85	89
Norman Wells (NWT)	°C	−29.8	−25.9	−19.8	−7.7	4.7	13.0	15.8	13.4	5.9	−4.7	−18.2	−26.3
64 m	mm	18	18	13	15	13	35	57	61	37	27	30	24
Prince George (BC)	°C	−10.4	−7.4	−1.8	4.5	9.9	13.2	15.2	14.0	10.2	4.9	−2.2	−7.1
676 m	mm	56	44	36	28	43	62	64	65	56	59	57	56
Regina (Sask)	°C	−16.9	−14.8	−8.1	3.4	11.2	15.3	19.3	17.8	11.9	5.1	−5.4	−12.3
574 m	mm	19	17	21	21	40	83	55	49	34	18	20	17
Toronto (Ont)	°C	−5.8	−5.4	−0.9	6.7	12.4	18.5	21.1	20.4	15.9	9.9	3.4	−3.2
176 m	mm	58	52	65	63	81	61	74	67	66	62	56	55
Vancouver (BC)	°C	2.3	4.2	5.8	9.1	12.6	15.2	17.6	17.0	14.3	10.1	6.0	3.9
0 m	mm	139	121	96	60	48	51	26	36	56	117	142	156
Whitehorse (Yukon)	°C	−18.1	−14.1	−7.6	0.1	7.5	12.6	14.2	12.4	7.9	0.7	−8.2	−15.1
698 m	mm	18	14	15	11	13	27	35	37	25	19	23	20
Winnipeg (Man)	C	−17.7	−15.5	−7.9	3.3	11.3	16.5	20.2	18.9	12.8	6.2	−4.8	−12.9
240 m	mm	26	21	27	30	50	61	69	70	55	37	29	22

United States of America

		J	F	M	A	M	J	J	A	S	O	N	D
Abilene (Tex)	°C	7.0	9.1	12.8	17.9	22.1	26.8	28.4	28.3	24.4	19.0	11.7	7.8
534 m	mm	22	28	26	58	110	68	58	37	53	72	28	32
Albuquerque (N Mex)	°C	1.7	4.4	7.9	13.2	18.4	23.8	25.8	24.8	21.4	14.7	6.7	2.8
1620 m	mm	10	10	12	12	19	14	30	34	24	19	10	12
Anchorage (Alaska)	°C	−10.9	−7.8	−4.8	2.1	7.7	12.5	13.9	13.1	8.8	1.7	−5.4	−9.8
40 m	mm	20	18	13	11	13	25	47	65	64	47	26	24
Asheville (NC)	°C	4.3	4.8	7.9	13.3	18.0	22.1	23.6	23.1	19.9	14.2	8.1	4.4
687 m	mm	81	77	95	81	73	89	109	92	71	63	56	74
Atlanta (Ga)	°C	7.1	8.1	11.1	16.1	20.9	24.9	26.0	25.8	22.8	17.1	10.6	6.7
315 m	mm	113	115	136	114	80	97	120	91	83	62	75	111

348

		J	F	M	A	M	J	J	A	S	O	N	D	Year
ow aska) 4 m	°C mm	-26.8 5	-27.9 4	-25.9 3	-17.7 3	-7.6 3	0.6 9	3.9 20	3.3 23	-0.8 16	-8.6 13	-18.2 6	-24.0 4	-12.4 110
narck Dak) 506 m	°C mm	-12.8 11	-10.8 11	-3.8 20	6.1 31	13.0 50	18.1 86	22.3 56	21.0 44	14.8 30	7.9 22	-2.0 15	-8.4 9	5.4 385
e (Idaho) 871 m	°C mm	-1.9 34	1.1 34	5.1 34	9.9 29	14.3 33	18.2 23	23.7 5	22.3 4	17.3 10	11.4 21	3.9 30	0.1 34	10.4 290
on (Mass) 9 m	°C mm	-1.2 100	-0.9 84	3.2 107	8.8 96	14.9 85	19.9 88	23.2 73	22.1 93	18.5 88	12.8 80	7.2 100	0.7 92	10.8 1086
bou aine) 91 m	°C mm	-11.9 54	-10.8 51	-5.1 60	2.4 67	9.9 77	15.0 103	18.1 103	17.0 93	12.1 90	6.1 85	-1.0 77	-9.2 62	3.6 922
ago (Ill) 190 m	°C mm	-3.3 47	-2.3 41	2.4 70	9.5 77	15.6 95	21.5 103	24.3 86	23.6 80	19.1 69	13.0 71	4.4 56	-1.6 48	10.5 843
mbus io) 254 m	°C mm	-0.6 80	0.1 59	4.4 80	10.7 89	16.7 102	21.8 106	23.8 100	22.9 73	19.1 67	12.9 54	5.7 64	0.3 59	11.5 931
ver lo) 1625 m	°C mm	-1.1 14	0.3 18	3.3 31	8.6 54	13.7 69	19.4 37	23.0 39	22.2 33	17.5 29	11.3 26	4.0 174	0.6 118	10.2 640
Moines wa) 294 m	°C mm	-5.9 33	-3.9 28	1.7 53	9.9 64	16.6 103	22.2 120	25.0 78	23.6 93	18.8 73	12.6 52	3.3 45	-3.1 29	10.1 771
ath (Minn) 432 m	°C mm	-12.9 29	-11.5 24	-5.7 41	3.1 60	9.8 84	15.2 108	18.9 90	17.9 97	12.6 73	6.7 55	-2.9 45	-10.0 29	3.4 736
banks aska) 138 m	°C mm	-23.9 23	-19.4 13	-12.8 10	-1.4 6	8.4 18	14.7 35	15.4 47	12.4 56	6.4 28	-3.2 22	-15.6 15	-22.1 14	-3.4 287
eras C) 3 m	°C mm	8.1 99	8.1 100	10.6 106	15.2 58	20.0 101	24.0 105	25.6 156	25.3 163	23.4 150	18.6 108	13.4 104	9.0 116	16.8 1384
olulu waii) 5 m	°C mm	22.5 96	22.4 84	22.7 73	23.4 33	24.4 25	25.5 8	26.0 11	26.3 23	26.2 25	25.7 47	24.4 55	23.1 76	24.4 556
Vegas v) 664 m	°C mm	6.4 13	9.1 11	12.9 9	18.3 6	23.2 2	28.6 1	32.3 13	30.9 12	26.9 9	19.5 5	11.7 8	7.3 10	18.9 99
e Rock k) 81 m	°C mm	4.8 133	6.9 110	11.0 122	16.9 125	21.4 134	26.1 92	27.7 85	27.4 72	23.5 82	17.3 73	9.7 105	5.5 104	16.5 1236
mi (Fla) 3 m	°C mm	19.4 52	19.9 47	21.4 58	23.4 99	25.3 164	27.1 187	27.7 171	27.9 177	27.4 241	25.4 209	22.4 72	20.1 42	23.9 1518
Orleans) 9 m	°C mm	12.3 98	13.4 101	15.8 136	19.4 116	23.3 111	26.4 113	27.3 171	27.4 136	25.4 128	21.1 72	15.3 85	12.7 104	20.0 1369
York (NY) 16 m	°C mm	0.9 84	0.9 78	4.9 107	10.7 91	16.7 91	21.9 86	24.9 94	24.1 129	20.4 100	14.8 86	8.2 91	2.4 86	12.6 1123
th Platte br) 849 m	°C mm	-4.4 11	-2.3 13	1.7 25	8.7 51	14.7 75	20.6 83	24.5 64	23.6 54	17.6 42	10.6 23	1.9 13	-2.6 10	9.6 464
land lif) 3 m	°C mm	8.9 97	10.4 82	12.0 61	13.7 35	15.4 17	17.1 3	17.9 1	17.9 1	18.4 5	16.2 20	12.6 44	9.7 91	14.2 455

		J	F	M	A	M	J	J	A	S	O	N	D
Oklahoma City (Okla)	°C	2.5	4.9	8.9	14.9	19.7	24.7	27.2	27.4	22.9	16.9	8.8	4.3
397 m	mm	33	35	50	79	132	114	60	64	77	64	40	36
Phoenix (Ariz)	°C	10.4	12.5	15.8	20.4	25.0	29.8	32.9	31.7	29.1	22.3	15.1	11.4
337 m	mm	19	22	17	8	3	2	20	28	19	12	12	22
Portland (Oreg)	°C	3.6	5.6	7.8	11.0	14.1	16.7	19.6	19.2	16.8	12.3	7.3	5.2
12 m	mm	136	107	97	53	51	42	10	17	41	92	135	162
Rapid City (S Dak)	°C	−5.6	−6.4	−0.5	6.9	13.2	18.3	23.2	22.2	16.4	10.0	1.7	−2.7
966 m	mm	9	12	26	42	68	78	45	31	24	20	10	8
St Louis (Mo)	°C	−0.1	1.8	6.2	13.0	18.7	24.2	26.4	25.4	21.1	14.9	6.7	1.6
172 m	mm	50	52	78	94	95	109	84	77	70	73	65	50
St Paul Island (Alaska)	°C	−3.7	−4.8	−4.3	−2.0	1.6	4.9	7.5	8.7	7.0	3.0	0.5	−3.1
9 m	mm	46	31	27	24	33	29	57	84	78	80	64	46
Salt Lake City (Utah)	°C	−2.1	0.6	4.7	9.9	14.7	19.4	24.7	23.6	18.3	11.5	3.4	−0.2
1288 m	mm	34	30	40	45	36	25	15	22	13	29	33	31
San Antonio (Tex)	°C	11.1	13.0	16.1	20.1	24.1	27.7	28.9	28.9	25.9	21.4	15.2	12.1
242 m	mm	44	42	42	72	88	75	53	60	89	64	35	44
San Diego (Calif)	°C	13.1	13.7	14.7	16.1	17.5	18.7	20.9	21.5	20.8	18.7	16.3	14.2
9 m	mm	51	55	40	20	4	1	0	2	4	12	23	52
Sault Ste Marie (Mich)	°C	−9.3	−9.3	−4.8	3.1	9.5	14.7	17.8	17.5	12.9	7.4	0.2	−6.4
221 m	mm	53	38	46	55	70	84	63	73	97	72	85	58
Sheridan (Wyo)	°C	−5.9	−4.6	−0.5	6.4	12.0	16.6	21.8	20.8	14.9	8.8	0.8	−3.2
1209 m	mm	16	19	36	55	65	65	30	23	30	29	20	16
Spokane (Wash)	°C	−3.7	−1.1	3.4	8.5	13.2	16.3	20.8	19.7	15.5	9.2	1.8	−1.3
721 m	mm	62	47	38	23	31	38	10	10	19	40	57	62
Washington (DC)	°C	2.7	3.2	7.1	13.2	18.8	23.4	25.7	24.7	20.8	15.0	8.7	3.4
20 m	mm	77	63	82	80	105	82	105	124	97	78	72	71
Wichita (Kans)	°C	0.0	2.4	6.9	13.7	18.9	24.7	27.2	27.1	21.8	15.5	6.9	2.1
408 m	mm	21	23	42	58	101	107	92	73	82	61	38	24
Winnemucca (Nev)	°C	−2.7	0.2	3.3	7.7	12.1	16.4	21.7	19.8	14.8	8.7	2.1	−1.2
1322 m	mm	27	24	21	21	24	19	7	4	9	21	20	24

Central America

Within the tropical zone, Central America has intensely hot summers and warm winters, often tempered by trade winds and generally cooler in the highlands of the interior. Backed by mountains, the coasts tend to receive heavy orographic rain throughout the year, with most of the heaviest downpours occurring in summer. Permanent or seasonal snow rests on many of the mountain peaks. The region's interior is drier and may even be short of water; for example, much of the Mexican upland is arid, with short and unreliable summer rains.

ze		J	F	M	A	M	J	J	A	S	O	N	D	Year
e	°C	23.5	24.8	26.1	27.2	27.6	28.3	27.6	28.3	27.4	28.1	26.1	24.7	26.6
m	mm	72	27	27	131	101	171	315	114	193	207	215	75	1648

ta Rica

osé	°C	22.0	22.8	23.5	23.8	23.1	22.5	22.5	22.5	22.3	22.0	22.1	22.1	22.6
158 m	mm	8	5	10	37	244	284	230	233	342	333	172	46	1944

alvador

Salvador	°C	22.1	22.4	23.5	24.2	23.7	23.1	23.0	22.5	22.5	22.4	22.0	22.0	22.8
89 m	mm	5	3	8	60	190	322	304	297	325	220	35	7	1775

temala

emala	°C	16.3	17.0	18.4	19.5	19.6	18.7	18.5	18.7	18.3	17.7	16.7	16.3	18.0
502 m	mm	3	2	7	19	141	265	211	187	257	159	23	7	1281

duras

Pedro

a	°C	23.1	24.5	25.9	27.4	28.1	27.9	27.1	27.6	27.7	26.3	25.2	23.7	26.2
'6 m	mm	74	49	47	37	93	148	154	122	206	166	132	104	1332

ico

ulco	°C	26.1	26.1	26.6	27.2	28.5	28.6	28.7	28.7	28.7	28.0	27.5	26.6	27.6
; m	mm	8	1	0	1	36	325	230	236	353	170	30	9	1401
atlán	°C	19.8	19.7	20.2	21.8	24.6	26.9	28.0	28.0	27.8	27.0	24.0	21.2	24.1
'8 m	mm	12	8	3	0	1	34	174	215	250	63	17	27	805
baya	°C	12.1	13.8	16.1	17.1	17.4	17.0	15.9	15.9	15.6	14.7	13.3	12.2	15.1
306 m	mm	8	5	10	23	55	118	160	145	129	49	17	6	726
pico	°C	18.9	20.3	22.0	24.7	26.8	28.0	28.0	28.3	26.5	25.6	22.0	19.7	24.2
3 m	mm	38	19	13	19	49	143	151	130	297	146	48	30	1083
cruz	°C	21.1	22.2	23.4	25.3	27.1	27.6	27.5	27.8	27.3	26.3	24.0	22.3	25.1
6 m	mm	22	16	14	19	65	263	358	283	353	175	76	26	1672
tecas	°C	9.5	10.8	12.9	15.1	16.7	16.1	14.5	14.8	13.8	13.1	11.4	10.0	13.2
2 m	mm	7	3	2	3	14	50	69	62	60	23	13	7	313

The Caribbean Islands

Blessed with constant sunshine and year-round trade winds, buffered by warm tropical seas, the Caribbean islands have stable, predictable climates, generally hot in summer and warm in winter, with high humidity throughout the year. Air temperatures seldom exceed 30°C (86°F) or fall below 20°C (68°F) – limits set by the surface waters. The low-lying islands tend to be dry; the higher ones attract rain from the constant winds, usually experiencing a peak of rainfall in summer. Cyclonic storms may swirl across the islands in late summer, occasionally causing serious damage to houses and crops.

GREATER ANTILLES AND BAHAMAS

Bahamas

		J	F	M	A	M	J	J	A	S	O	N	D
Nassau	°C	20.3	20.9	22.2	23.6	25.2	26.7	27.4	27.7	27.1	25.5	23.5	21.6
10 m	mm	36	43	45	78	117	159	150	135	165	164	85	39

Dominican Republic

		J	F	M	A	M	J	J	A	S	O	N	D
Santo Domingo	°C	23.9	24.0	24.5	25.3	25.9	26.5	26.7	27.0	26.8	26.4	29.6	24.6
14 m	mm	47	45	45	65	190	175	158	147	168	165	113	67

Jamaica

		J	F	M	A	M	J	J	A	S	O	N	D
Kingston	°C	25.4	25.4	25.9	26.7	27.6	28.0	28.3	28.5	28.2	27.6	27.1	26.1
12 m	mm	20	18	10	37	138	114	51	92	86	168	52	25

Puerto Rico

		J	F	M	A	M	J	J	A	S	O	N	D
San Juan	°C	23.6	23.6	24.1	24.7	25.9	26.7	26.9	27.2	26.9	26.7	25.7	24.6
19 m	mm	119	74	56	94	181	144	159	181	172	148	165	138

LEEWARD AND WINDWARD ISLANDS

Barbados

		J	F	M	A	M	J	J	A	S	O	N	D
Seawell	°C	25.2	25.1	25.9	26.3	26.8	27.1	26.8	27.1	27.1	26.7	26.3	25.9
56 m	mm	68	62	37	51	70	103	141	144	168	176	160	93

Curaçao

		J	F	M	A	M	J	J	A	S	O	N	D
Plesman	°C	26.3	26.2	26.5	27.2	27.8	28.1	28.1	28.5	28.8	28.4	27.8	26.9
0 m	mm	63	29	16	15	18	27	29	40	33	78	128	106

Guadeloupe

		J	F	M	A	M	J	J	A	S	O	N	D
Pointe-à-Pitre	°C	23.4	23.5	24.0	26.0	26.0	26.8	26.7	26.8	26.7	26.1	25.3	24.3
8 m	mm	91	66	66	86	135	148	179	244	196	229	231	143

Martinique

		J	F	M	A	M	J	J	A	S	O	N	D
Fort-de-France	°C	23.5	23.5	24.0	24.7	25.4	25.7	25.6	26.0	25.9	25.6	25.2	24.2
146 m	mm	96	68	58	82	126	160	214	227	232	221	230	126

South America

The northern half of the subcontinent is crossed by the Equator, the centre by the Tropic of Capricorn; all but the southern third of South America is tropical, with a variety of climates provided by local conditions. Northern lowlands are intensely hot, with mean temperatures exceeding 25°C (77°F) throughout the year, and mostly very wet, with inevitable daily convectional rainfall throughout the year; only parts of the Caribbean coast are semi-arid. The central region is also hot, though with marked seasonal cooling; rainfall is highest in the Andes, leaving little for the eastern plains and virtually no rain along the western seaboard. The south is temperate, with wet coastal forests in the west and dry pampas in the east. The highest Andean peaks are snow-capped even on the Equator; in the south they are heavily glaciated, with ice tumbling to sea level in southern Chile.

SOUTH AMERICA
Location of Climatic Stations

- Plesman
- Maracaibo
- Caracas
- Piarco
- Mérida
- Georgetown
- Bogotá
- Quito
- Guayaquil
- Manaus
- Belém
- Pôrto Velho
- Riberalta
- Lima
- Cochabamba
- Campo Grande
- Belo Horizonte
- Rio de Janeiro
- São Paulo
- Asunción
- Salto
- Mendoza
- Montevideo
- Buenos Aires
- Santiago
- Valdivia
- Comodoro Rivadavia
- Stanley
- Grytviken, South Georgia
- Ushuaia

World Climates

Argentina

		J	F	M	A	M	J	J	A	S	O	N	D
Buenos Aires	°C	23.7	23.0	20.7	16.6	13.7	11.1	10.6	11.5	13.6	16.5	19.5	22.1
25 m	mm	104	82	122	90	79	68	61	68	80	100	90	83
Comodoro Rivadavia	°C	18.6	18.2	16.0	12.7	9.4	7.0	6.9	7.6	9.6	12.8	15.4	17.3
61 m	mm	16	11	21	22	35	20	21	18	15	10	16	13
Mendoza	°C	23.7	22.5	19.6	14.8	10.9	7.7	7.4	9.7	13.0	16.6	20.0	22.6
827 m	mm	28	21	21	10	11	8	7	10	14	23	20	23
Ushuaia	°C	9.2	9.0	7.8	5.7	3.2	1.7	1.6	2.2	3.9	6.2	7.3	8.5
6 m	mm	58	50	57	46	48	45	47	49	38	37	50	49

Bolivia

		J	F	M	A	M	J	J	A	S	O	N	D
Cochabamba	°C	17.7	17.7	17.6	16.4	14.2	12.3	12.3	13.7	16.2	18.1	18.6	18.5
2570 m	mm	124	98	53	16	4	1	4	9	10	26	50	89
Riberalta	°C	26.4	26.5	26.6	26.1	25.9	25.3	25.2	26.6	27.7	27.3	27.1	27.0
172 m	mm	299	245	282	145	67	28	8	21	60	136	161	272

Brazil

		J	F	M	A	M	J	J	A	S	O	N	D
Belém	°C	25.6	25.5	25.4	25.7	26.0	26.0	25.9	26.0	26.0	26.2	26.5	26.3
24 m	mm	318	407	436	382	265	165	161	116	116	105	94	197
Belo Horizonte	°C	22.7	22.9	22.3	21.1	19.1	18.0	17.7	19.0	20.8	21.5	21.8	21.6
785 m	mm	268	194	165	77	22	10	7	9	38	113	215	354
Campo Grande	°C	24.3	24.2	23.8	21.9	20.3	19.3	19.1	21.1	22.8	23.5	24.0	24.5
552 m	mm	229	199	140	101	81	50	36	29	62	162	157	191
Manaus	°C	25.9	25.8	25.8	25.9	26.4	26.6	26.9	27.5	27.9	27.7	27.3	26.7
83 m	mm	276	277	301	287	193	99	61	41	62	112	165	228
Pôrto Velho	°C	25.0	25.1	25.2	25.2	25.2	25.0	24.8	26.2	26.4	26.0	25.7	25.4
105 m	mm	337	305	337	225	108	32	11	26	99	207	241	317
Rio de Janeiro	°C	25.9	26.1	25.5	23.9	22.3	21.3	20.8	21.1	21.5	22.3	23.1	24.4
27 m	mm	137	137	143	116	73	43	43	43	53	74	97	127
São Paulo	°C	21.1	21.4	21.3	19.5	17.3	15.8	15.0	16.5	17.3	18.7	19.5	21.1
801 m	mm	248	289	152	62	48	41	36	29	48	113	134	186

Chile

		J	F	M	A	M	J	J	A	S	O	N	D
Santiago	°C	20.5	20.0	18.1	15.3	11.7	8.6	8.9	10.3	12.2	14.7	17.0	19.4
520 m	mm	2	3	5	13	63	84	76	56	30	15	8	5
Valdivia	°C	16.9	16.7	15.0	15.0	9.7	8.3	8.1	8.3	9.7	11.9	13.1	15.3
5 m	mm	66	74	132	234	361	450	394	328	208	127	124	104

Colombia

		J	F	M	A	M	J	J	A	S	O	N	D
Bogotá	°C	14.2	14.7	14.7	15.0	14.7	14.4	13.9	14.2	14.2	14.4	14.4	14.2
2646 m	mm	58	66	101	102	114	61	51	56	56	108	117	66

Ecuador

		J	F	M	A	M	J	J	A	S	O	N	D
Guayaquil	°C	25.3	26.0	26.4	26.3	25.6	24.4	23.5	23.2	23.8	24.0	24.6	25.4
6 m	mm	212	289	292	207	54	11	4	0	0	1	2	28
Quito	°C	13.0	13.0	12.9	13.0	13.1	13.0	12.9	13.1	13.2	12.9	12.8	13.0
2812 m	mm	119	131	154	185	130	54	20	25	81	134	96	104

Guyana

		J	F	M	A	M	J	J	A	S	O	N	D
Georgetown	°C	26.3	26.4	26.8	27.1	27.0	26.7	26.2	27.7	27.7	27.7	27.4	26.7
1 m	mm	251	122	113	178	296	346	281	185	88	98	147	313

aguay		J	F	M	A	M	J	J	A	S	O	N	D	Year
ición	°C	28.8	28.2	26.8	23.1	20.9	18.9	18.2	20.1	21.7	23.7	25.7	27.9	23.7
4 m	mm	145	137	154	138	124	84	53	35	82	133	124	131	1340

u														
a	°C	21.5	22.3	21.9	20.1	17.8	16.0	15.3	15.1	15.4	16.3	17.7	19.4	18.2
55 m	mm	1.0	0.4	0.6	0.4	6	4	6	7	6	2	1	0.8	35

nidad and Tobago

co	°C	24.3	24.6	25.3	26.2	26.6	26.0	25.9	26.1	26.2	26.1	25.5	24.8	25.6
4 m	mm	79	51	26	55	131	291	252	236	159	142	198	152	1772

guay

tevideo	°C	22.5	22.2	20.3	17.0	13.7	10.9	10.5	11.1	12.8	15.1	18.3	21.0	16.3
2 m	mm	83	74	104	102	91	88	73	87	84	73	79	77	1014
	°C	26.2	25.2	22.9	18.4	15.5	12.8	12.5	13.7	15.4	18.4	21.9	24.4	18.9
6 m	mm	116	94	121	151	83	100	58	58	97	127	91	79	1175

ezuela

cas	°C	19.6	20.3	21.3	22.4	22.9	22.3	21.9	22.1	22.2	22.1	21.3	20.3	21.6
65 m	mm	23	3	13	27	75	151	109	120	115	104	74	40	854
acaibo	°C	26.5	26.7	27.1	27.8	28.4	28.6	28.5	28.7	28.6	27.9	27.8	27.1	27.8
8 m	mm	3	2	3	27	73	43	28	42	40	99	22	5	387
da	°C	17.5	18.0	18.9	19.2	19.3	19.1	18.7	19.3	19.4	18.9	18.4	17.9	18.7
498 m	mm	55	42	52	163	262	164	125	106	148	224	192	100	1633

AFRICA

Africa Northwest

Crossed by the Tropic of Cancer, northwestern Africa is an area of dry, stable continental air masses that block all other influences. Mean monthly temperatures exceed 25°C (77°F) over much of the Sahara even in winter, and summer means rise well above 30°C (86°F) in the hottest parts. Only along the Mediterranean coast, and in the coastal ranges of Morocco and Algeria, are ameliorating effects of the sea felt; cool sea breezes and trade winds bring both welcome relief from summer heat and reliable rains in winter. Inland the desert takes over, within a few dozen kilometres of the coast in Western Sahara, intensely hot by day, intensely cold at night, with little or no rain at any time.

eria		J	F	M	A	M	J	J	A	S	O	N	D	Year
rs	°C	10.3	10.8	13.0	15.2	18.0	21.8	24.4	25.1	23.1	18.9	14.9	11.7	17.3
5 m	mm	116	76	57	65	36	14	2	4	27	84	93	117	691
ar	°C	9.2	11.9	16.0	19.9	24.4	29.9	34.0	33.0	28.2	21.4	14.9	9.9	21.1
06 m	mm	7	9	13	8	3	2	0	4	7	14	13	10	90
	°C	12.5	15.5	19.9	24.7	29.4	33.5	33.5	32.7	30.7	26.0	19.9	14.4	24.7
50 m	mm	2	2	2	2	2	<2	<2	<2	2	<2	2	<2	18
	°C	12.2	13.3	14.7	16.6	19.1	21.6	24.4	25.5	23.3	19.7	16.1	13.0	18.3
I m	mm	71	48	51	30	20	5	<2	2	13	33	51	51	376

AFRICA
Location of Climatic Stations

kina Faso		J	F	M	A	M	J	J	A	S	O	N	D	Year
gadougou	°C	25.4	27.6	30.8	32.6	31.0	28.7	26.9	26.0	26.6	28.9	28.4	25.6	28.2
14 m	mm	0	3	8	19	84	118	193	265	153	37	2	0	879
i														
ako	°C	25.5	28.0	30.9	32.4	31.9	29.1	26.9	26.0	26.6	27.8	27.2	25.4	28.1
32 m	mm	1	0	3	15	60	145	251	334	220	58	12	0	1099
alit	°C	20.1	22.6	25.9	29.5	33.1	33.5	34.5	33.1	32.9	30.9	25.9	20.4	28.7
94 m	mm	1	0	1	0	2	7	23	55	27	1	1	0	118
buktu	°C	22.6	25.4	28.5	31.8	34.3	33.9	31.5	29.1	31.2	31.7	28.3	22.8	29.3
72 m	mm	0	0	0	1	3	19	65	95	37	5	0	0	225
rocco														
blanca	°C	12.4	13.0	14.7	16.1	18.0	20.5	22.5	22.9	21.8	19.4	16.3	13.4	17.6
8 m	mm	66	53	55	38	21	2	0	1	7	39	57	87	426
zazate	°C	9.2	11.4	14.8	18.3	22.0	26.7	29.8	29.2	25.0	19.5	14.0	9.4	19.1
136 m	mm	6	6	12	9	5	4	2	9	20	18	17	15	123
er														
lez	°C	20.1	22.7	27.1	30.7	33.0	33.0	31.3	29.8	30.7	29.2	24.4	20.7	27.7
00 m	mm	Tr	Tr	0	1	6	8	49	78	20	1	0	0	164
ney	°C	24.7	27.1	31.0	33.6	33.4	30.9	28.3	26.8	28.0	30.1	28.1	24.7	28.9
26 m	mm	Tr	0	1	3	46	79	181	206	101	21	0	0	636
isia														
s	°C	11.2	12.7	15.1	17.4	20.6	24.4	26.5	27.3	25.6	21.8	16.7	12.5	19.3
m	mm	17	17	17	17	9	2	0.3	1	14	41	30	19	183
s	°C	11.0	11.7	13.4	15.7	19.1	23.4	25.9	26.6	24.6	20.4	15.9	12.4	18.3
m	mm	70	47	43	42	23	11	1	11	37	56	57	70	466

Africa West

The bulge of western Africa lies mostly within the tropics and is hot through the year with little seasonal variation; even the coolest months have means exceeding 25°C (77°F). It spans two distinct rainfall zones, a factor immediately apparent from widely differing patterns of vegetation and human activity in the north and the south. In the north lies the Sahel, a broad zone of semi-desert bordering the Sahara, where rainfall is limited and generally unpredictable, and occasional spells of abundance may be followed by several rainless years. In the south is a narrower zone of abundant, reliable summer rains, increasing in amount from west to east – a zone of forests, rich pastures and plantations.

neroon		J	F	M	A	M	J	J	A	S	O	N	D	Year
la	°C	27.1	27.4	27.4	27.3	26.9	26.1	24.8	24.7	25.4	25.9	26.5	27.0	26.4
3 m	mm	61	88	226	240	353	472	710	726	628	399	146	60	4109
ua	°C	26.3	28.4	31.6	32.6	30.1	27.6	26.5	26.2	26.3	27.8	27.7	26.3	28.2
47 m	mm	Tr	1	4	35	135	157	159	199	220	76	2	2	990
na														
a	°C	27.3	27.7	27.8	27.7	27.0	25.7	24.6.	24.3	25.3	26.1	27.1	27.3	26.5
5 m	mm	16	37	73	82	145	193	49	16	40	80	38	18	787

		J	F	M	A	M	J	J	A	S	O	N	D
Kumasi	°C	25.2	26.7	26.9	26.7	26.4	25.4	24.2	23.6	24.8	25.4	25.9	25.4
293 m	mm	26	65	136	139	191	223	113	74	170	201	95	32

Guinea-Bissau

		J	F	M	A	M	J	J	A	S	O	N	D
Bissau	°C	24.2	25.7	26.6	27.0	27.4	27.2	26.3	25.8	26.4	27.1	26.9	24.8
40 m	mm	1	1	0	1	17	175	472	682	435	195	42	2

Ivory Coast

		J	F	M	A	M	J	J	A	S	O	N	D
Abidjan	°C	26.7	27.3	27.6	27.8	27.1	26.0	25.1	24.0	25.1	26.1	27.2	27.1
7 m	mm	26	42	120	169	366	608	200	34	55	225	188	111
Odienné	°C	25.6	27.8	29.0	28.8	27.6	26.3	25.3	25.0	25.4	25.8	26.2	25.0
434 m	mm	0	14	42	77	126	173	282	381	281	152	58	10

Nigeria

		J	F	M	A	M	J	J	A	S	O	N	D
Jos	°C	20.6	22.3	24.5	24.4	23.0	21.8	20.4	20.1	21.1	21.9	21.8	20.6
1285 m	mm	2	4	24	93	205	229	318	274	219	39	5	2
Kano	°C	21.4	23.9	28.2	30.6	30.2	28.1	25.7	25.1	25.9	26.8	24.8	21.8
481 m	mm	0	0.3	2	8	71	119	209	311	137	14	03	0
Lagos	°C	26.7	27.5	27.7	27.4	26.7	25.6	24.4	24.3	25.0	25.6	26.8	26.8
38 m	mm	40	57	100	115	215	336	150	59	214	220	77	41

Senegal

		J	F	M	A	M	J	J	A	S	O	N	D
Dakar	°C	21.1	20.4	20.9	21.7	23.0	26.0	27.3	27.3	27.5	27.5	26.0	23.2
23 m	mm	0	2	0	0	1	15	88	249	163	49	5	6

Sierra Leone

		J	F	M	A	M	J	J	A	S	O	N	D
Bonthe	°C	27.1	27.7	27.9	28.2	27.6	26.3	25.2	25.1	25.8	26.5	26.9	26.9
8 m	mm	17	21	49	112	267	570	882	755	616	351	179	67
Kabala	°C	24.7	26.7	27.6	27.4	26.0	25.0	23.9	23.5	24.5	25.0	25.1	24.1
464 m	mm	19	16	64	106	197	315	314	405	420	357	129	31

Africa Northeast

Much of northeastern Africa is intensely hot and dry, with little seasonal variation in temperature or rainfall. Exceptions are the coastal plains of the Mediterranean Sea and Indian Ocean, where cool, moist breezes temper the heat and occasionally bring rain, the coastal uplands of Libya, where rainfall is sparse but reliable, and southern Sudan where there is usually enough rain to support nomadic grazing. Exceptional too is the highland massif of Ethiopia, whose towering peaks temper the heat and catch rain in abundance, especially in summer. Much of the rain that falls on western Ethiopia flows northward in the Nile, providing floodwater for the valley farmers and ground-water for the desert oases.

Chad		J	F	M	A	M	J	J	A	S	O	N	D
Faya-Largeau	°C	20.4	22.7	27.0	30.6	33.8	34.2	33.6	32.7	32.6	30.5	25.5	21.3
234 m	mm	0	0	0	0	Tr	2	1	11	2	Tr	0	0
Ndjamena	°C	23.5	25.9	30.1	32.7	32.3	30.5	27.5	26.2	27.1	28.6	27.1	24.1
295 m	mm	0	0	0	5	36	66	156	257	104	23	1	0

		J	F	M	A	M	J	J	A	S	O	N	D	Year
ıouti														
outi	°C	25.0	25.5	26.9	28.6	30.9	34.0	36.7	35.7	33.9	29.4	27.1	25.7	29.9
) m	mm	13	7	24	11	6	0.1	7	8	3	13	30	13	133
˙pt														
andria	°C	14.4	15.0	16.9	19.1	21.9	24.4	26.0	26.9	26.3	24.1	20.8	16.6	21.1
˙2 m	mm	48	23	10	<2	<2	<2	<2	<2	<2	5	33	56	178
ân	°C	16.8	18.6	22.4	27.2	31.8	33.6	34.0	34.2	32.0	29.6	23.9	20.0	27.0
˙94 m	mm	Tr	Tr	Tr	Tr	1	0	0	0	Tr	0	Tr	Tr	1
˙o	°C	14.0	15.1	17.8	21.2	25.3	27.6	28.9	28.6	26.3	24.2	19.9	15.5	22.0
74 m	mm	4	4	3	1	1	0	0	Tr	0	1	1	7	22
iopia														
is Ababa	°C	16.1	18.2	19.0	19.2	19.8	18.1	15.1	15.0	15.4	15.3	14.9	15.0	16.8
˙360 m	mm	24	25	68	93	50	105	228	263	174	41	3	15	1089
˙ara	°C	14.2	15.5	17.1	18.0	18.6	18.2	16.0	16.1	16.5	15.4	15.0	14.0	16.2
˙321 m	mm	1	0	10	19	55	44	197	146	36	9	23	8	558
˙ya														
˙ghazi	°C	13.6	14.1	16.3	18.8	21.6	24.1	25.2	25.8	24.4	22.7	19.4	15.2	19.9
˙5 m	mm	66	41	20	5	2	<2	<2	<2	2	18	46	66	267
˙nah	°C	11.9	12.8	14.6	18.2	22.0	25.6	26.1	26.5	24.7	22.0	17.8	13.6	19.7
˙32 m	mm	67	23	15	6	3	0.2	0	0.4	0.1	22	28	66	231
˙a	°C	12.9	15.6	19.3	23.3	28.7	30.9	31.2	31.3	28.7	24.7	18.4	14.4	23.3
˙82 m	mm	0.1	0.1	0	0	0.4	0.1	0	1	0	0	0.1	0.4	2
ıali Democratic Republic														
adishu	°C	26.5	26.7	28.3	29.3	28.7	27.0	26.0	26.0	26.6	27.4	27.7	26.9	27.3
˙o m	mm	1	0	11	103	62	74	60	25	11	18	46	11	422
˙an														
	°C	27.4	28.4	28.5	27.5	26.2	25.3	24.2	24.1	24.9	25.7	26.3	26.6	26.3
˙57 m	mm	5	10	43	107	157	116	136	154	105	101	35	13	982
toum	°C	22.5	23.8	27.2	30.7	33.1	33.3	30.8	29.4	30.9	31.4	27.5	23.7	28.7
˙8o m	mm	0	0	0	1	5	7	48	72	27	4	0	0	164
Sudan	°C	24.4	22.9	24.1	26.3	29.4	31.8	33.7	34.2	31.9	29.3	27.4	24.8	28.3
˙ m	mm	4	1	1	1	2	0	9	3	0	12	52	25	110

Africa Central

Equatorial and southern tropical Africa is uniformly hot throughout the year, with mean monthly temperatures between 22°C (72°F) and 28°C (82°F) and little seasonal variation. The equatorial zone is also intensely humid, with year-round rainfall in the northwest and strong seasonal rains elsewhere, producing lush green rain forest and strongly-flowing rivers over most of the area. Further south rainfall is still plentiful, mostly in summer, with wet and dry seasons alternating. On the high southern plateau of Angola and Zambia temperatures are lowered by altitude, and rainfall is both seasonal and reduced. The west coast is also anomalously cool and dry, chilled by the cold Benguela current.

359

Angola

Luanda		J	F	M	A	M	J	J	A	S	O	N	D
Luanda	°C	25.9	26.6	26.9	26.4	25.0	22.2	20.2	20.3	21.8	24.0	25.2	25.6
70 m	mm	26	35	97	124	19	0	0	1	2	6	34	23
Malanje	°C	21.5	21.8	21.8	21.6	20.9	19.0	18.8	19.7	21.1	21.5	21.2	21.4
1142 m	mm	101	128	208	187	43	0	0	2	45	122	228	130
Namibe	°C	22.1	23.3	24.2	23.1	19.4	17.1	16.2	17.0	18.2	19.8	21.6	21.6
45 m	mm	8	15	14	7	0	0	0	0	0	1	2	2

Central African Republic

		J	F	M	A	M	J	J	A	S	O	N	D
Bangui	°C	25.9	27.3	27.4	26.7	26.6	25.8	25.1	25.2	25.4	25.5	25.5	25.5
381 m	mm	21	47	124	128	173	135	185	225	185	202	101	34
Ndélé	°C	26.8	27.8	28.8	28.8	27.4	25.9	24.9	24.8	25.3	25.7	26.0	26.3
510 m	mm	1	6	34	42	140	140	194	255	258	171	15	2

Congo

		J	F	M	A	M	J	J	A	S	O	N	D
Brazzaville	°C	25.6	25.8	26.2	26.2	25.4	23.0	21.7	23.0	24.8	25.6	25.5	25.5
314 m	mm	120	123	185	210	133	2	1	2	33	141	227	194
Ouesso	°C	25.6	26.0	26.2	26.5	26.1	25.2	24.7	24.8	24.8	25.0	25.0	25.2
351 m	mm	56	79	150	127	152	117	72	155	220	226	152	83
Pointe Noire	°C	26.2	26.6	27.0	26.8	25.6	22.7	21.2	21.5	23.4	25.2	25.7	25.9
17 m	mm	152	210	227	179	89	1	0	2	13	71	167	143

Gabon

		J	F	M	A	M	J	J	A	S	O	N	D
Franceville	°C	24.9	25.0	25.2	25.5	24.9	23.3	22.6	23.4	24.6	24.8	24.8	24.7
426 m	mm	160	191	217	210	205	32	7	21	107	265	255	193
Libreville	°C	26.7	26.8	26.9	27.1	26.8	25.2	24.1	24.4	25.5	25.8	26.0	26.4
10 m	mm	331	305	410	363	291	18	1	9	113	384	506	389

São Tomé e Principe

		J	F	M	A	M	J	J	A	S	O	N	D
São Tomé	°C	27.6	26.2	26.4	26.4	26.0	24.7	23.8	24.2	24.9	25.2	25.4	25.6
13 m	mm	82	84	132	120	113	16	0	1	18	108	100	98

Zaïre

		J	F	M	A	M	J	J	A	S	O	N	D
Lubumbashi	°C	22.0	22.2	21.9	20.8	18.6	16.3	16.1	18.0	26.3	23.5	23.3	22.2
1230 m	mm	267	244	213	56	5	0	0	<2	2	30	150	269
Kisangani	°C	25.8	25.8	25.8	26.0	25.5	25.2	24.1	24.1	24.7	24.9	24.7	24.9
418 m	mm	53	84	178	157	137	114	132	165	183	218	198	84

Zambia

		J	F	M	A	M	J	J	A	S	O	N	D
Kabwe	°C	20.9	20.8	20.7	19.9	18.0	15.7	15.4	17.8	21.8	24.6	23.2	21.4
1208 m	mm	226	207	121	20	1	Tr	Tr	2	2	18	96	232
Kasama	°C	19.8	19.9	20.2	20.4	18.9	17.1	16.9	18.8	21.7	23.6	21.9	20.3
1384 m	mm	266	250	258	71	8	Tr	Tr	1	1	17	137	236
Livingstone	°C	23.1	22.9	22.8	22.2	19.1	16.2	16.5	19.4	23.9	26.9	25.1	23.7
987 m	mm	186	175	101	28	4	1	0	Tr	2	26	92	164

Africa East

Much of eastern Africa stands on a high plateau; though situated between the Equator and the Tropic of Capricorn, its uplands have warm, bracing climates with hot sunny days and pleasantly cool nights. Only the coast remains torrid, though seasonally cooled and dampened by monsoon winds. In the far north the plateau is dry; northern Kenya and Uganda have little rain at any time and the country is mainly desert. Central and southern Kenya and Uganda, Tanzania and the small Rift Valley states have strongly seasonal rainfall, controlled by monsoon winds that bring welcome cloud and single or double wet seasons for the crops.

undi		J	F	M	A	M	J	J	A	S	O	N	D	Year
umbura	°C	23.1	22.9	22.2	22.8	23.2	23.0	22.1	23.0	24.2	24.6	23.5	23.5	23.2
783 m	mm	90	110	120	125	54	11	7	10	37	62	97	115	838
ıya														
var	°C	28.9	29.8	30.4	29.6	29.6	28.8	28.2	28.6	29.4	29.9	29.3	28.9	29.3
ɔ06 m	mm	8	5	22	41	25	10	15	9	4	7	7	10	162
ıbasa	°C	27.8	28.0	28.5	27.6	25.8	24.8	23.9	24.2	25.2	26.1	26.9	27.7	26.4
ɔ5 m	mm	30	14	59	192	319	100	72	69	71	85	74	76	1163
obi	°C	17.8	18.1	18.8	18.8	17.8	16.2	14.9	15.6	16.8	18.6	18.3	17.8	17.5
ɪ798 m	mm	45	51	101	206	160	46	19	26	26	54	109	82	926
lawi														
ıgwe	°C	21.2	21.0	20.7	19.7	17.4	15.3	15.0	16.7	19.7	22.6	22.9	21.8	15.8
ɪ136 m	mm	204	210	135	37	5	2	Tr	2	4	5	75	171	849
zambique														
uto	°C	25.4	25.6	24.8	23.4	21.0	18.7	18.4	19.6	20.8	22.3	23.5	24.7	22.4
ɔ9 m	mm	130	124	97	64	28	27	12	13	38	46	86	103	768
inga	°C	19.7	19.6	19.4	18.8	17.0	15.1	14.3	15.9	18.4	20.6	21.6	20.2	18.4
ɪ357 m	mm	262	259	173	103	26	6	1	3	3	22	37	224	1119
ızania														
es Salaam	°C	27.3	27.6	27.6	26.7	25.5	24.3	23.3	23.8	24.2	25.3	26.4	27.4	25.7
ɔ8 m	mm	58	68	128	264	219	33	21	24	28	48	68	83	1043
ɔra	°C	22.8	22.7	22.7	22.7	22.3	21.6	21.2	23.1	24.8	25.7	25.1	23.4	23.2
ɪ190 m	mm	135	126	170	133	34	3	0	1	5	14	81	181	882
ında														
bbe	°C	22.0	22.1	22.2	21.8	21.6	21.1	20.6	20.7	21.2	21.7	21.8	21.6	21.5
ɪ146 m	mm	79	85	170	278	279	113	73	84	77	84	137	115	1574
᷆	°C	24.4	24.8	24.6	23.7	22.8	22.3	21.6	21.7	22.3	22.8	23.2	23.4	23.1
ɪ109 m	mm	16	48	91	176	185	137	164	253	178	157	88	47	1540

Africa South

Below 15°S, and especially south of the Tropic of Capricorn, the African climate becomes progressively cooler and more seasonal; cooling is especially notable on the high central plateau of southern Africa and the uplands of Madagascar, but the coasts too are chilled by cool currents and frequent cool breezes from the south. With the sun almost overhead, mean January temperatures on the plateau reach 20° to 25°C (68° to 77°F); in winter they fall to a comfortable 15°C (59°F) or lower. Much of the area is dry; the plateau is semi-arid with meagre summer rains, and the western coast is a cool desert with only patchy and irregular rainfall. The south and east are damper with summer rains adequate for farming; the Cape itself has a Mediterranean climate with dry summers but plentiful winter rainfall.

Namibia

		J	F	M	A	M	J	J	A	S	O	N	D
Keetmanshoop	°C	26.6	25.5	24.1	20.8	16.5	13.5	13.2	14.8	18.8	21.2	24.3	25.5
1100 m	mm	22	31	35	13	5	2	1	1	2	4	14	17
Windhoek	°C	22.9	21.0	20.5	18.9	15.6	12.9	13.0	15.8	19.6	21.7	22.6	23.1
1700 m	mm	77	73	81	38	6	1	1	0	1	12	38	47

South Africa

		J	F	M	A	M	J	J	A	S	O	N	D
Cape Town	°C	20.3	20.0	18.8	16.1	14.0	12.6	11.6	12.3	13.7	15.0	17.6	19.3
0 m	mm	11	16	14	53	89	84	83	73	45	31	17	11
Durban	°C	23.4	23.8	23.2	21.2	18.9	16.2	16.3	17.2	18.4	19.9	21.2	22.5
0 m	mm	119	127	120	94	59	36	29	43	63	94	125	129
Kimberley	°C	24.5	23.3	21.4	17.3	13.1	9.9	10.1	12.4	16.4	19.8	22.2	23.6
1250 m	mm	53	61	71	43	19	9	6	11	11	30	45	58
Pretoria	°C	21.0	20.7	19.5	16.9	13.0	9.9	10.3	13.1	16.4	19.6	20.1	20.6
1400 m	mm	125	108	90	41	25	10	10	5	21	56	126	129

Zimbabwe

		J	F	M	A	M	J	J	A	S	O	N	D
Bulawayo	°C	20.9	20.8	19.9	18.9	15.9	13.4	13.6	15.9	19.3	22.1	21.6	21.3
1345 m	mm	134	111	65	21	9	3	Tr	1	5	25	89	125
Harare	°C	20.0	19.8	19.4	18.7	15.9	13.6	13.6	15.6	19.0	21.3	20.8	20.4
1479 m	mm	216	172	99	36	11	4	1	3	5	30	100	186

ISLANDS OF THE ATLANTIC AND INDIAN OCEANS

Atlantic Ocean Islands

Temperature regimes on oceanic islands are determined mostly by the surface temperatures of the surrounding waters, which tend to be stable and subject only to slow seasonal fluctuations. Few islands are big enough to generate climates of their own, though their altitude very often determines the amount of rain that falls upon them. The Cape Verde Islands are tropical, hot and dry throughout the year close to sea level, cooler and damper on the slopes of their volcanic uplands. Ascension Island is equatorial, with uniformly hot, dry coastal plains and rainfall mainly on Green Mountain, its single peak. St Helena is subtropical, with a high, damp interior tableland. The southern islands lie mostly in the zone of strong west winds, tending to be cold, cloudy and wet throughout the year; South Georgia, on the Antarctic fringe, is heavily glaciated down to sea level.

Cape Verde Islands

		J	F	M	A	M	J	J	A	S	O	M	D	
Praia	°C	22.5	22.2	22.8	23.3	24.2	25.0	26.1	26.7	26.9	26.9	25.6	23.9	
34 m	mm	3	Tr	Tr	Tr	0	Tr	5	97	114	30	8	3	2

Falkland Islands and Dependencies

		J	F	M	A	M	J	J	A	S	O	M	D	
Grytviken (South Georgia)	°C	4.4	5.3	5.0	3.0	0.8	−0.8	−1.5	−1.4	−0.1	2.0	3.5	3.5	
2 m	mm	118	115	139	126	174	123	113	121	102	89	92	119	1

		J	F	M	A	M	J	J	A	S	O	N	D	Year
t Stanley														
lkland Is)	°C	8.7	9.0	8.2	5.8	3.9	2.4	2.2	2.6	3.4	5.2	7.0	7.7	5.5
53 m	mm	79	55	44	46	58	47	50	42	36	34	41	72	598

Helena and Dependencies

		J	F	M	A	M	J	J	A	S	O	N	D	Year
nburgh (Tristan														
Cunha)	°C	17.4	18.2	17.0	15.7	14.3	13.2	12.0	11.8	11.8	12.8	14.2	16.3	14.6
23 m	mm	103	88	88	153	144	187	147	193	129	139	117	167	1655
rgetown														
cension Is)	°C	26.1	26.9	27.5	27.5	26.9	26.1	25.6	25.0	24.7	25.0	25.0	25.6	26.1
17 m	mm	5	10	18	28	13	13	13	10	8	8	5	3	132
estown														
Helena)	°C	23.6	24.2	24.7	24.2	21.9	20.8	19.7	19.7	19.7	20.3	20.8	21.7	21.7
12 m	mm	8	10	20	10	18	18	8	10	5	3	0	3	137

also Canary Islands (Spain, Europe Southwest) and Azores and Madeira
tugal, Europe Southwest).

Indian Ocean Islands

The tropical and subtropical islands of the Indian Ocean have uniformly warm, humid climates, with mean summer temperatures close to 25°C (77°F) and winters only slightly cooler. Cooled by trade winds and watered by year-round or strong summer rainfall, many were formerly forested and are now intensively cultivated with farms or plantations. Islands of the temperate zone lie within the belt of westerly winds and tend to be cool and blustery; those lying close to the Antarctic Convergence (the marine boundary between polar and subpolar waters) are cold, wet and windy and treeless, but clothed in tall tussock grass and snow-covered in winter.

		J	F	M	A	M	J	J	A	S	O	N	D	Year
tish Indian Ocean Territory														
o Garcia	°C	27.7	27.7	28.2	28.1	27.5	26.5	26.0	25.6	26.1	26.5	27.1	27.7	27.1
2 m	mm	322	233	228	212	141	183	140	161	180	233	218	211	2462
os (Keeling) Islands														
os Island	°C	27.1	27.3	27.4	27.4	27.1	26.4	25.6	25.8	26.1	26.4	26.8	26.8	26.7
5 m	mm	216	136	229	236	294	202	262	204	81	109	56	86	2108
noro Islands														
nde														
noro	°C	26.2	26.2	26.3	25.9	25.0	23.7	22.8	22.7	23.1	24.2	25.5	26.2	24.8
t7 m	mm	357	291	284	309	211	217	271	141	131	89	105	233	2639
dagascar														
nanarivo	°C	19.3	19.2	18.9	17.8	15.6	13.9	13.0	13.5	15.1	17.2	18.6	19.1	16.8
t310 m	mm	286	218	231	36	13	9	10	10	15	43	143	257	1270
iranana	°C	26.9	26.8	27.2	27.1	26.3	25.0	24.2	24.2	24.6	25.5	26.6	27.2	26.0
t05 m	mm	277	211	187	56	8	8	7	7	5	11	28	111	915

Mauritius and Dependencies

		J	F	M	A	M	J	J	A	S	O	N	D
Agalega Islands	°C	27.3	27.2	27.7	27.5	26.9	25.7	24.9	24.7	25.2	25.8	26.5	27.2
3 m	mm	272	198	195	168	175	83	90	87	91	143	113	225
Plaisance (Mauritius)	°C	26.0	25.8	25.6	24.3	23.0	21.3	20.7	20.6	21.1	22.0	23.5	25.0
57 m	mm	237	241	383	206	175	117	130	85	84	56	80	172
Rodriguez	°C	26.7	26.9	26.8	25.7	24.5	22.8	21.9	21.7	22.3	23.1	24.4	25.8
59 m	mm	170	126	117	164	147	78	79	74	49	52	52	97

Réunion

		J	F	M	A	M	J	J	A	S	O	N	D
St Denis	°C	26.0	26.3	25.8	24.5	22.9	21.6	20.7	20.6	21.3	22.2	23.6	25.2
12 m	mm	252	217	292	162	71	80	72	47	44	50	99	140

Seychelles

		J	F	M	A	M	J	J	A	S	O	N	D
Mahé	°C	27.3	27.3	27.9	28.3	27.9	26.7	25.9	25.8	26.1	26.5	26.9	26.9
3 m	mm	338	242	204	170	161	85	83	78	116	167	206	332

Marion Island

		J	F	M	A	M	J	J	A	S	O	N	D
Marion Island	°C	6.8	7.3	7.2	5.9	4.7	4.1	3.6	3.3	3.2	4.4	5.1	5.7
25 m	mm	194	185	216	221	235	221	228	178	190	167	190	226

ANTARCTICA

The Antarctic continent is uniformly cold but has many climates. Coastal temperatures are determined by the presence or absence of sea ice. Ice-free coasts and islands have summer temperatures close to freezing point and winters only slightly cooler; the open sea, though near to freezing point, has a warming effect. Shores invested by pack ice have colder winters and shorter summers, with mean temperatures seldom rising above freezing point even in January, the warmest month. Some coastal stations, especially on Antarctic Peninsula, are subject to depressions that bring heavy snow in winter and summer alike. The interior of Antarctica is very much colder and generally drier. On the high ice-capped plateau, site of the South Pole, mean summer temperatures stand about -30°C (-22°F), falling in winter to -60°C (-76°F) or below, with only a few centimetres of snow (mainly ice spicules) per year.

		J	F	M	A	M	J	J	A	S	O	N	D
Amundsen-Scott (South Pole) 2800 m	°C	−28.6	−40.3	−54.5	−58.6	−57.7	−56.9	−59.7	−59.3	−58.9	−52.2	−38.6	−27.4
Mawson 14 m	°C	−0.3	−4.0	−9.8	−14.4	−15.2	−16.3	−17.8	−18.7	−17.9	−12.9	−5.4	−0.7
McMurdo 45 m	°C	−3.3	−8.4	−18.1	−21.1	−23.7	−23.6	−26.3	−28.0	−24.7	−20.4	−9.1	−4.0

Section 4

Minerals, Crops and Animal Products

Minerals (including Fuels)

Apart from the products of animals and plants, almost every material useful to man is derived from minerals that originate in the Earth's crust. The diversity of mineral commodities makes generalization difficult. These tables include, for each commodity, all the countries that produce over 3 per cent of recorded world production, plus lesser producers where space allows. Unless otherwise indicated, figures for minerals refer to 1976–80 inclusive; for all other products means cover the period 1977–81. Wherever possible, figures have been given for the quantity of useful material produced rather than the quantity of ore.

In recent times industrial countries have become increasingly dependent on imported materials, many of which come from the less developed countries. Japan, for example, imports all its bauxite, over 90 per cent of its chromium, copper, iron ore, manganese and nickel. The EEC imports 95 per cent or more of its chromium, copper and manganese; the USA imports all its manganese and almost 90 per cent of its bauxite. Conversely the poorer countries have come to depend heavily on the export of raw materials to obtain the foreign exchange needed for the growth of their economies. The resultant network of interests and conflicts has focused attention upon the adequacy of world reserves of essential minerals. One crude measure of the probable future adequacy of supplies of a mineral is the ratio of reserves to production. Current ratios range from less than ten years for industrial diamonds, and less than fifty years for lead, tungsten, tin, zinc, mercury and silver, to over four hundred years for potash and over one thousand years for bauxite and phosphate. Such values depend on the interactions of technology, commodity prices and political forces and may change overnight; however, they reflect the diverse conditions associated with the provision and exploitation of minerals.

Coal, oil, natural gas and uranium are the major fuels, essential for almost every industrial process, and the basis of the high standards of living of the developed nations. While consumption of energy is greatest in the most highly developed countries, distribution of fuels is governed independently by geological factors. There is thus an important international trade in fuels. Approximately half the world's annual oil production and just under 10 per cent of the world's annual coal production are traded internationally.

During the 1960s world consumption of oil doubled; by 1970 total oil energy utilization exceeded that of coal. However, the rapid rise in the price of oil from 1973 to 1980 disrupted the energy economy of the world, and new patterns of energy consumption and trade are still emerging. Both the disposition and quality of the world's various fuel sources are very unevenly distributed. Whereas known coal reserves would last for over two hundred years if used at the rates which prevailed in the late 1970s, it is generally assumed that oil production will peak in the 1990s and dwindle rapidly in the first three decades of the 21st century. The data on uranium are the most speculative, and the energy value ascribable to reserves depends on the technology used in reactors. Spent mainly in conventional 'burner' reactors, world uranium reserves would be approximately equivalent in energy terms to world reserves of oil and gas. With 'breeder' reactors that generate more fuel as they operate, the energy available may be multiplied by a factor of fifty to a hundred.

METALS AND METAL ORES

Aluminium and Bauxite

The most abundant crustal metal, aluminium (Al) is produced mainly from bauxite, which forms a surface blanket where aluminium-rich clays have weathered under warm, moist conditions. Commercial deposits of bauxite contain 40 to 60 per cent of hydrated alumina ($Al_2O_3.2H_2O$); about four tonnes of good-quality bauxite produce one tonne of aluminium. Refining and production require large energy inputs, often beyond the capacity of the countries that mine the ore. About 90 per cent of world output of bauxite is used for aluminium production; small quantities are used for making refractory bricks, high alumina cements and abrasives. A derivative, alum, is widely employed in water-purification, paper-making and as a mordant in textile-dyeing. Aluminium alloys are widely used in aircraft, vehicles, as foil wrappings and in cans and containers, and aluminium is increasingly replacing copper in power-transmission cables.

Aluminium Production

Country	10^3 tonnes av. 1977–81
World Total	15,200
USA	4,435
USSR	2,334
Japan	1,023
Canada	1,015
West Germany	736
Norway	642
France	410
China	358
UK	354
Spain	293
Australia	292
Italy	272
Netherlands	256
Romania	222

Bauxite Production

Country	10^3 tonnes av. 1977–81
World Total	89,260
Australia	26,136
Guinea	12,686
Jamaica	11,680
USSR	6,540
Suriname	4,711
Brazil	3,865
Guyana	3,027
Greece	2,944
Hungary	2,937
Yugoslavia	2,801
France	1,985
India	1,764
USA	1,714
China	1,510

Cadmium

Cadmium is a rare metallic element most commonly obtained from the mineral greenockite (CdS), which occurs sparsely in association with zinc sulphide and ores of copper, zinc and lead. All commercial cadmium is recovered as a by-product of smelting such ores. Its major uses are as an electroplated protective coating for iron and steel, and in alloys used for brazing, electrical uses, and heavy-duty bearings. It is also used in rechargeable batteries, solar cells and to produce vivid yellow or red pigments for ceramic glazes.

Country	tonnes av. 1977–81
World Total	**18,200**
USSR	2,920
Japan	2,424
USA	1,731
Belgium	1,348
Canada	1,337
West Germany	1,210
Mexico	854
Australia	853
France	725
Poland	713
Finland	585
Italy	480
Netherlands	418
UK	332

Chromium

The major chromium mineral is chromite (FeCr$_2$O$_4$). Though widely used as an attractive, protective electroplated layer on metal objects, most chromium is used for making ferrous alloys. Chrome steels are used for cutlery, sinks, utensils and decorative trim. Exceptionally hard steels with resistance to high temperatues are made when chromium is alloyed in combination with iron, nickel, cobalt and tungsten. Chromium is used for the production of special refractory bricks, and chromium salts are used for tanning leather and making dyes.

Country	Ore 10^3 tonnes av. 1977–81
World Total	**9,300**
South Africa	3,103
USSR	2,346
Albania	1,028
Zimbabwe	557
Philippines	494
Turkey	490
Brazil	326
India	317
Finland	182
Iran	135
Madagascar	131
Greece	35
Cuba	26

Cobalt

Cobalt is produced mainly as a by-product from copper, nickel and silver ores, in which it occurs at low concentrations as sulphides and arsenides. It is a hard magnetic metal, used in the production of magnets and high-quality cutting tools. Alloyed with other metals it imparts resistance to corrosion and oxidation, and is used in gas turbines and jet engines. Cobalt pigments, ranging from blue to green, are used for colouring glass, enamels and ceramic glazes.

Country	tonnes av. 1977–81
World Total	**29,880**
Zaïre	12,511
Australia	3,321
New Caledonia	2,622
Zambia	2,564
USSR	2,050
Canada	1,658
Cuba	1,460
Finland	1,214
Philippines	1,195
Morocco	957
Botswana	240
Zimbabwe	85

Copper

Most of the commercially-worked copper deposits consist of low-grade (0.4–1.5%) sulphide ores. There are over a dozen commercial ores with two, chalcocite (Cu_2S) and chalcopyrite ($CuFeS_2$), accounting for about 75 per cent of all production. Copper is used for electrical and telegraphic cables, electrical apparatus and pipes, and in alloys such as bronze, brass and gun metal. The major importing nations are Japan, West Germany, Italy, France and the UK.

Country	10^3 tonnes av. 1977–81
World Total	**7,948**
USA	1,377
USSR	1,128
Chile	1,059
Canada	692
Zambia	619
Zaïre	468
Peru	361
Poland	314
Philippines	89
Australia	230
South Africa	200
Papua New Guinea	172
China	162
Mexico	137

Gold

Gold occurs widely in low concentrations, often as native metal. Commercially it is worked from veins, or from ancient or recent sedimentary deposits (placers): it is also recovered when certain copper, lead and zinc ores are refined. Gold is the traditional monetary standard, and is used in coins and jewellery (usually hardened with other metals) and as a dental alloy. Increasingly it is being employed as an infra-red filter, and for coating electronic components when corrosion resistance and low-noise electrical contacts are required.

Country	kg av. 1977–81
World Total	1,232,000
South Africa	687,287
USSR	256,000
Canada	51,339
China	39,400
USA	33,662
Papua New Guinea	19,685
Philippines	19,161
Australia	18,585
Zimbabwe	12,023
Ghana	11,828
Dominican Republic	11,296
Colombia	11,197
Brazil	9,585
Mexico	6,051

Iron and Iron Ores

Iron ores are widely distributed throughout the world in metamorphic, igneous and sedimentary rocks. The most important commercial ores – haematite (Fe_2O_3), magnetite (Fe_3O_4), siderite ($FeCO_3$) and limonite ($Fe_2O_3.H_2O$) – usually contain between 25 per cent and 60 per cent iron. Virtually all mined ore is used to make pig-iron. A wide range of ferro-alloys are manufactured from this basic product, including steel – a general term covering alloys which can be forged, drawn into rods and wires, rolled into sheets or machined. Much steel is derived from recycled iron.

Iron Ore Production

Country	10^3 tonnes av. 1977–81
World Total	877,200
USSR	243,462
Brazil	97,158
Australia	90,205
USA	74,341
China	70,000
Canada	50,986
India	40,468
France	30,454
South Africa	27,376
Sweden	24,461
Liberia	19,034
Venezuela	15,036
Mauritania	8,681
Spain	8,483

Production of Pig-Iron and Blast Furnace Ferro-Alloys

Country	10^3 tonnes av. 1977–81
World Total	**504,000**
USSR	108,423
Japan	83,077
USA	72,323
China	33,722
West Germany	32,018
France	18,520
Italy	11,788
Poland	10,915
Brazil	10,884
UK	10,486
Canada	10,308
Belgium	9,890
Czechoslovakia	9,782
India	9,165

Lead

Lead is obtained mainly from galena (PbS), which occurs in veins associated with sulphides of iron, zinc and silver. A ductile, extrusible metal which resists attack by dilute acids, lead is often used for lining chemical plant and as sheet-metal flashing for buildings. Lead-acid batteries are the major consumer of metallic lead, and much is converted to tetraethyl lead, a petrol additive. Small quantities are used in solder, babbit metal (for engine bearings), pewter and protective paints.

Country	10^3 tonnes av. 1977–81
World Total	**3,580**
USSR	593
USA	517
Australia	408
Canada	333
Peru	181
Mexico	162
China	155
Yugoslavia	125
North Korea	115
Morocco	110
Bulgaria	103
Sweden	82
Spain	75
Poland	55

Manganese Ores

Manganese (Mn) is a hard, brittle metal: its ores are frequently found in association with sedimentary iron ores. The main economically-exploitable sources are the minerals pyrolusite (MnO_2) and psilomelane. Over 90 per cent of production is used in the metallurgical industry, primarily in steel-making. Manganese is alloyed with iron, chrome and nickel to produce abrasion-resistant steels, and with aluminium to produce a range of tough, lightweight alloys. It is also used in dry batteries and inks, and as a decolorizer in glass production.

Country	10^3 tonnes av. 1977–81
World Total	24,760
USSR	9,359
South Africa	5,124
Brazil	1,974
Gabon	1,875
India	1,683
Australia	1,565
China	1,420
Mexico	505
Ghana	269
USA	202
Morocco	123
Japan	98
Hungary	94
Romania	82

Mercury

Mercury (Hg) is largely obtained from cinnabar (HgS) which occurs sparsely in several kinds of rock within volcanic and geothermal areas. The few large known reserves may be exhausted before the end of the 20th century. Mercury is the only metal that is liquid at normal temperatures; it has specialized uses in switches and thermometers, and as the cathode in industrial electrolytic cells. Most mercury, however, is consumed as compounds in the production of anti-fungal agents, anti-fouling paint, and detonators for explosives.

Country	10^3 kg av. 1977–81
World Total	6,400
USSR	1,900
Spain	1,273
USA	968
Algeria	864
China	700
Czechoslovakia	172
Turkey	169
Mexico	152
West Germany	81
Italy	54
Finland	47

Nickel

The major nickel ores are sulphides and oxides. Commercial deposits commonly contain 0.5 to 3.0 per cent nickel, together with copper and iron and small quantities of precious metals. Oxide ores generally occur in laterites (heavily-leached tropical soils). Most nickel is used in alloys, particularly in combinations with chrome and iron to produce high-strength steels, stainless steels, magnets, and electrical heating elements. Copper-nickel alloys have high resistance to corrosion and are widely used for coinage. The major importing nations are Japan, USA, UK, West Germany and France.

Country	10^3 tonnes av. 1977–81
World Total	718
Canada	166
USSR	141
New Caledonia	87
Australia	77
Philippines	37
Cuba	36
Indonesia	33
South Africa	24
Dominican Republic	19
Botswana	15
Zimbabwe	15
Greece	13
USA	12
China	10

Platinum Metals

Platinum metals, including platinum (Pt), palladium (Pd), iridium (Ir), rhodium (Rh), and ruthenium (Ru), are usually found together in basic igneous intrusions. Platinum is widely used in jewellery, but its principal use is as a catalyst in a range of chemical processes (for example the production of ammonia and nitric acids), and for refining petroleum spirit. Specialized applications make use of platinum's high melting point and high resistance to oxidation and attack by acids, for example in pyrometers, thermocouples and windings for electrical furnaces.

Country	kg av. 1977–81
World Total	206,750
USSR	98,040
South Africa	92,350
Canada	12,618
Japan	1,108
Colombia	462
Australia	341
USA	190
Yugoslavia	181

Silver

Silver (Ag) occurs mainly as the sulphide metal, argentite (Ag$_2$S), in veins or lodes together with sulphides of lead and copper. Most of the world's production is from ores mined and processed primarily for other metals. Alone, or alloyed with copper and other hardening metals, silver is coined and widely used in ornaments and jewellery. It has many commercial uses – in photographic films, as a catalyst in chemical processes, and in specialized batteries, electrical instruments and dental amalgams.

Country	10^3 kg av. 1977–81
World Total	**10,799**
USSR	1,560
Mexico	1,541
Peru	1,281
Canada	1,173
USA	1,172
Australia	802
Poland	686
Chile	280
Japan	279
Bolivia	191
Sweden	189
Yugoslavia	150
South Africa	150
Zaïre	85

Tin

Cassiterite (SnO$_2$), the main tin-bearing mineral, occurs in ores mineralized by acidic igneous magmas (molten rocks); often it has weathered from the veins where it formed, and concentrated in placer deposits; these provide most of the world's tin ore. Tin (Sn) is a soft, pliable, non-toxic metal, used as a protective coating for mild steel 'tin' cans, and for pliable tubes. Bronze, pewter, gun metal, bell metal and solders are tin alloys. Tin oxide is also used to produce a white glaze on ceramics.

Country	tonnes av. 1977–81
World Total	**224,200**
Malaysia	61,138
Thailand	30,702
Indonesia	30,112
Bolivia	29,643
USSR	17,200
China	14,120
Australia	11,830
Brazil	6,972
UK	3,409
Zaïre	3,025
South Africa	2,836
Nigeria	2,784
East Germany	1,580
Rwanda	1,427

Titanium

Titanium is obtained from ilmenite ($FeTiO_3$) and rutile (TiO_2) which are largely concentrated from sand deposits. Titanium metal, very resistant to corrosion, is as strong as steel but only half the weight. It is a high-cost metal, largely confined to uses in jet engines, aircraft, military hardware and in specialized chemical plant equipment. Titanium dioxide, a pigment of exceptional whiteness and opacity, is used in white paints and enamels.

Country	tonnes av. 1977–81
World Total	**6,089,000**
Australia	1,535,331
Canada	1,521,960
Norway	780,152
USA	530,842
USSR	422,800
South Africa	403,480
India	179,912
Malaysia	178,875
Finland	139,860
Sri Lanka	58,479
Brazil	36,427
Sierra Leone	20,747

Tungsten

Tungsten is obtained from wolframite (($FeMn)WO_4$) and scheelite ($CaWO_4$) which commonly occur associated with gold, tin, copper and other ores in acidic veins, contact metamorphic deposits and placer deposits. Tungsten metal has a high melting point (3410°C, 6170°F) and is used for light-bulb filaments, cathodes for X-ray tubes and sparking-plug electrodes. About 40 per cent of world production is used in making extremely hard, heat-resistant steels, which are used for razors, drills, hacksaw blades, engine valves and military hardware.

Country	tonnes av. 1977–81
World Total	**47,800**
China	12,600
USSR	8,590
USA	3,045
Australia	3,016
South Korea	2,701
Bolivia	2,542
Canada	2,373
North Korea	2,170
Thailand	2,008
Austria	1,619
Portugal	1,295
Brazil	1,178
Japan	723
Burma	635

Minerals (including Fuels)

Vanadium

Vanadium ores rarely occur in significant concentrations; most commercial supplies are obtained as by-products of other ore-processing – in the USA, for example, from processing the uranium-bearing mineral carnotite. Over four fifths of the vanadium produced is used in manufacturing tough, heat-resistant steels, which are made into high-speed tools, axles, springs and gears. Over 10 per cent is consumed in vanadium-aluminium alloys used in supersonic aircraft. Vanadium pentoxide is a catalyst used in the manufacture of sulphuric acid.

Country	tonnes av. 1977–81
World Total	33,975
South Africa	11,718
USSR	9,240
USA	4,758
Finland	3,249
China	2,920
Norway	510
Chile	482
Namibia	247

Zinc

The main commercial sources are sphalerite (ZnS), calamine ($ZnCO_3$) and hemimorphite (($ZnOH)_2 SiO_3$), which often occur in association with lead ores. Most zinc is used as a coating to protect steel from rusting: it is familiar as 'galvanized' buckets, wire, corrugated roofing sheets, bolts etc. Zinc is employed in dry batteries; its oxide as a pigment in white paints, its chloride as a wood-preservative and fireproofing agent. Zinc compounds are also used in medicines.

Country	10^3 tonnes av. 1977–81
World Total	18,240
Canada	1,180
USSR	1,020
Australia	501
Peru	445
USA	321
Japan	255
Mexico	241
Poland	221
Ireland	167
Sweden	164
China	153
Spain	149
North Korea	138
West Germany	110

NON-METALS

Asbestos

Commercial asbestos is obtained from a number of metamorphic minerals which possess long, fibrous crystals. Chrysotile ($2H_2O.3MgO.2SiO_2$) accounts for the bulk of production, though tremolite, crocidolite, amosite and other minerals are also worked. The minerals' long, strong, flexible and fireproof fibres possess low electrical and heat conductivity and are inert to many chemicals. Asbestos is used in brake and clutch linings, roofing materials, fireproof fabrics and ropes, filters for chemical plant and insulating materials.

Country	10^3 tonnes av. 1977–81
World Total	4,780
USSR	2,047
Canada	1,375
South Africa	280
Zimbabwe	256
China	240
Italy	144
Brazil	140
USA	86
Australia	66
Swaziland	35
Cyprus	33
India	27
Turkey	13
South Korea	11

Diamonds

The primary source of diamonds is a basic peridotite rock called 'blue ground' or kimberlite, which occurs as pipes and dykes. Weathered out of the kimberlite, diamonds are deposited with gravels and sands on river beds and beaches. Exceptional hardness and resistance to abrasion makes diamonds ideal for use in cutting tools, drills, dyes and styluses. Most of the world's diamonds are used industrially; only the finest, almost flawless stones are cut for gems.

Country	10^3 carats av. 1977–81
World Total	39,700
USSR	10,600
Zaïre	9,805
South Africa	8,360
Botswana	3,989
Namibia	1,672
Ghana	1,316
Angola	948
Venezuela	680
Sierra Leone	659
Brazil	517
Tanzania	330
Central African Republic	311

Fluorspar

Fluorspar or fluorite (CaF_2) occurs as a gangue mineral in veins of lead and zinc ores. It is used as a flux in steel-making and in the refining of copper, gold, silver and other ores. It provides the raw material for the production of hydrofluoric acid and for cryolite. Fluorine compounds are widely used as aerosol propellants and as refrigerants. A small amount of fluorspar is used in making enamel coatings for sanitary ware.

Country	10^3 tonnes av. 1977–81
World Total	4,720
Mexico	867
USSR	516
Mongolia	512
South Africa	443
China	440
France	266
Spain	262
Thailand	231
UK	184
Italy	171
USA	111
East Germany	100
Kenya	98
Czechoslovakia	96

Gypsum and Anhydrite

Gypsum ($CaSO_4.2H_2O$) and anhydrite ($CaSO_4$) occur as thick evaporite deposits in sedimentary rocks. Their principal use is for the production of plaster and plasterboard, for building and for use in special cements. Gypsum is also used as a flux for smelting nickel ores and as a filler in paper and paint. In the chemical industry anhydrite is used in manufacturing sulphuric acid and the fertilizer sulphate of ammonia.

Country	10^3 tonnes av. 1977–81
World Total	69,980
USA	12,117
Canada	7,610
Iran	6,980
France	6,318
USSR	5,360
Spain	5,309
Italy	4,190
UK	3,294
China	2,600
West Germany	2,241
Mexico	1,773
Australia	1,223
India	870
Austria	801

Kaolin

Kaolin or china clay is a simple clay mineral formed by the alteration of feldspars in granite. It is used for the production of ceramics, particularly porcelain and china. Large amounts are used as fillers in paints, rubber products and paper; smaller quantities are used in pharmaceuticals, and in polishes, where kaolin acts as a mild abrasive.

Country	10^3 tonnes av. 1977–81
World Total	**17,000**
USA	6,664
UK	2,840
USSR	2,440
Czechoslovakia	523
India	463
West Germany	396
France	365
Brazil	350
South Korea	319
Japan	206
Bulgaria	204
Spain	200
Yugoslavia	151
Mexico	145

Micas

Micas are layered silicates which split into very thin flexible plates. Muscovite (clear mica) and biotite (brown mica) occur in igneous and metamorphic rocks; the most valuable crystals occur in pegmatite veins. As mica is an extremely good electrical insulator, and can tolerate temperatures up to 500°C (932°F), it is widely used in electrical equipment. Small quantities of ground mica are used to give a lustre to paints and wallpapers, as a dry lubricant, and as a filler in rubber roofing compounds.

Country	10^3 tonnes av. 1977–81
World Total	**209**
USA	118
USSR	45
India	13
France	7
Norway	5
Spain	4
Brazil	3
South Africa	2
Zimbabwe	2
Argentina	1
Madagascar	1
Sudan	1

Phosphate

Phosphate rock occurs as sedimentary deposits of phosphatic limestone, guano and bonebeds, and as the igneous mineral, apatite. About three quarters of the phosphate rock quarried each year is consumed as fertilizer, generally after treatment with acid to produce 'superphosphate' and other water-soluble compounds readily available to plants. Phosphate rock is also used in the production of detergents, water-softeners, leavening agents for baking, toothpaste and metal alloys, including phosphor bronze.

Country	10^3 tonnes av. 1977–81
World Total	130,400
USA	51,388
USSR	24,690
Morocco	19,126
China	7,848
Tunisia	4,076
Jordan	3,016
South Africa	2,868
Togo	2,749
Senegal	1,839
Israel	1,818
Brazil	1,720
Nauru	1,708
Christmas Island	1,403
Vietnam	930

Potash

'Potash' in industry generally implies potassium oxide (K_2O), derived from such potassium salts as sylvite (KCl) that occur in sedimentary evaporite deposits. Potash is also obtained by the evaporation of natural brines. Most potash is used in fertilizer manufacture; a small amount is taken up in the formation of special cements, and high-grade glass and ceramics.

Country	K_2O equivalent 10^3 tonnes av. 1977–81
World Total	26,700
USSR	7,937
Canada	6,673
East Germany	3,365
West Germany	2,554
USA	2,220
France	1,937
Israel	755
Spain	743
UK	226
Italy	209
Chile	19
China	15

Salt

Sodium chloride (NaCl) or common salt is mainly obtained from rock-salt (halite) which occurs as sedimentary evaporite deposits. Small amounts are obtained from direct evaporation of brine. Widely used in preserving and flavouring food, it is also an important raw material for the chemical industry, being the source of sodium hydroxide and chlorine which are used in the production of glass, soap, baking-soda, bleaching agents, weed-killers, germicides, hydrochloric acid, pharmaceuticals and a host of other products. It is also spread as a de-icing agent on roads and used in glazing ceramic wares.

Country	10^3 tonnes av. 1977–81
World Total	**168,240**
USA	38,343
China	17,401
USSR	14,440
West Germany	13,404
UK	7,441
Canada	6,959
India	6,715
France	6,159
Mexico	6,056
Australia	5,353
Italy	5,153
Romania	4,810
Poland	4,397
Netherlands	3,408

Sulphur

Commercial sulphur (S) is obtained largely from sedimentary deposits of elemental sulphur; pyrites (FeS_2) and natural hydrogen sulphide gas (H_2S) provide other sources, and a small quantity is obtained from refining metallic sulphide ores. Though most is used for the manufacture of sulphuric acid, sulphur also plays a vital role in the production of superphosphate fertilizer, drugs, gunpowder, cosmetics, insecticides, dyes and a wide range of chemical products.

Country	10^3 tonnes av. 1977–81
World Total	**54,340**
USA	11,530
USSR	10,611
Canada	6,965
Poland	5,279
Japan	2,743
China	2,151
Mexico	2,091
France	2,041
West Germany	1,668
Spain	1,236
Iraq	692
Italy	616
South Africa	555
Saudi Arabia	242

Talc

Talc ($Mg_3Si_4O_{10}(OH)_2$) is a hydrated magnesium silicate mineral which occurs associated with metamorphic limestones and ultrabasic rocks (rocks poor in silica but rich in metallic oxides). It has a smooth unctuous feel, of value when talc is used as a dry lubricant in pharmaceutical and toilet preparations. Its most important applications are in priming paints, cosmetics and talcum powder. It is also used in the manufacture of specialized ceramics (e.g. high-tension electrical insulators), as a filler in the rubber and plastics industries, and in the formulation of insecticides and fertilizers.

Country	10^3 tonnes av. 1977–81
World Total	6,140
Japan	1,353
USA	1,201
South Korea	666
USSR	478
India	346
Brazil	345
France	285
Finland	262
Italy	163
North Korea	156
China	150
Australia	138
Austria	112
Canada	80

FUELS

Bituminous Coal and Anthracite

Bituminous coal and anthracite consist of vegetable remains which have been compressed, heated and metamorphosed to impure carbon within sedimentary rocks. Anthracites, most highly metamorphosed, have the highest energy content of all coals, but provide less than 10 per cent of world production. Bituminous coals account for just over half the world's total; these are the most abundant fossil fuels, and the ones most widely used for electrical power generation and metallurgical coke production.

Country	10^3 tonnes av. 1977–81
World Total	2,741,854
USA	689,811
China[1]	604,320
USSR	548,673
Poland	187,175
UK	123,303
India	109,286
South Africa	105,006
West Germany	86,139
Australia	78,933
North Korea	44,000
Czechoslovakia	27,917
France	19,263
Canada	18,530
South Korea	18,406

[1] Assumed bituminous.

Sub-Bituminous Coal and Lignite

Lignite and sub-bituminous coal are low-grade coals, commonly possessing about half the energy content of anthracite or high-quality bituminous coals. Both are used for power generation and general heating, usually only where higher-quality fuels are not readily available.

Country	10^3 tonnes av. 1977–81
World Total	915,745
East Germany	253,972
USSR	164,292
West Germany	127,502
Czechoslovakia	95,758
Yugoslavia	43,528
Australia	38,516
Poland	38,466
Bulgaria	27,462
Romania	25,105
Greece	23,880
Hungary	22,681
Turkey	16,883
Canada	15,231
India	4,193

Natural Gas

Natural gas and crude oil often occur together, both having formed from the decomposition of organic remains within sedimentary rocks. On average natural gas consists of 70 to 80 per cent methane, 10 to 20 per cent ethane, and 5 to 15 per cent nitrogen and other gases. Gas may be dissolved in oil, or form separate accumulations trapped within the interstices of rocks. Though the bulk of natural gas is burned as fuel, some is used for the production of carbon black, and as a source of hydrogen and general feedstock in the chemical industry.

Country	$10^9 m^3$ av. 1977–81
World Total	1,544
USA	572
USSR	405
Netherlands	91
Canada	88
UK	39
Romania	35
Mexico	26
Indonesia	25
West Germany	19
Norway	18
Venezuela	15
Iran	14
Italy	13
China	13

Petroleum

Crude petroleum oil is an organic deposit, which occurs in sedimentary rocks, principally in sandstones and limestones. According to the degree of modification of the original organic materials, oils may be either heavy and viscous or light and mobile. At oil-refineries the crude oil is converted into useful products such as petrol and diesel fuels, heating oils, lubricants and solvents, and organic chemicals.

Country	10^3 tonnes av. 1977–81
World Total	**3,013,000**
USSR	582,985
Saudi Arabia	466,379
USA	424,987
Iran	165,486
Iraq	117,622
Venezuela	116,279
China	102,216
Nigeria	96,143
Kuwait	93,945
Libya	86,985
Mexico	81,177
Indonesia	80,092
Canada	72,405
UK	66,742

Uranium

Uranium is widely distributed over the world in vein deposits, and disseminated through sandstones, limestones and conglomerates. Though several minerals are worked, pitchblende (uranite) is the major source of the metal. High concentrations are rare and typical ores contain only 0.2 per cent uranium oxide. Uranium's importance lies in its application for nuclear energy, both for power generation and weapons. Contemporary commercial power reactors utilize only the isotope U^{235}, though 'fast breeder' reactors can utilize the more abundant U^{238}.

Country	tonnes av. 1977–81
World Total	**37,460**
USA	14,322
Canada	6,720
South Africa	4,888
Namibia	3,374
Niger	3,122
France	2,359
Australia	1,199
Gabon	1,012
Argentina	170
Spain	162
Portugal	88
West Germany	32

Field and Plantation Crops

Protein crops form a significant component of the human diet, especially in poor countries where meat is scarce. The most concentrated source of vegetable protein is in legume seeds; the plants play a useful additional role in crop rotations by raising soil nitrogen levels and acting as break crops. Soya beans contain about four times as much protein as cereals; peas, beans and ground-nuts contain only twice as much. Soya beans are used in the manufacture of meat substitutes (textured vegetable protein); flour from the beans finds industrial application in fire-fighting foams and synthetic-fibre manufacture, and the oil is used in manufacture of paints, oilcloth and printing inks. Ground-nuts also yield a non-drying oil used in cooking and margarine, soap and cosmetics.

Cereals are grasses with starchy, edible seeds; every important civilization has depended on them as a source of food. The major cereal grains contain about 10 per cent protein and 75 per cent carbohydrate; the grains are easy to store, handle and transport, and contribute more than any other group of foods to the energy and protein content of the human diet. Intensively-grown cereals are among the most productive crops in terms of food production per unit of land; however, as may be calculated from the tables, yield per hectare varies considerably from country to country. If all the cereals grown were consumed directly by man, there would be no shortage of food in the world, but a considerable proportion of the total output is used as animal feed for the production of meat, fats, milk and eggs.

Starchy *tuber crops* or root crops, here represented by potatoes, yams and cassava, are second in importance only to cereals as staple foods; easily cultivated, they provide high yields of food for little effort, and store well – potatoes for up to six months, cassava for up to a year in the ground. Protein content is low (2 per cent or less), starch content high, with some minerals and vitamins present, but populations that rely heavily on these crops may suffer malnutrition, notably protein deficiency. Starchy root crops are also used as animal fodder, and their starch may be converted into industrial alcohol.

The *sugar* of commerce is sucrose ($C_{12}H_{22}O_{11}$); its main sources are tropical sugar-cane and temperate-climate sugar-beet. Growing mainly between $35°N$ and $32°S$, cane sugar dominates world trade, accounting for approximately two thirds of world production. Beet sugar is more expensive to produce; its cultivation is often subsidized by governments to promote local industry and avoid overdependence on the fluctuating cane-sugar market. Current world production of refined sugar approaches 100 million tonnes each year. A readily assimilated source of energy, sugar is consumed at a rate of 1 kg (2.20 lb) or more per person each week in affluent countries, providing about 20 per cent of dietary energy; far less is consumed in poor countries. Sugar is a preservative as well as a flavouring; jams contain 50 per cent or more by weight of sucrose. Minor sources of sugar are the sap of sorghum, maple trees and date palms; honey was used as a sweetening agent long before sugar.

Adults drink on average one to two litres (two to three pints) per day; even the poorest usually try to flavour their water intake, and several *beverages* have universal appeal. Tea, coffee, cocoa and wines include stimulants as well as flavouring, and there are many local variants that incorporate minerals and energy-producing substances. Ethyl alcohol, contained in beer and wines, provides significant energy for those who consume large amounts.

PROTEIN CROPS

Broad Beans

Broad, horse or fava bean (*Vicia faba*) is an erect annual up to 150 cm (60 in) high with a deep tap root, which is grown as a winter crop in Mediterranean climates and as a summer crop in cool-temperate areas. Though some varieties are frost-hardy down to $-5°C$ ($23°F$), they thrive best in areas where mean annual temperatures are 10° to 20°C (50° to 68°F) and yearly precipitation 60 to 80 cm (24 to 32 in). Containing about 25 per cent protein and 50 per cent carbohydrate, these beans are palatable to man and useful also as stockfeed.

Country	10^3 tonnes av. 1977–81	10^3 ha
World Total	**5,278**	**4,978**
China	3,720	3,480
Ethiopia	274	307
Egypt	246	108
Italy	210	166
Morocco	114	181
Spain	87	85
Czechoslovakia	82	44
Brazil	63	177
France	55	20
Turkey	52	30
Tunisia	44	69

Chickpeas

Chickpea or Bengal gram (*Cicer arietinum*), an erect, bushy annual 25 to 50 cm (10 to 20 in) tall, thrives in warm, sunny, dry climates. Though some cultivars can tolerate light frosts, optimum growing temperatures lie between 15° and 25°C (59° and 77°F). Annual precipitation in growing areas is usually between 20 and 70 cm (8 to 28 in). The crop matures in three to seven months, producing oblong pods that hold one or two seeds. Containing 17 to 23 per cent protein, the seeds are eaten boiled, fried, in soups and as flour.

Country	10^3 tonnes av. 1977–81	10^3 ha
World Total	**6,518**	**10,110**
India	4,916	7,472
Pakistan	529	1,301
Mexico	240	198
Turkey	234	195
Ethiopia	89	144
Burma	84	146
Spain	57	98
Iran	42	38
Bangladesh	41	57
Syria	38	54
Morocco	33	54
Nepal	32	67

Ground-nuts

Ground-nut or peanut (*Arachis hypogaea*) is a low-growing plant native to South America, which pushes its developing seed pod underground. Each pod contains two to five seeds. Grown from the tropics to warm temperate regions, ground-nuts require 40 to 60 cm (16 to 24 in) of rain and temperatures close to 23°C (73°F) during their four- to five-month growing season. Two thirds of world production is processed to obtain edible oils and protein-rich animal feed. Man eats ground-nuts fresh, roasted and as peanut butter.

Country	10^3 tonnes av. 1977–81	10^3 ha
World Total	**18,280**	**18,976**
India	5,852	7,244
China	3,030	2,349
USA	1,627	601
Sudan	864	989
Indonesia	754	504
Senegal	746	1,035
Nigeria	488	644
Argentina	434	333
Burma	414	527
Brazil	389	264
Zaïre	314	463
South Africa	305	232
Uganda	205	241
Malawi	175	250

Haricot Beans

The haricot, French, kidney or string bean (*Phaseolus vulgaris*) has both climbing and dwarf cultivars, which grow from subtropical to temperate areas. A frost-free growing season of three to five months is required. Monthly temperatures of 15° to 20°C (59° to 68°F) are optimal; the plants shed their pods if temperatures exceed 30°C (86°F). Immature green pods are eaten as green vegetables, or the dry beans may be harvested. A dwarf form, the navy bean, is used for the production of baked beans.

Country	10^3 tonnes av. 1977–81	10^3 ha
World Total	**13,247**	**24,268**
India	2,499	8,422
China	2,459	2,726
Brazil	2,194	4,603
USA	977	661
Mexico	950	1,635
Thailand	251	423
Argentina	191	202
Uganda	190	288
Burma	189	318
Rwanda	174	215
Burundi	168	257
Turkey	164	108
Tanzania	149	299
Yugoslavia	145	144

Peas

Peas (*Pisum sativum*) are annual bushy or climbing plants that require a cool humid climate with a growing season of two to three months. Best yields are obtained where growing season temperatures are between 13°C and 21°C (55° and 70°F) and annual precipitation is 80 to 100 cm (32 to 40 in). Temperatures over 30°C (86°F) are more damaging than slight frosts. Though fresh and frozen peas are widely consumed in the West, the data given refer only to dried peas, which constitute about 90 per cent of the world's pea production.

Country	10^3 tonnes av. 1977–81	10^3 ha
World Total	9,958	8,396
USSR	5,034	4,037
China	3,160	2,630
India	356	598
USA	154	84
Ethiopia	111	128
UK	109	36
Hungary	107	52
France	85	22
Poland	67	44
New Zealand	61	22
Czechoslovakia	59	28
Rwanda	48	61
Zaïre	47	73
Argentina	24	22

Soya Beans

Soya beans (*Glycine max*) grow on erect bushy plants 30 to 150 cm (12 to 60 in) high, yielding best in warm temperate regions with an annual rainfall of about 50 cm (20 in). They do not tolerate dry heat or severe cold. The beans contain 30 to 40 per cent protein and 14 to 18 per cent oil. In Asia they are eaten as sauces, pastes and bean sprouts. Most Western production is processed for vegetable oil and protein, food additives (for example lecithin) and animal feed. World production has tripled since 1950.

Country	10^3 tonnes av. 1977–81	10^3 ha
World Total	83,362	51,061
USA	52,920	26,387
Brazil	12,483	8,271
China	9,699	10,189
Argentina	2,974	1,464
Indonesia	622	724
Canada	611	268
USSR	533	831
Mexico	518	298
Paraguay	486	347
North Korea	330	300
India	326	410
Romania	304	269
South Korea	266	218
Japan	175	124

CEREALS

Barley

Barley (*Hordeum spp.*) requires a growing season of only eighty days, the shortest of all cool-temperate cereals. Though germination occurs at low temperatures, barley is not very frost-hardy and growing season temperatures above 15°C (59°F) are required. Tolerance of dry heat enables it to grow in the sub-arid tropics. Except in Africa and Asia, most is used as animal food rather than for direct human consumption. Special malting varieties are grown for beer and whisky production.

Country	10³ tonnes av. 1977–81	10³ ha
World Total	**169,148**	**86,300**
USSR	49,833	33,514
Canada	11,057	4,552
France	10,935	2,751
UK	10,095	2,350
China	9,460	6,690
USA	9,108	3,461
West Germany	8,377	1,959
Spain	6,826	3,429
Denmark	6,231	1,568
Turkey	5,188	2,737
East Germany	3,783	999
Poland	3,551	1,304
Czechoslovakia	3,505	936
Australia	3,234	2,657

Maize

Maize (*Zea mays*) originated in the New World. It requires temperatures over 19°C (66°F) during the summer and a rainfall of over 38 cm (15 in) during the growing season. In some poorer communities it is an important human food; in developed countries it is eaten as sweetcorn, cornflakes and cornflour, and used extensively in animal feeds. Maize also provides corn oil, starches, dextrin and adhesives.

Country	10³ tonnes av. 1977–81	10³ ha
World Total	**394,854**	**125,087**
USA	184,395	29,234
China	48,411	16,562
Brazil	18,113	11,425
Mexico	11,264	7,052
Romania	11,020	3,249
South Africa	10,648	5,940
France	9,381	1,749
Yugoslavia	9,331	2,230
Argentina	9,326	2,796
USSR	9,151	3,017
Hungary	6,646	1,317
India	6,319	5,793

Millet

The name 'millet' includes a number of distinct, small-grained cereal species, which grow in a range of environments. *Panicum miliaceum*, a temperate crop, has a very short growing season of seventy days, enabling it to thrive in continental areas with only a brief rainy season. Some tropical millets are very drought-resistant and grow in hot dry areas with only 25 to 40 cm (10 to 16 in) of rain per annum. Millets make good flour and meal and are fermented for alcoholic drinks.

Country	10^3 tonnes av. 1977–81	10^3 ha
World Total	30,944	47,327
India	9,641	17,955
China	7,953	8,057
Nigeria	3,100	5,000
USSR	1,826	2,863
Niger	1,197	2,893
Mali	877	1,407
Egypt	648	173
Senegal	605	951
Chad	576	1,142
Sudan	514	1,285
Uganda	475	393
North Korea	435	414
Cameroon	389	462
Burkina Faso	382	882

Oats

Oats (*Avena sativa*) are grown widely in maritime northwestern Europe, eastern Canada and the northeastern USA. Less resistant than wheat to cold, they tolerate humid, rainy late-summer conditions better than other temperate grains. Closely-related *Avena byzantina* grows best in areas with a Mediterranean climate. Oats are a valuable horse and general stock food containing 14 per cent protein, 7 per cent oil and 65 per cent carbohydrate; man eats them as porridge and oatmeal.

Country	10^3 tonnes av. 1977–81	10^3 ha
World Total	46,480	26,990
USSR	16,524	12,320
USA	8,243	4,258
Canada	3,499	1,753
West Germany	2,849	728
Poland	2,448	1,074
France	1,924	561
Sweden	1,557	458
Australia	1,361	1,245
Finland	1,130	439
China	780	620
UK	652	160
Argentina	543	417
East Germany	524	145
Spain	506	435

Rice

Rice (*Oryza sativa*) is the main cereal crop and staple food of millions of people in southeast Asia. There are thousands of varieties, and though most rice is grown standing in water, 'upland' types are grown on dry land where rainfall is heavy. Little rice grows where annual precipitation is under 100 cm (40 in). Rice tolerates high temperatures and humidity and maintains good yields under a system of continuous cultivation. Optimum temperatures are between 20° and 30°C (68° and 86°F) in the growing season.

Country	10³ tonnes av. 1977–81	10³ ha
World Total	**388,961**	**143,823**
China	140,611	35,518
India	77,031	39,933
Indonesia	27,638	8,823
Bangladesh	19,827	10,136
Thailand	16,715	8,634
Japan	14,663	2,491
Burma	11,630	4,971
Vietnam	11,186	5,388
Brazil	8,368	5,853
Philippines	7,455	3,507
South Korea	7,371	1,221
USA	6,312	1,230
Pakistan	4,789	1,976
North Korea	4,722	788

Rye

Rye (*Secale cereale*) is grown mainly in cool temperate areas on acidic soils of low fertility, for example sands. Used for making bread, rye whisky and fed to livestock, rye is nutritionally comparable with wheat. However, rye flour is inferior to wheat for baking, producing heavy, dark-coloured bread. The straw has little nutritional value and is used mainly for cattle bedding. Most of the world's rye is grown as an autumn-sown annual.

Country	10³ tonnes av. 1977–81	10³ ha
World Total	**26,398**	**15,538**
USSR	9,781	7,417
Poland	6,447	3,011
West Germany	2,187	589
East Germany	1,817	659
China	1,420	1,090
Turkey	591	465
Canada	589	331
Czechoslovakia	565	181
USA	513	319
France	385	127
Austria	348	108
Denmark	259	70
Sweden	250	74
Spain	241	225

Sorghum

Sorghum, Guinea corn or Kafir corn (*Andropogon sorghum*) is widely grown in hot, sub-arid areas. Optimum summer temperatures lie between 27° and 34°C (80° and 93°F), and most sorghum is grown where precipitation is 60 to 110 cm (24 to 44 in). Sorghum has a short growing season and is drought-resistant. Much is grown in the USA for livestock feed; in poorer areas it is a staple human food and used for brewing. Some varieties yield a sugary syrup.

Country	10³ tonnes av. 1977–81	10³ ha
World Total	66,200	49,651
USA	19,351	5,407
India	11,455	16,145
China	8,918	5,257
Argentina	6,128	2,027
Mexico	4,707	1,522
Nigeria	3,788	6,005
Sudan	2,401	2,998
Australia	961	514
Ethiopia	704	752
Burkina Faso	629	1,010
Yemen	625	751
South Africa	519	387
Niger	341	799

Wheat

Though there are several species of wheat, *Triticum vulgare* provides the bulk of world production. Wheat is grown under a wide range of climates but most varieties require growing seasons of over ninety days, with temperatures over 10°C (50°F) for three months. Very little grows where annual precipitation is below 25 cm (10 in); 80 cm (32 in) is optimal. Highest-quality bread wheats are grown in temperate grassland areas. Wheat is used mainly as flour for baking, but also converted to semolina, macaroni and breakfast cereals.

Country	10³ tonnes av. 1977–81	10³ ha
World Total	434,466	235,231
USSR	97,876	60,685
USA	60,613	27,339
China	54,178	31,680
India	32,911	21,859
France	20,861	4,339
Canada	20,373	10,903
Turkey	16,930	9,312
Australia	14,215	10,926
Pakistan	9,921	6,652
Italy	8,546	3,277
West Germany	7,976	1,629
Argentina	7,476	4,832
UK	7,198	1,327
Czechoslovakia	4,867	1,191

TUBER CROPS

Cassava

Cassava or manioc (*Manihot utilissima*) is a tropical shrub, 2 to 4 m (6 to 13 ft) high, which requires ten to thirty months to produce its large starchy tubers. The tubers are a basic food for many poor people in the tropical world, and a source of tapioca. Cassava requires a frost-free environment, deep soils and an annual precipitation of over 100 cm (40 in). Increasingly cassava is being used as cattle feed and for the production of industrial starch.

Country	10³ tonnes av. 1977–81	10³ ha
World Total	119,948	13,631
Brazil	24,942	2,117
Thailand	14,877	1,059
Indonesia	13,279	1,401
Zaïre	12,044	1,801
Nigeria	10,820	1,150
India	5,955	360
Tanzania	4,470	920
Vietnam	3,329	429
China	2,842	226
Mozambique	2,650	540
Philippines	2,062	191
Colombia	2,045	214
Paraguay	1,903	126
Ghana	1,811	231

Potatoes

Potato (*Solanum tuberosum*) is a plant grown for its edible tubers, which originated in the high Andes. Susceptible to damage by frost, it needs large amounts of water, and may fail to produce tubers if temperatures rise above 21°C (70°F); it is most commonly grown in well-watered temperate areas. For optimal yields it requires about 35 cm (14 in) of rainfall in the growing season and fertile soils. Though an important human food, potatoes are also used as an industrial source of starch and as an animal food.

Country	10³ tonnes av. 1977–81	10³ ha
World Total	263,420	18,190
USSR	79,951	6,973
Poland	41,271	2,368
USA	15,414	516
China	14,134	1,484
East Germany	10,609	548
West Germany	9,619	332
India	8,673	701
France	7,103	259
UK	6,730	209
Netherlands	6,212	167
Spain	5,638	364
Romania	4,288	295
Japan	3,375	126

Sweet-Potatoes

Sweet-potato (*Ipomoea batatas*) is widely cultivated throughout the tropical world. Optimum yields are produced in areas with annual rainfalls over 100 cm (40 in), abundant sunshine and well-drained soils. The crop is usually grown from stem cuttings. The potato-like tubers take four to five months to develop, and are prone to rotting and difficult to store. The leaves serve as a useful green vegetable, and if dried make excellent hay for livestock.

Country	10^3 tonnes av. 1977–81	10^3 ha
World Total	130,218	12,486
China	110,118	9,763
Indonesia	2,233	295
Vietnam	2,101	383
India	1,463	221
Japan	1,365	65
South Korea	1,357	63
Philippines	1,038	231
Brazil	978	103
Burundi	902	92
Rwanda	852	109
Bangladesh	784	72
Uganda	670	138
USA	588	45

SUGAR

Sugar-Beet

Sugar-beet (*Beta saccharifera*) is a low-growing temperate root crop which requires a five-month growing season. Seedlings are frost-sensitive; for best yield mean monthly temperatures should be above 17°C (62°F), and annual precipitation should exceed 40 cm (16 in). Temperatures over 30°C (86°F) decrease sugar yields. The beet's sugar content usually approaches 20 per cent by weight. Both the green leaves and the waste pulp from the sugar extraction factories are valuable animal feeds.

Country	10^3 tonnes av. 1977–81	10^3 ha
World Total	275,932	8,968
USSR	80,591	3,719
France	27,165	589
USA	22,407	487
West Germany	20,195	411
Poland	14,288	487
Italy	13,293	282
Turkey	8,919	282
Czechoslovakia	7,638	216
East Germany	7,571	259
Spain	7,304	211
UK	7,220	209
Netherlands	6,227	127
Belgium-Luxembourg	6,169	114
Romania	5,834	249

Sugar-Cane

Virtually all commercial cane sugar is obtained from the sap of *Saccharum officinarum*, a grass up to 4 m (13 ft) high which is grown throughout the wet tropics. Sugar-cane is susceptible to drought and requires over 100 cm (40 in) of well-distributed rain per annum and average monthly temperatures of 22° to 32°C (71° to 89°F). Frost is very damaging, and spells below 15°C (59°F) reduce yields. The first crop is cut fifteen to twenty-four months after planting, followed by 'ratoon' harvests taken at yearly intervals for three to five years.

Country	10^3 tonnes av. 1977–81	10^3 ha
World Total	745,790	13,384
India	152,196	2,872
Brazil	137,625	2,520
Cuba	66,017	1,312
Mexico	34,463	519
China	30,874	557
Pakistan	29,358	781
USA	24,891	301
Colombia	24,020	283
Australia	22,210	282
Philippines	20,740	461
Thailand	19,100	471
South Africa	17,313	230
Indonesia	16,010	158
Argentina	15,236	327

Honey

Commercial honey is virtually all produced by the domestic honeybee (*Apis mellifera*), which collects nectar from flowers and 'ripens' it into honey by reducing its water content and converting the sucrose into fructose and dextrose. The character of honey depends upon the type of nectar collected by the bees. Until the 18th century, when cane sugar became an important commodity in Europe, honey was the principal sweetening agent.

Country	10^3 tonnes av. 1977–81
World Total	897
USSR	188
China	160
USA	94
Mexico	60
Argentina	32
Canada	30
Turkey	23
Ethiopia	20
Australia	18
Angola	15
Romania	14
West Germany	11
Poland	11
France	9

BEVERAGES

Cocoa

Cocoa is obtained from the bean-shaped seeds of a tropical tree, *Theobroma cacao*, which grows in warm, humid, lowland areas between 20°N and 20°S. Commercial production requires minimum temperatures above 15°C (59°F) and at least 150 cm (60 in) of rainfall with no prolonged dry season. Cocoa has a high food value, containing 10 per cent protein and over 50 per cent fat (cocoa butter). Cocoa is used for the production of chocolate, cocoa drinks and as flavouring.

Country	10³ tonnes av. 1977–81	10³ ha
World Total	1,561	4,577
Ivory Coast	363	637
Brazil	291	459
Ghana	262	1,320
Nigeria	167	704
Cameroon	115	387
Ecuador	81	269
Dominican Republic	34	84
Mexico	33	67
Colombia	33	64
Papua New Guinea	30	71
Malaysia	27	60
Venezuela	14	67
Togo	14	35

Coffee

Coffee is the seed of a tropical tree. *Coffea arabica* produces the finest coffee though large quantities of *Coffea robusta*, which is hardier and tolerates higher temperatures, are used for the production of 'instant coffee'. Coffee trees are frost-sensitive, and no commercial coffee is grown outside the tropics. Commercial production occurs only where mean annual temperatures are close to 21°C (70°F) and there is a humid atmosphere, with 130 to 230 cm (52 to 92 in) of rain per annum.

Country	10³ tonnes av. 1977–81	10³ ha
World Total	4,876	9,619
Brazil	1,282	2,191
Colombia	697	1,061
Ivory Coast	272	1,010
Indonesia	235	394
Mexico	209	429
Ethiopia	191	694
Guatemala	156	247
El Salvador	154	165
Uganda	128	184
India	123	193
Philippines	113	100
Costa Rica	102	82
Cameroon	102	331
Kenya	86	120

Hops

Beer and similar beverages depend upon hops for their flavour. The hop (*Humulus lupulus*) is a temperate dioecious perennial vine which annually produces shoots up to 8 m (26 ft) long. Only the female flowers and their associated bracts contain the bitter substances which are used to flavour beer and improve its keeping qualities. The production of choice hops is difficult, as the slowly developing female flower structure is very sensitive to sun, wind, rain and extreme temperatures.

Country	10^3 tonnes av. 1977–81	10^3 ha
World Total	**111**	**83**
West Germany	31	18
USA	29	14
Czechoslovakia	10	11
UK	9	6
USSR	8	15
East Germany	2	2
Poland	2	2
Australia	2	1
Japan	2	1

Tea

Tea is the dried leaves of a low tree, *Camellia sinensis*, which is kept pruned to bush size to encourage the production of young growths. It requires frost-free, moist conditions, with temperatures between 13° and 32°C (55° and 89°F) and over 250 cm (100 in) of well-distributed rainfall. Black teas are produced by wilting and fermenting the leaves prior to drying, whilst green teas are heated before drying to prevent fermentation. The highest-quality teas are grown slowly at high altitudes.

Country	10^3 tonnes av. 1977–81	10^3 ha
World Total	**1,814**	**2,218**
India	565	371
China	311	1,002
Sri Lanka	203	243
USSR	120	78
Japan	102	60
Kenya	91	61
Indonesia	90	84
Turkey	85	49
Bangladesh	38	43
Malawi	31	17
Argentina	29	39
Iran	22	29
Tanzania	17	17

Wine

Wine is produced by fermenting juice crushed from grapes. During fermentation the sugars in the juice are converted to ethyl alcohol and carbon dioxide by enzymes produced in naturally-occurring wine yeasts. Normally the carbon escapes, but in champagne and other sparkling wines some of it is retained. In white wines only the juice of white grapes is used; for red wines, the skins, pulp and seeds of coloured grapes are present during fermentation to impart the desired colour, flavour and odour.

Country	10³ tonnes[1] av. 1977–81	10³ ha
World Total	**32,256**	**28,101**
Italy	7,659	6,414
France	6,459	5,256
Spain	3,504	2,182
USSR	2,980	3,070
Argentina	2,306	2,332
USA	1,549	1,418
Portugal	880	691
Romania	859	861
West Germany	746	956
Yugoslavia	675	630
South Africa	594	482
Chile	547	500
Hungary	535	562
Greece	488	400

[1] 1 tonne ≏ 1,000 litres.

Vegetables, Fruit and Nuts

Vegetables are the edible portions – leaves, stems, fruits and flowers – of herbaceous plants, especially bred and grown for their succulence and generally eaten fresh or lightly cooked. Some fruits (tomatoes, for example) are commonly regarded as vegetables because of their use in cooking. Most vegetables have a high water content and can be stored only for short periods. Their importance to human diet lies in their flavour and content of mineral salts, vitamins and other nutrients, and roughage. Much of the world's vegetable produce is consumed locally without reaching world markets, though increasing amounts are now being flown from centres of production to distant markets that are prepared to pay high prices for them. Statistics in these tables must be regarded as a minimal proportion of the total actually grown, referring only to recorded crops.

Fruits are the fleshy, edible portions of plants associated with seed development; most consist largely of water, but contain quantities of minerals, carbohydrates and proteins that help to make them palatable for man – as well as for the seed-dispersing insects, birds and mammals that they are usually intended to attract. Most are eaten raw and regarded as luxury or semi-luxury additions to diet, though they provide useful vitamins and roughage. A few, such as bananas and dates, may be important components of local diet. *Nuts* are seeds containing an embryo and fleshy storage tissues. Including all (except the water) that the seed requires to germinate and grow, nuts are often a source of concentrated, highly palatable food for man.

VEGETABLES

Aubergines

Aubergines or eggplant (*Solanum melongena*) are perennial, erect, bushy plants 1 to 2 m (3 to 6 ft) high, native to southeast Asia, which are usually grown as annuals for their fleshy 4 to 25 cm (1 to 10 in) long egg-shaped fruits. Aubergines are intolerant of frost and require a hot humid climate with a long growing season throughout which daily temperatures are between 22° and 32°C (71° and 89°F). The fruit, which may be dark purple or white, is usually boiled, baked or fried before being eaten.

Country	10³ tonnes av. 1977–81	10³ ha
World Total	4,362	317
China	1,416	152
Japan	645	21
Turkey	607	35
Italy	332	13
Egypt	291	14
Syria	157	8
Iraq	119	7
Spain	109	5
Philippines	100	17
Sudan	76	3
Greece	71	3
Thailand	58	10
Jordan	54	3

Cabbage

Cabbage (*Brassica oleracea* var. *capitata*) is a biennial plant grown as an annual for its large, 1 to 5 kg (2 to 11 lb) 'head' of fleshy leaves which are eaten raw, pickled or boiled, or used as livestock fodder. It stores well for up to a month. Cabbage grows best in cool, mild climates and is tolerant of moderate frosts (−5°C, 23°F); adaptable to a wide range of climates and soils, it is grown worldwide.

Country	10³ tonnes av. 1977–81	10³ ha
World Total	33,701	1,626
USSR	8,538	373
China	5,696	413
Japan	3,713	105
South Korea	2,400	61
Poland	1,551	57
USA	1,467	70
UK	896	39
Romania	852	25
Yugoslavia	737	47
Turkey	591	31
Italy	558	27
Spain	506	20
West Germany	484	11
India	460	77

Carrots

Carrots (*Daucus carota*) are biennial plants of temperate regions grown as an annual for the fleshy, sweet, conical tap roots which develop during the first year. Carrots grow best at temperatures between 15° and 20°C (59° and 68°F), in deep, moist, well-drained, friable soils. Young plants are sensitive to both frost and high temperatures. Hot weather produces coarse, strongly flavoured roots. The 5 to 25 cm (2 to 10 in) long slender roots store well for three to four months and are usually eaten raw or boiled, or used for livestock feed.

Country	10^3 tonnes av. 1977–81	10^3 ha
World Total	**10,249**	**479**
USSR	2,025	117
China	1,723	96
USA	905	29
UK	690	16
Japan	597	24
Poland	563	27
France	493	18
East Germany	311	9
Italy	273	8
Canada	225	6
Netherlands	156	3
Colombia	153	6
Czechoslovakia	134	6
West Germany	134	4

Cauliflowers

The cauliflower (*Brassica oleracea* var. *botrytis*) is a temperate biennial, grown as an annual for its compact terminal cluster of thick-stalked, partially-developed white flowers (curds) which develop in the centre of the plant. Cauliflowers are very exacting, requiring a cool, moist, frost-free growing season, with fertile, well-drained soils and mean monthly temperatures of 15° to 20°C (59° to 68°F) for good curd development. The curds are usually eaten boiled, served with a sauce, or pickled.

Country	10^3 tonnes av. 1977–81	10^3 ha
World Total	**4,389**	**335**
China	736	60
India	643	88
Italy	513	27
France	448	38
UK	309	15
Spain	202	8
USA	188	17
Poland	143	10
East Germany	126	5
Egypt	93	4
Japan	90	5
Australia	89	3
West Germany	82	4
Syria	71	3

Cucumbers and Gherkins

The cucumber (*Cucumis sativus*) is a tender, prostrate, branching vine, native to Asia, cultivated for its long (30 cm, 12 in) cylindrical watery-fleshed fruits, which are usually eaten raw in salads or pickled. The gherkin (*C. anguria*) is similar but smaller, and used almost exclusively for pickling. Both species are sensitive to drought and frost, for optimum production requiring temperatures of 18° to 25°C (64° to 77°F), and a growing season of two to three months. Cucumbers are grown intensively in hothouses near urban centres throughout northern Europe.

Country	10³ tonnes av. 1977–81	10³ ha
World Total	**10,362**	**795**
China	2,563	210
USSR	1,439	192
Japan	1,061	25
USA	842	70
Turkey	480	29
Netherlands	376	2
Poland	339	31
Spain	258	7
Egypt	256	16
Romania	241	24
Syria	220	21
Iraq	163	20
Indonesia	161	24
Mexico	153	9

Onions

Onions (*Allium cepa*) are hardy biennials, native to Asia, which are cultivated as annuals for their pungent edible bulbs. There are many varieties, each with specific day-length requirements. Most types require a growing season of four to six months and will not produce bulbs if temperatures rise above 30°C (86°F). Production of high-quality bulbs requires temperatures of 10° to 25°C (50° to 77°F) throughout the growing season. Most onions are harvested as bulbs and used either for flavouring or pickled.

Country	10³ tonnes av. 1977–81	10³ ha
World Total	**19,405**	**1,566**
China	2,581	209
India	1,616	217
USA	1,611	46
USSR	1,545	164
Japan	1,141	29
Spain	1,006	33
Turkey	931	70
Brazil	628	65
Egypt	607	23
Italy	521	21
Netherlands	476	11
Poland	366	24
Romania	360	39
South Korea	299	10

Peppers and Chillis

Sweet peppers (*Capsicum annum*) are annual plants, producing large, fleshy fruits to be eaten in salads or cooked as vegetables. They require temperatures of 20° to 30°C (68° to 86°F) throughout their short, two- to three-month growing season.

Red peppers or chillis (*C. frutescens*) are perennial plants, which are virtually confined to the tropics. The fruits are 'hot' to the taste and are powdered to produce cayenne pepper or for use in flavourings such as curry powder and tabasco sauce.

Country	10^3 tonnes av. 1977–81	10^3 ha
World Total	**6,790**	**914**
China	1,364	142
Nigeria	615	67
Turkey	536	43
Spain	535	28
Italy	469	19
Mexico	449	52
Yugoslavia	355	42
Bulgaria	283	18
USA	251	22
Indonesia	207	105
Romania	205	20
Hungary	174	17
Japan	167	4
Egypt	161	10

Plantains

Plantains (*Musa spp.*) are varieties of banana used for cooking. They are larger, coarser and have a higher starch content than normal bananas and are usually picked whilst still hard. Plantains fried, roasted or steamed are the staple food of people living in east Africa, and form a minor part of the diets of native peoples throughout the tropics. Details of their climatic requirements are given under bananas (*see* Fruits).

Country	10^3 tonnes av. 1977–81	10^3 ha
World Total	**21,057**	**19,536**
Uganda	5,320	3,100
Colombia	2,204	1,844
Nigeria	2,150	2,000
Rwanda	2,022	1,896
Zaïre	1,433	1,433
Sri Lanka	1,323	806
Ghana	973	1,100
Cameroon	972	950
Ivory Coast	795	750
Peru	761	700
Tanzania	759	746
Ecuador	751	770
Dominican Republic	583	531
Burma	435	501

Pumpkins and Squashes

Pumpkins and squash (*Cucurbita spp.*) are native to the Americas. Intolerant of frost, they grow best where the mean monthly temperature throughout their two- to three-month growing season is between 20° and 25°C (68° and 77°F). The distinction between marrows, pumpkins and squashes is inexact, though broadly, marrows and squash (*C. pepo* and *C. maxima*) have fine-grained flesh and a mild flavour and are used as cooked vegetables or for baking, whilst pumpkins (*C. mixta*) have a coarse texture and are mostly used as livestock feed.

Country	10^3 tonnes av. 1977–81	10^3 ha
World Total	**5,168**	**533**
China	904	79
Egypt	439	23
Romania	394	135
Turkey	341	22
Italy	329	13
Argentina	285	29
Japan	252	15
South Africa	216	12
Syria	161	14
Mexico	146	22
Chile	129	6
Spain	124	5
Bangladesh	101	15

Tomatoes

Tomatoes (*Lycopersicon esculentum*) are tender or half-hardy, 1 m (3 ft) tall, bushy or prostrate annuals, which originated in the New World. The plant is grown for its sweet fruits, which are eaten raw, fried, baked, stuffed or made into sauces and chutneys. Sensitive to drought and frost, tomatoes need temperatures between 10° and 27°C (50° and 80°F) for a four-month growing season. In northern Europe they are usually grown intensively in hothouses, giving very high yields.

Country	10^3 tonnes av. 1977–81	10^3 ha
World Total	**48,876**	**2,370**
USA	7,113	170
USSR	6,183	383
Italy	4,179	119
China	3,950	283
Turkey	3,430	108
Egypt	2,356	138
Spain	2,196	65
Greece	1,578	38
Brazil	1,453	52
Romania	1,421	74
Mexico	1,227	76
Japan	991	18
Bulgaria	856	30
France	764	21

FRUIT AND NUTS

Apples

Apples (*Malus spp.*) are the most important tree fruit of temperate regions. Over seven thousand varieties provide a wide range of fruit characteristics and tolerance to soils and climate. Though a cold period is necessary for fruit-bud development, temperatures below −20°C (−4°F) kill the trees, and frost during pollination severely reduces fruit production. 50 to 100 cm (20 to 40 in) of precipitation per annum, together with long sunny days, are desirable for commercial production. Different varieties are used for cooking, dessert and cider production.

Country	10^3 tonnes av. 1977–81
World Total	**33,384**
USSR	6,637
USA	3,523
China	2,701
France	2,388
Italy	1,875
West Germany	1,512
Turkey	1,221
Hungary	993
Spain	991
Poland	927
Argentina	893
Japan	891
India	732
East Germany	484

Apricots

Closely related to the plum, almond and peach, the apricot, *Prunus armeniaca*, is a stoned, temperate tree fruit, which originated in China. Being more frost-sensitive than the peach, but more drought-resistant, it is mostly grown in subtropical dry areas. The highly-flavoured, astringent, acid fruit is usually canned in sweet syrup or preserved by drying. The seeds contain about 40 per cent by weight of an oil which may be used as a substitute for almond oil.

Country	10^3 tonnes av. 1977–81
World Total	**1,520**
USSR	178
Turkey	159
Spain	145
USA	115
Italy	94
Greece	82
France	74
Morocco	61
Iran	57
Hungary	46
Syria	45
South Africa	36
Romania	36
Bulgaria	33

Bananas

Bananas (*Musa spp.*) are the fruit of a giant tropical herb (3 to 10 m, 10 to 32 ft, high), which is propagated from rhizomes. Banana plants produce large bunches of a hundred to two hundred individual fruits which develop nine to twelve months after planting; they continue to produce for five to twenty years. Bananas grow best in areas with mean monthly temperatures of 18° to 30°C (64° to 86°F), and 10 to 20 cm (4 to 8 in) of rain each month. Commercial production is virtually confined to within 30° of the Equator.

Country	10³ tonnes av. 1977–81
World Total	38,267
Brazil	6,431
India	4,197
Philippines	3,330
Ecuador	2,235
Thailand	1,948
Indonesia	1,899
Mexico	1,481
Honduras	1,299
Costa Rica	1,117
Colombia	1,115
Panama	1,043
Burundi	959
Venezuela	951
Papua New Guinea	900

Citrus Fruits

Citrus fruits (*Citrus spp.*) are the fruits of small evergreen trees which originated in subtropical Indo-China. Commercial production occurs between 20° and 40° north and south of the Equator, in areas with mean summer temperatures of 20° to 25°C (68° to 77°F) where the mean temperature of the coldest month is above 4.5°C (40°F) and frost rarely occurs. Citrus fruits tolerate a wide range of rainfall and are often irrigated. Oranges and tangerines provide over 80 per cent of world citrus production, whilst grapefruit and lemons each account for about 8 per cent.

Other citrus fruits

Country	Oranges 10³ tonnes av. 1977–81
World Total	35,735
USA	9,363
Brazil	8,007
Spain	1,895
Mexico	1,840
Italy	1,607
India	1,102
Egypt	966
Israel	929
China	749
Argentina	694
Morocco	692
Turkey	691
South Africa	553
Pakistan	516

	World Total
Grapefruits	4,398
Lemons and Limes	4,960
Tangerines etc.	7,332

Dates

Dates (*Phoenix dactylifera*) are the fruit of a tall (20 m, 65 ft), heat-loving palm which grows in dry subtropical areas. Though it tolerates temperatures down to 0°C (32°F) it requires a long, hot, dry period with ample soil water supplies for fruit production. A date palm will produce about 50 kg (100 lb) of fruit each year. The sweet fruit contain 70 per cent carbohydrate and are important in the diet of many desert peoples. Date seeds are used as camel fodder.

Country	10³ tonnes av. 1977–81
World Total	2,646
Egypt	436
Iraq	431
Saudi Arabia	397
Iran	298
Pakistan	202
Algeria	185
Sudan	111
Morocco	101
Libya	84
Yemen	77
Oman	54
Tunisia	46
United Arab Emirates	42
South Yemen	42

Grapes

Commercial grape production exceeds that of any other fruit. Grapes (*Vitis spp.*) require winter temperatures above −12°C (10°F), a good water supply during the spring, followed by warm sunny weather, with temperatures of about 18° to 22°C (64° to 71°F) to facilitate ripening and harvesting. They are not grown in the tropics as they usually need a dormant period for fruit-bud development. 80 per cent of production is used to make wine, the remainder being eaten as dessert fruit or as dried currants, sultanas and raisins.

Country	10³ tonnes av. 1977–81	10³ ha
World Total	61,814	10,065
Italy	12,037	1,406
France	9,736	1,215
USSR	5,833	1,309
Spain	5,572	1,674
USA	4,286	290
Turkey	3,475	808
Argentina	3,082	336
Greece	1,487	193
Romania	1,466	278
Yugoslavia	1,302	251
South Africa	1,078	115
Bulgaria	1,007	164
West Germany	983	89
Iran	941	183

Mangoes

The mango (*Mangifera indica*) is a very large tropical tree, grown for its delicious 250 to 500 g (9 to 18 oz) oblong fruits. Though it survives on rainfalls ranging from 25 to 250 cm (10 to 100 in) per annum and temperatures from 0° to 45°C (32° to 113°F), it grows best where mean monthly temperatures are between 23° and 27°C (73° and 80°F) and there is a well-distributed rainfall of 100 cm (40 in) each year. The fruit is generally eaten fresh but is also canned and made into jams and chutneys.

Country	10^3 tonnes av. 1977–81
World Total	13,372
India	8,619
Brazil	602
Pakistan	572
Mexico	543
Indonesia	359
Philippines	349
Haiti	308
China	252
Bangladesh	230
Dominican Republic	173
Tanzania	172
Madagascar	166
Zaïre	150

Melons and Cantaloupes

Melons (*Cucumis melo*) are annual trailing vines which are intolerant of frost and which require temperatures over 18°C (64°F), sunny dry conditions and plentiful water supplies. There are many varieties, grown from warm temperate to tropical regions. The main commercial types are the netted-skin or musk melon, the winter melon (honeydew), and the cantaloupe. Melon flesh is 94 per cent water and 5 per cent sugar and may be green, yellow, orange or pink. Melons are usually eaten raw, but when immature are sometimes used as vegetables.

Country	10^3 tonnes av. 1977–81	10^3 ha
World Total	6,312	471
China	1,418	83
Spain	751	85
USA	702	42
Iran	474	51
Italy	305	12
Mexico	289	23
Japan	287	14
Syria	212	26
France	188	14
Egypt	184	9
South Korea	160	10
Morocco	146	12
Chile	132	4
Romania	128	12

Peaches and Nectarines

Both the peach and the nectarine are forms of *Prunus persica*. Originating in China, the small tree (6 m, 19 ft, high) is now widely grown in Mediterranean climates and in sheltered parts of more temperate areas. Though tolerant of temperatures as low as −20°C (−4°F), the crop is severely reduced by frosts at blossom time. The fruit's orange flesh is usually sweet and juicy. Fruit is sold fresh, canned or dried. Clingstone peaches are widely used for canning as they handle well during processing.

Country	10³ tonnes av. 1977–81
World Total	7,003
USA	1,466
Italy	1,337
France	435
Greece	381
China	375
Spain	375
USSR	321
Japan	275
Argentina	255
Turkey	219
Mexico	190
South Africa	167
Brazil	119
Chile	119

Pears

Pears (*Pyrus spp.*) are hardy, temperate deciduous trees. Whilst most European pears are derived from *P. communis*, some North American varieties are cross-bred with the oriental pear *P. pyrifolia*. Pear trees are frost-hardy down to −20°C (−4°F) and require one thousand hours below 7°C (44°F) to break the winter dormancy of the fruit buds. However, they need warm conditions at blossom time and during the ripening of the fruit. Pears are eaten fresh, canned, and made into perry, an alcoholic drink.

Country	10³ tonnes av. 1977–81
World Total	7,995
China	1,225
Italy	1,186
USA	754
USSR	640
Japan	524
Spain	425
France	395
West Germany	332
Turkey	293
Argentina	151
South Africa	126
Austria	125
Australia	125
Switzerland	116

Pineapples

Pineapples (*Ananas comosus*) are strictly tropical, low-growing, herbaceous perennials which originated in South America. They grow best when temperatures are between 20° and 30°C (68° and 86°F), with 5 to 10 cm (2 to 4 in) of precipitation each month. Pineapples are usually propagated from suckers. Each plant produces one fruit. In commercial plantations an additional ratoon crop is taken before replanting. Large quantities of pineapples are canned, though air freight now enables them to be marketed fresh in Europe and North America.

Country	10³ tonnes av. 1977–81
World Total	**7,860**
Thailand	1,620
Philippines	795
USA	608
Brazil	577
China	537
Mexico	502
India	372
Ivory Coast	311
Indonesia	228
Vietnam	201
South Africa	199
Malaysia	193
Zaïre	156
Bangladesh	142 ·

Plums

Plums grow on frost-hardy deciduous trees in temperate and subtropical climates. The hardier varieties, derived from *Prunus spinosa* and *P. cerasifera*, originated near the Caucasus; those grown in warmer areas are largely descended from the Japanese plum, *P. salicina*. Many cultivars require a period below 4°C (39°F) to break flower-bud dormancy. Most grow best at temperatures of 12° to 22°C (53° to 71°F) with annual precipitation of 50 to 100 cm (20 to 40 in). Plums are eaten fresh, dried as prunes and used for brandy production in Eastern Europe.

Country	10³ tonnes av. 1977–81
World Total	**5,318**
Yugoslavia	685
USSR	666
USA	624
Romania	621
China	412
West Germany	394
Hungary	178
Poland	177
Bulgaria	171
Italy	159
Turkey	152
France	136
Austria	75
East Germany	67

Water Melons

The water melon (*Citrullus lanatus*) is an annual climbing or prostrate vine up to 5 m (16 ft) in length, native to tropical Africa, which is grown for its large (20 to 30 cm, 8 to 12 in, diameter), sub-spherical, red- or yellow-fleshed, sweet, watery fruit. It requires a growing season of at least four frost-free months with temperatures averaging 20° to 30°C, (68° to 86°F), well-drained moist soils, and low atmospheric humidity. Water melons are best eaten fresh as they do not store well.

Country	10³ tonnes av. 1977–81	10³ ha
World Total	24,505	1,879
Turkey	4,887	222
China	4,104	226
Egypt	1,245	51
USA	1,139	84
Japan	1,084	33
Iran	921	100
Italy	741	23
Syria	719	89
Greece	678	25
Iraq	641	50
Yugoslavia	620	46
Thailand	508	40
Spain	507	28

Nuts

Nuts usually contain 10 to 20 per cent protein and 40 to 70 per cent oil and fat. Hazelnuts, chestnuts, almonds, walnuts and pistachio nuts are grown in temperate or Mediterranean areas, whilst the cashew nut is produced in the tropics. Data on production are incomplete and under-recorded. In the table below the letters show where there are substantial outputs of six particular kinds of nuts. Total production covers these six varieties, plus brazil and pecan nuts. Ground-nuts are considered under Protein Crops, and coconuts under Vegetable Oils.

Country	10³ tonnes av. 1977–81	type of nuts
World Total	3,611	
USA	562	APHW
Turkey	535	APHWC
Italy	377	AHWC
China	332	WC
Spain	305	AHWC
India	186	WS
Mozambique	108	S
Brazil	108	S
Iran	107	APHW
Greece	88	APHWC
France	76	AHWC
USSR	75	AHWC
Tanzania	75	S
Japan	56	C

Key A = almonds; P = pistachios; H = hazelnuts; W = walnuts; C = chestnuts; S = cashews

Plant Products

Vegetable oils are pressed from the seeds of plants; though many kinds of plants produce oils, only about a dozen species are of commercial importance. Soya-bean and ground-nut oils are obtained from crops grown primarily for other uses (see Protein Crops); the oil content of soya beans is between 12 and 20 per cent, of ground-nuts between 40 and 50 per cent. Vegetable oils are used as human food and also in industry, where they are incorporated into paints, varnishes, inks and lubricants. Linseed, tung and castor oils are used almost entirely in industry, as are lower grades (often second pressings) of palm, coconut and other edible oils. Edible vegetable oils provide about 60 per cent of man's dietary needs for oil, the remainder coming from animal products. In warm countries fluid oils are used in cooking; in cool countries the oils are often hardened or emulsified into cooking fats, salad dressings and margarine.

Many natural *fibres* are of vegetable origin; the major producers are cotton, sisal, flax, jute and hemp, each with its unique combination of strength, flexibility and other qualities. Cotton and flax are used mainly in textiles, the coarser fibres in ropes, string, sacking, carpet-backing, etc.; weak fibres of short staple may be used as wadding and for upholstery. Recently, natural fibres have suffered competition from rayon, nylon and other artificial fibres, though they still account for over 60 per cent of the world's total fibre consumption.

Tobacco contains a drug, nicotine, of worldwide interest and importance that has secured it a place in world markets. Grown mainly in subtropical climates where the leaves can be dried in warm shade, there are many local varieties providing a range of flavours for blending.

Forest products include timber, firewood and pulp. The world's forests currently occupy about a quarter of the land surface (formerly much more). Most important commercially are the circum-polar coniferous forests of pine, spruce and fir, which extend through northern Europe into Asia and across Alaska and Canada; these and their southern extensions – planted by man in warmer regions – produce the so-called softwoods which provide about 80 per cent of the world's commercial sawn timber and pulp. Used in paper, cardboard and rayon manufacture, pulp is widely traded; several countries that do not appear in the table (for example Austria, Britain) manufacture paper from imported materials.

In warmer climates grow the temperate deciduous and tropical forests, producing mainly hardwoods. Much of the sawn timber from these areas is used in construction, especially of housing and furniture where strength, durability and beauty may be equally important. Typical temperate hardwoods include oak, maple, beech, elm and hickory. Tropical forests yield an enormous variety of hardwoods including teak, mahogany, afrormosia, sapele and iroko.

Forests also provide firewood (especially important in the poorer countries where other fuels are lacking), rubber (now mostly procured from plantations) and a range of other products including turpentine, cork, tannin, resins, camphor, quinine, chewing gum and foodstuffs.

VEGETABLE OILS

Castor oil

The castor bean (*Ricinus communis*), from which castor oil is obtained, is frost-sensitive and requires warm humid conditions. The beans have an oil content of up to 40 per cent, and the oil is used industrially and medicinally. The oil-cake is not suitable for cattle feed.

Country	10^3 tonnes av. 1977–81	10^3 ha
World Total	824	1,416
Brazil	304	389
India	212	452
China	105	190
USSR	44	168
Thailand	33	41

Coconuts

Coconuts are produced by *Cocos nucifera*, a palm tree widespread in coastal regions of the equatorial tropics. Temperatures between 22° and 32°C (71° and 89°F), with less than 10°C (18°F) daily range and precipitation of 150 to 200 cm (60 to 80 in) a year, provide optimum growing conditions. The figures below refer to whole nuts. Dried coconut flesh or copra constitutes only 12 per cent of the nut's weight. Copra yields 60 to 65 per cent coconut oil, which is used for shortenings, margarine and soap production.

Country	10^3 tonnes av. 1977–81
World Total	35,181
Indonesia	10,791
Philippines	9,978
India	4,383
Sri Lanka	1,627
Malaysia	1,177
Mexico	909
Papua New Guinea	810
Thailand	764
Mozambique	416
Tanzania	304
Vanuatu	288
Vietnam	272
Brazil	247
Fiji	240

Cottonseed

Cottonseed is essentially a by-product of fibre production; for growing conditions see under Fibres. Cottonseed oil, one of the world's most important industrial oils, ranks second only to soya-bean oil in terms of world production. The oil content of cottonseed ranges between 15 and 25 per cent. It is used for the manufacture of cooking fats, margarine and salad dressings. After oil extraction, the seed-cake residue provides a valuable supplementary protein feed for livestock.

Country	10³ tonnes av. 1977–81
World Total	26,673
USSR	5,994
China	4,852
USA	4,770
India	2,582
Pakistan	1,288
Brazil	1,061
Turkey	805
Egypt	790
Mexico	573
Argentina	304
Sudan	268
Guatemala	249
Greece	231
Syria	222

Linseed

Flax (*Linum usitatissimum*) produces both fibre and oil-yielding seed, though it is unusual for a single crop to give both. Grown in temperate climates, flax for linseed requires abundant rain and cool weather during the growing season, followed by a dry, warm spell for the harvest. The seed has an oil content of 30 to 40 per cent. Linseed oil dries on exposure to air, producing a flexible skin. It is used in the manufacture of putty, paints, varnishes, inks and soaps.

Country	10³ tonnes av. 1977–81	10³ ha
World Total	2,597	5,576
Argentina	667	847
Canada	596	619
India	435	1,868
USA	278	350
USSR	234	1,245
China	63	101
Romania	46	81
Uruguay	40	68
Poland	40	81
Egypt	33	27
France	32	49

Oil Palm

Oil palm (*Elaeis guineensis*) is confined to within 18° of the Equator. It requires a sunny, hot humid climate with a well distributed rainfall of over 150 cm (60 in) a year. Oil is obtained from both the soft flesh and the kernel of the fruit. One hectare (2.47 acres) of palms normally produces about 800 kg (1700 lb) of palm oil and 100 kg (220 lb) of kernel oil. Though used locally for cooking, palm oil is produced mainly for industrial purposes. Kernel oil is used in margarine, chocolate and pharmaceuticals.

Country	10^3 tonnes av. 1977–81
World Total	4,549
Malaysia	2,196
Nigeria	666
Indonesia	605
China	181
Zaïre	167
Ivory Coast	157
Cameroon	78
Colombia	52
Sierra Leone	48
Papua New Guinea	43
Guinea	40
Angola	40
Benin	30

Palm Kernels: World Total 1659

Olives

Olives are the fruit of *Olea europaea*, a tree of Mediterranean origins which cannot survive severe frosts. Average summer temperatures exceeding 18°C (64°F) and annual precipitation of 40 to 90 cm (16 to 36 in) are needed, with a dry autumn for ripening. The first pressings of the fruit produce the finest oil, which is used for salad dressings, cooking and for canning sardines. Lower-quality oil from later pressings is used for industrial purposes. One hectare (2.47 acres) of olives commonly yields 500 to 900 kg (1100 to 2000 lb) of oil a year.

Country	10^3 tonnes av. 1977–81
World Total	1,803
Italy	599
Spain	439
Greece	283
Turkey	139
Tunisia	125
Syria	58
Portugal	40
Morocco	32
Argentina	19
Libya	19
Algeria	15
Albania	7
Lebanon	7
Cyprus	4

Rapeseed

Rapeseed is the seed of several species of *Brassica*, but principally *Brassica napus*. The plant is a temperate annual growing up to 1 m (3 ft) tall, with bright yellow flowers. The long thin 'pods' (siliqua) contain small blackish-brown seeds which yield 35 to 40 per cent oil. Though the oil may be refined and used for culinary purposes (e.g. oiling baking tins), it is mostly used in lubricants, cutting oils, soap and candle-making, and for other industrial purposes.

Country	10^3 tonnes av. 1977–81	10^3 ha
World Total	**10,429**	**11,017**
Canada	2,631	2,242
China	2,409	2,925
India	1,747	3,558
France	730	329
Poland	538	302
West Germany	333	129
Sweden	313	156
East Germany	293	122
Pakistan	255	437
UK	223	82
Denmark	164	79
Czechoslovakia	162	78
Bangladesh	125	201
Hungary	88	54

Safflower

Safflower (*Carthamus tinctorius*) is a spiny annual plant, 1 to 1.5 m (3 to 5 ft) high, that grows in sunny dry areas. The oil is used for cooking and in paint and varnishes.

Country	10^3 tonnes av. 1977–81	10^3 ha
World Total	**985**	**1,371**
Mexico	496	422
India	246	704
USA	152	100
Ethiopia	30	64

Sesame

Sesame or benniseed (*Sesamum indicum*) is a 2 m (6 ft) high annual plant which takes three to five months to mature. Sensitive to low temperatures, it tolerates moderately dry conditions and is grown in areas of tropical, subtropical and Mediterranean climates. The seed has an oil content of 45 to 55 per cent, but overall yields are low. Oil from the first pressing is used for margarine manufacture, cooking oils and other culinary purposes. Sesame seed is also stewed and used in baking.

Country	10^3 tonnes av. 1977–81	10^3 ha
World Total	1,914	6,398
India	469	2,430
China	352	806
Sudan	214	863
Mexico	138	240
Burma	135	711
Nigeria	71	233
Venezuela	53	93
Uganda	45	130
Afghanistan	38	50
Ethiopia	38	66
Syria	27	42
Bangladesh	25	48
Turkey	24	40
South Korea	23	55

Sunflower Seed

Sunflower (*Helianthus annus*) is a tall annual grown mainly for its seed. Over 90 per cent of sunflower seed is grown for oil extraction. Though tolerant of light frosts, sunflowers require a growing season of 90 to 120 days with average temperatures over 10°C (50°F), and 30 cm (12 in) or more of precipitation. The seeds yield 25 to 30 per cent of a polyunsaturated oil which, because of its keeping qualities, is highly valued in cosmetics and cookery and as a base for margarine.

Country	10^3 tonnes av. 1977–81	10^3 ha
World Total	13,555	11,483
USSR	5,180	4,410
USA	2,085	1,491
Argentina	1,368	1,592
Romania	830	511
Turkey	571	451
China	533	416
Yugoslavia	433	221
Spain	430	628
South Africa	416	346
Bulgaria	408	240
Hungary	387	228
France	201	88
Canada	152	115
Australia	139	207

Tung

Tung or China wood oil is obtained from the seeds of a tree, *Aleurites fordii*. It is used in the manufacture of varnish and enamels and dries twice as fast as linseed oil.

Country	10^3 tonnes av. 1977–81
World Total	100
China	72
Argentina	12
Paraguay	12
Malawi	1

FIBRES AND TOBACCOS

Cotton

Cotton fibres are produced by the seed coat of *Gossypium* species. The plant is frost-sensitive and requires an 180- to 200-day growing season with temperatures averaging 21°C (70°F), abundant sunshine, and over 20 cm (8 in) of well-distributed rainfall. Commercial cotton, grown between 47°N and 32°S, is the leading natural fibre for textile production. Low-grade fibres are used for the production of felt, explosives, and high-quality paper. Cotton seed is a valuable source of vegetable oil and protein-rich cattle food.

Country	10^3 tonnes av. 1977–81
World Total	14,030
USA	2,905
USSR	2,696
China	2,426
India	1,291
Pakistan	644
Brazil	553
Turkey	503
Egypt	476
Mexico	363
Argentina	156
Guatemala	145
Sudan	142
Syria	131

Jute

Jute fibre is obtained from the stems of two *Corchorus* species which attain heights of 2 to 4 m (6 to 13 ft). Individual fibres may exceed 2 m (6 ft) in length. The plant requires a humid tropical or warm subtropical climate with high humidity (65 to 95 per cent), temperatures between 20° and 40°C (68° and 104°F) and 30 cm (12 in) of precipitation a month during the three- to five-month growing season. The fibres produce strong, bulky fabrics. 75 per cent of jute production is made into sacks and bags. Jute is also used for coarse twines and cordage, and as a backing for carpets.

Country	10^3 tonnes av. 1977–81	10^3 ha
World Total	4,121	2,752
India	1,427	1,245
China	1,055	296
Bangladesh	1,016	706
Thailand	271	221
Brazil	84	76
Burma	69	84
Nepal	56	45
USSR	44	17
Vietnam	37	21
Egypt	11	4
Indonesia	8	4
Cuba	7	7
Bhutan	5	5
Zaïre	1	5

Sisal

Sisal is obtained from the leaves of *Agave sisalana*. Though frost-sensitive and essentially tropical, the plant is hardy and can withstand dry periods. It requires well-drained soils and thrives best in hot areas where the precipitation is over 150 cm (60 in) a year, though it will grow with an annual rainfall of only 30 cm (12 in). The fibres, moderately resistant to rotting, are used for the manufacture of ropes, twines, cordage, bags, sacks and carpets, and in pulps for strong papers.

Country	10^3 tonnes av. 1977–81	10^3 ha
World Total	451	598
Brazil	226	287
Tanzania	94	121
Kenya	39	43
Madagascar	21	22
Angola	20	30
Mozambique	14	50
Haiti	11	20
Venezuela	9	7
China	8	8
South Africa	4	4
Morocco	1	2

Tobacco

The leaves of tobacco, *Nicotiana spp.*, are lightly fermented, dried and used for making cigars, cigarettes and snuff. Though tobacco originated in tropical America, the bulk of world production now comes from outside the tropics. Climate greatly influences the quality of the leaves. The plant is frost-susceptible and optimum temperatures for growth lie between 18° and 27°C (64° and 80°F). Some of the highest-grade tobaccos are grown in Cuba and Sumatra, though the USA dominates international trade.

Country	10^3 tonnes av. 1977–81	10^3 ha
World Total	**5,445**	**4,248**
China	935	668
USA	843	374
India	452	489
Brazil	391	310
USSR	296	170
Turkey	237	249
Japan	156	62
Bulgaria	134	113
Greece	123	96
Italy	120	59
Canada	104	46
Zimbabwe	95	54

FOREST PRODUCTS: RUBBER AND WOOD

Rubber

Over 95 per cent of the world's natural rubber is obtained by coagulating latex tapped from the trunks of *Hevea brasiliensis*, a tree native to tropical South America, but now grown throughout the wet tropical world. Commercial rubber trees require temperatures between 24° and 35°C (75° and 95°F), with a well-distributed rainfall of over 170 cm (68 in). A good plantation on fertile soil may produce 2 to 3 tonnes of rubber per hectare per annum. In the USSR some rubber is produced from the dandelion *Taraxacum keksaghyz*, the roots of which yield 5 to 10 per cent rubber.

Country	10^3 tonnes av. 1977–81
World Total	**3,745**
Malaysia	1,605
Indonesia	907
Thailand	491
India	147
Sri Lanka	144
Liberia	77
China	75
Philippines	60
Nigeria	52
Vietnam	44
Zaïre	28
Ivory Coast	20

Timber, Fuelwood, Pulp and Paper

Country	Roundwood[1] 10^3 m³ av. 1977–81	Industrial roundwood[2] 10^3 m³ av. 1977–81	Fuelwood and charcoal 10^3 m³ av. 1977–81	Wood pulp 10^3 tonnes av. 1977–81	Paper and paperboard 10^3 tonnes av. 1977–81
World Total	2,901,037	1,365,552	1,535,485	114,150	153,048
USSR	375,820	295,640	66,180	9,108	9,007
USA	333,851	319,697	14,154	41,072	51,955
China	205,791	58,673	147,118	1,883	7,176
India	205,290	13,501	191,830	—	—
Brazil	197,449	37,112	160,337	1,752	2,290
Indonesia	149,865	31,295	123,634	—	—
Canada	144,772	141,030	—	17,834	12,208
Nigeria	88,454	—	84,232	—	—
South Korea	65,443	—	62,396	—	1,081
Vietnam	60,246	—	57,658	—	—
Sweden	53,855	50,855	—	8,046	5,272
Turkey	41,056	—	33,276	—	—
Colombia	40,046	—	37,003	—	—
Malaysia	38,998	28,931	10,067	—	—
Finland	35,772	30,832	—	4,738	4,808
Thailand	35,557	—	30,460	—	—
Japan	35,337	27,722	—	9,357	15,811
Philippines	34,011	10,274	23,736	—	—
Tanzania	31,745	—	30,940	—	—
Sudan	31,701	—	30,256	—	—
France	30,141	27,221	—	1,863	4,732
West Germany	29,125	27,325	—	1,796	6,521
Mali	27,132	—	22,881	—	—
Kenya	24,487	—	23,398	—	—
Ethiopia	22,693	—	21,322	—	—
Poland	21,470	19,901	—	—	1,315
Romania	20,685	15,806	—	—	—

[1]Timber as felled.
[2]Saw-logs, veneer-logs, pit-props, pulp-wood and industrial wood.

Animals and Animal Products

Domestic animals traditionally browse, graze and scavenge on land that for one reason or another cannot be used for cultivation; their droppings provide fertilizer rich in nitrates, phosphates and minerals, and humus that improves soil quality, so their husbandry can be complementary to crop production. The cycle is broken where fuels are scarce; then cattle dung becomes an essential if wasteful household fuel. Free-ranging domestic animals are mostly slow-growing and low-yielding – well-suited to poor pastures. Where better ground is available, stock-improvement measures increase yields, though often at the risk of overgrazing and land deterioration. In many instances carrying capacity is limited by water availability.

In advanced countries, and in poorer countries where there are large urban markets to be satisfied, intensive methods replace outdoor husbandry; stock are maintained in sheds or feedlots where balanced feeding under controlled conditions gives high yields. The tables cover both kinds of husbandry.

Seas, lakes and rivers provide abundant food, from much-needed additional protein in a meagre, pastoral African diet to the main source of animal protein in the diets of some maritime peoples. Overfishing has led to dearth of the more popular species and substantial price increases; freezing technology has widened the market, so shrimps caught off Indonesia may sell at high prices in London or Toronto. World production of sea foods has levelled off, though there is a constant search for new stocks as the better-known ones are fished out.

POULTRY, EGGS AND POULTRY MEAT

Poultry Meat Production

Country	10^3 tonnes av. 1977–81	Country	
World Total	26,567		
USA	7,025	UK	738
China	3,130	Canada	556
USSR	2,002	Mexico	426
France	1,053	Romania	387
Brazil	1,026	Nigeria	181
Japan	1,002	India	108
Italy	976	Indonesia	101

Chicken Population

Country	10^3 av. 1977–81
World Total	6,309,701
China	1,044,507
USSR	890,012
USA	390,895
Brazil	365,531
Japan	280,107
France	174,189
Mexico	151,307
India	145,000
UK	128,395
Italy	113,398
Nigeria	111,000
Indonesia	104,289
Romania	89,492
Canada	79,244

Duck Population

Country	10^3 av. 1977–81
World Total	145,788
Vietnam	29,800
Bangladesh	18,855
Indonesia	15,603
Thailand	10,028
China	9,536
France	8,889
Brazil	4,937
Philippines	4,931
Poland	4,482
Burma	3,859
Romania	3,620
Egypt	3,440
Mexico	2,759

Hen Egg Production

Country	10^3 tonnes av. 1977–81
World Total	27,091
China	4,370
USA	4,023
USSR	3,631
Japan	1,989
West Germany	830
France	810
UK	800
Brazil	690
Spain	643
Italy	633
Mexico	542
Poland	483
India	474
Netherlands	463
Other Eggs: World Total	398

Turkey Population

Country	10^3 av. 1977–81
World Total	112,802
USSR	37,068
Mexico	13,109
France	12,653
Canada	9,487
USA	8,629
UK	6,021
Israel	4,740
Turkey	2,637
Brazil	2,153
Yugoslavia	1,830
Romania	1,600
Argentina	1,340
West Germany	1,329
Madagascar	1,310

LIVESTOCK AND LIVESTOCK PRODUCTS

Cattle and Beef Production

Country	Meat Production 10^3 tonnes av. 1977–81	Animal Population 10^3 av. 1977–81
World Total	46,083	1,205,930
USA	10,676	115,112
USSR	6,873	113,455
Brazil	6,242	90,800
Argentina	3,015	57,947
Australia	1,847	27,870
France	1,761	23,796
China	1,648	57,202
West Germany	1,453	14,877
Italy	1,091	8,663
UK	1,044	13,520
Canada	1,028	12,755
Poland	669	12,724
Mexico	598	30,213
Colombia	565	24,391

Animals Slaughtered:
World Total 234,243

Goats and Goat Meat

Country	Meat Production 10^3 tonnes av. 1977–81	Animal Population 10^3 av. 1977–81
World Total	1,922	448,413
China	335	75,539
India	273	71,086
Pakistan	165	27,995
Turkey	117	18,609
Nigeria	108	24,260
Ethiopia	55	17,150
Somali Dem. Rep.	52	16,240
Iran	44	13,541
Greece	43	4,553
Sudan	41	12,255
Bangladesh	41	10,363
USSR	39	5,673
Indonesia	38	7,734
North Yemen	38	7,580

Animals Slaughtered:
World Total 162,310

Pigs and Pig Meat

Country	Meat Production 10^3 tonnes av. 1977–81	Animal Population 10^3 av. 1977–81
World Total	52,402	756,333
China	15,547	304,039
USA	6,769	60,738
USSR	5,176	70,866
West Germany	2,642	21,908
France	1,811	11,494
Poland	1,636	20,561
Japan	1,350	9,293
East Germany	1,177	11,957
Netherlands	1,088	9,527
Italy	1,018	9,034
UK	918	7,795
Brazil	902	36,319
Romania	894	10,543
Denmark	884	9,166

Animals Slaughtered:
World Total 760,598

Sheep and Sheep Meat

Country	Meat Production 10³ tonnes av. 1977–81	Animal Population 10³
World Total	5,689	1,088,793
USSR	846	141,726
New Zealand	540	64,952
Australia	538	134,106
China	395	96,305
Turkey	289	44,562
UK	243	30,275
Iran	211	33,795
France	160	11,798
USA	145	12,628
South Africa	129	31,495
Spain	127	14,957
Argentina	125	33,588
Pakistan	125	24,345
India	119	40,970
Animals Slaughtered: World Total		374,857

Wool

Country	10³ tonnes[1] av. 1977–81
World Total	1,606
Australia	416
USSR	277
New Zealand	236
Argentina	88
China	76
South Africa	60
Uruguay	42
UK	36
Turkey	32
USA	24
Pakistan	23
India	22
Romania	22

[1] Scoured wool.

DAIRY PRODUCTS

Butter and Ghee

Country	10³ tonnes av. 1977–81
World Total	6,920
USSR	1,406
India	611
West Germany	557
France	544
USA	494
Poland	297
East Germany	278
Pakistan	227
Netherlands	191
UK	159
Denmark	123
Czechoslovakia	123
Turkey	120
Ireland	113

Cheese

Country	10³ tonnes av. 1977–81
World Total	11,037
USA	2,044
USSR	1,517
France	1,093
West Germany	746
Italy	585
Netherlands	434
Poland	380
Argentina	244
Egypt	238
UK	226
East Germany	207
Denmark	203
Canada	188

Milk

Country	Cows' Milk	Milked Cows
	10³ tonnes av. 1977–81	10³ head av. 1977–81
World Total	421,161	218,352
USSR	91,921	42,858
USA	57,050	10,857
France	31,957	10,085
West Germany	23,864	5,448
Poland	16,544	5,905
UK	15,780	3,315
India	11,770	23,425
Netherlands	11,494	2,302
Brazil	10,804	14,029
Italy	10,136	3,698
East Germany	8,236	2,128
Canada	7,745	2,263
New Zealand	6,415	2,030
Japan	6,283	1,273

FISH AND AQUATIC ANIMAL PRODUCTS

Though seas and oceans cover approximately 70 per cent of the Earth's surface, fish and marine animal products provide only about 4 per cent of the world's total protein and less than 1 per cent of its calories. Salt-water sources provided over 85 per cent of the world's 1980 recorded catch. Most of the world's major fishing grounds lie within the 200 nautical mile (370 km, 231 miles) exclusive economic zones claimed by maritime states, and deep ocean areas have little commercial importance. In terms of value, the most important fishing grounds are the northeast and northwest Atlantic and the northeast and northwest Pacific oceans.

Global fishery yields have changed only slightly during the last decade, rising from 69 million tonnes in 1969 to 72 million tonnes in 1980. However, this almost constant output is the product of a sharp decline in some traditional fisheries, such as the North Sea, and the development of new, deep-water fish stocks. The last decade has also witnessed the growth of fish-farming and other forms of mariculture, but these activities still produce less than 2 per cent of the world's total catch. In addition to the recorded fishery statistics, it is thought that some 5 to 7 million tonnes of fish are caught each year by subsistence fishermen.

Currently about 30 per cent of the world's commercial fish catch is directly reduced to fishmeal and similar products which are used for feeding pigs, poultry and other animals. The remaining 70 per cent of the catch nominally goes for human consumption, though the viscera and other wastes from the fish are also processed to form animal foods, so that in total roughly half of the world's fish catch is used to provide animal feeding stuffs. Oils and fats expressed from fish and other marine animals are used in the manufacture of margarine, soaps and other products.

Fresh Fish and Shellfish

Country	Fresh, Frozen and Chilled Fish 10^3 tonnes av. 1977–81	Crustacea and Molluscs 10^3 tonnes av. 1977–81
World Total	8,862	1,212
USSR	3,101	NA
Japan	2,775	274
USA	365	231
China	300[1]	NA
Canada	250	51
Spain	151	140
Norway	145	8
South Korea	145	26
Poland	139	3
Argentina	138	26
UK	125[2]	22
Denmark	123	13
South Africa	121	5
Iceland	119	3
Thailand	66[1]	51
India	NA	49
Mexico	28[1]	49
Indonesia	15[1]	38
Malaysia	NA	31

[1] Mean of 1977, 1979 and 1980 only.
[2] Mean of 1976, 1977, 1978 and 1979 only.
NA Data not available.

NA Data not available.

Dried, Salted and Smoked Fish

Country	10^3 tonnes av. 1977–81
World Total	3,807
China	982
Japan	783
USSR	673
Indonesia	322
Philippines	162
Norway	96
Iceland	74
Ghana	64
Canada	58
Spain	55
Poland	47

Fish Products

Country	Oils and Fats 10^3 tonnes av. 1977–81	Fishmeals and Animal Feeds 10^3 tonnes av. 1977–81
World Total	4,768	1,145
Japan	846	225
Peru	629	113
USSR	561	112
USA	432	110
Chile	390	78
Norway	377	208
Denmark	319	95
South Africa	180	35
Iceland	171	76
Thailand	145	NA
Ecuador	69	6
UK	68	3
Mexico	66	NA
Canada	65	12

Earth, Seas and World Population

The Physical World

Earth and Moon

The Earth is one of nine planets circling the Sun, forming our solar system. Fifth in order of size, its diameter is 12,756 km (7926.2 miles), about one eleventh that of the largest planet (Jupiter) and less than one hundredth that of the Sun itself. Third in distance from the Sun, it follows a slightly elliptical orbit of mean radius 149.6 million km (92.9 million miles), completing each circuit in 365.26 days. Distant Pluto takes 247.7 years to circle the Sun in a markedly elliptical orbit which can take it up to 7375 million km (4584 million miles) from the Sun.

Like several other planets the Earth has a natural satellite – the Moon. This gives the appearance of a large body, but is in fact much smaller than all the planets except Pluto, with a diameter of 3475 km (2159 miles). The Moon circles the Earth on a rather unsteady path, at an average distance of 384,392 km (238,850 miles), each orbit taking 27 days, 7 hours and 43 minutes to complete. The Sun is incandescent, radiating light, heat and other forms of energy into space. The Moon has little radiant energy of its own, but reflects light from the Sun to the Earth. The amount of light we receive from the Moon depends on the relative angles of Sun, Moon and Earth, giving the familiar succession of full, half and new Moon with all stages between. Both Moon and Sun exert gravitational pulls on the Earth, manifested most strongly in tidal movements of the oceans (see Seas and Oceans).

The Stars and Galaxies

The stars form patterns in the night sky which were grouped into constellations by ancient astronomers. Although they appear to be no more remote than the Moon or the planets, they are very much farther away; the nearest star (Proxima Centauri) lies some 40 million million km (24.8 million million miles) from the solar system, and Sirius, the brightest star, over twice as far. These distances, respectively a quarter and half a million times the distance of the Earth from the Sun, are usually expressed in light-years. One light-year is the distance (9.46 million million km, 5.88 million million miles) that light travels in a year, so Proxima Centauri is 4.2 light-years away, Sirius 8.6 light-years away.

The Sun too is a star, lying like Proxima Centauri and Sirius within a far-flung group of about one hundred thousand million years. Together they form a disc or galaxy over a hundred thousand light-years across, arranged in a pattern of spiralling spokes; Proxima Centauri, Sirius and the Sun lie somewhere near the edge. Looking up into the night sky and finding the Milky Way, where the stars appear densest, we are looking across and through the thickness of the galaxy, which is slowly rotating in space. Between the spokes of the galaxy are clouds of gas, much of it hydrogen, detectable by radio telescopes, and clusters of densely-packed stars are scattered around it. Countless millions of other galaxies have been observed, some much larger than ours and others relatively tiny, the farthest detectable over 4000 million light-years away and receding from us rapidly as the Universe expands.

The Seasons

Besides travelling around the Sun, the Earth rotates on its own axis, each complete rotation taking a day. The axis of rotation, which passes through the north and south geographic poles, is inclined at an angle of $23\frac{1}{2}°$ from the vertical to the plane of the Earth's orbit and the direction of the axis is fixed in space. Thus, in the course of a year, the poles take turns to incline toward the Sun and give rise to the cycle of seasons. While the North Pole faces towards the Sun, the northern hemisphere is in summer and the southern hemisphere in winter, and vice versa.

From this tilt or inclination of the Earth's axis of rotation comes the significance of the tropics of Cancer and Capricorn, respectively $23\frac{1}{2}°$ north and south of the Equator. Between their limits the Sun appears to be overhead at noon at some time of the year; it is overhead at the Tropic of Cancer during the northern summer solstice (about June 21), at the Tropic of Capricorn at the southern summer solstice (about December 21), and at the Equator midway between them at the equinoxes (about March 20 and September 23). Similarly the Arctic and Antarctic circles, respectively $23\frac{1}{2}°$ from their poles, are boundaries within which the midsummer Sun, even at local midnight, is above the horizon. At the poles themselves days and seasons merge; a six-month summer day is followed by six months of winter night.

Solar Radiation and Climate

Almost all the energy measured and heat felt at the Earth's surface comes from the Sun, only a tiny fraction seeping through from the Earth's own radio-active core. More than any other single factor, the angle of incidence of the Sun's rays determines the kind of climate that will be experienced in any part of the world. Polar regions always receive the incident rays obliquely, even at the height of summer, and are never warmed thoroughly. Tropical regions, well heated almost every day by a near-vertical Sun, are on average very much warmer. Temperate regions experience high sun in summer and low sun in winter, and in consequence have strongly seasonal climates.

The mean temperature of the Earth's surface, averaged over day and night, summer and winter, is about 14°C (57°F). How this varies with latitude and season in different parts of the world can be judged from the climatic tables of Section 3. Annual mean surface temperatures may lie above 20°C (68°F) in the tropics, or can be well below freezing point near the poles. Monthly mean temperatures vary widely in continental heartlands, hardly at all on oceanic islands where sea temperatures are a stabilizing influence.

Differential heating is responsible for the global pressure systems, which combine in turn with Coriolis forces (forces set up by the rotation of the Earth), topography and other factors to create prevailing winds and oceanic currents. These help to redistribute heat about the Earth's surface, carry water vapour from ocean to continent and deposit it as rain and snow, and produce the local and seasonal climatic effects with which we are all familiar.

The Structure of the Earth

The bulk of the Earth is a dense, iron-rich core of hot molten rock, in constant motion from swirling internal currents. Surrounding the core is a semi-molten mantle of peridotite – an oxide of iron, magnesium and silicon often found at the surface as a dark, crystalline rock. Outside core and mantle lies a thin casing of hard silicate rocks, chilled and crystallized by the Earth's restless journey through space. Under the oceans the crust is mostly wafer-thin, averaging 6000 m (19,700 ft), and covering the mantle like pack-ice on a polar sea. The continental crust is thicker, up to 35 km (22 miles) in depth, composed of paler, lighter rocks that 'float' like icebergs on the floes of sub-oceanic crust.

Slow swirling in the semi-molten material of the mantle, probably due to convection currents, causes the thin crust to fracture, and the resulting patchwork of plates to move horizontally over the Earth's surface. Some of the plates carry continental massifs, others not; many geologists recognize six major plates and several smaller ones, that shuffle and drift against each other with rates of movement of 1 to 4 cm (0.4 to 1.6 in) a year. Interactions of these plates are thought to be the cause of many of the world's major topographic features, and to explain the present distribution of continents and oceans.

Plate Tectonics

Where two plates are drawing apart (for example along the mid-oceanic ridges), molten rock wells up between them to form new crustal material, sometimes incorporating a record of magnetic orientation that allows different stages of fissure development to be dated accurately. Where plates collide (for example in the depths of submarine trenches), one disappears beneath the other to be melted back into the mantle, and lines of volcanoes, submarine and surface, may form along neighbouring cracks and zones of weakness; this explains the presence of interlinking arcs of islands along the far eastern shore of Eurasia, across the north Pacific Ocean, and perhaps in the eastern Caribbean Sea.

Sometimes the plates move together to form compression zones, crumpling the crust and its overburden of sediments into mountain ranges; the Himalayas of Nepal, northern India and China, the Rocky Mts and the Andes were all formed this way, and indeed are still rising under spasmodic pressures. Sometimes the cracks take in continental as well as oceanic plates: East Africa's Great Rift Valley is a classic example. Hot-spots below a moving plate may erupt at intervals, forming chains of volcanic islands with islands of decreasing age along the chain reflecting the movement of the plate over the hot-spot; the Hawaiian Islands can be interpreted this way. Some eruptions form isolated islands, like Ascension and St Helena in mid-Atlantic, St Paul and Amsterdam in the southern Indian Ocean, that erupt for a short period, perhaps over a few million years, and then seem to die.

Mineral Wealth

As prospectors are well aware, minerals are closely associated with particular geological formations, and the economic prospector is well advised to be an earth scientist as well. Many gemstones are linked with the heat and turbulence of vulcanism; iron ores and valuable phosphates are often concentrated within porous limestones, and hydrocarbons are generally found among sediments that represent former warm seas. Modern techniques of discovery, involving gravitational, seismic, magnetic and other forms of survey, help prospectors to diagnose what lies under the surface layers; deep drilling, today even in bedrock underlying turbulent shelf seas, confirms or denies what the preliminary surveys have indicated.

Seas and Oceans

Seas and oceans cover some 362 million km² (140 million sq miles) or 71 per cent of the Earth's surface. Except for such inland seas as the Caspian and the Sea of Galilee, they form a continuous mass of 1376 million km³ (330 million cubic miles) of water with a mean depth of 3800 m (12,467 ft). This represents about 98 per cent of all the water on Earth and in the enveloping atmosphere. Most of the balance is ground-water, locked away in the pores of sedimentary rocks and soils; a small fraction (a little over 1 per cent of the total) is in glaciers and ice sheets, and a fraction of 1 per cent forms rivers, lakes and atmospheric moisture, in constant exchange with the sea.

If the Earth's surface were perfectly smooth, the oceans would cover it in a layer some 2700 m (9000 ft) deep. As they stand, the continents rise high above sea level and the ocean floors descend to great depths; on average the oceans are 4.5 times as deep as the land is high, and the volume of ocean is roughly 11 times the volume of land above sea level. Everest, the highest mountain on dry land (8848 m, 29,030 ft), rises only three quarters as high as the greatest ocean depths. By human scales these heights and depths are considerable, but on a world scale they are trivial; on a model globe 2 m (6.6 ft) in diameter the seas would nowhere be more than 2 mm (0.08 in) deep, the land nowhere more than 1.4 mm (0.06 in) above the mean level.

The Ocean Floor

Surrounding the continents immediately beyond the shoreline are shelves of shallow water. Of mean width 60 km (37 miles), some are so narrow as to be hardly present at all, while several are wide enough to join parts of the continents to distant off-lying islands and to each other. Covered with shingle, sand and fine muddy sediments washed down from the land, the continental shelves slope gently seaward to depths of about 200 m (660 ft), forming the sea bed for shallow seas; Antarctica's shelves lie almost twice as deep, because of the depression of the continent by its load of ice. The so-called shelf seas (the North Sea and Sea of Japan are good examples) are characteristically enriched by run-off from the land (see below). They are correspondingly rich in marine life; some, like the North Sea, support huge concentrations of edible fish, shrimps, crabs and molluscs that generations of men have exploited.

All shallow seas close to human centres of population suffer pollution, for man dumps industrial effluents and wastes into both the seas and the rivers that feed them. Parts of the Baltic and North Sea are chronically poisoned; even the Arctic Ocean, far from human concentrations, suffers this insidious form of degradation.

Beyond the edge of the shelf the sea bed dips steeply down the continental slope, which is the true continental margin. This descends at a shallow angle of 3° to 5° to depths of 3000 to 5000 m (10,000 to 16,500 ft), where the sea bed flattens. Continental slopes are cut by deep ravines and canyons, thought to be caused by the downhill slumping and erosion of sediments from the land. The abyssal plains, generally far from land, carry deep accumulations of silt from the ocean surface, including the shells, bones, teeth and other hard parts of marine organisms that lived and died in the surface waters far above.

Beyond the base of the slopes lies a broad, undulating abyssal plain, punctuated by hills, ridges, submarine platforms, tall volcanic sea-mounts that sweep up towards the ocean surface, and taller cones that rise even higher to form oceanic islands. Several of the submarine ridges compare in length, breadth and height to some of the biggest mountain ranges on dry land. The Mid-Atlantic Ridge, for example, runs centrally down the ocean from arctic Iceland to ice-capped Bouvetøya in the Southern Ocean, rising high from the sea bed and penetrating the surface to form such isolated islands as the Azores, Ascension Island, Tristan da Cunha and St Helena. This ridge, like others of its kind, is formed by the splitting of the Earth's crust along a submarine plane of weakness, allowing molten rock to escape repeatedly and the ocean floor to expand.

There are also trenches in the abyssal plain, the deepest curving around the bases of island arcs; trenches off the Philippine, Aleutian and South Sandwich islands are good examples. These are sites where the sea floor is contracting, one section or plate of crust disappearing beneath another. They include the deepest corners of the oceans, several descending to depths of 11,000 m (36,000 ft) and more.

The familiar pattern of continents and oceans, once thought of as static and unchanging, is now known to be transient. The continents shift in relation to each other, splitting or moving apart here and colliding there, generating new shapes for seas and ocean basins (see The Physical World). Sea levels too have shifted radically; it is not long in geological terms since extensive glaciation held millions more tonnes of water captive in the northern hemisphere, causing many of the shallow seas on continental margins to dry out and disappear, and land bridges to form where there are now straits and shallows. On a longer time-scale mountains have arisen from the oceans, mainly under pressure from shifting continental blocks. Much of Everest and the neighbouring Himalayas, and most of the Alps, Andes and Rocky Mts were laid down as sediments on the sea floor; today's mountains are constantly being weathered and worn down by atmospheric processes and will in time return as sediments to the oceans. On another scale altogether the oceans themselves are in constant, slow interchange with each other, their waters circulating both horizontally and vertically. They also exchange in a never-ending cycle with the atmosphere and Earth, yielding up water vapour into the air above them and recruiting fresh water from rivers, icefields and rain.

Salts and Nutrients

Mean salinity of sea water is about 3.5 per cent, or 35 parts per thousand (ppt). Of the dissolved constituents sodium, magnesium, calcium, potassium, sulphate, bicarbonate and chloride together make up over 99 per cent of the total, with sodium and chloride together providing almost 30 ppt – hence sea water's salty taste. The *composition* of sea water (i.e. the relative proportions of the main constituents) is remarkably constant; *concentration*, however, varies considerably from sea to sea, being generally highest in the tropics where evaporation exceeds precipitation, and lowest in polar and subpolar regions where melting ice causes seasonal dilution. The normal range of salinities is 32 to 37 ppt. In the Red Sea and the Gulf surface salinities may rise to over 41 ppt, and in parts of the Baltic Sea during the spring thaw they may fall to 10 ppt and lower.

Some of the salts and other substances dissolved in sea water make it a nutrient broth capable of sustaining life. All life is thought to have begun in the sea, and a huge density and abundance of living creatures is still to be found there. Of particular importance to living matter are the gases oxygen and carbon dioxide, which dissolve from the atmosphere, and such familiar nutrients as phosphates and nitrates, which accumulate in the sea and are available for new life to assimilate. Absorbed by the microscopic plants that float near the ocean surface, these nutrients and their abundance may be limiting factors that determine the richness of plant life in a particular patch of ocean, and hence the numbers of shrimps, fish, whales, sea birds and other larger creatures that are found there.

Temperatures, Light and Life

Surface waters are warmed and lighted by the Sun and cooled by evaporation and radiation, their mean temperatures varying from over 30°C (86°F) in the hottest regions to −1.9°C (28.6°F) in the Arctic and Antarctic where sea ice is always present. Surface temperatures are an uncertain guide to temperatures deep down. In polar regions the sea is cold at all depths, for cold, dense water falls constantly from the surface to the deeper layers to spread far and wide across the ocean floor. In temperate and tropical habitats surface temperatures closely match those of the atmosphere above them, usually lagging slightly behind where there are seasonal changes. Below a relatively thin layer, however, the water is always colder. On the Equator temperatures may be 25°C (77°F) or more in the top 50 m (165 ft), falling to 8°C (46°F) at 500 m (1650 ft) and as low as 4°C (39°F) below 1000 m (3300 ft). Below about 1500 m (5000 ft) sea water in all latitudes is uniformly cold, generally at 3.5°C (38°F) or less.

Sub-surface layers of water are also in permanent darkness, for very little light penetrates below 150 m (500 ft) even in clear, sediment-free water. Life too becomes scarce; though living creatures occur at all depths, the greatest concentrations are found at the surface and on shallow sea floors, where the water is well lit and contains an abundance of life-sustaining gases, and food (i.e. other forms of life) is most plentiful. Below the photic (well-lit) zone the microscopic plant life, on which all else depends, cannot survive and multiply, nor can the tiny animals of the plankton which browse on them. There is a constant rain of dead and dying organisms from surface waters to the sea bed below, on which most of the sedentary animal life of deep waters depends.

Circulation

Temperature and salinity combine to produce distinctive water masses which keep their identity over long distances. Warm saline waters flowing westward from the Mediterranean Sea at a depth of 1000 m (3300 ft) can be detected by their temperature/salinity signature far out across the Atlantic Ocean; cold, dilute waters from the Arctic spread southward, remaining unmixed with neighbouring waters far south of Labrador, and the cold waters underlying the southern Atlantic and Indian Oceans are known from their signature to originate along the Antarctic shore. From such clues oceanographers over many years have built up a three-dimensional picture of ocean circulation, covering both horizontal and vertical movements of the major water masses.

Circulation is motivated mainly by winds and controlled by the shape of ocean basins, Coriolis forces, gravity and other factors. In each of the three main ocean basins (Indian, Pacific and Atlantic) surface waters move similarly in extensive gyres or circular paths, clockwise in the northern hemisphere and counter-clockwise in the south, driven by the trade winds in low latitudes and the prevailing westerlies of the cool-temperate zones. This circulation carries warm water poleward along the western flanks of the oceans, providing warm currents, for example, along eastern Australia, Brazil and southeastern USA. Correspondingly cold currents wash the western shores of South America, Canada, USA, Western Australia and Portugal.

The strong northern Atlantic gyre drives a flow of warm surface waters northeastward from the Gulf of Mexico; called the Gulf Stream or North Atlantic Drift, this brings anomalously warm winters to Iceland, Britain and Scandinavia. In the northeastern Pacific a similar but weaker flow warms the southern shores of Alaska. In equivalent latitudes of the southern hemisphere there is less land, and water-masses diverted south are driven eastward about the world by strong, unimpeded westerly winds, producing a continuous girdle of current in the Roaring Forties and Howling Fifties. Further south this changes to a westerly flow under the influence of easterly winds blowing from the Antarctic continent. There are many other surface currents and gyres in different corners of the oceans, strongly influencing local navigation, fishing and other human activities. Deep currents bear little direct relation to surface currents; indeed they may flow in opposite directions under completely different motivations, producing layers of different water-masses with radically different temperature and salinity signatures.

Waves and Tides

Waves are caused by friction between wind and ocean surface; the wind first corrugates the sea and then enhances the corrugations with further energy, building up the vertical oscillations called waves. Strong winds blowing over a wide stretch of sea build up massive waves, which travel far from their original source. Discernible only as harmless swell in the open ocean, their energy is manifest when they tumble as surf against distant coastlines. Wave action is a force to be reckoned with, constantly reshaping cliffs and beaches, eroding headlands, forming and destroying islands, and transporting billions of tonnes of material along the shore.

Tides are caused by the gravitational pull of Sun and Moon, which cause the sea surface to bulge in their direction. In fact two bulges are formed, on opposite sides of the Earth, and the rotation of the Earth beneath them results in two high and two low tides per day. There are many complicating factors, including the sizes and shapes of the ocean basins and their fringing seas, that modify the tides locally. Tides are generally small on oceanic islands; their effects are seen most strongly on continental coasts, where the difference between high and low tide may amount to several metres, and the inter-tidal zone (the coastal strip between high and low water) may be several kilometres wide.

Tides oscillate between 'springs' and 'neaps' on a lunar-monthly cycle. (The lunar month, the interval from new Moon to new Moon, is 29.5 days.) Spring or extreme tides (highest highs and lowest lows) occur two or three days after the full Moon and new Moon, when Sun and Moon pull together in the same direction; neap tides of lower range occur at other times of the month when Sun and Moon oppose each other. Times of tides at any point on the coast are generally predictable for years and months ahead; heights are predictable to some degree, but vary with wind strength and other factors. Freak tides, caused by winds or reduced atmospheric pressure, occasionally disrupt the tidal rhythm, lifting high tides several metres above normal and possibly flooding far inland. 'Tidal waves' are freak tide-like movements caused by waves of low amplitude and long wavelength, which travel across the oceans from sites of disturbance – often earthquakes or volcanic eruptions on the sea bed. The Japanese, who know them well, call them 'tsunami'; harmless in the open ocean, they generate huge surf on striking a coast, drawing back the sea and hurling it repeatedly at the land with devastating effect.

Biological Productivity

Oceans, like lands, show differing levels of biological productivity. Some areas are rich – the equivalent of well-watered pasture or agricultural land – supporting considerable plant and animal life. Other areas are as poor and unproductive as mountain fell, tundra or semi-desert. Shallow seas of temperate latitudes, which warm quickly in summer and have a good turnover of nutrients, are among the most productive waters, supporting rich plankton (the minute plants and animals that crowd surface layers) in spring and summer. Their prime wealth of plankton in turn supports shoals of fish, flocks of sea birds, herds of dolphins, seals and other predators, and a dense sea-bed fauna. Tropical seas are often poorer, lacking dissolved gases and nutrients; polar seas are surprisingly rich in summer, supporting considerable life even among and below floating pack-ice. In winter much of the polar plankton descends into deeper water, and the surface-feeding sea birds and other predators migrate to warmer seas until the spring thaw.

Some of the most productive patches of ocean are areas of upwelling, where prevailing winds, sea-bed topography and other factors bring nutrient-rich waters to the surface from layers beneath (see above). For example, strong winds off the western flanks of South America and South Africa push aside surface waters, allowing cool sub-surface waters to surge up in replacement. Nutrient-rich, these enhance local production of microscopic floating plants (phytoplankton), which support stocks of tiny crustaceans, larval fish, shrimps and other small floating animals. These in turn are eaten by larger fish, sea birds, seals, whales and other predators. Where plankton thrives the predators tend to gather, and man may benefit by hunting and fishing among them. Such locally-enriched areas include the Benguela, Peruvian and Falkland currents, all rich in small shoaling fish, and the whaling grounds east of South Georgia and the South Shetland Islands, in the southern Atlantic Ocean, which for a long time provided the world's richest whaling grounds.

Seas and Oceans

There is no universally recognized system of naming the seas and oceans. Most authorities agree to four major oceans (Arctic, Atlantic, Indian, Pacific), though some regard southern circumpolar waters as forming a separate Southern Ocean; between fifty and seventy separate seas (including large gulfs and bays) are commonly recognized. The following table covers the most important marine areas.

	Area km² (000)	sq miles (000)	Mean depth m	ft	Greatest depth m	ft	Remarks
tic ean	14,056	5,427	988	3,240	5,450	17,881	World's smallest ocean; permanently covered with shifting ice floes. Wide Siberian shelf; deep basins traversed by three parallel ridges.
ntic ean	82,217	31,744	3,900	12,796	9,560	31,366	Traversed N–S by Mid-Atlantic Ridge; very productive subpolar waters and coastlines with important inshore and pelagic fisheries. Considerable coastal pollution.
tic Sea	422	163	55	180	460	1,509	Salinities 5–15 ppt; surface frozen several weeks in winter. High productivity marred by industrial pollution.
ing Sea	2,269	876	1,400	4,593	5,121	16,802	Shallow Bering Shelf in NE half, deep Aleutian Basin in SW. Northern waters ice-bound in winter. High seasonal productivity, important fisheries.

435

Seas and Oceans

Name	Area km² (000)	sq miles (000)	Mean depth m	ft	Greatest depth m	ft	Remarks
Black Sea	461	178	1,300	4,265	2,245	7,366	Lower layers of water stagna unproductive; surface waters with important coastal fisher Seriously polluted.
Caribbean Sea	1,943	750	2,660	8,727	7,100	23,295	Complex sea bed with four ridges and basins; many cora fringed islands. Productive w with important coastal fisher Coastal pollution.
China Sea, East	1,248	481	350	1,148	999	3,278	Generally shallow shelf sea v deep trough bordering Ryuk Rich local and commercial fi at all levels. Coastal pollutio
China Sea, South	2,318	895	1,140	3,740	5,514	18,091	Wide continental shelf desce steeply to deeps. Very rich c and pelagic fishing, local and commercial. Coastal pollutio
Hudson Bay	1,233	476	112	367	259	850	Salinity less than 31 ppt; sur frozen December–May. High summer productivity, import local hunting and fishing.
Indian Ocean	73,481	28,371	3,900	12,796	9,000	29,529	Complex ocean bed with ma ridges, plateaus and island g Inshore fisheries locally impc large-scale pelagic commerci fisheries. Coastal pollution.
Japan, Sea of	1,008	389	1,350	4,430	3,743	12,281	Marginal shelves, deep centr Northern waters freeze November–April. High prod with rich inshore and pelagic marred by industrial pollutio
Mediterran-ean Sea	2,505	967	1,501	4,926	4,846	15,900	Almost tideless; salinity 38 p Divided into basins by comp ridges. Poor waters; small lo fisheries. Coasts heavily pollu
Mexico, Gulf of	1,544	569	1,500	4,921	4,377	14,361	Strong clockwise surface circ of warm, saline surface water generates Gulf Stream. Rich and pelagic fishing. Coastal pollution.
North Sea	575	222	90	295	661	2,169	Glacial deposits provide very sea bed, generally shallow bu off southern Norway. Rich s commercial fishing at all leve Severe coastal pollution.
Okhotsk, Sea of	1,528	590	972	3,192	3,475	11,401	Wide continental shelf: gene shallow in north, steepening toward the Kuril Basin in S Icebound and foggy: good fis

	Area		Mean depth		Greatest depth		Remarks
	km² (000)	sq miles (000)	m	ft	m	ft	
ıfic ean	165,384	63,855	4,300	14,108	11,524	37,810	Very complex bed with many island ridges, plateaus and sea mounts in western half. Rich fisheries, especially in cold northern waters and among islands.
Sea	438	169	538	1,764	2,246	7,370	Evaporation makes this the most saline sea (36–41 ppt); pools of hot brine (60°C, 140°F, over 250 ppt) in central deeps. Local fishing meagre but important. Some serious pollution.
ıow Sea	1,243	480	43	141	91	298	Waters silted yellow and diluted (31–33 ppt) by major rivers. Northern coastal areas freeze in winter. Rich seasonal commercial fishing at all levels. Coastal pollution.

World Population

Fossil Man

The fossil record shows that humans, or apes with many human characteristics, have existed on Earth for about ten million years. Their predecessors were similar creatures, more ape-like than man-like, which gave rise to several hominoid stocks. The record is far from complete and new fossils are being found every year, but creatures closely akin to our own species *Homo sapiens* seem to have come late on the scene, appearing in fossil deposits of the East Indies and eastern Africa about one and a half million years old. Their distribution suggests that the earliest true men were nomadic hunters of the plain and forest edge, living in warm climates. Short of stature and pigmy-like in their proportions, they seem to have wandered in small bands, without permanent homes but sheltering in caves and hollows. They were omnivorous, eating fruit and meat, probably including insects and any other small creatures they could catch. They would have needed to be adaptable in their constant search for food, and prepared to wander far as the seasons shifted. Some found their way to the coasts, living on fish and shellfish from the inter-tidal zone.

We know little of the demography or population structure of these early people. By modern standards they were no doubt short-lived, with few surviving even into their thirtieth year. They would have lived very much at the mercy of the environment, their wanderings limited at first to warm temperate regions where climatic conditions were favourable, food and water plentiful and natural predators scarce. If they were year-round breeders, bearing one offspring at a time like modern humans, their reproductive efficiency would have ensured rapid proliferation and population expansion when times were good.

Natural culling during periods of starvation, disease and inter-tribal hostilities, as well as climatic deterioration and other disasters, would have trimmed the population periodically, selecting only the most alert and adaptable to survive and reproduce further. Early man spread quickly about the world, crossing from Asia to the Americas during the glacial periods when the continents were connected by a land bridge, and spreading to the tip of South America, through the Pacific islands and even into the Arctic. We do not know the total size of population at any stage, but three to four million is probably a generous estimate for the world population of Stone Age man up to 100,000 years ago.

Population Expansion

Since Stone Age times the human population has expanded enormously – far faster than that of any other animal of comparable size. Widely dispersed across the length and breadth of the Earth, man has adapted to both tropical and polar regions, to mountains, forests and deserts. World population is still growing fast, and at a rate that has been increasing steadily over many decades. Currently it stands at about 4.5 billion (thousand million). It has doubled within the last forty years, trebled in the span of a human lifetime and almost quadrupled within a century; it could well double again within the lifetimes of many young people who are alive today.

Estimates for the future vary. We do not know which will prove correct because population patterns change quickly from decade to decade; birth rates and death rates in different parts of the world are shifting as we watch, and the rate of growth in many areas of the world is proving virtually unpredictable. But unless some worldwide catastrophe intervenes to reduce it, the human population can hardly fail to reach about six billion by the turn of the century – an increase of a quarter or more in twenty years.

Much of the vast expansion since the Stone Age has occurred recently. Human numbers probably remained steady at a few million, with births and deaths closely balanced, well into the New Stone Age some five to eight thousand years ago. The factor that first allowed population to expand was probably agriculture. When people began to settle and grow food instead of hunting it, and lived in small settlements rather than nomad camps, many uncertainties and hazards disappeared. Living conditions improved, and a slow but steady rise in population began.

With higher productivity from cultivated land, food became more plentiful and reliable. More children survived the rigours of infancy and, as life expectancy increased, more adults survived and lived on into middle age, producing more children to each generation. The villages and towns expanded with a new race of settled, domesticated folk, who felled the forests and cultivated the ground in ever-increasing areas about their settlements. There were still hard times when famine, pestilence and tribal warfare took their toll with undiminished ferocity. But civilization – the settled way of life – spread rapidly from several centres simultaneously, through North Africa, Asia and Europe, probably allowing world population to double every thousand to two thousand years. By medieval times there may well have been half a billion people spread across the world, with standards of living, security and longevity advancing slowly but surely in each successive generation.

The Explosion

A faster rate of increase was still to come, for human reproductive efficiency is remarkably high, and every slight rise in standards of living ensured a higher rate of survival. The most rapid increase in births over deaths began in Europe in late medieval times, when manufacturing developed alongside agriculture and Europe entered its industrial age. While societies reorganized themselves to absorb increasing wealth and productivity, life expectancy rose from two and a half to three or four decades. Though by modern criteria the standard of living of the majority of the population was still very low, and such factors as infant mortality remained high, nevertheless from late medieval times to the mid-19th century world population probably doubled from half to one billion, and waves of surplus humanity spread from Europe to colonize the still relatively empty lands of Africa, Asia and North America.

As more and more of the Earth's resources were mobilized for mankind, world population continued to increase at an accelerating rate. A revolution in medical and social care spread from industrial to underdeveloped countries, further improving the lot of millions who were still living only a little above subsistence level. Their populations too began to expand, breaching the natural controls that had hitherto held them in check. By the early 20th century world population had reached approximately the two billion mark, increasing to about four billion by 1975.

Overpopulation

As the tables of Section 2 show clearly, populations are still expanding in almost every country of the world, most rapidly in those with the lowest income per capita. It is not surprising that the poorest countries retain a high rate of increase, for their birth rates are invariably high, and survival rates still increasing through the effects of medical and other care.

Poverty and semi-starvation have little effect on fecundity; children are easily begotten in even the poorest communities, and probably most welcome among people who have little else to call their own. At subsistence level a family may survive better with children than without; even half-starving offspring are assets who will help with the stock, the crops and the water supplies, and care for aged parents whose working life is over. With high infant mortality, having four or five children helps to ensure that at least one or two survive.

For these reasons and several others, campaigns to limit family size make little headway in the poorest communities. They are more effective where standards of living are higher and anxieties for the future lower, and most successful of all where prosperity gives choice – hence the declining birth rates and low rates of population increase in nearly all the world's most advanced countries. The result in terms of numbers of rich and poor is inevitable. At present there are five people in the poor countries to every two in the rich. Within half a century, if current trends continue, the ratio of poor to rich will stand at seven to two or more, in a much larger world population. Poverty, malnutrition and starvation already blight the lives of millions in the poor communities; many see it as inevitable that millions more will be born to suffer in the world of the future.

Poverty, Wealth and Population

The division of the world into rich and poor is a relatively recent phenomenon. Until the Industrial Revolution almost everyone the world over was poor. Only very small, favoured minorities held riches, mostly through ownership of land and of rights over their neighbours, either by conquest or inheritance. Well into the 19th century, nine tenths of the world's population raised food for themselves and their families on rented or common land, by primitive techniques that gave them little more than a subsistence standard of living. In the poor countries, this is still the lot of the majority.

World Population

Advanced communities progressed to wealth through a fortunate combination of raw materials, surplus capital, energy and cheap labour, coming together at a critical period during the 18th and 19th centuries. These allowed them to embark on industrialization, a self-sustaining process that in turn generated more and more wealth, which was spread to varying degrees throughout the population. Societies that became rich in this way have usually managed to stay rich, raising and improving their living standards from year to year, attracting more and more of the world's resources to their markets, and stabilizing their position of economic superiority. Communities that missed the boat, for whatever reason, have tended to remain poor and undeveloped, caught in an economic trap from which escape seems to become progressively more difficult.

However, escape is not impossible, as several impoverished societies are in the process of showing, and a large population is not necessarily an impediment. China and Japan are heavily populated countries that, shredded by war little more than a generation ago, have hauled themselves up from poverty and chaos, in the case of Japan to become one of the leading countries of the Western world. By performing their miracles under diametrically opposite political regimes, they encourage those who believe that political ideologies are means rather than ends, and that no ideology holds a monopoly of truth.

The profiles of Section 2 show many underdeveloped countries, including several former colonies, that are climbing steadily to prosperity, whether hindered or helped by their large populations. Others less fortunate are foundering economically or slipping into political chaos, though warfare, civil strife, or the rapacity of their leaders are more obvious causes of trouble than the size of their populations.

Geographic Names and Features

Geographic Names and Features

A gazetteer of this length has necessarily to be selective. This listing includes all sovereign states with their capitals (with the exception of some smaller islands); major subdivisions of the world's largest countries, with capitals; all cities of over one million estimated population (1984); and commonly-used geographical features. The selection includes rivers over 1600 km (1000 miles); large lakes (over 1300 km², 500 sq miles); large islands (over 2600 km², 1000 sq miles); major mountain ranges and mountains over 5000 m (16,400 ft); gulfs, straits, seas and oceans.

Abbreviations

ASSR Autonomous Soviet Socialist Republic
I(s) Island(s)
L Lake
Mt(s) Mountain(s)
R River
Ra Range
Russian SFSR Russian Soviet Federative Socialist Republic
SSR Soviet Socialist Republic
St Saint
UK United Kingdom
USA United States of America
USSR Union of Soviet Socialist Republics

A

Abadan Island and city, SW Iran; oil terminus and refining centre.
Abidjan Capital city, Ivory Coast; shipping, manufacturing and agricultural centre.
Abkhaz ASSR Autonomous republic, SE USSR; capital Sukhumi.
Abu Dhabi Sheikhdom and city state on the Gulf, United Arab Emirates.
Abyssinia See Ethiopia.
Accra Capital city, Ghana; port and industrial centre.
Aconcagua Mountain (6960 m, 22,835 ft), Andes, SW Argentina; highest in southern hemisphere.
Acre State, W Brazil; capital Rio Branco.
Adana City, S Turkey; historic agricultural, commercial and industrial centre.
Addis Ababa Capital city, Ethiopia; agricultural and administrative centre.
Adélie Land See Terre Adélie.
Aden (1) Capital city, SW South Yemen, on Gulf of Aden; port, oil-refining and industrial centre. (2) **Gulf of**, formed by NW arm of Indian Ocean between S coast of Arabia and Somali Democratic Republic.
Adirondack Mts Isolated massif, NE New York, USA.
Admiralty I Island of Alexander Archipelago, SW Alaska, USA.
Admiralty Is Archipelago, Papua New Guinea.
Admiralty Ra Mountain range, Victoria Land, E Antarctica.
Adriatic Sea Extension of the Mediterranean Sea, bordered by Italy, Yugoslavia, Albania and the Balkan Peninsula.
Adzhar ASSR Autonomous republic, SE USSR; capital Batumi.
Aegean Sea Extension of the Mediterranean Sea, bordered by the Balkan Peninsula and Turkey.
Afghanistan Independent republic, Asia S; see Section 1.
Ahmadabad City, Gujarat, NW India; industrial and commercial centre.

Ajman Sheikhdom on the Gulf, United Arab Emirates.

Alabama State, SE USA; capital Montgomery.

Alagôas State, NE Brazil; capital Maceió.

Alai Mts Range, Kirgiz SSR, USSR; western end of the Tien Shan Mts.

Åland Is Archipelago of several thousand islands (about eighty inhabited), Finnish-owned, in Gulf of Bothnia.

Alaska State, NW USA; capital Juneau.

Alaska Ra Mountain range, central Alaska, USA, including Mt McKinley (see entry).

Albania Independent republic, Europe SE; see Section 1.

Albert, L See L Mobutu Sese Seko.

Alberta Province, W Canada; capital Edmonton.

Aleutian Is Volcanic island chain, N Pacific Ocean, SW Alaska, USA.

Alexander Arch Archipelago, N Pacific Ocean, SE Alaska, USA.

Alexandria City, N Egypt; historic port, agricultural and industrial centre.

Algeria Independent republic, Africa NW; see Section 1.

Algiers Capital city, Algeria; port, agricultural, industrial and commercial centre.

Allegheny Mts Range forming western flank of Appalachian Mts, E USA.

Alma Ata Capital city, Kazakh SSR, USSR; agricultural and industrial centre.

Alps Mountain complex, central Europe, extending from SE France to N Yugoslavia.

Alsace Region on Franco-German border; originally German, transferred to France 1648, held by Germany 1871–1918 and 1940–45, currently French.

Altai Mts Mountain range bordering S USSR, W Mongolia and NW China.

Amapá State, N Brazil; capital Macapá.

Amazon River (6280 km, 3920 miles), Peru and Brazil, flowing into the Atlantic Ocean; world's second longest.

Amazonas State, N Brazil; capital Manaus.

Ambon Island, Moluccas archipelago, Banda Sea, E Indonesia.

American Samoa Island group of SW Pacific; unincorporated US territory; see Section 1, Oceania Central.

Amman Capital city, Jordan; historic agricultural, manufacturing and commercial centre.

Amsterdam Capital city, the Netherlands; port, industrial and commercial centre.

Amu Darya River (2570 km, 1600 miles), central Asia, Afghanistan and USSR, flowing into the Aral Sea.

Amur River (2900 km, 1800 miles), central Asia bordering China and USSR, flowing into N Pacific Ocean.

Andaman and Nicobar Is Archipelago, E Indian Ocean; capital Port Blair; Indian Union Territory.

Andes Mountain range, W South America.

Andhra Pradesh State, SE India; capital Hyderabad.

Andorra Independent co-principality, Europe SW; see Section 1.

Aneto, Pico de Mountain (3404 m, 11,168 ft), NE Spain; the highest peak in the Pyrenees.

Angara River (1700 km, 1050 miles), E Siberia, USSR, flowing from Lake Baykal into the Yenisei R.

Angola Independent republic, Africa Central; see Section 1.

Anguilla British dependent territory, Leeward Is (West Indies); see Section 1.

Anhwei (Anhui) Province, E China; capital Hofei (Hefei).

Geographic Names and Features

Ankara Capital city, Turkey; administrative, commercial and cultural centre.

Annamese Cordillera Mountain range, Laos and Vietnam, SE Asia.

Annapurna Mountain ridge (8078 m, 26,502 ft), Himalayas, N Nepal.

Annobón I See Pagalu.

Antananarivo Capital city, Madagascar; commercial, manufacturing and education centre.

Antarctic Circle Latitude 66° 30′ S.

Antarctic Peninsula Northern extension of W Antarctica, separating the Weddell and Bellingshausen seas.

Antarctica Continent surrounding South Pole; see Section 1.

Anti Lebanon Mts Mountain range, Syria and Lebanon, SW Asia.

Antigua and Barbuda Independent island state, Leeward Is, E Caribbean Sea; see Section 1.

Antipodes Collective name for Australia and New Zealand.

Antwerp City, N Belgium; port, commercial and industrial centre.

Apennine Mts Mountain chain, Italy, extending from Ligurian Alps to Sicily.

Appalachian Mts Mountain range, E North America, extending from Quebec to Alabama.

Ararat Mountain (5165 m, 16,946 ft), E Turkey.

Aqaba Gulf on Red Sea, SW Asia.

Arabia Desert peninsula between the Gulf and Red Sea, SW Asia.

Arabian Gulf See The Gulf.

Arabian Sea NW corner of Indian Ocean, extending into the Gulf and Red Sea.

Araguaya River (2580 km, 1600 miles), S Brazil; tributary of Tocantins R.

Aral Sea Slightly saline lake (67,500 km², 26,000 sq miles), S central USSR.

Archipiélago de Colon See Galapagos Is.

Arctic Archipelago Group of large tundra-covered islands of Northwest Territories, N Canada.

Arctic Circle Latitude 66° 30′ N.

Arctic Ocean Northernmost of world's oceans, surrounding North Pole; see Section 5.

Argentina Independent republic, S South America; see Section 1.

Arizona State, SW USA; capital Phoenix.

Arkansas (1) State, S USA; capital Little Rock. (2) River (2330 km, 1450 miles), flowing from Rocky Mts, Colorado, to Mississippi R, USA.

Armenian SSR (Armenia) Republic, SW USSR; capital Yerevan.

Arnhem Land Northernmost part of the Northern Territory, Australia.

Ascension I Volcanic island, central Atlantic Ocean; dependency of St Helena; see Section 1.

Assam State, NE India; capital Dispur.

Asunción Capital city, Paraguay; river port, commercial and education centre.

Atacama Desert Cool desert of Chile and Peru, W of Andes; almost completely rainless, rich in minerals.

Athabasca Extensive lake (8080 km², 3120 sq miles) on borders of Alberta and Saskatchewan, Canada.

Athens Capital city, Greece; historic, cultural and administrative centre.

Atlanta State capital city, Georgia, USA; commercial, financial, industrial and communications centre.

Atlantic Ocean World's second largest ocean; see Section 5.

Atlas Mts Complex mountain chain of NW Africa; Morocco, Algeria and Tunisia.

Auckland Is Uninhabited islands 500 km (300 miles) S of New Zealand.

Australasia Unofficial grouping of SW Pacific countries including Australia, New Zealand, New Guinea and neighbouring islands.

Australia Commonwealth, Oceania SW; see Section 1.

Australian Antarctic Territory Sector of Antarctic continent facing S Indian Ocean; see Section 1.

Australian Capital Territory Enclaves of New South Wales, Australia, including Canberra and environs, and Jervis Bay.

Austria Independent republic, Europe Central; see Section 1.

Avalon Peninsula of SE Newfoundland, Canada.

Azerbaijan SSR Republic of SE USSR; capital Baku.

Azores Archipelago in N Atlantic Ocean; heavily-populated, Portuguese territory. See Section 1.

Azov, Sea of Sea, SW USSR, connected to Black Sea by narrow Kerch Strait.

B

Baffin Bay Arm of N Atlantic Ocean between Baffin I and Greenland.

Baffin I Largest island of Canadian Arctic Archipelago; mountainous, part-glaciated.

Baghdad Capital city, Iraq; agricultural, commercial and administrative centre.

Bahama Is Independent state, W Atlantic Ocean; see Section 1.

Bahia State, E Brazil, bordering Atlantic Ocean; capital Salvador.

Bahrain Independent sheikhdom on the Gulf, Asia SW; see Section 1.

Baja California (Lower California) Peninsula, NW Mexico.

Baku Capital city, Azerbaijan SSR, USSR; port, industrial (petroleum), agricultural and administrative centre.

Balearic Is Archipelago, W Mediterranean; major islands Majorca, Minorca, Ibiza; Spanish province, capital Palma (Majorca).

Bali Island and province, E of Java, Indonesia.

Balkan Mts Mountain range, SE Europe, extending from E Yugoslavia to Bulgaria.

Balkan Peninsula European peninsula including parts of Albania, Bulgaria, Greece, Romania, Turkey and Yugoslavia.

Balkhash, L Freshwater lake (17,300 km^2, 6679 sq miles), SE Kazakhstan, USSR.

Baltic Sea Shallow shelf sea, NW Europe; see Section 5.

Baltimore City, Maryland, E USA; port, manufacturing, and education centre.

Bamako Capital city, Mali; agricultural and administrative centre.

Banaba Coral island, Kiribati, central Pacific Ocean; source of phosphatic rock.

Bandung City, SW Java, Indonesia; cultural and education centre.

Bangalore State capital, Karnataka, central S India; communications and manufacturing centre.

Bangkok Capital city, Thailand; historic, marketing and industrial centre for SE Asia.

Bangladesh Independent republic, Asia S; see Section 1.

Bangui Capital city, Central African Republic; agricultural and administrative centre.

Bangweulu, L Lake (9800 km^2, 3800 sq miles), NE Zambia.

Banjul Capital city (formerly Bathurst), Gambia; port and administrative centre.

Barbados Independent republic, Windward Is (West Indies); see Section 1.

Barcelona City, Catalonia, NE Spain; provincial capital, port, commercial, industrial and administrative centre.

Barents I Ice-capped Arctic island, Svalbard archipelago; Norwegian territory.

Barents Sea Shallow Arctic sea between N Norway, Novaya Zemlya and Svalbard.

Bashkir ASSR Autonomous republic, S Urals, central USSR; capital Ufa.

Basque Provinces Provinces of Álava, Giupúzcoa and Vizcaya, N Spain; culturally and linguistically linked to Basque-inhabited departments of SW France.

Bass Strait Strait, 128 km (80 miles) wide at narrowest point, separating Australia from Tasmania, SW Pacific Ocean.

Baykal, L Freshwater lake (31,500 km², 12,162 sq miles) chiefly in Buryat ASSR, USSR; world's deepest lake.

Beaufort Sea Sector of Arctic Ocean N of Canada and Alaska, USA.

Bechuanaland See Botswana.

Beijing See Peking.

Beirut Capital city, Lebanon; port, commercial, financial and education centre.

Belfast Capital city, Northern Ireland; port, industrial, commercial and administrative centre.

Belgium Independent kingdom, Europe W; see Section 1.

Belgrade Capital city, Yugoslavia.

Belize Independent state, Central America; see Section 1.

Bellingshausen Sea Shelf sea bordering W Antarctic Peninsula.

Belmopan Newly-established capital, Belize.

Belo Horizonte State capital, Minas Gerais, Brazil; agricultural, mining, industrial and administrative centre.

Belorussian SSR (Belorussia) Republic, W central USSR; capital Minsk.

Bengal, Bay of Arm of Indian Ocean between India, Burma and Thailand.

Benin Independent republic, Africa W; see Section 1.

Bering I Largest of Komandorskiye Is, Bering Sea; USSR territory.

Bering Sea N extremity of Pacific Ocean, bounded by USSR (Siberia and Kamchatka) and USA (mainland Alaska and Aleutian Islands).

Bering Strait Shallow strait, 85 km (53 miles) wide at narrowest point, between Bering Sea and Arctic Ocean, separating USSR and USA.

Berlin City, former capital of united Germany; see East Berlin, West Berlin.

Bermuda Archipelago and British Crown Colony, W Atlantic Ocean; see Section 1.

Bern Capital city, Switzerland; industrial, administrative and educational centre.

Bhutan Independent kingdom, Asia S; see Section 1.

Biafra, Bight of N arm of Gulf of Guinea, off W African coast.

Bighorn Mts Range of Rocky Mts, Wyoming and Montana, USA.

Bihar State, NE India; capital Patna.

Bioko Island (formerly Macias Nguema) in Gulf of Guinea, W Africa; part of Equatorial Guinea.

Biscay, Bay of Shallow bay, E Atlantic Ocean off France and N Spain.

Bismarck Archipelago Group including New Britain and over two hundred other islands off NE Papua New Guinea.

Bissau Capital city, Guinea-Bissau.

Black Sea Almost enclosed sea, bounded by SW USSR, Turkey, Romania and Bulgaria; see Section 5.

Blanc, Mont Ice-capped mountain (4807 m, 15,771 ft) on border of France, Italy and Switzerland.

Blue Nile River (1600 km, 1000 miles) flowing through Lake Tana, Ethiopia, to join White Nile at Khartoum, Sudan. See also Nile.

Blue Ridge Mts Range of Appalachian Mts, extending from Pennsylvania to Georgia, E USA.

Bogotá Capital city, Colombia; agricultural, industrial and administrative centre.

Bolivár, Pico Mountain (5007 m, 16,428 ft), Cordillera de Mérida, Venezuela.

Bolivia Independent republic, South America; see Section 1.

Bombay City, NE India (India's second largest); capital, Maharashtra state; port, commercial and industrial centre.

Bonn Federal capital city, West Germany; light industrial, commercial and administrative centre.

Bophuthatswana Autonomous Bantu territory (homeland) within South Africa.

Borneo Island, SE Asia; divided between Indonesia, Malaysia and Brunei; world's third largest island.

Bosporus Strait up to 3 km (2 miles) wide, 30 km (19 miles) long, between Black Sea and Sea of Marmara, separating Asian and European Turkey; spanned by suspension bridge.

Boston State capital city, Massachusetts, E USA; historic port, industrial, commercial, financial and medical centre.

Bothnia, Gulf of Shallow N arm of Baltic Sea between Sweden and Finland.

Botswana Independent republic, Africa S; see Section 1.

Bougainville Island, Solomon Islands group, SW Pacific Ocean.

Bounty Is Uninhabited cool temperate islands off S New Zealand, SW Pacific Ocean.

Brahmaputra River (2900 km, 1800 miles) flowing from S Tibet through N India to join Ganga R in Bangladesh.

Brasilia Capital city, Brazil; begun 1956, administrative centre from 1960.

Brazil Independent republic, South America; see Section 1.

Brazzaville Capital city, Congo; industrial, market and administrative centre.

Bridgetown Capital city, Barbados, West Indies; port, commercial and tourist centre.

Brisbane State capital city, Queensland, Australia; port, industrial and commercial centre.

Bristol Channel Arm of E Atlantic Ocean between SW England and Wales, United Kingdom.

British Antarctic Territory Sector of Antarctic continent including Antarctic Peninsula and neighbouring islands.

British Columbia Province, W Canada; capital Victoria.

British Indian Ocean Territory Island group, W Indian Ocean; see Section 1.

British Isles Island group, W Europe, comprising Great Britain, Ireland and adjacent islands.

Brooks Ra Mountain range, central and N Alaska, USA.

Brunei Independent sultanate (recently British protectorate), NW Borneo, Asia SE; see Section 1.

Brussels Capital city, Belgium; industrial, commercial, cultural and administrative centre for Belgium and Europe.

Bucharest Capital city, Romania; river port, industrial, commercial, communications and administrative centre.

Budapest Capital city, Hungary; river port, industrial, commercial and administrative centre.

Buenos Aires Capital city, Argentina; port, industrial, agricultural and commercial centre; South America's largest city.

Buffalo City, New York state, NE USA; commercial and industrial centre.

Bujumbura Capital town, Burundi, E central Africa.

Bulgaria Independent republic, Europe SE; see Section 1.

Burkina Faso (formerly Upper Volta) Independent republic, Africa NW; see Section 1.

Burma Independent republic, Asia S; see Section 1.

Burundi Independent republic, Africa E; see Section 1.

Buryat ASSR Autonomous republic, SE USSR; capital Ulan Ude.

C

Cabinda Enclave of Angola N of Zaïre corridor.

Caicos Is See Turks and Caicos Is.

Cairo Capital city, Egypt; river port, industrial, commercial and administrative centre.

Calcutta City, NE India (country's largest); capital, West Bengal; historic industrial and commercial centre.

California (1) State, SW USA; capital Sacramento. (2) **Gulf of,** formed by arm of Pacific Ocean between Baja California peninsula and mainland Mexico.

Cambodia Independent republic, Asia SE; see Section 1.

Cameroon Independent republic, Africa W; see Section 1.

Canada Independent state, N America; see Section 1.

Canary Is Archipelago, E Atlantic Ocean; Spanish territory; see Section 1.

Canberra Federal capital city, Australia; commercial, cultural and administrative centre.

Cancer, Tropic of Latitude $23\frac{1}{2}°$N.

Canterbury Plains Plain along central E coast of South Island, New Zealand.

Canton See Kwangchow.

Canton I See Kiribati.

Cape Breton I Large island in Gulf of St Lawrence; part of Nova Scotia, E Canada.

Cape Town Legislative capital, South Africa; port, industrial, commercial and administrative centre.

Cape Verde Is Archipelago, central Atlantic Ocean; independent republic; see Section 1.

Cape York Peninsula N extension of Queensland, NE Australia.

Capricorn, Tropic of Latitude $23\frac{1}{2}°$S.

Caracas Capital city, Venezuela; commercial, industrial, administrative and cultural centre.

Caribbean Sea W arm of Atlantic Ocean bounded by West Indies and South, Central and North America; see Section 5.

Cariboo Mts Range of W British Columbia, Canada, between Rocky Mts and coast.

Caroline Is Archipelago, W Pacific Ocean; administered as US Trust Territory.

Carpathian Mts Alpine mountain range, E central Europe, extending from Czechoslovakia to SW USSR and Romania.

Carpentaria, Gulf of Shallow gulf of N Australia separating Arnhem Land and Cape York Peninsula

Casablanca Largest city of Morocco; port, fishing, commercial and industrial centre.

Cascade Ra Mountain range extending from S British Columbia, Canada to Washington and Oregon, USA.

Caspian Sea Enclosed saline lake (422,170 km², 163,000 sq miles), SW USSR and N Iran.

Castries Capital town, St Lucia, West Indies.

Catskill Mts Range of Appalachian Mts, New York, USA.

Caucasus Mountain system, SW USSR, extending between Black Sea and Caspian Sea.

Cayenne (1) Island of French Guiana and (2) capital city, French Guiana.

Cayman Is Archipelago, Greater Antilles (West Indies); British Crown Colony; see Section 1.

Ceará State, NE Brazil; capital Fortaleza.

Celebes See Sulawesi.

Central African Republic Independent republic, Africa Central; see Section 1.

Chad (1) Independent republic, Africa NE; see Section 1. (2) Shallow freshwater lake (up to 25,760 km², 9950 sq miles during rains) bordered by Chad, Nigeria, Cameroon and Niger, central Africa.

Changchun Capital, Kirin (Jilin) province, NE China; industrial, educational and administrative centre.

Channel Is Archipelago of four large islands (Jersey, Guernsey, Alderney, Sark) and several small islands off coast of Normandy, France; British dependencies.

Chatham Is Inhabited island group E of New Zealand, SW Pacific Ocean.

Checheno-Ingush ASSR Autonomous republic, SW USSR; capital Grozny.

Chekiang(Zhejiang) Province, E China; capital Hangchow (Hangzhou).

Chelyabinsk City, W Siberia, USSR; mining, smelting, industrial centre.

Chelyuskin, Cape Northernmost point of mainland Eurasia, N central USSR.

Chengchow (Zhengzhou) Capital, Honan (Henan) province, E central China; river port, industrial and communications centre.

Chengtu (Chengdu) Capital of Szechwan (Sichuan) province, SW China; river port, agricultural and commercial centre.

Chicago City, Illinois, central USA (second largest); lake port, manufacturing, commercial, industrial, communications and financial centre.

Chile Independent republic, W South America; see Section 1.

Chiloé Island, S Chile.

Chimborazo Mountain (6267 m, 20,562 ft), Andes, Ecuador.

China Independent republic, Asia E; see Section 1.

China, Republic of See Taiwan.

China Sea Arm of E Pacific Ocean consisting of the East and South China seas; see Section 5.

Chomo Lhari Mountain (7314 m, 23,997 ft), Bhutan and China.

Chongqin See Chungking.

Chugach Mts Coastal range, S Alaska, USA.

Chukchi Peninsula NE extremity of Eurasia, between Chukchi Sea and Bering Sea, E USSR.

Chukchi Sea Shallow sector of Arctic Ocean N of Bering Strait.

Chungking (Chongqing) City, Szechwan (Sichuan) province, SW China; river port, industrial, communications, mining and manufacturing centre.

Chuvash ASSR Autonomous republic, central USSR; capital Cheboksary.

Cincinnati City, SW Ohio, USA; river port, commercial and manufacturing centre.

Geographic Names and Features

Ciskei Autonomous territory (homeland) within South Africa.

Cleveland City, N Ohio, USA; port on Lake Erie, commercial and industrial centre.

Coast Mts Range along coast of W USA and Canada.

Coats Land Region of W Antarctica bordering Weddell Sea.

Cocos (Keeling) Is Coral atolls in SE Indian Ocean; administered by Australia; see Section 1.

Colombia Independent republic, NW South America; see Section 1.

Colombo Capital city, Sri Lanka; port, industrial and commercial centre.

Colorado (1) State, SW USA; capital Denver. (2) River (2300 km, 1440 miles) flowing from SW Rocky Mts through Colorado (Grand Canyon), Utah, Arizona and Mexico to Gulf of California.

Columbia (1) **District of** See entry. (2) River (1920 km, 1200 miles), flowing from Rocky Mts, SW British Columbia, Canada, through Washington and Oregon, USA, to enter Pacific Ocean.

Columbus State capital city, Ohio, USA; commercial and manufacturing centre.

Commander Is See Komandorskiye Is.

Comoros Is Independent republic, W Indian Ocean; see Section 1.

Conakry Capital town, Guinea.

Congo (1) Independent republic, Africa Central; see Section 1. (2) River (4700 km, 2900 miles), formed by confluence of Luapula and Lualaba Rs and known as Lualaba above Stanley Falls, flowing W through Zaïre as Zaïre R to estuary on Atlantic Ocean.

Connecticut State, E USA; capital Hartford.

Constantinople See Istanbul.

Cook Is Self-governing island group in free association with New Zealand, Oceania Central; see Section 1.

Cook Strait Strait, 23 km (14 miles) wide at narrowest point, between North and South Island, New Zealand.

Copenhagen Capital city, Denmark; port, industrial, cultural and commercial centre.

Copperbelt Mineral-rich region of N Zambia, central S Africa.

Coral Sea SW corner of Pacific Ocean.

Coromandel Coast SE coast of India.

Corsica Island, NW Mediterranean Sea; French territory.

Costa Rica Independent republic, Central America; see Section 1.

Cotopaxi Volcanic mountain (5896 m, 19,344 ft), N Ecuador.

Crete Island, E Mediterranean Sea; Greek territory, centre of Minoan culture.

Crimea Peninsula, N coast of Black Sea, S Ukraine, USSR.

Cuba Independent republic, Greater Antilles (West Indies); see Section 1.

Curaçao Island, largest of Netherlands Antilles, S Caribbean Sea.

Cyclades Archipelago, Aegean Sea, SE Greece.

Cyprus Independent republic, E Mediterranean Sea; see Section 1, Europe SE.

Czechoslovakia Independent republic, Europe Central; see Section 1.

D

Dacca Capital city, Bangladesh; river port, industrial, administrative and commercial centre.

Dagestan ASSR Autonomous region, SE USSR; capital Makhachkala.

Dahomey See Benin.

Dakar Capital town, Senegal; important strategic port.

Dallas City, Texas, S USA; industrial, commercial, financial and communications centre.

Damascus Capital city, Syria; historic administrative and commercial centre.

Danube River (2850 km, 1800 miles) flowing from Black Forest, SW West Germany, through Austria, Czechoslovakia, Hungary, Yugoslavia, Romania (Iron Gates gorge) to W Black Sea.

Dar es Salaam City (former capital), Tanzania; port and manufacturing centre.

Dardanelles Strait, up to 6 km (4 miles) wide, 61 km (38 miles) long, linking Sea of Marmara and E Mediterranean Sea, separating Asian from European Turkey.

Darwin Capital city, Northern Territory, Australia; port, communications and administrative centre.

Davis Strait Channel, 300 km (190 miles) wide at narrowest point, 650 km (400 miles) long, separating Greenland and Canada, NW Atlantic Ocean.

Dead Sea Saline lake some 400 m (1300 ft) below sea level on Israel–Jordan border.

Deccan Plateau region, central and S India.

Delaware State, E USA; capital Dover.

Delhi (1) Union territory, central N India, and (2) city, central N India, adjoining capital New Delhi (see entry); site of Mogul Red Fort and Rajghat shrine; historic market and commercial centre.

Denmark Independent kingdom, Europe N; see Section 1.

Denmark Strait Strait, 300 km (190 miles) wide, 500 km (300 miles) long, between SE Greenland and Iceland, N Atlantic Ocean.

Denver State capital city, Colorado, USA; commercial and industrial centre.

Detroit City, N central USA; river port, industrial, manufacturing and commercial centre.

Devon I Tundra-covered island, Canadian Arctic Archipelago, Northwest Territories, Canada.

Dinaric Alps Coastal range of Yugoslavia and Albania.

District of Columbia Federal territory of the US, containing federal capital of Washington, E USA.

Djakarta See Jakarta.

Djibouti (1) Independent republic, Africa NE, on Gulf of Aden; see Section 1. (2) Capital city, Djibouti.

Dnepr (Dnieper) River (2200 km, 1400 miles) flowing S through central Russia, Belorussia and Ukraine, USSR, into the Black Sea.

Dnepropetrovsk City on Dnepr R, Ukraine, SE USSR; river port, industrial and commercial centre.

Dodecanese Is Archipelago, SE Aegean Sea; Greek territory.

Dodoma Capital city, Tanzania.

Dogger Bank Shallow bank in W central North Sea; rich fishing ground.

Doha Capital city, Qatar.

Dolomite Alps Mountain range, NE Italy.

Dominica, Commonwealth of Independent state, Windward Is (West Indies); see Section 1.

Dominican Republic Independent republic, Greater Antilles (West Indies); see Section 1.

Don River (1900 km, 1200 miles) flowing S through SW USSR into Sea of Azov.

Geographic Names and Features

Donetsk City, Ukraine, SW USSR; river port, industrial and administrative centre.

Dover, Strait of Strait, 30–40 km (18–25 miles) wide, linking English Channel with North Sea, NW Europe.

Drakensberg Ra Mountains, SE South Africa and Lesotho.

Dubai Independent sheikhdom and city, United Arab Emirates.

Dublin Capital city, Republic of Ireland (Eire); historic port, industrial and administrative centre.

E

East Berlin Capital city, East Germany; industrial, communications and administrative centre.

East China Sea Shelf sea off E coast of China, W Pacific Ocean; see Section 5.

East Germany (GDR) Independent republic, Europe Central; see Section 1.

East Indies Historic name for islands of Malaysia and Indonesia.

Easter I Volcanic island, Oceania SE; noted for massive carved statues; Chilean territory; see Section 1.

Ecuador Independent republic, NW South America; see Section 1.

Edward, L Lake of Great Rift Valley (2150 km², 830 sq miles), Zaïre and Uganda, E Africa.

Egypt Independent republic, Africa NE; see Section 1.

Eire See Ireland, Republic of.

El Giza City on W bank of Nile R, Egypt; film-making centre.

El Salvador Republic, W Central America; see Section 1.

Elbert, Mt Highest mountain (4400 m, 14,436 ft) in Rocky Mts, Colorado, USA.

Elbrus, Mt Volcanic mountain (5633 m, 18,482 ft), Caucasus, Georgia, USSR.

Elburz Mts Mountain range, N Iran.

Elgon, Mt Volcanic mountain (4321 m, 14,177 ft), Kenya and Uganda.

Ellesmere I Ice-capped island, Arctic Archipelago, Northwest Territories, N Canada.

Enderby Land Sector of Antarctica facing Indian Ocean; Australian territory.

England Country of United Kingdom; see Section 1.

English Channel Arm of Atlantic Ocean separating Britain and France.

Equator Latitude 0°, equidistant from North and South Poles.

Equatorial Guinea Republic, Africa Central; see Section 1.

Erie, L Freshwater lake (25,670 km², 9911 sq miles), part of St Lawrence Seaway, Canada and USA.

Espirito Santo Atlantic seaboard state, E Brazil; capital Vitória.

Espiritu Santo Volcanic island, Vanuatu, SW Pacific Ocean.

Estonian SSR (Estonia) Republic of USSR on Baltic Sea and Gulf of Finland, NE Europe; capital Tallinn.

Ethiopia Independent republic, Africa NE; see Section 1.

Ethiopian Highlands Mountain ranges and high plateaus, NW Ethiopia, NE Africa.

Etna Active volcano (3340 m, 10,958 ft), NE Sicily, Italy.

Euphrates River (2700 m, 1700 miles) flowing from Turkey through Syria to Iraq, entering the Gulf through Shatt al Arab.

Everest, Mt World's highest mountain (8848 m, 29,030 ft), central Himalayas, Nepal and SW China.

Eyre (1) Saline lake (9600 km², 3700 sq miles), NE South Australia. (2) Peninsula, South Australia, forming W flank of Spencer Gulf.

F

Falkland Is Archipelago, Atlantic Ocean, British Crown Colony; see Section 1.

Falkland Islands Dependencies South Georgia and South Sandwich Is, Atlantic Ocean; see Section 1.

Faroe Is Volcanic archipelago, Atlantic Ocean; Danish territory; see Section 1, Europe N.

Fiji Republic and archipelago, Oceania Central; see Section 1.

Finland Independent republic, Europe N; see Section 1.

Finland, Gulf of Shallow E arm of Baltic Sea.

Flinders Ranges Mountain chains, S Australia.

Flores Island of Lesser Sunda Is, W Indonesia, SE Asia.

Florida State, SE USA; capital Tallahassee.

Formosa See Taiwan.

Fortaleza State capital city, Ceará, NE Brazil; important port.

Fort-de-France Capital city, Martinique, West Indies.

France Independent republic, Europe W; see Section 1.

Franz Josef Land Ice-capped archipelago, Arctic Ocean; USSR territory.

Freetown Capital city, Sierra Leone; port, commercial and administrative centre.

French Guiana Overseas Department of France, N seaboard South America; see Section 1.

French Polynesia Overseas Territory of France, Oceania SE; see Section 1.

Friendly Is See Tonga.

Fujiyama Volcanic mountain (3776 m, 12,389 ft), Honshu, Japan.

Fukien (Fujian) Province, SE China, on Strait of Taiwan; capital Foochow (Fuzhou).

Fukuoka City on Hakata Bay, N Kyushu, Japan; historic port, manufacturing and fishing centre.

Fundy, Bay of Bay between New Brunswick and Nova Scotia, E Canada (world's greatest spring tidal range, about 21 m, 70 ft).

Fushun City, Liaoning province, N China; coal-mining, oil-refining and industrial centre.

G

Gabon Independent republic, Africa Central; see Section 1.

Gaborone Capital city, Botswana; market and administrative centre.

Galapagos Is Volcanic archipelago, E Pacific Ocean; Ecuadorean territory.

Galilee, Sea of (Lake Tiberias) Saline lake (166 km², 64 sq miles), fed and drained by Jordan R, NE Israel; surface 200 m (656 ft) below sea level.

Gambia, The Independent republic, Africa W; see Section 1.

Ganga (Ganges) River (2500 km, 1560 miles), flowing from Himalayas S and E across N India, entering Bay of Bengal via extensive delta; sacred to Hindus.

Gansu See Kansu.

Geneva L Lake (581 km², 224 sq miles), SW Switzerland and E France.

Georgetown Capital city, Guyana; port, commercial and administrative centre.

Georgia State, SE USA; capital Atlanta.

Georgian SSR (Georgia) Republic, USSR; capital Tbilisi (formerly Tiflis).

German Democratic Republic See East Germany.

Germany, Federal Republic of See West Germany.

Ghana Independent republic, Africa W; see Section 1.

Geographic Names and Features

Gibraltar (1) Self-governing British Crown Colony, Europe SW; see Section 1. (2) **Strait of,** 14 km (9 miles) wide at narrowest point, linking E Atlantic Ocean and Mediterranean Sea.

Gilbert Is See Kiribati.

Gobi Desert, SE Mongolia and N China, central Asia.

Godthaab Capital town, Greenland.

Godwin Austen, Mt See K2.

Goiás State, W central Brazil; capital Goiânia.

Golden Gate Strait up to 3 km (1.8 miles) wide, 6.5 km (4 miles) long, at entrance to San Francisco Bay and harbour, USA.

Good Hope, Cape of Prominent cape near S extremity of South Africa.

Gorki City, Russian SFSR, W USSR; historic, industrial and administrative centre.

Gotland Island in Baltic Sea off SE coast of Sweden; Swedish territory.

Graham Land Part of Antarctic Peninsula, British Antarctic Territory, W Antarctica.

Gran Chaco Forested tropical plains fringing Andes, Argentina, Paraguay, Bolivia.

Grand Bank Extensive shallow banks SE from Newfoundland; important fishing grounds.

Grand Canyon Gorge in Colorado R, more than 1.6 km (1 mile) deep in places, NW Arizona, USA.

Grand Turk Capital settlement, Turks and Caicos Is; market and communications centre.

Great Australian Bight Bay on S coast of Australia.

Great Barrier Reef Semi-continuous coral banks off NE and E Australia.

Great Bear L Shallow lake (31,792 km^2, 12,275 sq miles), Northwest Territories; Canada's largest lake.

Great Britain Part of United Kingdom, including England, Scotland and Wales but not Northern Ireland.

Great Dividing Ra Mountain ranges, approximately NNW–SSE across E and S Queensland, NE Australia. Also known as Great Divide.

Great Lakes Five linked freshwater lakes, US-Canadian border (Superior, Michigan, Huron, Erie, Ontario).

Great Plains Sloping grassland plateau bordering E Rocky Mts, central Canada and USA.

Great Rift Valley World's most extensive rift running N–S through SW Asia and E Africa from Jordan to Mozambique; contains several deep lakes including Lake Tanganyika (world's second deepest).

Great Salt L Saline lake (approx. 2590 km^2, 1000 sq miles), N Utah, USA.

Great Slave L Deep freshwater lake (28,570 km^2, 11,031 sq miles), Northwest Territories, Canada.

Great Smoky Mts Ranges of S Appalachian Mts, Tennessee and North Carolina, USA.

Greater Antilles Archipelago, West Indies. See Section 1.

Greater Sunda Is See Sunda Is.

Greece Independent republic, Europe SE; see Section 1.

Greenland Ice-capped island (world's largest) and self-governing province of Denmark, N Atlantic and Arctic Oceans; see Section 1, Europe N.

Greenland Sea Sector of Arctic Ocean between Svalbard and Greenland.

Grenada Independent state, Windward Is (West Indies); see Section 1.

Grenadines Archipelago, S West Indies. See St Vincent and the Grenadines.

Guadalajara City, W Mexico; industrial, commercial and administrative centre.

Guadeloupe Island group, Leeward Is, West Indies; Overseas Department of France; see Section 1.

Guam Largest and southernmost island of Mariana Is, Oceania N; US territory; see Section 1.

Guangdong See Kwangtung.

Guangxi Zhuangzu See Kwangsi-Chuang.

Guangzhou See Kwangchow.

Guatemala Independent republic, Central America; see Section 1.

Guatemala City Capital city, Guatemala; market, industrial and administrative centre.

Guayaquil City, SW Ecuador; chief port and industrial centre.

Guernsey Island, second largest of Channel Is (see entry).

Guinea Independent republic, Africa W; see Section 1.

Guinea-Bissau Independent republic, Africa W; see Section 1.

Guizhou See Kweichow.

Gujarat State, W India; capital Gandhinagar.

Gulf, The Arm of Arabian Sea, SW Asia. Also known as Persian Gulf, Arabian Gulf.

Guyana Independent republic, NE South America; see Section 1.

H

Hague, The Seat of government, the Netherlands; historic, cultural, commercial and administrative centre; International Court of Justice.

Hainan Island in South China Sea off S coast of Kwangtung (Guangdong) province, SE China.

Haiphong Port on Red R delta, Gulf of Tonkin, N Vietnam; manufacturing, exporting and naval centre.

Haiti Independent republic, Greater Antilles (West Indies); see Section 1.

Halmahera Island, Moluccas, NE Indonesia.

Hamburg City, N West Germany; river port, industrial and commercial centre.

Hamilton Capital city, Bermuda; tourist, financial and commercial centre.

Hangchow (Hangzhou) Capital city, Chekiang (Zhejiang) province, E China; historic port, industrial and tourist centre.

Hanoi Capital city, Vietnam; historic river port, commercial, administrative and industrial centre.

Harare Capital city, Zimbabwe; agricultural, mining, commercial and administrative centre.

Harbin Capital city, Heilungkiang (Heilongjiang) province, NE China; historic river port, commercial and administrative centre.

Haryana State, central India; capital Chandigarh.

Harz Mts Mountains on border, East and West Germany.

Havana Capital city, Cuba; historic port, commercial and industrial centre.

Hawaii Archipelago, N central Pacific Ocean; state of USA, capital Honolulu.

Hebei See Hopei.

Hebrides Archipelago, NW Scotland.

Heilungkiang (Heilongjiang) Province, NE China; capital Harbin.

Helsinki Capital city, Finland; Baltic port, commercial, cultural and administrative centre.

Geographic Names and Features

Henan See Honan.

Himachal Pradesh State, NW India; capital Simla.

Himalayas Chain of mountain ranges extending from Pakistan to S China, S Asia; includes world's highest peaks.

Hindu Kush Mountain range, Afghanistan and Pakistan.

Hispaniola Island, West Indies; includes Haiti and Dominican Republic.

Ho Chi Minh City (Saigon) Former capital city, South Vietnam; river port, industrial, commercial, communications and administrative centre.

Hokkaido Island, N Japan.

Honan (Henan) Province, E China; capital Chengchow (Zhengzhou).

Honduras Independent republic, Central America; see Section 1.

Hong Kong Self-governing British Crown Colony, off coast of SE China, Asia E; see Section 1.

Honolulu State capital, Hawaii (on Oaku I), USA; port, manufacturing, tourist and administrative centre.

Honshu Largest of the four chief islands of Japan.

Hopei (Hebei) Province, NE China; capital Shihkiachwang (Shijiazhuang).

Horn, Cape Southernmost extremity, South America.

Houston City, SE Texas, USA; canal port, petroleum-refining, industrial, financial and commercial centre.

Huascara Volcanic peak (6768 m, 22,206 ft), Andes, Peru.

Hubei See Hupei.

Hudson Bay Shallow inland sea, NE Canada; see Section 5.

Hunan Province, central China; capital Changsha.

Hungary Independent republic, Europe Central; see Section 1.

Hupei (Hubei) Province, central China; capital Wuchan.

Huron, L Second largest of Great Lakes (59,829 km^2, 23,100 sq miles), USA and Canada.

Hwang-ho (Huang) River (4800 km, 3000 miles), flowing E from Kunlun Mts to Yellow Sea.

Hyderabad Capital city, Andhra Pradesh state, S India; historic commercial, communications and administrative centre.

I

Iberian Peninsula Peninsula including Spain and Portugal, SW Europe.

Ibiza Island, one of three main Balearic Is, W Mediterranean Sea; Spanish territory.

Iceland Independent republic, N Atlantic Ocean; see Section 1, Europe N.

Idaho State, NW USA; capital Boise.

IJsselmeer Freshwater lake (1200 km^2, 460 sq miles), remnant of reclaimed Zuider Zee, NW Netherlands.

Illinois State, N central USA; capital Springfield.

Ilmen, L Freshwater lake (up to 2100 km^2, 810 sq miles), NW Russian SFSR, USSR; drains into Lake Ladoga.

India Independent republic, Asia S; see Section 1.

Indian Ocean Third largest ocean; see Section 5.

Indiana State, N central USA; capital Indianapolis.

Indianapolis State capital city, Indiana, USA; industrial and communications centre.

Indonesia Independent republic, Asia SE; see Section 1.

Indus River (3000 km, 1900 miles), flowing from Tibet, S China, through NW India and Pakistan to Arabian Sea.

Inland Sea Shallow, island-studded sea between S Honshu, Shikoku and Kyushu Is, S Japan.

Inner Mongolian Autonomous Region (Nei Monggol) Region of NE China; capital Huhehot (Hohhot).

Ionian Is Archipelago off SW Greece, central Mediterranean Sea; Greek territory.

Ionian Sea Sector of Mediterranean Sea between SE Italy and SW Greece.

Iowa State, central USA; capital Des Moines.

Iran Independent republic, Asia SW; see Section 1.

Iraq Independent republic, Asia SW; see Section 1.

Ireland (1) Westernmost island of British Is, W Europe; includes Republic of Ireland (Eire) and British province of Northern Ireland; (2) the Republic of Ireland, Europe W; see Section 1.

Ireland, Northern See Northern Ireland.

Irian Jaya Indonesian sector of New Guinea.

Irish Sea Shallow sea separating Ireland from Great Britain, NW Europe.

Iron Gates Gorge and rapids, Danube R, Yugoslavia and Romania.

Irrawaddy River (2100 km, 1300 miles), flowing from N Burma to large delta on Gulf of Martaban, NE Indian Ocean.

Irtysh River (3500 km, 2200 miles) flowing from Altai Mts, Mongolia, NE through NW Kazakh SSR to join Ob R in W Siberia, USSR.

Islamabad Capital city, Pakistan; administrative and commercial centre.

Israel Independent state, Asia SW; see Section 1.

Issyk Kul Freshwater lake (6332 km^2, 2445 sq miles) high in Tien Shan Mts, Kirgiz SSR, USSR.

Istanbul City, NW Turkey, spanning Bosporus Strait; historic port, commercial, cultural, tourist and communications centre.

Italy Independent republic, Europe SE; see Section 1.

Ivory Coast Independent republic, Africa W; see Section 1.

J

Jakarta Capital city, Indonesia; historic port (formerly Batavia), commercial and administrative centre.

Jamaica Island and independent republic, Greater Antilles (West Indies); see Section 1.

Jammu and Kashmir State, NW India; capital Srinagar; part-occupied by Pakistan (Azad Kashmir). Commonly known as Kashmir.

Jan Mayen Tundra-covered uninhabited island, Arctic Ocean; Norwegian territory; see Section 1, Europe N.

Japan Independent state, Asia E; see Section 1.

Japan, Sea of Semi-enclosed sea between E Asian coast and Japan; see Section 5.

Japura See Yapura.

Java Forested volcanic island, SW Indonesia.

Java Sea Semi-enclosed sea between Java, Sumatra and Borneo, Indonesia.

Jersey Largest island of Channel Is, NW Europe (see entry).

Jerusalem Capital city, Israel; historic, religious, cultural, tourist and administrative centre; Jewish, Arab and Christian shrines.

Jiangsu See Kiangsu.
Jiangxi See Kiangsi.
Jilin See Kirin.
Jinan See Tsinan.
Johannesburg City, NE South Africa; gold-mining, industrial and commercial centre.
Jordan Independent kingdom, Asia SW; see Section 1.
Juan de Fuca Strait Strait up to 27 km (17 miles) wide, 160 km (100 miles) long, between Vancouver I and British Columbia mainland, W Canada.
Juan Fernandez Forested volcanic islands, SE Pacific Ocean; Chilean territory.
Juba River (1600 km, 1000 miles) flowing from uplands on Ethiopia–Somalia border through Somalia to Indian Ocean.
Julian Alps Mountain ranges, Italy–Yugoslavia border.
Jungfrau Mountain (4158 m, 13,642 ft), Bernese Alps, S Switzerland.
Jura Mts Mountain range, Franco–Swiss border.
Jutland Peninsula forming mainland of Denmark, and part of West Germany, NW Europe.

K

K2 (Mt Godwin Austen) Mountain (8611 m, 28,253 ft), Karakoram Range, Pakistan; world's second highest peak.
Kabardino-Balkar ASSR Autonomous republic, Caucasian region, SW USSR; capital Nalchik.
Kabul Capital city, Afghanistan; river port, commercial, administrative and cultural centre.
Kaiser Wilhelm's Land Coastal sector, E Antarctica, facing Indian Ocean; Australian administration.
Kalahari Desert Cool desert region, Botswana, Namibia, South Africa.
Kalimantan Indonesian sector of Borneo.
Kalmyk ASSR Autonomous republic, Caspian Sea region, USSR; capital Elista.
Kamchatka Peninsula, NE USSR, between Sea of Okhotsk and Bering Sea.
Kampala Capital city, Uganda; lake port, commercial, communications and transport centre.
Kampuchea See Cambodia.
Kanchenjunga Mountain (8598 m, 28,210 ft), E Himalayas, Nepal and Sikkim, India.
Kanpur (Cawnpore) City, Uttar Pradesh, N central India; river port, industrial and commercial centre.
Kansas State, central USA; capital Topeka.
Kansu (Gansu) Province, NW China; capital Lanchow (Lanzhou).
Kansas City (1) City, Kansas state, central USA, adjoining Kansas City, Missouri at Kansas–Missouri border; industrial, commercial and communications centre. (2) City, Missouri state, central USA, adjoining Kansas City, Kansas.
Karachi City (former capital), Pakistan; port, industrial, commercial and financial centre.
Kara Kalpak ASSR Autonomous republic, central Asian region, USSR; capital Nukus.
Kara Kum Sandy desert, Turkmen SSR, S USSR.

Kara Sea Sector of Arctic Ocean between Novaya Zemlya and Asian mainland.

Kaohsiung (Gaoxiong) City, SW Taiwan; major port, petrochemical, manufacturing and fishing centre.

Karakoram Ra Mountain range, India and Pakistan; part of Himalayas including K2 (world's second highest mountain) and other high peaks.

Karelian ASSR (Karelia) Autonomous republic, NW region, USSR; capital Petrozavodsk.

Karelian Isthmus Former Finnish, now Soviet territory E of Gulf of Finland, NW USSR.

Karnataka State, SW India; capital Bangalore.

Kashmir See Jammu and Kashmir.

Katmandu Capital city, Nepal; historic market, commercial and communications centre.

Kattegat Channel between North Sea and Baltic Sea, separating Denmark and Sweden.

Kawasaki City, Honshu, Japan; industrial and commercial centre.

Kazakh SSR (Kazakhstan) Republic, central Asia, USSR; capital Alma Ata.

Kazbek, Mt Mountain (5047 m, 16,559 ft), Georgia, USSR.

Kentucky State, E central USA; capital Frankfort.

Kenya (1) Independent republic, Africa E; see Section 1. (2) Volcanic peak (5199 m, 17,058 ft), central Kenya.

Kerala State, SW India; capital Trivandrum.

Kerguelen Glaciated archipelago, S Indian Ocean; French territory.

Kharkov City, Ukraine, W USSR; historic river port, industrial and cultural centre.

Khartoum Capital city, Sudan; river port, administrative and communications centre.

Kiangsi (Jiangxi) Province, SE China; capital Nanchang.

Kiangsu (Jiangsu) Province, E China; capital Nanking (Nanjing).

Kiev Capital, Ukrainian SSR, W USSR; historic river port, industrial, commercial and administrative centre.

Kigali Capital town, Rwanda.

Kilimanjaro Volcanic mountain (5895 m, 19,341 ft), Kenya and Tanzania; Africa's highest peak.

King William I Tundra-covered island, Canadian Arctic Archipelago.

Kingston Capital city, Jamaica; historic port, commercial and industrial centre.

Kingstown Capital city, St Vincent and the Grenadines, West Indies.

Kinshasa Capital city, Zaïre; river port, industrial and commercial centre.

Kirgiz SSR (Kirgizia) Republic, SE USSR; capital Frunze.

Kiribati Island republic, Oceania Central; see Section 1.

Kirin (Jilin) (1) Province, central China, capital Changchun, and (2) city (former provincial capital), Kirin province; industrial centre.

Kitakyushu City, N Kyushu, Japan; shipbuilding, fishing and heavy-industry centre.

Kivu L Lake (2700 km^2, 1042 sq miles), Great Rift Valley, Rwanda-Zaïre border.

Kobe City, Honshu, Japan; port, industrial, commercial and education centre.

Kodiak I Forested island of S Alaska, USA, NE Pacific Ocean.

Koko Nor Saline lake (6000 km^2, 2300 sq miles), Tsinghai (Qinghai) province, NW China.

Kola Peninsula Arctic peninsula between White and Barents seas, NW USSR.

Kolyma River (2100 km, 1300 miles) flowing N from Kolyma Range, NE USSR to Arctic Ocean.

Komandorskiye Is Archipelago of tundra-covered islands, NW Pacific Ocean and Bering Sea; Soviet territory.

Komi ASSR Autonomous republic, NW USSR; capital Syktyvkar.

Korea, Democratic People's Republic of See North Korea.

Korea, Republic of See South Korea.

Kowloon (1) Peninsula, part of New Territories, Hong Kong. (2) City on W shore of Kowloon peninsula; commercial centre, connected by rail to Kwangchow (Guangzhou) on Chinese mainland.

Krakatoa Volcanic island, Sunda Strait, SW Indonesia; renowned for destructive implosion of 1883.

Kuala Lumpur Federal capital, Malaysia; river port, marketing, communications and industrial centre.

Kunlun Mts Mountain range, N Tibet (Xizang) and central Tsinghai (Qinghai) province, NW China.

Kunming Capital city, Yunnan province, SW China.

Kuril Is Volcanic island chain, Kamchatka to Hokkaido; Soviet territory, in part claimed by Japan.

Kuwait (1) Independent state, Asia SW; see Section 1. (2) Capital city, Kuwait.

Kuybyshev City on R Volga, E central USSR; river port, industrial and communications centre.

Kwangchow (Guangzhou) Capital city, Kwangtung (Guangdong) province, S China; delta port, industrial and commercial centre. Formerly Canton.

Kwangsi-Chuang (Guangxi Zhuangzu) Autonomous region, S China; capital Nanning.

Kwangtung (Guangdong) Province, S China; capital Kwangchow (Guangzhou).

Kweichow (Guizhou) Province, SW China; capital Kweiyang (Guiyang).

Kyoto Capital city, Honshu prefecture, Japan; religious, cultural and light industrial centre.

Kyushu Southernmost large island, Japan.

L

La Paz Capital city, Bolivia; commercial and administrative centre.

Labrador See Newfoundland and Labrador.

Ladoga, L Lake (17,678 km^2, 6825 sq miles), NW USSR.

Lagos Capital city, Nigeria; port, commercial, industrial and administrative centre.

Lahore Capital city, Punjab province, E Pakistan; commercial, communications, market and administrative centre.

Lanchow (Lanzhou) Capital city, Kansu (Gansu) province, W China; petrochemical, industrial and administrative centre.

Laos Independent republic, Asia SE; see Section 1.

Lappland Tundra-covered area, N Norway, N Sweden, N Finland and NW USSR, inhabited by nomadic Sami (Lapps).

Latvian SSR (Latvia) Republic, NW USSR; capital Riga.

Lebanon Independent republic, Asia SW; see Section 1.

Lebanon Mts Mountain range, formerly forested, running parallel to coast, Lebanon.

Leeward Is Northernmost islands of Lesser Antilles, West Indies.

Lena River (4500 km, 2800 miles), flowing N from central Siberia to Arctic Ocean.

Lenin Peak Mountain (7134 m, 23,407 ft), Trans-Altai Range, SE USSR.

Leningrad City, NW USSR (former Russian capital); historic river port, commercial, industrial, administrative and cultural centre.

Lesotho Independent kingdom, Africa S; see Section 1.

Lesser Antilles Archipelago of West Indies; see Section 1, Leeward and Windward Is.

Lesser Sunda Is See Sunda Is.

Lhotse Mountain (8500 m, 27,890 ft), China and Nepal.

Liaoning Province, NE China; capital Shenyang.

Liberia Independent republic, Africa W; see Section 1.

Libreville Capital city, Gabon; river port, timber, marketing and administrative centre.

Libya Independent republic, Africa NE; see Section 1.

Liechtenstein Independent principality, Europe Central; see Section 1.

Ligurian Sea Sector of Mediterranean Sea between Corsica and N Italy.

Lilongwe Capital city, Malawi; marketing and administrative centre.

Lima Capital city, Peru; historic commercial, industrial and administrative centre.

Limpopo River (1600 km, 1000 miles), flowing from Transvaal, South Africa, N and E along Botswana and Zimbabwe borders, SE through Mozambique to Indian Ocean.

Lisbon Capital city, Portugal; river port, historic commercial and administrative centre.

Lithuanian SSR (Lithuania) Republic, NW USSR; capital Vilnius.

Llanos Extensive plains stretching across Venezuela and Colombia, N South America.

Llullaillaco Mountain peak (6723 m, 25,058 ft), Chilean Andes, South America.

Lofoten Is Archipelago of tundra-covered islands off N Norway.

Logan, Mt Mountain (6050 m, 19,850 ft), SW Yukon; Canada's highest peak.

Lomé Capital city, Togo; port, marketing, communications and administrative centre.

London Capital city, United Kingdom; historic river port, commercial, financial, administrative, cultural and industrial centre.

Los Angeles City, SW California, USA; port, industrial, commercial, financial, communications and cultural centre.

Louisiana State, SE USA; capital Baton Rouge.

Low Countries Collective name for the Netherlands, Belgium and Luxembourg.

Lower California See Baja California.

Luanda Capital city, Angola; port, petroleum, industrial and administrative centre.

Lucania, Mt Mountain (5227 m, 17,149 ft), St Elias Mts, Yukon, NW Canada.

Lusaka Capital city, Zambia; commercial, industrial, communications and administrative centre.

Lu-ta (Lüda) City, Liaoning province, NE China (including former Port Arthur and Dairen); naval port, commercial and industrial centre.

Luxembourg (1) Independent Grand Duchy, Europe W; see Section 1. (2) Capital city, Luxembourg; river port, historic cultural, communications, administration and industrial centre.

Luzon Largest island, Philippines archipelago.

Lyons City, E central France; river port, historic, commercial, manufacturing and communications centre.

M

Macau Portuguese overseas province, Asia E; historic city, gambling, tourist and manufacturing centre; see Section 1.

Mackenzie River (2000 km, 1250 miles) flowing from Great Slave Lake, Northwest Territories NW to Beaufort Sea, NW Canada.

McKinley, Mt Ice-capped mountain (6194 m, 20,322 ft), Alaska Range, S Alaska, USA; North America's highest peak.

Macquarie I Isolated tundra-covered island SSW of New Zealand; Australian territory.

Madagascar Island, SW Indian Ocean (former Malagasy Republic); see Section 1.

Madeira (1) Volcanic archipelago, NE Atlantic Ocean; Portuguese territory; see Section 1. (2) River, South America, 3200 km (2000 miles) long, flowing NE from confluence of Mamoré and Beni Rs at Brazil–Bolivia border to join Amazon at Manaus, N Brazil.

Madhya Pradesh State, central India; capital Bhopal.

Madras Capital city, Tamil Nadu state, S India; port, industrial, commercial and administrative centre.

Madrid Capital city, Spain; historic cultural, commercial, communications and administrative centre.

Madura Island off NE coast of Java, Indonesia, SE Asia.

Magdalena River (1600 km, 1000 miles), flowing from Central Cordillera, Andes, in SW Colombia N to Caribbean Sea.

Magellan's Strait Passage up to 32 km (20 miles) wide, 560 km (350 miles) long, between S South American mainland and Tierra del Fuego.

Maharashtra State, W India; capital Bombay.

Maine State, NE USA; capital Augusta.

Majorca Island, largest of Balearic Is, W Mediterranean Sea; Spanish territory.

Makalu Mountain (8475 m, 27,806 ft), E Himalayas, China.

Malabo Capital town, Equatorial Guinea.

Malacca Strait Seaway up to 300 km (190 miles) wide and 800 km (500 miles) long, between Malay peninsula and Sumatra, SE Asia.

Malagasy Republic See Madagascar.

Malawi (1) Independent republic, Africa E; see Section 1. (2) Lake (29,640 km², 11,444 sq miles) of Great Rift Valley system, Malawi, E Africa; also known as Lake Nyasa.

Malaysia, Federation of Independent republic, Asia SE; see Section 1.

Malay Peninsula Peninsula, SE Asia, comprising West Malaysia and SW Thailand.

Maldive Is Archipelago and independent republic, N Indian Ocean; see Section 1.

Mali Independent republic, Africa NW; see Section 1.

Malta Independent island republic, Mediterranean Sea, Europe SE; see Section 1.

Maluku (Moluccas) Group of islands between Sulawesi and New Guinea, SE Asia; a province of Indonesia.

Man, I of Island dependency, Irish Sea, NW Europe; British territory.

Managua Capital city, Nicaragua; industrial, commercial and administrative centre, subject to earthquakes.

Manama Capital city, Bahrain; port, commercial and administrative centre.

Manchuria Area of NE China comprising the three provinces of Heilungkiang (Heilongjiang), Kirin (Jilin) and Liaoning.

Manila Capital city, Philippine Is; port, historic commercial, financial and industrial centre.

Manipur State, NE India; capital Imphal.

Manitoba (1) Province, central Canada; capital Winnipeg. (2) Large shallow lake (4706 km², 1817 sq miles), SW Manitoba, Canada.

Maputo Capital city, Mozambique; port, mining, commercial, industrial and administrative centre.

Maracaibo, L Saltwater lake (13,500 km², 5212 sq miles), centre of petroleum industry, Venezuela.

Maranhão State, NE Brazil; capital São Luís.

Mari ASSR Autonomous republic, central USSR; capital Yoshkar-Ola.

Mariana Is Island chain, W central Pacific Ocean; US Trust Territory; see Section 1, Oceania N.

Mariana Trench World's deepest (11,040 m, 36,220 ft) submarine trench, SW of Mariana Is, W central Pacific Ocean.

Marion I Tundra-covered volcanic island, S Indian Ocean; South African territory.

Maritime Provinces New Brunswick, Nova Scotia and Prince Edward Island, E Canada.

Marmara, Sea of Sea linking Black and Mediterranean seas, Turkey, SW Asia.

Marquesas Is Volcanic archipelago, central Pacific Ocean; French territory.

Marseilles City, SE France; historic port, industrial, commercial, military and naval centre.

Marshall Is Coral archipelago, central Pacific Ocean; US Trust Territory.

Martinique French Overseas Department, Windward Is (West Indies); see Section 1.

Maryland State, E USA; capital Annapolis.

Mascarene Is Mauritius, Réunion and Rodriguez Is, SW Indian Ocean.

Maseru Capital city, Lesotho; market, communications and administrative centre.

Massachusetts State, NE USA; capital Boston.

Massif Central Upland plateau region, S central France.

Mato Grosso State, W central Brazil; capital Cuiabá. (2) Plateau in E central Mato Grosso state.

Mato Grosso do Sul State, W central Brazil; capital Campo Grande.

Matterhorn Mountain (4479 m, 14,695 ft), Switzerland and Italy.

Mauna Kea Volcanic peak (4208 m, 13,806 ft), Hawaii, N Pacific Ocean.

Mauna Loa Volcanic peak (4170 m, 13,680 ft), Hawaii, N Pacific Ocean.

Mauritania Independent republic, Africa NW; see Section 1.

Mauritius Independent island state, Mascarene Is, Indian Ocean; see Section 1.

Mayotte Island of the Comoro group, Indian Ocean; French territory; see Section 1.

Geographic Names and Features

Medellín City, NW Colombia; manufacturing and education centre.

Mediterranean Sea Large enclosed sea between Africa and S Europe; see Section 5.

Meghalaya State, NE India; capital Shillong.

Mekong River (4000 km, 2500 miles) flowing S from S China along Burma–Laos border through Laos, Thailand, Vietnam to South China Sea.

Melanesia Island region, SW Pacific Ocean, including New Guinea, Bismarck Archipelago, Solomon Is and Vanuatu.

Melbourne Capital city, Victoria, Australia; port, industrial and commercial centre.

Melville I Tundra-covered island, Canadian Arctic Archipelago; natural gas source.

Mesa Central Plateau, central Mexico.

Mesopotamia Historic region between the Tigris and Euphrates Rs, SW Asia, site of early civilizations of Babylonia and Assyria; now part of Iraq.

Messina Strait, 3–16 km (2–10 miles) wide, 32 km (20 miles) long, between S Italy and Sicily, central Mediterranean Sea.

Mexico Independent republic, Central America; see Section 1.

Mexico City Capital city, Mexico; historic, commercial, administrative and manufacturing centre.

Mexico, Gulf of Northern extension of Caribbean Sea; see Section 5.

Miami City, SE Florida, USA; port, tourist, commercial and manufacturing centre.

Michigan (1) State, N central USA; capital Lansing. (2) SW lake (57,760 km², 22,301 sq miles) of Great Lakes system, N central USA.

Micronesia Island region, W central Pacific Ocean; includes Caroline, Marshall and Mariana Is, Kiribati, Nauru.

Mid-Atlantic Ridge Ridge running centrally down N–S axis of the Atlantic Ocean, the crest of which forms several island groups; see Section 5.

Milan City, N Italy; historic cultural, communications, manufacturing and commercial centre.

Milwaukee City, Wisconsin, N central USA; lake port, manufacturing, commercial and industrial centre.

Minas Gerais State, E Brazil; capital Belo Horizonte.

Mindanao Island, second largest of Philippines.

Minneapolis-St Paul City, Minnesota, N USA; river port, commercial and industrial centre.

Minnesota State, N central USA; capital St Paul.

Minorca Island, Balearic Is, W Mediterranean Sea; Spanish territory.

Minsk Capital city, Belorussian SSR, USSR; historic, industrial, commercial and administrative centre.

Mississippi (1) State, S USA; capital Jackson. (2) River (3780 km, 2350 miles) flowing from Minnesota S to Gulf of Mexico, USA.

Missouri (1) State, central USA; capital Jefferson City. (2) River (3700 km, 2350 miles) flowing from Rocky Mts SE to join Mississippi R at St Louis, Missouri, USA.

Mobutu Sese Seko, L Freshwater lake (5333 km², 2059 sq miles), Great Rift Valley, Uganda and Zaïre, E Africa.

Mogadishu Capital city, Somali Democratic Republic; port, historic market and commercial centre.

Mojave Desert, S California, USA.

Moldavian SSR (Moldavia) Republic, SW USSR; capital Kishinev.

Moluccas See Maluku.

Monaco Independent principality, Europe W; see Section 1.

Mongolia Independent republic, Asia E; see Section 1.

Monrovia Capital city, Liberia; port, shipping, commercial, industrial and administrative centre.

Montana State, SW USA; capital Helena.

Monterrey Capital city, Nuevo León state, Mexico; smelting, industrial, communications and commercial centre.

Montevideo Capital city, Uruguay; river port, commercial and industrial centre.

Montserrat Island of Leeward Islands (West Indies); British territory; see Section 1.

Montreal City, Quebec, SE Canada; river port, commercial, manufacturing and cultural centre.

Mordovian ASSR Autonomous republic, W USSR; capital Saransk.

Morocco Independent kingdom, Africa NW; see Section 1.

Moscow Capital city, USSR; historic industrial, commercial, cultural, communications and administrative centre.

Mozambique Independent republic, Africa E; see Section 1.

Mozambique Channel Seaway up to 1000 km (600 miles) wide, 1600 km (1000 miles) long, between southern Africa and Madagascar.

Munich City, Bavaria, West Germany; historic cultural, commercial and manufacturing centre.

Murray River (2600 km, 1600 miles) flowing from Australian Alps W to Great Australian Bight.

Muscat Capital city, Oman; port, petroleum terminus, market and commercial centre.

N

Nagaland State, NE India; capital Kohima.

Nagoya City, Honshu, Japan; port, industrial and commercial centre.

Nairobi Capital city, Kenya; commercial, communications and administrative centre.

Namib Coastal desert, Namibia, SW Africa.

Namibia UN mandated territory under South African control, Africa S; see Section 1.

Nanda Devi Mountain (7817 m, 25,648 ft), Himalayas, N India.

Nanga Parbat Mountain (8126 m, 26,661 ft), Himalayas, NW India.

Nanking (Nanjing) Capital city, Kiangsu (Jiangsu) province, E China; historic river port, cultural, communications, industrial and commercial centre.

Naples City, S central Italy; port, industrial, cultural and commercial centre.

Nassau Capital city, Bahamas; port, tourist resort, financial centre.

Nauru Independent island republic, Oceania SW; see Section 1.

Ndjamena Capital city, Chad; river port, marketing and administrative centre.

Nebraska State, central USA; capital Lincoln.

Negev Desert, S Israel.

Negro, Rio River (2000 km, 1250 miles) flowing from Andes, Colombia, across Brazil to join Amazon R at Manaus.

Nejd High desert plateau, central Saudi Arabia.

Nepal Independent kingdom, Asia S; see Section 1.

Netherlands, The Independent kingdom, Europe W; see Section 1.

Netherlands Antilles Two island groups administered as part of the Netherlands, Windward Is (West Indies); see Section 1.

Netzahualcóyotl City, suburb of Mexico City, central Mexico; Mexico's second largest city.

Nevada State, SW USA; capital Carson City.

New Britain Island, Bismarck Archipelago, SW Pacific Ocean.

New Brunswick Province, E Canada; capital Fredericton.

New Caledonia Volcanic island, Oceania SW; French territory; see Section 1.

New Delhi Capital city, India, in federal territory, N central India; administrative, communications and manufacturing centre. See also Delhi.

New England Historic name for states of Connecticut, Maine, Massachusetts, New Hampshire, Rhode Island and Vermont, NE USA.

New Guinea World's second largest island, SW Pacific Ocean; includes Irian Jaya (Indonesia) and independent Papua New Guinea.

New Hampshire State, NE USA; capital Concord.

New Hebrides See Vanuatu.

New Ireland Volcanic island, Bismarck Archipelago, SW Pacific Ocean.

New Jersey State, E USA; capital Trenton.

New Mexico State, SW USA; capital Santa Fe.

New Orleans City, S Louisiana, USA; port, communications, industrial, manufacturing, cultural and commercial centre.

New South Wales State, SE Australia; capital Sydney.

New York (1) State, E USA; capital Albany. (2) City (USA's largest), New York state, E USA; river port, commercial, financial, manufacturing and cultural centre.

New Zealand Independent state, Oceania SW; see Section 1.

Newfoundland Large island, former colony, E Canada.

Newfoundland and Labrador Province, E Canada; capital St John's.

Nicaragua Independent republic, Central America; see Section 1.

Nicobar Is See Andaman and Nicobar Is.

Nicosia Capital city, Cyprus.

Niger (1) Independent republic, Africa NW; see Section 1. (2) River (4000 km, 2500 miles) flowing from eastern mountains of Guinea NE, E and S through Mali, Niger and Nigeria to Atlantic Ocean.

Nigeria Independent republic, Africa W; see Section 1.

Nile River (6690 km, 4180 miles, world's longest); Blue Nile (flowing from Ethiopia) joins White Nile (from Lake Victoria, Uganda) at Khartoum, Sudan, continuing N to Egypt and delta on Mediterranean Sea.

Ningsia Hui (Ningxia Huizu) Autonomous Region, N China; capital Yinchwan (Yinchuan).

Norfolk I Volcanic island, SW Pacific Ocean; Australian territory.

North Carolina State, E central USA; capital Raleigh.

North Dakota State, N central USA; capital Bismarck.

North European Plain Plain spreading from European Alps E to Ural Mts in USSR, across N West and East Germany, Poland and W USSR.

North Island Northernmost of the two main islands forming New Zealand, S Pacific Ocean.

North Korea Independent republic, Asia E; see Section 1.

North Ossetian ASSR Autonomous republic, SW USSR; capital Ordzhonikidze.

North Sea Shallow extension of NE Atlantic Ocean; see Section 5.

Northern Ireland Province of United Kingdom, NE Ireland; capital Belfast.

Northern Territory State, N Australia; capital Darwin.

Northwest Territories Region, NW Canada, including large area of mainland and Arctic Archipelago; capital Yellowknife.

Norway Independent kingdom, Europe N; see Section 1.

Norwegian Sea Part of Arctic Ocean between Greenland and Iceland.

Nouakchott Capital city, Mauritania.

Nova Scotia Province, E Canada; capital Halifax.

Novaya Zemlya Two large islands in Arctic Ocean off N coast of USSR, separating Barents Sea and Kara Sea.

Novosibirsk City, Russian SFSR, central USSR; river port, communications and industrial centre.

Nullarbor Plain Stony plateau and desert, SW South Australia.

Nunivak I Volcanic tundra-covered island, Bering Sea, W Alaska, USA.

Nyasa, L See Lake Malawi.

O

Oahu Main island, Hawaiian archipelago, N Pacific Ocean.

Ob River (3500 km, 2200 miles) flowing N from Altai Mountains through central Siberia to Arctic Ocean.

Ocean I See Banaba.

Oceania Island region, S and central Pacific Ocean, including Australasia, Polynesia, Melanesia, Micronesia.

Ogaden Desert, SE Ethiopia and Somalia.

Odessa City, S Ukraine, USSR; major port, fishing, and industrial centre.

Ohio State, N central USA; capital Columbus.

Ojos del Salado Mountain peak (6863 m, 22,517 ft), Argentine Andes, South America.

Okavango River (1600 km, 1000 miles) flowing from central Angola SE to Okavango Swamp, Botswana, S Africa.

Okhotsk, Sea of Shelf sea between Kamchatka and E Siberia, NW Pacific Ocean.

Oklahoma State, SW USA; capital Oklahoma City.

Öland Island, SE Sweden, Baltic Sea.

Olenek River (2200 km, 1400 miles) flowing from central Siberia E and N to Laptev Sea, Arctic Ocean.

Olympus Mountain (2917 m, 9571 ft), N Greece.

Olympic Mts Coastal range, Washington, NW USA.

Oman (1) Independent sultanate, Asia SW; see Section 1. (2) Gulf formed by NW arm of Arabian Sea between N Oman and SE Iran, SW Asia.

Omsk City, W Siberia, USSR; river port, industrial and administrative centre.

Onega, L Freshwater lake (9720 km², 3753 sq miles), NW USSR.

Ontario (1) Province, E central Canada; capital Toronto. (2) Freshwater lake (19,550 km², 7548 sq miles), smallest of Great Lakes, part of St Lawrence Seaway, SE Canada.

Oporto City, NW Portugal; historic port, commercial, fishing and manufacturing centre.

Orange River (2100 km, 1300 miles) flowing from N Lesotho SW and W through South Africa to Atlantic Ocean.

Ore Mountains Mountain range, Czechoslovakia and S East Germany.

Oregon State, W USA; capital Salem.

Geographic Names and Features

Orinoco River (2150 km, 1350 miles) flowing from Serra Parima mountains, S Venezuela, NW, N and NE to Atlantic Ocean.

Orissa State, E India; capital Bhubaneswar.

Orizaba Volcanic peak (5700 m, 18,700 ft), S Mexico.

Orkney Is Archipelago, N of Scotland; British territory.

Osaka City, Honshu, Japan; industrial, commercial and financial centre.

Oslo Capital city, Norway; port, historic commercial and industrial centre.

Ottawa Capital city, Canada; administrative, commercial and manufacturing centre.

Ouagadougou Capital city, Burkina Faso (formerly Upper Volta), W Africa; marketing, communications and manufacturing centre.

Owen Stanley Ra Mountain range, Papua New Guinea, SW Pacific Ocean.

Ozark Mts Mountain plateau, Missouri and Arkansas, SE central USA.

P

Pacific Islands, US Trust Territory of Mariana, Caroline and Marshall Is, Oceania N; US administration; see Section 1.

Pacific Ocean World's largest ocean; see Section 5.

Pagalu (formerly Annobón I) Small mountainous island in Gulf of Guinea, W Africa; part of Equatorial Guinea.

Pakistan Independent state, Asia S; see Section 1.

Palestine Historic region, SW Asia, including Syria, Lebanon, Jordan, Sinai, Israel; see country entries, Section 1.

Palk Strait Seaway up to 137 km (85 miles) wide, 137 km (85 miles) long, between SE India and Sri Lanka.

Pamir Mts Mountains, Tadzhik SSR, S central USSR.

Pampas Plains of Argentina extending S from lower Paraná R to Gulf of San Matias.

Panama (1) Independent republic, Central America; see Section 1. (2) Capital city, Panama; historic commercial and administrative centre.

Panama Canal Waterway linking Pacific Ocean with Caribbean Sea, Panama, Central America.

Papeete Capital town, French Polynesia, on Tahiti I, Society Is; port and commercial centre.

Papua New Guinea Independent state, New Guinea, Oceania SW; see Section 1.

Pará State, N Brazil; capital Belém.

Paraguay (1) Independent state, S central South America; see Section 1. (2) River (2560 km, 1600 miles), central South America, flowing S from SW Brazil to join Paraná R at SW corner of Paraguay on Argentinian border.

Paraíba State, NE Brazil; capital João Pessoa.

Paramaribo Capital city, Suriname; seaport.

Paraná State, S Brazil; capital Curitiba. (2) River (4000 km, 2500 miles) flowing from confluence of Rio Grande and Paranaiba R, central Brazil, W and S along Argentina–Paraguay border to Rio de la Plata.

Paris Capital city, France; cultural, communications, administrative, industrial and commercial centre.

Patagonia Grassland and semi-desert plateau region, S Chile and Argentina, South America.

Peace River (1900 km, 1200 miles) flowing from Rocky Mts NE through British Columbia and Alberta to join Slave R, Canada.

Pechora River (1800 km, 1120 miles) flowing from E central Ural Mts N through USSR to Barents Sea.

Peking (Beijing) Capital city, China; historic, cultural, administrative, commercial, communications and industrial centre.

Peloponnesos Peninsula, S Greece.

Pemba Island, coast of Tanzania, W Indian Ocean.

Pennine Alps Mountains, Switzerland and Italy.

Pennsylvania State, E USA; capital Harrisburg.

Pernambuco State, NE Brazil; capital Recife.

Persian Gulf See The Gulf.

Peru Independent republic, W South America; see Section 1.

Philadelphia City, Pennsylvania, E central USA; river port, industrial and commercial centre.

Philippines Independent republic, Asia SE; see Section 1.

Phnom Penh Capital city, Cambodia; river port, marketing, commercial and administrative centre.

Phoenix State capital city, Arizona, SW USA; river port, tourist, manufacturing and agricultural centre.

Piauí State, NE Brazil; capital Teresina.

Pilcomayo River (1600 km, 1000 miles), S central South America, flowing SE from Bolivian Andes to form part of boundary between Argentina and Paraguay and joining Paraguay R at Asunción, Paraguay.

Pindus Mts Mountains, S Albania and Greece, SE Europe.

Pitcairn I British Crown Colony, Oceania SE; see Section 1.

Pittsburgh City, SW Pennsylvania, E USA; major river port, industrial and communications centre.

Plata, Rio de la Estuary separating Argentina and Uruguay, SE South America.

Poland Independent republic, Europe Central; see Section 1.

Polynesia Island region of the central and eastern Pacific Ocean, including Tonga, Samoa, Tuvalu, Society and Tuamotu Is.

Popocatepetl Volcanic peak (5452 m, 17,888 ft), central Mexico.

Port-au-Prince Capital city, Haiti; port, commercial and administrative centre.

Port Moresby Capital city, Papua New Guinea; port, commercial and administrative centre.

Port of Spain Capital city, Trinidad; industrial, commercial and administrative centre.

Portland City, NW Oregon, NW USA; port, commercial, industrial and education centre.

Pôrto Alegre State capital city, Rio Grande do Sul, S Brazil; port, commercial and manufacturing centre.

Porto Novo Capital town, Benin; historic port, commercial and administrative centre.

Portugal Independent republic, Europe SW; see Section 1.

Prague Capital city, Czechoslovakia; river port, historic communications, commercial, industrial and administrative centre.

Pretoria Administrative capital city, South Africa; administrative and industrial centre.

Pribilof Is Volcanic island group, Bering Sea, SW Alaska.

Prince Edward I Province, E Canada; capital Charlottetown.

Prudhoe Bay Centre of offshore petroleum discoveries, N Alaska, USA.

Puerto Rico Island, Greater Antilles (West Indies); US territory; see Section 1.

Pune (Poona) City, Maharashtra state, W India; manufacturing, communications, military and administrative centre.

Punjab (1) Historic region, NW Indian subcontinent; divided between India and Pakistan. (2) State, NW India; capital Chandigarh.

Purus River (3150 km, 2000 miles) flowing from Andes, E central Peru, NE through Brazil to Amazon R.

Pyongyang Capital city, North Korea; mining, industrial and administrative centre.

Pyrenees Mountain range, NE Iberian Peninsula; Spain and France.

Q

Qatar Independent state, Asia SW; see Section 1.

Qattara Depression Saltmarsh, 130 m (430 ft) below sea level, N Egypt.

Qingdao See Tsingtao.

Qinghai See Tsinghai.

Quebec (1) Province, E Canada, and (2) provincial capital city; river port (St Lawrence Seaway), historic, cultural, commercial, administrative and industrial centre.

Queen Charlotte Is Archipelago, W British Columbia, Canada.

Queen Elizabeth Is N islands of Arctic Archipelago, Northwest Territories, N Canada.

Queensland State, NE Australia; capital Brisbane.

Quezon City City, Luzon I, Philippines; former capital, adjoining NE Manila (current capital).

Quito Capital city, Ecuador; historic, cultural, manufacturing and administrative centre.

R

Rabat Capital city, Morocco; port, historic marketing and manufacturing centre.

Rand See Witwatersrand.

Rajasthan State, NW India; capital Jaipur.

Rangoon Capital city, Burma; river port, historic, marketing, administrative and commercial centre.

Recife Capital city, Pernambuco state, NE Brazil; port, industrial and cultural centre.

Red Sea Narrow sea between Saudi Arabia and NE Africa; see Section 5.

Reindeer, L Freshwater lake (6400 km², 2450 sq miles), Saskatchewan–Manitoba border, central Canada.

Réunion Island, Mascarene Is, SW Indian Ocean; French Overseas Territory; see Section 1.

Reykjavik Capital city, Iceland; commercial, industrial and administrative centre.

Rhine River (1320 km, 820 miles) flowing from Grisons, Switzerland, N and W through Liechtenstein, Austria, West Germany, France and the Netherlands into the North Sea.

Rhode Island State, NE USA; capital Providence.

Rhodes Island, Dodecanese group, NE Mediterranean Sea; Greek territory.

Rhodope Mts Mountain range, Balkan peninsula, SE Europe.

Riff (er Rif) Mountains, part of Atlas Mts, NE Morocco.

Rio de Janeiro (1) State, SE Brazil, and (2) state capital city; port, cultural, administrative, recreational and industrial centre.

Rio Grande River (3000 km, 1875 miles) flowing from San Juan Mts, Colorado, S through SW USA to Gulf of Mexico.

Rio Grande do Norte State, NE Brazil; capital Natal.

Rio Grande do Sul State, S Brazil; capital Pôrto Alegre.

Rio Muni Mainland territory of Equatorial Guinea, W Africa.

Riyadh Capital city, Saudi Arabia; communications, commercial and administrative centre.

Rocky Mts Mountain ranges, extending from Mexican frontier to Arctic, W Canada and USA.

Rodriguez Island, Mascarene Is, SW Indian Ocean; dependency of Mauritius.

Romania Independent state, Europe Central; see Section 1.

Rome Capital city, Italy; river port, historic, commercial, administrative and tourist centre.

Rondônia State, N Brazil; capital Pôrto Velho.

Roraima State, N Brazil; capital Boa Vista.

Roseau Capital town, Dominica, West Indies.

Ross Dependency Sector of E Antarctica S of Australasia; New Zealand administration.

Ross Sea Arm of S Pacific Ocean between Victoria Land and Edward VII Land, Antarctica.

Rotterdam City, W Netherlands; historic port, industrial, commercial and communications centre.

Rub al Khali (The Empty Quarter) Desert region extending across S Arabian peninsula, SW Asia.

Rudolf, L See Lake Turkana.

Russian SFSR (Russia) Largest republic, USSR; capital Moscow.

Ruwenzori Mountain range, Uganda and Zaïre, E Africa.

Rwanda Independent state, Africa E; see Section 1.

Ryukyu Is Archipelago, volcanic and coral islands, S Japan, NW Pacific Ocean.

S

Sabah N sector of Borneo, Malaysia, SE Asia.

Sahara Sandy and stony desert, world's largest; N Africa.

Saharan Atlas Mountains, S arm of Atlas Mts, Algeria, NW Africa.

Sahel Semi-arid region S of Sahara desert, W Africa.

Saigon See Ho Chi Minh City.

St Christopher-Nevis See St Kitts-Nevis.

St Croix Island, largest of US Virgin Is, West Indies.

St Elias, Mt Mountain (5489 m, 18,009 ft), St Elias Mts, Alaska, USA and Canada.

St Eustatius Island, Netherlands Antilles, West Indies.

St George's Capital town, Grenada, West Indies; port, marketing and administrative centre.

St George's Channel Channel up to 150 km (90 miles) wide and 160 km (100 miles) long between NE Atlantic Ocean and Irish Sea, separating S Ireland and S Wales, UK.

Geographic Names and Features

St Gotthard Mts Mountain range, Alps, central Switzerland, W central Europe.

St Helena Island, Atlantic Ocean; British colony; see Section 1.

St John's Capital city, Antigua, West Indies; port, tourist and marketing centre.

St Kitts-Nevis Independent island state, Leeward Is (West Indies); see Section 1.

St Lawrence River (1300 km, 800 miles) flowing from Lake Ontario E to Gulf of St Lawrence and Atlantic Ocean, E Canada and USA; see St Lawrence Seaway. (2) **Gulf of** Deep gulf of Atlantic Ocean between Newfoundland I and Canadian mainland.

St Lawrence Seaway System of canals and locks linking Gulf of St Lawrence with Great Lakes, E Canada and USA.

St Louis City on Mississippi R, Missouri state, S central USA; river port, industrial, manufacturing, communications and education centre.

St Lucia Independent island state, Windward Is (West Indies); see Section 1.

St Martin Island, Leeward Is, West Indies; part French territory (Guadeloupe), part Netherlands (St Maartens, Netherlands Antilles).

St Paul Volcanic island, S Indian Ocean; French territory.

St Pierre and Miquelon Island group, North America; French territory; see Section 1.

St Thomas Island, most heavily populated of US Virgin Is, West Indies.

St Vincent and the Grenadines Independent island state, Windward Is (West Indies); see Section 1.

Sajama Volcanic mountain (6520 m, 21,400 ft), Bolivia, South America.

Sakhalin Mountainous island off E USSR, Sea of Okhotsk, NW Pacific Ocean.

Salton Sea Saline lake (958 km², 270 sq miles), S California, SW USA.

Salvador City, Bahia state, E Brazil; port, commercial, manufacturing, tourist and naval centre.

Salween River (2900 km, 1800 miles) flowing from E Tibet, SE China, S through Burma to Gulf of Martaban, NE Indian Ocean.

San Antonio City, S central Texas, S USA; river port, commercial, manufacturing, military and tourist centre.

San Bernardino Mts Mountain range, Coast Range, California, SW USA.

San Diego City, S California, SW USA; port, manufacturing and tourist centre.

San Francisco City, W central California; port, industrial, commercial and cultural centre.

San José Capital city, Costa Rica; commercial and industrial centre.

San Juan Capital city, Puerto Rico, West Indies; port, historic marketing, manufacturing, and administrative centre.

San Marino Independent republic, Italy, Europe SE; see Section 1. (2) Capital city, San Marino.

San Salvador Capital city, El Salvador; manufacturing, marketing and administrative centre.

Sana Capital city, Yemen; historic commercial centre.

Santa Catarina State, S Brazil; capital Florianópolis.

Santiago Capital city, Chile; commercial, manufacturing, communications, cultural and administrative centre.

Santo Domingo Capital city, Dominican Republic, West Indies; port, historic marketing and commercial centre.

São Francisco River (2900 km, 1800 miles) flowing from Minas Gerais, S Brazil, NE through E Brazil to Atlantic Ocean.

São Miguel Island, largest of Azores archipelago, N Atlantic Ocean.

São Paulo (1) State, SE Brazil, South America, and (2) state capital city; industrial, commercial and manufacturing centre.

São Tomé e Principe Independent republic, Africa Central; see Section 1.

Sapporo City, Hokkaido, Japan; industrial, commercial and tourist centre.

Sarawak NW sector of Borneo I, Malaysia, SE Asia.

Sardinia Island, N central Mediterranean Sea; Italian territory.

Saskatchewan Province, central Canada; capital Regina. (2) River (2000 km, 1250 miles), including confluent S and N arms, flowing E from central and S Alberta through Saskatchewan to Lake Winnipeg, Canada.

Saudi Arabia Independent kingdom, Arabian peninsula, Asia SW; see Section 1.

Sawatch Mts Mountain range, Rocky Mts, Colorado, W USA.

Sayan Mts Mountain ranges, Siberia–Mongolia border, S central USSR and W China.

Scandinavia Region, NW Europe, including Sweden, Norway, Finland, Denmark, Iceland.

Scilly Is Archipelago off SW Cornwall, UK, Europe W.

Scotland Kingdom, part of UK, Europe W; capital Edinburgh.

Seattle City, Washington, NW USA; port, commercial, industrial, financial and tourist centre.

Selkirk Mts Range of Rocky Mts, British Columbia, W Canada.

Senegal Independent republic, Africa W; see Section 1. (2) River (1600 km, 1000 miles) flowing from confluence of Bakoy and Bafing Rs in Mali, W Africa, NW along Mauritania–Senegal border to Atlantic Ocean.

Seoul Capital city, South Korea; river port, communications, manufacturing and administrative centre.

Sergipe State, NE Brazil; capital Aracajú.

Seychelle Is Independent island republic, W Indian Ocean; see Section 1.

Shaanxi See Shensi.

Shanghai City, Kiangsu (Jiangsu) province, E China; port, industrial, commercial, financial and cultural centre; China's largest city.

Shansi (Shanxi) Province, N China; capital Taiyüan.

Shantung (Shandong) Province, NE China; capital Tsinan (Jinan).

Sharjah Independent emirate, United Arab Emirates, SW Asia.

Shatt al Arab Estuary of Tigris and Euphrates Rs, Iraq, flowing S into the Gulf.

Shenandoah River with N and S arms in valley between Blue Ridge Mts and Allegheny Mts, Virginia, E USA.

Shensi (Shaanxi) Province, E central China; capital Sian (Xi'an).

Shenyang Capital city, Liaoning province, NE China; river port, railway junction, commercial and industrial centre.

Shetland Is Archipelago off N Scotland, UK, Europe W; British territory.

Si Kiang (Xi-Jiang) River (2000 km, 1250 miles) flowing from Yunnan province E to South China Sea.

Sian (Xi'an) Capital city, Shensi (Shaanxi) province, E central China; industrial, manufacturing and communications centre.

Siberia Region, central Asia E of Ural Mts to E coast.

Sichuan See Szechwan.

Sicily Island, central Mediterranean Sea; S region of Italy.

Geographic Names and Features

Sierra Leone Independent republic, Africa W; see Section 1.
Sikkim State, NE India; capital Gangtok.
Simpson Desert Stony desert, central Australia.
Sinai Peninsula, E Egypt, SW Asia.
Sinaloa State, W Mexico; capital Culiacán.
Singapore (1) Independent republic, Asia SE; see Section 1. (2) Capital city, Singapore.
Sinkiang-Uighur (Xinjiang Uygur) Autonomous region, NW China; capital Wulumuchi (Urumqi).
Skagerrak Strait 130–145 km (80–90 miles) wide, 240 km (150 miles) long, linking North Sea with Kattegat and Baltic Sea, NE Europe.
Snake River (1700 km, 1060 miles) flowing from NW Wyoming W across NW USA to join Columbia R.
Snowy Mts Ranges of Australian Alps, New South Wales, E Australia.
Society Is Archipelago, S central Pacific Ocean, including Windward and Leeward Is; French territory.
Socotra Mountainous island, Gulf of Aden, NW Indian Ocean; South Yemen territory.
Sofia Capital city, Bulgaria; industrial, manufacturing, administrative and cultural centre.
Solomon Is Independent state, Oceania SW; see Section 1.
Somali Democratic Republic (Somalia) Independent republic, Africa NE; see Section 1.
South Africa Independent republic, Africa S; see Section 1.
South Australia State, S central Australia; capital Adelaide.
South Carolina State, SE USA; capital Columbia.
South China Sea Shelf sea between China, Vietnam and Philippines, W Pacific Ocean; see Section 5.
South Dakota State, N central USA; capital Pierre.
South Georgia Glaciated island, S Atlantic Ocean; dependency of Falkland Is, British territory.
South Island Southernmost of the two main islands forming New Zealand.
South Korea Independent republic, Asia E; see Section 1.
South Orkney Is Glaciated islands NE of Antarctic Peninsula, W Antarctica; British territory.
South Sandwich Is Glaciated volcanic islands, S Atlantic Ocean; dependencies of Falkland Is, British territory.
South Shetland Is Glaciated islands NW of Antarctic Peninsula, W Antarctica; British Antarctic Territory.
South West Africa See Namibia.
South Yemen Independent republic, Asia SW; see Section 1.
Southampton Island Tundra-covered island, Hudson Bay, Northwest Territories, N Canada.
Southern Alps Mountain ranges, SW and central South Island, New Zealand.
Southern Ocean Belt of ocean surrounding Antarctica.
Spain Independent kingdom, Europe SW; see Section 1.
Spencer Gulf Large bay, southern Australia.
Spitzbergen Largest island of Svalbard archipelago, Arctic Ocean; Norwegian administration.
Sri Lanka Independent republic, Asia S; see Section 1.

Steele, Mt Mountain (5010 m, 16,438 ft), St Elias Mts, NW Canada.

Stewart I New Zealand's southernmost inhabited island.

Stockholm Capital city, Sweden; port, commercial, financial, industrial and administrative centre.

Sudan Independent republic, Africa NE; see Section 1.

Suez Canal Waterway, NE Egypt, linking E Mediterranean Sea with Red Sea.

Sulawesi Largest of islands forming Indonesia, SE Asia.

Sumatra Mountainous island, Indonesia, SE Asia.

Sunda Is Malay archipelago forming part of Indonesia, SE Asia; divided into Greater Sunda Is (Java, Sumatra, Borneo, Sulawesi and adjacent islands) and Lesser Sunda Is (island chain from Bali to Timor and Alor Is).

Superior, L Freshwater lake (82,414 km^2, 31,820 sq miles), Great Lakes system, Canada and USA; world's largest lake.

Surabaya City, E Java, Indonesia; port, industrial, commercial and naval centre.

Suriname Independent republic, NE South America; see Section 1.

Svalbard Glaciated archipelago, Arctic Ocean; Norwegian administered; see Section 1, Europe N.

Sverdlovsk City, E Urals Mts, USSR; industrial, manufacturing and railway centre.

Swaziland Independent kingdom, Africa S; see Section 1.

Sweden Independent kingdom, Europe N; see Section 1.

Switzerland Independent state, Europe Central; see Section 1.

Sydney Capital city, New South Wales, Australia; port, manufacturing, industrial, administrative and cultural centre; Australia's largest city.

Syr Darya River (2200 km, 1400 miles) flowing from Uzbekistan N and W to Aral Sea, S USSR.

Syria Independent republic, Asia SW; see Section 1.

Szechwan (Sichuan) Province, SW China; capital Chengtu (Chengdu).

T

Tadzhik SSR Republic, S central USSR; capital Dushanbe.

Tahiti Volcanic island, Windward Is, S Pacific Ocean; French territory.

Taimyr Peninsula Northernmost mainland peninsula, USSR.

Taipei Capital city, Taiwan; manufacturing, industrial and administrative centre.

Taiwan (Formosa) Large island, Asia E; governed by Republic of China; see Section 1.

Taiyüan Capital city, Shansi (Shanxi) province, N China; industrial, administrative and cultural centre.

Tamil Nadu State, SE India; capital Madras.

Tampa City, W central Florida peninsula, SE USA; port, manufacturing and tourist centre.

Tananarive See Antananarivo.

Tanganyika, L Freshwater lake (32,893 km^2, 12,700 sq miles), Great Rift Valley, E central Africa, Burundi, Tanzania, Zaïre, Zambia.

Tanzania Independent republic, Africa E; see Section 1.

Tashkent Capital city, Uzbek SSR, S USSR; historic, industrial, commercial and administrative centre.

Tasman Sea Sector of SW Pacific Ocean separating New Zealand and Australia.

Geographic Names and Features

Tasmania Island state, SE Australia; capital Hobart.

Tatar ASSR Autonomous republic, central USSR; capital Kazan.

Tatra Mountains, W Carpathians, Czechoslovakia and Poland, E central Europe.

Taurus Mts Mountain range, S Turkey.

Tbilisi (formerly Tiflis) Capital city, Georgian SSR, SW USSR; industrial and cultural centre.

Tegucigalpa Capital city, Honduras; marketing, manufacturing and administrative centre.

Tehran Capital city, Iran; commercial, industrial, administrative and cultural centre.

Tel Aviv-Jaffa City, Israel, including former city of Jaffa; port, industrial, commercial, financial and tourist centre.

Tenerife I Volcanic island, largest of Canaries group; Spanish territory.

Tennessee State, SE USA; capital Nashville.

Terre Adélie Sector, E Antarctica, S of Australia; French-administered.

Texas State, SW USA; capital Austin.

Thailand Independent republic, Asia SE; see Section 1.

Thorshavn Capital city, Faroe Is; port, fishing, manufacturing and administrative centre.

Tianjin See Tientsin.

Tibesti Mts Isolated mountain range, Chad and Libya, N central Africa.

Tibet (Xizang) Autonomous region, SW China; capital Lhasa.

Tien Shan Mts Mountain ranges, NW China and S USSR, central Asia.

Tientsin (Tianjin) City, Hopei (Hebei) province, NE China; river port, industrial, and manufacturing centre.

Tierra del Fuego Archipelago, S South America; Chilean and Argentine territory.

Tigris River (1850 km, 1150 miles) flowing from S Taurus Mts, Turkey, S through Iraq to join Euphrates R in Shatt al Arab, ending in the Gulf.

Timor (1) Island, Lesser Sunda Is, Indonesia, SE Asia. (2) Sea, part of SE Indian Ocean between NW Australia and Indonesia.

Tiranë Capital city, Albania; industrial, manufacturing, administrative and commercial centre.

Titicaca, L Freshwater lake (8300 km^2, 3205 sq miles), Andes, Bolivia and Peru, W South America.

Tocantins River (2700 km, 1700 miles) flowing from Serra Dourada, central Brazil, N to estuary on Rio do Pará, NE Brazil coast.

Togo Independent republic, Africa W; see Section 1.

Tokelau Is Island group, Oceania Central; see Section 1.

Tokyo Capital city, Japan; port, manufacturing, industrial, commercial, financial and cultural centre.

Tonga Independent island kingdom, Oceania Central; see Section 1.

Tonkin, Gulf of W sector, South China Sea, bordered by Vietnam and S China.

Tonlé Sap Freshwater lake (up to 10,000 km^2, 4000 sq miles), central Cambodia.

Toronto Provincial capital city, Ontario, central Canada; industrial, commercial, cultural and financial centre.

Torrens, L Saline lake (5776 km^2, 2230 sq miles), South Australia.

Torres Strait Island-strewn channel, 160 km (100 miles) wide, linking Arafura Sea and Coral Sea, between Cape York Peninsula, N Australia, and Papua New Guinea.

Transkei Autonomous Xhosa state (homeland) within South Africa.
Trinidad and Tobago Independent island state, West Indies; see Section 1, South America.
Tripoli Capital city, Libya; port, commercial and historic centre.
Tripura State, NE India; capital Agartala.
Tristan da Cunha Volcanic island, S Atlantic Ocean; dependency of St Helena; see Section 1.
Tsinan (Jinan) Capital city, Shantung (Shandong) province, E China; historic commercial, industrial and manufacturing centre.
Tsinghai (Qinghai) Province, W central China; capital city Sining (Xining).
Tsingtao (Qingdao) City, Shantung (Shandong) province, E China; port, industrial and manufacturing centre.
Tsin Ling Shan Mountain chains, Shensi (Shaanxi) province, central China.
Tuamotu Archipelago, French Polynesia, S Pacific Ocean.
Tunis Capital city, Tunisia; historic port, administrative and tourist centre.
Tunisia Independent republic, Africa NW; see Section 1.
Turin City, N Italy; industrial, commercial and communications centre.
Turkana, L (Rudolf) Lake (6405 km^2, 2473 sq miles), Great Rift Valley, N Kenya, E Africa.
Turkey Independent republic, Asia SW; see Section 1.
Turkmen SSR (Turkmenistan) Republic, SW USSR; capital Ashkhabad.
Turks and Caicos Is Archipelago, Greater Antilles (West Indies); see Section 1.
Tuva ASSR Autonomous republic, SE USSR; capital Kyzyl.
Tuvalu Is Independent state, Oceania Central; see Section 1.
Tyrol Mountainous region, Austria and Italy, central Europe.
Tyrrhenian Sea Sector of Mediterranean Sea between Italy, Sicily and Sardinia.

U

Ucayali River (1600 km, 1000 miles) flowing N along E flank of Andes, Peru, to join Marañon and Amazon Rs.
Udmurt ASSR Autonomous republic, central USSR; capital Izhevsk.
Uganda Independent republic, Africa E; see Section 1.
Ukrainian SSR (Ukraine) Republic, SW USSR; capital Kiev.
Ulan Bator Capital city, Mongolia; marketing, communications, administrative and manufacturing centre.
Ulster (1) Historic region of nine northern counties of Ireland, (2) currently used for the six counties of Northern Ireland (see entry).
Umm-al-Quaiwain Independent emirate, Asia SW; see United Arab Emirates, Section 1.
Union of Soviet Socialist Republics (USSR) Independent state, Asia N; see Section 1.
United Arab Emirates Independent confederation of seven emirates, Asia SW; see Section 1.
United Kingdom (UK) Independent kingdom, Europe W; see Section 1.
United States of America (USA) Independent republic, North America; see Section 1.
Upper Volta See Burkina Faso.
Ural River (2500 km, 1560 miles) flowing from SW Ural Mts S through SW USSR to Caspian Sea.

Ural Mts Isolated N–S mountain range, central USSR.

Urmia, L Lake (6000 km², 2316 sq miles), Iran, SW Asia.

Uruguay Independent republic, South America; see Section 1.

Utah State, W USA; capital Salt Lake City.

Uttar Pradesh State, N India; capital city Lucknow.

Uzbek SSR (Uzbekistan) Republic, S central USSR; capital Tashkent.

V

Vaduz Capital town, Liechtenstein; market, tourist and administrative centre.

Valletta Capital city, Malta; port, tourist and administrative centre.

Vancouver City, SW British Columbia, W Canada; port, industrial, communications, manufacturing and cultural centre. (2) **I** Large mountainous island off coast of British Columbia, W Canada.

Vänern, L Lake (5600 km², 2160 sq miles), SW Sweden; largest Swedish lake.

Vanua Levu Volcanic island, second largest of Fiji Is, SW Pacific Ocean.

Vanuatu Independent republic (formerly New Hebrides), Oceania SW; see Section 1.

Vatican City Independent Papal state, Rome, Europe SE; see Section 1.

Vatnajökull Largest ice mass in Europe, SE Iceland; includes several active volcanoes and Iceland's highest peak, Öraefajökull (2119 m, 6952 ft).

Venezuela Independent republic, N South America; see Section 1.

Vermont State, NE USA; capital Montpelier.

Vesuvius Volcanic mountain (1277 m, 4190 ft), Bay of Naples, SW Italy.

Victoria (1) State, SE Australia; capital Melbourne. (2) Capital city, Seychelles, W Indian Ocean. (3) Provincial capital city, British Columbia, W Canada; port, manufacturing and naval centre. (4) Freshwater lake (68,422 km², 26,418 sq miles), Great Rift Valley, Uganda, Kenya, Tanzania; Africa's largest lake.

Victoria I Tundra-covered island, Arctic Archipelago, Northwest Territories, N Canada.

Victoria Land Sector of E Antarctica bordering E Ross Sea; New Zealand administered.

Vienna Capital city, Austria; river port, industrial, manufacturing, commercial, cultural and administrative centre.

Vientiane Capital city, Laos; river port, commercial and administrative centre.

Vietnam Independent state, Asia SE; see Section 1.

Virgin Is Archipelago, Greater Antilles (West Indies); see Section 1 (Virgin Is (British) and Virgin Is (US)).

Virginia State, E central USA; capital Richmond.

Viti Levu Volcanic island, largest of Fiji group, SW Pacific Ocean.

Volga River (3700 km, 2300 miles) flowing from Valdai Hills, NW USSR, SE through several lakes to Caspian Sea; longest river W of Ural Mts.

Volta River system (c. 1600 km, 1000 miles); Black Volta and White Volta flow south from Burkina Faso (formerly Upper Volta) to join in Ghana, continuing through Lake Volta to Gulf of Guinea.

Vosges Extensive mountains and uplands, E France.

W

Waddenzee Shallow sector of North Sea between Frisian Is and mainland, Netherlands, NW Europe.

Walcheren I Low-lying island, Scheldt River estuary, the Netherlands, NW Europe.

Wales Principality, western sector of UK, Europe W.

Wallis Archipelago Island group, Oceania Central; see Section 1.

Walvis Bay Bay, central coast of Namibia.

Warsaw Capital city, Poland; historic cultural, communications, industrial and manufacturing centre.

Wasatch Mts Mountain range, W Rocky Mts, Utah and Idaho, W central USA.

Washington State, NW USA; capital Olympia.

Washington DC Federal capital city of USA, District of Columbia, E USA; administrative, cultural and tourist centre.

Weddell Sea Ice-filled sector of Southern Ocean (SW Atlantic Ocean), E of Antarctic Peninsula.

Wellington Capital city, New Zealand, port, commercial, communications, manufacturing and administrative centre.

West Bengal State, NE India; capital Calcutta.

West Berlin City, enclave in East Germany, state of West Germany; manufacturing, cultural and tourist centre.

West Germany Independent republic, Europe Central; see Section 1.

West Indies Archipelagos, Caribbean Sea, including Greater and Lesser Antilles and Bahamas; see Section 1.

West Virginia State, E USA; capital Charleston.

Western Australia State, W Australia; capital Perth.

Western Sahara Disputed territory, Africa NW; see Section 1.

Western Samoa Independent state, Oceania Central; see Section 1.

White Mts Granitic mountains, NE Appalachians, New Hampshire and Maine, NE USA.

White Nile See Nile R.

White Sea Shallow S sector of Barents Sea, NW USSR.

Whitehorse Capital town, Yukon Territory, NW Canada; communications, mining and marketing centre.

Wight, I of Island, English Channel, off S coast of England, UK, NW Europe.

Wilkes Land Sector of E Antarctica S of Australia and E Indian Ocean.

Willemstad Capital city, Netherlands Antilles, Curaçao I; port, petroleum, commercial, administrative and tourist centre.

Wilson Mt Mountain (1880 m, 6170 ft), San Gabriel Mts, S California, SW USA; observatory site.

Windhoek Capital city, Namibia; communications, manufacturing and administrative centre.

Windward Is Chain of volcanic islands forming S section of Lesser Antilles, West Indies.

Winnipeg Provincial capital city, Manitoba, central Canada; agricultural, market, commercial and communications centre. (2) Extensive lake (24,514 km², 9465 sq miles), S central Manitoba, S Canada.

Wisconsin State, N central USA; capital Madison.

Witwatersrand (Rand) Gold-mining district, Transvaal, South Africa.

Wrangel I Tundra-covered island, Chukchi Sea, NE USSR.

Wrangell Mts Mountain chain, SE Alaska, USA.

Wuhan Provincial capital city, Hupei (Hubei) province, central China; river port, industrial, commercial, communications and administrative centre.

Wyoming State, W central USA; capital Cheyenne.

X

Xi Jiang See Si Kiang.
Xingu River (2000 km, 1250 miles) flowing from Serra da Chapada, central Brazil, N to Amazon R.
Xinjiang Uygur See Sinkiang-Uighur.
Xizang See Tibet.

Y

Yakut ASSR Autonomous republic, E USSR; capital Yakutsk.
Yangtze Kiang River (5000 km, 3100 miles) flowing from E Tibet S and E through Szechwan (Sichuan), Hupei (Hubei), Anhwei (Anhui) and Kiangsu (Jiangsu) provinces to the East China Sea; world's third longest river.
Yaoundé Capital city, Cameroon; commercial, industrial and communications centre.
Yapura River (1800 km, 1100 miles) flowing from confluence of Caqueta and Apaporis Rs, SE Colombia, E through Brazil to Amazon.
Yellow Sea Shallow sea between China and Korea.
Yellowknife Capital city, Northwest Territories, N Canada; mining, communications and administrative centre.
Yemen, Arab Republic of (N Yemen) Independent republic, Asia SW; see Section 1.
Yemen, Democratic Republic of See South Yemen.
Yenisei River (4000 km, 2500 miles) flowing from N central Mongolia N through central and N Siberia to Arctic Ocean.
Yerevan Capital city, Armenian SSR, USSR; industrial and historic cultural centre.
Yokohama City, Honshu, E Japan; port, industrial, manufacturing and cultural centre.
Yucatán Peninsula Limestone peninsula between Gulf of Mexico and Caribbean Sea, E Mexico.
Yugoslavia Independent federal republic, Europe SE; see Section 1.
Yukon River (2500 km, 1550 miles) flowing from N British Columbia N and NW through Yukon Territory and Alaska to Bering Sea.
Yukon Territory Province, NW Canada; capital Whitehorse.
Yunnan Province, S China; capital Kunming.

Z

Zagros Mts Oil-rich mountain range, W Iran.
Zaïre (1) Independent republic, Africa Central; see Section 1. (2) River; see Congo R.
Zambezi River (3500 km, 2200 miles) flowing from E Angola to Indian Ocean.
Zambia Independent republic, Africa Central; see Section 1.
Zanzibar (1) Island, E coast of Tanzania, SW Indian Ocean, and (2) city, Zanzibar I; historic marketing, administrative and cultural centre.
Zhejiang See Chekiang.
Zhengzhou See Chengchow.
Zürich City, N Switzerland; industrial, financial, communications and tourist centre.
Zimbabwe Independent republic, Africa S; see Section 1.

International Organizations and Affiliations

Geological Periods

Conversion Tables

Map Index

International Organizations and Affiliations

African Development Bank (ADB) Association of African countries to provide development funds on favourable terms within the African community.

ANZUS (Security Treaty between Australia, New Zealand and United States of America) Coordinates defence and security in Pacific area.

Arab Bank for Economic Development in Africa (ABEDA) Organization of Arab League countries, providing financial aid to distressed African countries.

Arab Fund for Economic and Social Development (AFESD) Association of Arab countries to provide financial and technical help in the Arab community.

Arab League See League of Arab States.

Association of South East Asian Nations (ASEAN) Association of Indonesia, Malaysia, Philippines, Singapore and Thailand to promote prosperity and stability.

Bank for International Settlements (BIS) Swiss-based bank for promoting cooperation and easing transactions among international banking community.

Benelux Economic Union Promoting economic association and ultimately union of Belgium, Netherlands and Luxembourg.

Caribbean Community and Common Market (CARICOM) Association of Caribbean states to promote common market facilities among its members, and political cooperation.

Central American Common Market (CACM) Association of Costa Rica, Guatemala, El Salvador, Honduras and Nicaragua to promote common market facilities.

Centre for Educational Research and Innovation (CERI) Responsible for technical and educational development in Organization for Economic Cooperation and Development (see entry).

Colombo Plan for Cooperative Economic and Social Development in Asia and the Pacific (Colombo Plan) Association of Commonwealth and other countries in Pacific and Indian Ocean areas, promoting economic and social development.

Committee on Space Research (COSPAR) International committee of International Council of Scientific Unions (see entry), for promoting and coordinating research in space.

The Commonwealth Association of forty-eight nations, formerly or currently British possessions, for mutual support and cooperation.

Council for Mutual Economic Assistance (CMEA, COMECON) Association of ten communist states for economic cooperation and development.

Council of Europe (CE) Association of European countries promoting the ideals and principles of their common heritage (including human rights and freedoms), encouraging common legislation and intergovernmental cooperation.

Danube Commission Association of Danube countries (Austria, Bulgaria, Czechoslovakia, Hungary, Romania, USSR, Yugoslavia) to promote effective navigation.

Economic and Social Commission for Asia and the Pacific (ESCA) UN regional commission studying economic development, industry, population and other issues in the region.

Economic Commission for Africa (ECA) UN regional commission promoting economic policies and development in African countries.

Economic Commission for Europe (ECE) UN regional commission studying economic and technological issues relating to European economic development.

Economic Commission for Latin America (ECLA) UN regional commission promoting economic development and planning in South and Central America.

Economic Commission for Western Asia (ECWA) UN regional commission studying economic development problems in SW Asia.

Economic Community of West African States (ECOWAS) Association of sixteen West African states to promote trade and economic cooperation.

European Atomic Energy Community (EAEC, Euratom) Component body of European Economic Community (see entry), with particular responsibility for promoting peaceful uses of nuclear power.

European Coal and Steel Community (ECSC) Component body of European Economic Community (see entry), with particular responsibility for promoting and administering common market facilities for coal and steel.

European Economic Community (EEC, Common Market) Association of European countries to promote common economic policies and political unity.

European Free Trade Association (EFTA) Association of non-EEC European countries to promote free trade and economic cooperation.

European Trade Union Confederation (ETUC) Association of trade unions from twenty European countries.

Food and Agriculture Organization of the United Nations (FAO) Promotion and support of forestry, fisheries and agriculture, especially in undeveloped countries.

General Agreement on Tariffs and Trade (GATT) UN-sponsored agreement; regulates international trading, reducing trade barriers and promoting trade of developing countries.

International Atomic Energy Agency (IAEA) UN-sponsored; promoting peaceful uses of atomic energy.

International Bank for Reconstruction and Development (IBRD, World Bank) Providing loans, advice, technical help for undeveloped countries, in cooperation with UN.

International Chamber of Commerce (ICC) Private international business organization promoting interests of world commerce and trade.

International Civil Aviation Organization (ICAO) UN-sponsored; coordinates, regulates and promotes international civil aviation.

International Confederation of Free Trade Unions (ICFTU) Promotion of free trade unionism, especially in developing countries.

International Cooperative Alliance (ICA) Official body promoting and coordinating international cooperative movement.

International Council of Scientific Unions (ICSU) Worldwide affiliation of scientific unions to promote and coordinate national and international research.

International Court of Justice (ICJ) International court of fifteen judges, supported by UN, working in accord with UN Charter.

International Development Association (IDA) World Bank and UN affiliate, providing loans to developing countries.

International Energy Agency (IEA) Responsible for developing energy policies within Organization for Economic Cooperation and Development (see entry).

International Finance Corporation (IFC) Invests funds provided by member countries in private companies of developing countries; affiliate of World Bank and UN.

International Fund for Agricultural Development (IFAD) UN-sponsored; association for developed countries to provide loans for food-producing schemes in less developed countries.

International Labour Organization (ILO) UN agency; improvement of employment conditions and living standards; promotion of employment.

International Maritime Organization (IMO) UN-sponsored; forum for discussion and action on shipping, safety and pollution at sea.

International Monetary Fund (IMF) Promotes international coordination in monetary matters; advises and makes loans available; mutual cooperation with UN.

International Narcotics Control Board (INCB) UN agency; monitors effective application of drug-control treaties and agreements, attempts to limit drug production and encourage control of supplies.

International Olympic Committee (IOC) Coordinates activities of National Olympic Committees in promoting sports and four-yearly Olympic Games.

International Red Cross Coordinating body for International Committee of the Red Cross and League of Red Cross Societies, promoting worldwide humanitarian, relief, health and welfare activities.

International Telecommunication Union (ITU) UN agency; coordinates radio-frequency allocation, telecommunications charges, safety functions, information.

International Union for the Conservation of Nature and Natural Resources (IUCN) Scientific advisory body determining priorities for worldwide conservation measures.

International Union for the Protection of New Varieties of Plants (UPOV) Promotes and provides model legislation for registering new breeds of plants, and securing property rights for breeders.

League of Arab States (LAS, Arab League) Association of Arab states to develop links and coordinate policies within the Arab community.

Nordic Council (NC) Advisory council promoting objectives of Treaty of Helsinki for economic, social and other cooperation among Scandinavian community.

North Atlantic Treaty Organization (NATO) Association of W European and North American states, to promote regional cooperation in defence, political, economic and scientific issues.

Nuclear Energy Agency (NEA) Body responsible for nuclear energy policies in Organization for Economic Cooperation and Development (see entry).

Organization for Economic Cooperation and Development (OECD)

Association of twenty-four states, mainly European and non-communist, promoting economic and social-welfare development.

Organization of African Unity (OAU) Association of fifty African states to promote common policies of unity, independence and solidarity, eliminate colonialism and defend sovereignty.

Organization of American States (OAS) Association of USA with Central and South American states to promote peace, security and cooperation.

Organization of Central American States (OCAS) Association of Costa Rica, El Salvador, Guatemala, Honduras and Nicaragua to promote peace and common development.

Organization of the Islamic Conference (OIC) Association of over forty Moslem states to promote solidarity, cooperation and common aims.

Organization of the Petroleum Exporting Countries (OPEC) Association of thirteen petroleum-exporting countries in South America, Africa and S Asia to coordinate production and sales policies.

Scientific Committee for Antarctic Research (SCAR) Committee of the International Council of Scientific Unions (see entry) for promoting and coordinating Antarctic research programmes.

Scientific Committee on Oceanic Research (SCOR) Committee of the International Council of Scientific Unions (see entry) for promoting and coordinating oceanographic research.

United Nations (UN) Association of 155 states, signatories to UN Charter, dedicated to maintaining international peace and security.

United Nations Capital Development Fund (UNCDF) Provides loans and grants to support small-scale development projects.

United Nations Children's Fund (UNICEF) Promotes child welfare programmes in distressed countries.

United Nations Conference on Trade and Development (UNCTAD) Permanent secretariat and board, frequent conferences on international trade policies.

United Nations Development Programme (UNDP) Administers technical and development assistance to developing countries.

United Nations Disaster Relief Office (UNDRO) Coordinates international relief programmes and preventative measures in disaster areas.

United Nations Educational, Scientific and Cultural Organization (UNESCO) Promotes international collaboration in education, science and culture.

United Nations Environmental Programme (UNEP) Promotes international cooperation in conserving, improving and protecting the human environment.

United Nations High Commissioner for Refugees (UNHCR) International protection, resettlement and rehabilitation programmes for refugees.

United Nations Industrial Development Organization (UNIDO) Promotion and development of industries, improvement of industrial conditions, in developing countries.

United Nations Relief and Works Agency for Palestine Refugees in the Near East (UNRWA) Long-term relief and rehabilitation of displaced Palestinians.

Universal Postal Union (UPU) UN-related; promotes international collaboration in postal services.

Warsaw Treaty Organization (WTO, Warsaw Pact) Association of seven communist countries to promote defence and other mutual interests.

Western European Union (WEU) Defence union between UK, France, the Netherlands, Belgium, Luxembourg, West Germany and Italy to control and coordinate arms policies.

World Bank See International Bank for Reconstruction and Development.

World Council of Churches (WCC) International association of over 260 Christian churches and denominations.

World Confederation of Labour (WCL) Association of trade unions, with worldwide religious affiliations.

World Federation of Trade Unions (WFTU) Mainly communist association of trade unions.

World Food Council (WFC) UN-associated; developing worldwide strategy of food production and distribution.

World Food Programme (WFP) UN-sponsored; provides and facilitates food supplies and encourages new food policies for countries in need.

World Health Organization (WHO) Coordinates worldwide programmes for improvements in health standards, initiating and stimulating research, advice etc., in cooperation with the UN.

World Intellectual Property Organization (WIPO) UN agency; coordinates and encourages international cooperation in protecting copyright, performing rights etc.

World Meteorological Organization (WMO) UN agency; promotes worldwide network of weather stations, coordinating data collection, research, training etc.

World Wildlife Fund (WWF) International charity, raising funds for protection and conservation of wildlife and wildlife habitats.

Geological Periods

Million years ago			
Pre-Cambrian	4,600–570	Triassic	225–190
Cambrian	570–500	Jurassic	190–136
Ordovician	500–430	Cretaceous	136–65
Silurian	430–395	Tertiary	65–present (c. 10,000 years ago)
Devonian	395–345	Eocene	65–38
Carboni-		Oligocene	38–12
ferous	345–280	Miocene	12–7
Permian	280–225	Pliocene	7–2.5
		Pleistocene	2.5–present (c. 10,000 years ago)

Conversion Tables

Note These figures have been rounded off to three decimal places.

Length

To convert	multiply by	or divide by
inches to metres	.025	39.370
feet to metres	.305	3.281
miles to kilometres	1.609	.621
metres to inches	39.370	.025
metres to feet	3.281	.305
kilometres to miles	.621	1.609

Area

To convert	multiply by	or divide by
sq feet to metres^2	.093	10.764
sq yards to metres^2	.836	1.196
acres to hectares	.405	2.471
sq miles to hectares	259.2	.0038
sq miles to kilometres^2	2.590	.386
metres^2 to sq ft	10.764	.093
metres^2 to sq yards	1.196	.836
hectares to acres	2.471	.405
hectares to sq miles	.0038	259.2
kilometres^2 to sq miles	.386	2.590

Weights

To convert	multiply by	or divide by
lbs to kilograms	.454	2.205
tonnes to kilograms	1,000.0	.001
tonnes to long tons	.984	1.016
tonnes to short tons	1.102	.907
kilograms to lbs	2.205	.454
kilograms to tonnes	.001	1,000.0
long tons to tonnes	1.016	.984
short tons to tonnes	.907	1.102

Temperatures

To convert	
°C to °F	multiply by 1.8 and add 32
°F to °C	subtract 32 and multiply by .556

Map Index

Abbreviations

Arch Archipelago
B Bay
cont Continent
G Gulf
I(s) Island
L Lake
Mt(s) Mountain
NZ New Zealand
Penin Peninsula

R River
Ra Range
reg Geographical region
Rep Republic
Russian SFSR Russian
  Soviet Federative
  Socialist Republic
SSR Soviet Socialist
  Republic

St Saint
Str Strait
UK United Kingdom
USA United States of
  America
■ Country
□ Administrative
  subdivision of a country

489

Index

Index

Index

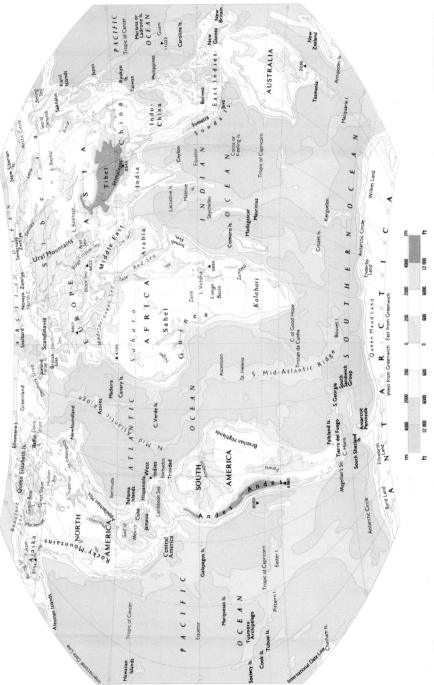

Projection: Hammer Equal Area

Projection: Hammer Equal Area

3

ARCTIC OCEAN

Novaya Zemlya
North C.
Severnaya Zemlya
New Siberian Is.
Murmansk
Arkhangelsk
Ob
Yenisey
Lena
Arctic Circle
Bering Sea
Sea of Okhotsk

UNION OF SOVIET SOCIALIST REPUBLICS

Stockholm
Leningrad
Moscow
Gorki
Sverdlovsk
Novosibirsk
L. Baykal
Chita
Sakhalin
Kuril Islands

Warsaw
Kiev
Kharkov
Omsk
Irkutsk
Amur
Vladivostok

Budapest
Odessa
L. Balkhash
Ulan Bator
Urumchi
MONGOLIA
Harbin
Shenyang
JAPAN

Black Sea
Istanbul
Baku
Aral Sea
Tashkent
Lu-ta
Seoul
Tokyo

Athens
TURKEY
Tehran
CHINESE
Peking
Tientsin
Yokohama
Osaka

CYPRUS SYRIA
ISRAEL
Baghdad
IRAN
Kabul
Lahore
Delhi
REPUBLIC
Nanking
Wuhan
Shanghai
Chungking

Alexandria
Cairo
EGYPT
Medina
SAUDI
Mecca
ARABIA
Karachi
INDIA
Kwangchow
Ryukyu Is.
PACIFIC
Tropic of Cancer

LIBYA
OMAN
Bombay
Calcutta
BURMA
Hong Kong
TAIWAN (FORMOSA)
Mariana or Ladrone Is.
OCEAN

AFRICA
NIGER
CHAD
Khartoum
SUDAN
Aden
SOUTH YEMEN
Hyderabad
Madras
THAI.
(SIAM)
Bangkok
VIET-
NAM
Manila
PHILIPPINES
Guam (U.S.)

Addis Ababa
SOMALI REP.
ETHIOPIA
Lakshadweep Is.
(Laccadive Is.)
(India)
Phnom Penh
Ho Chi Minh City
Caroline Is.
(U.S. Trust Territory)

NIGERIA
CAMEROON
CENTRAL AFRICAN REP.
Zaire
(Congo)
UGANDA
KENYA
Mogadishu
Colombo
Maldive Is.
SRI LANKA
Equator
MALAYSIA

GABON
ZAIRE
Kinshasa
L. Victoria
Nairobi
Mombasa
Zanzibar
Dar-es-Salaam
Seychelles
Chagos Arch.
INDIAN
Sumatra
Singapore
Borneo
INDONESIA
New Guinea
PAPUA NEW GUINEA
New Britain

ANGOLA
ZAMBIA
Lusaka
Comoro Is.
OCEAN
Cocos or Keeling Is.
(Australia)
Jakarta
Surabaya
Java
Darwin
Cairns

NAMIBIA
BOTSWANA
ZIMB.
Beira
MADAGASCAR
Mauritius
Tropic of Capricorn
AUSTRALIA

Johannesburg
Maputo
SOUTH AFRICA
Durban
Brisbane

Cape Town
Good Hope
Port Elizabeth
Crozet Is.
(Fr.)
Kerguelen
(Fr.)
Perth
Fremantle
Adelaide
Sydney
Canberra
Auckland
NEW ZEALAND

Bouvet I.
(Norway)
SOUTHERN OCEAN
Melbourne
Tasmania
Hobart
Wellington
Christchurch

Antipodes Is.
(N.Z.)

Antarctic Circle
Enderby Land
Wilkes Land
Macquarie I.
(Australia)

Maud Land
DEPENDENCY
from Greenwich
AUSTRALIAN DEPENDENCY
ANTARCTICA
ROSS DEPENDENCY

G H J K L M N

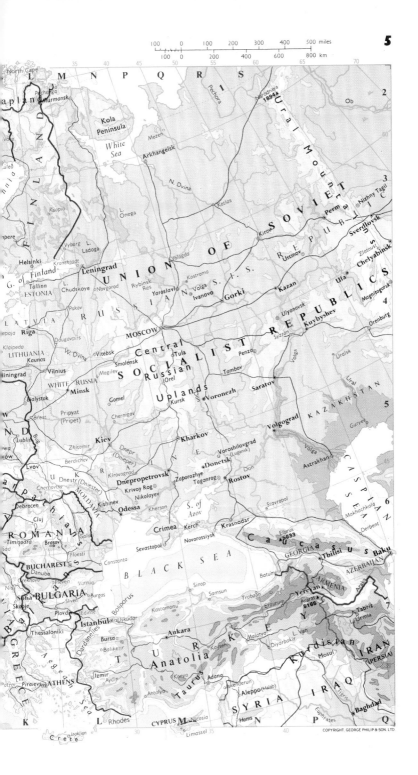

5

100   0   100   200   300   400   500 miles
100   0   200   400   600   800 km

L M N P Q R S

North Cape
Lapland   Pechenga   Murmansk
Petsamo

Kola
Peninsula

White
Sea

Arkhangelsk

Mezen

N. Dvina

Katlas

Pechora   1   Narodnaya
                18944

Ural Mountains

Ob   2

FINLAND
Kuopio

L. Onega

Kotlas

Perm   Nizhny Tagil
Kirov   Ustinov   Sverdlovsk   3
                              Zlatoust

Helsinki   Vyborg   L. Ladoga
Kronstadt

UNION   OF   SOVIET

Ula   Chelyabinsk

Magnitogorsk   4

Tallinn
ESTONIA   L. Chudskoye   Novgorod   Rybinsk Res.   Kostroma
                                                   Yaroslavl

Leningrad

Vologda

Gorki

Kazan

R U S S I A N   S.F.S.   R.   REPUBLICS

Pskov   Volga

Ivanovo

Ulyanovsk   Kuybyshev

Orenburg

LATVIA   Riga   Daugavpils
W. Dvina   Vitebsk

MOSCOW

Central
Russian
Uplands

Tula

Penza

Syzran

Uralsk

KAZAKHSTAN   5

LITHUANIA   Klaipeda
Kaunas   Smolensk   Mogilev   Orel

SOCIALIST   REPUBLICS

Volga

Ural

WHITE RUSSIA   Minsk
Vilnius   Gomel

Kursk   Voronezh

Saratov

Tambov

Volgograd

Guryev

Bialystok
Brest   Pripyat
(Pripet)   Chernigov

Kharkov

Don

Astrakhan   45   C A S P I A N

POLAND   Lublin   Bug

Kiev   Dnepr
(Dnieper)

U K R A I N E

Voroshilovgrad
(Lugansk)

Stavropol

Makhachkala

Derbent

S E A

Lvov   Zhitomir   Berdichev   Kirovograd   Dnepropetrovsk   Donetsk
Krivoy Rog   Zaporozhye   Taganrog   Rostov

Chernovtsy   U   K
Dnestr (Dniester)

MOLDAVIA   Kishinev   Nikolayev
Odessa   Kherson

S. of
Azov

Krasnodar

Debrecen   Carpathians   Cluj   Galati
ROMANIA
Timișoara   Brasov
BUCHAREST   Ploesti
Danube   Constanta

Crimea   Kerch

Sevastopol   Novorossiysk

Elbrus
5633   C a u c a s u s
GEORGIA   Tbilisi   Baku
Batumi   AZERBAIJAN
ARMENIA
Trabzon   Erzurum   Yerevan   Ararat   Tabriz
                              5165   Urmia

Nis   Krushevo   Pleven   Varna
Sofia   BULGARIA   Sliven   Burgas
Skopje   Plovdiv   Edirne

B L A C K   S E A

Sinop

Samsun

Kastamonu   Ankara

TURKEY

Kayseri   Malatya   Diyarbakir   Van

Kurdistan   Mosul

IRAN
(PERSIA)   7

Thessaloniki   Istanbul   Uskudar
Bursa   Balikesir

Anatolia

Konya   Adana

Tigris

GREECE   Izmir   Aydin
Piraievs   ATHENS   Taurus   Antalya
Iraklion   Iskenderun

Aleppo (Halab)

SYRIA   Homs

IRAQ   Baghdad   Q

Rhodes   CYPRUS   Nicosia
Crete   Limassol

COPYRIGHT. GEORGE PHILIP & SON. LTD

6   ASIA

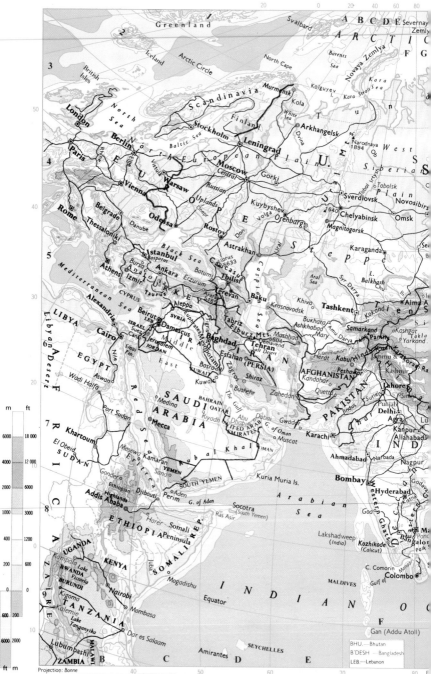

Projection: Bonne

m ft
6000 18 000
4000 12 000
2000 6000
1000 3000
400 1200
200 600
0 0
600 200
6000 2000
ft m

Greenland
Svalbard
A B C D E Severnaya
Zemly
A R C T I C
F G
Iceland
Arctic Circle
North Cape
Barents
Sea
Novaya Zemlya
Kolguyev I.
Kara Strait
Kara Sea
Murmansk
Kola
T
u
n
British
Isles
North
Sea
S c a n d i n a v i a
Finland
White
Sea
Arkhangelsk
Dvina
Narodnaya
1894
U.
West
Siberian
S
S
London
Baltic Sea
Stockholm
Leningrad
Moscow
Central
Russian
Gorki
Tobolsk
Sverdlovsk
Plain
Novosibirsk
Berlin
N o r t h   E u r o p e a n   P l a i n
Warsaw
Vistula
Kuybyshev
Volga
Orenburg
1640
Chelyabinsk
Omsk
Paris
Rhine
E
U
Vienna
Uplands
Russian
P
E
S
t
e
p
p
e
Rome
Belgrade
Danube
Odessa
Dnepr
Rostov
Don
Astrakhan
Ural
Magnitogorsk
Karaganda
Se
Thessaloniki
B l a c k   S e a
Elbrus
5633
C a u c a s u s
L.
Balkhash
Athens
Istanbul
Bosporus
Ankara
Erzurum
Batumi
Tbilisi
Aral
Sea
Syr Darya
Chu
Tashkent
T
i
e
n
Alma-
Izmir
Anatolia
T U R K E Y
Taurus
Ararat
5165
Tabriz
Elbruz Mts.
5604
Caspian
Sea
Khiva
Krasnovodsk
Bukhara
Amu Darya
Samarkand
Pamir
Kashgar
Yarkand
Takla
S
i
CYPRUS
Mediterranean Sea
Aleppo
SYRIA
Damascus
Euphrates
Baghdad
Mesopotamia
Tehran
I R A N
Demavend
5604
Mashhad
Salt Desert
Herat
Kabul
Hindu
Jammu
Kashmir
&
Alexandria
LIBYA
Beirut
LEB.
ISRAEL
Jerusalem
JORDAN
Middle
Esfahan
Zagros
Qom
2181
Peshawar
Lahore
Cairo
EGYPT
Suez
Sinai
Pen.
East
Basra
KUWAIT
Kuwait
Shiraz
Bushehr
Zahedan
AFGHANISTAN
Kandahar
Quetta
PAKISTAN
Indus
Sutlej
Simla
Libyan Desert
Nile
Aswan
Wadi Halfa
Red
Sea
Medina
BAHRAIN
QATAR
Riyadh
Abu
Dhabi
Dubai
Gwadar
Punjab
Delhi
Agra
Kanpur
Allahabad
Lu
Khartoum
El Obeid
SUDAN
Port Sudan
Mecca
SAUDI
ARABIA
UNITED ARAB
EMIRATES
The Gulf
G. of Oman
Muscat
OMAN
Karachi
Ahmadabad
Narbada
Nagpur
I N D I A
Kassala
Gonder
Atbara
Kamaran
Sana
YEMEN
R u b   a l   K h a l i
Bombay
Godav
Hyderabad
Eastern Ghats
Goa
Ma
Bangalo
Addis Ababa
Ethiopian
Highlands
Djibouti
Perim
SOUTH YEMEN
Aden
G. of Aden
Socotra
(South Yemen)
Ras Asir
Arabian
Sea
Kuria Muria Is.
Lakshadweep
(India)
Kozhikode
(Calicut)
Paik
UGANDA
Kampala
Lake
Victoria
RWANDA
BURUNDI
KENYA
Juba
SOMALI REP.
ETHIOPIA
Harer
Somali
Peninsula
C. Comorin
Colombo
Gulf of M
Western Ghats
Nairobi
Mombasa
Mogadishu
Equator
MALDIVES
T A N Z A N I A
Kigoma
Kalemie
Lake
Tanganyika
Dar es Salaam
I N D I A N
O C
Gan (Addu Atoll)
Lubumbashi
MALAWI
ZAMBIA
Amirantes
SEYCHELLES
BHU. — Bhutan
B'DESH — Bangladesh
LEB.—Lebanon
A F R I C A

20 0 20 40 60 80
50
40
30
20
10
0
10
40 50 60 70 80 E

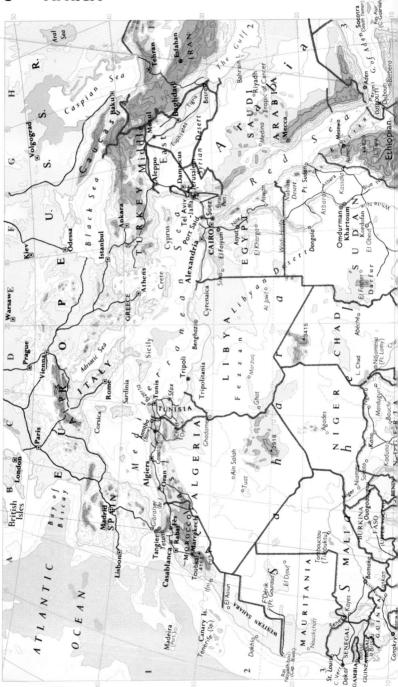

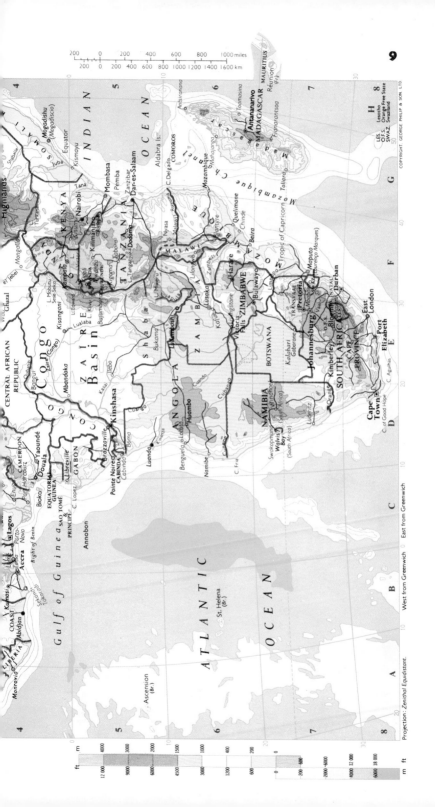

9

Projection: Zenithal Equidistant.

West from Greenwich 0 East from Greenwich

| 200 | 0 | 200 | 400 | 600 | 800 | 1000 miles |

| 200 | 0 | 200 | 400 | 600 | 800 | 1000 | 1200 | 1400 | 1600 km |

H
LES. Lesotho
O.F.S. Orange Free State
SWAZ. Swaziland

INDIAN OCEAN

ATLANTIC OCEAN

Gulf of Guinea

MADAGASCAR

MAURITIUS
Réunion (Fr.)

COMOROS
Aldabra Is.

Mozambique Channel

Tropic of Capricorn

Equator

SOMALI

KENYA
Nairobi
Mombasa
Pemba
Zanzibar
Dar-es-Salaam

TANZANIA
Kilimanjaro
Dodoma

Kampala
L. Victoria
L. Edward
L. Kivu
Bujumbura
L. Tanganyika

ZAÏRE Basin
Kisangani
Lualaba
Lomami
Mbandaka
Kinshasa
Boma

CONGO
Brazzaville
Pointe Noire
CABINDA

GABON
Libreville
C. Lopez

EQUATORIAL GUINEA
SÃO TOMÉ & PRINCIPE
Annobon

CAMEROON
Douala
Yaoundé
Bioko
Port Harcourt

CENTRAL AFRICAN REPUBLIC
Bangui

Lagos
Porto Novo
Accra
COAST
Abidjan
Monrovia
Kumasi

LIBERIA
IVORY

Mogadishu (Mogadiscio)
Juba
Kismayu
Tana

Highlands

MALAWI
L. Nyasa
L. Malawi
Lilongwe
Blantyre

ZAMBIA
Lusaka
L. Mweru
Lubumbashi
Shaba
Kasai
Kabompo
Zambezi
Victoria Falls
Livingstone
Kafue

ZIMBABWE
Harare
Bulawayo
Limpopo

MOZAMBIQUE
Quelimane
Chinde
Beira
Maputo (Lourenço Marques)
C. Delgado

ANGOLA
Luanda
Benguela
Lobito
Huambo
Namibe
Cuango
Cuanza
Cuando
Cubango

NAMIBIA
Windhoek
Walvis Bay (South Africa)
Swakopmund
Lüderitz
Orange

BOTSWANA
Gaborone
Kalahari

SOUTH AFRICA
CAPE PROVINCE
Cape Town
C. of Good Hope
C. Agulhas
Kimberley
Johannesburg
TRANSVAAL
Pretoria
O.F.S.
Bloemfontein
NATAL
Durban
East London
Port Elizabeth
Vaal

Ascension (Br.)

St. Helena (Br.)

ft	m
12 000	4000
	3000
9000	2000
6000	1500
	1000
3000	400
1200	200
600	0
0	

m	ft
200	600
2000	6000
4000	12 000
6000	18 000

Lombok
Sumbawa
Sumba
INDONESIA
C Timor
D

Arafura

E

Melville I.
P. Darwin
Darwin
Arnhem Land
Pine Creek
Katherine
Roper
Birdum
Daly Waters

NORTHERN
L. Sylvester

TERRITORY

Macdonnell Ranges
Alice Springs

Amadeus
Ayers Rock
867
Musgrave Ranges
Mt. 1549
Woodroffe
Finke

Oodnadatta
SOUT
E

Ashmore I.

Timor
Sea

C. Londonderry
Cambridge G.
Wyndham

Victoria

Ord

King Sound
Kimberley
Dampier Land
Derby
Fitzroy
Hall's Creek
Broome
Sturt
Woods
L.

INDIAN

OCEAN

P. Hedland
Dampier Arch.
Dampier
Roebourne
Preston
Fortescue
Hamersley
Home Sta.
N.W. Onslow
Cape
Mt. Enid
Mt. Bruce
Price
Mt. Tom 1226
Ashburton
Mt. Augustus
1105

Mt. Goldsworthy
Marble Bar

Great
Sandy Desert

L.
Mackay

Hamersley Ra.
Mt. Nicholas
Mt. Whaleback
WESTERN
L. Disappointment

L. Macdonald

Gibson Desert

Gascoyne
Carnarvon
Shark B.

Steep Point

Murchison
Meekathara
Wiluna

L. Carnegie

AUSTRALIA

L. Austin
Mt. Magnet
Sandstone
Laverton

L. Barlee

Geraldton

Bonnie Rock
Coolgardie
Kalgoorlie
Boulder
Northam
Hyden
Perth
Fremantle
Darling Range
Narrogin
Esperance
Geographe B.
C. Naturaliste
Bunbury
Augusta
C. Leeuwin
Albany

Norseman

Great Victoria Desert
Ooldea
AUSTR
L. Te

Loongana
Deakin
Nullarbor Plain
Eyre

Penong
Ceduna
L. Gairdner
Gawle

Great Australian Bight

Eyre
Pen.
P. Lincoln
Spencer
We

Kangar

SOUTHERN

ft   m

6000   2000

3000   1000

1200   400

600   200

0

200   600

2000   6000   40

m   ft

Projection: Bonne

115
120
125
130
135

East from   Gre

A   B   C   D   E

11

100   0   100   200   300   400   500 miles
100   0   200   400   600   800 km

PAPUA NEW GUINEA
On same scale as general map

Torres Str.
Thursday I.
C. York

Arnhem
Cape
York
Peninsula

Gulf of
Carpentaria

K   **L**   **M**

Admiralty Is.

Wewak Sepik   Schouten Is.   Bismarck   New
                                Archipelago Ireland   **8**
                                             Rabaul
NEW   Madang   Kokopo

Muller Ra.
GUINEA   Lae Huon G.   New Britain   **9**
                        Wau
Fly   *Gulf of*   Owen Stanley Ra.
           Papua   Mt. Victoria
                        4035   D'Entrecasteaux
           Daru   P. Moresby   Is.
                                    Samarai China Str.

G   **H**   **K**   **L**   **M**

Cooktown
Cairns
Great Barrier Reef
Laura
Mitchell
Gilbert
Normanton
Croydon   Georgetown
Forsayth
Dobbyn
Flinders   Burdekin   **Townsville**

Mt. Isa
Cloncurry   Charters
Dajarra   Towers
            QUEENSLAND   Mackay
apricorn   Winton

Longreach   **Rockhampton**
        Barcoo   Mt.   Gladstone
Yaraka   Mackenzie   Morgan
                            Bundaberg
Charleville   Great Divide   Sandy C.
Quilpie   Gympie **Maryborough**
Thargomindah   Warrego Culgoa Ipswich
        Cunnamulla Darling **Toowoomba** **Brisbane**
Dirranbandi   Downs
                Warwick   C. Byron
Barwon Walgett   Lismore
Bourke   New England Ra.
    Darling   Tamworth Round Mt. Grafton
Cobar   1615 Armidale
        Macquarie
NEW SOUTH
Bathurst Lithgow W. Maitland
Katoomba **Newcastle**
WALES Blue Mts. Parramatta
Hay   **Sydney**
Murrumbidgee Botany Bay
Riverina Goulburn **Wollongong**
Albury Wagga Wagga Jervis Bay
        Canberra
Mildura Lachlan Austral.Cap.Terr.
Murray   Mt. Kosciusko
        VICTORIA 2230
Maryborough Bendigo Australia Bombala
Ballarat   C. Howe
Geelong **Melbourne** Orbost
Portland Port Phillip B.
Warrnambool Port Albert
        Wilson's Promontory
King I. *Bass Strait* Flinders I.

TASMANIA
Mt. Ossa Launceston
1617
Queenstown
Hobart

Coral Sea

PACIFIC

OCEAN

P   **Q**
C. Maria van Diemen
North C.   Russell
    Whangarei Gt. Barrier I.
Kaipara   Hauraki Gulf
Harb.
    Auckland Thames Bay of Plenty
        Hamilton   East C.
    NORTH
    ISLAND
New Plymouth   L. Taupo **Gisborne**
Mt. Egmont   Ruapehu Mahia Pen.
2518   2796   Napier
Wanganui   Hawke B.
Palmerston N. Hastings
C. Farewell **Wellington**
Nelson Cook Strait C. Palliser
Picton
Greymouth
Hokitika   *PACIFIC*
SOUTH
ISLAND Canterbury Plains
Mt. Cook 3764 **Christchurch**
        & Lyttelton   *OCEAN*
    Southern Alps Bank's Pen.
Timaru
Waitaki
Doubtful Oamaru
Sd.
West C.   **Dunedin**
Te Anau   & P. Chalmers
Foveaux Strait **Invercargill**
Stewart I. Bluff Hr.
Southwest C.

NEW ZEALAND
On same scale as main map

COPYRIGHT. GEORGE PHILIP & SON. LTD

13

PACIFIC OCEAN

UNITED STATES

WEST INDIES

ATLANTIC OCEAN

BAHAMAS

C U B A

CARIBBEAN SEA

GULF OF MEXICO

MEXICO

Sierra Madre

Lower California

G. of California

Revilla Gigedo Is.
(Mexico)

Tropic of Cancer

CENTRAL AMERICA

GUATEMALA
HONDURAS
NICARAGUA
COSTA RICA
EL SALVADOR
BELIZE

PANAMA

SOUTH AMERICA

COLOMBIA

VENEZUELA

ECUADOR

PERU

BRAZIL

Galapagos Is.
(Ecuador)

Equator

HAITI
DOM. REP.
PUERTO RICO (U.S.)
Hispaniola

JAMAICA

San Francisco
Oakland
San Jose
Los Angeles
San Bernardino
Anaheim
San Diego
Phoenix
Tucson
Albuquerque
Santa Fe
El Paso
Denver
Colorado Springs
Pueblo
Cheyenne
Salt Lake City
Great Salt Lake
Sacramento
Reno
Omaha
Des Moines
Wichita
Kansas City
Topeka
Oklahoma City
Dallas
Fort Worth
Houston
San Antonio
Corpus Christi
Galveston
Shreveport
Austin
Baton Rouge
New Orleans
Memphis
Little Rock
Pine Bluff
Nashville
Chattanooga
Birmingham
Montgomery
Mobile
Atlanta
Macon
Savannah
Charleston
Columbia
Charlotte
Jacksonville
Tampa
St. Petersburg
Daytona Beach
Orlando
Miami
Nashville
Louisville
Cincinnati
Indianapolis
Peoria
St. Louis
Chicago
Richmond
Washington
Baltimore
Norfolk
Cape Hatteras

Monterrey
Saltillo
Torreón
Nuevo Rosita
Chihuahua
Ciudad Juárez
Hermosillo
Guaymas
Mazatlán
La Paz
Guadalajara
León
Mexico
Puebla
Acapulco
Veracruz
Tampico
Mérida
Yucatán

Havana
Matanzas
Santa Clara
Camagüey

Kingston

Guatemala
San Salvador
Tegucigalpa
Managua
San José
Colón
Panamá

Barranquilla
Cartagena
Medellín
Manizales
Cali
Bogotá
Quito
Guayaquil
Iquitos
Caracas
Maracaibo
Bucaramanga
Barquisimeto

Bermuda

Projection: Bonne

West from Greenwich